THE YEAR OF DECISION:

1846

BOOKS BY
BERNARD DeVOTO

THE CROOKED MILE

THE CHARIOT OF FIRE

THE HOUSE OF SUN-GOES-DOWN

MARK TWAIN'S AMERICA

WE ACCEPT WITH PLEASURE

FORAYS AND REBUTTALS

MINORITY REPORT

MARK TWAIN AT WORK

THE YEAR OF DECISION

THE LITERARY FALLACY

MOUNTAIN TIME

ACROSS THE WIDE MISSOURI

THE WORLD OF FICTION

THE HOUR

THE COURSE OF EMPIRE

THE JOURNALS OF LEWIS AND CLARK

THE EASY CHAIR

THE COVER DESIGN IS BY SAMUEL HANKS BRYANT. FOR THE BACKGROUND, THE DESIGNER HAS USED A RETROSPECTIVELY ORNAMENTAL WOOD ENGRAVING THAT APPEARED IN *Harper's New Monthly Magazine* IN 1867 AND WAS ENTITLED "THE COURSE OF EMPIRE."

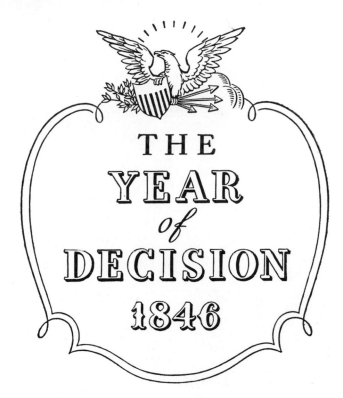

THE YEAR of DECISION 1846

BY BERNARD DeVOTO

WITH AN INTRODUCTORY ESSAY ON THE AUTHOR
BY CATHERINE DRINKER BOWEN

Sentry Edition 1961

HOUGHTON MIFFLIN COMPANY · BOSTON
The Riverside Press Cambridge

The Riverside Press
CAMBRIDGE • MASSACHUSETTS
PRINTED IN THE U.S.A.

DEDICATION

Dear Kate:

While I was writing this book you sometimes asked me what it was about. Reading it now, you will see that, though it is about a good many things, one theme that recurs is the basic courage and honor in the face of adversity which we call gallantry. It is always good to remember human gallantry, and it is especially good in times like the present. So I want to dedicate a book about the American past written in a time of national danger to a very gallant woman,

TO

KATHARINE GRANT STERNE

Yours,

Benny

BERNARD DeVOTO
HISTORIAN, CRITIC, AND FIGHTER

BY CATHERINE DRINKER BOWEN

BERNARD DeVOTO was my valued friend. I am among the host of writers who came to him for advice, for criticism, and for general renewal of spirit. In letters and by word of mouth DeVoto and I shouted at each other. But always, in the end, I sat still and listened to what he had to say. And after each encounter, I came away rejoicing in the existence of that vivid, generous, and diabolically intelligent presence.

Mr. DeVoto had much influence on me as a writer. He still has. Very often, when I have composed a page on which I look with favor, I hear a voice within. "What," it asks, "would DeVoto think of that?" He is looking over my shoulder, his big spectacles level with my eye. I go back, rewrite the passage — an exercise known to DeVoto as "just running it through your typewriter again." Out come the adjectives, the passive verb turns active, the sentences tighten and compress. As we grow older, DeVoto told me, our style becomes simpler, or it should. Age, he said, reduces us to the ultimate simplicities. There is not time left for frill and ornament. When he died he was only fifty-eight, and when he spoke to me of age he could not have been more than fifty-five.

What a handsome shelf of histories DeVoto has given us! *Mark Twain's America* — which surely must be counted as history — *The Year of Decision, Across the Wide Missouri, The Course of Empire*. And finally, his superb edition of *The Journals of Lewis and Clark*. Critics have grouped the three central books as a trilogy; DeVoto himself referred to them that way. For my part I cannot separate them from the others. I see the five books as composing the wide arc and panorama of DeVoto's thesis: the westward movement of a people, the settling and seeding of a continent, the culture that flowered therefrom, and the slow, episodic acceptance of the federal idea. From the Atlantic to the Pacific, a federal union — impossible, romantic, necessitous conception which today we know as the United States of America. Nobody thought we could do it; in Europe it had not been achieved on anything approaching such a scale. Even Thomas Jefferson supposed that, following the Louisiana Purchase, we might be needing two republics, one east of the Rocky Mountains and one west. "As a historian," wrote DeVoto, "I have interested myself in the growth among the American people of the feeling that they were properly a single nation between two oceans; in the development of what I have called the continental mind."

Bernard DeVoto was haunted by that idea and by his vision of how it came to pass, geographically, culturally, agriculturally, anthropologically. The continental reality, he called it. He thought and wrote of this reality in terms of history, biography, fiction, poetry (written when he was very young). He even composed a play about the Mormons. And there is, it may be said, another word for the condition of a haunted man. Some people call it inspiration.

As for DeVoto's "place among American historians," let me say at once that he is not to be placed, classified, or categorized. There is no historian like him and no histories like his. His thinking was direct, ruthless, wholly his own, and because of it, less original men feared him. He was a fighter for public causes, for conservation of our natural resources, for freedom of the press and freedom of thought. The world knew him better in that guise, perhaps, than as a historian. I shall make it my business to speak of DeVoto the fighter. For this trait — call it pugnacity, call it passion, hot blood, or a high-beating heart — this trait it is which informs and animates DeVoto's historical writing, from his early essays on the Mormons to his last words about the great captains, Lewis and Clark.

When DeVoto said the word "west," he meant the desert west, the arid, thin-soiled Rocky Mountain west which begins, he said, "at that place where the average annual rainfall drops below twenty inches." Most of his books are concerned with the movement west. *Mark Twain's America* announced his lifelong theme. It opens in 1835 with "The New Jerusalem," as DeVoto called it — that western Zion envisioned by men of piety and men whose god was gold. Mark Twain's parents left their eastern home to settle there. "The migration," wrote DeVoto, "was under way. Its great days were just around the turn of spring — and an April restlessness, a stirring in the blood, a wind from beyond the oak's openings, spoke of the prairies, the great desert, and the western sea. The common man fled westward. A thirsty land swallowed him insatiably. There is no comprehending the frenzy of the American folk-migration. God's gadfly had stung us mad."

After *Mark Twain's America,* eleven crowded years went by before DeVoto wrote his second volume of social history. *The Year of Decision* is perhaps the most absorbing of DeVoto's books, with its account of the Donner Party's fearful march across the desert and Rocky Mountains, a story of starvation, courage, bestiality, faith, and almost incredible endurance. *Across the Wide Missouri* came next. Magnificently illustrated with colored reproductions of contemporary paintings by Alfred Jacob Miller, it won both the Pulitzer and the Bancroft prizes. *Across the Wide Missouri* sets out to tell of the early fur trade — "how it helped to shape our heritage," writes DeVoto, "what its relation was to the western expansion of the United States, most of all how the mountain men lived."

This "most of all" is what brings the book alive. And it is an extraordinary reconstruction. Mountain men, free trappers, the long hunter and the hapless tenderfoot — we see them, hear them talk, share their camp, their appalling meals of buffalo guts raw or roasted, their dangers and their hero-sized sprees when the trail ends in safety. We learn more about Indians than we thought we cared to know. Warriors and their squaws confront us, not as Uncas or Hiawatha or Minnehaha, Laughing Water, but as they were actually seen, heard, and smelled by travelers in the wagon trains. Trappers traded furs with the tribes, killed them skulking at night beyond the campfire, or bought the favors of the young squaws. DeVoto hated romanticism about Indians, "the squash blossom in the hair and talk about the plumed serpent." It did not help, he said, "to be precious about the rain dance and the mystical awareness that neolithic savages are supposed to have." He hated also the over-intellectual approach and declared that "anyone who thinks of Indians as the Amerinds is not going to add much to our literature."

These are gorgeous books, all three. No less a word will do. They are rich, strong, filled with color and movement. Also they are long books, jammed with fact. Not infrequently there is repetition, a page or two or three which the reader is inclined to skip. This is a fault of all long books; I am not even sure that it is a fault. DeVoto, going over a lengthy book manuscript of mine, told me not to worry about including a dull page now and then, of connective matter or exposition or suchlike. "Give the reader time to breathe," he said. Actually, DeVoto's method achieved an even more subtle purpose. His books of history have — as Alfred Knopf once pointed out — an interwoven architecture, a deliberate movement from theme to theme. The narrative could have proceeded in a straight line, direct from start to finish. But DeVoto chose the more difficult and far more effectual method of taking several stories or themes and carrying them along, parallel. This does not make for careless reading. He who wishes to travel with DeVoto will have to keep his head; the journey will not be easy. In *The Year of Decision,* DeVoto confesses his purpose: to tell the "story in such a way that the reader may realize the far western frontier experience, which is part of our cultural experience, as personal experience."

Let readers say if he succeeded. I know one reader who has had to put these books aside at times, when the terror and the suffering needed surcease. There is small doubt about this being a shared experience. From Massachusetts, from Virginia, we travel with these humble men and women as they launch their wagon trains over the Alleghenies, through the forests and grasslands to where the trails run west from Council Bluffs or Independence — across the Blue, across the Nishnabotna, across the wide Missouri.

Throughout the books I have discussed, DeVoto's history has been frankly episodic, sectional, a string of vivid anecdotes comprising in space a continent and in time a generation or two. But in his next and fourth volume, *The Course of Empire,* DeVoto swings far backward in chronology and ties the long threads together. Boldly his narrative opens in the eighth century with that missionary archbishop who set out over the Atlantic — the Sea of Darkness — and founded, on the legendary island of Antilia, the seven radiant cities of God. The narrative ends in the year 1806, and there is quoted a line from the diary of Captain Clark, Meriwether Lewis' partner. On a rainy November morning, Captain Clark looks westward from his mountain camp and writes, in his own phonetic spelling, "Ocian in view! O! the joy."

After this book, DeVoto was bound to edit *The Journals of Lewis and Clark.* And by now, he knew these journal writers and these journeys as he knew the back of his hand or the Wasatch Mountains and Weber Canyon, where he roamed as a boy. In the summer of 1946 he had even followed, in person, the actual trails taken by Lewis and Clark. His edition of the journals is authoritative and final. And it is the best kind of historical reading, notes and all. An introduction, vigorous, thick-packed, explains Jefferson's purpose in dispatching the expedition and the political and social urgencies involved. Published in 1953, the book's final chapter is called "The Home Stretch." One could wish that the title had not proved, for DeVoto himself, so tragically symbolic.

How did DeVoto come to write these books? What conditions of birth, background, and experience shaped his style and caused him to be a man thus haunted? In truth one felt behind this man a compulsion so strong that, but for an essential health and integrity

— and a wife like Helen Avis MacVicar DeVoto — his talent might have torn him wide apart.

DeVoto's father, Florian Bernard DeVoto, of Ogden, Utah, was the son of an Italian cavalry officer; his mother was the daughter of a Mormon pioneer. (DeVoto liked to say that he was born of an apostate Mormon and an apostate Roman Catholic.) At high school he had a job as a reporter for the Ogden *Evening Standard.* When he was sixteen the paper published his first printed piece, which bore no less a title than "The Reasonableness of World-Wide Conciliation." DeVoto entered the University of Utah, but when four members of the faculty were dismissed for unorthodox opinions, the young sophomore left and finished his education at Harvard. He came west again to teach in Illinois, but in his late twenties picked up and migrated eastward to Cambridge, Massachusetts, where he spent the rest of his life, except for two years in New York as editor of the *Saturday Review of Literature.* To my best knowledge and belief he never went farther from the borders of the U.S.A. than a few miles into Canada.

For me, the significant facts of this brief biography are, first, that DeVoto was born and raised in Utah; and, second, that he was a novelist before he was a historian. DeVoto was conscious of his debt to this literary apprenticeship. The forematter to *The Year of Decision* carries a page and a half of thanks to those men and women who helped with its preparation — scholars, librarians, critical readers of manuscript. "Finally," says DeVoto, "I acknowledge that I could not possibly have written the book if I had not had periodic assistance from Mr. John August."

John August was the pen name signed by DeVoto to four novels, all of them serialized in *Collier's Magazine.* Perhaps DeVoto meant financial assistance. John August, he used to say, paid the rent. But I prefer to read further into that wry little statement. Four novels signed by John August, five signed by DeVoto. I have read them all, from *The Crooked Mile* (1924) to *Mountain Time* (1947). I do not care for them, except as their writing taught DeVoto to write history, gave him facility, cut the bonds imposed by the academic training and tradition, and allowed him to move freely and exuberantly within the prescribed circle of historic fact. DeVoto is not the first historian nor the last to come to his craft by way of fiction writing.

He was early aware of his confessed literary aim — to make America realize the western pioneer experience. Very likely he thought, at the outset, that it could best be done by fiction. DeVoto wrote novels periodically from 1924 to 1947, meanwhile casting about for other ways to express his theme. When he was engaged in a novel DeVoto never talked to me about it; our conversations concerned historical writing. Therefore I am only guessing when I say that I think he suffered during the composition of these novels. When he fell short of aim DeVoto knew it; he did not spare self-criticism. In 1934, I was trying to buy his early novels and he wrote me, "Be warned, my juvenilia are ungodly lousy, and *The Crooked Mile* is the most terrible and amusing of them all." Twenty years later, DeVoto told a friend that he had solved his life once he gave up fiction writing.

Yet it was his novels, I believe, which taught DeVoto how to lead his readers through the wilderness of historical fact. The writing of fiction is a relentless discipline, and in its exercise an author learns techniques which can serve the historian well. He learns, for instance, to manipulate scene and time, learns how to move his characters about, get them from the back porch into the kitchen. He learns how to arrange his material into a pattern or "plot," so that the reader can follow. History also has its patterns, implicit in the material and only awaiting the artist's eye to perceive and bring them out. In the management of historical time, DeVoto was especially skillful. Let me recommend to you page sixty-four of *The Course of Empire,* where DeVoto ranges freely across four hundred years, philosophically as well as chronologically — a difficult thing to do without throwing the reader into hopeless confusion. The page in itself is material for a chapter, almost for a book. We travel from 1540 to 1605, back to the medieval mind and forward to the twentieth century. Yet we emerge exhilarated by the journey and quite clear as to where we have been.

Or let us observe a still different manipulation and effect, from *Mark Twain's America.* The narrative begins and ends with Halley's comet. For DeVoto it was sheer luck that Samuel Clemens was born with the comet in 1835 and died with its return in 1910. But it was the kind of luck which comes only to the initiated, to an artist who is so absorbed in his subject that everything feeds it. Everything such a man sees, reads, hears is referred to that subject — rejected if immaterial, and if pertinent, retained with almost insane tenacity until the moment for its proper use.

Beginning and ending *Mark Twain's America* with the comet had nothing to do with historiography or scholarship. It had to do with the art of writing; it was a writer's device. Good art, the best art, is full of such devices — circus turns and sleights of hand which invariably succeed. They come off: five rabbits emerge from the hat when we looked for only one; the colored balls fly through the air and land, each in its cup. It requires technique as well as talent to break the barriers between ourselves and the past. By the time I met him in 1934, Benny DeVoto was an old pro and proud of it. By no means a professional historian, but a professional writer who referred to himself in print as "a historian, riding on the commuter's local." Not, DeVoto implied, a dweller in the sacred city, in the pure temple of the guild historian. And indeed DeVoto wandered far beyond the historian's conventional territory. For twenty years he supplied *Harper's Magazine* with monthly pieces for its department called "The Easy Chair." The Stanford University Library has a list of his published articles and editorials that covers fifty-one sheets of typewriter-sized paper. DeVoto taught at Harvard, and it was not history he taught, but writing; he taught also at the Bread Loaf Writers' Conference in Vermont. "I am," he told his wife once, "a literary department store."

He had learned how to write by writing and his experience in the field was wider than most men's. Novelists are commonly more skillful than historians in describing individuals. It is a novelist's nature to be interested in people. And his descriptions have to start from scratch. His characters are created out of air, with no contemporary portraits to help, such as the historian has — no descriptions in diaries or family correspondence. The novelist simply sits down and sweats it out until his man comes alive on the page.

DeVoto knew this. When he had a historical character to describe he assembled the documents, absorbed them thoroughly, and then started again from the beginning, *ab ovo,* as it were. Read his description of "that gnarled grizzly-hunter, Joe Meek." Or of Jim Bridger, mountain man, called Old Gabe, whose habit it was to wake in the night, throw buffalo ribs on the fire, eat hearty, and "sing Injun to himself with a tin pan accompaniment." (Captain Humfreville read *Hiawatha* aloud by the campfire and Old Gabe hated it; he never seen no Indians like them, he said.) Read DeVoto's description of the Reverend Samuel Parker, gentle scholar bound west by pack train from Middlefield, Massachusetts. Or his paragraph about the two first white women ever to cross America. Eliza Spaulding, "in heavy boots and swathed by yards of skirt," riding sidesaddle on the South Pass when trappers and Indians galloped whooping down to greet the caravan. "Eliza," writes DeVoto, "tall, naturally thin and emaciated by travel and illness, dark-haired, sallow under tan, frightened and appalled by the uproar of hospitality. And Narcissa Whitman who was neither frightened nor appalled — she was delighted. A smaller woman than Eliza but by no means emaciated, the period's ideal in womanly curves, blue-eyed, tanned now but memorably blond. Men always remembered her face and red-gold hair. Men in fact remembered Narcissa, and though she was dedicated to God's service she was charged with a magnetism whose nature no one could mistake."

For a historian, this is emancipated language. DeVoto is riding the commuter's local. We see these young women, we know them after a few sentences. DeVoto could do it more subtly when he chose, and when the occasion called for subtlety. Hear him on the flaming orator of the 1890's, William Jennings Bryan. Many historians had already described Bryan, who therefore could be disposed of with one hand. "Six years earlier," writes DeVoto (it does not matter in what connection), "the sonorous, fraudulent voice of an eater of wild honey in the hills had quieted a Chicago convention hall . . . 'You shall not crucify mankind upon a cross of gold.' "

That is all, and it is enough. It assumes a certain amount of historical knowledge on the reader's part. But even without such knowledge, one catches DeVoto's meaning. "An eater of wild honey in the hills." DeVoto's early training in the Bible served him well. Years ago, I wrote him, "Those black-haired people who brought you up must have read Scripture to you, Benny. What else would put such a roll, such a punch into your sentences?"

It is when DeVoto writes of the Mormons that his Biblical phraseology serves him best. Joseph Smith he called a man "drunk on God and glory"; Brigham Young, "an organizer of the kingdom on this earth . . . the one Mormon of history who knew how to laugh." When finally the Mormons triumphed over hardship and over continued hostility, and their city was secure and their credit good, "The Saints," wrote DeVoto, "had come into the inheritance promised them, their rivals had fallen away, their enemies had been trodden under foot or converted into business partners, their wars were ended forever, Israel was secure, the stake of Zion had been driven fast."

The DeVoto vocabulary was wide and he liked to use it; the tools of his trade felt good to his hand. The word "parallax" was a favorite, the word "eidolon," and terms like "mitosis" from the biologist's lexicon. Mark Twain he spoke of as "a maculate and episodic genius," and a certain phrase which DeVoto disliked carried, he said, "a slight taxonomic emphasis on the adjective." Yet

DeVoto was never carried away by his own virtuosity. He did not succumb to the temptation to be abstruse, to skip three arguments and confuse his readers with the clever man's ellipses. DeVoto wrote history in a conversational style, always colorful, often polemical, very difficult to achieve, and wonderfully adapted to what he had to say. There was no room for pompousness. He addressed his readers as if they were his equals — even when he was blasting off at the enemy, which was not infrequent. When occasionally he did slip into one of those large, neophilosophical statements that make for pomposity, DeVoto recognized his error and pulled up short. "The genius of the American people. . . ." Thus, in "The Easy Chair," he began a paragraph — and quickly corrected himself. "No," he wrote, "start that one over. The vigor of our democratic system and the size and richness of our continental empire. . . ."

The writing of history needs humor, and humility. And it needs affection, a fellow-feeling for mankind, a perception of motivation in human beings. It needs, in short, the novelist's eternal preoccupation with the whys and wherefores of men's actions. DeVoto had this preoccupation. Catch him any time when he was not working and he was ready to talk for hours about why a woman had said a certain thing to her child, or why a young man had not defended himself against attack. His books speak often and lovingly of "the damned human race" — a phrase he got from Mark Twain. And it was a phrase neither comic nor ironic. Man's fate is hopeless, he is doomed, and he endures his fate with valor. This is DeVoto's belief, the point of his departure and of his return. And it is the point where his fever rises when he sees this belief questioned, as with Sinclair Lewis, "who spent his talents," said De Voto, "in writing fiction that was conceived to show the contemptibility of American life." *Mark Twain's America* is a fighting book, a book with a thesis. DeVoto has an ax to grind and he grinds it till the wheel screams. His pugnacity has been deplored by his admirers as well as by his detractors. He himself admitted in print that one day he might rewrite *Mark Twain's America* and leave out the blasts against Mr. Van Wyck Brooks. I am glad he never did, because I believe that without anger this book would have fallen short of greatness. Anger drives these pages forward. Anger brings the book to life.

What was Bernard DeVoto mad at? His critics protested that they did not know, they could not find out. DeVoto, they implied, was just plain born angry, and arrogant, and insulting. What, they demanded, was his thesis? What was he defending and why did it need defense? "Has he a secret?" Edmund Wilson asked, in the

New Republic. "If so, let him stand and unfold himself. What does he want?"

DeVoto made plain enough what he wanted. I fail to see why Edmund Wilson didn't recognize it, and Sinclair Lewis, when he wrote, in the *Saturday Review of Literature,* the diatribe entitled "Fools, Liars and Mr. DeVoto." Bernard Augustine DeVoto of Ogden, Utah, born January the eleventh, 1897, wanted the facts of history told upon the printed page. He wanted to see history written from fact, not from intuition or from deduction or from the argument a priori and the flowery heights of what he castigated as "the literary mind."

It all began, of course, with DeVoto's defense of the frontier and the frontiersman. Various writers, Van Wyck Brooks among them, had intimated that life on the American frontier possessed a certain aridity. To live there would stifle artistic talent in anybody, let alone in Samuel Clemens. The frontiersman was said to be crude, subsisting at a rudimentary animal level; his life lacked every good thing which civilization possesses. From Mormon to mountain trapper, the westerners were nothing more than transplanted Puritans, with the Puritan's hatred of beauty, art, and love.

It was enough to make a Utah man shrink in his bones, or burst the boundaries of Rocky Mountain profanity. "The frontier is not a person," DeVoto retorted indignantly. "A historian does not speak of the frontier's tastes and preferences. The historian sees the frontier as many different places, in many different stages of development, inhabited by many people with many different kinds and degrees of culture, intelligence, racial tradition, family training, and individual capacity. He cannot speak of the life of the frontier, for he knows many kinds of frontiers and many kinds of people living many kinds of lives." If these literary historians would examine the facts, they would discover, for one thing, that the American people were "incurably musical. Working westward they carried fiddles and a folk art. Catgut strings were an article of commerce in the fur trade. . . . And there might be music near the three Tetons in the country of the Blackfeet."

"We must be accurate," he said further. "We must make our descriptions exact, verify our conclusions, we must avoid certainty and the loaded dice. Metaphysics is not experience and the philosophy of history is not history."

It infuriated DeVoto to have a so-called historian prefer the *must be* and the *ought to be* to the cold fact. History is not made by "thinking it out." Writers "mistake the quirks of their own emotions for the contours of objective fact." They write about the American mind, about Puritans or the frontier without having studied America, Puritans, or the frontiersman. "Authority is not born full grown," he wrote, "in any mind, nor can any one come to it by staring into his own soul, or at his navel, or into the high priest's emerald breast-plate." DeVoto could not endure man-made utopias, gospels, prophecies. He said he had had his fill of them in his youth. "Absolutes," he wrote, "are a mirage. And in my desert country, mirages are a commonplace." DeVoto, an expert on the religious sects that blossomed in the American forties of the last century, was at his ironic best when describing them. Always, when he says the word "Mormon," the pressure rises. "The Underwriters of Salvation," he called them. Mormonism was "the most colorless of American heresies," and Zion, city of the Saints, in the end "became a successful business venture, blended with the map and joined hands with the damned."

Small wonder that Ogden, Utah, did not welcome its native son on the few occasions when he returned there. In boyhood, Benny must have been a difficult child, precocious, disconcertingly quick, disconcertingly inquisitive and critical. In 1943, on my way east from Oregon, I stopped off at Ogden to see what I could find about that boy and that young man. (Even then, I wanted to write about him.) DeVoto's Aunt Martha — Mrs. Grey — told me that as a child Benny was aloof. Not a country boy by nature, but studious. His brilliant father, Florian, insisted that he study. Florian DeVoto, by the way, read Latin and Greek for his entertainment until he died. When Benny was four he could read *Hiawatha*. As a young man he was bored, his aunt said, if people talked about ordinary things. "Come down to earth," she used to tell him. "Just listen and be interested."

Before I went to Ogden I had read an early article of DeVoto's, published in the *American Mercury* when its author had not yet gone east to live. The piece opens with a discouraged tourist, descending from the Overland Limited at Ogden. I, too, stepped from that train and walked out of a station which DeVoto had called "hideous." I was confronted, as his tourist had been, with a wide flat street between ugly houses. And then I, too, looked up and saw, at either end of the street, the mountains, red, pink, yellow, and dusted with snow — mountains, DeVoto had written, "on which the gods of the Utes walked in the cool of the day."

The stories that I heard in Ogden were diverse. Some were mere gossip, all were amusing. As a child, it seems, Benny was beautiful — black-haired, with fine features; at the age of six he won a beauty contest. Then, said his Aunt Martha, he climbed on the roof and fell off and broke his nose. His friends and his enemies had been hospitable to me; one can have a good time in Ogden. But after three clear and pleasant days in the city and environs, I could see why it was that a man of intellect and imagination had to leave Ogden, had to climb onto the Overland Limited, head east, and shake the dust of Utah from his shoes. Yet I saw also how, for the rest of his life, no matter where that Ogden boy might travel, to the Ultima Thule or the seven radiant cities of Antilia, he could not forget those startling deep canyons, that mountain air, and the glowing peaks where walked the gods of the Utes. Born and raised among those dry hard mountains a man must live haunted, his life dedicated to recounting the story of that country and of the caravans which traveled to it from the east.

Bernard DeVoto lived with history, read history at night and in the morning, talked history, and was restless when other people did not want to talk history. When I began to write about John Adams, I asked him if I should buy the *Dictionary of American Biography*, known to historians as the *D.A.B.* There are twenty-one volumes and it is not cheap. DeVoto was surprised at my question and surprised that I did not already own the volumes. "Of course, buy it," he said. "It's good to read in bed at night before you go to sleep."

DeVoto lived with history and he lived with maps. I never saw such a man for maps. His last four books of history have maps for end papers; maps lined his study walls when he was working. In 1947, DeVoto came to stay with us in Bryn Mawr, Pennsylvania; he was to give a lecture on those doubtful historical characters, "The Welsh Indians." He arrived with a suitcase full of maps, big folded maps of the United States, mostly west of Council Bluffs, Iowa. He spread them on the floor of our living room and we crawled from map to map, with Benny talking, until our knees were sore and our minds enlarged with names like Ogallala, Little Blue, Three Forks, Elephant Butte, the country of the Mandans, the Arikaras, and the Blackfeet. When he left our house DeVoto gave us, as guest present, a beautiful book about maps. And he never ceased to urge upon me, to my great advantage, the study of maps — though during all those years I happened to be investigating not river, sea, and landfall but the geography of men's minds and the cosmography of their laws and constitutions.

DeVoto was generous to other writers — not a common trait among members of the union. When a manuscript needed editing he was ready with time and effort. And he was a believer in good editing; he knew there is more than one way to compose a sentence and that the right way may take some seeking. He did not spare those who came to him. The treatment was rough, and sensitive souls have been known to turn and flee at his approach. Yet he understood the writer's psychology, I think, as few men have understood it, although he declared that he seldom knew the right thing to say to authors. "They bleed on," he wrote, "from wounds healed long ago, which began by seeming mortal but turned out only to need a Band-aid or five pages of type."

Once DeVoto wrote a paragraph to me, about American history and his feeling toward it. (I have quoted this in my last book, but it's worth repetition.) The words came, remember, from a man tough-minded, who professed to write history from the facts and the facts alone. I was working, at the time, on our revolutionary period, and I had been challenged by a scholar who declared that my view of American history was too romantic altogether. The men who composed our United States Constitution were interested not in ideals but in property — their own property and its protection. George Washington only went into the army to recover his lands along the Shenandoah, and so on. In distress I wrote DeVoto, telling my chagrin because I had not made adequate rebuttal. He wrote back at once. Here is what he said:

Sure you're romantic about American history. What your detractor left out of account was the fact that it is the most romantic of all histories. It began in myth and has developed through centuries of fairy stories. Whatever the time is in America it is always, at every moment, the mad and wayward hour when the prince is finding the little foot that alone fits into the slipper of glass. It is a little hard to know what romantic means to those who use the word umbrageously. But if the mad, impossible voyage of Columbus or Cartier or La Salle or Coronado or John Ledyard is not romantic, if the stars did not dance in the sky when our Constitutional Convention met, if Atlantis has any landscape stranger or the other side of the moon any lights or colors or shapes more unearthly than the customary homespun of Lincoln and the morning coat of Jackson, well, I don't know what romance is. Ours is a story mad with the impossible, it is by chaos out of dream, it began as dream and it has continued as dream down to the last headlines you read in a newspaper. And of our dream there are two things above all others to be said, that only madmen could have dreamed them or would have dared to — and that we have shown a considerable faculty for making them come true. The simplest truth you can ever write about our history will be charged and surcharged with romanticism, and if you are afraid of the word you had better start practising seriously on your fiddle.

Contents

Contents

Acknowledgments

THE writing of history is a co-operative enterprise. Many people have helped me write this book by providing information, by directing me to the sources of information, by answering my questions, by discussing matters with me, by clearing up ambiguities, by finding ways through difficulties that had delayed me. It is impossible for me to thank them individually or even to make a full list of them. I want, however, to express my obligation to a number of them whose help has gone beyond the ordinary courtesy of the republic of letters.

Five people in particular have given me extraordinary aid. Therefore, first of all, my thanks to:—

Charles L. Camp and Dale L. Morgan, specialists, who have patiently answered innumerable questions, put their knowledge at my disposal, empowered me to publish results of their work, and made special searches for me that encroached upon their leisure time and proper interests.

Madeline Reeder, who found a way for me through a barrier that had stopped me cold and read my manuscript with critical attention to detail.

Rosamond Chapman, who began working with me on the material of this book in 1935, and has ever since been the custodian of my accuracies and my handy guide to research in the West.

Arthur M. Schlesinger, Jr., who toured the West with me in the summer of 1940 and argued out most of the book with me before it was written, who has put his own researches at my disposal, has shaped or modified many of my ideas, has critically read my manuscript, and has saved me from making a good many errors I should certainly have made except for him.

If a number of my friends who are professional historians read the book I have so insistently talked over with them, they will probably experience something halfway between shock and horror. I formally absolve them from all responsibility for anything printed in it but must insist that, by boring them for many years with talk about the West, I have formed my own ideas through friction with theirs. To Paul Buck, Arthur M. Schlesinger, Sr., Frederick Merk, Perry Miller, and Kenneth Murdock: thanks, this is in part your book, and you will see in it a part I was to build of a structure we planned together as a common job, a long time ago when I was a colleague of yours.

My thanks for help freely given to: Garrett Mattingly, Donald Born, Samuel E. Morison, Randolph G. Adams, Lewis Gannett, Franklin J. Meine, Mary Brazier, Wallace Stegner, Eleanor Chilton, Elaine Breed, Henry Canby, Edward Eberstadt, Charles P. Everitt, Mason Wade, George Stewart, Elmer Davis, Dr. Henry R. Viets, Dr. George R. Minot, Dr. William G. Barrett, Dr. Lawrence S. Kubie, Dr. Robert S. Schwab, George Stout; to the officers and employes of the Harvard College Library, the New York Public Library, the Library of Congress, the Missouri Historical Society, the Bancroft Library, and the State Library of Illinois; also to many local librarians in the West and to many Westerners whose names I do not even know, who made a summer tour fruitful in the study of history.

Quotations from *James Clyman: American Frontiersman* are by permission of Charles L. Camp and the California Historical Society.

Quotations from the unpublished notebooks of Francis Parkman are by the courtesy of Mason Wade and the permission of the Massachusetts Historical Society.

Finally, I acknowledge that I could not possibly have written the book if I had not had periodic assistance from Mr. John August.

B. DV.

Preface

THE purpose of this book as stated in the opening pages is a literary purpose: to realize the pre-Civil War, Far Western frontier as personal experience. It is, however, considerably longer than it would have been if fulfilling that purpose had not proved to involve a second job. I found that my friends and betters, the professional historians, had let me down. One who wanted to study the Far West at the moment when it became nationally important and to study it in its matrix could turn to no book that would help him very much. His only recourse was Paxson's encyclopedic treatment of the whole frontier from 1763 to 1893. Since Turner's great beginning the frontier has been a favorite subject of the profession and yet there is no unified study of the area in which this book is set in relation to its era. There are a great many specialized studies and a vast accumulation of monograph material — both of which, however, have left wholly untouched a number of matters treated herein which I have had to settle for myself. But there is no synthesis of them. The profession, in short, has broken up this phase of our history into parts; it has carefully studied most but by no means all of the parts; it has not tried to fit the parts together. And the stories I wanted to tell could not be told intelligently unless their national orientation was made clear. So perforce I have had to add to my primary job another job which it was reasonable to expect the historians would have done for me.

My hope is that, in combining the two jobs, I have not bungled both. I write for the nonexistent person called the general reader. He is here promised that, once it gets under way, my text does not long depart from actual events in the lives of actual men and women. In getting it under way I have chosen the stern but kinder way of throwing at him a first chapter of grievous weight. If he survives that, he will find things happening from then on.

By the end of the first chapter, also, the method of the book will be clear. The actual narrative is always rigorously chronological, and the parts of the book are kept as close to a chronological order as the multiplicity of stories will permit. In passages designed to illustrate or interpret the narrative, however, I range forward and backward in time as far as the end in view requires. Thus the narrative of my first chapter covers the month of January, 1846, but some of the quotations from Walt Whitman belong to 1847 and some of those from Thoreau date back to 1843 and forward to 1849. Similarly, I not only allude to the Presidential campaign of 1844 but follow some of its issues back to La Salle and on to 1942. Usually such departures from chronology are immediately self-apparent; where they are not, I have called attention to them.

Acknowledgments and a statement about bibliography are made separately.

BERNARD DEVOTO

CAMBRIDGE, MASSACHUSETTS
February 12, 1942

Calendar for the Years 1846–1847

[1846]

JANUARY	5	Resolution to terminate joint occupation introduced in Senate.
	7–10	Frémont at Sutter's Fort.
	12	Word received of Slidell's rejection by Mexico.
	13	Taylor ordered to the Rio Grande.
	24–27	Frémont to Monterey.
FEBRUARY	3	Taylor receives orders.
	4	Mormons begin crossing the Mississippi.
	13	Polk's interview with Atocha.
	22	Frémont starts for the coast.
	22	Gillespie embarks at Mazatlán.
MARCH	1	First Mormon wagons start across Iowa.
	3	Burning of the Phalanstery at Brook Farm.
	5–9	Frémont at Gavilán Peak.
	8–11	Taylor starts for Rio Grande.
	20	Slidell notified of Mexico's refusal to negotiate.
	21	Frémont reaches Sutter's Fort.
	28	Taylor reaches the Rio Grande.
	30	Frémont reaches Lassen's ranch.
APRIL	7	Polk learns Slidell will not be received.
	5–11	Frémont to Mt. Shasta and return.
	17	Clyman meets Hastings.
	17	Gillespie reaches Monterey.
	19	Taylor orders the Rio Grande blockaded.
	23	"Termination" passes Congress.
	24	Frémont starts for Oregon.
	25	First hostilities on the Rio Grande.
	29	Hastings-Clyman party starts over the Sierra.
MAY	8	Battle of Palo Alto.
	9	Battle of Resaca de la Palma.
	9	News of hostilities reaches Washington.
	9	Gillespie overtakes Frémont.

	13	Polk signs resolution that a state of war exists.
	15	Boggs and Thornton parties reach the rendezvous.
	18	Taylor occupies Matamoros.
	22	National Fair opens.
	24	Frémont reaches Lassen's ranch on way south.
	31	Clyman and Hastings reach Great Salt Lake.
June	7	Clyman and Hastings reach Fort Bridger.
	10	Bear Flaggers capture Castro's horses.
	11	Susan Magoffin sets out from Independence.
	12	Congress votes to accept 49th parallel.
	14	Attack on Sonoma and birth of the "California Republic."
	14	First Mormons reach the Missouri.
	15	Parkman reaches Fort Laramie.
	16–29	Army of the West leaves Fort Leavenworth for Santa Fe.
	18	Clyman reaches South Pass.
	25	Frémont arrives at Sonoma.
	26	Russell-Reed-Donner-Boggs train reaches Fort Bernard.
	27	Thornton, Clyman and Parkman reach Fort Bernard.
July	2	Sloat arrives at Monterey.
	2	Clyman meets the Mississippi Mormons.
	6	Taylor starts up the Rio Grande.
	9	Sonoma taken over by the United States.
	16	Parkman rejoins the Oglala village.
	17	Bryant reaches Fort Bridger.
	18	Thornton crosses continental divide.
	19	Frémont marches into Monterey.
	20	Bryant and Hudspeth leave Fort Bridger.
	21–22	Mormon Battalion starts for Fort Leavenworth.
	26	Susan Magoffin reaches Bent's Fort.
	26	Frémont dispatched to San Diego.
	26	Bryant reaches Great Salt Lake Valley.
	28	Donners reach Fort Bridger.
	28–30	Army of the West reaches Bent's Fort.
	29	Frémont raises flag at San Diego.
	31	Taylor takes Camargo.
	31	Donners leave Fort Bridger.
August	1	Mormon Battalion reaches Fort Leavenworth.

1–2 Kearny leaves Bent's Fort.
3 Bryant crosses the Salt Desert.
3 Fall of Paredes government.
3 Parkman returns to Fort Laramie.
6–11 Donner party in camp on the Weber.
7 Thornton reaches Fort Hall.
8 Frémont starts north from San Diego.
8 Wilmot Proviso introduced.
12 Cooke and Magoffin reach Santa Fe.
12–27 Donner party crosses the Wasatch.
13 Mormon Battalion leaves Fort Leavenworth.
14 Frémont and Stockton occupy Los Angeles.
16 Santa Anna arrives at Vera Cruz.
18 Kearny occupies Santa Fe.
19–25 Taylor reaches Cerralvo.
20 Parkman at Pueblo.
22 Thornton reaches the Humboldt.
26 Bryant crosses the Sierra.

SEPTEMBER 1 Bryant reaches Sutter's Fort.
5 Carson starts east with Stockton's report.
3–8 Donner party crosses the Salt Desert.
17 Remaining Mormons driven from Nauvoo.
20–24 Battle of Monterrey.
23–25 Wool leaves San Antonio for Chihuahua.
25–28 Kearny leaves Santa Fe for California.
30 Donner party reaches main trail.

OCTOBER 4 Gillespie evacuates Los Angeles.
circa 5 Harlan-Young party crosses the Sierra.
6 Kearny meets Kit Carson.
9–12 Mormon Battalion reaches Santa Fe.
9 Susan Magoffin starts south.
19 Stanton returns to the Donner party.
19 Mormon Battalion leaves Santa Fe.
27 Stockton reaches San Pedro.

NOVEMBER 1, 3, 12, 21 Unsuccessful attempts by Donner party to cross the divide.
13 Mormon Battalion leaves the Rio Grande.
15 Conner captures Tampico.
16 Taylor occupies Saltillo.
17 "Sick detachment" joins the Mississippi Saints at Pueblo.

	18	Thornton reaches the Willamette Valley.
	18	Scott given command of Vera Cruz expedition.
	20–22	Rendezvous of Doniphan's detachments at Bear Spring.
	22	Kearny reaches junction of Gila and Colorado.
	27	Last refugees from Nauvoo reach Winter Quarters.
December	2	Kearny reaches Warner's ranch.
	5	Wool occupies Parras.
	6	Battle of San Pascual.
	9	Mormon Battalion reaches the San Pedro.
	12	Kearny reaches San Diego.
	12–23	Doniphan's command assembles at Doña Ana.
	16	Mormon Battalion reaches Tucson.
	16	The "Forlorn Hope" sets out.
	25	Battle of El Brazito.

[1847]

January	10	Los Angeles reoccupied.
	10–11	Mormon Battalion crosses the Colorado.
	17	Eddy reaches the settlements.
	19	Revolt at Taos.
	29–30	Mormon Battalion reaches San Diego.
February	4	Reduction of the pueblo at Taos.
	4	First Relief leaves Johnson's.
	5	Doniphan leaves El Paso for Chihuahua.
	22	First Relief starts back over the Sierra.
	22–23	Battle of Buena Vista.
	28	Battle of the Sacramento.
March	1	Second Relief reaches Donner cabins.
	1–2	Doniphan occupies Chihuahua.
	11–17	Third Relief.
	23	Fourth Relief starts.
	29	Surrender of Vera Cruz.
April	7–15	Mormon pioneers rendezvous at Elkhorn River.
	8	Scott advances into the interior of Mexico.
	13–25	Final relief expedition, under Fallon.
	16	Pioneer party starts west.
	18	Battle of Cerro Gordo.
	25–28	Doniphan marches from Chihuahua.
May	15	Scott occupies Puebla.

JUNE	1	Pioneer party reaches Fort Laramie.
	16	Kearny starts east.
	22–28	First Missouri discharged at New Orleans.
	26–27	Pioneer party crosses South Pass.
	28	Pioneer party meets Bridger.
	30	Sam Brannan meets the pioneer party at Green River.
JULY	14	Kearny meets first westward-bound emigrants.
	21	Pratt and Snow reach Great Salt Lake Valley.
	22	Main party arrives.
	24	Brigham Young arrives.
AUGUST	19–20	Battles of Contreras and Churubusco.
SEPTEMBER	14	Fall of Mexico City.

Invocation

WHEN I go out of the house for a walk, uncertain as yet whither I will bend my steps, and submit myself to my instinct to decide for me, I find, strange and whimsical as it may seem, that I finally and inevitably settle southwest, toward some particular wood or meadow or deserted pasture or hill in that direction. My needle is slow to settle — varies a few degrees and does not always point due southwest, it is true, and it has good authority for this variation, but it always settles between west and south-southwest. The future lies that way to me, and the earth seems more unexhausted and richer on that side. The outline which would bound my walks would be, not a circle, but a parabola, or rather like one of those cometary orbits which have been thought to be non-returning curves, in this case opening westward, in which my house occupies the place of the sun. I turn round and round irresolute sometimes for a quarter of an hour, until I decide, for the thousandth time, that I will walk into the southwest or west. Eastward I go only by force; but westward I go free. Thither no business leads me. It is hard for me to believe that I shall find fair landscapes or sufficient wildness and freedom behind the eastern horizon. I am not excited by the prospect of a walk thither; but I believe that the forest which I see in the western horizon stretches uninterruptedly toward the setting sun, and there are no towns nor cities in it of enough consequence to disturb me. Let me live where I will, on this side is the city, on that the wilderness, and ever I am leaving the city more and more and withdrawing into the wilderness. I should not lay so much stress on this fact if I did not believe that something like this is the prevailing tendency of my countrymen. I must walk toward Oregon, and not toward Europe.

HENRY THOREAU

THE YEAR OF DECISION:
1846

I
Build Thee More Stately Mansions

THE First Missouri Mounted Volunteers played an honorable part in the year of decision, and looking back, a private of Company C determined to write his regiment's history. He was John T. Hughes, an A.B. and a schoolmaster. Familiarity with the classics had taught him that great events are heralded by portents. So when he sat down to write his history he recalled a story which, he cautions us, was "doubtless more beautiful than true." Early in that spring of 1846, the story ran, a prairie thunderstorm overtook a party of traders who were returning to Independence, Missouri, from Santa Fe. When it passed over, the red sun had sunk to the prairie's edge, and the traders cried out with one voice. For the image of an eagle was spread across the sun. They knew then that "in less than twelve months the eagle of liberty would spread his broad pinions over the plains of the west, and that the flag of our country would wave over the cities of New Mexico and Chihuahua."

Thus neatly John T. Hughes joined Manifest Destiny and the fires that flamed in the midnight sky when Caesar was assassinated. But he missed a sterner omen.

The period of Biela's comet was seven years. When it came back in 1832 many people were terrified for it was calculated to pass within twenty thousand miles of the earth's orbit. The earth rolled by that rendezvous a month before the comet reached it, however, and the dread passed. In 1839 when the visitor returned again it was too near the sun to be seen, but its next perihelion passage was calculated for February 11, 1846. True to the assignment, it traveled earthward toward the end of 1845. Rome identified it on November 28 and Berlin saw it two days later. By mid-December all watchers of the skies had reported it. The new year began, the year of decision, and on January 13 at Washington, our foremost scientist, Matthew Maury, found matter for a new report.

Maury was a universal genius but his deepest passion was the movement of tides. In that January of '46 he was continuing his labor to perfect the basis for the scientific study of winds and current. Out of that labor came the science of oceanography, and methods of reporting the tides not only of the sea but of the air also that have been permanent, and a revolution in the art of navigation. But he had further duties as Superintendent of the Naval Observatory, and so by night he turned his telescope on Biela's comet. That night of January 13, 1846, he beheld the ominous and inconceivable. On its way toward perihelion, Biela's comet had split in two.

This book tells the story of some people who went west in 1846. Its purpose is to tell that story in such a way that the reader may realize the far western frontier experience, which is part of our cultural inheritance, as personal experience. But 1846 is chosen rather than other years because 1846 best dramatizes personal experience as national experience. Most of our characters are ordinary people, the unremarkable commoners of the young democracy. Their story, however, is a decisive part of a decisive turn in the history of the United States.

Sometimes there are exceedingly brief periods which determine a long future. A moment of time holds in solution ingredients which might combine in any of several or many ways, and then another moment precipitates out of the possible the at last determined thing. The limb of a tree grows to a foreordained shape in response to forces determined by nature's equilibriums, but the affairs of nations are shaped by the actions of men, and sometimes, looking back, we can understand which actions were decisive. The narrative of this book covers a period when the manifold possibilities of chance were shaped to converge into the inevitable, when the future of the American nation was precipitated out of the possible by the actions of the people we deal with. All the actions it narrates were initiated, and most of them were completed, within the compass of a single calendar year. The origins of some of them, it is true, can be traced back as far as one may care to go, and a point of the book is that the effects of some are with us still, operating in the arc determined by 1846. Nevertheless, the book may properly be regarded as the chronicle of a turning point in American destiny within the limits of one year.

This is the story of some people who went west in 1846: our focus is the lives of certain men, women, and children moving west. They will be on the scene in different groupings: some emigrants, some soldiers, some refugees, some adventurers, and various heroes, villains, bystanders, and supernumeraries. It is required of you only to bear in mind that while one group is spotlighted the others are not isolated from it in significance.

Our narrative will get them into motion in the month of January, 1846. But the lines of force they traveled along were not laid down on New Year's Day, and though our stories are clear and simple, they are affected by the most complex energies of their society. They had background, they had relationships, and in order to understand how an inevitability was precipitated out of the possible, we must first understand some of the possibilities. We must look not only at our characters but at their nation, in January, 1846.

The nation began the year in crisis. It was a crisis in foreign relations. The United States was facing the possibility of two wars — with Great Britain and with Mexico. But those foreign dangers had arisen out of purely domestic energies. They involved our history, our geography, our social institutions, and something that must be called both a tradition and a dream.

Think of the map of the United States as any newspaper might have printed it on January 1, 1846. The area which we now know as the state of Texas had been formally a part of that map for just three days, though the joint resolution for its annexation, or in a delicate euphemism its "reannexation," had passed Congress in February, 1845. Texas was an immediate leverage on the possible war with Mexico. Texas had declared itself a republic in 1836 and ever since then had successfully defended its independence. But Mexico had never recognized that sovereignty, regarded Texas as a Mexican province, had frequently warned the United States that annexation would mean war, and had withdrawn her minister immediately on the passage of the joint resolution which assured it.

In the far northwestern corner our map would tint or crosshatch a large area to signify that it was jointly occupied by the United States and Great Britain. This area would include the present states of Oregon, Washington, and Idaho, and small parts of Montana and Wyoming lying west of the continental divide. It would also include a portion of Canada, extending northward to agree with the political sentiments of the map maker, perhaps as far north as a line drawn east from the southern tip of Alaska. The whole area was known simply as "Oregon" and it was an immediate leverage on the possible war with Great Britain. For the President of the United States had been elected on a platform which required him to assert and maintain the American claim to sole possession of all "Oregon," clear up to 54° 40′, that line drawn eastward from southern Alaska,* and on January 1 the British press was belligerently resenting his preparations to do so.

West of Texas and south of Oregon, from the Pacific Ocean to the continental divide and the Arkansas River, was a still larger area which our map would show as Mexican territory. This area included the present states of California, Nevada, Utah, Arizona, New Mexico, and parts of Wyoming and Colorado. It was composed of two provinces, "California" and "New Mexico," but no American map maker could have approximated the theoretical boundary between them. It too was a powerful leverage, though not often a publicly acknowledged one, on the possible war with Mexico.

It is of absolute importance that no map maker of any nationality, even if he had been able to bound these vast areas correctly, could have filled them in. Certain trails, certain rivers, long stretches of certain mountain ranges, the compass bearings of certain peaks and watersheds, the areas inhabited by certain Indian tribes—these could have been correctly indicated by the most knowledgeful, say Thomas Hart Benton and the aged Albert Gallatin. But there were exceedingly few of these and the pure white paper which the best of them would have had to leave between the known marks of orientation would have extended, in the maps drawn by anyone else, from the Missouri River and central Texas, with only the slightest breaks, all the way to the Pacific. That blank paper would almost certainly have been lettered: "Great American Desert."

The Great American Desert is our objective—"Oregon," "New Mexico," and "California"—the lands lying west of the Louisiana Purchase. Like the Americans who occupied them, however, we must also deal with Texas, the newly annexed republic. The sum of these four geographical expressions composed, on January 1, 1846, the most acute crisis in foreign relations since the Treaty of Ghent had ended the second war with Great Britain in December, 1814, and they were bound together in what can now be understood as a system of social energies. Just how they were bound together will (the hope is) be clear by the end of this book, and we must begin by examining some of the far from simple reasons why they had produced the crisis. It will be best to lead into them by way of the man who in part expressed and in part precipitated the crisis, the President, hopefully called by some of his supporters "Young Hickory," James K. Polk.

* Really from the southern tip of Prince of Wales Island.

Two years before, in the summer of 1844, the first telegraph line brought word to Washington that the Democratic convention, meeting in Baltimore, had determined to require a two-thirds vote for nomination. The rule was adopted to stop the comeback of ex-President Martin Van Buren, who had a majority. That it was adopted was extremely significant — it revealed that Van Buren had defeated himself when he refused to support the annexation of Texas. The convention was betting that the spirit of expansionism was now fully reawakened, that the annexation of Texas was an unbeatable issue, that the Democrats would sweep the country if factionalism could be quelled. Smoke-filled rooms in boarding houses scorned President Tyler (whose renomination would have split the party in two), and would not take General Cass, John C. Calhoun, or Silas Wright, all of whom were identified with factions that were badly straining the party. Factionalism, it became clear, was going to be quelled by the elimination of every prominent Democrat who had ever taken a firm stand about anything. So presently the telegraph announced that George Bancroft, with the assistance of Gideon Pillow and Cave Johnson and the indorsement of Old Hickory in the Hermitage, had brought the delegates to agree on the first dark horse ever nominated for the Presidency, Mr. Pillow's former law partner, James K. Polk.

"Who is James K. Polk?" The Whigs promptly began campaigning on that derision, and there were Democrats who repeated it with a sick concern. The question eventually got an unequivocal answer. Polk had come up the ladder, he was an orthodox party Democrat. He had been Jackson's mouthpiece and floor leader in the House of Representatives, had managed the anti-Bank legislation, had risen to the Speakership, had been governor of Tennessee. But sometimes the belt line shapes an instrument of use and precision. Polk's mind was rigid, narrow, obstinate, far from first-rate. He sincerely believed that only Democrats were truly American, Whigs being either the dupes or the pensioners of England — more, that not only wisdom and patriotism were Democratic monopolies but honor and breeding as well. "Although a Whig he seems a gentleman" is a not uncommon characterization in his diary. He was pompous, suspicious, and secretive; he had no humor; he could be vindictive; and he saw spooks and villains. He was a representative Southern politician of the second or intermediate period (which expired with his Presidency), when the decline but not the disintegration had begun.

But if his mind was narrow it was also powerful and he had guts. If he was orthodox, his integrity was absolute and he could not be scared, manipulated, or brought to heel. No one bluffed him, no one moved him with direct or oblique pressure. Furthermore, he knew how to get things done, which is the first necessity of government, and he knew what he wanted done, which is the second. He came into office with clear ideas and a fixed determination and he was to stand by them through as strenuous an administration as any before Lincoln's. Congress had governed the United States for eight years before him and, after a fashion, was to govern it for the next twelve years after him. But Polk was to govern the United States from 1845 to 1849. He was to be the only "strong" President between Jackson and Lincoln. He was to fix the mold of the future in America down to 1860, and therefore for a long time afterward. That is who James K. Polk was.

The Whigs nominated their great man, Henry Clay. When Van Buren opposed the annexation of Texas, he did so from conviction. It was only at the end of his life, some years later, that Clay developed a conviction not subject to readjustment by an opportunity. This time he guessed wrong—he faced obliquely away from annexation. He soon saw that he had made a mistake and found too clever a way out of the ropes which he had voluntarily knotted round his wrists. Smart politics have always been admired in America but they must not be too smart. The Democrats swept the nation, as the prophets had foretold. It was clear that the Americans wanted Texas and Oregon, which the platform had promised them. Polk, who read the popular mind better than his advisers did, believed that the Americans also wanted the vast and almost unknown area called New Mexico and California.

They did. Polk's election was proof that the energy and desire known as expansionism were indeed at white heat again, after a period of quiescence. This reawakening, which was to give historians a pleasant phrase, "the Roaring Forties," contained some exceedingly material ingredients. Historians now elderly made a career by analyzing it to three components: the need of certain Southern interests and Southern statesmen to seize the empty lands and so regain the power which the increasing population of the North was taking from them, the need of both Northern and Southern interests to dominate the Middle West or at least maintain a working alliance with it, and the blind drive of industrialism to free itself to a better functioning.

Now all those elements were certainly a part of the sudden acceleration of social energies signified by the election of 1844. But society is never simple or neat, and our elder historians who thus analyzed it forgot what their elders had known, that expansionism contained such other and unanalyzable elements as romance, Utopianism, and the dream that men might yet be free. It also contained another category of ingredients — such as the logic of geography, which the map of January 1, 1846, made quite as clear to the Americans then as it is to anyone today. You yourself, looking at a map in which Oregon was jointly occupied by a foreign power and all the rest of the continent west of Texas and the continental divide was foreign territory, would experience a feeling made up of incompletion and insecurity. Both incompletion and insecurity were a good deal more alive to the 1840's than anything short of invasion could make them now. And finally, expansionism had acquired an emotion that was new — or at least signified a new combination. The Americans had always devoutly believed that the superiority of their institutions, government, and mode of life would eventually spread, by inspiration and imitation, to less fortunate, less happy peoples. That devout belief now took a new phase: it was perhaps the American destiny to spread our free and admirable institutions by action as well as by example, by occupying territory as well as by practising virtue. . . . For the sum of these feelings, a Democratic editor found, in the summer of '45, one of the most dynamic phrases ever minted, Manifest Destiny.

In that phrase Americans found both recognition and revelation. Quite certainly, it made soldiers and emigrants of many men (some of them among our characters) who, without it, would have been neither, but its importance was that it expressed the very core of American faith. Also, it expressed and embodied the peculiar will, optimism, disregard, and even blindness that characterized the 1840's in America. As we shall see, the nation which believed in Manifest Destiny came only by means of severe shock and after instinctive denial to realize that Manifest Destiny involved facing and eventually solving the political paradox, the central evasion, of the Constitution — slavery. But it is even more indicative of the 1840's that those who rejected the innumerable statements of Manifest Destiny, repudiated its agencies, and denied its ends, believed in Manifest Destiny. Let Brook Farm speak for them — Brook Farm, the association of literary communists who had withdrawn from the world to establish Utopia a few miles from Boston.

For the Brook Farmers, certainly, did not speculate in Western lands and so cannot come under the economic interpretation of expansionism. Neither were they the spirit of industrialism: they had organized with the declared purpose of nullifying industrialism. Nor were they political adventurers, conspirators, or opportunists: they had formally announced their refusal to adhere to the American political system. But Manifest Destiny had no clearer or more devout statement, and the 1840's had no more characteristic expression, than the editorial which the Brook Farmers published in optimism's house organ, *The Harbinger,* when the curve of the year 1846 began to be clear: —

> There can be no doubt of the design being entertained by the leaders and instigators of this infamous business, to extend the "area of freedom" to the shores of California, by robbing Mexico of another large mass of her territory; and the people are prepared to execute it to the letter. In many and most aspects in which this plundering aggression is to be viewed it is monstrously iniquitous, but after all it seems to be completing a more universal design of Providence, of extending the power and intelligence of advanced civilized nations over the whole face of the earth, by penetrating into those regions which seem fated to immobility and breaking down the barriers to the future progress of knowledge, of the sciences and arts: and arms seem to be the only means by which this great subversive movement towards unity among nations can be accomplished. . . . In this way Providence is operating on a grand scale to accomplish its designs, making use of instrumentalities ignorant of its purposes, and incited to act by motives the very antipodes of those which the real end in view might be supposed to be connected with or grow out of.

Thus the literary amateurs: it violates our principles but is part of a providential plan. As Providence's instrumentality Polk was much less woozy. Shortly after he was inaugurated, he explained his objectives to George Bancroft, the scholar, historian, and man of letters who had been a Democratic Brain-Truster since Jackson's time, and whom Polk would make acting Secretary of War, Secretary of the Navy, and finally Minister to Great Britain. His objectives were: the revision of the protective tariff of 1842, the re-establishment of the independent treasury, the settlement of the Oregon question, and the acquisition of California. He was to achieve them all.

Of the four objectives which Polk named to Bancroft, the one that immediately concerns us was the acquisition of California. He understood that there was a possibility of war with Mexico over Texas. But he hoped to avoid that war and to use Texas, instead, as a step toward the acquisition of California. He hoped to move on the vast Western area, that is, by way of opportunities which had been provided by the annexation of Texas.

The naïve mythology called economic determinism has provided an outline of the earlier history of Texas which is still too widely accepted in our thinking. This outline describes Texas as a kind of American Sudetenland. It goes something like this: —

At the height of the last great surge of western expansion, a colony of American expatriates was planted in the unsettled territory of Mexico. The Mexican government welcomed them; it required them to become citizens and Catholics but otherwise granted them greater autonomy and more privileges than the generality of Mexicans possessed. The colonists came mainly from the Southern states and the surge that carried them to Texas was the same one that peopled the lush cotton lands of the states variously called the New South or the Old Southwest. They took to Texas with them the institutions of Protestant America. Among these institutions were land banks, land loans (with their speculative possibilities), and African slavery; the first two foreign to the Mexican economy, the third forbidden by Mexican law. The colony flourished in a fat land, carefully observed by the proprietors of certain American interests who clearly understood that new slave territory would be required to balance the rapidly filling areas which, because they were north of the Missouri Compromise line, were free territory. In due time the Mexican government perceived that the Texans, instead of being assimilated, had become the spearhead of an all too probable invasion. Thereupon it tried to repair its mistake, it tried to govern Texas. But Mexico had awakened too late. The Texans intended to preserve their institutions (primarily slavery) and they intended to join themselves to the sovereignty of the United States. They declared themselves independent, and after some fighting made good. The revolution was assisted by money, arms, munitions, and volunteers from the United States — on the specious excuse that Americans were being oppressed in a foreign land, were denied civil and religious liberties there, and were being massacred by a despotic power. American help was decisive and the imperialists, both American and Texan, were due to cash in on their speculation soon afterward, with the annexation to the United States of a territory large enough to make four or five slave states.

But here, the naïve mythology says, annexation ran into a double barrier. The manufacturing interests of the North (using the Abolitionists as a screen) opposed the spread of the slave economy, and the panic of 1837 made it impossible to finance the war which, so Mexico warned us, annexation would precipitate. So down to 1844, while the American economic system stumbled, sprawled, staggered toward equilibrium, and repeatedly collapsed, the republic of Texas had to exist unannexed but under an undeclared American protectorate, and had to fight an intermittent guerrilla war with Mexico. This war also was supported with money, men, and munitions by the Southern interests, which were only waiting their time. Meanwhile those same interests took care to distribute the bonds of Texas and its land-purchase scrip so widely in the United States that opposition to annexation disappeared from large areas. By 1844 bonds and scrip had modified the sentiments and American economy was expanding, so that it was possible to try again. There remained a good device, an appeal to the liveliest American sentiment. Texas threatened to form an alliance with France or Great Britain, and even to accept a protectorate under either. This was a threat to cotton and slave labor, and so would kill whatever opposition might exist in the South. It was also a threat to cotton manufacture and it meant the repudiation of the Monroe Doctrine; so it ought to force the North to accept Texas. If any opposition should remain in the North, however, it could be ended by coupling Texas with the acquisition of Oregon, which would gratify imperialists and pacify Abolitionists. It was enough, the myth says. The pieces were fitted together, the campaign was fought in '44, and the expansionist Democratic Party came into power.

It makes a pretty picture and most separate parts of it are in some degree true, but the picture is false. There was, to begin with, no conspiracy. There was a noisy bloc of pro-slavery expansionists who openly wanted more slave territory and openly agitated for it, as they had every right to do. They were by no means in control — it was not till the mid-1850's that the South could organize a really powerful expansionist movement for more land. They were opposed by other blocs fully as vociferous, among them many slave owners and many spokesmen of other Southern interests. It is true that some of the excited oratory reported in the *Congressional Globe* does represent more or less directly the ownership of Texas bonds and land scrip. But the sum of both could hardly have bought the support of one of the midwestern counties which actually turned the scale (counties which, moreover, risked their spare cash on their own land banks), and the farm boys who hurried to die in Mexico owned no Texas scrip. Again, if the colonization of Texas was a spearhead, then it penetrated not a populous, developed, and organized civilization but an empty waste. Few Mexicans lived there in '46, practically none when the colony was made. The occupation of Texas neither usurped nor absorbed a community, a culture, or an economy. Instead, it created all three.

Moreover, it is a fundamental mistake to think of Mexico, in this period, or for many years before, as a republic or even as a government. It must be understood as a late stage in the breakdown of the Spanish Empire. Throughout that time it was never able to establish a stability, whether social or political. Abortive, discordant movements of revolution or counter-revolution followed one another in a meaningless succession, and each one ran down in chaos from which no governing class ever arose, or even a political party, but only some gangs. Sometimes the gangs were captained by intelligent and capable men, sometimes for a while they stood for the merchants, the clergy, the landowners, or various programs of reform, but they all came in the end to simple plunder. Furthermore, the portions of Mexico with which we are concerned, Texas, New Mexico, and California, were precisely the portions where Spain's imperial energy had faltered and run down. To this frontier Great Spain had come and here it could go no farther, here it began to ebb back. It had succeeded most in the genial California lands, but not much and long ago, much less in New Mexico, least of all in Texas. Stephen W. Kearny and Alexander Doniphan brought more safety, stability, and hope to the New Mexicans in two months than Spain had found for them in two centuries, or Mexico after Spain. The annexation of Texas was a tragedy to some Mexicans but it was not a tragedy for Mexico. It was the last episode in the erosion of an empire.

When Polk took office, in March, 1845, his narrow, clear mind harbored no doubts about Texas. He accepted the orthodox Democratic position. Our theoretical "right" to Texas rested on claims that ran clear back to La Salle—and may possibly have been clear once. We had ceded away our right in 1819, but that was a blunder in statesmanship. But, whatever the legal claim, Texas was independent; Mexico did not recognize the independence but it was a fact. Finally, by the time Polk was inaugurated all discussion of claims and rights and sovereignties had become academic. President Tyler had correctly interpreted the election of Polk as a mandate for annexation. He failed to get a two-thirds vote in the Senate by treaty, but, in the closing hours of his administration, he put it through by joint resolution. (The same difficulty is a fixed pattern of our history.) Though Texas did not ratify it until July and was not formally a state of the Union till December, Polk regarded it, on March 4, 1845, as a part of the United States and as such entitled to protection.

If Texas was in danger, and the warmth of Mexican resentment indicated that it was, then to defend it was certainly Polk's duty. Since we had annexed a boundary dispute as well, there remained the question of just what Texas was. Part of that intricate and ancient question involved a strip one hundred and twenty miles wide between the Nueces River, on the north, and the Rio Grande. Texas claimed this almost uninhabited strip but had made no attempt to occupy it. Mexico, which did not recognize Texas as either independent or annexed, claimed that the strip belonged to the states of Tamaulipas and Nuevo León. The Texas claim had no substance; it was purely metaphysical. But it had great value and high potentialities for Polk, who was thinking well beyond Texas. That claim could be used as a move in the game of high politics whose objective was the acquisition of California. The first thing to do was to assert it.

Therefore in mid-June, 1845, a month before Texas ratified annexation, six months before it became a state, Polk had William Marcy, his Secretary of War, order the army under Zachary Taylor to take a position south of the Nueces — cautioning him, however, to treat any Mexican troops he might encounter with punctilious courtesy. Between three and four thousand troops had been concentrated at Fort Jesup, Louisiana, for some time, with precisely this step in mind. By the end of July Taylor got his forces to Corpus Christi, a minute Mexican seacoast village just inside the disputed strip. Polk's intention was clear: this was a show of force intended to give the Mexicans a sense of reality in the settlement of various matters he now intended to take up, among them the purchase of California. But, though a show of force, it was not, in Polk's mind, an invasion. It was a protective occupation. Whatever the right term may have been, the army was at Corpus Christi still on January 1, 1846.

. . . All the military operations of the ensuing three years, excepting only those commanded by Winfield Scott and Stephen W. Kearny, are iridescent with what must be called fantasy. One encounters it at once in Old Rough and Ready, as newspaper correspondents were soon to call Zachary Taylor. And the army was composed of the kind of men who could be induced to join it at a time when it was held in popular contempt, when Congress thought of it as a mere posse and paid it badly and barely equipped it at all, and when any capable male who could speak English could get a job or a farm almost anywhere. Dispersed in squads and platoons over half a continent, it had had two jobs: to transfer Indians to worse lands when the frontier wanted their homesteads, which it usually contrived to do, and to defeat them when they went on the warpath, which it could seldom do without the help of militia. Staffed in the upper ranks by oratorical veterans of 1812, some of them approaching senility, it had a good many brilliant younger officers who had been well trained at West Point and were now to serve an apprenticeship that would fit them for the more serious business that was to follow fifteen years later.

And it had Ethan Allen's grandson, who was to be Taylor's executive brain, as W. W. Bliss, soon to be his son-in-law, at once became his military brain and political manager. Lieutenant Colonel Ethan Allen Hitchcock commanded the 3d Infantry and, effectively, the encampment at Corpus Christi. He succeeded in giving a destitute mob far from its base something like food and shelter, something like organization, and even something like discipline, if not much like it. He could not give Taylor intelligence, however, and our first Expeditionary Force knew nothing of its prospective enemy's whereabouts or intentions, tried to learn nothing about them, and hardly patrolled its own camp. Nor could he give the army morale. They drank bad water and sickened; they drank bad whiskey and brawled. Their rations gave them scurvy, the food they bought from sutlers and Mexicans gave them dysentery. Two thousand camp followers, gamblers, and whores got their money. Officers made themselves, in Hitchcock's words, a "public scandal." He dealt with them as he could, treated his own severe illness (which Dr. Beaumont, the famous observer of Alexis St. Martin's gastric juice, had been unable to cure in St. Louis), and pursued his studies in mystical philosophy.

This extraordinary man had no illusions about the invasion and used no euphemisms. He had written that Polk's election meant "a step towards the annexation of Texas first and then, in due time, the separation of the Union." He tranquilly maintained that conviction while he labored to get food and self-respect for his troops. He court-martialed officers for publicly consorting with prostitutes and made notes on the hermetic mysteries. He wrote on New Year's Day, 1846, that it went as other days did, "drinking, horse-racing, gambling, theatrical amusements," and stayed in his tent reading Mrs. Shelley's *Rambles in Germany and Italy,* in which he saw "no evidence of talent." Through January he buried the dead, fed the living, heard rumors of war with Mexico and war with England, read Spinoza's *Ethics* and copied out in longhand his brother's translation of it. And from the swamps of Corpus Christi he began a correspondence with Henry Wadsworth Longfellow about the writings of the mystics whom Rossetti had translated. . .

In June of '45 Polk did not think of a protective occupation as war. He thought clearly about many things but never about war. Sixteen years short of Fort Sumter, there were few people anywhere in America who thought clearly about it. War was militia muster-day, it was volunteers shooting Seminoles in the Florida swamps, it was farmers blowing redcoats to hell from behind stone walls, most of all it was embattled frontiersmen slaughtering Wellington's veterans at New Orleans. It was rhetoric, a vague glory, and at bottom something that did not imply bloodshed. Polk, who was deliberately risking two wars at once, believed that the Americans could win both without fighting either one. He believed that the Texas question could be settled without fighting — that the settlement of it, in fact, could be used as a leverage for the acquisition of California. He was thinking about California with the greatest clarity. War would be the direct way to get it and as a last recourse he was quite willing to fight for it, but he thought that even a bloodless war would be unnecessary.

While he was preparing the show of force, he called on the diplomatic arm. The Mexican minister had demanded his passports immediately on the passage of the joint resolution for the annexation of Texas. Soon after he was inaugurated, Polk sent an emissary to inquire whether Mexico would receive an envoy. The emissary was to make clear that the contemplated negotiations would not involve any payment for Texas, which had been annexed in strict accordance with the usages of nations — but he was to intimate that a reasonable gratuity to ease the Mexican grief at parting could be arranged in due time. In August the emissary reported that the Mexican government would probably receive a commissioner. Commodore Conner, who commanded a squadron that had been sent to conduct practice maneuvers in Mexican waters, confirmed his belief. So in November, '45, Polk appointed John Slidell envoy extraordinary and minister plenipotentiary to Mexico.

Slidell was to explain the propositions which covered Polk's intentions and desires. The Monroe Doctrine was to be reaffirmed throughout the hemisphere. (This was in response to persistent British attempts to impede or prevent the annexation of Texas and, in some degree, in response to vaguer aggressions, French as well as British, farther south. In December, '45, Polk's message to Congress would for the first time make the Monroe Doctrine a genuine force in the international relationships and would add to it an express prohibition of protectorates in the New World. This addition, which pivoted squarely on Texas and California, is sometimes called the "Polk Doctrine.") Also, Mexico was to pay the long unpaid claims against her made by the American citizens, which a commission had adjudicated. The Rio Grande was to be acknowledged as the boundary and the disputed strip thus given to Texas. Once more it was to be made clear that we would not pay a cent for Texas. But, when the claims should be acknowledged and the Rio Grande accepted as the boundary, the United States would assume the claims and pay them. Furthermore, if Mexico would accept the Rio Grande as the boundary throughout its length, east as well as north, thus adding half the present state of New Mexico to the area of Texas, the United States would add a further tip of five million dollars.

These propositions were extremely sophisticated. The claims, which could serve as a legal case for waging war, were an adjudicated two million dollars out of a much larger sum which American citizens said they were owed, mostly for damage, confiscations, and loss of life during a quarter century of revolutions. Mexico, being forever bankrupt, could not pay them in cash but only in land. But any Mexican government which might cede territory to the United States would, as the Herrera government did at the end of December, '45, stop governing at once. The bland offer for the eastern half of New Mexico was a mere talking point, and an atrociously forced one at that. The idea that Texas extended west as well as south to the Rio Grande was not even metaphysical. The Texans had positively asserted it just once, in 1841, when they sent a diplomatic, military, and marauding expedition toward Santa Fe. (Including some American volunteers and newspaper correspondents.) The New Mexicans cut it to pieces, slaughtered some of its members, imprisoned others, and nailed the ears of still others to the Governor's Palace. There followed guerrilla episodes which made the word *Tejano* as odious in Santa Fe as it was south of the border and were to keep New Mexico quite uninterested in the solicitations of the Confederate States of America in '61.

Clearly there was room here to swing a cat in. The cat was not New Mexico, though New Mexico was thus publicly joined to the Texas settlement for the first time. It was another, carefully unmentioned province, California. So we must now glance at the golden shore.

We have noted the extent of California on a map dated January 1, 1846—with New Mexico, it included the present states of California, Nevada, Utah, Arizona, New Mexico, and parts of Wyoming and Colorado. We have also noted the extent of "Oregon" on such a map — Oregon, Washington, Idaho, parts of Wyoming and Montana, and northward into Canada, perhaps as far as 54° 40′. Well, in 1844, Sam Houston, then ending his second term as president of Texas, drew a map. It showed the domain his nation was eventually to occupy, the extent of its manifest destiny, if the movement for the annexation to the United States should fail. Houston's map has its merit as prophecy. If Texas could not be American, then Texas was eventually to include Oregon, New Mexico, and California — as defined above. It was also to include the Mexican state of Chihuahua and thence westward to the Pacific. And it was to include Arkansas, Louisiana, Tennessee, Mississippi, Alabama, Georgia, Florida, the Carolinas, and Virginia. That is, the republic of Texas was to cover, besides some territory which is Mexican today, precisely the extent of the Far West and the Confederate States of America.

Probably there were, on January 1, 1846, a few members of the slavery bloc who hoped to approximate Houston's map. Just before

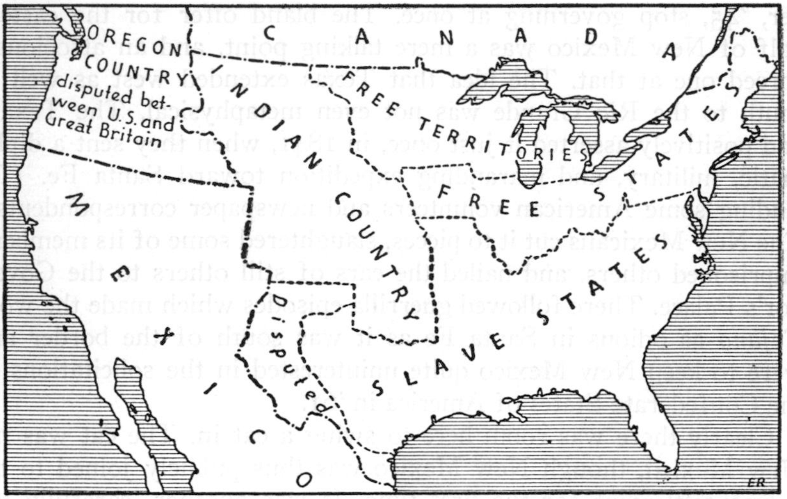

Free and Slave States in 1846

the peace treaty of 1848 a considerable agitation broke out, North as well as South, to seize large areas of Mexico, even all of it. By the middle of the 1850's, Southern Democrats could demand Mexico and Cuba as a right implicit in the order of nature, and by the end of the decade they were adding Central and South America. But in '46, even the few who looked toward more of Mexico than Polk did hardly knew what they meant by California. It is not clear that Polk knew what he meant by it. Expansionism, North or South, included California, but this meant little more than a recognition of Monterey, where the trade in hides centered, and a lively realization of the geographical importance of San Francisco Bay.

Benton, Allen, all the warhawks, wanted California. John Quincy Adams, who had said that there were laws of politics as fixed as the laws of mechanics and they would bring Cuba tumbling in our lap like Newton's apple — Adams had wanted California and had warmly advocated acquiring it till, like some other expansionists, he had a premonition of its linkage with slavery. Andrew Jackson had tried to buy California. When he failed, his envoy advised him to take it by guile or force. Hardly a year passed without some enthusiast repeating the suggestion in the Senate or the House.

But this California was almost entirely dream, a dream vague but deep in the minds of a westering people. Slowly it had begun to be more than dream. Yankee shipowners had long ago established the trade in hides and tallow which still flourished and about which Richard Henry Dana had written his masterpiece. Yankee merchants had followed them, to provide the province with its only merchandise, most of its currency, and a picturesque if precarious sliver of the old China trade. A few of these had acquired large land grants from the somnolent government or married into families that held such grants, and had been completely absorbed in the native way of life. Yankee whalers put into Monterey and, once the Russians had withdrawn from it, the Bay of San Francisco. There were a few runaway sailors, a few fugitives from justice, a few romantics and dream-drugged escapists; these mingled with their like from other nations and the large tolerance of the Californians welcomed them all. Finally, the last four years had seen an entirely different, more purposive kind of arrival — small handfuls of John Does in white-tops who had turned off the Oregon trail at the Bear River and headed southward for the Sacramento.

In spite of all this, it would be difficult to overstate the ignorance of California in the United States. Oregon, which was wilderness with a thin population of immigrants, where there were only the fur trade and the small, precarious trade which the immigrants had been able to organize — Oregon was known thoroughly. It had had years of sedulous advertising by missionaries, military explorers, traders, merchants, sailors, trappers, propagandists, and such publicists as Hall Kelley. Benton, Linn, and their fellow expansionists had its history, geography, and statistics by heart — if attractively colored by their private fantasies. Polk need only send to the Library of Congress for any information he might want. But California was universally unknown. Of all the vast space east of the Sierra it was impossible to know anything except for the records of the fur trade and the few trails scratched across the deserts — and it does not appear that anyone now in official life except Benton knew any useful part of this. Even the great valleys between the Sierra and the sea, even the genial, pastoral, hospitable life of the Californians, were little known. As late as '46 no detailed, dependable map of California existed. There were few trustworthy descriptions, in English, of any part east of the coastal towns. Newspapers published letters from shipmasters or their passengers who touched the coast — romantic, flamboyant, packed with fable and misunderstanding. The War Department had a handful of reports, fragmentary, in great part inaccurate, ignored by everyone but Benton: it is not certain that Polk had ever heard of them. There were half a dozen books: the President had not read them. Lately the State Department had made a shrewd and intelligent merchant, Thomas O. Larkin, consul at Monterey. His reports were the one dependable source of information.

Polk, who intended to acquire California, and by war if necessary, knew little about it. He was the dream finding an instrument. . . . As he opened the great game, an anxiety hurried him. The tension over Texas might develop into war with Mexico, quite apart from the great game — and California remained bound to Mexico by a gossamer only, if at all. If the war should come, might not California seek a protectorate under Great Britain? It seemed possible, even likely — and a French or a Prussian protectorate was not inconceivable. The State Department learned that small native movements for independence and other movements for a foreign protectorate showed themselves from time to time. That was ominous — and there was something else. We were preparing to face and force the Oregon question. Might not Great Britain actually seize California, to strengthen both her military and her diplomatic position in Oregon? Plenty of sober minds besides Polk's thought she might, and behind that fear was one which the new nation had inherited in 1785 and as far back as there had been white men in America, the dread that Europe might set a limit to our development. It was playing its last stand now, continentally at least, and in fact there had ceased to be any basis whatever for it. A British government which was eager to settle the Oregon question and promote free trade with the United States had no designs on California. Nevertheless Polk's anxiety was genuine and understandable.

In any event, measures looking toward the outbreak of war, if war should come, had to be prepared. So in June, 1845, almost simultaneously with Marcy's orders to Taylor, Bancroft, the Secretary of the Navy, sent secret and confidential instructions to Commodore John D. Sloat, an elderly fuss-budget who commanded the Pacific Squadron. If Sloat should learn that Mexico and the United States were at war, he was to seize the harbor of San Francisco (the only part of California whose importance was clearly understood) and to blockade the other ports. Meanwhile, whether or not war should come, there were other expedients. So in October, James Buchanan, the Secretary of State, sent secret and confidential instructions to Thomas Larkin at Monterey, who had been made consul for exactly this purpose. They came to this: Larkin was to take advantage of any native revolutionary movements he might nose out (there were always a number) and was to do everything in his power to induce the Californians to break the gossamer that held them to Mexico and set up for themselves; then he was to guide them into asking for annexation to the United States. Texas series, second impression.

Everything in this book is under the iron domination of time and distance. There was no telegraph except a few miles on the Atlantic Coast. There was no radio, no Western railroad, no air mail. On the Pacific Coast and in Willamette Valley there was mail only by sailing ship or by courtesy of ox train overland.

Buchanan's instructions to Larkin were sent in the frigate *Congress* by way of Cape Horn and the Sandwich Islands. Also a copy of them was intrusted to Lieutenant Archibald H. Gillespie of the Marine Corps, who was ordered to travel by ship to Vera Cruz, overland across Mexico to the Pacific, and then to Honolulu and on to Monterey. At 8 P.M. on October 30, 1845, Polk had a "confidential conversation" with Lieutenant Gillespie at the White House. What he said during that conversation was not entered in his diary and historians have been arguing about it ever since. (Later entries, however, prove that Polk gave Gillespie no additional instructions.) Gillespie sailed four days later and, though no one knew it, Polk least of all, the conquest of California had begun.

Furthermore, Lieutenant Gillespie was instructed to seek out Brevet Captain John Charles Frémont, of the United States Topographical Engineers, who was expected to be in or near California, at the head of an exploring expedition, and who was the son-in-law of Senator Benton. He carried private letters from Benton and Frémont's wife.

Frémont had left St. Louis in June of '45 on his third exploration of the West, instructed to map the central watershed of the Rockies, to complete his examination of Great Salt Lake, and to obtain information about the Cascade and Sierra Nevada Mountains. (In that third requirement, the War Department was planning to reduce the difficulties of emigrants on the last stage of the Oregon trail, and, much farther along, we shall see Jesse Applegate doing what Frémont had been ordered to do.) He would thus be on the frontiers of Oregon and California at a time expected to be critical, and if there seems to be a certain convenience in having an army officer and sixty armed men on hand there, let it stand.

A similar convenience attended two other expeditions sent out by the War Department during that same summer of '45. Lieutenant Abert of the Topographical Engineers was ordered to explore northwestern Texas and northeastern New Mexico, either on or near the route to Santa Fe. There could be no pretense of exploring the trail between Fort Leavenworth and South Pass, which was as well marked as Pennsylvania Avenue, so Colonel Stephen Watts Kearny, the ablest frontier officer, and five companies of his crack regiment, the First Dragoons, were sent to awe the Indians . . . along the trail by which not only emigrants but armies as well, if armies should be needed, would move to Oregon.

With Oregon we have reached our third objective, the last political preliminary we must scrutinize, and the portion of the crisis in foreign relations which, on January 1, 1846, was felt to be most immediate and most dangerous. Through the month of January, '46, readers of *Niles' Register* might study a department called "Are We to Have Peace or War?" very much as readers of *Time,* through the summer of 1939, studied a department called "Background for War." The war which *Niles' Register* was talking about was war not with Mexico but with Great Britain, and the news magazine, in common with most informed people, considered this war much the more likely of the two. If war with Great Britain should break out, it would be precipitated by the Oregon question. That question was at boiling point in January, and had been at boiling point since the preceding August. In fact, it was on August 26, 1845, that

President Polk began to keep a diary of his administration. He opened it with notes on a Cabinet discussion of the Oregon question. The Oregon question was a question of the extent of Oregon.

For our purposes, that ancient and extremely involved controversy can be reduced to a simple statement. Russian claims to any part of the West Coast south of 54° 40′ (the southern tip of Alaska) had been extinguished in 1824 and 1825, by treaty. All Spanish claims to land north of 42° had been ceded to the United States in 1819. The conflicting British and American claims to the lands between those boundaries and west of the continental divide had not been settled. By the Convention of 1818, renewed in 1828, that settlement was in abeyance and the lands were jointly occupied, each nation having the right to renounce the convention at a year's notice. The extreme American position held that Oregon was ours to the boundary of the Russian lands, 54° 40′. The extreme British position was that we had no valid claim north of the Columbia River. What had prevented the British from accepting the several times offered compromise boundary of the 49th parallel was that this would have cut them off from the southern end of Vancouver Island and denied them access by the strait of Juan de Fuca. (They also wanted the right to navigate the Columbia.) What had lately made 54° 40′ a battle cry was the reawakened energy of expansionism.

Polk appears to have been willing to fight for "all of Oregon" when he was elected but by Inauguration Day he was not so sure. Closer thought about Mexico had cooled Polk down but among the people the momentum of campaign emotions was not easily braked. Orators who had twisted the lion's tail on the stump went on twisting it in Congress, the press could not be called off, and the electorate which had been told that Oregon was ours up to 54° 40′ kept on clamoring for 54° 40′. Rhetoric had succeeded much too well, the British press was roaring back, and Polk was already embarrassed. His inaugural address delicately receded from the campaign. Our title, he said, was "clear and unquestionable." What title? "Our title to the country of Oregon." Not to the campaign slogan, "all of Oregon." The difference was big enough to let a weasel through.

It was not wide enough for the British press, however, nor even for the Peel government. That government had readily abandoned its intrigues in Texas as soon as annexation was accomplished. It was doing its best to negotiate a tariff agreement with the United States. It had one Irish problem on its hands and, as the potato crop began to fail, foresaw that it would soon have another one.

As a little-England government, it had no dialectical desire for Oregon. Furthermore, it had a sheaf of recent reports which added up to the double conclusion that the Americans had established themselves in Oregon beyond any hope of getting them out and that Oregon was certainly not worth fighting for. (Just for good measure, as soon as it had negotiated a settlement it got another report from an investigating commission which had had to live under canvas, had found the country insufficiently supplied with hot water for bathing, and wanted nothing whatever to do with Oregon.) But the torchlight procession and campaign oratory over here had roused the hair-trigger contempt of the English for Cousin Jonathan, the late provincial. There was a popular uproar which the government could not disregard. The right questions were asked in Parliament and there was a bustle of activity in naval ports.

This badly frightened James Buchanan, the gentleman politician who had the greatest possible shrewdness but no backbone whatever. It also salted Polk's ideas with realism. A President who had already sent to Mexico stipulations likely to be unacceptable and had arranged to occupy California with a small and antique navy, if the stipulation should prove unacceptable, would find himself inconvenienced if he had to fight a skirmish with the mistress of the seas. In this clearer state of mind, he saw that relations with Great Britain had drifted into a crisis and must not be allowed to drift any longer. He moved to settle them. The campaign pledge of 54° 40′ could be avoided by pointing out that the President was bound to renew the offers of his predecessors. They had all tried to compromise the conflicting claims with the 49th parallel, which was the boundary from the Great Lakes to the continental divide. So through the summer of '45 Polk tried to negotiate a settlement at the 49th parallel. But Pakenham, the British minister, not only understood the powerful leverage of the intensifying Mexican crisis, but in the natural course of things was bound at first by the traditional policy of his country: when an opponent offers concessions, you can get bigger ones by holding out. Pakenham would not close for 49°.

British firmness threw Buchanan into a panic and from then on he was for appeasement, though his attitude swung in a small arc as he maneuvered his most abiding interest, a nomination to the Supreme Court as a step toward the Presidency. He felt that negotiations could be continued only if Pakenham's demands were met, that anything else would mean war. Polk was not frightened, and Pakenham's adroitness had made him mad. He saw that the minister was playing diplomatics by the textbook, and he too knew the rules. So in late August of '45 he forced the timorous Secretary of State to notify Pakenham that, following the refusal of Her Majesty's government to accept the compromise, the President no longer felt himself bound by the policy of his predecessors and from now on would not be interested in any offer short of the whole of Oregon, up to 54° 40′. When Pakenham promptly tried to reopen with a bid for 49°, provided only that the President would openly invite the concession, Buchanan all but wept with relief. The President was not interested, and he remained uninterested through the autumn, while the press of both countries screamed. Then on December 2, in his message to Congress, he played his ace. When the conflicting claims to Oregon had been stabilized *in statu quo,* both countries had accepted a joint right of occupation. This "joint occupancy" had been renewed ten years later but the treaty provided that it could be ended on formal notification one year in advance. In his message to Congress, Polk asked that the one year's notice be sanctioned now. He went on to advise that American legal jurisdiction be extended over Americans in Oregon (as they had been vehemently demanding for more than two years), and that land grants be made at the expiration of the stated year. He summarized his efforts to settle the controversy, rehearsed the British refusals to compromise, repudiated the British claim to the territory north of the Columbia River, and took occasion to restate the Monroe Doctrine at such length that, acquiring additional point from Texas and California, it began to develop the binding force it has been exercising ever since. And he said that we had "reached a period when the national rights in Oregon must either be abandoned or firmly maintained." Also that "they cannot be abandoned without a sacrifice of honor and interest."

That was war talk, and it was received as such at home and abroad. British cartoonists promptly drew Cousin Jonathan licked and cowering, and Congress resounded with sixty years of British perfidy. Mass meetings blossomed across the country. Polk was a hero in the Middle West for the first time, and the War and Navy Departments consulted with Congressional committees to prepare war measures. (They made no preparations, however.) In the Senate Lewis Cass shouted that it was better to fight for the first inch of territory than for the last, and Allen of Ohio, Chairman of Foreign Affairs and the most extreme warhawk, rejoiced that his candidate was holding fast to his pledge after all and would procure his war. Even the Western Whigs rejoiced likewise, though

Daniel Webster perfectly expressed the ideas of the manufacturing interests, saying that Oregon was too far away for either us or the English to make anything of it — its destiny was to be an independent Anglo-Saxon republic. (Herman Melville could not approve of Allen. In *Mardi* he appears as Alanno of Hio-Hio, an "unfortunate lunatic" who is "ferociously tattooed" and has "his hands full of headless arrows." "Laboring under violent paroxysms" in the Temple of Freedom, Alanno repeatedly breaks loose from his guards to "burst anew into his delirium," though no one pays much attention to him. Yet, for all his derision of Alanno and of a colleague in tail twisting, Nulli-Calhouni, a "cadaverous ghost-like man" lashing the back of Hamo's tribe, Melville also was building a more stately mansion to the westward. Farther to the westward, in fact, than his nation has got so far. He believed that "America can hardly be said to have any western bound but the ocean that washes Asia.")

On January 5, 1846, a resolution to terminate the joint occupation of Oregon was introduced in the Senate, and now all the forces were committed, all the movements were under way, from here on there could be no turning back. Buchanan's alarm had steadily increased and he warned the President that the country, which was supporting 54° 40′ with a sustained roar, would not support it. And on January 4, Representative Black of South Carolina, as perturbed as Buchanan, had called at the White House to say that the war fever of the Western Congressmen had alarmed the following of Mr. Calhoun, who would therefore vote against termination. He pleaded with the President to recede from his stand. Polk replied to Mr. Black

> that the only way to treat John Bull was to look him straight in the face; that I considered a bold & firm course on our part the pacific one; that if Congress faultered or hesitated in their course, John Bull would immediately become arrogant and more grasping in his demands & that such had been the history of the Brittish Nation in all their contests with other Powers for the last two hundred years.

One goal to the President. Polk had reached bedrock in British-American relations. It may be said that he not only looked John Bull in the face but struck him in the head with a blunt instrument, but he had the right idea. While Buchanan trembled and a second thought began perceptibly to sober Congress and the press, he tranquilly waited for England to settle on his original terms. He prepared one of the ingenuities that enable Presidents to back down without losing face. When John Bull was ready to accept 49°, Polk would, he decided, invoke a clause of the Constitution which it is usually the first concern of the administration to avoid. He would submit the anticipated offer to the Senate, not for its "consent" but for its "advice." By that time developments in Mexico could be counted on to put the Senate in a mood to advise the compromise.

So his diary is untroubled throughout January. His days are broken by the office seekers, "more importunate than meritorious," whom the uncomplicated Republic had not yet dared to bar from the executive office. He sits for his portrait to Mr. Healy, sent by France to immortalize both him and Old Hickory. Very bored, he conscientiously spends two hours at the Jackson Day banquet, his party's annual debauch of oratory. He attends the Presbyterian Church with Mrs. Polk and their nieces, but is scrupulous to honor Justice Catron by attending Catholic services on one Sunday. He wins two skirmishes with the Senate, over appointments.

Another skirmish develops serious trouble when the Senate rejects his nomination of George W. Woodward as Associate Justice of the Supreme Court. At first the villain responsible seems to be Mr. Cameron of Pennsylvania, who may have been piqued by Polk's failure to appoint Mr. John M. Read. But Polk had unanswerable reasons for not appointing him. Mr. Read was once a Federalist and it is the President's duty to protect the purity of our judicial institutions. Polk records an observation: he has never seen a Federalist who professed to change his opinions later than the age of thirty who did not revert to "broadly Federal and latitudinarian" opinions as soon as he received a life appointment. Presently, however, the carefully begotten rumors of Washington inform the President that not Mr. Cameron swayed the Senate but Mr. Buchanan: the city hears that the Secretary of State is going to get the appointment. So there is intrigue in the Cabinet — and perhaps that explains Buchanan's timidity. And clearly Buchanan is violating the pledge he signed before his appointment, to which Polk made all the Cabinet sign their names, not to use his office to advance himself toward the Presidency. Polk's integrity is affronted: if it shall prove that Buchanan has worked against Woodward's appointment, he will dismiss him. Buchanan glooms like Hamlet at Cabinet meetings, then sulks and opposes frivolous or capricious objections to the Oregon policy. Now the rumors begin to hint that he will break with the administration and resign. But "Mr.

Buchanan will find that I cannot be forced to act against my convictions, and that if he chooses to retire I will find no difficulty in administering the Government without his aid."

In fact, the President's emotions were so roused by Buchanan's intrigue that he did not record in his diary the arrival in Buchanan's department of news from Mexico which, the event proved, was much more important than the intrigue or than any news from England. A report came from Slidell, the minister plenipotentiary, informing his chief that the Herrera government, to which he was accredited, had fallen on December 31 and a junta had appointed General Paredes y Arrillaga, who had once deposed Santa Anna, president *pro tem.*

This was one more gang revolution, arranged in the name of patriotism and deriving its force from the supreme Mexican contempt of Americans. (For if a certain condescension toward Mexicans is discernible in Polk's attitude and his assumption that they would not fight, all classes and degrees of Mexicans despised the Yankees and knew that they neither would nor could fight.) The Herrera government had lately been infected with a little realism and had shown signs of being willing to negotiate with the United States about the boundary of Texas. The army officers who overthrew it were laying a bet on war, on the cowardice of Yankees, and on the illusory hope that Great Britain would support them against us. Crowds were sent shouting through the streets, the signs of American merchants were pulled down, bells rang, musketry was fired, and Paredes went in. . . . In Mexico City a traveler in mufti who was using an alias found his journey delayed by these demonstrations. Deeply impressed, Lieutenant Gillespie of the Marine Corps committed to memory the confidential dispatches he was carrying, destroyed them, and as soon as the city grew quiet under its new jingo hurried on to Mazatlán. The impression which these firecrackers made on him was the second step in the conquest of California.

Slidell told his government that Paredes, who stamped into office with some gorgeous rhetoric and an appeal to the consciences of France and England, would neither care nor dare to receive him. (He was right. Paredes could hold his office only by accepting war.) He retired to Jalapa to await word from Paredes and instructions from home.

Those instructions were prepared at the end of January. Slidell was told to demand his passports if he should not be duly received. For (this is eight weeks after Polk's irretrievable defiance of Great Britain in his message to Congress, three weeks after the irretrievable resolution was introduced in the Senate) "the cup of forbearance will then have been exhausted. Nothing can remain but to take the redress of the injuries of our citizens and the insults to our Government into our hands." It had taken two weeks to prepare this gambit in diplomacy. But it took less than twenty-four hours to open with the military. On the day after Slidell's dispatch was received, the Secretary of War initiated another irretrievable sequence of actions by sending orders to General Taylor, in command of the protective occupation. Taylor, at Corpus Christi, was just south of the Nueces River, just inside the strip of disputed territory. His new orders bade him march to the boundary in dispute,· the Rio Grande (as Taylor had been clamoring to do), and to take up a position there. However, Secretary Marcy enjoined him to show a scrupulous regard for the invaded Mexicans. Let him do nothing whatever to antagonize them.

But, he was further cautioned, it might be a good idea to post sentinels. The Mexicans, who were known to be a hotheaded people, might make some retaliation.

We have stated a number of political forces — primarily political forces, that is — which in January, 1846, were focused on the lands we are concerned with. In that January between two thousand and twenty-five hundred Americans, variously distributed through the States, knew that they would begin a journey across the Great American Desert, toward Oregon and California, as soon as the prairie grass should freshen. Between fifteen and twenty thousand others knew that, at some time during the year now beginning, they would be forced to abandon their homes (in Illinois mostly) and begin a journey toward an undetermined destination somewhere in the Great American Desert. These people knew — or thought they knew — something of what the year held in store for them. Thousands of other Americans would be soldiers this year because these forces would make them soldiers. Many thousands would cross Texas to invade Mexico, several thousand would cross a portion of the Great American Desert bound for New Mexico and beyond, and still others, crossing that desert or sailing round the Horn, would be dispatched to occupy California.

Yet to represent even the energies so far named as purely political would be to misrepresent Manifest Destiny. In separating out the political strains from that great composite we have already done violence to the early morning vigor of the time. Perhaps the best recourse would be to forgo analysis altogether and to take refuge in the phrase which Dr. Holmes would not make into a poem for ten years yet, the phrase prefixed to this chapter of analysis. For, looking at the Americans in the year of decision, one sees them primarily engaged in building more stately mansions, at least in intent. Yet that would be to shirk a plain necessity and before we can be free to start our emigrants, refugees, and soldiers westward we must state at least one other energy that was operating on them. It too is subtly misrepresented when it is isolated from the system of energies of which it was a part, but be assured that it too had a direct bearing on Oregon, New Mexico, and California.

There were sixteen inches of ice on Walden Pond, and it undulated under a slight wind like water. Mornings, Henry Thoreau woke with a feeling that he had not answered some question asked him during sleep, but there was no question on Nature's lips. He took an axe and chopped through snow and ice but, before drinking, gazed at the sandy bottom where "waveless serenity reigns as in the amber twilight sky." Heaven, he decided, is under our feet as well as over our heads. He watched men fish through the ice for pickerel and went about a job he had set himself, to plumb the bottom of Walden, which was locally believed to have no bottom. He found it at one hundred and two feet, then, after plotting a chart, discovered that the line of greatest length intersected the line of greatest width exactly at the point of greatest depth. Might this not correspond to the law of average? Might not the two diameters of a man's thought similarly be used to determine exactly how and where his depth went down? Henry thought so, and he went on to see whether White's Pond would show the same regularity. It did.

He had cleared his plot above the lake front the preceding spring, while Polk pushed his foreign policy in the direction of war. He had planted his beans and raised the walls of his shack while Frémont and Kearny headed west, had mortared his chimney while Buchanan prepared Gillespie's instructions, and had plastered the walls while Pakenham fished through the President's ice to determine how much he must concede. These things had no present notice in Henry Thoreau's mind. He was conducting an experiment in economy. He had looked at the twin wonders of the age, the developing industrial system and the certainty of universal moral reform, and had seen no need to pay tribute to either. The first chapter of *Walden* accurately analyzes the bank failures, bond repudiations, mortgages, farmsteads, and factories of the thirties and forties, but Thoreau's experiment dealt with a preliminary, or antecedent, problem, the survival of the mind's integrity in such a system. In Arcadia he had seen no one pounding stone, and he wanted to free himself from subjection to horses, plowing, and the day's waste—as the system would have to do if it were to inclose his loyalty. His house cost him twenty-eight dollars and a shilling; at the end of a year he had needed $25.21¾ to live on. (He appears not to have discussed capitalization with the Provident Institution.) Meanwhile he had written *A Week on the Concord and Merrimac Rivers,* beginning it, very likely, during the January of Mr. Buchanan's insubordination, and had begun the notes that were to acquire form in *Walden.* He had also acted as inspector of snowstorms and rainstorms, and had proved conclusively that "it is not necessary that a man should earn his living by the sweat of his brow, unless he sweats easier than I do." . . . What else he had proved we shall see.

There was a further element in Thoreau's expatriation from Concord. The village had reached a tension of conversational reform. Emerson had observed that "Mr. Alcott and Mr. Wright cannot chat or so much as open the mouth on aught less than a new solar system and the prospective education in the nebulae." Thoreau, though he inexplicably thought Alcott so great a man that nature could not let him die, began to repudiate his conversation as soon as the Walden pines shut off the rhythms of that noble drool. Henry had stayed too long among the pure and garrulous; he felt that his manners had "been corrupted by communication with the saints." Concord had suggested to him that the reforms and liberations it exhaled in sitting rooms might not be a cure of the world's ills but only for dyspepsia. "What so saddens the reformer," he had come to think, "is not his sympathy with his fellows in distress but, though he be the holiest son of God, is his private ail." Truly, wailing did come up from Southern plains, but was it the wailing alone of blacks, and just how shall we begin to act on it? Just what intemperance and brutality would best serve for the beginning of redemption? "If anything ail a man, so that he does not perform his functions, if he have a pain in the bowels even, for that is the seat of sympathy, he forthwith sets about reforming — the world."

Here Henry was glancing at Harvard Village, ten miles northwest of Walden, where at Fruitlands the pain in Mr. Alcott's bowels had not succeeded in bringing in the rule of right reason, though it had reformed the world for some months. More particularly, toward West Roxbury, where the far happier Brook Farmers, in smocks, ignorant of the catastrophe preparing for them, hated Polk but praised Providence for using him as an instrument, and spent the January evenings chatting and munching apples before log fires, reading *Consuelo* for beautiful sentiments and, as preparation for the more stately mansion they were building, Fourier's *Theory of the Human Passions.*

The smock wearers also were making an experiment in economy, and they were very happy. The newest Newness made amazing progress, they loved one another and humanity, the children did so marvelously well in the progressive school. Everything was so clear, so easily hand-tinted with pretty words, though it was among the benefits of Association that they came less and less to need words, the twitch of an eyebrow conveying a philosophy and the intuitions so sharpening that they could read letters by simply pressing the envelope against the forehead. This showed how their "right development" refined the passions. Wrong development, which the world's people suffered, produced selfishness, injustice, duplicity; but right development produced harmony, justice, unity. Charles Fourier told them so, who was part Alcott and part Marx. Under Association, which was Fourier's principle of economy, right development would go farther still. It would soften and regulate the temperature (a desirable achievement in January at West Roxbury) and increase the warmth at the poles, correct the heat of the equator, bring on eternal springtime, fertilize the desert, and prevent the drying up of streams. Moreover, it would domesticate the beaver and the zebra to man's uses and increase the fish in lakes and rivers some twenty-fold. (Thus Mr. Albert Brisbane, translating Fourier. He omitted Fourier's further promise that lions would turn into anti-lions, a soothed, humanitarian species, other savage carnivores into playful anti-beasts, and the great sea itself into soda pop.) Association would also put an end to larceny, there would be no theft, no sharp business practices; nine tenths or more of the diseases that afflict man under incoherence or Civilization would disappear, and men would live three times as long. Moreover, Zachary Taylor's profession would be obsolete and fleets and armies would wither away So much for Polk.

(Right development had not yet, however, produced the anti-cow. Nathaniel Hawthorne, who had bought two $500 shares in Brook Farm and would later sue to get his money back, had had to flee Association because he could no longer bring himself to fork the bright, symbolic gold out of the stalls.)

Two months short of final extinction, there burned here more appealingly than anywhere else a hope that had built more than two score communities in the last two decades, most of them already dead. It was the design of Brook Farm: "1. To indoctrinate the whole people of the United States with the principles of associative unity. 2. To prepare for the time when the nation, like one man, shall reorganize its townships on the basis of perfect justice." Thus American millennialism had changed its phase: it had given up Christ in favor of Refined Passions and Virtuous Labor. In the earlier phase, the expectation of perfect sainthood in the immediate (or the oncoming) Kingdom of God had begotten such associations as the Shakers, the Latter-day Saints, the Rappites, and the Disciples of Christ. In the new phase a different perfection was expected, perfect justice as an outgrowth of perfect co-operation — the co-operation, that is, of literary people.

Industrialism had spread its first great wave across the countryside, and a misunderstood abhorrence of its bleak factories oppressed sensitive spirits. The sensitive found only two courses: they could flee from industrialism or they could master it with virtue. The first era of Brook Farm, now over, had attempted flight: the literary raking hay in yellow pantaloons, a small but elevated company baking their bread from their own handmade flour to Plato's dream, presumably as an inspiration to greasy mechanics and stunted factory girls. There were many similar companies of the sensitive, and they had reached perihelion at Fruitlands, where the Great Inane voiced thoughts while Mrs. Alcott and the children gathered in the barley, a poor wench was excommunicated for eating a shred of vile flesh, and in the end Alcott turned his face to the wall and hoped to die because virtue had failed. Of forty such congregations, John Humphrey Noyes, who may be granted authority, said that they failed because right reason was not a working substitute for the grace of God, and because you could not defeat industrialism with plow and scythe.

For the others, those who would master industrialism with virtue, Charles Fourier was the way and the light, and the second era of Brook Farm was dedicated to him. Fourier promised the sensitive that the hideous factories could be transformed into beauty. You refined the passions. You dignified and ennobled labor. You made industry the more attractive as its operations were the more laborious and unpleasant. You put Corinthian columns round the prison house of labor and built it in "fields beautifully laid out and diversified by clusters of fruit and forest trees, flower beds, and fountains." You supplied band concerts and bright uniforms and a series of Eagle Scout badges for the ennobled mechanics. You beguiled the children by inducing them to play in little workshops with little tools. And again and always you refined the passions, inviting mankind to change its heart, to enter into the womb and be born again a second time, to sink the brute and bring the angel in.

Yet mortgages had to be paid, the brute lingered and the angel delayed, and the literary ended in despair. Between Charles A. Dana of Brook Farm, going out to sound Association's trumpet call by lecturing on "Reform Movements Originating among the Producing Classes," and Charles A. Dana of the *Sun,* the century's ablest public disbeliever in mankind, is just the paradox that in all ages overcomes the literary dream. The literary will accept no hybrid of brute and angel; they desire Utopia and will not settle for the human race. They love the people but they hate the mob. On George Ripley's word, and he was the founder of Brook Farm, mankind is dwarfed and brutish. In that common despair ended all that Association had to say.

We are to see several answers to George Ripley worked out to the westward. And at Walden another answer was worked out, to Ripley and to all the decade's reforms as Henry Thoreau saw them. Might not the pain in a reformer's bowels, Thoreau wondered, be just an egoism that debauched his cause? It was necessary to rescue the drowning but also you must tie your shoestrings. Most men lived lives of quiet desperation, and Thoreau could not see that they grew more desperate in factories than on farms, in colleges, or at reason's feast in Mr. Alcott's house. He went down to talk to the Irishmen who were building the Fitchburg railroad, whose whistle he welcomed without a shudder. The railroad was industrialism but also it was making toward Oregon. He anticipated Mr. MacLeish in perceiving that "the rails are laid on them and they are covered with sand, and the cars run smoothly over them." But he would waste no sorrow on them so long as farmers must be subject to their cattle or any man whatsoever was involved in "bankruptcy and repudiation, the springboards from which much of our civilization vaults and turns its somersets."

In short, Thoreau believed that the factory could not be fled from and that it could not be beautified by refining the passions. Labor was dignified only as the laborer was not thought dwarfed and brutish but granted membership in the human race. And with the race, he told his listeners, you must go much farther back than you have ever dreamed. He who wants help wants everything. Nothing can be effected but by one man. You may begin by sawing the little sticks, or you may saw the great sticks first, but sooner or later you must saw them all. So on the banks of Walden he sat him down, "in the Presidency of Polk, five years before the passage of Webster's Fugitive Slave Bill," to grow his beans and write his book. It was not by chance that when Henry Thoreau went out to walk his needle settled west.

American literature gained a flowerier Brook Farm, this spring of '46. The minister in London who was interpreting the Peel government and the jingo press to Buchanan was Louis McLane. A Tammany technician who had assisted the campaign was sent with him as secretary of legation. In May Buchanan was to receive a letter from McLane earnestly desiring the removal of his secretary of legation, "for the sake of the honor as well as the interest of the country." Mr. Gansevoort Melville, the secretary in question, had taken to London with him the manuscript of a younger brother's book about the Marquesas Islands. Gansevoort had sold it and now *Typee* was being printed in both England and America. Sweet, artless, prismatic with an aspiration that was not Concord Village nor the United States Senate nor the Oregon emigration but partook of all three, it described a poet's stay among some gentle cannibals. Chatting with his Mehevis and Kory-Kory's, Melville feels a splendid scorn for Alcott's orphic platitudes and the colonists sweating with hayforks at West Roxbury. Better in coral bays to swim with islanders uncorrupted by reason, to sleep beside them under thatched palm leaves unregardful of factories, to dine on pork in the pi-pi where the gorged chiefs smoke their coconut-shell pipes. The city of Lowell is obliterated altogether and nothing need be considered but sunrise and violet lagoons and the surf coming in. Moreover Fayaway's shoulders wear epaulettes of tattoo, her tappa skirt ends at the knees, and her tunic makes no effort to conceal her young breasts. . . . This mansion opening to the westward, though built of dream, is also part of expansionism, and though Melville might despise Alanno of Hio-Hio, he breathed the same air.

(But Fayaway's breasts were too sweetly displayed, her olive-tinted thighs were bare when Melville swam with her, and many readers exercised their privilege of conjecture. Moreover, Melville had denounced the missionaries, who were too much debauching paradise with a sense of shame and the city of Lowell's cotton cloth. The nation would hear no criticism of righteousness, and his publishers hurriedly altered such sheets as were not yet bound and rushed another printing which omitted comment on the godly. Meanwhile, in early '46, he sat down to write *Typee's* successor, in Lansingburg, New York, and began to court the daughter of Lemuel Shaw. In the end he married her and found no tattooing on her shoulders; if she had breasts, no one crushed flowers between them. She is implacable in our literature. Her husband's work turned aside, after *Omoo,* into phantasies of incest and at last an orphic impotence that has too much in common with Bronson Alcott's noblest thoughts.)

Mr. Hawthorne was back in Salem, where a happy marriage had freed him of the old phobia that had kept him from coming outdoors by day. He was writing to his friend George Bancroft, Secretary of the Navy, in hope of the Salem post office, and was due, by summer, to get the customhouse where he was to meet certain ghosts and in old papers was to find a scarlet initial embroidered with threads of gold. Mr. Emerson was finishing his lectures on Representative Men in Boston and making notes quite as acute as Thoreau's about Fourier, reform, politicians, and slavery. Though he was whiggish, he was no Whig. "These rabble at Washington are really better than the snivelling opposition. They have a sort of genius of a bold and manly cast, though Satanic. They see, against the unanimous expression of the people [the seer was wrong, here, and would amend that judgment before the spring was out], how much a little well-directed effrontery can achieve, how much crime the people will bear, and they proceed from step to step. . . ."

Longfellow heard Emerson lecture and worked on *Evangeline,* the second canto, where the lovers' marriage contract is signed in Acadia just when the English ships "ride in the Gaspereau's mouth with their cannon pointed against us." The menace of those guns or something graver oppressed him through January and he could not shake off a heaviness of spirit. Perhaps his gloom was just the Cambridge winter: "This dull dismal cold crushes me down, as if the sky were falling; or as if I were one of the four dwarfs of the northern mythology, who uphold the dome of heaven upon their shoulders." Or maybe it was a poet's premonition as, foreboding but helpless, he saw his country moving inexorably toward war. And, seeing, could remember what he had written four years before: —

> There is a poor, blind Samson in this land,
>   Shorn of his strength and bound in bonds of steel,
> Who may, in some grim revel, raise his hand,
>   And shake the pillars of this Commonweal,
> Till the vast Temple of our liberties
> A shapeless mass of wreck and rubbish lies.

Walking to Boston with Longfellow, hoping to lighten his dull mood, James Russell Lowell felt the pillars of the commonweal begin to shake. It was a literary achievement of Polk's election that it had stiffened a dilettante into a serious writer. Lowell had written when the Democrats triumphed: —

> Careless seems the great Avenger; history's pages but record
>   One death-grapple in the darkness 'twixt old systems and the Word;
> Truth forever on the scaffold, Wrong forever on the throne,
>   Yet that scaffold sways the future and, behind the dim Unknown,
> Standeth God within the shadow, keeping watch above his own.

Thereafter he could not be satisfied with the sweet-lavender asininity of Brook Farm; he had found steel and an edge. Since writing it he had married his beloved bluestocking, Maria White, had honeymooned in Philadelphia, had done some prentice work writing tracts for the Abolitionists, and now had come home to Elmwood. On the last day of '45 his daughter Blanche was born and James is seen briefly in January dreaming of a time when she will be "a great, strong, vulgar, mud-pudding-baking, tree-climbing little wench" . . . and beginning some articles for a London paper that will be Lowell taking up arms and going forth to war.

But do not suppose that Mr. Polk lacked literary support. The Democratic Party had an organ in Brooklyn and now there began to resound from it the barbaric if adolescent yawp of Mr. Walter, as he still signed it, Whitman.

Whitman could discern no danger to the eastward: "As for the vaunted ocean-sway of Great Britain, we laugh it to scorn! It can never compete with us, either in time of peace or war. Our Yankee ingenuity has built better ships and manned them with hardier crews than any other nation on earth." A flag goes up on the *Eagle* building, and "Ah! its broad folds are destined to float yet — and we, haply, shall see them — over many a good square mile which now owns a far different emblem." Where? "The more we reflect on the matter of annexation as involving a part of Mexico, or even the main bulk of that Republic, the more do doubts and obstacles resolve themselves away, the more plausible appears that at first glance most difficult consummation. . . . Then there is California, in the way to which lovely tract lies Santa Fe; how long a time will elapse before *they* shine as two new stars in our mighty firmament?" Expansion finds its incident: "Mexico, though contemptible in many respects, is an enemy deserving a vigorous 'lesson.' We have coaxed, excused, listened with deaf ears to the insolent gasconnade of her government, submitted thus far to a most offensive rejection of an ambassador personifying the American nation, and waited for years without payment of the claims of our injured merchants." And Manifest Destiny its broadest sentiment: "It is from such materials — from the Democracy, with its manly heart and its lion strength spurning the ligatures wherewith drivellers would bind it — that we are to expect the great FUTURE of this Western World! a scope involving such unparalleled human happiness and rational freedom, to such unnumbered myriads, that the heart of a true *man* leaps with a mighty joy only to think of it!"

Adolescent but perfectly expressive of Walter Whitman's countrymen, in January, 1846.

California, January 24, 1846.

"Many weeks of hardships, close trials, and anxieties have tried me severely, and my hair is turning gray before its time. But all this passes, *et le bon temps viendra.*" Thus Childe Harold's American heir, writing to his wife from Yerba Buena, on the Bay of San Francisco. And, receiving that letter of January 24 in Washington and learning that a Mr. James Magoffin (who will be an actor in our drama) can take an answer to Bent's Fort on the Arkansas, whence it will be forwarded to California, Jessie Benton Frémont grieves: "Poor papa, it made tears come to find that you had begun to turn gray. [He was thirty-three.] You must have suffered much and been very anxious 'but all that must pass.' . . . I have not had so much pleasure in a very great while as today. The thought that you may hear from me and know that all are well and that I can tell you again how dearly I love you makes me as happy as I can be while you are away."

Young Francis Parkman found it natural to prefix quotations from *Childe Harold* to the chapters of *The Oregon Trail.* But it was in the person of John Charles Frémont that the nation's enthusiasm for the poetry of Lord Byron found a career. We are to follow him through knotty and hardly soluble controversies. They will be less obscure if it is kept in mind that Frémont was primarily a literary man . . . who had a literary wife.

Greatness was a burden on Childe Harold's soul but nature kept the lines a little out of drawing. Born in high romance outside the law, he had grown up a young Rousseau. He had found a profession plotting the wilderness for the Topographical Corps. His native poetry responded to the solitudes and he had mastered the skilled crafts of living there. If his father's romance was out of Alexandre Dumas, his own was out of Italian opera. It rose in a fine cadenza when, secretly married to Jessie, the beautiful, bluestocking daughter of Thomas Hart Benton, he stood before the Senator to announce defiance of his will. Benton's rage had been known continentally ever since he had shot it out with Andrew Jackson in a community brawl. It now turned on Frémont but to violins Jessie stepped forward and sang her aria, "Whither thou goest I will go, and where thou lodgest I will lodge." Benton, who was one of the best-educated men in Congress, surrendered to a literary allusion.

An obscure lieutenant of topographical engineers had become the son-in-law of the most powerful Senator, of the Senator, furthermore, who was the greatest expansionist, whose lifelong vision it had been to make all the West American. Also, greatness had secured the assistance of a national spotlight. Benton and his colleague Linn had Frémont put in command of two explorations of the West whose sole purpose was to advertise the Oregon country. The first took him to South Pass and a little beyond; the second to Oregon and, looping back, to California by a spectacular if injudicious winter crossing of the Sierra. He proved himself a first-rate wilderness commander, learning his new trade from two of its masters, Kit Carson and Tom Fitzpatrick. He traveled little country that his instructors had not had by heart for twenty years, blazed no trails, though the Republicans were to run him for the Presidency as the Pathfinder, and did little of importance beyond determining the latitude and longitude of many sites which the mountain men knew only by experience and habit. But he learned mountain and desert skills well, was tireless in survey and analysis, and enormously enjoyed himself.

Also he was a literary man and the Thunderer was his father-in-law. Benton roared in the Senate, the other expansionists chimed in, and Frémont had given the West to the American people. With Jessie's eager help he wrote his two reports, which were far more important than his travels. The government printed them, first separately, then together, and sowed them broadcast. The westering nation read them hungrily. Frémont chasing buffalo, Galahad Carson reclaiming the orphaned boy's horses from the Indians, Odysseus Godey riding charge against hordes of the red butchers — there was here a spectacle that fed the nation's deepest need. They were adventure books, they were charters of Manifest Destiny, they were texts of navigation for the uncharted sea so many dreamed of crossing, they were a pageant of daring, endurance, and high endeavor in the country of peaks and unknown rivers. With Benton's advertising, they made Frémont a popular image of our Western wayfaring. Now he could come downstage center with the light on him and begin his role as a hero of romantic drama.

We have noted the start of his third expedition, from St. Louis, in June, 1845. Carson was his adjutant again. Fitzpatrick was with him for a while but was detached to accompany Lieutenant Abert on that other subtly motivated "exploration" to the Southwest. He had such other mountain men as Dick Owens, Lucien Maxwell, Basil Lajeunesse, Alexis Godey, and Joe Walker. The usefulness to Polk of this third expedition, its part in the great game, is clear. While the crises with Mexico and Great Britain were intensifying, on the frontier of Oregon and California there would be an army officer and sixty armed men, most of them thirty-third-degree mountain men. . . . Now there was making toward him a lieutenant of marines vastly impressed by anti-American demonstrations in Mexico City. The lieutenant had been ordered to show him instructions directing the consul at Monterey to procure a peaceful revolution in California, and also carried private letters from Benton and Benton's daughter. In January, Lieutenant Gillespie was crossing Mexico with exceeding slowness, to sail for Honolulu on February 22.

In January greatness burgeoned in Frémont's soul. He had reached his stage and time was on the march. It might be that some great deed could be done. And from then on to the end of his life he was to go, always subtly, astray. Nothing came out quite the way it should have done. Lord Byron, who had imagined him, could not make him rhyme.

He had reached Sutter's Fort (the site of Sacramento) on December 9 of '45, after the outstanding exploration of his career which broke a trail across the Salt Desert west of Great Salt Lake to Ogden's or Mary's River, which Frémont renamed the Humboldt. . . . Well, not quite the first passage of that white waste, though Frémont sincerely believed that it was. Jedediah Smith, the great mountain man, had crossed it from the west, east, south of Frémont's trail, in 1827. Carson seems not to have known of Smith's crossing, though both he and Joe Walker should have known, and it was indicated on at least two well-known maps with which it was Frémont's business to be wholly familiar. No matter, that crossing (under Walker's guidance) was notable enough, and so was the earlier stretch (under Carson's guidance) which had brought the party from the Grand River to the White River and on to the Green.

At the Humboldt Frémont sent the larger part of his force into California under Joe Walker. Then, after another valuable survey, he divided his force again and led a picked party in a forced winter crossing of the high Sierra. The venture was foolhardy, was disapproved by Carson, served only Frémont's consciousness of brave deeds — and beat the snows by just a little while. He and his gaunt companions came down into the great green valley. Sutter fed them and they waited for Walker's party to join them.

Walker delayed, having mistaken the rendezvous appointed. Frémont had now reached his theater and he was restless. He marched his little group vaguely toward Oregon, whither he had been ordered, turned back to Sutter's again (past a site on the American River where Sutter had considered building a sawmill), and on January 14 started south to find his larger party. He met some of the California Indians who lived on horses stolen from their decayed relatives, the mission peons. So he redressed an injury they had done him on his last visit, two years before. Owens, Carson, and the Delaware scouts got fresh scalps for their leggings in three sharp, unnecessary skirmishes. It was at least a theatrical deed but it was not judicious. There had arrived in California, from a Mexican government that feared war, orders to warn out of the province all foreigners who were not licensed to hold land. The warning had not been issued but the orders directing it had begot suspicion and unrest. And now a foreigner, accompanied by the mountain men whom the Californians knew from years of forays against their horse herds, was marching through their province killing Indians. To what end? If he meant nothing worse, did he mean to stir up an Indian war?

Frémont went back to Sutter's Fort. He got a passport from Sutter and went to Yerba Buena, where he wrote the letter quoted above. Then he moved down the coast to Monterey, the seagirt town where Richard Henry Dana had first sent down a royal yard and heard the mate's "Well done" with as much satisfaction as ever he had felt in Cambridge on seeing a "*bene*" at the foot of a Latin exercise. Here he called formally on the consul, Larkin, to whom Gillespie was bringing secret instructions.

Sea and sky are pleasant at Monterey, and Frémont stayed on drinking the excellent native wines and talking with the shrewd, hard-bitten consul. On January 29 the prefect, Don Manuel Castro, inquired through Larkin what errand had brought an American army officer to the golden shore. Frémont answered that though he was an army officer his errand was not military but peaceful, to determine the best trade route to the Pacific, and that his company were not soldiers but civilians. That was true. He was a touch diplomatic, however, when he added that he had left his party on the frontier — he did not know where they were but did know that they were moving through the interior — and that he had come to Monterey for supplies. Then another Castro, Don José, the military commander of California (who was bickering with the governor, Don Pío Pico, and whom Larkin had cozened a good way toward revolution), gave Frémont permission to winter in the valley of the San Joaquin. Frémont told Don José that, eventually, he would want to go home along the southern route, up the Gila River.

But he did not go to the San Joaquin Valley, which was east of the coastal mountains and distant from the settlements. He stayed on where he was. Later he was to explain that he had lingered here like any tourist, in the hope of finding a place to build a house for his mother. Maybe. But he was hearing stories from resident Americans. And destiny was stirring in his soul.

On January 14 James Clyman, encamped in the mountain chaos of northern California, wrote in his journal: —

> Heard that Mr. Fremont had arived at suitors Fort and still more recently that Mr. Hastings and Party had likewise arived Both from the U. States. But no information has yet arived of the Politicks in the states in fact information of all Kinds Travels slow and is very uncertain when it has arived you know nothing certain unless you see it yourself.

Jim Clyman, a master mountain man, thus notes the coming of two California authors. Clyman's own role in our story will unfold presently; his immediate convenience here is that he also had literary moments. He had written into his journal a treatise on the hunting of grizzly bears and, just before it, a more extended one on California and the Californians. He found the latter "a proud Lazy indolent people doing nothing but ride after herds from place to place without any appearent object," whose labor and drudgery were done by Indians "kept in a state of Slavery haveing or Receiving no compensation for their labour except a scanty allowance of subsistence . . . and perhaps a cotton Shirt and wool sufficient to make a coarse Blanket." Their government was a series of revolutions, "every change for the worse," and the change meaning merely that "the revenue has fallen into other hands." And "in fact the Military and all parts of the Government are weak imbecile and poorly organized and still less respected."

Jim Clyman, however, liked the California scenery. And he was quite clear about such countrymen of his as he met there. "The Forigners which have found their way to this country are mostly a poor discontented set of inhabitants and but little education hunting for a place as they [want] to live easy only a few of them have obtained land and commenced farming and I do not hear of but one man that has gone to the trouble and Expence to get his title confirmed and fixed beyond altiration and dispute."

Clyman lingered along the Putah and other mountain creeks during January, chronicling the rains and watching the lush spring come on. And, doubtless, remembering his past. It was his private past, but to saturation it was the American past also.

January in California was already spring. The rains had wrought their resurrection and Jim Clyman "noticed the manseneto trees in full Bloom . . . an evergreen shrub growing in a thick gnarled clump . . . and would make a beautiful shade for a door yard." The season was "fine growing weather verry much resembling a Missouri April or an Eastern May."

But in Missouri and the East January was still winter, an uncommon hard winter. The prairies were deep under snow, frost sank deep in the ground, the wind whistled by from the north and the boughs of trees fired pistol shots when they moved in it. It was a season suspended, a time to finish jobs while the stock stamped in the barn all day long, a time for talking.

They talked in country stores, at the post offices, in the kitchens of farmhouses — along the Sangamon, in the Western Reserve, in the bluegrass country, under the shadow of Mount Equinox. The little weeklies — *Journal, Sentinel, Freedom's Herald* — reprinted what the Washington *Union* said about Texas, the *National Intelligencer's* appraisal of the British fleet, a summary of the impending crisis based on *Niles' Register*. Gittin' on to war, I guess. Polk's bound to take no sass from Johnny Bull, no, nor the Greasers, neither. Or Polk's set to make us fight a war if he can't get slave territory noways else. ("They just want this Californy So's to lug new slave states in, to abuse ye an' to scorn ye', An' to plunder ye like sin.") They talked very much like Benton, Buchanan, Webster, Lincoln, Whitman, Emerson, Dana, Thoreau. Fist on the table, Pa brought the verdict in. Dave listened and had his say but would not mention a young dream of Her Majesty's frigate striking her colors in humiliation or dark-skinned lancers dying in the Halls of Montezuma while a Hoosier farm boy waved an unfamiliar sword. And Ma looked at Dave, a firstborn son whom President Polk might send to war.

But to a long-peaceful nation war was an unreal haze on the far horizon. Whereas here at hand, in the Sangamon country or in the Green Mountains, next to Perkins' store or half a mile up the crick, someone who might be named, say, Bill Bowen had sold his place. Bill and Mother, the girls, and three of the boys were going west.

Strange paraphernalia gathered in the Bowen barn and the Bowens were preparing a granary that would have seen the family through a famine year. At least two hundred pounds of flour or meal per person, the *Guide* said, *The Emigrants' Guide to Oregon and California* by Lansford W. Hastings, whose arrival in California Jim Clyman had recorded. All the Bowens thumbed that small volume, arguing, checking, refuting. Twenty pounds of sugar, ten pounds of salt . . . everyone will require at least twice as much as he would need at home, since there will be no vegetables . . . some buffalo can be counted on — and along the icebound Sangamon Bill Bowen sees himself riding down a shaggy beast straight out of fable . . . such goods for the Indian trade as beads, tobacco, handkerchiefs, cheap pantaloons, butcher knives, fish hooks — so young Bill and Nancy and Henry Clay and Joe will truly trade fish hooks for moccasins with a feathered topknot beside streams that are also straight out of fable. That topknot looks just like Tecumseh or Pontiac, and the streams of fable, the Platte, the Snake, the Green, are just such known rivers as the Sangamon, the Connecticut, the Maumee. While the north wind howls over the rooftree, it seems impossible that, come summer, Bill and Nancy Bowen will be unyoking the oxen while the "caral" forms on the banks of the Sweetwater, but they will be, for on page 147 Mr. Hastings says so.

This Hastings was a Frémont in miniature. He is an elusive soul, not much can be said about him with certainty. A young man on the make, he was at this moment engaged in a grandiose and still wholly theoretical real-estate enterprise on the golden shore, and he was the local agent of a bigger one managed from Washington which was a kind of gaudy bet on an insider's guess that there would be war. But he also had speculations — or visions — more gaudily ambitious. He may have meditated another overlordship on the frontier of empire, like the one which Sutter had actually established at New Helvetia. He may have seen himself — he would only have been one of a good many — as a kind of Sam Houston, president of another Lone Star Republic. He may have intended to utilize the opportunities provided for a smart man with nerve — precisely as Frémont did. Rumors connected him — loosely — with the Mormons and, on grounds that are apparently more substantial, with one of the current revolutionary intrigues. Whatever was in his mind, he did not have quite enough stuff. Put him down as a smart young man who wrote a book — it is not a unique phenomenon in literature — without knowing what he was talking about. As the first head of the California Chamber of Commerce, the first Booster on the golden shore. He went from his home town, Mount Vernon, Ohio, to Oregon in 1842 with Elijah White's famous caravan. He found no opening for his talents in that sober commonwealth and moved on to California. He liked what he saw, he perceived there were opportunities for smart men, so he wrote a prospectus and took it east in 1844. It was published at Cincinnati in 1845 and Hastings went back to California. Jim Clyman heard of him just when the Bowens and the Smiths and the Does were reading it. And while they were reading it Mr. Hastings formed a new design, one which shifted him from merely mischievous advertising to really dangerous activity. As, farther along, we shall see.

"Here perpetual summer is in the midst of unceasing winter; perennial spring and never failing autumn stand side by side, and towering snow clad mountains forever look down upon eternal verdure." That strain was not as familiar in '46 as the years have made it now. Bill Bowen, who has to plunge between frozen walls of snow to lug in endless armfuls of hickory lengths, reads with an understandable fascination that no fires are needed in California except to cook by, and those usually outdoors. Mother's knuckles are gnarled and stiff with rheumatism begotten by prairie winters —

but by that violet sea it is warmer in winter than in summer, and even in December vegetation is in full bloom. (My sakes! hollyhocks, sweet william, carnation pinks at Christmas time in your own dooryard!) Aunt Esther is racked by chills and fever every autumn, her thin shoulders wrapped with a shawl even in August. But "there being no low, marshy regions, the noxious miasmatic effluvia . . . is here nowhere found" and "while all this region . . . is entirely exempt from all febrific causes, it is also entirely free from all sudden changes and extreme variableness of climate or other causes of catarrhal or consumptive affections." So Aunt Esther can ease her tired old bones in California, and Nancy will not sniffle all winter long, and pink will come back to little Bob's cheeks, they will not have to watch him die of lung fever, after all.

And such farms! Young Bill, chipping at the frozen droppings of the cows, may meditate on the information that California stock require neither feeding nor housing, nor other care, nor any expense. Moreover, Mr. Hastings has seen oats half an inch thick through the stalk and eight feet high, thousands of acres at a stretch. Clover grows to five feet, covering the hills with natural hay. A single stalk of wheat forms seven heads and the grain runs four pounds to the bushel heavier than any the Bowens know. Seventy bushels to the acre, often up to a hundred and twenty bushels — and next year sixty-one bushels spontaneously, with no sowing at all. Also two crops in one twelvemonth, and up to sixty bushels of corn per acre, and wild flax waves as far as the eye can see, and the soil grows everything, tobacco, rice, cotton, crabapples, plums, strawberries the largest and most delicious in the world, peaches blossoming in January, such grapes as you cannot believe in.

Bill Bowen had no reason to know that there were optimisms in Hastings' book. The advertiser told him too candidly that there was no scarcity of fuel east of the Platte River, that all the streams he would cross were easily fordable, that buffalo would be plentiful for hundreds of miles beyond the Rockies, that they could be herded like cattle, that the California Indians were inoffensive, and so on. Publicity is an art of omission — and Hastings' need was to trump Oregon, which drew most of the emigration. There were few difficulties, he said, till you reached the place where the road forked. On the fork that led to Oregon the travel became dreadful and hazardous at once — and even if you survived it you would have only unfruitful Oregon for all your labors. Some remarks here about five months of rain and sleet, whereas rain in California was California rain. They read this in the Sangamon country. They also read the barker's light suggestion that a fine way to shorten the trip would be to try a route which Mr. Hastings had so far not bothered to try (and no one had yet broken), a possible cutoff from Fort Bridger (which Hastings had barely seen) to the southern end of Great Salt Lake and thence due west to Ogden's River (country about which Hastings knew nothing whatever). The saving of several hundred miles seemed promising on a winter evening in the kitchen.

Much more widely read, Frémont's was a much better book. It knew what it was talking about, and when Bill Bowen read that there was wood or water in a given place, or good soil, or difficult travel, he could count on it. The myth of the Great American Desert went down before this literary man's examination — and before his vision (like his father-in-law's) of cities rising in wasteland and the emptiness filling with fat farms. It was filled with solid facts that solid minds could use: it told about the winds, the water, the timber, the soil, the weather. It was extraordinarily seeing and intuitive, remarkably accurate. In the book he wrote, Frémont deserves well of the Republic.

But the book had a much greater importance than this: it fed desire. The wilderness which was so close to Frémont's heart that he has dignity only when he is traveling it was the core of the nation's oldest dream. Kit Carson, Tom Fitzpatrick, Alexis Godey, Basil Lajeunesse, his mountain men, were this generation's embodiment of a wish that ran back beyond Daniel Boone, beyond Jonathan Carver, beyond Christopher Gist, innumerable men in buckskins, forest runners, long hunters, rivermen, *gens du nord*, the company of gentlemen and adventurers of the far side of the hill. Something older than Myles Standish or Captain John Smith fluttered a reader's pulse when the mountain men worked their prodigies before Frémont's admiring eyes. It responded to his exaltation when, pounding his rifle on the saddle to seat a fresh load, he charged through dust clouds at the snorting buffalo. It quickened when he reached the highest peak of the Wind River divide and there pressed between leaves of his notebook a honey bee that was making westward. He went on — across deserts, through untrodden gulches, up slopes of aspen, over the saddle, along the ridge, down the far side. He smelled sagebrush at dawn, he smelled rivers in the evening — alkali in sun-hardened earth when a shower had passed, pines when the pollen fell, roses and sweet peas and larkspur, carrion, sulphur, the coming storm, greasewood, buffalo dung in the smoke of campfires. He saw the Western country with eager eyes — saw it under sun, bent and swollen by mirage, stark, terrible, beautiful to the heart's longing, snow on the peaks, infinite green and the night stars.

That was what the pulse answered in Frémont's book. And, looking at Bill Bowen, asking why this settled citizen of Sangamon County or Brattleboro or the Mohawk Valley was selling out and heading west, one finds no dependable answer except in that answering pulse. Now it is true that Bill Bowen, reading Frémont by candlelight beside the Cumberland or the Delaware, could jot down a well-considered memorandum that there was first-rate farm land along the Willamette. It is true that the dispossessed Mormons, scrutinizing in their beleaguered city every page he wrote and every similar page they could find, could plot an itinerary toward a destination unknown but known to offer their only chance of surviving. But that is of the slightest importance, and it is not what a young man named Francis Parkman read painfully, with eyes beginning to be diseased, that winter in Boston. Or a boy named Lewis Garrard, reading him in Cincinnati and tossing away his schoolbooks because "the glowing pages of Frémont's tour to the Rocky Mountains . . . were so alluring to my fancy that my parents were persuaded to let me go westward." Or a thousand men named Bill Bowen, from Missouri eastward to the state of Maine.

It was certainly an important, an irrevocable climax when Bill Bowen sold his place, and certainly there went into it the hardest, most reasoned motives. Bodies bent by the labor of New England farms would find a longing crystallized in the tidings that the Oregon soil was deep and without stones, in gentle weather, beside broad waters, below the brows of timbered hills. Bodies sapped by malarial autumns and prairie winters would feel the tug of a California where there was neither cold nor hard work nor any distempers of the flesh. Furthermore, the prairie crops had slackened for the past several seasons and over a wide area had failed — and, on Mr. Hastings' promise, crops never slackened or failed where rolled the Sacramento. Also, neither the tariff of '42 nor all the rhetoric of Congress had succeeded in fully restoring the farmers' market which had been shattered in '37 — and there was a belief that in Oregon the trade with China and the Sandwich Islands would absorb all crops that could be grown, a knowledge that there was a great grazing industry in California, a promise that the same great herds could be developed in Oregon. We may also make the conventional genuflection to the texts which tell us that the victims of industrialism's earliest American failures were going westward in new hope — though, after due search, exceedingly few of them have been found in any of the events we deal with and none at all along the Western trails. Finally, those Congressmen who talked so gloriously about stretching the eagle's wing across the setting sun were talking about a fundamental reality, a belief that plumbed deep in Bill Bowen's heart. Bill Bowen had long believed and now believed more passionately than ever before that the Americans must occupy their continent, and if others won't do it while there is yet time, maybe I'd better start right now.

Nevertheless, when all these reasons are totaled up they make a sum far from large enough to explain why, suddenly, the Americans were marching on their last frontier — to explain the evening talk in farm kitchens in January, 1846. One comes much closer to the truth with Boone and Carver and Gist, with the venturers crossing the fixed frontier of Sudbury toward the new land in the Connecticut bottoms — with all those who in two and a quarter centuries had moved up to the Fall Line and beyond it, across to the Mississippi, and, a few years since, beyond that. . . . When Bill Bowen sold his house a national emotion welled in the secret places of his heart and he joined himself to a national myth. He believed with Henry Thoreau in the forest and in the meadow and in the night in which the corn grows. Eastward Thoreau went only by force, but westward, ever since Columbus dared the Ocean Sea, westward he had gone free. The lodestone of the West tugged deep in the blood, as deep as desire. When the body dies, the Book of the Dead relates, the soul is borne along the pathway of the setting sun. Toward that Western horizon all heroes of all peoples known to history have always traveled. Beyond it have lain all the Fortunate Isles that literature knows. Beyond the Gates of Hercules, beyond the Western Ocean, beyond the peaks where the sun sinks, the Lapps and the Irish and the Winnebago and all others have known that they would find the happy Hyperboreans — the open country, freedom, the unknown. Westward lies the goal of effort. And, if either Freud or the Navajo speak true, westward we shall find the hole in the earth through which the soul may plunge to peace.

These people waiting for spring to come are inclosed by our myth. But think of them as hard-handed, hard-minded Americans seeking a new home in the West. Think of them also as so certain in their desire that James K. Polk's war seems trivial and wasted. . . . If the dream filled the desert with a thousand brooks like the one that tinkled in the north pasture, built in the Rocky Mountains a thousand white cottages like those that line a New Hampshire common, sowed alkali plains with such crops as the oak openings knew in Michigan, and sketched on the unknown a familiar countryside of rich green slopes, farm cattle lying in noon shade beside familiar pools, and the jeweled miniature of neighbors striking whetstone to scythe within a shout's reach of one another — why, they would learn about the West soon enough.

II
The Mountain Man

THERE were between six and seven thousand Americans in Oregon, most of whom had traveled there by white-top in the last four summers. Most of them were in the Willamette Valley, practically all the rest along the Columbia west of The Dalles. They had built sawmills and flour mills, had established a considerable commerce in cattle, were beginning to export lumber and grain. There were perhaps eight hundred Americans all told in California, thinly scattered, in the Sacramento Valley, in Napa Valley, nearer Monterey, at Monterey, along the Bay of San Francisco, a few elsewhere. Not all of them were genuine emigrants; most had come by sea; most of those who had come overland had arrived in the last two years. Some had been completely assimilated in the leisurely, gracious, pastoral society of the Californians, a happy and indolent people who raised great herds of cattle in a fat land. Some were drifters, refugees, deserters, younger sons, remittance men. Some were agents of the Yankee commerce. Some, and these the arrivals of the last two years, were like the Oregonians, movers seeking a new home in the West. Most of the currency in the province came from the trade in hides and tallow, which centered at Monterey and San Diego. A few coasters traded northward to the Columbia or Puget Sound; there was a small triangular trade with China and the Sandwich Islands. The sea otter was still hunted and so there was trade with Russia as well as China. But the Russians were out of San Francisco Bay and, ever since their withdrawal, American whalers had been putting in there, with Daniel Webster keeping an eye on them for his principals.

Eastward from the coastal ranges and the Cascades, all the way to the Missouri River was a big unknown. This was the country they argued about in Congress. Benton knew a great deal about it, as a lover and a scholar — as one knows who reads and dreams but has never seen his desire. Polk had some knowledge of it, thin and inaccurate, at fourth hand. Webster was very clear about the Bay of San Francisco and could make speeches dizzy with the future of a sister republic somewhere in the Great American Desert, but had never bothered to find out what he was talking about. Thoreau felt this empty land as a question asked while he slept. Whitman read about it in the Washington *Union* and the lesser party press, Longfellow in Frémont, * thousands of others in Frémont and in Farnham, Wyeth, Hall, Kelly, Nuttall, and similar narratives, and they also had love but not knowledge. The archives at Washington, London, Paris, Madrid, and St. Petersburg held reports on it, properly filed. . . . And the Oregon, California, and New Mexico of Polk's war and a westering people were only a quickening pulsebeat, type in slugs, movement of the vocal cords, a pulsation without substance.

Substance begins when we mention some names: the states of Washington, Oregon, Idaho, California, Nevada, Utah, Arizona, New Mexico, and parts of Colorado, Wyoming, and Montana. Add the rest of the last three and add the Dakotas, Nebraska, and Kansas. Now across the blank paper outlined by those names, sketch in some rivers: the Pecos, Gila, Rio Grande, Arkansas, Red, El Rio de las Animas Perdidas en Purgatoire (call that one the Picketwire), the Missouri, Blue, Vermillion, Platte, Niobrara, Cheyenne, Milk, Marias, Musselshell, Yellowstone, Jefferson, Madison, Gallatin, Okanagan, Columbia, Snake, Sacramento, Feather, San Joaquin, Humboldt, Virgin, Bear, Green, Grand, Colorado of the West. Now from a station high above Long's Peak observe those streams emptying the fundamental watershed, the snows of a few square miles diversely rolled down the Madison to the Gulf of Mexico, down the Colorado to the Gulf of California, down the Snake to the Pacific, down the Bear to Great Salt Lake, down the Humboldt to the alkali desert. From that same station sketch on the blank paper the continental divide from Canada to Mexico and attach to that spine various peaks and ranges: the Flatheads, the Big Belts, the Absarokas, the Tetons, the Wind Rivers, the Laramies, the Medicine Bows, the Black Hills, the Rabbit Ears, the Sawatch, the San Juan, the Cochetopas, the Sangre de Cristo, the Spanish Peaks, the Ratons, the Sierra Blanca, the Los Piños, the Tulerosas, the Piloncillos, the Blacks, the Sierra Nevada, the Coast Range, the Cascades, the Blues, the Seven Devils, the Bitterroots, the Sawtooths, the Wasatch, the Uintas.

There remain other names to be lettered along these waters and between these ridges: deserts, passes, forests, plains, plateaus, sunken canyons, salt flats, lakes, divides. Such names sounded like whispers

* From his journal, December 3, 1846: "In the evening F. read Frémont's Expedition to the Rocky Mountains in 1842; highly interesting and exciting. What a wild life, and what a fresh existence! But, ah, the discomforts!"

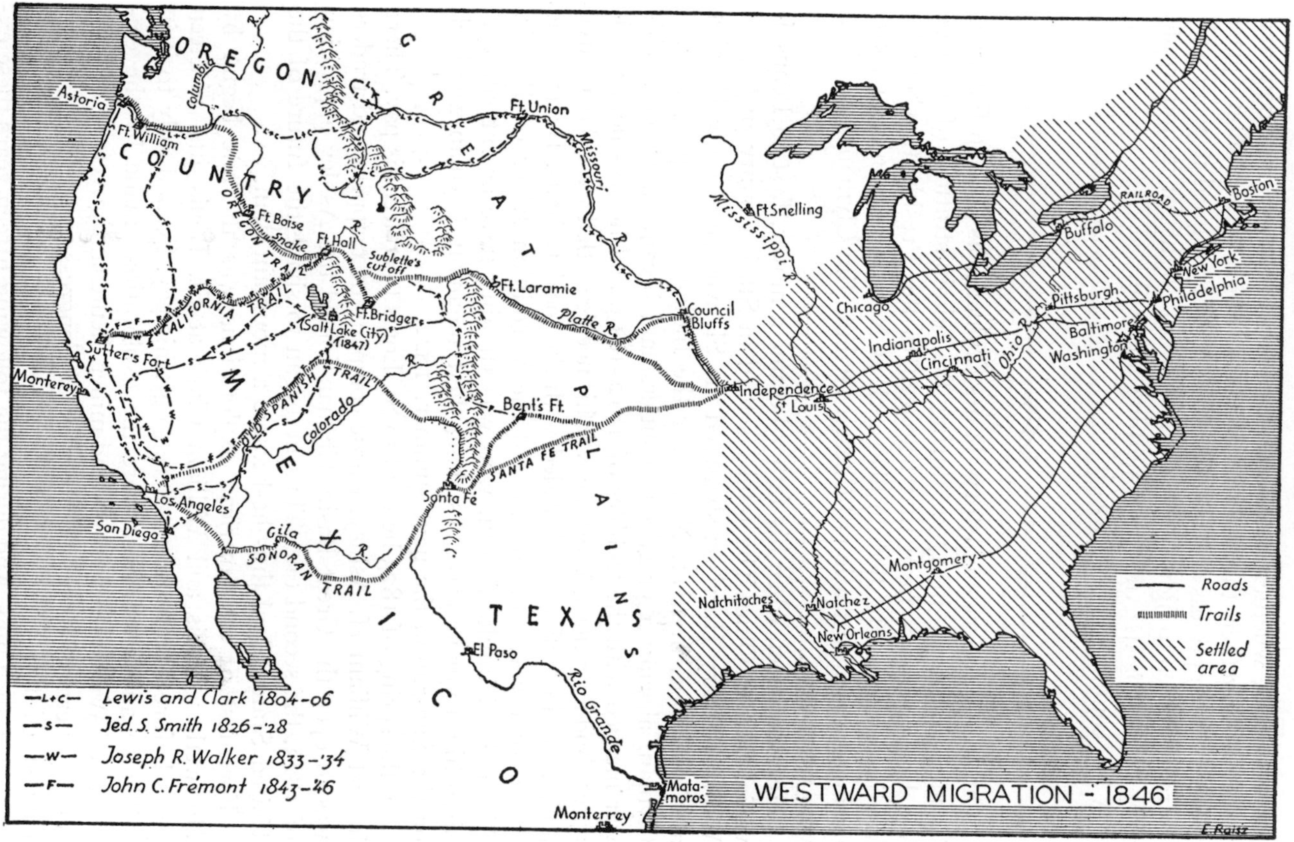
WESTWARD MIGRATION - 1846
OREGON COUNTRY
GREAT PLAINS
MEXICO
TEXAS
Astoria
Ft. William
Columbia R.
Ft. Boise
Snake
Ft. Hall
OREGON TRAIL
Sublette's cut off
Ft. Union
Missouri R.
Ft. Laramie
Platte R.
Council Bluffs
Ft. Bridger
Salt Lake City (1847)
CALIFORNIA TRAIL
Sutter's Fort
Monterey
OLD SPANISH TRAIL
Colorado R.
Los Angeles
San Diego
Gila R.
SONORAN TRAIL
Santa Fe
SANTA FE TRAIL
Bent's Ft.
El Paso
Rio Grande
Matamoros
Monterrey
Ft. Snelling
Mississippi R.
Independence
St. Louis
Chicago
Indianapolis
Cincinnati
Ohio R.
Pittsburgh
Baltimore
Washington
Philadelphia
New York
Buffalo
RAILROAD
Boston
Montgomery
Natchitoches
Natchez
New Orleans
Roads
Trails
Settled area
L+C Lewis and Clark 1804-06
S Jed. S. Smith 1826-'28
W Joseph R. Walker 1833-'34
F John C. Frémont 1843-'46
E. Raisz

in a few ears, whether in Washington or along the Sangamon, and heaped up together, they mean a big land. Short of a million square miles, a big emptiness and a big unknown. They argued it, were willing to send men to fight for it, were willing to fight for it, and would have a war for it. And knew nothing about it.

A big country. Whose was it?

Outline of American history. James Clyman was born in Fauquier County, Virginia, in 1792, during the administration of George Washington, on a farm that belonged to the President, whom he saw in the flesh. He died on his ranch at Napa, California, in 1881, during the administration of Chester Arthur. Jim Clyman was a man who went west.

He was fifteen when his father became a mover, first to Pennsylvania, then to Ohio. The family settled in Stark County just when William Henry Harrison shattered the Shawnee under the Prophet at Tippecanoe, in 1811. Next year the Indians were up again, and Clyman, already a practised frontiersman, became a ranger. This war merged with the troubles of 1812–1814, and he was both a volunteer and a regular. After the war his needle settled west. He cleared a planting in Indiana and traded with the local Indians. By 1821 he was a surveyor, working toward the Vermillion River of Illinois. Alexander Hamilton's son, who was running government surveys, hired him to make traverses along the Sangamon. Clyman was back on the Sangamon the next summer, 1822.

In the spring of 1823 he went to St. Louis to collect his pay. There he met William H. Ashley, whose company of trappers and traders was to open the Great Basin. Clyman joined the Ashley expedition of 1823, the second one. Thus he began to shape the future of the United States. And thus he became a mountain man.

Foremost of all American explorations was the one begun by Meriwether Lewis and William Clark at St. Louis just nineteen years before Clyman went there to get his pay. Second only to it in brilliance and importance were the explorations made by the employes of William Ashley — lead miner, lieutenant governor of Missouri, general of its militia, member of Congress, student and propagandist of the West, expansionist — during the two years after Clyman joined him. And during the following fifteen years these explorations became, as Ashley's employes bought him out, set up their own businesses, and interchanged and joined other firms, the discovery, the exploration, and the possession of the big unknown. Of the country we have sketched in names.

Between Benton or Polk or Longfellow and the West stretched a black curtain of the unimaginable, but the mountain men knew the country. They took Frémont across it in comfort, showing the Pathfinder paths they had had by heart for twenty years. They took Lansford Hastings through the West, and Kearny, Abert, Cooke, all the officers, all the travelers. They made the trails.

From 1823 to 1827 Clyman was in the mountains with Ashley's men. He fought in the battle with the Aricara that made Ashley determine to forsake the known road to the West, the river route which Lewis and Clark and their successors had traveled, and to blaze a trail south of the dangerous Indians,[1] an overland trail, the trail up the valley of the Platte by which the entire emigration was to move. He was with Jedediah Smith and Thomas Fitzpatrick when they made such a trail possible by finding South Pass, the one opening through which wagons could cross the mountains, the door to Oregon and California, the true Northwest Passage.[2] He was one of the party of four who paddled round Great Salt Lake, and so laid forever the old myth of the River Buenaventura which was supposed to flow salt water westward to San Francisco Bay — though the Pathfinder still half believed it twenty years later. . . . But these are details and the whole is vastly greater than its parts. From 1823 to 1827, Clyman was a mountain man and a good one, a peer of Carson, Fitzpatrick, Bridger, Harris, Provost, Ogden, the Sublettes, Fontenelle, or any of the other resounding names. It is enough to say, without decoration, that he was a mountain man.

Unlike most of his fellows he saved money and came out of the mountains. He bought a farm near Danville, Illinois, and set up a store. This is the phase of prairie farming while the land fills up. Then Illinois rose to the Black Hawk War, and Clyman joined Captain Early's company. This is an outline of American history: another private in Captain Early's backwoods fusileers was named Abe Lincoln. Still another private of that company is a person of our drama, James Frazier Reed. Born in Ireland of a noble Polish line, Reed settled near the Sangamon, made money, and in 1846 helped a townsman of his, George Donner, organize a wagon train for California. In June we shall see Clyman, moving eastward, meet him after fourteen years, in a moment of decision at Fort Laramie.

There was dysentery but no battle during the glorious two years of the Black Hawk War. When it was over the country had filled up and the mountain man's blood was uneasy. . . . In July, '46, having said good-bye to Reed, Clyman moved eastward along the trail he had helped to blaze and came to the grave of Reed's mother-in-law, who had died when her family neared the Blue on its westward journey. He meditated beside the grave: "This stone shews us that all ages and all sects are found to undertake this long tedious and even dangerous Journy for some unknown object never to be realized even by those the most fortunate. And why? because the human mind can never be satisfied never at rest always on the strech for something new some strange novelty.". . . Black Hawk's fangs drawn and Illinois getting crowded, Clyman's mind was on the "strech" in 1835.

That year they were opening up Wisconsin. Clyman filed a claim where Milwaukee was to sprout. But settlers rushed in and he fled northward to the shadowy timber along Green Bay. He had fought the Blackfeet in their forbidden lands and all the shock troops of the plains — Aricara, Sioux, Pawnee, Kiowa. None had counted *coup* on him. Compared to them, the Winnebago were sissy Indians but now a Winnebago counted *coup* — shooting Clyman with his own gun and driving him into a forty-eight-hour flight through rain and forest. But he survived.

There followed six peaceful years on his timber claim and at his Danville store. He was called "Colonel," the settlements rightly conferring the command of a regiment on anyone who came back from the West. Odysseus was back in Ithaca and had before him the years when the American dream gathered its harvest, the homestead growing in productivity, one's age secure, and one's sons and grandsons sharing the increase. But Odysseus had no sons, he had seen the far side of the hill, and that seventeen years had passed since he came out of the mountains meant nothing, for he had drunk the waters of Manitou which, the Ute said, would call one back again.

Clyman was fifty-two and had half a volume of American history behind him. He caught a cold, there was no healing for it in the Wisconsin winter, and as the spring of '44 came on, taking his water spaniel with him, he set out on horseback from Milwaukee to seek recovery in softer weather. His needle settled southwest, he rode into Independence, and the incantation of the Manitou water was fulfilled. There had been no Independence in his time, at best only some scattered cabins in the Indian country. But the Independence he saw in '44 was a frontier metropolis, rich, noisy, cosmopolitan, lively with the commerce of the prairies. It was boiling with an energy new under the sun, families with their oxen and their kine forming wagon companies to cross the mountains to a new home in the

West. He found two old companions, Ashley's men both, serving these companies in a new role, as guides. Bill Sublette, whom the Indians called Cut Face, was taking a party of invalids to Brown's Hole, in the heart of the mountain man's domain. That was astonishing, but there was greater astonishment in Black Harris' engagement to pilot Nathaniel Ford's company of five hundred all the way to the mouth of the Columbia.

These signs said that the mountain man's empire had fallen. The tenderfoot would move down the trails the trapper had broken, few beaver plews would be taken from creeks that would now water crops, and plows would bring up the bones of the disregarded who had taken an Indian or two with them when they died, to make sure that those plows might break the soil. So Jim Clyman signed up with Manifest Destiny. ("It appears there has been a great Troubling & striving of the elemints the mountain having at last brot forth J. K. Polk & the invincible Henry Clay as candidates for the Presidency. go it Clay. Just whigs enough in camp to take the curse off.") He signed with Ford's company and was off for Oregon, composing an epitaph for his messmate: —

> Here lies the bones of old Black Harris
> who often traveled beyond the far West
> and for the freedom of Equal rights
> He crossed the snowy Mountain hights
> was free and easy kind of soul
> Especially with a Belly full

We need not follow that westering. Clyman got to Oregon. He spent some months inspecting the country and the settlements which, having organized themselves as a fragment of the United States floating in space, were clamoring to be moored to the United States. But there were new lands to visit . . . "I never saw a more discontented community. . . . Nearly all, like myself, having been of a roving discontented character before leaving their eastern homes. The long tiresome trip from the States has taught them what they are capable of performing and enduring. They talk of removing to the Islands, California, Chili, and other parts of South America with as much composure as you in Wisconsin talk of removing to Indiana or Michigan."

So in July of '45 Clyman went south to California. He took letters from Elijah White concerning the murder of a Wallawalla brave by an American: a fuse burned here which would at last set off the first uprising of the Oregon Indians and the murder of Marcus Whitman. He joined one of the companies that were trying to build a road. This is still an outline of American history: one of his companions was James Marshall, unknowingly heading for the sawmill which Sutter hoped to build on American Fork. He reached Sutter's Fort at New Helvetia, made note of the fleas, and went on to Monterey to talk to Larkin. He turned north to Yerba Buena, spent about three months there, and in December plunged into the mountains on a bear hunt. We have seen him camped on Putah Creek, watching the spring come on.

In a little while he will write a letter to Captain Frémont, join Hastings, and start eastward along the trail down which the emigration is moving west.

Jim Clyman was a mountain man. That is the proudest of all the titles worn by the Americans who lived their lives out beyond the settlements.

History does not tell us whether Eric the Red and his successors traded with Indians for furs. If they got to Minnesota, as the legends say, they had to when the winter closed in. Besides strange birds and herbs and carvings, there may have been furs in the wealth that the Admiral of the Ocean piled in Queen Isabella's throne room. Certainly, before Spain or France or England sent explorers up the tidal rivers, coasting fishermen from overseas made deals for furs with the native savages. Furs were a principal object of all explorations, no matter if one also sought Cibola or the Northwest Passage or some other sunny myth, and the Captain John Smith who took skins home to his queen got them along trade routes already old. Then half a dozen countries planted colonies in the New World, and from all these plantations men went up the rivers — whether a few miles up the James or by the St. Lawrence to the Lakes and then by portage to the Wisconsin and so down the Mississippi — to trade with Indians for the only wealth the Indians had. It was these men who made the unknown known.

Plantations grew to empires and on the farthermost frontier of New France some of the *coureurs du bois* fell into contention. Some lost out and two of the disgruntled came in due time to the court of Charles II of England, then withdrawn to Oxford because there was plague in London. The court was bored in that provincial community, no one more bored than the King's mistresses, whose great silken sleeves could be attractively lined with the beaver, mink, and otter which Radisson and Groseilliers heaped at their feet. So plague and boredom conferred a monopoly on the King's cousin, the Governor and Company of Adventurers of England trading into Hudson's Bay. From that moment it was inevitable that two empires in the New World would come to grips. New France went down.

Meanwhile in all the colonies the Indian trader pushed up the streams, over the divides, and down into the new country. He was the man who knew the wilderness and he held the admiration of the settlements. Let there follow after him the men who built cabins; his was the edge and the extremity. The settlements saw his paddle flash at the bend or sun glint on his rifle at the edge of the forest, and then there was no word of him till his shout sounded from the ridge and he was back, with furs.

He had to live in the wilderness. That is the point. Woodcraft, forest craft, and river craft were his skill. To read the weather, the streams, the woods; to know the ways of animals and birds; to find food and shelter; to find the Indians when they were his customers or to battle them from stump to stump when they were on the warpath and to know which caprice was on them; to take comfort in flood or blizzard; to move safely through the wilderness, to make the wilderness his bed, his table, and his tool — this was his vocation. And habits and beliefs still deep in the patterns of our mind came to us from him. He was in flight from the sound of an axe and he lived under a doom which he himself created, but westward he went free.

Thus the Long Hunter. On May 25, 1804, Lewis and Clark, ascending the Missouri River toward the mountains, passed the mouth of La Charette Creek and a settlement "of seven small houses and as many poor families . . . the last establishment of whites." Here, in 1804, ended the fringe of civilization and the lifelong westering of "Colonel" Daniel Boone, seventy years old, his back to the wall, unable to go farther. The Long Hunter's farthest west . . . Lewis and Clark went on up the river, to winter near the Mandan villages at the Great Bend. So far the pirogues of rivermen were familiar and the trails were known. The next spring they went on, and to about the mouth of the Yellowstone they still traveled where the *voyageurs* had gone before them, but somewhere hereabout the known ended. Doubtless an occasional pirogue had passed beyond the Yellowstone and there is always some phantom Spaniard, a memory in an Indian narrative, who had come up from Taos to leave his scalp, his bridle, and perhaps his bastard in this country. Nevertheless, somewhere on this side of the Shining or Stony Mountains they were seeking,

Lewis and Clark brought a white man's eyes for the first time to the big unknown. They went on into the mountains, over the divide, down the Snake to the Columbia, and on to the Pacific. The next year they were coming back along their own trail—and met fur hunters already following it toward the mountains. The Astorians moved in, the North West Company worked westward through the English lands, and Americans and Mexicans came up from a third base at Taos or Santa Fe. The era of the mountain man began.

The frontiersman's craft reached its maximum and a new loneliness was added to the American soul. The nation had had two symbols of solitude, the forest and the prairies; now it had a third, the mountains. This was the arid country, the land of little rain; the Americans had not known drouth. It was the dead country; they had known only fecundity. It was the open country; they had moved through the forests, past the oak openings, to the high prairie grass. It was the country of intense sun; they had always had shade to hide in. The wilderness they had crossed had been a passive wilderness, its ferocity without passion and only loosed when one blundered; but this was an aggressive wilderness, its ferocity came out to meet you and the conditions of survival required a whole new technique. The Long Hunter had slipped through forest shadows or paddled his dugout up easy streams, but the mountain man must take to horse in a treeless country whose rivers were far apart and altogether unnavigable. Before this there had been no thirst; now the creek that dwindled in the alkali or the little spring bubbling for a yard or two where the sagebrush turned a brighter green was what your life hung on. Before this one had had only to look for game; now one might go for days without sight of food, learn to live on rattlesnake or prairie dog, or when those failed on the bulbs of desert plants, or when they failed on the stewed gelatine of parfleche soles. Moreover, in that earlier wilderness, a week's travel, or two weeks' travel, would always bring you to where this year's huts were going up, but in the new country a white man's face was three months' travel, or six months', or a year away. Finally this was the country of the Plains Indians, horse Indians, nomads, buffalo hunters, the most skillful, the most relentless, and the most savage on the continent. . . . Mountain craft was a technological adaptation to these hazards.

The Ashley party to which Jim Clyman was attached spent the winter of 1823–1824 in a valley north of Frémont's Peak in the

Wind River Mountains. In February they tried to cross the range but could not and moved southward looking for a gap. (This was the trip that, as an incident merely, was to reveal South Pass.) One morning Jim and the Bill Sublette whom he was to meet again at Independence in '44 saddled their winter-worn horses and went out to hunt. Nothing showed in that arctic air till at sundown they sighted some buffalo. Their horses were too broken-down to make a run and they had to crawl on their bellies for nearly a mile over frozen snow. The buffalo scented them and bolted but they wounded one. Sublette went back for the horses and Clyman followed the wounded buffalo, finally killing it in a small arroyo, whence he could not get it out alone. Sublette came up at nightfall, they got a small fire going, and were able to butcher some meat. But a blizzard came out of the north. There was no wood and but little sage; their fire was blown away. They pulled their robes over them and the gale battered them till morning. At daylight Clyman was able to pull some sage but they could not ignite it, either by flint and steel or by rifle fire. Jim got the horses. Sublette was too weak to mount. Jim found a single live coal left from their fire of the night before and got the sage lighted. They warmed themselves and Sublette was able to mount his horse — but soon turned numb and began to die. Jim dismounted and led his friend's horse through snow a foot deep into the teeth of the gale. Four miles away he found a patch of timber where one wall of an Indian bark lodge was standing. Behind this shelter he got a fire going at last, then "ran back and whoped up my friends horse assisted him to dismount and get to the fire he seemed to [have] no life to move as usual he laid down nearly assleep while I went Broiling meat on a stick after awile I roused him up and gave him his Breakfast when he came to and was as active as usual."

Jim says, "I have been thus particular in describing one night near the sumit of the Rockey mountains allthough a number simular may and often do occur."

The following June, coming east, Clyman pushed ahead of his companions, among them Fitzpatrick, and moved down the Sweetwater to wait for them on the Platte. Near Devil's Gate he suddenly found Indians on all sides. He holed up like a prairie dog in the rocks for eleven days, the Indians having set up their village. Then he "began to get lonesome." He had "plenty of powder but only eleven bullets." Since this was a wholly new country he did not know "whether I was on Platt[e] or the Arkansas," but he decided to get out. Note his course: "On the 12th day in the afternoon I left my lookout at the mouth of Sweetwater and proceeded downstream knowing that civilization could be reached Eastward." Eastward about six hundred miles in an air line.

He started out. He killed a buffalo. He kept close to the streams. He found an abandoned bull boat and so knew that either whites or Indians had passed this way. Once he saw some martins and lay listening to them—"it reminded me of home & civilization." Encountering some wild horses, he tried to crease one but broke its neck. Some Indians overtook him, robbed him of his blanket, powder, and lead, and bore him to the village, intending to kill him. But a friendly chief led him out of camp, restored his rifle, and gave him some parched corn. Game failed, water failed, and Clyman grew weak. He saw two badgers fighting. His gun misfired but he picked up some bones, "horse brobly," and killed the badgers. It rained for some days and the wet grass made walking easier but brought out the prairies' deadliest wild life, the mosquitoes. The going was harder, food scarcer, time stretching out:—

I could not sleep and it got so damp I could not obtain fire and I had to swim several rivers at last I struck a trail that seamed to lead in the right direction which I determined to follow to its extream end on the second day [on this trail] in the afternoon I got so sleepy and nervous that it was with difficulty I kept the trail a number of times I tumbled down asleep but a quick nervous gerk would bring me to my feet again in one of these fits I started up on the trail travelled some 40 rods when I hapened to notise I was going back the way I had come turning right around I went on for some time with my head down when raising my eyes with great surprise I saw the stars and stripes waving over Fort Leavenworth [really Fort Atkinson, 150 miles up the Missouri from Fort Leavenworth] I swoned emmediately how long I lay unconscious I do not know. . . .

So there entered into Captain Bennett Riley's quarters a bearded, hatless, all but starved mountain man, his buckskins and moccasins in tatters, his powder used up, after eighty days and at least seven hundred miles of solitary journeying. Ten days later Fitzpatrick and two others reached the fort after even harder going. . . . This was misadventure after accident, a commonplace risk in the mountain trade.

Much of the routine could be repeated here from Clyman's recollections: drifting downstream with a log to escape the Aricara, watching a Dakota tear the flesh of a dead enemy with his teeth, sewing Jedediah Smith's scalp and ear in place after a grizzly had lacerated them, starving in winter canyons, purged by alkali water, feasting with the Crows on a buffalo hunt, battling the Arapaho on Green River, captured by the Blackfeet but escaping them. But the routine may be assumed.

Of the Ashley expedition which he joined Clyman said that "Falstaf's Battallion was genteel in comparison." Yet it included some men whose distinction did not rest entirely on their craftsmanship. There was Jedediah Smith, the Yankee whose ambition was to be a geographer, who first crossed the desert to California and first made contact northwestward with the Hudson's Bay Company, whose reports it would have been sensible of both Polk and Frémont to look up — a Christian gentleman who became an explorer of the first rank. There were Pierre Louis Vasquez, the Spanish gentleman of St. Louis; Robert Campbell, who was to become a great Western merchant; Andrew Henry, who, like Campbell, was a true empire builder. Elsewhere in the mountain trade there were men like them: Joe Meek, whose cousin by marriage, Jim Polk, was President of the United States in '46; Lucien Fontenelle, in whose veins flowed the royal blood of France; Peter Skene Ogden, from a family that had been loyalist in the Revolution and was now important in Canada; Manuel Lisa, whose life was ambiguous and shadowed but who came from the Spanish aristocracy; "Captain William George Drummond Stewart, seventh Baronet of Grandtully," trapper, traveler, big-game hunter, and novelist-to-be. There were other sprigs of British, French, and Spanish nobility, remittance men or younger sons or just the restless seeking a new title. There were British army officers who had tasted the life on frontier garrison duty and liked it, men like George F. Ruxton, Lieutenant of Her Majesty's 89th Regiment, whom we shall meet in Mexico. There was the Irish romantic, American journalist, and European revolutionary, Mayne Reid.

Against such mountain men may be set off such others as Edward Rose, the crossbred white, Negro, and Cherokee, who had been a river pirate and became a Crow chief. Or another riverman, Mike Fink, who is immortal in our folklore. Or another Crow chief, the mulatto Jim Beckwith, who went up the river as Ashley's blacksmith and gave our literature its goriest lies. Or Bonneville's partisan, Joe Walker, who broke part of Frémont's trail, who wiped out Diggers as he would have stepped on piss-ants, and who, following the lead of Ewing Young, opened a trade in stolen California horses and so gave the mountains another routine of simple theft, complicated though not made hazardous by the murder of Californians. Such irreproachables as Frémont and Kit Carson were to follow him in this commerce.

And there were those whose distinction was wholly of the trade itself. There was the French strain: Frémont's Alexis Godey and Basil and François Lajeunesse, the Cerrés, the various Robidoux, Godin, Gervais, La Bonte, Etienne Provost. There were the Canadians and Scots of the North West Company and the Hudson's Bay outfit that absorbed it. More particularly there were the Americans, mostly Missourians, Kentuckians, and Virginians: the Sublettes, John Gant, Drips, Vanderburgh, Peg-leg Smith who cut off his own leg and whittled a stump to take its place, Black Harris, Old Bill Williams who had been a Methodist preacher and served as fiction's first image of the mountain man,[3] David Jackson, Dick Owens, Dick Wooton, Doc Newell, Hugh Glass, Greenwood, Fallon, Rube Herring, Long Hatcher — to the number of a good many hundred. And finally the great triumvirate must be named: Kit Carson, the Little Chief; Tom Fitzpatrick, White Head or Broken Hand; and, with drums and trumpets, Old Gabe, Jim Bridger.

So reads a short catalogue of Clyman's peers. A few of the names still clang a little, and at least Kit Carson and Jim Bridger have found a permanent place in our legends. But the catalogue does not disclose the history coiled within it or the era they began and ended within the span of a single lifetime.

They were the agents of as ruthless a commerce as any in human history; they were its exploited agents. The companies hired them — or traded with the highest order of them, the free trappers, such as have been named above — on terms of the companies' making, paid them off in the companies' goods, valued at the companies' prices deep in the mountains. They worked in a peonage like the greasers they despised, the freed Negroes of the South, or the sharecroppers of our day. The companies outfitted them and sent them out to lose their traps, their horses, and frequently their scalps — to come back broke and go deeper into debt for next year's outfit. Their trade capitalized starvation, was known to practise land piracy, and at need incited Indians against competitors. It made war on Indians who traded with competitors and debauched the rest with the raw alcohol that was called whiskey in the mountains. There was no problem in the Indian trade which firewater could not solve; so the fixed policy of the business that made rich men of the Astors, Chouteaus, McKenzies, Ashleys, and Campbells perfected the methods begun by coasters along the Atlantic littoral. The Indians went down before tin tubs curved to fit a packsaddle and filled with alcohol at fifty cents a gallon. . . . And, as they went down, took with them through the hole in the earth the scalps of mountain men.

"Adventure, romance, avarice, misanthropy, and sometimes social outlawry have their influence on enticing or driving these persons into the savage wilderness," Edwin Bryant wrote, who learned to respect them but observed that they lived in savagery. To Francis Parkman they were "the half-savage men who spend their reckless lives in trapping among the Rocky Mountains," and he could live with them as he never brought himself to live with the "offscourings of the frontier," those sallow-faced and inquisitive people who were moving on toward Oregon. He even came to call one of them a friend, Henry Chatillon, who chaperoned him through the prairies, whom he found noble and true-hearted, "a proof of what unaided nature will sometimes do." Chatillon interpreted them and so he could associate with others, till at last he could lie in camp with them at the mouth of Chugwater and listen with unalloyed admiration to their stories, and "defy the annals of chivalry to furnish the record of a life more wild and perilous than that of a Rocky Mountain trapper."

The savagery thus alleged was that of the Indians, a neolithic people. Jim Beckwith, who knew, said that though the Indian could never become a white man, the white man lapsed easily into an Indian. The mountain man's eye had the Indian's alertness, forever watching for the movement of boughs or grasses, for the passage of wild life downwind, something unexplained floating in a stream, dust stirring in a calm, or the configuration of mere scratches on a cottonwood. His ear would never again hear church bells or the noises of a farm but, like the Indian's, was tuned to catch any sound in a country where every sound was provisionally a death warning. He dressed like an Indian, in blankets, robes, buckskins, and moccasins, and it was sometimes his humor to grease his hair and stripe his face with vermilion. He lived like an Indian in bark huts or skin lodges, and married a succession of squaws. He thought like an Indian, propitiating the demons of the wild, making medicine, and consulting the omens. He had on call a brutality as instant as the Indian's and rather more relentless. The Indians who had proved themselves his friends were his friends just so long as they seemed to be; all others were to be shot and scalped at sight. It was the Indian law, no violence to be left unavenged.

He might winter at Taos, that first of Wild Western towns; he might bring his or the company's furs to St. Louis after the fall hunt, when the town would roar with mountain war cries, rock with the pleasures of behemoths, and grow quiet toward dawn when he spread his robes in some alley under the sky. But mostly he wintered at a log stockade a thousand miles from the Planters' House — Bent's Fort, Fort Union, Fort Pierre, Fort Laramie; or hutted up in some basin under the peaks — Brown's Hole, Ogden's Hole, Jackson's Hole, Pierre's Hole, Bayou Salade. Mostly his only touch with the settlements was an annual debauch when the caravan came to buy his furs and get the purchase price back in tobacco and alcohol at two thousand per cent advance. For the rest, in small parties he was on the creeks and among the mountains. His legs stiffened from the icy waters where he trapped beaver. Behind any ridge Blackfeet or Arapaho might be waiting for him. From the dark behind any fire he lighted might come the ultimate arrow. Any sleep might end in the rush of stampeded horses and a gurgle in his partner's throat. He had ahead of him only more years of unintermitted struggle against a savage country, unending warfare against a savage race, the long stretch against starvation, solitude, loneliness, and some final effort that would be not quite enough. Comparatively few lived to settle down as permanent colonels in the tamed West; the trade did not last long enough for many to grow old in it.

True enough . . . But the back trail was always there and need only be followed eastward. Few ever took it. They were, by God! the mountain men. The companies might exploit them but they were free and masters. Folks might call them Indians but they were better Indians. They had usurped the Indian's technology and had so bettered it that they could occupy the Indian's country and subdue the Indian. They had mastered the last, the biggest, and the hardest wilderness. Give any of them a horse and a pack mule, a half-dozen traps, a couple of robes, a bag of possibles, and a rifle — and he could live comfortably among privations that broke the emigrants' spirit and safe among dangers that killed soldiers like flies in the first frost. They had learned not only to survive the big lonesome but to live there at the height of function.

The waters of Manitou held freedom and desire, both inappeasable in the American consciousness. Why else the everlasting myth of the West? From Eric the Red to Jim Clyman, from the Atlantic fall line to the Pacific littoral, from *The Adventures of Emmera* to this week's horse opera issuing from Hollywood. The seed of expansion, to answer the tug, to push over the ridge, to go it alone. To the destructive element submit yourself and with the exertions of your hands and feet in the water make the deep, deep sea keep you up.[4] To be a man and to know that you were a man.

And to be a free man. At any evening fire below the Tetons, if they had paid civilization its last fee of contempt they had recompense in full, and Henry Thoreau had described it. They made their society, and its constraints were just the conditions of nature and their wills, the self-reliance in self-knowledge that Mr. Emerson commended. At that campfire under the Tetons, in the illimitable silence of the mountain night with the great clouds going by overhead, one particular American desire and tradition existed in its final purity. A company of free companions had mastered circumstance in freedom and their yarns were an odyssey of the man in buckskins who would not be commanded — what scalps had been taken along the Yellowstone, who counted *coup* in Middle Park, what marvels had been seen in John Colter's Hell or where the stone trees lie beyond the Painted Desert or where the waters of Beer Spring make the prettiest young squaw quite unattractive for a surprising time. The stories came from a third of a continent and summed up something more than two centuries of the American individual.

Finally there was the beauty of this last wilderness, added upon all the unspoiled natural beauties through which the individual had passed in his two centuries. The land of little rain, the Shining Mountains. It was theirs before the movers came to blemish it — rivers flowing white water, peaks against the sky, distances of blue mist against the rose-pink buttes, the canyons, the forests, the greasewood flats where the springs sank out of sight. They were the first to pass this way and, heedless of the eagle's wing which they stretched across the setting sun, they stayed here. God had set the desert in their hearts.

Their era was ending when Jim Clyman got to Independence in '44 and found Bill Sublette, who had first taken wagons up the Platte Valley in 1830, now taking invalids to Brown's Hole for a summer's outing. It was twenty-one years since Jim had first gone up the Missouri, forty years since Lewis and Clark wintered at the Mandan villages, thirty-three years since Wilson Hunt led the Astorians westward, twenty years since Clyman with Smith and Fitzpatrick crossed South Pass, eighteen years since Ashley, in the Wasatch Mountains, sold his fur company to Smith, Sublette, and

Jackson. Thirty-two years ago Robert McKnight had been imprisoned by the Spanish for taking goods to Santa Fe. Twenty-three years ago William Becknell had defied the prohibition and returned from Santa Fe in triumph. Eighteen years ago the Patties had got to San Diego by the Gila route and Jed Smith had blazed the desert trail to San Bernardino Valley; fourteen years ago Ewing Young, with Kit Carson, had come over the San Bernardino Mountains, making for the San Joaquin. There had been a trading post at the mouth of Laramie Creek for just ten years. Bent's Fort was fifteen years old.

Now the streams were trapped out, and even if beaver should come back, the price of plews would never rise again. There were two or three thousand Americans in Oregon, a couple of hundred in California, and in Independence hundreds of wagons were yoking up. Bill Sublette and Black Harris were guiding movers. Carson and Fitzpatrick were completing the education of John Charles Frémont.

Forty years since Lewis and Clark. Think back to that blank paper with some names sketched in, the Wind River peaks, the Tetons, the Picketwire River, the Siskidee, names which, mostly, the mountain men sketched in—something under a million square miles, the fundamental watershed, a thousand mountain men scalped in this wilderness, the deserts crossed, the trails blazed and packed down, the mountains made known, the caravans carrying freight to Santa Fe, Bill Bowen selling his place to go to Oregon, half a dozen wagonwrights setting up at Independence . . . and, far off, like a fly buzzing against a screen, Joe Meek's cousin, Mr. Polk, preparing war.

Whose country was it?

III
Pillar of Cloud

ALL through February Congress debated the resolution to terminate the joint occupancy of Oregon, and by its deliberation, Polk thought, informed the British that we were irresolute. The Whigs had a cold choice: they had to oppose termination because it was an administration measure but, except for New England, the country seemed to be approving it. Webster, who was daily galled by seeing Buchanan in the post designed by Providence for Webster himself, felt sure that the President would compromise on 49°, and, brushing away the war talk, John Quincy Adams told his journal the same thing. Well, you could embarrass the President by publicly assuming that he meant to compromise, and the Whigs clamored for the question to be reopened. They found an ally in the Democracy. Mr. Calhoun had taken the election of '44 and even Polk's nomination as a signal that the Democratic Party had now conformed to his desire and become a party of the South, but the President understood otherwise and, besides, listed Calhoun high among his distrusts. So Calhoun would use the spur: with his junior, McDuffie of South Carolina, he began to organize a bloc against termination. Senator Haywood of North Carolina panted to the White House with word that Calhoun would demand reopening the negotiations for Oregon, that he favored giving Great Britain anything she might ask. Benton, who knew more about Oregon than all the rest of them together, said ominously little about it on the Senate floor — that chilly forum where statesmen shook off their shawls and rugs to thrust stately sterns to warm at the hickory fires. Benton worked behind the scenes with a quiet effectiveness and allowed Polk to understand that though he favored termination he would back the claim no farther than he thought it just. The best administration speech was by John A. Dix of New York and, when it was finished, Benton concurred without revealing his position. He told the warhawks that they had no claim to the Frazer River, but no matter: Cass would bleed or die before one inch should be surrendered south of 54° 40′, Allen drummed a vast resonance from his chest, and Hannegan rushed off to stiffen Polk's spine whenever there was rumor that he would compromise or even receive proposals from Great Britain. Or thought he stiffened it — for no one smoked Polk out. His ideas had been plainly expressed in his message, he told everyone, and if the Senators did not abide by them they would ruin the party. McLane's reports from London described an increasing preparation for war, but the Cabinet met it only with discussion and nothing happened.

The Indians had not been notified that they had a new White Father and so the President sat for another portrait. It would be stamped on the medals distributed to the chiefs by all administrations. Office seekers went on consuming public time, and Polk had to receive the French minister, bearing documents which certified that Louis Philippe had been blessed with two sons, a ceremony that "has always appeared to me to be supremely ridiculous." And one evening Mrs. Polk summoned him from a conference with the erupting Allen to a party in the East Room, where Herr Alexander was performing "tricks of slight of hand." The President's nieces and some forty or fifty guests watched the professor exhibit "his art greatly to their wonder and amusement, but as I think not much to their edification or profit."

But now the President encountered a juggler from the big time. On February 13 a Colonel Atocha obtained audience at the White House. This was a Spaniard who had once lived in New Orleans but whose immediate importance was that he had later been an associate and now was probably an agent of General Antonio López de Santa Anna.

Santa Anna is the set piece of Mexican history, complete with rockets, pinwheels, Greek fire, and aerial bombs. He had been president of Mexico, dictator, commander in chief, much too often and too variously for specification here. He had contrived to persuade a good many different factions that he was their soul, and had never betrayed any of them till he had got their funds. He was enormously rich — on the invasion, Lieutenant Colonel Ethan Allen Hitchcock was to inspect his abandoned castle and remark in his journal on the luxurious hangings and fine art it was packed with, and no sign of cloth or furniture or picture that had been made in Mexico. He had the national genius for oratory and manifesto, and a genius of his own for courage, cowardice, inspiration, and magnificent graft. He had massacred hundreds of Texans at Goliad, the Alamo, and elsewhere. He had been well licked by them at San Jacinto and, captured, had conceded their independence. Since then he had procured further revolutions at home, had lost a leg defending his country against a French invasion, had established a new dictatorship, and had been overthrown by the uprising that put Herrera in power. His impeachment for treason and his banishment had followed. Now he was in Havana with a beautiful young wife, intriguing on a scale not to be matched again, even in Mexico, before the arrival there of Leon Trotsky. Nothing could be of greater interest to Polk than Santa Anna's relations with the Paredes government, which seemed ambiguous.

On behalf of this cosmic scoundrel, Colonel Atocha proceeded to explain Mexican politics to Mr. Polk. Above all things, it appeared, Santa Anna desired tranquillity for Mexico, and he held that peace with the United States was a necessary condition. Furthermore, he recognized the logic of geography and so would concede that Texas extended westward to the Rio Grande — thus handing half of New Mexico to Mr. Polk — and the "Colorado of the West down through the bay of San Francisco could be the Mexican line on the North." [1] Let us frankly face the fact, however, that this cession would necessitate a certain expense: thirty million dollars would probably be required. Any Mexican government that got hold of thirty millions could firmly establish itself. But Atocha made clear that the patriotic Mexicans would not consent to any government's selling them out; the cession must appear to be forced. He would suggest that Washington take stronger measures. Taylor's army should invade Mexico (Polk did not tell him it had been ordered to), the fleet should concentrate off Vera Cruz, and Minister Slidell, then waiting at Jalapa (Santa Anna's home town) for word from Paredes, should go on board a warship and peremptorily demand payment of the American claims. Such action would convince both the clergy, whose interests would be imperiled, and the common people, who needed the discipline of a scare, that the United States was in earnest. Santa Anna would return to power in April or May and, if given such strong measures for a leverage, would conclude the treaty that was as close to his heart as to Polk's. He and Paredes, by the way, could facilitate the business if they had some cash in hand — say half a million dollars. . . . Before leaving, Colonel Atocha put out another teaser: the loyalty of two of the northern provinces, Nuevo León and Tamaulipas, was uncertain and Polk could annex them easily.

Splendid! and an excellent simplification of a tiresome problem. Polk took Atocha to be thoroughly unreliable but nevertheless laid his suggestions before the Cabinet in good faith, got the Cabinet's approval, and from then on believed that he could buy a peace. He proposed to instruct Slidell exactly as Atocha had suggested, but omitted clapping him on the warship when the actual instructions were prepared. Thereafter no matter how many armies he raised, no matter what appropriations he asked of Congress to support them, he kept in mind the chance that he could fight the war with bribes. . . . With the result that his hope of waging a bloodless war, already sufficiently dangerous to the success of the war, intensified. Neither he nor his Cabinet seems to have appreciated that Santa Anna's proposal was one of the most outrageous in the history of nations. Worse, they were unaware that they were being used as aides to gang politics in Mexico — in plain American, that they were being played for suckers to assist in the overthrow of Paredes. What the Americans of '46 thought of the Mexicans shows quite clearly — and the decay of American statesmanship.

Jim Clyman watched the California earth swell like a sponge in the spring rains and then burst open with beets, cabbages, onions, radishes, turnips — the peaches beginning to bud, the willows reddening along the creeks, "the native grasses and wild oats ancle high." On February 18 he decided that the rainy season was over. The lower slopes began to dry out and one could find a bottom beneath the valley mud. He heard talk of a party getting ready to go to Oregon, whence he had come, and another one forming for the States. Both journeys must be made over "long, tiresome and somewhat dangerous routs." But Jim had been in California for quite a spell and the spring fret came over him. Might be a good notion to move on somewheres else.

As Clyman's record of it shows, the winter had been near its end when Brevet Captain Frémont asked permission of the authorities to spend it in the San Joaquin Valley. No matter. He settled down to spend the winter on the deserted Laguna Seca *rancho* near San Jose, two mountain ranges, two valleys, and a good many miles west of the San Joaquin. Still, the bulk of his party, whom he had sent round the mountains (and whom he told the authorities he had punctiliously left at the frontier), were now tramping down the San Joaquin Valley — trying to find him. They joined him near San Jose at last, on February 15. Sixty extremely tough foreigners commanded by a foreign army officer were now where they had no permission to be, where they had promised not to be, and where they had no instructions from their government to be.

Frémont speaks favorably of the spring weather at San Jose, and his command had a good time. Their camp attracted all resident and transient Americans, who talked industriously about this province, its inhabitants, and the rumors of war and revolution. The amiable Californians visited too, pleased by these strange, hairy *americanos* who were such miraculous marksmen. They had some prodigies of their own, and were glad to exhibit feats of horsemanship which were amazing even to men who knew the Ute and the Comanche. With ropes also the Californians were unsurpassed. Moreover they had the strangest native cookery, hot with chili but very grateful after the rations of an exploring trip. Amiable, sunny, slothful, in the opinion of the Americans a lot of stinking greasers, something of a sideshow or even a zoo. But their good nature was attractive, so were their women, and the native wines were bland.

The Californians were of two factions, a revolution having occurred just a few months before. (California revolution: by proclamation. No unthrifty waste of gunpowder, no indecorous bloodletting, just some heroic marching and a fierce barrage of rhetoric. But it had had the assistance of some Americans on the make. And it was the sort of thing Larkin had been instructed to facilitate.) Excuse the authorities, particularly Don Pío Pico, the nativist revolutionary governor, if they anticipated that Frémont's force, whose presence here violated a formal agreement, might try to make headway by stirring up the outs. Frémont had already shot up some Indians, and no Indians cared in the least what white men they murdered in satisfaction of other white men's deeds. And the authorities were under notice from Mexico City that trouble with the United States was brewing and all foreigners were to be carefully watched. But as yet the governor merely cautioned Don José Castro, the *comandante,* not to go to sleep.

Frémont was outfitting his party — with, among other things, fresh horses. One of the principal personages of the Santa Clara Valley, Don Sebastian Peralta, believed that he saw some horses from his own great herd at the American camp, and they had certainly not been purchased. He made claim for them and was told to go to hell. He went instead to the alcalde of San Jose and filed a complaint. On February 20 the court summoned Frémont to answer it.

Why, good God! A greaser presume to hold John Charles Frémont to account? (It was the more galling in that Sutter had just written Frémont asserting that some of the horses which Frémont's men had stolen from the Indians had been, perhaps previously, stolen from New Helvetia.) Frémont, a literary man, sat down to express himself. Don Sebastian, he told the alcalde, was lucky not to have been horsewhipped out of camp. The captain of topographical engineers would hereafter not even write a letter, and "you will readily understand that my duties will not permit me to appear before the magistrates of your towns on the complaint of every straggling vagabond who may chance to visit my camp." As for the alcalde's threat to forward the complaint to the governor if Frémont did not answer it, why, Childe Harold's cloak thrown over one shoulder, let the alcalde make sure, when he should forward it, to "enclose to his Excellency a copy of this note."

A touch of paranoia? Hardly. Just a man great with destiny and labor coming on. Frémont's dignity was always on a hair trigger (he was a South Carolinian) and even an obscure official of a declining power in a far province could discharge it. And he had not had an audience for a long time. His literary batteries were overloaded.

The alcalde sent the complaint on to the governor, obediently forwarding a copy of Frémont's letter with it. And on February 22 (the same day when, at last, Lieutenant Gillespie sailed from Mazatlán for Honolulu) Frémont got his expedition moving. His instructions from Washington were to explore the way to Oregon through the Cascades. (Others with a better sense of practical needs would presently begin doing just that.) And he had suggested to the California authorities that he might want to survey a road out of the country southeastward, by way of the Gila. He neither obeyed his orders nor followed his own suggestion. Instead, without permission or purpose, he moved west across the Santa Cruz Mountains to the coast and then south in the direction of Monterey.

No reason. But he believed in his star. There was no way of knowing what had been happening in the States — the present status of the contention with Mexico or of the contention with Great Britain. But the most recent news in California, Consul Larkin's a month ago, showed both contentions accelerating, and — what is much more important — Frémont had been talking with the resident Americans. The golden shore was, even to a calm eye, a province drifting in anarchy, the Mexican hold on it slackening, the natives divided by factions, wild rumors of European grabs widely believed, and some vigorous, not to say violent, Americans, some of whom had been trying for years to seize it for the flag, worried because more had not happened and eager to help out if anything should start to happen. Frémont's hour might well be on the march; if only he stayed here he might soon be able to do a great deed. The stage was ready, the hero was at hand, and it might turn out to be a very great deed.

About fifty miles north of Quincy, Illinois, a point of land thrusts out into the Mississippi. It looks across the cocoa-colored water to Lee County, Iowa, twelve miles above Keokuk. It is about a hundred miles west northwest of Springfield on the Sangamon, where Jim Clyman had run his traverses, where in this winter month a friend of Clyman's, James Frazier Reed, was settling his affairs before moving west, and where an army messmate of both, A. Lincoln, was practising law and moving his pieces toward the Whig nomination for the House of Representatives. On this peninsula, marshy at the riverside but rising to high bluffs with prairie land beyond them, there had been built in 1839 the city of the Lord God Jehovah, King of Kings. It was called Nauvoo and its name, we are instructed, meant "Beautiful Place." Now in February, 1846, it was fallen — that great city.

Acres of ice floated in the river and a wind out of the north tossed the makeshift ferries about, that first day, February 4. The ferries were jammed with men, women, children, horses, oxen, cows, swine, chickens, feather beds, Boston rockers, a miscellany of families and goods hastily brought together in the fear of death. The boats dumped them on the Iowa shore and turned back for other, identical freights — American refugees fleeing a city under threat from an enemy. They landed, hitched up such equipage as they had, and moved out on the frozen prairie. Nine miles inland they reached a timbered stretch, on Sugar Creek, and here they pitched a camp. The timber made a windbreak; they chinked it with such wagons and carts as they had been able to cross; some tents went up; those who had neither wagon nor tent hurried to raise huts of bed quilts, logs, bark, or brush. Men felled trees to make great fires, the logs sizzling as the hard snow crust melted. Winter night came up beyond the grove. Supper was whatever you had brought with you, cooked in pans held out to the fires.

Afterward, they sang hymns, prayed, and listened to instruction from the elders. They stayed by the fires while they could, then huddled under stiff blankets in the tents or on the snow. Many women, most of the children, were sick — undermined by months of terrorism, by farewells and the bitter crossing, by the unknown.

There was need to bring more than one screaming child out from the blankets, to warm him and show him familiar faces at the fires which the men kept going all night. There was more urgent need for the fires: that night on Sugar Creek nine babies were born, their squalling a muted note against the winter wind.

The ferries ran all day when weather permitted. Gales tossed them about, terrified oxen kicked holes in them, unskillful piloting swamped them. Hosea Stout, crossing his family, saw a boat go under, felt that the Destroyer brooded over the land, and "remembered the revelation which Said the Lord had cursed the watters in the Last Days and Said in my heart it was verily true." Then on February 13 the river froze clear to Iowa and families could begin crossing on the ice. Some eight hundred such families were on Sugar Creek when Brigham Young, President of the Quorum of the Twelve Apostles, crossed on February 15. Five years before, the word of the Lord to the prophet Joseph had told Israel to build a city here and name it Zarahemla, in commemoration of the great city which Israel's precursors, the Nephites, fresh from Jerusalem, had built in Central America ages ago. Trouble and strife had kept Israel from obeying the commandment, however, and this was just a camp on a frozen creek, the first station on a journey west. They did what they could, plastered the bark huts with mud, thickened the brush walls, made some ineffective attempts at sanitation. The temperature fell to twenty below, moderated long enough for great snows to bury the huts, went down again. Lean-tos and cabins went up, some shelter could be had for the dying, and the camp grew along the creek as people kept coming from Nauvoo. Lee County was settled, if only thinly, and many brethren went out to look for work, splitting rails or chopping firewood mostly, to be paid in grain. However destitute, these were Israel's richest and they did not too greatly suffer for food, though sometimes many fed on no more than a gruel of corn meal, sometimes there was envy when a brother whose heart had hardened tapped a crate of hams and bacons for his private use, sometimes a newborn child must turn crying from a breast gone dry.

Newcomers kept arriving. The Twelve met in council, the bishops anointed the sick and made assignments for the common labor, by night there were prayer meetings and hymn festivals. By night also there were dances to the music of Captain Pitts's brass band, which had been converted as a group in England to praise Israel's God. Blacksmith shops were set up; the wagons and the stock were being readied for the journey. In Brother Markham's buggy, an old-fashioned foot warmer under her blankets, Eliza Snow, secretly a widow of the martyred prophet Joseph and soon to be a wife of the prophet Brigham, wrote her poetry.

They renamed Sugar Creek the Brook Kedron. Hosea Stout gathered the Temple guards into a new organization and cleared a parade ground for them in the snow. As colonel of this regiment he raised a white flag above his tent. "But it refused to waive in the air notwithstanding there was a light breeze, which seemed to say that it would not proclaim peace in the United States when there was nought but oppression and tyranny towards the people of God by rulers of this government and the Saints fleeing from her borders to the wilderness for safety and refuge from her iron yoke."

In the East, Elder Priddy Meeks learned that Exodus had begun, and came hurrying home to Nauvoo. He had to pass through Carthage, the seething stronghold of the anti-Mormons. Men shouting obscene oaths surrounded him, took his horse, swore to carve his heart out, and on no charge flung him into Carthage jail. It was a small jail: he had to look at a dark stain on the floor, the unavenged blood of the prophet Joseph Smith and his brother Hyrum. A sheriff sympathized with him, procured a doubtful bond, and got him out of town on a borrowed horse. At Nauvoo Brother McCleary had been building a wagon for him on shares, but Brother Meeks now had to trade his interest in it for a barrel of flour. He still had a small, one-horse wagon in good shape; he swapped it for a larger one in execrable shape. To this he hitched a pair of "three-year-old, unbroke bullocks" and was able to borrow a yoke of oxen to drive ahead of them till they were gentled.

Elder Meeks was a man of property. He owned an interest in Brother McCleary's wagon shop, which he bade McCleary sell to anyone who would help the less fortunate cross the river. He owned the horse which had been stolen from him at Carthage; he assigned it to Lawyer Edmunds, who was defending him. He owned a small flock of sheep; there was no time to sell them and no one to buy them, so he just let them stray. He owned a house and lot; houses and lots in Nauvoo were selling for whatever a buyer cared to offer and no one was interested in his. He left it there, with furniture and books which any anti-Mormon in a thrifty mood could cart away. His disintegrating wagon packed with as much as it could carry, he and his family crossed the river. He thought that twenty dollars would repair it enough to travel to the Missouri, if not the Rocky Mountains, whither, he knew vaguely, Israel was to travel. They were safe on the Iowa shore — safe at least from mobbers.

He did not know what might lie ahead, except that the Lord had said to Joseph the Seer, "Thou mayest go up also unto the goodly land, to possess thine inheritance." Maybe he remembered the goodly land that had been Israel's inheritance in Missouri and now Illinois. But, turning his back on the river, Elder Meeks laid the gad to his unbroken bullocks. They moved off toward Sugar Creek, the rachitic wagon groaning. The road sloped upward and they came to a small hill. He looked back to the ferry landing, across the water, to the roofs of Nauvoo, to the edifice that dominated the city, the temple reared to the Lord God Jehovah.

And send ye swift messengers [the Lord had commanded Joseph], yea, chosen messengers, and say unto them: Come ye, with all your gold, and your silver, and your precious stones, and with all your antiquities; and with all who have knowledge of antiquities, that will come, may come, and bring the box tree, and the fir tree, and the pine tree, together with all the precious trees of the earth;

And with iron, with copper, and with brass, and with zinc, and with all your precious things of the earth, and build a house to my name, for the Most High to dwell therein.

Israel had begun a house for the Most High and had gone on building and furnishing it with antiquities after the murder of the prophet, during the tumult of the Burnings, and up to now. It was still unfinished but for some months it had been acceptable unto the Lord and the priesthood had been conferring the endowments in it — to Elder Meeks and as many more as there was time for. So he looked back at God's house. His marriage ceremony had been repeated there in the new and everlasting covenant, and there he had been baptized many times, as proxy for ancestors who had lived during the darker centuries when the priesthood was withdrawn from the earth. The tabernacle of the mysteries, built to His holy name on the high hill, Israel's morning star and a beacon to the peoples of the earth. God had promised that it would endure, but Israel had learned in suffering that His ways were mysterious altogether, and Elder Meeks's heart darkened. He looked once more at his home and the altar of his pieties, then went on westward, toward Sugar Creek.

So came to climax in civil war and the flight of American citizens as other refugees have fled Attila or Hitler — so came to climax thirteen years of contention between the Church of Jesus Christ of

Latter-day Saints and their neighbors on the middle border. The climax had been preceded by two years of terrorism, arson, and gang warfare. It cannot be justified or palliated. But it has to be explained.

In a mob uprising, the citizens of Hancock County, Illinois, had murdered Joseph Smith, Jun., and his brother Hyrum, in Carthage jail, on June 27, 1844, at "about five o'clock, P.M." That was supposed to settle matters forevermore but it settled nothing. When the lynchers killed that poor crazed man they had murdered a prophet but had not destroyed a church.[2] Instead they had halted its certain break-up from within and given it immortality with that surest of fertilizers, the blood of the martyrs. For a while chaos did indeed seem likely to destroy it, as various pretenders reached for Elijah's mantle. Sidney Rigdon told the terrified Saints of a vision that made him guardian of the Church; a small fragment accepted it as from God and followed him counter-clockwise to Pennsylvania. James Jesse Strang produced a letter from Joseph (not in the Seer's handwriting) and a signed revelation from God, very much like Joseph's, appointing him to rule over Israel. This was a much more serious heresy, which reached its height during the spring and summer of '46 while Israel was actually on the march, and for a while seemed likely to be victorious. But, though it captured many of the Eastern stakes of Zion, it lost the all-important battle for the missions in England. So it waned and was soon a mere parody of Mormonism with Strang the anointed King of Beaver Island, practising polygamy, announcing the wildest revelations, and making the enemies who finally murdered him in what was, for Mormon martyrdoms, privacy. The nuclei of at least three more schismatic sects formed at Nauvoo between the Martyrdom and the Exodus; still another small one split off as the Saints crossed Iowa; all told these half-dozen, dividing by mitosis, were to form over twenty minute churches, each one the true apostolic succession from the martyr.

They did not matter in the least. While Sidney Rigdon wailed his vision from the back of a wagon in the grove at Nauvoo, a master was listening to him. After a little work behind the scenes, Brigham Young called the Saints together. And the Saints beheld a transfiguration. That pudgy body suddenly became the tall, handsome, commanding body of the martyred prophet; from Brigham's throat came the very voice of Joseph. While Brigham was telling them that the Twelve Apostles, of whom he was the head, would rule over Israel, the Saints believed that a miracle had brought Joseph back from the grave. In miracle they found the courage that united them again, but they had never been farther from the truth. This was a much greater man than Joseph. Instead of a man drunk on deity whose mind swooned with apocalyptic splendors but who could produce no effective leadership, no effective government, no effective social organization, there had come to lead the Church out of the land of Egypt one of the foremost intelligences of the time, the first American who learned how to colonize the desert.

Young had the help of a few first-rate men: George Q. Cannon, Willard Richards, Charles Coulson Rich, Orson and Parley Pratt. He had the help, possibly more valuable, of such more rugged, more tireless, if less intelligent men as Orson Hyde, Heber Kimball, Jedediah Grant, Lorenzo Snow, John Taylor, Wilford Woodruff, various other dedicated souls. But their sum was small. It was Young who saved the Saints. Without him Mormonism would have become exactly what its heresies became, a series of dividing sects dwindling to handfuls of gaffers remembering Joseph in their sorrow and waiting for the sky to open and show him come again.

He had to unify Israel, give it courage and hope. He had to defend it against such heresiarchs as Strang. How he achieved these ends is not our present concern but how he saved his people from Illinois and Missouri. The society surrounding the Mormons was anarchy. No court had authority, no peace officer was obeyed, sheriffs were mobbers or Mormons and acted according to their affiliation, the militia was only the mob given leaders. In the fall of 1844, four months after the death of Smith, it was possible for an invitation to circulate through the surrounding countries, summoning fanciers to a wolf hunt. Wolf hunt meant burning the Mormons' houses, running off their stock, and killing a good many of them. The formal hunt did not come that year or the next, but informal terrorism continued. The Saints rode and raided and stoned and shot in turn. The Gentiles (the word means anyone not a Mormon) plundered still more and grew more scared of reprisals, circulated and believed rumors that the Mormons intended to massacre them, called on the state and national governments to subdue them. The demand was, as Governor Thomas Ford says, a demand for a military dictatorship in Illinois. The Mormon counter-demand for the same dictatorship as a protection seems more reasonable.

The Illini were asking the extermination of the Mormons and beginning to achieve it piecemeal. By '45 they had become more realistic and recurred to the earlier compromise of the Missourians, asking only the expulsion of the Mormons. At first Young had stood on the Constitution and the Bill of Rights, but he recognized the inevitable, accepted it, and began to prepare his church to move west. Throughout '45 Nauvoo and the lesser stakes of Zion were a workshop making ready the emigration of a people — some fifteen or twenty thousand. But you do not loose such emotions as the Illini had been feeling for nearly two years without paying for them. The Mormons were leaving, were they? — then whoop it up. There was a chance to pay off old scores, to avenge floggings and knivings and murders, to have some fun, to make a profit. To make a profit, most of all. The real and personal property of the Saints now came into a buyers' market, a market systematically made more favorable for buyers. Crowd the seller for time and scare him: Economics A, first proposition.

So the "Burnings" began. System was introduced into an activity that had been haphazard and sporadic. The mobbers "worked quietly and methodically. They would call upon a farmer, state the object of their visit and would then assist the family in removing their household effects to a safe distance. They would then set the torch to the house and, watching it until it burned, they would leave behind them a bed of glowing embers, a jag of furniture, and a weeping family with broken hearts. It was then easy to convince the family that it was time for them to leave Illinois." Such mobbers were well-behaved, if perhaps not quite so courteous as the United States Army moving Cherokees off their lands to accommodate the Georgians. Sometimes the decorous ones encountered opposition, however, and there were others who enjoyed being tough.

If here and there a voice was raised against them and if a genuine outrage was expressed in the press at a safe distance, nothing was done locally to stop them except what the Mormons could do in self-defense. So mob rule, terrorism, expropriation, and occasional murder went on in the soundly American state of Illinois. And precisely the same thing had happened to the Saints twice before in Missouri. They had been driven out of Jackson County, into less settled lands, and in 1838 they had been driven out of those lands with greater violence and bloodshed than they were experiencing now in Illinois. Why?

The answer is not single but multiple, and begins with the cliché which the Mormons have applied to themselves for a hundred and ten years, "We are a peculiar people." Most of that peculiarity was stamped on them by the aberrations of Joseph Smith. At all times the generality of Saints have been sincere, kindly, God-fearing, hard-working people. But from the beginning they have had the complete smugness of a people on whom a monopoly of truth and virtue was conferred by Almighty God. And in their earlier decades that monopoly was further certified by God's assurance, to a people who would not dream of questioning the least, literal syllable of it, that they would dominate the whole world almost at once. That they would, by divine violence chiefly but not without the co-operation of human violence, triumph over the Gentiles and possess their "inheritance," in plainer words, their property. This highly inflammable assurance permeated a society which, at the base and in detail, was incompatible with the society it tried to live in. Twice in Missouri and once in Illinois there came into a frontier community a co-operating group who believed that Judgment Day was close at hand, that it would initiate their domination of the whole earth, that their actions were in obedience to God's commands, that their neighbors were without God and so against God.

Various payments were being collected on one of history's due bills. American evangelism, from the Great Awakening on, had ended by igniting the vast camp meetings at the turn of the nineteenth century, which burned eastward from Kentucky. From the soil thus burned over had sprung both the thousands of believers who could accept a prophet and the psychotic boy who took his puberty walking in the woods and there talked with God, various patriarchs, angels, and demons. The cheap story of the golden plates and the colonization of the American continent by emigrants from Jerusalem, the mumbo-jumbo of illiterate, semi-Biblical, degraded Masonic rituals, the apocalyptic nonsense of the Mormon metaphysics — such things were in themselves enough to cause trouble on a frontier enthusiastically Methodist and Presbyterian. Communities much less ready to settle a contention by violence than the still early stages of this frontier culture could easily be touched off by the presence of a loud and numerous sect which held that it was in communication with God and that God promised it early, complete, and all too literal triumph. In addition, almost from its earliest year, Mormonism had taught and practised the doctrine of polygamy, if secretly.[3] The sexual mores of the frontier were exceeding free but, as in all the rest of America, the monogamous family was at the core of its institutions. In Putney, Vermont, a much less turbulent society than the Mormons found in Missouri and Illinois, the mere rumor that John Humphrey Noyes's handful of perfectionists were talking beyond monogamy sufficed to expel them to the

York State forest. On the frontier polygamy was dynamite with the fuse burning.

There was an even more powerful explosive in the economic system which the Church was developing. For two things the Mormons of today can be profoundly grateful, that though their forefathers did fall among Missourians and Illini they did not come in conflict with the Texans, and that Brigham Young, who could make the system work, did not rise to power in time to direct it in a settled community. Either event would have insured the extermination they escaped.

Mormonism was a great catch basin of evangelical doctrine. Everything ever preached by any Protestant heresy in America, always excepting celibacy, was at one time or another preached if not adopted in Mormonry. Smith's vertiginous mind wove the total into a crazy quilt of dogma. But also that mind worked on other flotsam that drifted within its reach, including the strivings of the little associations. If the Beehive House,* Brigham Young's wifery in Salt Lake City, was to see experiments in "rational dress" and calisthenics, that strain entered Mormonry in its earliest years, and came from the reformers whom Henry Thoreau repudiated. If the streets of Utah towns are true with the compass and so wide that Young seems to have foreseen the automobile, such city-planning floated through the Mormon daydreams long before Nauvoo, and got into them from Owen's New Harmony and other attempts of nature to anticipate Lewis Mumford and the General Motors Futurama. On February 27, 1833, the Lord spoke unto Joseph at Kirtland, Ohio, announcing the revelation still known as the Word of Wisdom, which commands the Saints to abstain from wine and hard liquor, from tobacco (though Young eventually ruled that snuff and chewing tobacco were exempt from the prohibition), from tea, coffee, and hot drinks generally, and in the summertime from animal food. And God was quoting Sylvester Graham, who was reverenced at Brook Farm, and a medley of other American reformers.

In this wise there came into Mormonism — directly from the Campbellites, the Shakers, the Rappites, New Harmony, and other sects and communities, indirectly from several decades of American thought at large — a stream of associative communism. In its earliest hours the Church instituted the United Order, a practical working communism (theocratic model) which was to hold the

* The beehive, which is a device of Mormon iconography and appears on the state seal of Utah, was a Fourierist symbol.

property and the labor of the Saints in common. Like the Shakers, like Zoar, Oneida, and others. It failed at once — because it was wholly unadaptable to the place and time and people, and for the further reason that Brigham Young had not come to take charge of it. Nevertheless by commandment of God it remained Israel's goal. Theoretically, though the practice was suspended, every Saint lived (and still lives) in the United Order, his labor and property at the disposition of the Trustee, and some day the Order will spread across the world. And though it failed in Missouri it accelerated the developing control of a united people by an oligarchy. Under the priesthood the Church acted far more like a co-operating unit than anything the middle border had ever seen. As Gentile opposition sharpened, co-operation increased.

So that in Missouri and Illinois alike, a sizable and growing body of people who obeyed the priesthood and were building up the kingdom in a highly literal way came into conflict with as vigorous and jealous a set of individualists as have ever lived anywhere. Furthermore, the Mormons had the edge. They could strongly influence and frequently control trade, real estate, and finance — in all of which their reputation was already bad. The economic power of masses arbitrarily controlled — a foreshadowing of Young's eventual autarky — was what first turned the Missourians against the Saints. The emotions of an individualist who has been bludgeoned by a monopoly are not soothed, moreover, when the monopolist explains that God Himself has commanded the assault. In Mormon eyes sharp business practices were as logical a part of the Kingdom being built up against the Terrible Day to come as fasting and prayer. No wonder that their opponents came to make no distinctions among real-estate speculation, the keys of prophecy, co-operative landholding, and the holy languages of Heaven.

We may also remember the motto of Captain Simon Suggs of the Tallapoosy Vollantares: "It is good to be shifty in a new country." A fixed part of the frontier experience was the inevitable conflict between the "butcher-knife boys" and the elements of respectability, the pitched battle between the lawless of the frontier and the frontier as a developing social stability. It seems certain that, in Missouri and Illinois both, the first violence between Mormons and Gentiles broke out among the butcher-knife or squatter elements, the unstabilized, the incompletely absorbed. It was in a sense close to the action of those Regulators and night riders who are usually to be found at this stage of the frontier, all the way from the Alleghenies to the Indian Territory. The squatter element was present alike among the Saints and their enemies. Unquestionably some portions of Israel spoiled the Gentiles by theft, burglary, and fraud, and found protection in the holy city. There was counterfeiting. There were various kinds of sucker-baiting to the greater glory of God. There were shady banking and shady credit manipulation. And wildcat real-estate operations reached as high as the Prophet Joseph himself, who inflated land prices so systematically that one must not too greatly sorrow over their collapse when Nauvoo fell.[4]

Finally, the greatest offense of the Mormon system was its political cohesion. The frontier took its democratic elections with the greatest possible seriousness — and Joseph Smith voted his church for whoever would pay most for the vote. The Church was a bloc that could turn the balance of power. It was the foolish use of this power in Illinois — quite as foolishly purchased by both Democrats and Whigs in turn — that finally exploded the dynamite which the other peculiarities of the Saints had heaped up. The one-party system is what drove Mormonism out of Illinois. (The Saints repeated this mistake blatantly in Iowa, California, and Nevada. It was at least as powerful an irritant as polygamy in the conflict between Utah and the national government down to statehood. It is the principal source of friction with Gentiles today.)

A note on Missouri, to introduce two persons of our drama. It was Lillburn W. Boggs who, as governor of the state, had loosed six thousand militia on the Mormons when, in 1838, Carroll and Davies Counties flared with precisely the same mob violence we have seen at Nauvoo. The Gentiles were howling that the Mormons must be expelled, the Mormons howling that the Lord had loosed His people to vengeance. There were night riding, burnings, floggings, lonely murder, and occasional attacks in force. Finally Governor Boggs directed the general of his militia, "The Mormons must be treated as enemies and must be exterminated or driven from the State if necessary for the public peace — their outrages are beyond description." That was the "Extermination Order" of October, '38, and the Mormons have not forgotten it to this day, quite rightly. So in 1842 O. P. Rockwell, one of the Sons of Dan (the "Destroying Angels" of ten-cent fiction), crept up to a window in Boggs's house and shot him — not quite fatally. Under the charter granted Nauvoo by an Illinois legislature eager for Mormon votes neither Rockwell nor the prophet who had inspired the assault could be held to answer for it — and that immunity helped to keep alive in Missouri the hatred that had been lighted by the guerrilla wars. . . . Boggs was a person moving west in '46, appropriately. He had moved from

Kentucky to St. Louis. There he married a sister of the brothers Bent who maintained far up the Arkansas a trading post that was one of the most famous and influential institutions of the mountain trade. He moved again, to the far frontier of Missouri, and set up in business at Independence, outfitting Santa Fe traders and venturers to the mountains. At this far outpost town, which lived on the traffic of the wilderness, his wife died. He married Panthea, a granddaughter of Daniel Boone. She and three of her brothers (their father was also an outfitter at Independence) went with him when he pulled up stakes for California.

One of his militia commanders in 1838 was Alexander Doniphan. He was a famous jury lawyer, probably the best in all Missouri, and it followed naturally that he commanded six militia regiments. He was a mighty man — and a righteous one. So when General Lucas captured Joseph and other leaders of the Church and, in obedience to Boggs's Extermination Order, tried them by court-martial and ordered them to be shot for treason in the public square at Far West, Doniphan took a stand. Called upon to execute the condemned, he refused. "It is cold-blooded murder," he wrote his general. "I will not obey your order. My brigade shall march for Liberty tomorrow morning at 8 o'clock, and if you execute these men I will hold you responsible before an earthly tribunal, so help me God." His troops marched, the order was not executed, and the chastened general, after holding the condemned prisoners over the winter, finally arranged for them to escape.[5]

Even before that, Doniphan had tried to deal justly with the Mormons. When they got into trouble at their earliest Missouri settlements, in Jackson County, Doniphan, as a member of the Legislature, had put through the bill which set off two new counties, Davies and Caldwell, in the unoccupied part of the state and arranged for the Mormons to take one of them. He had also represented Joseph in various suits brought against him; during one of them it had been the prophet's whim to study law under him. . . . He was very much of Benton's type, a crammed, insatiable mind, a conspicuous integrity. This is the image of the leader in frontier democracy, the kind of man who was called an empire-builder before the phrase lost its meaning. He also was to go west in '46.

By revelation Jackson County, Missouri, from which the Saints were first expelled, was to be the eventual gathering place of the saved in the Last Days. They were commanded to build a city there, and a temple. Others have built the city and they had not even started the temple when they were driven out. (Israel cannot even buy from the tiny, obstinate schism that owns it, the site revealed for it by God Himself.) They went to Clay and Caldwell Counties and when they were driven thence, they went to Nauvoo. . . . So that when Joseph was killed in Carthage jail there had been eleven years of fluctuating strife between Mormons and Gentiles. It is a long time for violence to go hunting on both sides of a dogma. The glory of God, revenge, eternal right, economic monopoly, political necessity, mob panic and mob ecstasy — they make a strong brew. Murder in Carthage jail and the Burnings were the climax of a debauch.

But it must not be forgotten that, during the last two years of his life, Joseph's paranoia had increased. He had always been drunk on glory, now he was drunk on power. His fury fell alike on those who questioned him within the Church, the Missouri Pukes, and the Congress and President of the United States. In musical-comedy uniforms, he was lieutenant general of the Nauvoo Legion; its rituals were fantastic but its muskets were just as usable as any the Pukes had. He had announced himself as a candidate for President against Polk and Henry Clay — his platform was mostly apocalypse but included a plank for the seizure of the West — and several hundred missionaries were stumping the East to get him votes. He had dropped some of the secrecy that had hidden the doctrine of polygamy; he and many of his hierarchy were practising it with a widening range that could not be altogether covered by denials.

All these were blunders; the last was the worst blunder. There had always been dissent in Israel, backsliders, apostates, a sizable if futile bulk of opposition. Suddenly opposition to polygamy crystallized in a revolt led by men of courage and genuine intelligence. They struck hard, establishing in Nauvoo a newspaper which denounced Joseph. He struck back, and the newspaper printed one issue only. Joseph's marshal, assisted by Joseph's Legion, pied its type and pounded its press to pieces in the street. The rebels fled. The Illini, especially the politicians who had been sold out, needed just this to produce their own uprising. Illinois had had enough of the Mormons, the mob rose, and Joseph was killed.

Brigham Young inherited. After some effort to prevent the inevitable, he accepted it. Israel would leave Illinois — would go west. So while mob and Mormons took pot shots at one another and both sides spread rumors of massacre which might easily have come true, Brigham and his counselors met with a commission which Governor Ford named to procure peace. The commission required the Mormons to get out, in return for which it would secure their safety while making preparations to go. If they refused to go, the commission said, it seemed certain that they would be exterminated. The commission included Stephen A. Douglas, the Little Giant, and John J. Hardin, lately member of Congress from Illinois, now canvassing for the same seat in competition with Lincoln, eventually to die in command of the First Illinois Volunteers at Buena Vista. There were no better citizens; if their terms were harsh, they were also realistic. Mormonism could no longer exist in Illinois; if it had tried to, James K. Polk would have had a fair-sized civil war on his hands.

Through 1845, then, the Saints sent broadcast over the world a literature describing their oppression, and memorialized all governing and religious bodies, but also they prepared the Exodus. (Meanwhile, for the fulfillment of prophecy, they rushed the completion of the Temple. Workmen had to keep their rifles near at hand, lest the mob come. But God's pleasure was manifested: sometimes "a flame of fire was seen by many to rest down upon the Temple." By the end of January enough was finished so that the ordinances could begin — sealing in marriage for eternity and baptism for the dead.) They made thousands of wagons — collecting all the seasoned timber they could, hastily kiln-drying more, pickling still more in a half-effective brine. The forges beat out tons of tires and ironwork. Agents bought rifles, pistols, revolvers, shotguns, muskets, and all the supplies they had money for. The Eastern and European missions sent what cash they could raise to help out. The brethren built and assembled equipment. The sisters made clothes, tents, wagon covers; preserved fruit, corned beef, pickled pork, dried beef, parched corn, put out potatoes and pumpkins to dehydrate in the sun, even parched the crusts left over at mealtime. Everything they had that could not be used on the journey was offered for sale, and the Gentiles picked up excellent bargains in land, houses, furniture, farm implements, and stock. They kept the prices good by means of the Burnings. Guilt mingled with avarice, their consciences were uneasy, and rumors began to run again. Maybe the Mormons weren't going to leave after all, or maybe they intended to work a final bloody revenge before leaving. So, though the peace commission had guaranteed them security till spring, it seemed expedient to get them started earlier. There was some more musketry, an indictment charged Brigham and some of his Twelve with counterfeiting, various marshals and posses came into the city hunting arms and Apostles. It sufficed. On February 4 the first ferries pushed through floating ice and grounded on the Iowa shore.

God had anciently spoken unto Moses: "For Pharaoh will say of the children of Israel, they are entangled in the land, the wilderness hath shut them in."

When the first wagons started west from Sugar Creek (on March 1), Lorenzo Snow wrote that they "were moving to — we know not where." He was telling the truth — and he was high in the government of the Church. Israel had a marching song, "O Upper California, that's the land for me," but in the States Upper California meant anywhere south of Oregon and west of the divide. Word reached Sutter's that the Mormons might come to New Helvetia, even that Lansford Hastings was acting as their agent, and it scared the settlement badly. Some Saints believed that they would end in Texas, where in fact Lyman Wight's small schism did settle, and some of the Apostles had discussed going there. A more important idea was to settle on Vancouver Island. This seemed likely to be forever outside the jurisdiction of the United States, which throughout 1845 was considered to be leagued with Satan in hostility to the Church. (When Elder Little called on President Polk to ask for help he found that the idea of a Mormon colony at Vancouver Island was a powerful leverage on the President's goodwill.) Still other destinations were rumored, from Mexico, where the ancient Church had had great cities, to the Sandwich Islands. Yet most Saints believed that Zion was to rise somewhere in the Rocky Mountains, and they were right. The Twelve knew as much when the emigration started. Brigham Young could even specify the interior basin.

It was inevitable that the Mormons should go west. Israel's needle had pointed that way from the beginning. It had moved westward from Palmyra to Kirtland and on to Independence, though it had taken the back trail to Nauvoo. Doctrine held that the Indians, or Lamanites, were the decayed survivors of the earlier Church, and the Dispensation of the Fullness of Time, which Joseph Smith had instituted, was required to bring them back to grace. The first mission to Jackson County had gone there to convert the Lamanites. In Missouri the Saints were always in touch with Indians, mountain men, traders, all the traffic and impetus of the far frontier. At intervals, when Satan raged, Joseph dreamed of the Rocky Mountains. The dream flickered in his sermons, so that the Saints were habituated to it — though both the Garden of Eden and the gathering place of the Saints in the Last Days continued to be Missouri. Shortly before his death, he had ordered Brother James Emmett to go to the mountains and find a resting place for Israel, though Emmett did not begin his reconnoissance till after the martyrdom. Joseph had even started west himself, on the wild flight before he decided to surrender to his persecutors at Carthage, and in his panic vision the Church was to follow him. Yet this was as irresponsible as all Joseph's ideas during his last years. The only genuine action he ever took was to ask President John Tyler for authority to enlist a mere matter of "one hundred thousand armed volunteers" for the conquest of the West. Or the Prophet, Seer, and Revelator, Lieutenant General Smith of the Nauvoo Legion, at the head of as many troops as Polk raised all told for the Mexican War, and eight or ten times as many as any officer commanded in it.

Brigham Young was a realist. Texas was out of the question; it was square in the path of empire, and if the Saints could not survive among Illini and Missourians, they had still less chance to survive among Texans. California was no better. The notion of settling at or near the mouth of the Colorado (we shall see Cooke suggesting it to the Mormon Battalion) was considered and rejected. Israel would not be a buffer state between the Americans and the Mexicans, though the idea of maintaining an outpost there seems to have developed very early. By 1846 it was clear that northern California was also a Gentile terminus; a large emigration was preparing for it and anti-Christ in person, ex-Governor Boggs, was going to go there. The golden shore, as either an independent republic or a territory of the United States, was certain to fill up with Israel's enemies, and this fact was quite clear to Young before the migration started. The two hundred and thirty-eight Mormons who sailed with Sam Brannan in the *Brooklyn* on February 4, the day when the first ferries crossed to Iowa, expected that the main body of the Church would join them west of the Sierra, and many of the Battalion, who started west six months later, shared that belief. But even before the *Brooklyn* sailed, Young was thinking of its company as only an outpost — which, in the San Joaquin Valley, is what it became.

It may have been Stephen A. Douglas who initiated the idea of Vancouver Island. That was a politician's happy solution but Young appears not to have taken it seriously, except that another outpost there would be a good thing and it could be colonized with converts from the British Isles. (As late as November, '46, the Church was memorializing the British government for help in establishing such a colony. Nothing came of it.) Douglas shifted and recommended Oregon, which the Saints had considered much more seriously. But Oregon also was impossible — whether as the United States or as the Republic of the West which Daniel Webster and so many others envisioned. Young had rejected it before 1846. Oregon also was square in the path of empire, it had ten times as many Americans as California, five times as large an emigration was preparing to go there in '46, and it would certainly come under the flag.

Mormon legend has it that when, on July 24, 1847, Brigham Young, weak with mountain fever, came jolting in a white-top over the last summit in the road down Emigration Canyon and gazed over the sagebrush flat toward the Dead Sea, he spoke with the power of revelation and said "This is the place." Brigham, however, held it irreligious to call upon the Lord until you had first exhausted your own resources. Long before that day he had determined on Great Salt Lake Valley. He had, in fact, decided on that general vicinity sometime in 1845.

Throughout 1845 the destination of the Saints was constantly discussed by the leaders who would have to manage the emigration, and they made the most minute study of the available literature. It is not clear that Frémont's second report was decisive. They used it with exceeding care to rough out an itinerary, but they could get little more from his account of the Great Salt Lake country than that the lake did not have the mysterious whirlpool which legend attributed to it, that its islands were barren, and that the canyons which ran down to it from the east were well timbered. It seems likely that Young knew more details about Zion by the end of 1845 than Frémont had observed there. Certainly he knew much more by the end of 1846.[6]

It is clear that Young had decided on the Great Basin, rather than Oregon or coastal California, by midsummer of 1845. It was an inevitable decision: there was, in fact, nowhere else to go. Israel could survive only if left to itself long enough for Young to organize and develop its institutions. That meant that it must find a place where the migrating Americans would not be tempted to settle. That, in turn, meant the Great Basin. But also, as Young seems to have understood quite clearly, Israel must be near enough the course of empire to sustain itself by trading with the migration. And that meant the northern portion of the Great Basin. It meant, in fact, one of no more than three places, Bear River Valley, Cache

Valley, and Great Salt Lake Valley. All three places seem to have been in his mind in '45, and there are still references to Bear River Valley late in the autumn of '46, but the actual choice proved to be between the other two. Later we shall see the choice being made.

In March of 1846, then, Young and the Apostles knew that Zion was to rise somewhere in the Great Basin. They knew that certainly; they were less clear about the site of Zion and still less certain when they could get there. As late as January 1, 1847, at Winter Quarters, Hosea Stout, who was in the confidence of the Twelve, heard that a pioneer company was to push out from the Niobrara River to the headwaters of the Yellowstone to put in a crop. (Faulty information: crops could not be raised there.) Such a pioneer party, to go ahead of the Church proper and select Zion and put in crops, was discussed throughout 1845 at Nauvoo, and actual preparations for it were made, in the expectation that it could start late that summer. After the Saints began leaving Sugar Creek in March of '46, another call for such a party was made. (Actually the company under the unruly individualist Bishop George Miller did pull ahead of the main body with an intention of going all the way, as we shall see.) But neither Brigham nor his counselors could determine, at the beginning, whether any could cross to the mountains this year, or if any could, how many could be spared. It was the principal question to be answered while Israel toiled through the mud.[7]

"West Side of the Mississippi, Feb. 19th, 1846," Eliza Snow dated her poem, huddled with a foot warmer in Elder Markham's buggy. And the poetess wrote:

The Camp, the Camp — its numbers swell —
Shout! Shout! O Camp of Israel.
The King, the Lord of Hosts is near,
His armies guard our front and rear.

Chorus

Though we fly from vile aggression,
We'll maintain our pure profession,
Seek a peaceable possession
Far from Gentiles and oppression.

The ridgepole of Sister Green's tent broke under the weight of snow, and she and the children were half-buried. All their clothes got wet. All the clothes of all the children were wet all the time; fingers, toes, cheeks, were discolored with frostbite; children were lethargic, cried easily, played little in the wind, gave out at their chores. There was so little to eat! Sister Green was pregnant but the family could apportion her a daily ration of less than half as much bread and milk as she needed. There were, however, enough wild onions for them all, chipped from the frozen soil.

The Saints kept arriving from Nauvoo. Tents, wagons, huts, spread over the discolored snow. Great portions of the grove had been felled, Sugar Creek was overcrowded, some of the faint-hearted were trying to return to Nauvoo, and clearly it was time for the Mormons to go. Orson Pratt's thermometer did not fall below zero for several days. So Young organized his people as the Camp of Israel and, on the model of Joseph's nightmare expedition against the Missourians years ago, set "captains of tens" and "captains of fifties" over them. (The entire scheme of organization used here and revealed in January '47 as the Lord's plan for the journey had been worked out in Nauvoo in '45.) Elder Markham, who had succeeded in trading his buggy for a wagon, took a hundred pioneers to prepare the road. "Colonel" Hosea Stout commanded a guard of a hundred riflemen, and "Colonel" John Scott with two more fifties watched over the artillery, which was mostly homemade and had been hidden under lumber piles in Nauvoo. And on March 1, the first detachment started west, between two and three thousand of them, about five hundred wagons of all kinds, in all conditions of repair. The first day they made five miles. Day by day behind them other detachments left Sugar Creek and others arrived there from Nauvoo to follow after, till by late spring about fifteen thousand Saints were on the march.

They were a full two months ahead of the time when, as the mountain men and the Santa Fe traders knew, it was safe for caravans to cross the prairies. Apart from sudden whirlwinds of sleet out of the north the snows were over now, but the rains had come. Rain nearly every day for about eight weeks — a chill, monotonous downpour that soaked everything and brought out mildew in the center of packed crates. It saturated the prairies; after saturation, it turned them into a universal shallow lake. Through that slough the horses and oxen, gaunt after the winter, had to haul the unwieldy wagons, frequently with men and women helping at the wheels. The season was significantly known on the prairies as "between hay and grass." Prairie craft forbade you to travel before the grass came, but Israel had to travel and so the stock grew weak. A wagon would mire to the hubs or deeper. Then neighbors must help out, double or triple teaming, perhaps hitching on a couple of the family cows. If there was brush at hand, it could be cut and spread under the wheels. The wagons would be sucked out to a somewhat firmer stretch, the extra teams unyoked, the slow, sodden progress resumed. Babies howled under drenched blankets. Everyone who could walk slithered through the mud, "shoe-mouth deep," boot-top deep sometimes, clinging in five-pound masses to each foot.

Six miles was a big day, one mile a not uncommon one. Prairie creeks that would be five feet wide in July were now five rods wide, bottomless, swift, and impassable. Reaching one, a "fifty" — or a whole caravan — would have to camp beside it till it should subside or a ford be found, which might be two weeks. If there were no timber, then there might be no fires for two weeks, no cooked food, no dry clothes or bedding except as the sun might come out for an hour or two. No brush, either, to spread a bed on or to build a hut for an obstetrical ward. The historian Tullidge has a tableau: blankets stretched to poles and roofed over with bark, a woman in labor within, and intent sisters holding tin pans to catch the rain that leaked through the bark.

Supplies were scanty, though this first group was better off than any that followed it. They were feeding the stock on cottonwood bark, when they could get it, and they themselves were living on what they had amassed in Nauvoo. Hunters ranged the prairies for deer, turkeys, grouse, but the season was too early. Terror, winter, rain, and malnutrition now assessed their tax and the Saints sickened. Frostbitten feet could become gangrenous, knees and shoulders stiffened with rheumatism, last autumn's agues were renewed. William Clayton's legs pained him so that he could hardly walk; he tried to restore their function by jumping and wrestling but made himself sicker and had to go to bed. Heber C. Kimball, one of the Apostles, caught a fever and took to the swaying wagon, where a sick wife and two sick children, one of them only a few days old, were alternately shaking and burning; an older child could work a little but was too weak to carry a two-quart pail.

Sister Ann Richards' husband, who had already served five missions in the United States, was called to a mission in England. He had to leave his family a few miles from Sugar Creek and go "without purse or scrip" to bear his testimony overseas. This was Franklin D. Richards, a nephew of Apostle Willard Richards who had been with the prophet Joseph when he was killed in Carthage jail. A brother of Franklin's had been killed by the Missourians at the Haun's Mill massacre, and another one would die on the march of the Mormon Battalion. He had married Sister Ann four years before, had been sealed to her in the temple in the everlasting covenant, just this January, and a week later had taken Sister Elizabeth McFate as his second wife. Sister Ann had her two-year-old daughter, Wealthy Lovisa, with her in the wagon — and Sister Ann was big with another child and her hour was near. There was no suitable food for her or Wealthy Lovisa. Many days they could not have a fire, either because night overtook them in the open prairie or because, if they got one started, the rain put it out. But sometimes they managed to keep one going and then Sister Ann could brew a pinch of tea from the pound which a neighbor had given her before she left Nauvoo. The Word of Wisdom forbade it but she could warm her body and cheer her mind with it, and "through sickness and great suffering [it] was about all the sustenance I had for some time."

Twenty days out from Sugar Creek her term was full. The wagons stopped and a midwife was summoned, a Gentile whom the Saints had heard about. The hag demanded a fee in advance; Sister Ann had no money; a woolen bedspread would do, and "I might as well take it, for you'll never live to need it." Little Isaac was born, and he died at once. The priesthood anointed the small body and buried it; the wagons got started again. Little Wealthy Lovisa had been sick when they left Sugar Creek, and week by week her strength failed. Presently she was altogether listless on a roll of blankets in the wagon, and could not be induced to eat. Once, however, they passed a prairie farm and Wealthy revived enough to ask for some potato soup. Her grandmother went to the house, but the farm wife had heard the stories. "I wouldn't sell or give one of you Mormons a potato to save your life," she said, and set the dog on the grandmother. Wealthy lived till they got to the Missouri River, and then died. Brigham told Sister Ann, "It shall be said of you that you have come up through much tribulation."

But the summer was past and September had come when Wealthy Richards died. Many other children and many men and women had died too. All this time Saints had been coming across the Mississippi and taking to the trail. And Israel's outlook was not hopeful.

The emigration had begun too soon, was insufficiently prepared and inadequately financed. A family had what equipment it could get, and no matter how much the Saints might help one another, there were the most serious inequalities. The wealthiest among them might have three or four wagons and a sizable herd of cattle. Even such as these suffered severely, and Apostles Pratt, Kimball, and Richards had to see their families weakening with a never-satiated hunger. But also a family might have only one wagon and no cattle, or merely a light cart, perhaps merely a buggy. Many a Saint trundled his entire possessions westward in a wheelbarrow — a sack of meal or flour, a roll of blankets, a change of clothing for the children.

Moreover, this was the migration not of certain individuals coming together in a temporary organization while they crossed the plains but of an entire people. The Camp of Israel was the Church of Jesus Christ of Latter-day Saints, past, present, and to come. The Mormons carried with them not only their goods but also their church and social institutions — the hierarchy, the various priesthoods, the rituals and sacraments, the co-operative associations, the United Order, the mission system. An Oregon train had no social fabric to preserve, and when it reached the Willamette its members had crossed the country once and for all. No other train had any relation to it; the country closed in behind with no marks except the litter of the nightly camp. But Israel had to maintain its nervous system and could support its venture in the West only by constant accessions. It had to be a continuing emigration.

So for the sake of many who could go no farther, of those still in Nauvoo, and of the as yet unconverted all over the world, facilities of some permanence had to be provided. The problem had to be solved at once; Brigham solved it. His little eyes lacked the gift Joseph's had, of piercing the heavens and beholding the glories there, but it is exceedingly unlikely that Joseph could ever have got his people beyond Sugar Creek.

At Richardson's Point, fifty-five miles from Nauvoo, they built a permanent camp, which would always have a garrison. Companies coming in from the east would find wood, supplies, blacksmithing tools, experienced help — and the priesthood making sure that they "accepted counsel," obeyed, kept discipline, and lived their religion. Another one was established farther on, at a crossing of the Chariton River, and here the first crops were sowed. The first companies planted crops, a permanent personnel cultivated them, later arrivals would harvest them. There were other farms on the way and other permanent camps on Locust Creek, at Garden Grove on Grand River, and lastly "Mount Pisgah," a hundred and forty miles east of Council Bluffs. At Winter Quarters on the west bank of the Missouri and near Council Bluffs on the east bank much more ambitious camps were built, permanent settlements really, with a vigorous trade, large herds of horses and cattle, and farms of several thousand acres worked by hundreds of the Saints. All these plantations except those on the Missouri made crops in '46. Even before Brigham led his people to the mountains in '47, they were making the land in part support them as they traveled.

The prairies dried out. Clothing and bedding were dry at last, but now there were other plagues. The prairie mosquitoes settled in solid layers on men and oxen. The prairie rattlesnakes terrified everyone and killed many cattle. If there was now purchase for the wheels there was not yet fodder for the oxen, which grew still weaker on a diet of buds and twigs. The hunters could not get game enough; they were hundreds of miles east of the buffalo that the other movers could count on. Each permanent camp was a hospital, its garrison composed of those who were too weak, too sick, or too poor to go farther.

But this was the Church of Christ. They were escaping from their oppressors, Moses had led them out of the land of Egypt, they were going to establish Zion and build up the Kingdom. Eliza Snow's heart was merry, and in Brother Markham's wagon she easily flowed into song.

> And it matters not where or whither
>   You go, neither whom among,
> Only so that you closely follow
>   Your leader, Brigham Young.

Captain Pitts's band was a great solace — and a help with the Gentiles. One day, after traveling eight miles, it split a hundred and thirty rails before dark and traded them to a farmer for corn, then gave a concert in the evening. Throughout the settlements it played wherever Gentiles would gather and for any fee, a pail of honey, eight bushels of corn, seven dollars in one place where the parsons opposed it, twenty-five dollars and meals for everyone at another place, and once for ten dollars and ten cents contributed to it by a village of awed, admiring Indians. Still more helpfully, it played for the Saints — Israel's hymns, the current balladry, quadrilles and minuets and hoedowns. For Israel danced every night. The wagons made their rough park, the fires blazed up and supper was prepared, then the band got out the instruments and by firelight and after prayer the pudgy, rubicund prophet clapped his hands and sashayed up to some favored sister, while Israel formed sets under the stars.

This was the English band, the largest one. Behind it smaller ones did the same service for other parts of Israel. (There were so many

Saints and they were so far from the Indian country that there was no need to organize the trains tightly.) There were many fiddles too, and their music might rise above the wheels' shrieking on the march. There were glee clubs, quartettes, choirs. Parties freckle all the journals, at night when the wagons halt in the rain, in the huts of the permanent camps, and in "boweries" or arbors when there is a few days' pause. News came from the other divisions, from Nauvoo, from the European missions. The "teachers" called their groups together to study the everlasting mysteries, praise Joseph, and curse his murderers. The priesthood quorums met for their rituals. And the vigilant mothers in Israel extemporized their schoolrooms; many a Mormon child learned his alphabet to the turning wheels and practised it in a hornbook at night, scrawling the misspelled word ten times over before he was permitted to crawl into the blankets.

They were prodigious, the mothers in Israel. They trudged through mud or dust or, a sick child on their knees, drove teams when father had been drafted to build a bridge or cut grass. They sewed, knitted, patched, spliced, while the wagons bumped and swayed. They spun and wove, and even found time to make the dyes and color the homespun. They learned to let the wagon's jolting churn a pail of cream to butter. They learned to identify edible prairie roots and make them palatable. They learned to extemporize a household economy in wagons and to maintain family order on the march. And if by night father left them after a patriarchal prayer, to visit another wagon or go back ten miles on the trail to where another, younger wife prayerfully awaited him, why that also was their portion and they learned to live their religion.

And the brethren also were performing prodigies. Universal human cussedness, pricked by hunger and doubt, had Brigham and his lieutenants thundering at them a good part of the time. They would not accept counsel, they would fight for position and advantage, they kept tumbling by scores into the stupidest predicaments. But, spread out over Iowa, they were laboring strenuously if not concertedly for the Lord. They prepared the permanent farms and wagon shops, dug wells, got the crops planted. They found time to make nails, burn charcoal, shape oxbows, and manufacture harness and even wagons as they traveled. At farms and little settlements they would hire out for any job at any wage. Some Gentiles were friendly, some suspicious, some hostile. Some had to be overawed by a show of pistols; but the Lord moved others to pity and contributions. Sometimes the brethren held instruction for them, expounding the holy mysteries. . . . And always there were the endless harangues and reorganizing that Israel had found essential. A brother might prove false in that he outbid another brother for corn or refused the use of a team which a Seventy wanted to borrow. Then Brigham or some minor prophet opened the floodgates of exhortation. Much refreshed, this particular division of the Camp of Israel accepted counsel and got going again.

And Brigham and his staff were learning to manage an emigration while doing their other jobs. The journal of William Clayton, who was clerk of the Camp, shows the headquarters at work. An immense bookkeeping, a constant dispatch and arrival of couriers, an almost nightly convocation of the counselors, the prophet's fingers on the controls of an organization that stretched from the Missouri River all the way eastward across America and halfway across Europe. The largest mission, the one in the British Isles, was reorganized while the Camp crossed Iowa. Treaties and arrangements with local officials had to be made. Nearly half the Camp were sick; they must be ministered to somehow, medicine and care must be got for them, they must be buried when they died.[8] Supplies dwindled; they must be replaced somehow, bought, bartered for, worked for, begged, freighted endless miles going and coming. Weak, shoddy, and ill-built equipment was giving out; it must be restored or replaced somehow, more wagons brought up, more stock, more tools, bedding, ammunition.

And Satan was hard at work. While Israel plodded westward the recreant William Smith was rousing the Gentile wolf pack and the Strang heresy was winning the Eastern stakes. Strang had cozened away important leaders and was filling the land with abuses, as a heresiarch's demonic energy carried him raging through the undefended sheepfolds. Even in the Camp itself there was apostasy. Just as February ended and the migration began Apostle John E. Page had to be disfellowshiped for obstructing counsel; a small group followed him to Strang's kingdom at Voree, Wisconsin. Halfway across Iowa, another apostate group split off and headed toward Texas, where another Apostle, Lyman Wight, had set up his community. If two Apostles, why not another one? Why not, indeed, any casual enthusiast who might tap the source of private revelation after a night of hunger and ecstasy, and convince others that his inspiration was superior to Brigham's? Why not a really formidable, perhaps fatal secession? There was much grumbling, quarreling, and despair, many were obstinate, many on the verge of open rebellion, many were terrified by the unknown ahead, many were too selfish to share their goods, many too willful to accept counsel. Israel had not shaped into an obedient instrument, the Saints were not welded together.

All this tried Brigham's genius and dismayed his counselors. Moreover, the news from Nauvoo grew ominous: the mob was more demanding and seemed likely to close in for the kill. Also rumors about the Missourians to the southward grew urgent. They were said to be raising armies and posses, determined to seize this chance to wreak the extermination they had been refused eight years ago. There were repeated alarms; the guards were always turning up some fancied spy or outpost; there was always some new plot on foot. Young took the rumors so seriously that he ordered the Saints never to fire a gun except when hunting, never to flourish or even display a rifle, pistol, or sword in the presence of Gentiles but to keep them hidden in the wagons. They were to be kept charged while hidden, however, and Hosea Stout was ordered to drill his command in the old Danite tactics.

All this made a sufficient test of leadership, organization, and public control, not to mention prophecy. But there was a still greater anxiety, the finances. At the sacrifice of their property the Mormons had raised all the money they could. The Eastern and European stakes had sent all the money they could raise. Missionaries and special couriers went about the land gleaning their petty pence, stripping the faithful still further, calling on all Gentile agencies that could be moved to contribute. The sum was short of what Israel must have in order to reach the mountains. Brigham held fast to his intention of getting an advance party to Zion in this summer of '46. But it became increasingly clearer to him that he could not get the main body of the Church farther than the Missouri River this year. There was before his mind the possibility that he might not get them beyond it in '47 or even in '48. On reaching the Missouri they might truly find that the wilderness had shut them in.

Well, he would get them to the Missouri. Richardson's Point, the Chariton, Garden Grove, Mount Pisgah, and at last Council Bluffs.[9] The pioneer company reached the river on June 14, the last refugees from Nauvoo on November 27. Through eight months, continuously across more than four hundred miles, the Iowa prairies witnessed such a pageant as no one had seen since the Goths moved on Rome — and moved on it inward from the frontier, not outward toward it. Between fifteen and twenty thousand people uprooted from their land and seeking a new land. Thousands of wagons, tens of thousands of oxen, horses, mules, milch cattle, beef cattle, neat cattle, sheep, goats. Chickens, geese, turkeys, guinea fowl, ducks, pigeons, parrots, love birds, canaries. Seedlings with their roots bound in sacking, slips from the shrubbery back home, seeds for the harvest to come, the disassembled machinery of flourmills and sawmills, a college, the mysteries of Heaven, the keys to eternity, the Dispensation of the Fullness of Time. Through sleet and rain, through drouth and prairie summer, half-starved and half-sick, dispossessed, believing, and faithful unto the last, Israel traveled the unknown, toward the land of Canaan, in God's faith and for His glory and under the shadow of His outstretched hand, to build Zion and inherit the earth.

Before they got to the Missouri a pattern began to shape out of the undetermined, the filings formed along the lines of force. On June 28, Clayton, who was traveling in the rear of the headquarters, noted in his journal that some United States Army officers had come up the trail from the east and gone on ahead to find Brigham at Mount Pisgah, eight miles farther on. They — or rather he, for there was only one, though he had three troopers with him — had roused terror and rebellion all along the emigration, for the Saints supposed that the army had been ordered to head them off, perhaps to massacre them. But the truth was far different. Mr. Polk's war had caught up with the Mormons and they were going to be solicited, ever so courteously, to take a patriotic part in it.

IV

Equinox

ON Sunday the younger Channing told the Brook Farmers to be pure unto their mission. As the crusaders sacrificed so much to restore the tomb of the buried Lord, how much more ought George Ripley's phalanx to sacrifice, whose work it was to restore the whole earth. As the monks and nuns withdrew from the world to be free from temptations and sin and to become pure, how much greater need had the phalanx of earnest devotedness, whose work it was to regenerate and purify the world.

On Monday carpenters went to work on the Phalanstery again, resuming after the winter's lull. It was not such a mountainous edifice as the "Palaces" which Fourier's trance reared against the clouds — twenty-two hundred feet long, wings five hundred, grand square twelve hundred, with parallel ranges of outbuildings and columned porticos passing among trees and shrubbery.[1] It was just a three-story frame structure, as formless as a summer hotel in the White Mountains, a hundred and seventy-five feet long, but it was the Farm's most ambitious undertaking. The attic was a hive of single rooms, the second and third floors were divided into fourteen family apartments, and the ground floor held a kitchen, a vast dining room, "two public saloons, and a spacious hall and lecture room." Also it was mortgaged. Some of the Farmers felt that it was badly planned and cheaply built, others that the community was unwise to sink so much capital in it. But, designed to be the nerve center of the community, it was the embodiment in fragrant white pine of the Brook Farm vision and the symbol of the hope to be.

Tuesday evening there was dancing in the Hive, the original farmhouse — cotillions, waltzes, hops, the blue and brown blouses pleasant in the dining room. They were a high-spirited company, the Archon, the Poet, the Hero, the Time-Keeper, the Admiral, the General, the Parson — the Farming Group, the Amusement Group, the Dormitory Group, the Kitchen Group. Their genial and very learned repartee flashed through the candlelight, and doubtless one heard above the music the terrible puns that Association had come to love. (Is Mr. —— much of a carpenter? not a *bit* of it, that's *plain.*

These Grahamites will never make their ends *meet,* you may *stake* your reputation on that. Italics supplied without fee.) . . . The dance was to celebrate resumption of work on the Phalanstery. And, passing the Phalanstery, Mr. Salisbury saw a light in an upper window. A moment later the revels at the Hive were halted by an awful cry: "The Phalanstery is on fire."

They saved the Eyrie, the little square house near by, though its paint blistered. They could not save the Phalanstery. They could only watch it burn. Marianne Dwight, the artist, noted the liquid turquoise and topaz of the flames, and John Codman, the florist, how his camellias and azaleas were "glorified in the transcendent light." Crowds gathered from as far away as Cambridgeport; the Dedham engine got stalled in a snowdrift; rivals from Jamaica Plain, Newton, and Brookline could only soak the embers after the walls fell in. Only two hours of transcendental flame, then the thing was over and there were guests to feed. The colonists "made coffee, brought out bread and cheese and feasted about 200 of the fatigued, hungry multitude," and Mr. Orange ran about West Roxbury borrowing milk. Then the world's people departed and darkness closed over the faithful. Marianne Dwight saw the calm radiance of Orion and was reminded of the unchanging, the eternal.

There was an ecstatic renewal of devotion, but the burning of America's first Phalanstery brought a belated realism to Brook Farm. John Codman's family called him home. The General left, Peter Baldwin the baker, saying that the new order had not succeeded—and the Association lost a humble worker who had done much for it. The Poet was next, John Sullivan Dwight, ex-minister, fine teacher, fine musician, a sweet and troubled soul. He left to lecture and teach and raise money, intending to send it back to the Farm. But before he could begin his remittances Brook Farm was ending: after the first fissure it split rapidly. By October there were only the children's school and the *Phalanx* left of all that aspiration. Just a year after the fire the farm was for rent at $350 a year, and two years later the City of Roxbury bought it at auction for $19,150—$1704 above the mortgage.

They had lived in dream and they had lived on capital. Gifts from admirers, the board bills of transcendental visitors, and a trickle of profits from the industries had a little slowed the steady consumption of the paid-in shares, but they had been consumed and all the Yankee inheritance of the Associates knew that spending capital was the unforgivable sin. They kept asserting that if they had had more capital they could have succeeded, and seem neither to have seen the paradox in joint-stock exploitation of "a radical and universal reform" nor to have understood that there was not enough capital in "Incoherence or Civilization" to support their experiment.

Their aim was to destroy (by developing past it) the competitive organization of industry. But in withdrawing from the system, they had to premise the continuation of competition to support them. They had to compete with the competitive order, and competed with it on hopeless terms — gentle, unskilled, literary amateurs against "the dwarfed and mutilated" who had been shaped to win. As the paradox hardened they could by successive "retrenchments" reduce their living fare to little more than bread, cheese, and beautiful ideas, but they got no farther and wondered why the paying guests fell off. And though they began by sawing the little sticks they must, as Henry Thoreau told them, sooner or later saw the great sticks too. The biggest stick of all was that they had to produce. It was all very well to establish an eight-hour day for winter and a ten-hour day for summer — but if there was still hay to rake after ten hours, there would be more hay to buy out of capital next winter. They could paint wildflowers on lampshades for Boston stores and so raise the equivalent of a parish sewing society's fund for a new melodeon. They could set up a workshop to make sashes and blinds, a hothouse for the cultivation of flowers, a truck garden, similar attractive "industries" for which they felt one or another of Fourier's passional attractions. But philosophers achieved a low index of production relative to that of journeyman cabinetmakers, and they had to incorporate in their group an alien element of the skilled who worked for profit and did not share, or only partly shared, the vision. Once that began, it was no longer possible to maintain the subterfuge. Frankly, they could not love the hard-handed and malformed as they loved one another. Brook Farm endured as the communion of amateurs, as the ineffectiveness of amateurs it ended, and Mr. Emerson wrote an indorsement in his journal: —

> Tell children what you say about writing and laboring with the hands. I know better. Can you distil rum by minding it at odd times? or analyze soils? or carry on the Suffolk Bank? or the Greenwich Observatory? or sail a ship through the Narrows by minding the helm when you happen to think of it? or serve a glass-house or a steam-engine, or a telegraph, or a railroad express? or accomplish anything good or anything powerful in this manner? Nothing whatever. And the greatest of all arts, the subtlest and most miraculous effect, you fancy is to be practised with a pen in one hand and a crowbar or a peat-knife in the other.

They were even amateur reformers. It is significant that of the generation's men and women who accomplished something toward the reduction of social chaos and the furtherance of justice, opportunity, and good sense — of the effective reformers, only one or two were Brook Farm associates and they but briefly. The Associators were, in a word, generous, high-minded, self-sacrificing people, literary folk mostly, who felt the world's pain and lacked a sense of reality. Like most literary dreams, Brook Farm was a flight, a withdrawal from the dust and wounds. The destructive element did not bear them up because they did not submit themselves to it.

But Marianne Dwight wrote, after gazing at the charred beams of hope's Phalanstery, "It does seem as tho' in this wide waste of the world, life could not possibly be so rich as it has been here." She was right. Though they were amateurs, though all their activities bring to mind young Francis Parkman's sneer at them, "the she-philosophers of West Roxbury," nevertheless they had been members one of another. Probably nothing they did left any mark, except that their school for children picked up education where Alcott's had left off, substituted some intelligence for the traditional stupidities, and so, as the children grew up, left an expectation here and there that better things could be. But they had so good a time that all of them, even the agnostic Dana (who, like thirteen others, found a wife there), always looked back on West Roxbury as the time of idyl and belief, the planting and the spring.

So much laughter, so much honest weariness after work, so much dreaming together! The time when Mr. Allen brought back an orphaned child and many of the colonists caught the smallpox, and the women waiting on the sufferers in the Hive. The day the bull broke loose and chased an ox out of the barn. The sweet grave face of the Dwight girl at her wedding, when all the colonists made a ring round her in the Pilgrim House. Always the singing — in the fields, at supper, at the shocking, in the long winter evenings. The poet Cranch's gifted imitations of animal cries. The search by night for a rumored highwayman through the woods at Muddy Pond. Spring festival with roses and jasmines from the greenhouse and the great name FOURIER on the wall with his beehive, and the Archon making a splendid speech. The long hours of talking together while we raked hay or sewed bonnets for the industries and the heart swelled with generous indignation for the poor — and Mr. Brisbane's eloquence a fierce flame, and the dream stretching out till God was almost come again. And over all the great hope so near fulfillment, "the light of universal principles in which all differences, whether of religion, or politics, or philosophy, are reconciled, and the dearest and most private hope of every man has the promise of fulfillment" — the great belief that "the Infinite Power ordained social laws so universal and equitable that the fulfillment of them would make all unqualifiedly happy, and that it is the mission of this race of beings to be attracted to this earth, to this universe, until their happy human destiny is accomplished."

They were fly specks on the periphery of a globe which was swelling out in tidal promontories as a wandering sun drew near and pulled it out of shape — under the omen of a comet that had split in two. They have an essential innocence, asserting in blue tunics universal principles of benevolence at a moment when the disregardful country was pushing through the desert to its last boundary, when the newly manned machines were loosing a new and irresistible energy across the country they hoped to master with some gracious wishes, and when the armies formed for a war of which this year's war would be only a prologue. And yet they were members one of another. Something in the moment of their experience brought it partly out of dream. The American nation has formed so very slowly, for such brief times, in such haphazard symmetry! For a moment not pathetic only because it was ridiculous, the nation formed here, on some pleasant farmland a mile from West Roxbury, where some ineffective literary people worked, sacrificed, and dreamed together. It was not lost altogether and its small deposit is laid down. . . . Only, the nation needed hotter fires than the flame that consumed the Phalanstery. Only, welded in such fires, the Mormons, for one group, were members one of another much more truly than Brook Farm — and may leave our history the moral that Association needs the lowest social denominator. And, of course, Bill Bowen and his tribe watched the frost come out of the ground and turned westward.

Through March the inner tensions of the Democratic Party heightened so that the skin was like to burst, but in Congress everything was Oregon. Mr. Polk's design to reduce the tariff of '42 was in danger of getting lost from inattention, and the President reminded his callers that they were accountable. Mr. Calhoun, the metaphysician, twisted on the inadvertent rack. He had no simple emotions and if any of his ideas were simple they have been clear to no one else. And all his stands were at the third remove of calculation. But, without enthusiasm for Oregon and committed to appeasement by his negotiations as the previous Secretary of State, he had guessed that the party would plump for peace and he had had some hope of seizing its leadership. But it was now clear that the country wanted Oregon in earnest. He had to hedge and would not head the Democracy this year. (Here was the surface of deeper conflicts in Mr. Calhoun himself. He was committed to expansion as the hope and glory of the South, yet had some dim premonition that expansion must reduce the price of cotton forever and so destroy the economy of the Southern seaboard if not of the entire South. He was now logically committed also to the separation of the South, to secession, but saw drifting down that path ahead of him the specter of Great Britain. Even to the metaphysician it was clear that to divide the Union was to make Great Britain supreme in this hemisphere.) Others besides him read the nation's desire, and opposition to Polk's Oregon policy all but disappeared before the triumphant oratory of the Western states. But at the same time, the majority warhawks began to quarrel. They had to be vigilant against compromisers who might find a parliamentary or a sectional leverage and use it. Haywood, Cass, Hannegan, Allen shouted in the Senate all day, then rushed to the White House to sound out Polk. He would not be sounded but grew irritated, for delay in terminating Joint Occupancy would be plain evidence to London that we were irresolute. He now felt that Allen and Cass, if not the others, were maneuvering not so much for Oregon as to succeed him in the White House. Buchanan's unsleeping candidacy had also got the idea: at Cabinet meetings he was suddenly firm about Oregon. And Walker, the Secretary of the Treasury, impartially considering candidates for the Presidency, had begun to see excellent material in himself. So the month ran out in oratory and intrigue and the resolution to terminate Joint Occupancy did not come to a vote.

Toward the end of the month, Mexico came downstage. The President had been meditating on Colonel Atocha's suggestion; even with an army marching south, purchase would be such an agreeable way out. He mentioned to Mr. Ingersoll, the chairman of the House Committee on Foreign Affairs, the convenience of providing the Executive with a secret fund of one million dollars. Remember, Mr. Jefferson had twice had such funds voted him, and from one of them had come Louisiana. Mr. Ingersoll agreed and would send up a trial balloon. This conversation was on March 25. On the twenty-eighth dispatches arrived from Slidell, saying that Paredes seemed likely to receive him as minister. That looked as if Santa Anna, as reported by Atocha, knew what he was talking about and the plan was going well. Slidell would propose the treaty of cession as soon as he was received, and "if our minister could be authorized upon the *signing* of the Treaty to pay down a half million or a million dollars, it would enable Gen'l Paredes to pay, feed, and clothe the army, and maintain himself in power until the Treaty could be ratified by the U. S." Everything Polk wanted — California, New Mexico, Texas to the Rio Grande — appeared to be on the counter, for cash.

This made it Polk's turn to sound out his party leaders. Mr. Benton would vote the money. Mr. Houston, newly returned as Senator from Texas to the Washington that had been a stage for his romantic heartbreak, would vote it. Mr. Allen likewise, but he foresaw trouble with Calhoun. Summoned to the White House, Calhoun would be glad to pay up to $25,000,000 for the Western lands, but saw an opening and had his price. The existence of a secret fund would be public knowledge, he said, and would embarrass the Oregon negotiations. Wherefore the President would be wise to compromise on 49°, Calhoun's own stand. The President said hotly that Great Britain would not compromise even on 49° unless the Senate speedily passed the pending resolution. He went on lining up Senators behind his secret fund.

Too bad. Just a week earlier Slidell had been notified that he would not be received. The Paredes government had decided that it could not maintain itself if it made a move for peace. Mexico was for war, Mr. Slidell had asked for his passports, and his dispatch conveying the decisive news was on its way to Washington.

Diplomacy, however, had already been superseded. Marcy's order of January 13 — which had only recently been made known to Congress — directing Taylor to march to the Rio Grande had reached Corpus Christi on February 3. A number of reasons had prevented Taylor from obeying it promptly — among them his failure to organize his command for maneuver and his failure to investigate the country which it would have to cross. Taylor bought mules and wagons frantically, prepared to transfer his sea base to Point Isabel near the mouth of the Rio Grande, and hurried out the cavalry to reconnoiter. On March 8, the Dragoons and some artillery marched out of Corpus Christi, and by the eleventh Taylor's whole army was under way.

It was about 4000 strong, less those who had taken fevers at Corpus Christi and those who had deserted through the swamps. As it marched, two of the senior officers, Brevet Brigadier General Worth and Colonel Twiggs, quarreled fiercely over seniority, and the quarrel had already aligned their juniors in cliques and given Polk his first military headache. The question was whether a brevet (honorary) promotion enabled a man to rank one who was his senior in the line. General Scott, the head of the army, had decided in favor of the brevet rank, and from Corpus Christi Lieutenant Colonel Hitchcock had published a letter supporting the line, firing by battery at Scott and denouncing all Congressmen who had taken Scott's side. . . . The army was badly supplied, the insufficient trains trailing far behind it. It had little discipline, its equipment was scanty and shoddy, and its arms were a chaos of diverse and mostly obsolescent models — smoothbore muskets, flintlock and percussion-cap rifles, a handful of Hall's breech-loaders, a good many of the "Harpers Ferry" rifles mostly made by Eli Whitney, Jr., and even a few repeaters. It had never moved as an army. Neither Taylor nor any of his juniors could maneuver it. Textbooks of drill and tactics were in everybody's saddlebags, for consultation en route, and Taylor had a healthy democratic contempt of the West Pointers who knew the things he badly needed to know.

But anything was better than the stagnation of Corpus Christi, and they were off for the Halls of Montezuma. There were swamps at first, then a waterless stretch, finally the chaparral country. Food was bad and there was never enough water under the Southern sun. It was a land rich only in rattlesnakes, which buzzed by the hundred underfoot and slid into blankets by night. Mirages flared across the horizon and there were more rumors than rattlesnakes and mirages lumped together.

On March 20 the advance reached the Arroyo Colorado, a salt pond, where General Mejía, who commanded at Matamoros, drew up some skirmishers and informed the Americans that if they came any farther they would begin a war. The advance splashed through; the first headlong flight of the Mexican army was well started before they reached the farther bank. Three days later Taylor took part of his force off at an angle to Point Isabel and got there just as his transports and supply ships made harbor. He ordered the place fortified and started back toward his army. Under General Worth (the leader of the brevet faction, next to Scott the best-dressed man in the military establishment, and the most contentious of all that quarrelsome crew) it had reached the Rio Grande opposite Matamoros on March 28.

They ran the flag up opposite the town on the north bank of the river, which either was or was not foreign soil, and the Army of Occupation had become the American Expeditionary Force. With less haste than dignity Taylor began to fortify his camp, and to write Marcy demanding reinforcements. He needed them. Also he began to exchange letters and proclamations with Mejía, soon to be superseded by General Ampudia, who had more rank and a longer record. It was a kind of warfare in which Old Rough and Ready was under a handicap, the Mexicans having a far more formidable rhetoric. He was at the further disadvantage of having to represent his presence here as entirely benevolent. Theme: the A. E. F. had come to co-operate with the Mexican army in keeping the uninhabited frontier quiet while their governments were negotiating. Not too good. What Taylor needed was the baroque style of Winfield Scott.

At first the Mexicans, who were winning the manifestoes paragraph by paragraph and had no orders from Paredes, let the situation stand. When a patrol captured a couple of dragoons, Mejía punctiliously returned them, with his card.

In all this Lieutenant Colonel Hitchcock saw nothing to admire. He was so sick that he had done most of the march in an ambulance, though resolved to lead the 3d Infantry in person if action should come. If it should come, he thought, the enemy would have a walkaway. Hitchcock's brigade commander could not give the simplest command except at an adjutant's prompting. None of the brigades had been maneuvered; of the regiments only his own had been trained as a unit. "General Taylor knows nothing of army movement," and the camp site could not have been more dangerously exposed if the enemy engineers had chosen it in advance. No systematic reconnoissance was made but the air vibrated with rumors. Maybe a rumored force in the rear was going to attack; maybe it consisted of disaffected troops who were waiting a favorable moment to join the invaders as allies. Maybe a *levée en masse* was preparing, the whole countryside to rise and throw the gringos out. Or maybe, since this was "Northern Mexico," which was known to be on the edge of revolt, the states of Tamaulipas and Nuevo León were going to secede and come under the flag now brought to their border. Was this enterprise war or was it peace? Whichever it was, "my heart is not in this business; I am against it from the bottom of my soul as a most unholy and unrighteous proceeding." For, finally, "It looks as if the government sent a small force on purpose to bring on a war, so as to have a pretext for taking California and as much of this country as possible; for, whatever becomes of this army, there is no doubt of a war between the United States and Mexico."

At the beginning of March, Frémont was continuing his northward progress toward Oregon by moving west over the Santa Cruz Mountains and south toward Monterey. In violation of his agreement and in defiance of the authorities. They now took action. On March 5, at the Hartnell ranch near Salinas, an officer of the California militia rode into his camp and gave him letters from the prefect and the *comandante.* Both directed him to take his force out of the department at once. The hero worked on a hair trigger. He ordered the lieutenant out of camp with a red-fire message for his superiors, moved hastily into the hills, set up a breastwork of logs on the top of Gavilán Peak, nailed Old Glory to a pole, and prepared to be sacrificed. "If we are unjustly attacked," he wrote to Larkin, "we will fight to extremity and refuse quarter, trusting our country to avenge our death. . . . If we are hemmed in and assaulted here, we will die, every man of us, under the flag of our country." . . . He had been told to get out, on the ground that he had broken faith with the officials, lied about his instructions and intentions, broken the law, defied the courts, and condoned the misbehavior of his men. There had been no thought of killing him.

Nobody was ready to confer martyrdom on him, and though his mountain men were hot for a go with the greasers he got nothing for his brave words except an artist's pleasure in the style. Consul Larkin found so little intelligence in his actions that he supposed Frémont could not have understood the official orders and wrote explaining them — meanwhile asking Don José Castro not to get rough but to talk things over with the hero in simple language. Also, seeing his patient intrigue all but ruined by this dramaturgy, he hastily asked for a man-of-war at Monterey, to persuade all parties to dampen their powder. As for Don José, he mustered what militia he could, circularized an already agitated countryside with proclamations, and paraded his forces under the spyglasses trained on them from Gavilán Peak. That was the traditional way of using force in California.

It worked. In his lofty fortress Frémont reverberated with the most dramatic emotions but his position was impossible in both law and tactics, as he realized when the McGuffey phase had passed. He was here without the slightest authority of his government, which could only disavow him, and the Californians had ordered him out on sufficient grounds and altogether within their rights. They were unlikely to attack him on the Gavilán and, if they had attacked, his mountain men could have shot them to pieces. But they must eventually have starved him out and then ridden him down with the long lances that were to win them San Pascual. However stirring his compositions and however humiliating the retreat, no great deed was possible and he had to get out. After three days of Hollywood fantasy, his flagpole fell down and he told his men that this showed they had done enough for honor. He moved out, most slow and dignified.

He went at last to the San Joaquin Valley, and from there moved to the Sacramento, reaching Sutter's Fort again on March 21. (On that day Jim Clyman wrote to him and, at Jalapa, Slidell was notified that Mexico would not receive a minister from Mr. Polk.) There was nothing to do but refit his party at Sutter's and carry out his original instructions. Heading toward Oregon, he got to Neal's ranch on Butte Creek, March 28 (Neal had come out as his blacksmith on the Second Expedition and had stayed), and on the thirtieth reached Peter Lassen's place on Deer Creek, some two hundred miles out from Sutter's. . . . He took a frustrated spirit with him. The attitudes of a romantic hero must succeed altogether or they will be merely funny, and the greasers had dented this one so badly that it could hardly be refurbished even for Jessie's eyes, not to mention the great audience. And after the dream of glory a routine exploration would be an anticlimax. It would end in a drab return to the States, a party coming ingloriously home at a time when, Frémont was tormented by suspecting, officers of the army would be making glorious reputations in the Halls of Montezuma. Circumstance had turned against Childe Harold and his fate was more than he could bear.

Behind him Don José was jubilant, the war having gone according to ritual. Rhetoric had blown El Gringo away, which called for some more. "Compatriots, the act of unfurling the American flag on the hills, the insults and threats offered to the authorities, are worthy of execration and hatred from Mexicans; prepare, then, to defend our independence in order that united we may repel with a strong hand the audacity of men who, receiving every mark of true hospitality in our country, repay with such ingratitude the favors obtained from our cordiality and benevolence." The ungratefuls were already repelled but Don José had a warrior's license. Don Pío Pico, the governor, reproved him for usurping the privilege of manifesto, a civil monopoly, but the Californians took him quite seriously — and why shouldn't they? They knew mountain men as highwaymen and horse thieves. They knew Frémont as an army officer and knew that his country and theirs were on the verge of war. He had violated the terms agreed on for his visit, defied the alcalde's court, roused the Indians, flouted the authorities, and raised a hostile flag. Their clarity of understanding amounted to prescience.

There were about eight hundred Americans in California. Jim

Clyman did not think much of them and his doubts hold for the majority. They varied from worthless beachcombers, deserters from the ships, resident horse thieves, and Diana's foresters up to a small, respectable, and potentially valuable company of ranchers, merchants, and traders. This last was the seed of the plantation to come, from the same winnowing as the emigration soon to leave the frontier, but they were joined to the rest in a common contempt of the Californians. This languorous society where no one worked hard, not even the Indian slaves, where no one set much value on wealth, industry, or sober righteousness, where the standard of living was far below the standard of manners, where progress was unheard of and the principles of *laissez faire* governed everything except the commerce to which they should apply only — in this society there was nothing whatever that the expansionist Yankees of the 1840's could admire. Furthermore they were committed to an implicit revolution; they were invaders and their land titles hung on the whim of a nation which had made an open move to dispossess them. They knew how brittle were the few remaining bonds that held the province to Mexico. They knew and freely assisted the vague apprehensions that one or another nation half the world away would hold out a hand to catch it as it fell. They knew that a sizable number of Californians, and those among the most substantial, hoped it would be an American hand and preferred that sovereignty to the grafters sent from Mexico to collect the revenue, the convicts sent to maintain them, and the native picaros who formally contended with both. . . . A mixed solution had reached the point of saturation; shake it ever so slightly and something must crystallize out.

"Facts more terrible than thunder, lightning, hurricane, volcanic eruptions!" This was the news of the tableau on Gavilán Peak reaching John Marsh, A.B., Harvard '23, George Ripley's classmate, M.D. by apprenticeship, veteran of the Black Hawk War, itinerant Rousseau, eccentric, landowner, colonizer by intention, and one of a good many who could see themselves as president of a California republic. Less than a year ago he had been up to his ears in the native revolution and had composed a manifesto calling on the Americans to unite, watch, and pray. For years he had been intriguing with native intenders and pretenders — and had the hour now struck? He could not tell but walked warily round Frémont's drama, and a good many compatriots walked with him, but under the unpleasantness that they suspected one another. . . . The ship *Moscow* lay at Monterey, taking on hides. The news reached her captain in even more urgent form, and he sent a courier galloping after Frémont to offer him sanctuary. And on his mountain creek at the head of Napa Valley,

Jim Clyman heard on March 17 "that Capt. Fremont has raised the american flag in Monteray and all good citizens are caled on to appear forthwith at Sonoma armed and Equiped for service . . . to defend the rights and priviledges of Mexican citizens." He understood that the trouble had been provoked by Frémont's refusal "to apeare before some of the so caled Legal authorities," for whom Jim had no deep respect. Four days later he heard that Castro had four hundred troops, so his duty was clear. He wrote to Frémont offering his rifle and a serviceable collection of others.

Frémont's reply shows romantic glory at its ebb mark, the hero marching northward with his back to the foe and nothing done.[2] (And part of its gloom springs from the fact that so few others had volunteered support.) He was, he confessed, in a peculiar position. "The Californian authorities object to my presence here and threaten to overwhelm me. If peace is preserved I have no right or business here [The furious Orlando had contrived to forget that all winter]; if war ensues I shall be out numbered ten to one and be compelled to make good my retreat pressed by a pursuing enemy. . . ." So, summing up these phantom dangers to assuage his hurt, he refused the alliance and dragged northward toward Oregon, a bedraggled knight with some tail feathers plucked, through chilly rain.

Well, all right, fight or fandango. Jim had offered his support and, since it was not wanted, would go on with his plans. He dried more meat and made packsaddles for the journey. Ready at last, he started down Napa Valley on March 31. He was turning back along the line of emigration and he had closed, or begun, another chapter in the outline of American history. For Jim Clyman's letter to Frémont is the first click of a completed circuit, the sign that the mixed brew of California affairs was ready to crystallize out the Bear Flag Revolt.

Down South crops were already out of the ground; in Texas Taylor's army suffered from the heat. Rain drenched the prairies and there was no bottom to the mud the Mormons trudged through. In New England it was not yet even mud time. They were plowing along the Sangamon, however, by the end of March, green streaked the yellow Missouri grass, and there were fruit blossoms in the Shenandoah Valley. But, snow, rain, or seed time, the sunwise turn had come; spring was at hand. April would see all the Bill Bowens on the move.

And by the end of March one of them had already begun his journey. Twenty-two years old, an A.B. and LL.B. of Harvard, Francis Parkman was back from a winter trip to scenes in Pennsylvania and Ohio that would figure in his book and now he started with his cousin, Quincy Adams Shaw, for St. Louis. He was prepared to find it quite as alien to Beacon Hill as the Dakota lands beyond it, whither he was going. He was already an author (a poet and romancer), had already designed the great edifice his books were to build, and already suffered from the mysterious, composite illness that was to make his life a long torture. He hoped, in fact, that a summer on the prairies might relieve or even cure the malady that had impaired his eyes and, he feared, his heart and brain as well. He had done his best to cure it by systematic exercise, hard living in the White Mountains, and a regimen self-imposed in the code of his Puritan ancestors which would excuse no weakness.

But more specifically Parkman was going west to study the Indians. He intended to write the history of the conflict between imperial Britain and imperial France, which was in great part a story of Indians. *The Conspiracy of Pontiac* had already taken shape in his mind; beyond it stretched out the aisles and transepts of what remains the most considerable achievement by an American historian. So he needed to see some uncorrupted Indians in their native state.

It was Parkman's fortune to witness and take part in one of the greatest national experiences, at the moment and site of its occurrence. It is our misfortune that he did not understand the smallest part of it. No other historian, not even Xenophon, has ever had so magnificent an opportunity: Parkman did not even know that it was there, and if his trip to the prairies produced one of the exuberant masterpieces of American literature, it ought instead to have produced a key work of American history. But the other half of his inheritance forbade. It was the Puritan virtues that held him to the ideal of labor and achievement and kept him faithful to his goal in spite of suffering all but unparalleled in literary history. And likewise it was the narrowness, prejudice, and mere snobbery of the Brahmins that insulated him from the coarse, crude folk who were the movement he traveled with, turned him shuddering away from them to rejoice in the ineffabilities of Beacon Hill, and denied our culture a study of the American empire at the moment of its birth. Much may rightly be regretted, therefore. But set it down also that, though the Brahmin was indifferent to Manifest Destiny, the Puritan took with him a quiet valor which has not been outmatched among literary folk or in the history of the West.

V

Spring Freshet

ON his way out of Napa Valley, Jim Clyman met the party of young men whom he had heard about, preparing to go back to Oregon — "Quite wiling to return to whare the manners and customs of the inhabitants is more in unison with civilization than can be found in this half Barberous half Indian population." Their intention made sense to Jim but his stick floated another way. Since there was no present disposition to take the province from the half-Barberous inhabitants, he was for the States. There was plenty of time; he moved slowly through the lush California spring, making notes on the flowers and crops and drying more meat for the journey. Word reached him that the party he was seeking were to rendezvous at William Johnson's ranch on Bear Creek. He got there on April 16, and "Mr. Hastings welcomed us to his camp in a warm and Polite manner and we unpacked under the shade of a spreading oak tree." He had caught up with the publicity man.

Lansford Hastings' bright, deluded mind was a-boil. He was fresh from helping John Bidwell lay out a theoretical town called Sutterville, which could use buyers. He was the local representative of an even gaudier speculation in real estate. California was ripe to the sickle . . . and rich with rumors. Castro was going to revolt against Pico. Pico was going to make war on Castro. Mexico was going to order all foreigners out. Mexico was going to expropriate the lands it had granted to Americans. Mexico was going to sell California to England — to France — to Russia — in order to prevent the United States from seizing it on the outbreak of war. Great Britain was going to occupy California to use it as a counterweight in the Oregon controversy. Vallejo was going to turn it over to the United States, Pico to England, Castro to France, Prince Henry of Spain was to rule over it. . . . And ten thousand Mormons were coming, either at Sutter's invitation or in defiance of him (and in some rumors at the instigation of Hastings himself), to settle at New Helvetia. And a great, a vast emigration was even now gathering on the Missouri — so vaguely vast that it was pulling Hastings' mind to the upper strata of fantasy.

Something had to be done about that emigration. (It might buy lots at Sutterville.) The fabulous province was slipping its moorings, ready to be taken, likely to be lost. It must not be!—or there would be no future for a young man who knew it was good to be shifty in a new country and Lansford Hastings would not rise to glory in California. In his mind this year's emigration from the frontier became decisive for the destiny of the word. There must be enough stout hearts, if they could be joined with those already in California, to save the dream. But the greater part of them, indifferent to Hastings' book, would go to Oregon. Unless they were stopped. So he would stop them. Reveille at dawn and Hastings in the saddle once again. He would go forth to meet them and at some high pass take his stand, summoning them for God and country to seize their hour.

It was not a new idea, though given a varnish of urgency and empire. The previous summer Sutter had sent out Caleb Greenwood, a mountain man almost immemorially old but still tough as ironwood, to travel eastward along the trail and persuade the Oregon-bound to come to California. And Sutter was sending him out again. With two of his innumerable half-breed sons (one of them happily named Governor Boggs), he had joined Hastings' party on the same errand before Clyman came up. Hastings' immediate partner, however, was James M. Hudspeth.

Jim Clyman did not share Hastings' delusion or his hope. The golden shore was, in his opinion, hardly worth the taking. Its vehement spring loosed a rough poetry in his journal but it was not a country for Americans. Jim was going back to the States, his mind fed on geography, and he had not crossed the Sierra, which stood "in cold and awful grandeur" just ahead. After he had crossed it, his judgment, which was that of a thirty-third-degree mountain man, would so violently dissent from Hastings', which was that of a real-estate booster selling lots to suckers, that he would set up as a one-man bureau of more reliable information. But Hastings would do to travel with. They stayed in camp on Bear Creek till April 23, when Jim and five others impatiently set out, only to decide that the party was too small to dare the snows. They camped and waited for the rest to come up, fretting at the delay. Jim complained about the coyotes that chewed the lariats at night, and restlessly climbed the ridges to scan the tumbled chaos of the peaks. On April 28 the entire party was together again, nineteen men, three women, and three children. On the twenty-ninth they started out and toiled through snowdrifts and spring floods to the

Yuba, "roring through its snowy bed."[1] The next day they went on. Spring had made the drifts too sodden to support them, and all the land was mud. The horses stuck repeatedly, the packs loosened, and they made three miles. That took them to the head of the valley and tomorrow they must tackle the main ridge.

The beginning of a curious and momentous trip, against the current — Lansford Hastings and Jim Clyman moving east.

For the week of April 18, fifty-nine steamboats docked at the port of St. Louis, forty from the upper Mississippi, Illinois, and Missouri rivers, thirteen from the Ohio, six from New Orleans. Six thousand passengers arrived on them, and freight from all the world. Spring reached the metropolis of the Western waters in an immense commerce of bales, crates, implements — steamboats, broadhorns, scows — wagons, Indians, traders, trappers, Negroes, and Bill Bowen. It was April 28 when the steamboat *Radnor* backed out of her slip in a cloud of pitch-pine smoke and turned northward to make the Missouri passage. She was loaded so deep that the water broke over her guards. And she carried Francis Parkman. He had seen the multicolored romance of St. Louis. He had met Henry Clay and a passed midshipman of the navy, Selim Woodworth, who was taking dispatches to Oregon. He had called on the oldest surviving Chouteau, provided himself with letters to American Fur Company representatives in the mountains, and hunted down all legends about Pontiac. Now he noted that the *Radnor's* upper deck was covered with wagons for the Santa Fe trade and her hold filled with goods to go in them. There were also a party of Oregon emigrants, horses and mules and harness, and some mountain men. A few days later he began to see on the banks "signs of the great western movement that was then taking place."

For this was April. All across America the crops were in and for more than two thousand adventurers who would not concern themselves with this year's crops it was time to start. The Mormons labored through the still bottomless mud of Iowa and their stock gaunted because the grass had not yet come. But the grass would soon freshen, now, and must not be lost: the trains would form in May. The wayfaring was ready to begin. One's good-byes were said. One took passage on the cars or a steamboat for St. Louis, and from there one went by boat like Parkman, or bought wagons and traveled overland to the frontier.

The "Great Migration" of the histories is variously the first big push toward Oregon in 1843 or the more populous one of '45. The phrase is rightly used in that, as the texts say, those years made Oregon American soil no matter what might be said in Congress or Downing Street. Yet the migration of '46 was the decisive one — this was the year of decision — and though Parkman failed to understand it, he was right in calling it great.

Here it is convenient to examine some of the people who went west in '46.

The wagons which Parkman saw on the *Radnor's* deck were destined for the trade to Santa Fe and Chihuahua.[2] Frequently illegal in the early days and sometimes broken off, it had now been regularized for twenty-three years and had grown steadily. This year, ahead of the armies, beside them, and behind them, a good deal more than a million dollars' worth of goods, St. Louis wholesale, would move down the trail. The trade had already riveted New Mexico to the American economy and it paid a rich profit (from fifty per cent upward) in spite of risk, redskins, graft, and competition. Mexico had been unable to organize a commerce with its northern provinces; New Mexico and Chihuahua could buy goods freighted to them from Independence more cheaply than any that came up from the interior. Many a Yankee, in fact, moved south or southeast from Chihuahua to undersell local merchants near the seacoast and the capital. It was a varied trade and the most unpredictable ventures might succeed, but the bulk of the freight was cotton goods, prints, cutlery, light hardware, and the miscellaneous cheap household goods of the new industrialism. The traders took back with them a little wool, a scattering of small handicraft goods, the mules that had already got themselves identified with Missouri, and hard cash.

The goods moved by boat this April from St. Louis to Independence and Westport, where established firms were getting ready for the start in May. We have seen Jessie Frémont preparing to send a letter to Bent's Fort by James Magoffin. This was "Don Santiago," a veteran of the trade, born in Harrodstown when it was still a frontier station, of the big-boned Ulster stock who helped to subdue the Dark and Bloody Ground. This year he would travel light and fast on a diplomatic mission and the wagons of his firm would be captained by his brother Samuel. As the freight was sorted for the start, Samuel Magoffin brought to Independence, to continue her honeymoon on the trail, the eighteen-year-old Susan Shelby whom he had married six months ago. . . . Another Kentuckian outfitted traders at Independence and would take some wagons of his own to Santa Fe, Samuel C. Owens. His half-sister Mary had visited in New Salem in 1836, had been courted by a Springfield lawyer whose melancholy troubled her heart, and had been rejected by him in a wry, ambiguous heartbreak that foreshadowed A. Lincoln's panic on approaching marriage with Mary Todd. . . . Messrs. Webb and Doan used the security, in this troubled year, of an English connection, and Albert Speyer, another well-established trader, traveled under the protection of a Prussian passport, whereas the Armijo brothers of Santa Fe relied on their connection with the governor of New Mexico. Speyer was a Prussian Jew and the diversity of the trade shows in part of his lading and in a guest who traveled with him. He was taking two wagonloads of arms and powder which the governor of Chihuahua had had the foresight to order and his guest was Dr. Adolphe Wislezenus, who needs a word of his own. Wislezenus was an M.D. of Zurich, having had to flee his native Germany because of political liberalism. He had practised in Paris and New York, then moved to Illinois and later Missouri. A competent geologist and a naturalist of high standing, he had made the Oregon passage as far as Fort Hall some years ago and had written a book about that venture which is today one of the standard sources. Now he had chosen the spring of '46 to investigate the flora and fossils of the Southwest, and we shall meet him at Chihuahua. . . . Kentuckians, Missourians, Mexicans, a Prussian Jew, a German scientist, an enchanting girl — they sufficiently represent the traders and travelers of the Santa Fe trail. There were many others, for the million-dollar trade was in small holdings. These were the proprietors to whom were attached the annual miscellany of amateurs, vacationists, adventurers, invalids, young gentlemen on tour, and smart men looking for an opening. And for whom worked the bullwhackers, immeasurably skilled, oratorical, unbreakable, and bellicose — members in good standing of an American line that had included the drovers, the keelboaters, the canawlers, the stagers, and the Allegheny packers. They have not yet had a celebrant.

A much larger and more various company was crossing Missouri for the western passage. Bill Bowen to the number of about twenty-five hundred, disregarding the already opened Wisconsin, unfilled Iowa, untouched Kansas, all but unknown Minnesota, and upper Michigan where some Scandinavians were just beginning to fell trees and the great copper deposits were just beginning to be mined. Bill Bowen was mostly for Oregon but was seven hundred strong, or a little less, for California. Mostly he came from Missouri or Illinois or the states that immediately bordered them, but all states were represented and much of Europe as well. He was mainly a farmer and of the haves rather than the have-nots, but the states poured into this retort a complete democracy, all classes and conditions, backgrounds, moralities, philosophies, and cultures. Look at some individuals.

We have seen Lillburn Boggs start out for Independence: former governor of Missouri, former trader to Santa Fe, Beelzebub to the Mormons, brother-in-law to the Bents, also brother-in-law to the grandsons of Daniel Boone, three of whom traveled west with him. On April 18, Mr. Edwin Bryant, a transplanted Yankee, left his newspaper in Louisville and, with Mr. R. T. Jacob and Mr. R. Ewing, started for Independence. He did not know that he would be joining Lillburn Boggs, could not foresee that he would presently be joining Brevet Captain Frémont and Colonel Stephen Watts Kearny also, or that he would be made alcalde of a village that was not yet called San Francisco. In April Mr. Jessy Quinn Thornton left Quincy, Illinois, for Independence. He was an asthmatic and something of a hypochondriac, and his wife, Nancy, had even worse health. They hoped that the mountains or Oregon would restore them and they too, without knowing it, were traveling to join Lillburn Boggs. Thornton was thirty-five, a traveled and educated man, a correspondent of Horace Greeley's, a friend of Benton and Stephen Douglas. Born in Virginia, he had grown up in Ohio, studied law in London, practised in Virginia and later in Missouri (Nancy was born in Hannibal), then moved to Quincy. The Thorntons were a perfect flowering of the bourgeoisie that had already risen on the middle border and Mark Twain has drawn a dozen portraits of their kind: genteel, unbelievably refined, pious, narrow, of an overwhelming respectability and sentimentality — the people of the gift books and the novel in pantalettes. Set off against them another who also moved, this April, to an unpremeditated rendezvous with Boggs and Bryant, William Henry Russell. He had a title, but not so much because he had served in the Black Hawk War as because he was the mint-image of a type already fixed in our theology, the Kentucky Colonel. Tall as Doniphan, big as Benton, he was a hell-roaring orator and once had been secretary to Henry Clay. He had been opportune rather than shifty in Missouri, eloquent on the hustings, a holder of political jobs. Noisy, affable, and commanding, he was certain to be chosen captain of this wagon train, and just as inevitably a worshiper and appointee of Captain Frémont.

Some called him Owl Russell. The story ran that once he heard owls who-whooing from the woods and, mistaking the lament for an inquiry, stood up and roared into the dark, "Colonel William H. Russell of Kentucky — a bosom friend of Henry Clay."

They will do as samples: a Kentucky colonel, a monument of Illinois respectability, a Yankee editor, and the grandson-in-law of Daniel Boone. But certain others, just as typical, must be introduced, since the West was preparing a special destiny for them while they traveled across Missouri to join this wagon train.

A. Lincoln attended the sessions of the Tazewell Circuit Court at Tremont, Illinois, from April 8 to 15, and when it closed went on to the Woodford Circuit at Metamora. So he was not in Springfield on April 15 when there rendezvoused there, and camped on the site of the present Statehouse, a party of thirty-two[3] emigrants from Sangamon County who had spent the preceding months getting ready for California. We have already glanced at two of those who spent that April night in Springfield — anticipating the day in June when Jim Clyman is to meet James Frazier Reed near Fort Laramie and the day in July when he is to meditate beside the grave of Mrs. Sarah Keyes, who was Reed's mother-in-law. That night in Springfield, she had just a month to live.

A family ready for the decisive break with the past. Reed, forty-six, noble Polish blood mingling in his veins with that of the log-cabin pioneers, well-to-do, luxuriously outfitted for the passage, bearing credentials of character and position signed by Thomas Ford, the governor of Illinois. His wife, Margaret, thirty-two. Their children, Martha (Patty), eight years old; James, five; Thomas, three. Margaret Reed's daughter by an earlier marriage, Virginia Backenstoe, thirteen. Margaret's mother, Mrs. Sarah Keyes, feeble and failing but resolved to live till she might meet her son, who had gone to Oregon two years before and was supposed to be coming back along the trail this year. And some employes — one hardly knows the right term for hired companions, since "servant" will not do. These were Baylis Williams, twenty-four years old, and his sister Eliza, twenty-five; they were young country folk going west to better their estate. There were Milt Elliott, twenty-eight; James Smith, twenty-five; Walter Herron, twenty-five; these three, known as Reed's teamsters, like the two Williamses came from Sangamon County, neighbors working their way to a new start on the golden shore.

The families of two friends of Reed, with employes, came to that rendezvous on April 15, to complete the party. These were portions of the patriarchal tribes of two brothers, George Donner who was sixty-two and Jacob Donner who was sixty-five. Tamsen was George Donner's third wife. None of the children of his first marriage, who were now mature and settled for themselves, went with him. Two daughters of his second marriage, aged fourteen and twelve, however, and Tamsen's three daughters, aged six, four, and three, were with them. George's second wife, the mother of the two older girls, had been a sister of Elizabeth, who was the wife of Jacob Donner. She had been Elizabeth Hook in an earlier marriage, and two sons of that marriage, fourteen and twelve, were with her now, besides her children by Jacob Donner, a seven-year-old daughter and boys of nine, five, four, and three. With the Donner families were also four teamsters working their way west: Hiram Miller; Noah James, twenty years old, from the immediate neighborhood (see how the talk of winter evenings had struck fire from the neighbors); Samuel Shoemaker, twenty-five, who had reached the Sangamon from Springfield, Ohio; and John Denton, twenty-eight, a gunsmith, who had come a longer journey to this rendezvous, all the way from Sheffield, England . . . and who was to die in the snow-choked valley of the Yuba toward which Jim Clyman was heading when Denton camped with his employer in A. Lincoln's home town.

Like Reed, the Donners were well-to-do; they had already reached the happy ending of the American success story before the spring fret came over them. George Donner had broken prairie soil a few miles out of Springfield in the town's earliest days. Before that he had moved from North Carolina, his birthplace, to Kentucky, on to Indiana, to Illinois, to Texas, and back to Illinois. There his land and his brother's grew in value and their speculations were happy. George Donner's older children (in three marriages he had thirteen all told) were already giving him grandchildren to make the house merry on Thanksgiving Day, and were richly established on the homesteads he had set off for them from his large holdings, reserving a hundred and ten acres for the younger ones he took to California, in case they might sometime want to come back home. They were going to California in the mood of Bill Bowen, but consciously to live out their days in the languorous, winterless country that seemed so much like the Marquesas of Herman Melville's nostalgia. The younger children would grow up in a softer, more abundant life — and their gentility would not be impaired. Tamsen took with her "apparatus for preserving botanical specimens, water colors and oil paints, books and school supplies . . . for use in the young ladies' seminary which she hoped to establish in California." Touch of the invincible New England aspiration: Tamsen, a Yankee, was a schoolteacher and something of a writer for the ladies' press, and made notes for a book as she traveled. (She also sewed ten thousand dollars in bank notes in a quilt, and that was by no means all the reserve cash that went with the Donners.) The Donners had three wagons apiece, one packed with goods to set up trade and housekeeping in California, one with supplies for the journey, and one to live in; Reed also had three wagons, one of them a great, ungainly ark, double-decked and outfitted with bunks and a stove. The wagons were packed not only with the necessities but with a rich and dangerous bulk of comforts, luxuries, and indulgences. Reed, a gourmet, carried wines and brandies toward the vineyards of the province. Moreover, they had faithfully obeyed Lansford Hastings' directions to take goods for the Indians, and were even supplied with better goods to barter for land in California. . . . Not a people moving west like the Mormons, but some families — who carried with them a culture, an expectation, and the warm, habitual affections of a patriarchal life.

This is not the roster of "the Donner party," as that title comes down in history. Others were added along the trail, who will be noted later on. But, to exhibit one more specimen of the migration, we must mention another family who joined them at Independence on May 11 or 12, after they had encountered Jessy Quinn Thornton and had accepted his advice to hurry on and join the wagon train that was forming under the command of Colonel William Henry Russell, the friend of Henry Clay. This was the family of Patrick Breen, from Ireland by way of Keokuk, and his wife Peggy. They had six sons, John, Edward, Patrick, Simon, Peter, and James, ranging from fourteen years to four, and a daughter, Isabella, just a year old. Patrick Breen's friend went with him, Patrick Dolan, a bachelor who was also from Keokuk and Ireland. They were successful farmers and Breen, like Reed and the Donners, started from Independence with three wagons, plus a sizable herd of horses and milch cattle besides his oxen.

But they had not heard of the Breens when they camped at Springfield — nor of Jessy Quinn Thornton, Edwin Bryant, or Colonel Russell. Abraham Lincoln, Stephen A. Douglas, Governor Tom Ford, and ex-Congressman Hardin were familiar names to them; doubtless they had listened to them all, may have known some of them personally. The story of Joseph Smith was common talk among them, and they had their own ideas about Brigham Young and probably about Lillburn Boggs, who would eventually be their captain. They knew that the Mormons were moving west and heard that they would massacre as many Gentiles as they could on the way. They did not know about the maneuvers of Taylor's army at the Rio Grande and did not guess what was said of it in Polk's Cabinet meetings. Sam Houston was a shining name to them. Possibly they had heard about Slidell, but certainly not about Atocha or, since the Alamo and San Jacinto, about Santa Anna. They had read Frémont and Lansford Hastings. Reed knew Jim Clyman but had heard nothing about him since they had been in the same company with A. Lincoln in the Black Hawk War fourteen years ago.

On the morning of April 16, they yoked up the oxen to nine wagons and made their start — for the West. That day Jim Clyman reached Lansford Hastings on Bear Creek and was welcomed under a spreading oak in "a warm and Polite manner" . . . the Bear Creek they were to be brought down to — some of them — from the snows. There were thirty-two in the combined parties that left Springfield that morning. One of them was to leave the party just beyond Fort Laramie and Mrs. Keyes was to die when Colonel Russell's wagon train reached the Big Blue, at the beginning of the journey. Of the thirty others, thirteen were to die this side of Bear Creek because they trusted the publicity man, Lansford Hastings, who as April ended would start east to meet them and make sure of their fate.

On the day after they left Springfield, an American who had crossed the plains the year before sat down in California to write a letter to the folks back home in Springfield. This was William L. Todd, son of the high-born Dr. Todd and nephew of Mrs. Abraham Lincoln, and the *Journal* would publish his letter in early August. What young Todd had to say on April 17 is exceedingly interesting.

> . . . If there are any persons in Sangamon who speak of crossing the Rocky Mountains to this country, tell them my advice is to stay at home. There you are well off. You can enjoy all the comforts of life — live under a good government and have peace and plenty around you — a country whose soil is not surpassed by any in the world, having good seasons and yielding timely crops. Here everything is on the other extreme: the government is tyrannical, the weather unseasonable, poor crops, and the necessaries of life not to be had except at the most extortionate prices, and frequently not then. . . .
>
> I do not, however, believe there was ever a more beautiful climate than we have in this country. During the whole winter we have delightful

weather except when it rains. . . . Most all day long we could be seen in winter with our coats off, walking in the neighborhood of our cabin, except when we were off hunting for a term of four or six days.

The Mexicans talk every spring and fall of driving the foreigners out of the country. They must do it this year or they can never do it. There will be a revolution before long and probably the country will be annexed to the United States. If there, I will take a hand in it.

Mr. Todd exactly and almost completely expressed the majority beliefs of Americans in California, a month short of May. In exactly that state of mind, Jim Clyman had offered to raise filibusters for Frémont. In exactly that state of mind, John Marsh, who for years had agitated for an uprising of Americans and had assisted various native revolts, had expected a "revolution" some months before. In exactly that state of mind several hundred others felt that their hour was at hand. They believed most of the rumors that circulated in the province of anarchy, and some that were too absurd for belief they propagated as useful. Few of them understood the way of life around them, fewer respected it. The Californians were *pelados,* greasers: different from the Yankees and therefore contemptible, little interested in money, negligent of land, without thought of the morrow, abandoned to popish superstitions. And, of course, immoral.

A correspondent of the *National Intelligencer* adds an involuntary postscript, a few days later: —

Most of the inhabitants are great scamps; many not only confess they steal horses and cattle but they boast of it. I bought a horse this morning that the man is to steal for me in a day or two. You will think this strange conduct, but this same man was not only robbed but beaten by the other; and there is no law to punish them, so that he has to make himself whole in the coin of his opponent. The Spanish portion of the inhabitants are a thieving, cowardly, dancing, lewd people, and generally indolent and faithless.

Sermon on a moral text.

There is no awareness in Hastings' book that California was not an American possession, but the realization that it was not had begun to grow acute among the resident Americans. War was at hand and California would not survive it as a province of Mexico. Whatever happened, they would be exposed to material damage. Mexico or an autonomous California could expropriate their lands, to which only a few of them had any title. Cession to or seizure by a foreign state was intolerable to their patriotism and distasteful to their sense of real estate. Under any efficient foreign government most of them would have no status. Whereas an American occupation — which, always remember, had the plain logic of the map behind it — would probably obliterate the inconveniences of the established land system. They had interpreted Frémont's arrival in the light of their hopes and holdings. With Frémont gone and the hope withdrawn, they were again at the mercy, if not of the greasers at least of the land system — and what had they come for if not for land? (Well, some for health, some for adventure, some as deserters or fugitives, some merely as flotsam.) They ought to do something about it.

Besides, there would be glory for those who wanted glory. Also positions: something like a spoils system if not a civil service. Also, in the vision of the wooziest, a chance to repeat the heroic pattern of the Americans, free an enslaved people, set up the institutions of the eagle, and establish a gaudy if rather illiterate parody of Brook Farm.

It was the peculiar fortune of the Americans to find revolutions going on wherever they invaded Mexico. But if one is to sympathize with the Californians, it must be only a nostalgic sympathy, a respect for things past. This coming autumn Lieutenant Ruxton of the British Army would find some of the Plains Indians possessed by a stoic melancholy which issued from a conviction that their day was over and the white man could not be stayed. Similarly, California was suffused with a knowledge that there was no help for it. Its golden age had ended. No one could govern it from Mexico; no one could govern it at home. Its feudal organization, feeble at best, had broken up into cliques which lowered the standard of public honor and responsibility, enfeebled the society, and drained it alike of money and belief. An era was closing in regret; an order of mankind, a phase of society, in many ways a happy phase, was collapsing. This much the Californians knew. They felt diversely about it, as men do when the sanctions bred in them have broken. Some of them would welcome anything that would restore stability to the no longer stable — France, England, the United States — nor was it hidden from many landholders in this country of vast landholdings that real estate would be most valuable under the United States. Some dreamed of restoring the allegiance to Mexico which had never quite existed. Some dreamed, instead, of going it alone. A good many, and they likely to be the best, would do what they could, not much in any event, to hold together while the flood closed over them. After all, it was their country.

They were, of course, caught in the requirements of Mexican rhetoric and hindered by the heritage from Spain of interior dissents. This April the immemorial conflict between the north and the south, between San Francisco and Los Angeles, was shaping to a crisis. There was a species of representative assembly at Los Angeles, controlled by Pico, the governor. Nominally it was the civil power. In the north there were the two Castros, prefect and *comandante,* who nominally represented the military power. Neither Spain nor Mexico had ever been able to fuse the two powers in this province, but the contention between them now was only a facet of collapse. Clyman saw it as a contest for control of the revenues, but it was only a contest for the titles of office, which were resounding, and the real trouble between Pico and Castro was that neither could vote the other out. Castro formed a junta at Monterey, to consider the state of the nation and the danger of conquest, calling on Pico in excellent prose to abandon partisanship and co-operate with him. But to Pico and his assembly the Monterey junta looked like a committee of revolution, and as April ended each side was raising forces against the other. Forces? Well, both sides were raising horsemen but they were several hundred miles apart, and the likelihood was that this campaign, one more installment in a long serial, would confine itself to the methods of its predecessors, pageantry and syntax.

However, one item of the routine was to lead to results which were not contemplated and had no precedent. Castro sent north for horses to equip his levies, and northward were the jittery but opportunistic Americans.

None of this escaped the observation of Thomas Larkin. He saw that political control was dying in California. He was under orders to foment a revolution and one might develop from this new strife. In two years more the society would be altogether broken down — perhaps in one year, say by the spring of '47. . . . The trouble was time and events. His orders were five months old now and already obsolete. Frémont had attended to that; after the drama of Gavilán Peak Larkin would need time to persuade Castro that the United States was interested in his well-being. More time than he or Secretary Buchanan, months away by messenger, was to get.

And Frémont had been humiliated. Early in April he moved up the Sacramento from Lassen's ranch toward the Cascades, whither he had originally been ordered. He got past Mount Shasta but spring snow fell in the peaks and Frémont — who had twice crossed the Sierra in winter — turned back again to Lassen's, where he stayed till April 24. His father-in-law would describe to a spellbound Senate how Frémont had suffered in the harsh weather, but the truth is that he could not bring himself to leave his stage. The drama of Gavilán had come to nothing, to worse than nothing. The hero had neither conquered nor died: he had retreated. Behind him were the triumphant sneers of the Californians — and with him traveled the caustic doubts of his mountain men, who had never before seen him outfaced, and his own gnawing frustration. His image of himself had been impaired by a conflict with reality; the hero had been scaled down to life size. There was no vindication at Lassen's, however, and ultimately there was nothing to do but go on. So he started out again on the twenty-fourth, a momentous day elsewhere, toward Oregon.

Back at Monterey, the U. S. sloop *Cyane* dropped anchor on April 17 and Lieutenant Gillespie repeated to Consul Larkin the instructions he had memorized at Mexico City. He had been just short of six months on his way. Larkin presented him as an invalid traveling for his health, and he rode north to Yerba Buena and the vice consul. From there he set out to overtake Frémont.

April produced the President's triumph. Final word came from Slidell on the seventh that Paredes had refused to receive him, and the Cabinet had moved so steadily that Polk found no opposition in it to the strongest measures — to war with Mexico. However, he would not recommend them to Congress just yet, for the Oregon question was at last coming to a head. Congress must now reach a decision, and could not like the necessity. The administration drove its forces with whip, spur, and nosebag. Mr. Polk believed that he could best control the Northern members with patronage, whereas with Southerners the appeal to principle was better. But the best talent of the Whigs was opposition, Polk's own party was half a dozen factions precariously held together, and both parties were looking not only at Oregon and Great Britain but two years ahead. Neither 49° nor 54° 40′, his diary noted in disgust, meant so much to even the Democratic Senators as '48 and the election.

Mr. Calhoun was trying to find leverage in Polk's proposal for a secret fund to buy a treaty from Mexico. He blew hot and cold and persisted in mentioning it inadvertently when he called to suggest that the way out of the Oregon impasse was to have the foreign ambassadors propose a negotiation — which was suggesting that Polk admit defeat. The Whigs liked the tactics that circumstances had imposed on them; they would not dissent from Termination, which the country obviously wanted, but, to make sure of their position if it should beget trouble, they would put the entire responsibility for it on the President. Enough Democrats had factional axes to grind to help out, and as the debates reached climax, that was the shape it began to take.

The House resolution instructed the President to "cause notice to be given" to Great Britain. The Senate resolution advised negotiation in its preamble and declared merely that the President was "authorized at his discretion" to give the notice — a much weaker platform for him to dive from. The Senate resolution was passed first, on April 16, and went to the House for concurrence. The House amended it so that the vital clause read that the President was "authorized and directed," and here for an anxious moment the whole thing seemed likely to stall. The first objective of the administration was imperiled for, Polk believed, the Senate was so divided on factional cleavage lines that it would, if given a chance, gladly let the resolution perish. His journal filled with intense, precise resentments, he hurried out the party chiefs in both Houses, sent his Cabinet cracking down, and labored with his own full strength. He yielded to the inevitable and let the Senate throw out the word "directed," thus losing his last chance to present Termination as the united will of the country, and there he dug his heels in. His all-out effort succeeded. The House accepted the Senate's modification and on April 23 the resolution "to abrogate the convention of 1827" passed both Houses. Polk signed it the next day, the notice of termination had already been prepared, and on April 28 Polk sealed it with the Great Seal of the United States and sent it by special packet to the sovereign of Great Britain. Joint Occupation of Oregon was over and Mr. Calhoun, the Whigs, and whoever might be interested, would now see who was bluffing.

It was a great victory. The President had put through the first of his measures, and he was confident that it would do the job, that Great Britain was the party running a bluff. The administration felt very good indeed but its exhilaration was premature. For though the hidden realities had not come to the surface during the Oregon debate they were on their way up, the inner tensions had been increased and half revealed, the opposition had found a tactic, and pressures were rising that must soon explode. He had won handsomely but he had almost lost, his party was breaking up and the wind was rising. One trouble with decisions is that they necessitate other decisions.

But, his Oregon position carried and the "Brittish" notified, he could turn to Mexico with a tranquil and cunning mind. We see him on April 30 amazed and touched by a delegation from the new school for the blind, twenty or thirty exhibiting their pitiful accomplishment, one "a female named Bridgman who had been taught by signs with the hands and fingers to understand and communicate ideas and to write." Polk's victorious month ended with that curiously symbolical note but it was five days earlier, on the twenty-fifth, three days before he dispatched the joint resolution, that it reached its climax. On April 25, after telling the Cabinet that the notice would go to Victoria in person on May 1, he announced that it was time to deal with Mexico. We must treat all nations alike, great or small, Great Britain had the gauntlet now and here was Mexico: Mr. Polk favored "a bold and firm course." The Cabinet understood and the Secretary of State spoke the right phrase: the President should recommend a declaration of war. "The other members of the Cabinet did not dissent, but concurred in the opinion that a message to Congress should be prepared and submitted to them in the course of the next week." Very well. The President would outline the points to be presented, and Mr. Buchanan would please collect the materials and sketch out a message.

That was April 25. On the same day the fuse that was burning at the Rio Grande reached powder.

7th. Apr. General Taylor made me a long visit this a.m. He told me General Worth is to leave here tomorrow. He added that, on tendering his resignation, General Worth had asked a leave of absence as soon as his services "could be *dispensed with,*" but he determined to relieve Worth at once. So Worth leaves us while the very atmosphere is animated with rumors of attacks upon us, and he had just obtained from a spy of his own the most distinct threats from the other side of the river. I cannot help asking myself what would have been thought of the patriotism of a revolutionary officer who had abandoned his post in the presence of the enemy on an alleged grievance which, in the opinion of almost everybody, is without any proper or defensible foundation.

Colonel Hitchcock, who was confined to his tent, thus interrupted his notes on Swedenborg to criticize Brevet Brigadier General William Jenkins Worth, veteran of Chippewa, Niagara, and Lundy's Lane, conqueror of the Seminoles, and victim of Marcy's order which had reversed Scott's ruling and given the line priority over brevet rank. Worth's long quarrel with Twiggs was thus settled unfavorably, and he now went home in almost Aztec splendor. He would be back again before long, making more trouble. He was an excellent commander in battle and did some of the best fighting of the war, but he suffered from ego, malice, and purple prose. He sowed letters broadcast, explaining the jealousy of his successive commanders, and at last Scott had to order him, at the war's end, into well-merited arrest — and so gave Polk an opening and produced one more unhappy turbulence in the military biography of Winfield Scott.

Taylor had crudely fortified Point Isabel, at the mouth of the river, but the bulk of his force was in the vicinity of Fort Brown, a set of textbook field works which he had built opposite Matamoros, on a site no textbook would have approved. Hitchcock calls it a cul-de-sac, it commanded nothing but a stretch of river, it was open to enfilade from three sides, and any competent enemy could have pinched it off from the rear. All that prevented its capture now and hereafter was a Mexican incompetence as resplendent as Taylor's own. Hitchcock was too feeble from disease to undertake the security of an army but wrote gloomily that if Taylor were to succeed it must be by accident. Taylor had not yet received the young engineers who had learned an alphabet at West Point and were eventually to save him at the extremity. Worth and Twiggs, who had some mental life, were too busy fighting over rank to take thought of war, but it is hard to see why Bliss did not do something about the camp site.

It gratified Taylor, however, and he sat down to his principal enjoyment, letter writing. He shared that taste with all our other generals (Kearny is the exception), and if the campaigns of this war were inactive for long stretches, there was never a pause in the correspondence. It had two departments. One stream of letters flowed back home, to Congressmen and newspaper editors, impugning the motives and competence of all rivals and superiors and presently giving Polk, no small-time resenter himself, one of the most serious problems of the war. The other stream inundated the enemy with addresses, proclamations, and manifestoes, and drew from them an equally resounding counter-barrage. Neither side really won, but it is only simple justice to say that Taylor's proclamations were no sillier than those his opponents published.

The enemy won some points at the very beginning. On both of the two days preceding his remarks about Worth, Hitchcock notes that American deserters had been shot while crossing the Rio Grande. Probably they were just bored with army rations but there was some thought that they might be responding to a proclamation of General Ampudia's which spies had been able to circulate in camp. Noting the number of Irish, French, and Polish immigrants in the American force, Ampudia had summoned them to assert a common Catholicism, come across the river, cease "to defend a robbery and usurpation which, be assured, the civilized nations of Europe look upon with the utmost indignation," and settle down on a generous land bounty. Some of them did so, and the St. Patrick Battalion of American deserters was eventually formed, fought splendidly throughout the war, and was decimated in the campaign for Mexico City — after which its survivors were executed in daily batches. . . . This earliest shooting of deserters as they swam the Rio Grande, an unwelcome reminder that war has ugly aspects, at once produced an agitation. As soon as word of it reached Washington, the *National Intelligencer* led the Whig press into a sustained howl about tyranny. In the House J. Q. Adams rose to resolve the court-martial of every officer or soldier who should order the killing of a soldier without trial and an inquiry into the reasons for desertion. He was voted down but thereafter there were deserters in every Whig speech on the conduct of the war, and Calm Observer wrote to all party papers that such brutality would make discipline impossible. But a struggling magazine which had been founded the previous September in the interest of sports got on a sound financial footing at last. The *National Police Gazette* began to publish lists of deserters from the army, and the War Department bought up big editions to distribute among the troops.

Taylor sat in his field works writing prose. Ampudia's patrols reconnoitered the camp and occasionally perpetrated an annoyance. Taylor badly needed the Texas Rangers, a mobile force formed for frontier service in the Texas War of Independence and celebrated ever since. It was not yet available to him, however, and he was content to send out a few scouts now and then. So Colonel Truman Cross, the assistant quartermaster general, did not return from one of his daily rides. He was still absent twelve days later, and Lieutenant Porter, who went looking for him with ten men, ran into some Mexican foragers and got killed.

Meanwhile another proclamation from Ampudia was brought to camp and Taylor found himself under twenty-four hours' notice to take his army back to the Nueces. He elegantly replied that "the instructions under which I am acting will not permit me to retrograde from the position I now occupy." Nothing happened, and on April 19 it occurred to him to have the brig *Lawrence* and the revenue cutter *St. Anna* close the mouth of the Rio Grande to Mexican supplies. This was a blockade, as Ampudia instantly designated it in a moving protest which ended "God and Liberty!" but Taylor saw it, like all his earlier steps, as "a simple defensive precaution."

Paredes, however, looked on it as king's pawn to king's fourth. Two days before Polk's Cabinet discussion, he announced that the United States had begun hostilities — remarking also that American troops were threatening Monterey (news of the Gavilán tableau thus acknowledged) — and ordered the defense of Mexican territory to begin. That was April 23. The next day General Arista, who had reached Matamoros and outranked Ampudia, crossed the Rio Grande to catch Taylor between two forces. He also sent Taylor a private letter full of the courtliest expressions.

That day at the American camp they were burying Colonel Cross, whose body had at last been found. The ceremonial volleys clattered over the river, and by nightfall there were rumors that the enemy was coming. The next morning, April 25, the rumors persisted and Taylor sent out Captain Thornton with some sixty dragoons to see what they were all about. (The second in command was that Hardee who would later write a treatise on cavalry tactics.) Thornton rode up the river some twenty-five miles and was told by a native that General Anastasio Torrejon with his command was near by. Knowing the Mexicans to be liars, Thornton determined to verify the information at the first rancho. He led his horsemen into a chaparral-walled inclosure, knocked courteously at the door — and the better part of Torrejon's sixteen hundred cavalry opened fire on him. Thornton was wounded and Hardee charged to the riverbank, where he surrendered. Sixteen dragoons were killed or wounded, the rest were prisoners of war, and, as Taylor wrote to Polk, hostilities had begun.

On the day before, Frémont had started north from Lassen's and Gillespie, posting after him, had reached Yerba Buena. On the day of Thornton's capture Polk told the Cabinet he must lay the Mexican affair before Congress, Buchanan agreed to draft a war message, and the President summarized in a thousand words a talk he had had with Allen of Ohio about a rumored intrigue to restore Francis Preston Blair, who did not admire him, to the editorship of the administration newspaper. At the foot of the Sierra Jim Clyman and Hastings decided to wait a few days before "we attact the region of all most Eternal snow and ice." Francis Parkman was at St. Louis, waiting for the *Radnor,* Edwin Bryant was ahead of him, six days short of Independence, and the Donners, the Breens, Lillburn Boggs, Jessy Quinn Thornton, and Owl Russell were moving across Missouri. Lieutenant Colonel Hitchcock, invalided home, had reached New Orleans, bought passage on the steamer *Louisiana,* and begun to read a manuscript translation of Spinoza's *Tractatus.*

Polk had lost the mid-term elections and the House was Whig when, on December 22, 1847, the gangling Representative from the Seventh District of Illinois stood up at his desk, number 191, in the back row, to move eight resolutions which called on the President to inform the Congress about the first hostilities. They were more than a shade canny but had some points to make, and the fifth of them asked "Whether the people of that settlement [where Thornton was attacked], or a majority of them, or any of them, have ever submitted themselves to the government or laws of Texas or of the United States, by consent or by compulsion, either by accepting office, or voting at elections, or paying tax, or serving on juries, or having process served on them, or in any other way."[4] And on the twelfth of the following month A. Lincoln stood up again to explain his now tabled resolutions and to give the President what-for. It was quite a speech, and — with the rest of his war record — it retired Lincoln to private life. In the course of it he again called on Polk to locate the first bloodshed geographically. If Polk, Lincoln said, "can show that the soil was ours where the first blood of the war was shed — that it was not within an inhabited country, or if within such, that the inhabitants had submitted themselves to the civil authority of Texas or of the United States, and that the same is true of Fort Brown — then I am with him for his justification."

He was gratuitously offending the Seventh District, which by then had lost some sons in war, and he might have been content to stand on his party's record. For nine days before, on January 3, 1848, by a strict party vote and a majority of one, the House of Representatives had adopted another resolution, by George Ashmun of Massachusetts, which formally decided that war had been "unnecessarily and unconstitutionally begun by the President of the United States."

INTERLUDE

Doo-Dah Day

ON April 27, '46, the Virginia Minstrels of Edwin P. Christy played in New York for the first time, at Palmo's Opera House. The date will do as well as any to fix a fact: that American drama had matured its first native form. For at least four years now such companies as Christy's, or the Kentucky Minstrels, the Congo Melodists, White's Serenaders, the Sable Harmonizers, Campbell's Minstrels, with such artists as Daddy Rice, Dan Emmett, Cool White, Master Juba, Dan Bryant, had been appearing in the full-length, standardized variety performance in blackface known as the minstrel show. It was already universally popular and its popularity was to increase for nearly a half century and to decline only slightly before the twentieth century was well along.

The minstrel show was a species of vaudeville, a succession of gags, dances, and songs, interspersed with acrobatics, dramatic sketches, and what are now known as blackouts. It rested solidly on the awesome convention of the stage Negro and developed out of a full quarter century's elaboration of that caricature. Already such songs as "Jump Jim Crow," "Ol' Dan Tucker," and "Such a Gittin' Upstairs," from that convention, had impressed themselves permanently on the national memory. They in turn had come — a rather long way — out of the genuine singing of uncaricatured Negroes, who also contributed to democracy's new art form a rich variety of dances and songs — levee songs, work songs, jubilees [1] — all of them turned to caricature by the minstrels. But many other kinds of music went into this flowering. "The Sacred Harp," just now being printed for the first time, contributed its characteristic melodies and harmonies. The kind of fiddling called folk music, such as fox-hunting keens, "The Arkansas Traveler," and "Frog Went a-Courting," was incorporated, and any tune detective can untangle innumerable airs from the balladry which we still know in "Springfield Mountain," "Hand Me Down My Walkin' Cane," "She'll Be Comin' Round the Mountain," "Weevily Wheat," "Rosin the Bow," and a thousand others. Moreover the lush pathos from England, where the Queen's taste was refining sentiment, was breaking over us in a great wave at this very hour, and, joined to the music of acrobatic trills and cadenzas typified by Ole Bull, found welcome and transposition on the minstrel stage. The world's most musical people had a sudden focus for their music.[2]

A Tin Pan Alley had arisen to give the minstrels songs, and the best of the songsmiths was only two years away from the beginning of his service to Christy and the others. In March of '46 a twenty-year-old Pittsburgh youth failed of appointment to West Point, and so at the end of the year he went to keep books in his brother's commission house at Cincinnati. He took with him the manuscripts of three songs, all apparently written in this year, all compact of the minstrel-nigger tradition. One celebrates a lubly cullud gal, Lou'siana Belle. In another an old nigger has no wool on the top of his head in the place whar de wool ought to grow, and you heard your grandfather, as your children's grandchildren will hear theirs, telling the chorus to lay down de shubble and de hoe for poor old Ned has gone whar de good niggers go. And in the third American pioneering was to find its leitmotif for all time: it was "Oh Susanna!"

Stephen Collins Foster himself need not occupy us very long. He was different from fifty contemporaries, and his songs were different from theirs, only in that the obscure chemistry of genius concentrated an era and a society in him. He was as Bohemian as Edgar Poe, Fitz-James O'Brien, Mayne Reid, or the first period of Walt Whitman. He took no thought of the morrow, could not make a marriage work, lived precariously, accepted the tinsel of the cheapest theater, came to the proper end of pathetic artists — and said perfectly what his people felt. He wrote well over two hundred songs, most of them quite dead now. He took what pleased him, from his friends if research was too troublesome. He repeated himself and his rivals monotonously. And the difference between him and everyone else was that he made a final music. A hundred years after him you need only play the opening bars of "My Old Kentucky Home" or "The Old Folks at Home" to stir in any American the full nostalgia of things past or to bind any audience, be it naturalized Czechs or the Daughters of the American Revolution, South Carolina Consistory, in the unity of a nation that knows itself. Art is the unpredictable, the miraculous and undefined, but if that be art which a people take most closely to their bosoms and hold there most tenderly and longest, then Stephen Foster is incomparably the greatest American artist.

He dreamed of Jeanie with her light brown hair, floating like a vapor on the soft summer air. The joys of other days oppressed him, he could not sing tonight, and why should the beautiful ever weep, why should the beautiful die? He supped sorrow with the poor, dreaming of a once happy day, and with the gentle voices gone he had no friend left but in Old Dog Tray. He roamed with gentle Annie mid the bowers but would never hear her winning voice again, the happy dream had passed like a fleeting beam with sweet Laura Lee, and the bell must toll for lubly Nell, his dark Virginny bride. The emotion twists to the period's refined lust and gone are the cares of life's busy throng, beautiful dreamer awaken to me; light is the young heart, so come where my love lies dreaming the happy hours away. It changes to a jig and here is Susanna — de buckwheat cake was in her mouth, de tear was in her eye, and he was off to Alabama wid his banjo on his knee. It becomes a cakewalk, the buck and wing, and turnabout and jump Jim Crow — de Camptown race-track five miles long, gwine to run all night, gwine to run all day, he bet his money on de bobtail nag, somebody bet on the bay. But it is surest in that limpid pathos. I cannot work before tomorrow cayse de tear drop flow. Gone are the days when my heart was young and gay, where are the hearts so happy and so free? — I heard those gentle voices calling "Old Black Joe." All de world am sad and dreary, ebrywhere I roam, hard times come again no more, the head must bow and the back will have to bend wherever the darky may go — a few more days for to tote the weary load, no matter, 'twill never be light, a few more days till we totter on the road, then for Foster and millions of Americans who have answered with an unmistakable assent to a feeling only started, not expressed, by the music, my old Kentucky home, good-night. He made the Americans members one of another.

Between the America of the 1840's and the America we belong to a century has built a barrier which can be penetrated only with the greatest difficulty. What is called the modern temper has complexities, ambiguities, and tentatives that the forties did not know. We persuade ourselves that our consciousness is tragic. That may be; certainly the American consciousness of the forties lacked the sense of tragedy. It had achieved only pathetics. But no one will understand the decade in whose mind that assertion is tinctured with reproof or superiority. Where would you find tragedy in, say, American literature of the time? Not in Walt Whitman, not in Hawthorne's exquisitely engraved melancholy, not in the cheap gloom of Edgar Poe. Melville was making toward it through a misunderstood underbrush that was half false, but the event was still to come and would be disfigured when it arrived. Yet the white-robed maiden who died in gift books, annuals, and the mortuary poems of Mark Twain's aristocrats (whose date is '45) is not to be understood as a grotesque but as a limpidity. What makes her distasteful or even emetic to us is not insincerity or sentimentality in the emotion that lamented her, but a neutral-colored thing that has been added unto us and is called, without value, sophistication. The emotions of the forties were simpler than our own, more limpid, more absolute, and more forthright.

That, at least, is where one man comes out after years of trying to understand these people by way of what they did, what they believed, and what they felt — by way of their literature, their journalism, their religion, their causes, their institutions, their dreads, hopes, pleasures, and ambitions. They were an inchoate people between two stages of the endless American process of becoming a nation, with their heads down and their eyes resolutely closed to the desperate realities which a few years would force them to confront in the deadliest of awakenings. They were a people without unity and with only a spasmodic mutual awareness, at this moment being pulled farther asunder by the centrifugal expansion of the frontier and the equal explosiveness of the developing industry — both of which would turn back again in the nation-making curve, but not for a long while yet. A people going blithely into a war of conquest whose certain ending few tried to foresee. A people divided by racial differences, sectional cleavages, cultural antipathies, an enormous disparity of assumption, expectation, hope, and philosophy. A people united only by a political system and tradition which were nearing the deadly test, by habits of democratic association — and by a common readiness and reality of feeling which few took conscious thought of. That commonalty of feeling, in its simplicity, sincerity, and high potential, is the one feasible way into them. Stephen Foster caught it at dead center — the maiden's grave under the willows, the old times that come again no more, the Camptown races, Susanna's immortal quickstep — the ready regret, the instantaneous and immortal confidence that was bred in the bone and acknowledged if only half realized in a joke. A forthright people, with a readiness of sincere tears and an energy that could be neither measured nor stayed. The way to understand the persons who were about to fight an unpremeditated war and by building new homes in the West push the nation's boundary to the Pacific — is to steep yourself in Stephen Foster's songs.

VI

Oh Susanna!

THOUGH it was to be a drouth summer throughout the West, the prairies had one of their wettest springs. The citizenry of Independence had built six miles of macadam road to the Missouri in order to keep their commerce, but had omitted grading their own streets. It was still raining in early May, wagons bogged to the hubs, and one waded to Colonel Noland's tavern or Robert Weston's blacksmith shop through a knee-deep solution of red Missouri clay. Either was worth the miring, however. Weston's was the most celebrated of the frontier's smithies, though only one of a dozen or more in Independence, all overburdened with this spring's preparations. Smallwood Noland's inn was even more famous, the westernmost hotel in all America, the last one this side of the Sandwich Islands, with accommodations for up to four hundred guests if they didn't mind sleeping two or more in a bed.

Franklin had slid into the Missouri and there was only Westport, some ten miles away (now a part of Kansas City), to challenge the priority of Independence in the Western trade. This year a few wagon trains moved west from St. Joseph, and in the future Leavenworth, Atchison, Plattsmouth, and finally Council Bluffs would feed traffic to the trail. But Independence was the traditional jumping-off place, the beginning alike of New Mexico and Oregon and romance, fully as important in history as it has become in legend.

Quite properly, a son of Daniel Boone was the first white man to visit it. He named it Eden and was later confirmed by inspiration. "The land of Missouri," God revealed to Joseph the Seer in 1831, "is the land which I have appointed and consecrated for the gathering of the Saints. Wherefore this is the land of promise and the place for the city of Zion. . . . Behold, the place which is now called Independence is the center place [of the earth and of the starry universe as well] and a spot for the temple is lying westward upon a lot which is not far from the court house." Round that courthouse and that still vacant Temple Lot the Saints were to gather when the Latter days should become the Last days, and they are still to gather there when prophecy shall be fulfilled. But though Joseph acquired his most industrious murderer at Independence, Porter Rockwell, Israel's enemies prevailed and the Saints were driven from their gathering place to the less sanctified lands of Clay County. Later still and suffering another persecution, Joseph, in jail at Liberty in 1838, foresaw God's vengeance on Independence. Do not accept some Jackson County land, offered in payment of a debt, he told Alexander Doniphan, his attorney. For "God's wrath hangs over Jackson County. God's people have been ruthlessly driven from it and you will live to see the day when it will be visited by fire and sword. The Lord of Hosts will sweep it with the besom of destruction. The fields and farms and houses will be destroyed, and only the chimneys will be left to mark the desolation." So Doniphan is said to have told a friend in 1863, soon after a Union army swept through the county burning out the guerrillas who had been ravaging it for eighteen months.

But in '46 neither the gathering of the Saints nor the besom of destruction menaced Independence. It was still Eden but with metropolitan additions, and the flood poured through it. All conditions of mankind were there, in all costumes: Shawnee and Kansa from the Territory and wanderers of other tribes, blanketed, painted, wearing their Presidential medals; Mexicans in bells, slashed pantaloons, and primary colors, speaking a strange tongue and smoking shuck-rolled cigarettes; mountain men in buckskins preparing for the summer trade or offering their services to the emigrant trains; the case-hardened bullwhackers of the Santa Fe trail in boots and bowie knives, coming in after wintering at the other end or preparing to go out; rivermen and roustabouts, Negro stevedores, soldiers from Fort Leavenworth, a miscellany of transients whose only motive was to see the elephant wherever the elephant might be. Freight poured in from the steamboat landings, the great wagons careened through the streets, day by day the freshet of movers came in from the east, the lowing of herds pullulated over the town, the smithies and wagon shops rang with iron, whooping riders galloped their ponies through the mud, the groggeries were one long aria, and out from town the little clusters of tents grew and grew.

The town was a first violent shock of the strangeness which was a primary condition of the emigration. From now on the habits within whose net a man lives would be twisted apart and disrupted, and the most powerful tension of pioneering began here at the jumping-off. Here was a confusion of tongues, a multitude of strange businesses, a horde of strangers — and beyond was the unknown hazard. For all their exuberance and expectation, doubt of that unknown fermented in the movers and they were already bewildered. They moved gaping from wheelwright's to blacksmith's, from tavern to outfitter's, harassed by drovers and merchants trying to sell them equipment, derided by the freighters, oppressed by rumors of Indians and hostile Mormons, oppressed by homesickness, drinking too much forty-rod, forming combinations and breaking them up, fighting a good deal, raging at the rain and spongy earth, most of them depressed, some of them giving up and going ingloriously home.

They in turn were passing strange to Francis Parkman. He thought the Mexicans' tongue outlandish and he heard with an intense distaste the high Tennessee whine, the Illinois nasals, the cottonmouth Missouri drawl, the slurred syllables, the bad grammar, the idioms and slang of uncouth dialects. The emigrants were loud, rowdy, carelessly dressed, and unmistakably without breeding. They waited for no introduction before accosting a grandson of a China merchant and his cousin whose triply perfumed name was Quincy Adams Shaw — slapping them on the back, prying into their lives and intentions. "How are ye, boys? Are ye for Oregon or California?" None of their damned business: would not have been on Beacon Hill and certainly was not since they were coarse, sallow, unkempt, and dressed in homespun which all too obviously had been tailored for them by their wives. "New England sends but a small proportion but they are better furnished than the rest," he wrote in his notebook — and in his book set down that the movers were "totally devoid of any sense of delicacy or propriety." They would not do. He was perplexed by "this strange migration" and wondered whether mere restlessness went into it, or "a desire of shaking off restraints of law and society," or "an insane hope of a better condition of life." But with that wonder his interest in them reached a full stop. Manifest Destiny was taking flesh under his eyes, his countrymen were pulling the map into accord with the logic of geography, but they were of the wrong caste and the historian wanted to see some Indians.

He could not suffer the Pukes or the Suckers. So he joined three Englishmen whom he had met at St. Louis, preparing for a summer on the plains, and who also wanted no truck with the "Kentucky fellows." They were three of God's innocents and one of them had high ranking among God's bores. Captain Chandler had retired from Her Majesty's Army on a competence; he had his brother with him and a Mr. Romaine. This was a faintly literary gentleman who bossed everything, knew nothing, was inept in all things, and expressed his type at the very beginning by leading them off the trail for a full week. Yet he had to be accorded a certain authority since he had been on — and survived — a mountain expedition in 1841.[1] Parkman had hired his mountain man, Henry Chatillon, and a humble Canadian pork-eater named Delorier; the Britishers had three *engagés.* Ten strong altogether, with twenty-three horses and mules, they fled the movers into the prairies, where there would be no worse affliction than the Pawnee. They intended to travel a long way, the Englishmen to the Pacific and Parkman as far as need be to find the noble savage in his unspoiled state. One supposes that Henry Chatillon assumed they must soon join a wagon train; otherwise, to take so small a party west was folly.

Parkman had taken care, however, to provide himself with such safeguards as the American Fur Company, the law west of the Missouri, could offer. He had met the principal Chouteau at St. Louis, and had previously met Ramsay Crooks, the New York head. In March Crooks had sent him the necessary letters "to facilitate your contemplated excursion, and by requesting these friends to give you introductions to others on your way to, or in the interior of the country, they will no doubt do so." In St. Louis he had obtained from the Chouteau company, the actual management, a letter, dated April 25 and signed J. B. Clapp. It commended Parkman and Shaw to all employes of the company, wherever they might be met, and ordered given to them any services, supplies, or assistance they might require. It was countersigned by Shaw and Parkman, for recognition. (The Chouteaus had also engaged Chatillon for them.)

The Britishers dressed in the fearful costumes of their kind and were equipped with expensive sporting arms. Parkman and Shaw wore the prairie uniforms supplied by correct outfitters and had the conventional weapons. They packed their miniature train and were off, after calling on the Kickapoo trader, in whose house Parkman saw a loaded pistol resting on the poems of John Milton. At Fort Leavenworth Colonel Stephen Watts Kearny of the First Dragoons (he was clearly a gentleman) had no hint of what the summer was preparing for him, talked of steeplechases and buffalo hunting, and pledged them with a bottle of Madeira. And so westward — if, as a result of British confidence, at first not on the trail.

Alone of the year's travelers who described their journeying, Parkman called this lush country the Great American Desert. He observed at once, however, that "the clouds in this region are afflicted with incontinence of water." The phrase was a trifle high and what survived in his book was a remark that the climate made New England's seem "mild and equable." He was right. It buffeted him, the Mormons, the Santa Fe traders, and the emigrants with a violent succession of deluges, thunderstorms, northers, freezes, and heat waves. Oxen might die of heat beside streams made impassable by yesterday's rain while their owners sniffled with the colds produced by day before yesterday's norther. Sudden gales blowing out of nowhere flattened the tents, barrages of thunder that lasted for many hours might stampede the stock, and Parkman remarked that his bed was soft for he sank into it. Nevertheless the life was enchanting at once: this was a camping trip many times enlarged. He equably accepted the rains, the continual miring and occasional breakdown of the cart, the deadly mosquitoes, the dor bugs, and the ineptitudes of the British. It was wild, free, and rewarding, an intensification of the tramps and canoe trips through upper New England that had laid the ground plans of the books he would write. He quickly learned the knacks of prairie travel, could pitch camp, hitch a pack, find wood or water, track a strayed horse, extricate the mired cart.

They got back on their course after a lost week's travel — they had been trying to strike the new trail from St. Joseph [2] — and reached the Oregon trail proper near the crossing of the Blue in late May. The next month was pleasant, routine travel, and exciting only as climate. They got through the Pawnee country without the pillage to which their defenselessness exposed them, and such specimens of these prairie pirates as they met only delighted Parkman. There was little game at first — as the Mormons to the eastward had already found — but the prairies were populous. They met parties on their way back from the mountains, Papin the bourgeois of Fort Laramie with eleven bullboats of furs precariously navigating the Platte (he gave them a letter to his understudy at the fort), a half-dozen Canadian *engagés* of some other fur company who gathered round their fire in a desolate rain. Nearly every day there were companies of emigrants, whom Parkman could not love. The notebook records a girl at the head of one of them on horseback, delicately holding a parasol, various quarrels and debates along the trail, "a true specimen of the raw Western way, 'Hullo boys — where do you water your horses?' " But he could commend the appearance of one group who, though as inquisitive as the rest, came from "one of the least barbarous of the frontier counties" and were "fine looking fellows with an air of frankness, generosity and even courtesy." That was a sizable admission and presently he was able to accept without too much distaste the small band of movers who joined his party on Mr. Romaine's invitation — four wagons, ten men, one woman, and a child. These traveled with or just ahead of them for two weeks, and though Parkman fumed he spent part of the night with one of them on guard duty and found him not too bad. The young man had an intelligent face and his manners and conversation showed the essential characteristics of a gentleman. He was not, however, an Indian.

Good fun, good food, the nightly ritual of camp and fire. The rains ended, though there was a vicious sleet storm in June. Vegetation grew sparse, the land sloped and broke up. Traveling grew monotonous but had a pleasant languor. Parkman had some symptoms of illness but did not realize how ominous they were. His notebook says occasionally that he was "hipped," meaning the fits of depression that were to grow stronger and darker in his middle years.

Then they met the buffalo and the fantasy of all American boys was fulfilled. Parkman's horse, which he had duly named Pontiac, was not broken to buffalo running but he made a frenzied and ecstatic chase. Drenched with sweat, his heart pounding, armed only with a saddle pistol, he missed his first one and nearly got lost in the prairie sea to boot, but before long he was a veteran. By June 10 he and Shaw had had all they could stand of British fumbling and bumbling. "The folly of Romaine — the old womanism of the Capt. combine to disgust us" is one notebook entry. They decided to go it alone. There would be only four of them — and they were now at the Lower California Crossing of the Platte — but that would be all right. Pretty soon they would find some Indians.

And pretty soon they did. Something was coming down a butte on the horizon and Parkman took it to be a file of buffalo. But Henry Chatillon shouted that it was Old Smoke's village of Sioux.[3] Shortly a young buck in robe and moccasins, with bow and quiver, an eagle-bone whistle thrust in his topknot, gorgeously rode up and Parkman had a foretaste of his desire. The visitor rode on with them, the village was camped at Horse Creek, and here was Old Smoke in person, and Old Smoke's youngest squaw was a beauty in fringed and beaded white deerskin, her cheeks vermilioned. Here were other chiefs in a tableau of savage dignity, formally posed, with their robes thrown over their shoulders like Roman knights. Squaws and children boiled about, hundreds of dogs were howling, and the old women, "ugly as Macbeth's witches," worked feverishly and added a high screaming to the mingled noises that made Parkman's heart run over. He had reached the threshold of adventure.

He noted an emigrant train, "dragging their slow, heavy procession" across Horse Creek at that moment. The thought struck him that these people and their descendants would finish the Western Indians in the course of a century.

He gave a noon feast for some chiefs and camped on the Platte that night, within sight of the Sioux. The next day, June 15, he hurried on to Fort Laramie and began to make arrangements. Leave him there for a while.

The emigration moved beside Parkman, ahead of him, and behind him. We will follow it mainly in the experiences of several persons, already introduced, who started a little after him. In early May an enormous wagon train was forming at Indian Creek, a few miles out of Independence. We are concerned with its itinerary and experience, though this narrative calls at need on the whole summer's movement and on what is typical in the history of such travel. This particular train was nearer the eastern than the western end of the long line of wagons that stretched in its entirety for several hundreds of miles, making from the Missouri to the Pacific in this summer of '46. It was not to be a unit for very long and the units that formed of its components were themselves to shift, interchange, break up, and reunite. Ahead of it moved at least twenty trains that had left Independence, Westport, and St. Joseph as units, and these too underwent similar fractures and transformations. Behind it were an undetermined but smaller number of similar trains which had a similar history. . . . Remember that this was a drouth year already in the mountains and would soon become one on the plains. Earlier trains had diminished the originally plentiful grass, and the trail, where it was fixed, was dusty from the wheels of those that had gone before. The prairie air was full of rumors, and there was doubt of one's welcome in Oregon, which might be British when one arrived, or in California, which might be at war.

Edwin Bryant, the transplanted Yankee, left Independence with his two companions [4] for the rendezvous on May 5. They had hired a sub-mountain-man named Brownell to drive for them, had bought and outfitted an emigrant wagon, and had provided it with three yoke of oxen at $21.67 per span.[5] The asthmatic Thornton had already been nominated a colonel, probably because he used such beautiful language, when he left Independence with his Nancy and two hired drivers on May 12. He joined Governor Boggs's party and when they reached the rendezvous, the fifteenth, they brought its census to 72 wagons, 130 men, 65 women, 125 children. For a brief space it was to be more than twice as large as that. A few days later Reed and the Donners came up, and the populous Breens had joined them. They were probably the most luxuriously equipped emigrants on the plains that summer, and an undercurrent of resentment began. One of Reed's wagons was not only outsize but had been filled with bunks, cushions, a stove, and various contrivances for comfort. Virginia Reed's blooded riding mare was envied. The Donners had three spare yoke of oxen, more milch cows than seemed necessary, some yearlings for beef, and five saddle horses. An even more ambitious effort was made. Messrs. J. Baker and David Butterfield undertook to make the crossing with a herd of 140 cattle.[6] After a few days they were required to leave the train, on the formal verdict that so large a herd would be a danger when they should reach the desert country, but more likely because they refused to butcher their calves.

Parkman's judgment on these people, that of a tory and a Brahmin, has been quoted. Thornton, who was a Virginian by origin, something of a cosmopolite, and as genteel as possible, did not agree.[7] "The majority were plain, honest, substantial, intelligent, enterprising, and virtuous," he says. "They were indeed much superior to those who usually settle in a new country." Both halves of his judgment are unquestionably correct. A frontier that could be reached only by eighteen hundred miles of hard travel was not an easy recourse for brush dwellers, squatters, and butcher-knife boys. From the Connecticut and the Kenawha on to the Missouri the "new country" had always offered opportunities to the shiftless and the shifty, but this was different. The migration was drawn from the stable elements of society, if only because the stable alone could afford it. A customary family outfit had a value of from seven to fifteen hundred dollars. The only way in which a really poor man could make the passage was to hire out as driver or helper.[8] Most trains had a number of such young men (and sometimes, as with the Donners, young women) who were working their passage, but the bulk were, at least in a moderate degree, men of property and therefore substantial citizens. A certain fraction, of course, if not "squatters" (generically, "poor whites") were of the butcher-knife type, and the fraction increased as travel cheapened. (In the last stages of the Gold Rush it got fairly large.) A good many had the Big Bear of Arkansaw exuberance that distressed Parkman, but even they were likely to be farmers who had sold their farms at a profit. Farmers predominated but it was a heterogeneous mass. The train we are following included lawyers, journalists, students, teachers, day laborers, two ministers of the gospel, a carriage maker, a cabinet-maker, a stonemason, a jeweler, a gunsmith, and several blacksmiths. It had Germans, Hollanders, Frenchmen, and Englishmen, but was native American in the overwhelming majority. Companions of Thornton's alluded to in a few successive entries of his journal are named Crump, Clark, Lard, Van Bibber (Lazarus!), Mootrey, Savage, Croiyers, Dunbar, Luce, Hill, Norris, Perkins, and Burns. It is a voting list of any town from Concord to Sedalia.

They were Americans and would therefore organize. An impressive staff of officers — captain, vice captains, secretary, treasurer, judges, committees of appeal, and so forth — was proposed and these honors implied electioneering. Candidates mounted stumps or wagon boxes to confess their personal excellences and praise the patriotism of emigration. Cliques formed, votes were cast, and whoever lost began to store up resentment that would make trouble later on. The committees could meet by night and make recommendations, which one obeyed at his pleasure but was more likely to disregard. The captain's duties were large but his authority was theoretical; everyone had the inalienable privilege of dissent and especially of criticism. Few trains ever got to South Pass, and still fewer to the Pacific, under the same officers or even the same organization they had voted in at the start. But organizing was fun and as native as a town meeting.

The election went to Owl Russell, described at this very moment as a tall man in a panama hat which had an oiled-silk cover, "courteous to all around him — how kindly he takes every man who is introduced to him by the hand, exceedingly delighted to have the privilege of meeting him."[9] He was a mighty orator and therefore a predestined captain. The stock had exhausted the near-by grass and he got his unwieldy train in motion — somehow, by sections mostly — and the start was made. It was too big, and it had a fundamental inner conflict in that some of the Osnaburg wagon-covers had "California" painted on them and others "Oregon," "The Whole or None," or "54° 40′." They waddled through the mire, the oxen unused to the routine and stubborn and stupid, the horses alert to slip away and turn back to the settlements, no order of camp life yet established, and the movers rebellious, vociferous, and bewildered by the strangeness of the country.

As they started, rumor raised up sizable dangers. The Kansa were supposed to be mobilized beside the trail, waiting to slaughter the emigration — a degenerate tribe fluent at theft but no longer hardy enough to make trouble. Bryant heard that a party of five Englishmen were moving down the trail on Her Majesty's business, to incite all Indians between here and the Pacific "to attack [the] trains, rob, murder, and annihilate them." This was the passage of Francis

Parkman among the half barbarous, or it was mere air — though it is true that a surprising number of British Army officers went out to hunt buffalo or commune with the prairie gods while Oregon and California hung in the balance. More immediate was the threat of the Mormons who were now loose beyond the frontier, five or ten or twenty thousand of them, with "ten brass field pieces" and every man "armed with a rifle, a bowie knife, and a brace of large revolving pistols." Their homes having been burned behind them, it seemed likely that they intended slaughter and neither mob nor police would head them off. "No one," Parkman said, "could predict what would be the result when large armed bodies of these fanatics should encounter the most impetuous and reckless of their old enemies on the prairie." Here were many Illini and more Missourians and here, specifically, was Lillburn Boggs, who had ordered his militia to exterminate them, who was responsible for the massacre of their relatives, who had sought the death of their prophet, and who had his share in producing that martyrdom by keeping alive the prosecution of Porter Rockwell, the Destroying Angel who had filled him with buckshot in his own home. The worst seemed exceedingly likely. The emigrants kept their rifles primed and their suspicions at half cock — and sent an express to Colonel Kearny at Fort Leavenworth, asking his advice and protection. Kearny answered that they need fear no trouble if they behaved themselves. (He repeated the suggestion to other trains which expressed the same anxiety.) But the emigrants were not reassured till the border was far behind them, and whenever Parkman approached a train hard characters with their rifles cocked were apt to ride out on the chance that this descendant of John Cotton and son of the pastor of the New North Church might be a Mormon. Parkman suffered no greater indignity anywhere in the West.

(Meanwhile, making a few weary miles a day across Iowa, a hundred miles north and a good way east of the emigration, the Mormons kept their guns loaded but hidden, in fear that, now they were beyond the settlements, the Missourians would annihilate them. They walked warily and behaved themselves, but they had bad dreams. So did the Missourians, to whom a hundred miles of prairies seemed an insufficient buffer. They kept memorializing the Adjutant General, the Secretary of War, and President Polk himself. Why, they demanded, were the Saints "armed to the teeth and supported by batteries of heavy ordnance?" Why were they without their families? — this, when the discreet Mormon Battalion was marched toward Fort Leavenworth to get its equipment. They meant no good to Missouri and had already given the neighboring Indians "a more savage bearing and more bold assurance." They were "depredating" Missouri property and were, in the belief of the memorialists, "British emissaries, intending by insidious means to accomplish diabolical purposes." So it was clearly the duty of the President, "in defence of 'the brave and hardy men of the frontier' to take the necessary measures to disarm them and expel them from our border." In short, the brave and hardy men of the frontier had a bad conscience and a violent scare. . . . And not only in Missouri. As far south as Texas it was believed that the Mormons were coming with sword and firebrand, various Californians were panicky with the same expectation, even Larkin was uneasy, and dispatches were hurried eastward calling on Polk in much the same vocabulary. These representations had a part in Polk's decision to raise a new regiment of Mounted Rifles for border duty. Also, the moment he had a war on his hands, the Camp of Israel, pitched far out in the country that was his main objective, acquired an importance that his best humanitarian rhetoric had not previously attributed to it.)

As soon as Colonel Russell got his train moving, the Reverend Mr. Dunleavy was dissatisfied, and turned back to await more congenial companions. Five days later, Mr. Gordon decided that the going was too slow for him and persuaded a total of thirteen wagons to strike out ahead. Four days after that, Governor Boggs, Reed, George Donner, Bryant, and Thornton (probably the best minds in the train) convened beside the swollen Big Blue to take counsel on disorder and delay. So the next morning (perhaps further exasperated by the tumultuous storm of the same night) one hearty democrat who had aspired to office and been defeated assailed Russell and his lieutenant with violent language. All other activity stopped while the protestant demanded that the whole corps of officers be tried for misfeasance and malfeasance. The officers submitted their resignations. Voted to accept. Debate followed, and second thoughts. Voted to reinstate the officers.

Already there had been absorbing incidents. On May 19, several wagons stayed behind, so it was delicately explained, to "hunt cattle." Dr. Rupert of Independence, who had ridden out for a last few days with a consumptive brother traveling to California for his health, stayed with them and presently delivered Mrs. Hall of twin boys. The Thorntons would be cooing about them for weeks to come. That day Mr. Burns got himself plentifully lost in the prairies and established a precedent that the greenhorns would act on till they learned better.

And on May 16 they got the last news from the States that they would hear until they reached the Pacific. A horseman hurrying to catch up with a train ahead of them brought a copy of the St. Louis *Republican* containing word of hostilities in Mexico. The next day Mr. Webb, the editor of an Independence newspaper, rode into camp to confirm the story. On the Rio Grande a Captain Thornton of the Dragoons had been attacked and his command had been captured after a great loss of life, and the situation of Zachary Taylor was said to be extremely perilous. Excitement stirred among those who were bound to California — and the success of Lansford Hastings was now assured — but Bryant noted that no one thought of giving up the emigration. And Jessy Thornton, experiencing an access of patriotism exactly like that which had foamed up in the States, knew what to do. He felt that Old Rough and Ready (who was about to receive that title) would come through and "add additional luster to a name already greatly endeared to his admiring countrymen." Therefore, on the right bank of the Kansas, he nominated Zachary Taylor to be President of the United States.

These people were greenhorns: what the West came to call tenderfeet. Most of them were schooled in the culture that had served American pioneering up to now. The unfitness for the West of that experience shows at the beginning of the journey. The Oregon and California emigrants had a much harder time of it than they would have had if they had understood the conditions. They did not have to face the cholera that made the Gold Rush and certain later passages hazardous, or the Indian troubles that began in the fifties and lasted as long as there were Indians along the trail. But they experienced hardships, disease, great strain, and aimless suffering of which the greater part was quite unnecessary. The mountain men avoided it almost altogether.

We have already seen them breaking up and without trail discipline. A caravan of mountain men passing this way was an efficient organization. The duties of every member were stated — and attended to in an awareness that both safety and comfort depended on their being done right. The fur caravan was a co-operative unit, the emigrant train an uncohesive assemblage of individualists. The mountain men had mastered the craft of living off the country, finding grass and water, managing the stock, making camp, reading buffalo sign and Indian sign. All such matters were hidden from the

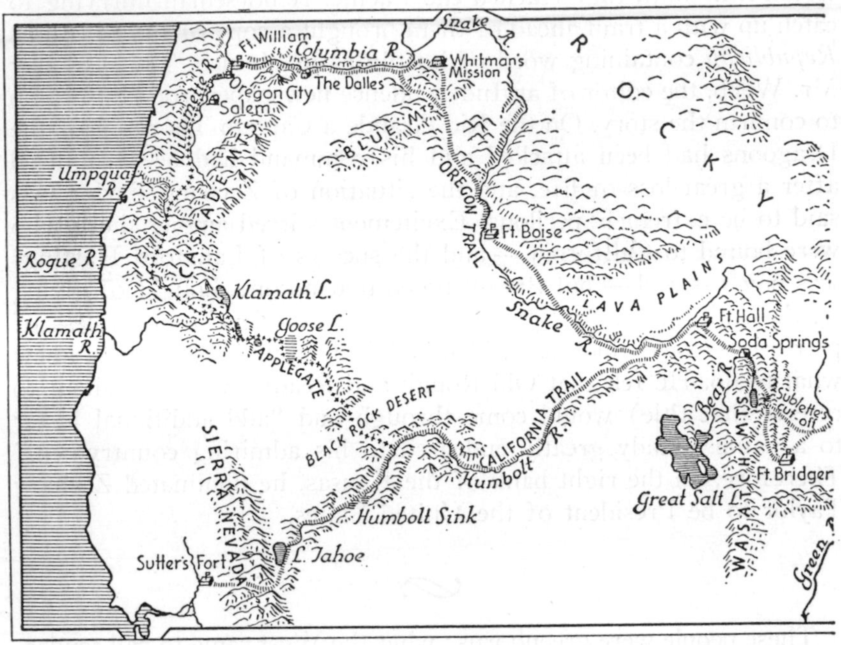

The Oregon and

emigrants, who besides were tired men at the end of any day and prone to let someone else do the needful tasks. So their wagons were not kept up, horses and oxens strayed, and many hours, counting up to many days, were squandered. This added to the delay and we have already seen them moving much too slowly even at the beginning of the trip. The passage must be made with the greatest possible speed consonant with the good condition of the animals — but the movers dallied, strolling afield to fish or see the country, stopping to stage a debate or a fist fight, or just wandering like vacationists. It was necessary to press forward, not only because the hardest going of the whole journey was toward the western end and would be far worse if they did not pass the mountains before snowfall, but also because every day diminished the food in the wagons, wore down the oxen by so much more, and laid a further increment of strain on man and beast. They lingered. And also, expert as they might be at living healthfully in the oak openings, they did not know how to

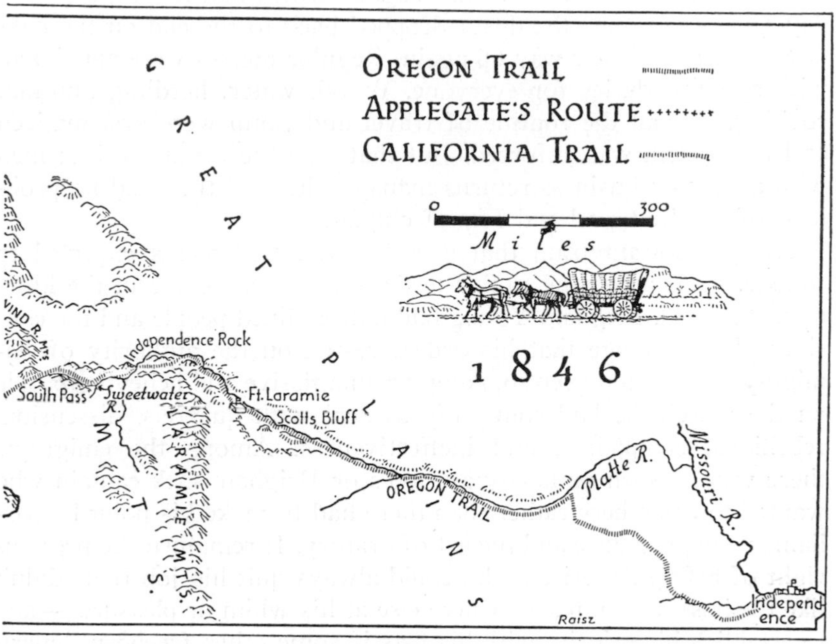

California Trails

take care of themselves here. The mountain men suffered bountifully from scalping but you seldom hear of one who is sick, and when you do he is suffering from a hangover or a decayed tooth. Whereas from the first days on, the emigrants are preyed upon by colds, agues, and dysenteries that are their own damned fault. . . . All this has its part in the stresses put on human personality by emigration.

The train is moving along the Oregon trail. But the movement must not be thought of as the orderly, almost military procession of spaced wagons in spaced platoons that Hollywood shows us, and the trail must not be thought of as a fixed avenue through the wilds. The better discipline of the freight caravans on the Santa Fe trail did impose a military order of march. On the southern trail wagons moved in something like order; in single file where the route was narrow, in columns of twos or fours when there was room for such a formation and it was needed for quick formation of the corral in case of Indian attack. Every night they were parked in a square or circle, the stock was driven inside after feeding, guard duty was enforced on everyone in his turn. Wagons which had led a file on one day (and so escaped the dust) dropped back to the end on the next day and worked their way up again. Regular messes were appointed, with specified duties for everyone. Wood, water, herding, hunting, cooking, and all the routine of travel and camp were systematized and the system was enforced. But that was the profit motive; men with an eye on business returns managed it. And they had no problems of family travel and few of cliques.

Every emigrant train that ever left the settlements expected to conduct itself according to this tested system. None except the Mormons ever did. Brigham Young had a disciplined people and the considerable advantage that his orders rested on the authority of Almighty God — and even so, among a submissive and believing people on the march, he had constantly to deal with quarrels, dissension, rebellions, complaints, and ineffectiveness. Among the emigrants there was no such authority as God's or Brigham's. A captain who wanted to camp here rather than there had to make his point by parliamentary procedure and the art of oratory. It remained the precious right of a free American who could always quit his job if he didn't like the boss, to camp somewhere else at his whim or pleasure — and to establish his priority with his fists if some other freeborn American happened to like the cottonwood where he had parked his wagon. Moreover, why should anyone take his appointed dust when he could turn off the trail? Why should he stand guard on the herd of loose cattle, if he had no cattle in it? . . . They combined readily but with little cohesiveness and subdued themselves to the necessities of travel only after disasters had schooled them. They strung out along the trail aimlessly, at senseless intervals and over as wide a space as the country permitted. So they traveled fewer miles in any day than they might have, traveled them with greater difficulty than they needed to, and wore themselves and the stock down more than was wise. They formed the corral badly, with too great labor and loss of time, or not at all. They quarreled over place and precedence that did not matter. They postponed decisions in order to debate and air the minority view, when they should have accepted any decision that could be acted on. Ready enough to help one another through any emergency or difficulty, they were unwilling to discipline themselves to an orderly and sensible routine.

The trail, in long stretches, was more a region than an avenue, especially in those earlier portions. Where the prairie was open and the streams easily fordable, it might be many miles wide and a train would fan out at the individual's judgment or whim. Farther west, it narrowed at the dictation of hills, rivers, and grass, though there were alternative crossings, fords, and passages through badlands. The valley of the Platte varies from five to fifteen miles in width and there are many places where choice was free. At Scott's Bluff, for instance, some clung to the riverbank but others, like Thornton, detoured several miles to the south in hope of less precipitous going. Wherever there were steep hills or mountains, the trail contracted still more, and these are the places where it was worn in a few parallel pairs of ruts, or a single pair, so deeply that it can still be followed today.

In general, the route from Independence lay along the Santa Fe trail some forty miles, to the present site of Gardner, Kansas, where the famous sign pointed its finger northwest with the legend, "Road to Oregon." It crossed to the Waukarusa and then to the Kansas, which it forded near the present Topeka and followed some miles farther before striking overland to the Little Vermillion and then the Vermillion. On to the Big Blue, the Little Blue, and so to the Platte, which was usually reached at or near Grand Island. Here was the great conduit to the West and for many days the wagons groaned up the long slope which became increasingly arid. The valley was an oasis in what seemed to be truly the Great American Desert, the scenery got more alarming as the going got dryer, and the river was one of the most preposterous in the world, a bottomland through which a mile-wide trickle of water you had to chew made its way among cottonwoods and quicksands. Where the river forked, the trail struck up the South Platte, then crossed to the North Platte by several alternative routes. The Lower California Crossing was near the modern town of Brule, Nebraska, and trains which crossed there usually reached the North Platte at the famous Ash Hollow. The Upper California Crossing was thirty-five miles farther up the South Platte. Once it reached the North Platte, the trail followed it to well beyond Fort Laramie, then left it for good and struck out for the Sweetwater. Before this happens, however, geography will become important to our narrative and will be treated in detail.

The menace of Indians remains to be mentioned. The earliest stretches of the trail ran through the country of the missionized Shawnee and the decayed Kansa (Kaw); potential thieves and persistent beggars, they made trouble for no one who kept an eye on his property. It then passed into the country of the Pawnee — and they were different. They had been a formidable tribe till recently, and later on the government would recruit some of its best scouts, or scabs, from among them; now they were expert thieves, cattle raiders, and banditti who tried to levy blackmail on all passers-by. They got a steady harvest of strayed and stampeded cattle from the emigrant trains, they demanded tribute and usually got it, and they robbed and sometimes murdered stragglers. It was of the first importance not to wander alone in the Pawnee country.

Some ten days before our emigrants reached their country, in fact, the Pawnee had macerated a train. They swept down on the herd and drove it off, netting something over a hundred horses and oxen. Some of the movers quit right there and hurried back to the States. Others kept going — and kept splitting up into smaller groups. They also kept trying to recover their stock. So they lost some more of it. And one day four of them, armed only with black-snake whips, set out to retrieve some animals which the Pawnee had driven off the night before. The Pawnee killed two of them and took over their riding horses and would have killed the other two except that help arrived. . . . The second moral was, don't leave camp unarmed. If they had carried rifles they would probably not have been attacked. . . . In their little fragments, these movers kept going, though some of them turned back still later. The Graves family, who joined the Donners in the Wasatch Mountains, had started out with this train and one of their companions, a man named Trimble, was one of those killed by the Pawnee.

It was exceedingly intelligent not to straggle from the train at any place on the trail, though the danger lessened beyond South Pass, but the train itself, in spite of the movers' anxiety, was always safe. No train was attacked during the period we are dealing with. On the Santa Fe trail the Comanche would take on anybody when the mood was on them: during the first half of this summer they were raiding Texas and northern Mexico and solemnly meeting with United States commissioners to assert their purity, but they got back in time to plunder the Quartermaster Corps. But the emigrants faced no actual danger once they were beyond the Pawnee. The pressure that was forcing the Sioux southwest was forcing them toward this country but it was still a kind of Indian no man's land, a hunting ground not dominated or even claimed by any particular tribe. The Sioux, the Crows, the Arapaho, and the Cheyenne all bordered on it, the Shoshoni (Snakes) regularly came into it from the west, and a good many other tribes might occasionally be encountered there. But of these, all but the Arapaho were still well disposed, and the Arapaho (whom Parkman took the greatest care to avoid) saw no profit in raiding well-armed trains.[10] Year by year the increasing emigration narrowed the buffalo range and eroded the economy of the tribes who had to live on it; year by year the Indian danger got greater. Finally the Sioux and the Cheyenne rose as nations and made the trail terrible, but there was no premonition of that in the summer of '46. The risks now were that stragglers might be killed for their arms and equipment, that venturesome young bucks might raid the horse herd for glory, or that the antic Indian humor might stampede the oxen. Indians did not covet the ungainly tamed buffalo that drew the white-tops, but it was fun to see them run, especially with some arrows sticking in them.

Fear of Indians was chronic with every train that went west this summer and with most of them it sometimes grew acute — a frantic corralling of wagons when dust swirled up on the horizon or a frantic assembly of the men by night when a guard fired at a bush or the echo of his own footstep. All of them blended with their anxiety a compound of rumors, legendry, and the desperate loneliness of the wilds. But the alarms were not justified. True, not even the Crows, who had a long record of friendship with the whites, were trustworthy when someone strayed. True, the Sioux were feeling very great indeed this summer. When Parkman met the great war parties at Fort Laramie they were swelling with an almost Teutonic brag, beating their chests in the stateliest of furies and telling everybody that they were going to destroy all the whites who had invaded their *Lebensraum*. But the Sioux were merely making a play for greater blackmail and in fact were genial, inquisitive, and hungry for gifts. They still looked on the movers as a kind of circus parade, rich with goods but fundamentally comic.[11]

At first the country was lush and fragrant, almost overpoweringly beautiful as the rains ended and the prairie spring came on. Bryant traveled it in amazement. He thought the soil the richest in the world and the scenery — on a scale not imaginable in the settlements — the most magnificent he had ever seen. His fantasy reared great cities here, and farms richer than any in the world, and a race living gorgeously in this electric air. The Thorntons oozed a single, uninterrupted exclamation. The high grass was frequently crowded down by wildflowers. They were more vividly colored than those to the eastward, their perfume hung in the morning air, and Thornton, who had edited James's *Rocky Mountain Plants,* was dazzled to see its sketches realized before his eyes. On his word, Nancy was "an ardent lover of nature." Her journal filled with a noticeably amorous prose and she botanized furiously. So did Tamsen Donner, that staunch New England schoolmarm who was writing a book, and a good many other ladies of the train, wandering through the grass at nooning or after camp was made, to get these gorgeous blooms and press them for their albums. Such birds, too! — and, seeing two hummingbirds kissing each other, Thornton is almost blasphemous in praise of the Creator's forethought, who had given him an exquisite soul. Flowers, birds, sky, clouds, rivers, willows, cottonwoods, zephyrs — the Thorntons were enraptured and Jessy almost forgot the bundle of sermons he had got from the American Tract Society to distribute among the emigrants. So far he had conferred them only on a Kansa squaw, the wife of the ferryman at the first crossing.

It was one of the great American experiences, this first stage of the trail in the prairie May. It formed the symbols we have inherited. The ladies knitted or sewed patchwork quilts. They extemporized bake ovens for bread, made spiced pickles of the "prairie peas" and experimented with probably edible roots, gathered wild strawberries to serve with fresh cream. They shook down into little cliques, with a chatter of sewing circles, missionary talk, and no charity for any nubile wench who might catch a son's eye. Tamsen Donner wrote home — there was a pause for letter writing whenever someone moving eastward was encountered — that linsey proved the best wear for children. They put a strain on clothes — this was a fairy tale for children: the absorbing train, the more absorbing country, bluffs to scale, coyote pups to catch and tame, the fabulous prairie dogs, the rich, exciting strangeness of a new life with school dismissed. The sight of the twisting file of white-tops from any hill realized all the dreams of last winter along the Sangamon, and the night camp was a deeper gratification still. The wagons formed their clumsy circle, within reach of wood and water. Children whooped out to the creek or the nearest hill. The squealing oxen were watered in an oath-filled chaos, then herded out to graze. Tents went up outside the wagons and fires blazed beside them — the campfire that has ritual significance to Americans. The children crowded back to stand in the perfume of broiling meat. The most Methody of them were singing hymns — Parkman walked into a search party who were settling the question of regeneration while they hunted their oxen. Glee clubs sang profaner songs, sometimes organized by the most meticulous choirmasters. An incurable Yankeeness extemporized debates, political forums, and lectures on the flora of the new country or the manifest destiny of the American nation. Oratory pulsed against the prairie sky. Be sure that nature was served also and the matrons who distrusted the unmarried girls had cause. This was the village on wheels, and the mind and habit of the village inclosed it, beside those carmine fires which Hollywood need only show us against white canvas to awaken our past. The fires lapsed, the oxen came grumping into the inclosure, and one fell asleep hearing the wolves in endless space. . . . This is what the grandfathers remembered when they told us stories.

Nevertheless, already something too subtle to be understood was working a ferment. We have seen Mr. Dunleavy's and Mr. Gordon's groups slip off. The train had both grown and lessened since then (at one time it had numbered almost three hundred wagons), and now a dissension that had simmered from the first boiled over. The train split in halves. The Oregon wagons formed their own train — Thornton belonged to it — and the others, including Bryant, Boggs, the Boone grandsons, and the Donner party, were for California. Bryant saw women weeping at the parting, after only three weeks' association. From now on the two divisions, though they kept on fragmenting and regrouping, traveled more or less on this basis, and the women's tears were premature. They were seldom more than a day's journey apart and visited one another freely.

This division had more behind it than difference of destination, debate over methods, and personal rivalry. It had been preceded by a fist fight between two ordinarily peaceful men, and they drew knives before they could be separated. They were parted when the train split, but immediately there were fist fights and brandished knives and pistols in both halves. From now on the companions of the trail would quarrel violently on the minutest provocation. . . . Cumulative shock. The strains of travel were bad enough. Drenched blankets, cold breakfasts after rainy nights, long hours without water, exhaustion from the labor of double-teaming through a swamp or across quicksands or up a slope, from ferrying a swollen river till midnight, from being roused to chase a strayed ox across the prairie two hours before dawn, from constant shifting of the load to make the going better. Add the ordinary hazards of the day's march: a sick ox, a balky mule, the snapping of a wagon tongue, capsizing at a ford or overturning on a slope, the endless necessity of helping others who had fallen into the pits which your intelligence or good luck had enabled you to avoid. Add the endless apprehension about your stock, the ox which might die, every day's threat that the animals on which your travel depended might be killed by disease or accident or Indians, leaving you stranded in the waste. Such things worked a constant attrition on the nerves, and God Himself seemed hostile when there was added to them a bad storm or some neighbor's obstinacy that reacted to the common loss. The sunniest grew surly and any pinprick could be a mortal insult. The enforced companionship of the trail began to breed the hatred that is a commonplace of barracks. Your best friend's drawl or innocent tic was suddenly intolerable.

Beyond this, which could be understood, was the unseen, steady seepage of the life you had been bred to. The tax of strangeness grew heavier. This was not your known pastureland. The very width and openness of the country was an anxiety. It had no bound; the long heave of the continent never found a limit, and in that waste, that empty and untenanted and lonely waste, the strongest personality diminished. There was no place to hide in, and always there was the sun to hide from, further shrinking the cowering soul. Consciousness dwindled to a point: the little line of wagons was pygmy motion in immensity, the mind became a speck. A speck always quivering with an unidentified dread which few could face and which the weaker ones could not control. The trail bred a genuine pathology, a true *Angst,* proper material for psychiatry to work on. The elements of human personality were under pressure to come out of equilibrium. There was a drive to phobia or compulsion or fugue or dissociation. Some survived it unchanged or strengthened in their identity; some suffered from it, inflicting it on their families, for the rest of their lives. And it grew as the trip went on. Worse country lay ahead and the drained mind was less able to meet it.

Moreover, the trail had begun to collect its toll. The unfit oxen sold to greenhorns at Independence were dying of heat. (What did you do when an ox died? If you had no spare, you yoked up a cow, when you had one; otherwise you threw out Mother's chest of drawers and went on.) But not only the oxen. Parkman passed a plank set up in the prairie and crudely lettered: "Mary Ellis. Died May 7th, 1845. Aged two months." Surprisingly, it was legible after a year. One night Bryant noted the death of Judge Bowlin's child in a train ahead. Thornton passed the graves of two other children, one with a cross on it, "the other with a stone bearing the simple inscription, 'May 28, 1846' — (mercury at sunrise 46°; sunset, 57°)." And his own train already, before it divided, had dug and marked the grave we have seen Jim Clyman looking at while he thought long thoughts. . . . Mrs. Sarah Keyes, the mother-in-law of James Frazier Reed, had hoped to reach Fort Hall. The doctors told her that she had not long to live but she was resolved to make this journey. She would not be left behind to die in Illinois when Jim and Peggy started, for her son Caddan had gone to Oregon a couple of years before and this year would be coming back. She would go to meet him — surely God would let her live till they could meet at, say, Fort Hall. But she endured just over two weeks of travel, dying on May 29, when they reached the Big Blue. They dug a grave under an oak some sixty yards off the trail. The Reverend Mr. Cornwall prayed over it in prairie sunlight and in the Western silence, and John Denton, the young Englishman who was traveling with the Donners, cut the stone that Clyman read.

Many of them were sick. The Thorntons' uncertain health failed periodically, Nancy languishing in the wagon and Jessy's asthma sometimes so bad that he could not drive. Northers and the rains gave many colds, bronchitis, even pneumonia. Others found the ague that lingered in their blood unseasonably awakened. Their diet was bad and some of them got scurvy.[12] Epidemics of diarrhea raged repeatedly. Some of this dysentery was the result of dirty utensils, some was amoebic, more was the natural result of bad cooking and poorly kept food, more still was an endless physicking by drinking water impregnated with Epsom and Glauber's salts. The sun was an additional strain both constitutional and nervous. And as they got to thinner air they encountered a new malady, a prostrating seizure of nausea and violent headaches, frequently complicated by still another kind of dysentery. Bryant, who was stricken with it, attributed it to excessive drinking of milk from cows which had been made unhealthy by overwork and had drunk alkali water and eaten noxious weeds. But it was really "mountain fever," a process of adjustment to diminished oxygen which most people repeat today when they go to high altitudes.

Bryant had studied medicine (of the homeopathic school) before taking up journalism. Word of his experience was carried to near-by trains, and anxious men frequently rode in for miles to implore him to attend someone who had been stricken. Thus, on June 14, moving up the South Platte, he met three men who had come from a train some twenty-five miles ahead to ask him to amputate the leg of a nine-year-old boy who had fallen under a wagon nine days before. Thornton's train had camped near theirs to spend the Sabbath resting and on their way they made the same request of Thornton, presumably because he used good English. Forgoing his pleasure in hearing Mr. Cornwall preach a sermon, Thornton rode over to the train and saw that the boy was dying. The wound was a compound fracture and gangrene had set in. A Canadian drover who had been a hospital servant was whetting butcher knives for the operation; they were giving the boy laudanum without effect and had bound him to a packing case. Thornton directed them to wait for Bryant. Getting there, Bryant saw that an operation would be wasted agony and refused to perform one, telling the frantic mother that her child should be permitted as painless a death as possible. She rejected his advice and the drover began to operate. Someone held camphor to the boy's nostrils and an incision below the knee freed a gush of pus. The drover started again, above the knee this time, and hacked through the bone with a common handsaw. After an hour and three-quarters of bloody effort, he was starting to close the wound with a flap when the child died.

Bryant stepped past the bereaved mother to diagnose her husband, who had lain for four weeks in the jolting wagon, prostrated by rheumatic fever. Bryant left him some attenuated solutions and enjoined him to take them as they were, for "the propensity of those afflicted with disease on this journey is, frequently, to devour medicines as they would food, under the delusion that large quantities will more speedily and effectually produce a cure." He then visited a woman who had thus dosed herself for "intermittent fever" and sunk near the point of death, and a young man whose ailment he diagnosed as heart disease. He told the last sufferer that he could do nothing for him but gave him leave to hope that the journey would effect a cure. He visited and prescribed for "some four or five other persons" who were less seriously ill, and then accepted Thornton's invitation to visit his former companions at their camp.

Reunion on the trail. They were glad to see him, and Nancy ("a lady of education and polished manners," he remarked) spread her white linen tablecloth on the grass. She brought savories from her store and was able to serve roast antelope and stewed buffalo, which the precise Thornton insisted on calling bison, since that was its proper name. Old friends gathered to tell stories and toward nine o'clock the Sabbath had a fitting climax, after rest and general wash-day. The emigrants gathered at the tent of Mr. Lard, where the Reverend Mr. Cornwall married Mr. Lard's daughter Mary to young Mr. Riley Septimus Mootrey. The women had got out their finery, had found candles and made a wedding cake. Thornton could not much approve this marrying on the trail. "It looks so much like making a hop, skip and jump into matrimony" — and like a licensing of human desire. But after all it was an occasion of sentiment and he found the bride fair, said some of the younger women were "dressed with a tolerable degree of taste and even elegance," and could praise the males for having shaved and changed to clean pantaloons. Village mores under desert stars.

The guests formed a procession behind a fiddler and conducted Mr. and Mrs. Mootrey to the nuptial tent. A mile away they saw faint sparks moving by twos in another procession, torches lighting the dead boy's body to its desert grave. A mile or so in the opposite direction still a third train was camped, and there at that same moment a dozen desert-worn women were ministering to one of their sisterhood who writhed and screamed under a dusty wagon cover. They did for her what centuries of old wives' wisdom prescribed for those in travail, and in due time her child was born.

They were in the sagebrush and alkali country now. Thornton observed "a remarkable peculiarity in the atmosphere, which made it impossible for me to judge with any tolerable degree of accuracy as to the distance of objects." He meant that sun and thin air made distances deceptive. Thornton speaks of the "white efflorescence of salts" but does not set down how it makes one squint, how it glares like snowfields under the sun, how it glimmers and quivers in the snaky heat waves and fills the plain with lakes that quench no thirst. The sage smelled like turpentine to Thornton; it smells so still but he might have mentioned its rich, aromatic perfume in the dawn wind, the pungency it gives to campfires, and the tang that grilled meat picks up from it. Mirages flickered across the plain in that terrible sun and he noted them with scholarly glosses on the Specter of the Brocken and the distant prospect of Dover Castle. They were another strangeness in a country that grew increasingly to look like Hell. On the horizon they thrust up peaks or pinewoods or blue New England ponds, where there were no mountains and no lakes or forests, either.

For some time now the emigrants had been making their nightly fires out of what Thornton calls the dried excrement of the bison. Children ranged out from the plodding train to collect it in gunnysacks, and it made red coals for cooking in long, shallow pits. Moreover, they were well into the arid country, in a summer drier than usual. The never-ending wind of the plains blew up dust from the wheels in twisting columns that merged and overspread the whole column in a fog and canopy that moved with it. It "filled the lungs, mouth, nose, ears, and hair, and so covered the face that it was sometimes difficult to recognize each other," and "we suffered from this almost insupportable flying sand or dust for weeks if not for months together." Thornton had neglected to supply himself with goggles which "can be purchased in the United States for thirty-seven and a half cents"; near Independence Rock he would have given fifty dollars for a pair. Right. The tortured eyes tortured the brain. The immense sun, the endless wind, and the gritty, smothering, inescapable dust reddened and swelled the eyes, granulated the lids, inflamed the sockets. The excited nerves make shadows horrible — such shadows as there are — and produce illusions of color and shape. The illusions are not less disturbing in that the heat mirage distorts size and pattern so that a healthy eye may see a jack rabbit as a buffalo at a hundred yards or a clump of sage at half a mile as mounted Indians charging down. Trachoma was endemic among the Indians, a number of emigrants went blind, and few came through this country without eye trouble of some sort. The medicine chests held solutions of zinc sulphate, which was proper, but simple boric would have been better for it was alkali that made the dust corrosive. It was also driven into the skin by the daily wind. Most of the movers were burned black now; the rest were burned a less comfortable, fiery red; their cheeks peeled and their lips were deeply cracked by what is, after all, simple lye. . . . When you read of cowboys buying canned tomatoes and laving their cheeks with juice, you observe an elementary reaction in household chemistry.

The hundredth meridian of west longitude, a geographer's symbol of the true beginning of the West (meaning the point beyond which the annual rainfall is less than twenty inches), strikes the Platte near the present town of Cozad, Nebraska, well east of the Forks. The trail up the North Platte moved mainly west or a little north of west to a point opposite the present town of Ogallala, Nebraska, where it took the due northwest bearing it would maintain for hundreds of miles. And between the sites of the present towns of Broadwater and Bridgeport, Nebraska, it struck the Wildcat Range. Here the scattered buttes and bluffs which had been growing common for a considerable distance became a true badlands. The scenery was spectacular but spectacle was only a momentary solace to the emigrants, who had now reached truly tough going — with cumulative fatigue, anxiety, and mental conflict piling up. In early June the desert still had the miraculous brief carpeting of flowers that delights travelers to this day, but it was late June when the emigrants got there, a wholly different season, and '46 was now a drouth year.[13]

The slow pitch of the continent which they had been climbing toward the ridgepole so slowly that they seldom felt the grade here lost its monotony. The gentle hills that bordered the valley of the Platte, known as the Coast of the Nebraska, suddenly became eroded monstrosities. Jail Rock, Courthouse Rock, Chimney Rock, Scott's Bluff, were individual items in creation's slag heap that had got named, but the whole formation was fantastic. The learned Thornton called it Tadmor of the Desert and sketched a gift-book description of ruined cities, defeated armies, and ancient peoples put to the sword. (But exactly opposite Chimney Rock one of his hubs locked for want of grease and he had to interrupt his poetry.) Even such prosy diarists as Joel Palmer and Overton Johnson were startled into rhetoric, the realistic Bryant saw Scott's Bluff against the green and purple murk of an oncoming storm and committed phrases like "ruins of some vast city erected by a race of giants, contemporaries of the Megatherii and the Icthyosaurii," and Frémont composed a resounding *tutti* passage about "The City of the Desert."

The emigrants had had premonitions and foretastes. As far back as Ash Hollow our travelers had met stalled parts of the train which the Pawnee had broken up, the survivors abandoning half their possessions and combining what was left of their teams. (Parkman also met these unfortunates, farther east.) At the Forks still another train was near dissolution. In Bryant's train the orotund Russell had been deposed from the captaincy, though his constituents allowed him to save face by resigning on the plea that his ague had returned. Governor Boggs had been elected in his place and there was also a new legislature and judiciary on whom resentment could now focus. Russell, probably a better than average captain, was just a victim to the heightened tensions of the trip. A good many dissenters had broken away to catch up with, or wait beside the trail for, other trains in the hope that the going would be more companionable and pleasant with them. It never was. The same bickering and atomization was occurring in the Oregon train, where some wagons departed for Boggs's or other companies and, one day, Thornton's Dutch driver suddenly conspired with Mr. Dunbar, who had succeeded the earlier captain, and laid claim to owning two yoke of Thornton's oxen. The scholar, whose asthma had been so galled by the dust that he lay in the wagon spitting blood, chased the Dutchman through camp with one of Mr. Colt's patent five-shooters and reclaimed his property.[14] Since his other driver had joined the rebellion, he would hereafter try to manage alone, but his neighbors frequently had to do his work for him. . . . By now they had met a good many parties coming east along the trail, full of information. One of these included Joel Palmer in person, going home to write his book and also to meet the party which had been raided by the Pawnee, on the strength of which he would fill the settlements with stories of Indian depredations and movers scared into going home again. (By the end of July the St. Louis *Republican* would falsely report that some sixty emigrants to California, including a Mr. Cunningham, had "starved on the route, having lost their way and run out of provisions.") They had also met one sizable wagon train of permanent re-emigrants. Also they were close to the main buffalo herds, had got sophisticated about them, and, developing several mighty hunters, had learned efficient butchering and connoisseurship about the cuts.

The grade was steep now, and once they were in the badlands the trail narrowed and was frequently precipitous. Crazy gullies and canyons cut every which way, and whoever gave up in anger and tried to find better going elsewhere only found worse troubles. The ropes came out and wagons had to be lowered by manpower down a steep pitch or hauled up over the vertical side of a gully or between immense boulders — while those not working sat and swore in level dust and intolerable sun, far from water. When they moved, the dry axles added a torturing shriek to the split-reed soprano of the wheels and the scrape of tires on stone or rubble. Dry air had shrunk the wheels, too, and without warning tires rolled off or spokes pulled out and the wagon stalled.[15] The same brittleness might make a wagon tongue break, which was disastrous unless a spare pole had been slung beneath the bed, and the violent stresses sometimes snapped the metal hounds, the side bars which connected tongue and fore-carriage to reach and hind-carriage. Sometimes the ropes broke at a cliff or pulled off the snubbing post, and a wagon crashed. Or crazed oxen capsized one, or defective workmanship or cheap material could stand no more and the thing went to pieces like the one-hoss shay. Sometimes half a wrecked wagon could be converted by desert blacksmithing into a cart; sometimes a sound wagon had to be so converted because some of the oxen had died. In any event, here was where the "ancient claw-footed tables, well waxed and rubbed" which Parkman saw began to litter the trail, along with "massive bureaus of carved oak." Parkman speculated on these "relics of ancestral prosperity in the colonial time." He saw them as cherished through successive periods of decline (from the grace of the seaboard) as their owners took them across the Alleghenies to

Kentucky and on to Illinois or Missouri. . . . Allocate the abandoned household goods as another stress of desert travel, for something of personality and spiritual heritage died when they had to go. Their owners were in the grip of necessity. The desert beat triphammer blows, an overmastering realism, on one's soul, and something permanent came from that forging, the old confirmed forever or the new, frequently the lesser, formed forever.

In sun and dust they went on, the daily distance shortening and no end to the country ahead. They were not yet to South Pass, not yet halfway to the Pacific! Horses and oxen bloated from foul water; many of them died. Their hooves swelled and festered. Even the soundest grew gaunt as the grass diminished: sparse along the upper Platte at any time, it had failed quickly in the drouth summer and many trains had cropped it before our travelers. Men got as gaunt as their stock, in this country, and alkali water was just as bad for them. They saw suddenly that food was limited, and there was an anxious computation of the days ahead, with Hastings' or Frémont's or Parker's mile-by-mile itineraries reckoned over and over. Add to the increasing strain the altitude making the nerves tauter. Though the violent sun was hot and the dust pall breathless, there were sudden viciously cold days too and all nights were cold. Water froze in the pails — and you remembered how early snow fell in the mountains that were still so far ahead. . . . It was the triphammer, the test itself. You stood it. You went on. Sometimes, in the badlands, you remembered the moist coolness by the elm-bordered pool in the east pasture back home, and how the brook sang falling into it.

Bryant's mind strained toward California and chafed as the train fell steadily farther behind the schedules printed in the books. He talked it over with some friends; they decided that, on reaching Fort Laramie, they would trade their wagons for a mule pack-outfit and press on by this more rapid means. Nine of them rode out ahead. They rolled up the tape of trains that had unrolled ahead of them, now broken up in fragments, among them the seceders from their own train whom Mr. Gordon had led and who were now led by Mr. Dickinson. From one train Bryant was able to replace a tin cup he had lost: strange how valuable the wilds could make a simple, cheap cup. At Horse Creek the drouth was broken by a short, torrential downpour which saturated their outfit and left them to a freezing night. A cold mist hung over the valley the next morning but they got a fire going and managed coffee and bacon for breakfast. They hurried on up the Platte, much contracted in the badlands, and at about two in the afternoon sighted the first building they had seen since they left the border.

It was the half-finished trading post maintained by the Richard brothers, in a loose association with Pratte, Cabanne & Company, as a local opposition to the American Fur Company's Fort Laramie, which was some six or eight miles away. It stood on the flat ground where Laramie Creek empties into the Platte, where various other short-lived forts had been located, and was called Fort Bernard. Traders from Taos were there, having recently arrived with mules and goods and Taos Lightning for the summer trade, and Bryant had a letter to Richard, the bourgeois, who invited the party to spend the night. But they hurried on to Fort Laramie. He made it 642 miles out from Independence.

Another violent storm broke before they got there, just at sunset. And, coming out of the trees that lined Laramie Creek for their first sudden glimpse of the famous trading post, they saw that the plain beneath the bluffs and in the *V* between the rivers was crawling with Indians. At least six hundred lodges were pitched there. A war dance was ending when Bryant reached the fort, and the whole Sioux nation, bucks and squaws, were working up an ecstasy. They rode whooping everywhere, they shouted their personal histories of *coups,* they beat skin rattles and invoked their deities for scalps. For, Bryant found, they were preparing to take to the warpath, maybe against those routine villains, the Crows, certainly against the Snakes, one of whose hunting parties had encountered a band of Sioux, last year, and cleaned it up.

Bryant was dazzled. Hundreds of yelling Indians tricked out for war and now met suddenly in the desert stunned him, and he gaped. Wild and savage as the bucks were, he found them not merely impressive but genuinely handsome too. Distaste of the squaws, who were drunk with dancing and fell into attitudes bordering on the indecent, yielded to admiration. They were graceful, their complexions were surprisingly fair — except when they were, as Bryant put it, rouged. Their limbs were seductively rounded, their feet small, their robes clean, and their beadwork beautiful.[16] . . . He marveled but their horses had cleaned the grass round the fort, so he went six miles farther and camped for the night.

He came back to Fort Laramie, the next morning, among still more panoplied bucks and beautiful maidens with delicate hands riding prancing steeds — or so the yellowback novels would be saying in another year or two. There were more villages at the fort and others were coming in. He dined with the bourgeois on corned beef, biscuit, and milk — no one raised vegetables at Fort Laramie — and then retraced his path to Fort Bernard. It too was now crawling with Sioux on their way to the rendezvous. One party camped just outside the stockade, displaying twenty-five Pawnee scalps which they had taken on a recent foray. Two emigrant trains crawled up and formed their corrals. The Sioux settled on them like locusts, demanding a feast, which Captain Casper provided. The next day the plain filled with entertainment, both Indians and movers displaying their skills, and there was a shooting match, firearms against bows. Some of the movers had Mr. Colt's revolvers, for which the Indians had already learned a profound respect. Meanwhile Bryant and his companions bargained with the Taos trappers for mules. It was a realistic trade. Seven hundred miles from the border, coffee, sugar, and tobacco were a dollar a pound, whiskey a dollar a pint, flour fifty cents a pound — and those prices would worsen fast during the next few days. After prolonged talk, Bryant and his partner Jacob exchanged their wagon and oxen (still behind them with the train) for seven mules and packsaddles. Their companions made similar terms. So they settled down at Fort Bernard, in a village fair of Indians and emigrants, to wait for the wagons to come up.

All this time, Hastings and Jim Clyman had been coming east. Over the Sierra on May 1, down to Truckee Lake, along the Truckee in bitter cold with Diggers skulking just out of range, and on to the Humboldt Sink. (Before they reached it, the little spaniel who had slept on Jim's buffalo robe every night since he left Milwaukee in '44 dashed into a spring for a drink. It was a boiling spring and the dog died.) They started up the Humboldt. It was a new country to Jim, fearfully barren; he studied it and did not like it. The mules sneezed in the alkali and the going got tougher. They reached the place (near Halleck, Nevada) where Frémont's trail of 1845 made a straight line eastward while the established trail swung northeast toward Fort Hall. Some of the party wanted to keep to the safe, familiar way. But Hastings was hurrying to change the destiny of nations: the empire-builder felt that the Conquest of California might hinge on his choice of a route. In his book he had said that the straight line from the Humboldt to Great Salt Lake and thence to Fort Bridger was the best, easiest, and quickest California trail. When he commended this trail to the public he had never seen it. In fact, there was no trail in any proper sense and it seemed a good idea, since he was going to recommend it to this year's emigrants, to see what it looked like. He won. The party moved on to the Salt Desert.[17]

It is the ghastliest country in the United States, but they found, as Frémont had found, more oases — more wood and drinking water — than could reasonably have been expected.[18] They got across it without incident, except exhaustion, heard a bird singing on May 30, reached the Great Salt Lake on the next day and Jordan River on June 2. They went up Parley's Canyon and struck the Weber on June 4, Jim making prophetic notes on the difficulty of this country. On the fifth they reached Bear River and on the seventh their first grand objective, Fort Bridger. But the place was empty and Jim would not see his old companions. Vasquez was to the eastward, bringing trade goods, and Bridger himself, Old Gabe, was off with his Shoshoni, making a hunt.

There was consternation in the little party, and a far more realistic understanding of their situation than the emigrants could feel made Jim Clyman grave. He had expected to find at this miserable little log stockade not only friends but food and companions for his trip through the Indian country. Somehow (and it would be interesting to know just how) he had learned that the Sioux were up. That could be difficult — and it might explain Bridger's absence, maybe the Sioux had got Old Gabe at last. (He had got plenty of them in his time.) Furthermore, Hastings and Hudspeth intended to set up headquarters hereabouts, to turn the emigration to California, whereas Jim and the rest wanted to get supplies and then move on the States. There was a long argument in the pleasant valley,[19] then the parties separated. Jim and his party — "4 men of us one woman and one boy" — turned northwest in hope of meeting an eastern-bound party on the older stretch of the Oregon trail in the valley of Bear River.

Hastings and Hudspeth struck northeastward, to reach the Oregon trail sufficiently near South Pass to be east of any new "cut-offs" that might attract emigrants to Oregon. There they set up their service of information (false) and alarm (meretricious and pumped up). They were going to get recruits for the California revolution, if fate should provide it, and in any event they were going to get prospects for the California real-estate business. No innocent emigrant had to travel ignorantly to disappointment in the uninhabitable, un-Californian province of Oregon — not while Lansford Hastings lived. The high-pressure salesman camped beside the trail to save the emigration from disaster. If the young man, stuffed with vision, ignorance, and the will to lie for empire's sake has had any romantic appeal so far, he now loses it.[20]

Jim Clyman found him less than appealing. Jim had just traveled with him the route he intended to recommend to the emigrants. To Jim's intelligence — undeluded, far greater than Hastings', and weathered by a lifetime of pioneering — it was an extremely dangerous route. The mountain man's eyes, faded by years of scanning horizons under desert sun, must have hardened. He also had a duty to the emigration and with his handful of companions he started out to meet it.

He was still hoping to increase the size of his party. A Shoshoni came into camp and said that no one had yet come east along the trail this summer, which, of course, was a thumping error. On one of the alternate stretches of the trail they found signs that a large party had traveled eastward a few days before, and finally, on June 11, near Bridger's hunting camp (not the fort), they met the members of the original party who had stayed behind in the Sierra to await the melting of the snows, and who had taken the orthodox trail by way of Fort Hall. The parties united and moved eastward.[21]

They crossed La Barge Creek where in 1825 Jim had been attacked by Arapaho and got a shot through his coat, seen a companion axed, and killed one of the attackers. They rafted their small outfit across Green River, moved on to the Big Sandy, and on June 18 they reached South Pass. End of a circle. He was in the Northwest Passage again, moving eastward, against the current, twenty-two years after he and his companions under Jedediah Smith had found it. And now the promise of that spring morning was in course of fulfillment. He and Smith and Fitzpatrick had found the road of empire, the only route to the West that wagons could take, and now, after traversing the Northwest Passage, he met the westering trains.

Jim had the continental mind: he was on Atlantic waters now and had an invigorating sense of having reached home. The Wind River Mountains were in sight to the north, "the back bone of North America," and the scene of his starving with Bill Sublette. On the Sweetwater the horses stampeded, so maybe there were Indians about. No sign in the morning, however, and they kept on, reaching Independence Rock on June 21. On the next day they judged by the actions of buffalo that they were near the emigration. Sure enough: they crossed toward the Platte on June 23 and — here came the wagons! The old order, traveling counter to the sun, met the new — "eleven wagons nearly oposite the red Butes." [22] And "when we came in sight of N. Platte we had the Pleasant sight of beholding the valy to a greate distance dotted with Peopl Horses cattle wagons and Tents their being 30 wagons all Buisily engaged in crossing the River which was found not to be fordable and with the poor material they had to make rafts of it took two trips to carry over one waggon with its lading we however ware not long in crossing as we threw our baggage on the returning rafts and swam our animals over and encamped onc more in the Buisy humm of our own Language." America had come out to meet him.

Next day, June 25th, he went on down the Platte and, company by company, it was "all most one continual stream of Emigrants winding their long and Tedious march to oregon and california." From any bluff, that length of punctuated dust would come out of one horizon and twist its slow, agonized, sunbeaten course to the other while the wheels shrieked and the mirage wavered above the greasewood. Jim wanted to tell "these honest looking open harted people" certain hard facts about their destination and, though he says he hurried on, doubtless he told some of them. Certainly he made occasion to discourse that night and the succeeding two nights. When it was time to camp, they found a small stream where still another company was corralled, "and they came to us with Pail fulls of good new milk which to us was a treat of greate rarity after so many long tiresome days travel." The next day was June 26 and they met six companies, a hundred and seventeen wagons all told. They camped that night with another California company, who "kept us in conversation untill near midnight."

So on June 27 he came eastward along the bluffs that border the Platte and saw, far off, the whitewashed adobe walls of Fort Laramie. He had paused there in August of '44 on his way west, had been unable to buy meat, and had been charged mountain prices for flour and whiskey. It had been pretty lonesome then; it wasn't now. Between the ford of the Platte and the arc of cottonwoods along Laramie Creek (about a mile due west) he saw innumerable white-tops with their herds compactly grazing under guard. Between the post itself and the ridge of barren hills about two miles to the northwest, the entire plain was populous with Sioux lodges, many hundreds of them, innumerable Indian herds everywhere, a vast movement and shift of herders and riders. It was a stranger, more imposing rendezvous than any he had seen before.

He got from Judge Morin of Thornton's train the first cup of coffee he had had since early winter. And sometime that afternoon, moving on to Fort Bernard, he met a man he had read about and also, in the same company of California-bound emigrants, an old friend. They would want information from the mountain man and he camped with them, ex-Governor Boggs and his fellow veteran of A. Lincoln's company in the Black Hawk War, James Frazier Reed. "Several of us," Jim sets down for history to read, "continued the conversation until a late hour."

On June 27, Francis Parkman also rode back to Fort Laramie and on to Fort Bernard. He had reached Fort Laramie on June 15, had stayed there till the twentieth, and then had gone to camp on Laramie Creek at the mouth of the Chugwater. "Arid and desolate, broken with precipitous buttes — Black Hills in the distance — wild sage, absanth, wild tansy, and a variety of strange plants." It was from this camp on the Chugwater that he rode back to the Fort on June 27.

We left him riding toward Fort Laramie from the east on June 15. The night before, a compliment had been paid him. A buck who was called the Hog because of his vast size was wealthy in horses and coveted Parkman's mount, Pontiac. He offered one of his daughters in matrimony. Good omen, even though Parkman declined the match. It showed that Beacon Hill could establish impeccable social relations with the Sioux.

He stopped at Fort Bernard to smoke a ceremonial pipe with Richard, the bourgeois, in "a log room with a rock fireplace and hung with rifles and their equipments, *fanfaron* bridles, garnished buckskin dresses, smoking apparatus, bows & quivers etc." He bought a pair of moccasins from Richard's squaw and punctiliously invited the residents to drink coffee with him. While they got ready, Parkman and Shaw prepared for the more elegant society of Fort Laramie by washing up and taking their first shave in six weeks. After entertaining Richard, they hurried on. The hills opened out, Laramie Peak stood up, they passed the ruins of Sybille & Adams' old post, and here at last was the fort, people already climbing its wall to welcome them. Henry Chatillon recognized Vasquez, Bridger's partner, and some others. Laramie Creek was bank-full but they found a ford and splashed through with water up to their saddles. The place was in charge of one Bordeau for the bourgeois Papin was, as we have seen, taking robes and furs to St. Louis.[23] Bordeau suspected that Shaw and Parkman might be rival traders and had no hospitality till they showed him Papin's letter. Then he took them to Papin's room, furnished chiefly with a couple of chairs, a crucifix, and the scalp over which the Sioux were preparing to make war. However, it was the first room the travelers had seen since they left Fort Leavenworth and seemed luxurious. They arranged their possibles, and "two eyeballs and a visage as black as night looked in on us," an Indian entered and squatted on the floor with a grunt. One by one others came in, grunted, and formed a semicircle on the floor. (They were relatives of squaws who were living with *engagés* on the post.) They pawed over all of Parkman's equipment but the Brahmin sachem was undisturbed. He lighted a pipe and started it round the circle.

. . . Fort Laramie, the American Fur Company's [24] post near the junction of Laramie Creek and the Platte, was by far the largest and most celebrated post in this region and was only less important to the mountain trade than Bent's Fort on the Arkansas. The confluence of these creeks was extremely important in the fur trade. It was central in the no man's land described above, where the plains and mountains meet, at a decisive curve in the route to South Pass, near the immemorial trade route, and within reach of a number of Indian tribes. The Rocky Mountain Fur Company, Astor's principal rivals, had built a post there, named Fort William after Bill Sublette. It passed to various successors and finally was sold to the American Fur Company, which named it Fort John. Neither name ever stuck — it was always Fort Laramie in the trade. It had recently been torn down and rebuilt on a larger scale a mile or so farther up Laramie Creek, and this later building is the one which our travelers saw, which had become vitally important to emigrants, and which, three years later, was sold to the government as the nucleus of the military establishment that rose on the site.

Thornton has a poetic engraving of it, as regular as a military fortress, prettily buttressed with shrubbery and Indian lodges, and Laramie Peak rising up behind. It stood a few yards up from Laramie Creek and, like all mountain trading posts, had the form of a hollow square. Fifteen-foot walls of adobe formed the square which Thornton estimated at a hundred and thirty feet a side. The customary blockhouses stood at opposite corners, an inner square was formed by the various living rooms, storerooms, and blacksmith shops, and beyond that was a corral into which stock could be driven at need. As at Bent's Fort, the entrance, which led down a corridor between apartments, had gates at each end, so that Indians who came to trade could be denied admission to the interior and dealt with in safe handfuls. . . .

Parkman was all eyes, drinking in strangeness. And the next morning Old Smoke's village, the first of the Sioux, swarmed through Laramie Creek and spread out over the flat — hundreds of horses, hundreds of dogs with laden travois, warriors galloping, squaws perched on top of packsaddles, "the slender figure of some lynx-eyed boy clinging fast behind them," babies solemn and scared in their baskets. Dogs howled, the old hags screamed at unmanageable colts, the squaws got to work and sixty or seventy lodges rose on the plains. Old Smoke and some of his warriors put on their costumes and came into the fort to make a ceremonial petition for presents. Some of the bucks had blacked their faces to commemorate a victory over some Pawnee. By nightfall Parkman could hear the shrill, ululant monotony of medicine songs. . . . His heart swelled and pounded. His dreams had not been too romantic.

But there was an anticlimax. Bordeau looked through a spyglass — and here were "the families." An emigrant train crawled out of the hills, wagon after wagon jolted down the bank, lurched through the creek, strained up the far side, and went on under dust to form the circle a quarter of a mile from the magnificent Sioux. Soon "tall, awkward men in brown homespun, women with cadaverous faces [no gorgeous squaws here] and long lank figures came thronging in together and, as if inspired by the very demon of curiosity, ransacked every nook and cranny of the fort." Parkman and Shaw fled to their room but these gaunt hags were "without scruple or reserve," not to be snubbed by a withdrawal. Some of them "appeared at our door but were immediately expelled." The humble and ungainly might not aspire to the privilege granted the Sioux.

However, for a moment Parkman almost felt the emigration and again one aches for the book that might have been added to our literature if God had a little thawed the Brahmin snobberies. He saw the "perplexity and indecision" of the families — always at its worst at this pause in the trail — and rightly interpreted it. They were bred, he says, to the forest; in the high, dry country they were out of their element. They were right to be suspicious of the fort, for it unmercifully fleeced them, and their perturbed state of mind could not be cowardice for they were of the same stock as the volunteers for Mexico. He pondered. Though his journal shows that he himself had several times been "hipped" — sunk in depression — he had no premonition of the *Angst,* akin to the emigrants' anxiety, that would shadow his middle years with the fear of insanity. . . . The moment's sympathy lapsed. The movers were rude and ignorant, they pried into privacies, and there is an exquisite climax when he reproaches them for knowing nothing of the country and for — looking on Francis Parkman with suspicion. The historian succumbed to a parochialism of his class and we lost a great book.

But he could love the Oglala and every day withdrew from the coarse pioneers to Old Smoke's lodge. He sedulously practised the Indian amenities, made himself a bottomless inquiry, and filled his journal with notes on Indian ways, beliefs, and traditions. He observed the cuisine, the games, the jurisdictions and authorities, the old men talking, the young men at their courting. Shaw treated cases of inflamed eyes. The warriors postured, the squaws gabbled, the lodges etched unforgettable patterns against the sunset. And finally he established citizenship: one of Old Smoke's squaws gave a dog feast, he was able to belch his satisfaction, and he can no longer be called a greenhorn.

He stayed for six days (on one of which the dim-brained Englishmen passed westward), smoking out the plans for war. The scalp that hung in his apartment had belonged to the son of a minor "chief," whom Parkman calls the Whirlwind. With nine others it had been taken in the buffalo country by the Shoshoni, the preceding summer. Parkman says that, scared by their own rashness, the Shoshoni had thereupon asked Vasquez to intercede for them with the Whirlwind and to propitiate him had left his son's scalp at Fort Laramie.[25] The Whirlwind, however, would not be appeased, and this summer he had stirred up most of the Teton Sioux to take the warpath. They would avenge this wrong on the Shoshoni, and incidentally could clean up any Crow hunting parties they might meet. Many villages of them were to rendezvous farther west, where La Bonte Creek flows into the Platte, and by a happy coincidence Henry Chatillon had a squaw and children in the Whirlwind's village.

Parkman rejoiced. The history he had set himself to write required him to understand the Indian character, and now he could see most of a nation gathered together, their "vices and virtues . . . their innate character . . . their government, their superstitions, and their domestic situation." He planned to travel with Old Smoke's village to the rendezvous at La Bonte Creek, but an impressive young buck rode into the fort with word that, at the Whirlwind's village, Henry Chatillon's squaw was very sick. Parkman decided to ride straight to that village so that Henry might see her. He hired another *voyageur,* a numbskull named Raymond; and one Reynal, a trader, joined the party with his squaw and some of her relatives. On June 20 they rode out to find the Whirlwind.

Before he reached Fort Laramie Parkman had had a mild dysentery. At the fort that curse of prairie travel struck him in earnest, prostrating him. He had taken six grains of opium without arresting it, and was so feeble that he could hardly sit his saddle. But his Puritan heritage forbade him to be deterred by a weakness of the flesh. Giddy, frequently doubled up in agony, he went out to find his Indians. From then on for a long time there were periods when a quality of nightmare colored his mind, distorting the day.

They could not find the Whirlwind and so camped on Laramie Creek at the mouth of the Chugwater, a site which the Indians would probably pass on their way to the rendezvous. Chatillon sent the messenger back to tell his squaw to come to meet him. They stayed here for a week. They fished, smoked, talked, Parkman lying on a robe trying to recruit his strength. It would have been a charming, lazy interlude — except that Parkman's illness would not abate. One night they were saved from a marauding band of Crows only because a mist came up in time. Henry's squaw did not come in, and, worst of all, there was no sign of the Sioux.

Parkman chafed and fretted. Was he, on the brink of satisfaction, to lose his chance? One evening the messenger came back. The Whirlwind's village, he said, was moving slowly and would not arrive for a week — and Chatillon's squaw was dying. The news was intolerable. The next morning, leaving the Reynal family to guard the camp, Shaw rode out with Chatillon to find his squaw, and Parkman, to prevent *cafard,* rode back to Fort Laramie. It was June 27th.

So here is Francis Parkman, a Brahmin snob and our greatest historian, his strength undermined by a dangerous illness, riding toward history through the Bessemer heat of a June morning in the Wyoming badlands, some miles to the southwest of Fort Laramie. There are cottonwoods along Laramie Creek, the tree of the barrens; wherever a minute stream slinks for a few miles through desolation, their twisting scrawl of green rises against the dead land to refresh his heart. Cottonwoods: the desert-born remember them, needing only to see the movement of their leaves on a movie screen to be drawn back again to childhood, blue shade cool on parched skin, and the smell of water. For the rest there is only olive-dun sage in the long thrust toward the foothills, heated by the sun and a stench in Parkman's nostrils. West of him the ridge of the Laramie Mountains (then called the Black Hills) is notched unevenly below the flattened pyramid-top of Laramie Peak. Northward a scroll of cottonwoods loops along the base of jagged buttes beyond the Platte. The badlands close in round him, open out, are regrouped as he rides, upthrust fingers, elbows, domes, flying buttresses, haystacks, human breasts, some yellow or red, some gray or white or brown, some black with cedar, but mostly the nameless desert color. They flicker and change under the twitching membrane of heat mirage, and a hot wind driving hot alkali into the skin comes out of them from the west. The sky has turned from blue to powdered gray, which burns the color of steel in the sun's quarter. Where the sage has a dot of shadow round its roots, that shade has a queer, flat tinge of smoke in it and a transparent, unreal brown. There is no perspective; the assaulted eyes can hardly tell whether an object at a distance moves or holds still, whether it is half a mile away and small or ten miles away and gigantic. There is no way for the eye to turn, no way for the mind to turn, but inward. . . . Summer morning in the desert, June 27, 1846.

At Fort Laramie Parkman learned of a ball the emigrants had given. "Such belles!" he wrote in his notebook. But "one woman, of more than suspected chastity [be sure that the Sioux maidens, those of good family at least, were chaste] is left at the Fort and Bordeaux is fool enough to receive her." He met Paul Dorion, to whom he had traded Pontiac, a week before, for a little mare whom he named Pauline. This was the son of the half-breed Pierre Dorion who, for a brief space, had assisted the labors of Sacajawea on the Lewis and Clark expedition and later, with his Iowa squaw Marie, had shared the long privation of the Astorians' trip west under Wilson Hunt. (Marie Aioe is remembered with only less respect for courage and kindness than Sacajawea herself. The child she bore on the trail was Paul Dorion's brother.) Parkman had read about the Dorions in Irving's book, had talked with Paul in a mixture of French and English, had found him a complete Indian and so respected him. The Sioux at Fort Laramie had not made up their airy minds. Dorion said that another great band had arrived at Fort Bernard, where there were also many new emigrants. He wanted to trade Pontiac there. So Parkman rode on with him.

Well, there proved to be only a few Sioux as yet at Fort Bernard, they were Oglala like Old Smoke, but two large villages of their Minneconjou cousins were expected during the day. The emigrants were camped a little in front of the fort. "Some fine-looking Kentucky men," he wrote in his journal, "some of them D. Boone's grandchildren — Ewing, Jacobs [whom he had met in St. Louis] and others with them — altogether more educated than any I have seen." And, in his book he said that the Boones had "clearly inherited the adventurous character of that prince of pioneers [their grandfather] but I saw no signs of the quiet and tranquil spirit that so remarkably distinguished him." At Fort Bernard, no. For the camp was drunk and getting drunker. This California party—he learned it had been captained by Russell, but was now led by Boggs—was lightening its load. It would sell what goods it could to the traders and would sell some of its whiskey to the Indians and would drink the rest. The Indians were drunk already, so were the fort's garrison, so were the traders and the hangers-on—"maudlin squaws . . . squalid Mexicans . . . long-haired Canadians and trappers, and American backwoodsmen in brown homespun, the well-beloved pistol and bowie-knife displayed openly at their sides." The chinked-log, unfinished fort resounded with a clamor offensive to well-born ears, and he had never looked on such a miscellany of casehardened men. Men filthy with dust, smelling for want of soap, bearded, their homespun or buckskins in tatters from the trail, some singing Injun, some shouting the frontier balladry, all making what sound they could. . . . They had come a long, hard way, some of their companions had died and more were broken, they had found the country in nothing like the quiet pastures back home, and now for a day or two beside water and within the sound of leaves they could take their ease. So they roared a little, having reached the West.

And here was "a tall, lank man with a dingy broadcloth coat," extremely drunk, drunk as a pigeon the notebook says, and making an oration. On one forearm and crooked elbow, thumb through the handle, he cradled a whiskey jug which was empty now but which from time to time he swung to his mouth with the immemorial deftness. The other hand made stately passages while the oration boomed its periods over the fort's uproar. Richard, the bourgeois, formally presented to this personage making a big drunk the scion of John Cotton and Elias Parkman, grandson of Samuel Parkman the China merchant, son of the Reverend Francis Parkman of the New North Church, Francis Parkman II, A.B. Harvard '44, LL.B. Harvard '46. The personage in liquor recognized another personage, seized the fringe of Parkman's buckskin shirt, and made another speech, with pauses, fist doubled and swung, affecting pathos, and hiccoughs. He had been captain of this train, sir, but a mutiny of envious small men had turned him out. Nevertheless, sir, his was the superior intelligence, instinctively recognized by all men, as all men knew Hector when he passed, sir, and he still commanded, sir, in all but name he was still chief . . . Some threads had come together at Fort Bernard, and Francis Parkman had met Colonel William H. Russell of Kentucky, a bosom friend of Henry Clay.

The splendor was more than he could bear and, calling Dorion, he rode back to Fort Laramie. But on the way, "met a party going to the settlements, to whom *Montalon had not given my letters.* Sent them by that good fellow Tucker. People at the fort a set of mean swindlers, as witness my purchase of the bacon, and their treatment of the emigrants." A slight swindle thus linked him for a moment with the coarse and ungainly and this brief entry in his notebook ends so. But he had stopped to talk with a party going eastward to the settlements, between Fort Laramie and Fort Bernard, past midafternoon of June 27, and the entry should have had a few lines more. For Francis Parkman had met a genius of the mountains, perhaps had talked with him, had seen a greatness he was not able to recognize. . . . That was Jim Clyman's party.

Parkman reached Fort Laramie just after Bordeau had been defied by one of his own men. The rebel, one Perrault, shouted insults at his scared bourgeois, then in disgust packed up his possibles and started off alone through the Sioux for Fort Union. Just an incident in the mountain trade.[26] Parkman spent the night there — the night of June 27 — and the next morning found that the Whirlwind, the focus of his desire, had come to Fort Laramie.

At once things looked bad. For Bordeau, the bourgeois, had been trying to turn the Whirlwind's heart from the warpath, since fighting would have a bad effect on the trade — and on the emigration. To Parkman's alarm, he had made serious headway, and a newly arrived trader reported that six other villages were now talking of going to the La Bonte rendezvous only on the ominous condition that there should be buffalo there, which was unlikely at this season. Worse still, an Indian rode in from Fort Bernard and revealed that the emigrants' whiskey and the traders' Taos Lightning had debauched the Minneconjou, whose villages had arrived after Parkman left. Like Owl Russell they had made a big drunk — and it had done the job. They had shrieked and howled all night, had fallen to quarreling, had worked up a typical Indian contention, beaten and stabbed one another, and losing their purpose had called off their splendid military parade. Racked by hangover, they had abandoned the warpath and were now, at this moment, working back homeward to the Missouri. No Shoshoni scalps for the Minneconjou Sioux.

Pretty serious. (Parkman did not realize that so large a body of Indians could not possibly have held to any purpose, least of all a warlike one.) He understood that the abandonment of the warpath might mean that his life had been saved, but what counted more was that, if it should spread to the Oglala, as the Whirlwind's growing timidity threatened, he would lose his chance. Was he not to see the Indian "under his most fearful and characteristic aspect" after all this travel? Grave and foreboding, he saddled Pauline and started back to his camp at the mouth of the Chugwater. He must wait there for Shaw and Chatillon and hope for the Oglala. As he left the fort, a trapper told him that word had come of the murder of two mountain men, Boot and May, by the Arapaho. As he rode up Laramie Creek, two emigrants shouted at him, suggesting that he keep his eye peeled.

Fort Bernard, on the North Platte, below the mouth of Laramie Creek. Saturday, June 27, 1846.

On June 24 Edwin Bryant, his partner Mr. Jacob, and those who had decided to join their sprint by pack train had arranged to trade their wagons to the Taos men for mules, and had determined to stay at Fort Bernard till the train should come up. It came up on June 26, under Governor Boggs (*vice* Colonel Russell, deposed, who now determined to go with Bryant) — with the Donners, James Frazier Reed, and the rest. (Small fragments of the original train were several days ahead; some nearer, at Fort Laramie, where Parkman had seen them.) It was the established custom of the emigrants to pause at or near Fort Laramie to recruit their stock, repair the wagons, and lighten loads and reorganize after the desert just passed and before the desert just ahead. Word that the Sioux had used up the grass at Fort Laramie was what halted the California train here, where the bottom land along the Platte had not been grazed.

Boggs and the California-bound reached Fort Bernard on June 26. At about noon on June 27, the Oregon train with which Thornton was traveling (at this stage, captained by Rice Dunbar) pulled in and camped near by. So they were neighbors again, the two largest fragments of the big train which Owl Russell had led west from Indian Creek. At midafternoon or a little later, Parkman, resentful of drunks, emigrants, and Kentucky colonels, turned his back on Fort Bernard, riding back to Fort Laramie. A few minutes later the Minneconjou began to come in, from the northeast. A little later still a party from the west arrived, nine or ten men, two women, two children, and appropriate horses and packs — Jim Clyman keeping an appointment with destiny.

. . . We must look at the trail again: at three large detours. Make a capital cursive letter *S* with the curves long but shallow, and turn it on its back. This represents the trail from Fort Laramie to South Pass, with the middle curve of the *S* reaching its highest (northernmost) point at the present city of Casper, Wyoming. The route obeyed the inexorable conditions of geography. You had to follow the Platte north and northwest to Casper because a more direct route west would have had to cross the waterless desert between the Platte and the Medicine Bow National Forest of today. It would also have had to cross the Medicine Bow Mountains. Beyond Casper (a little west of which you would leave the Platte at last), you had to strike for the one opening through the continental divide by which wagons could be crossed, the South Pass which Jim Clyman and Jed Smith and Tom Fitzpatrick had first used. But you could not go straight west of Casper or even southwest: the desert and mountains (the Rattlesnake Range) of the present Natrona County and the still trackless desert of eastern Fremont County forbade. So the trail took the western half of our recumbent *S,* bent sharply south of southwest, moved by Fremont's Island and Independence Rock to Devil's Slide and the Sweetwater River, and then up the Sweetwater to South Pass.

Although the last stretch before Fort Laramie had been hard going, all emigrants knew that this next stretch, to South Pass, would be worse. So anxiety sharpened, especially the worry of falling behind schedule, the chance of getting caught in winter snows. We have observed how at Fort Laramie one suddenly realized that time was getting short. The realization especially galled those who were going to California because of the roundabout loops which the California trail made west of South Pass.

The trail came out of the Pass and made due west to Little Sandy Creek (for convenience, the present town of Farson, Wyoming). All the rest of Wyoming was desert; the only possible routes, not many and not much different from one another, were determined by small streams and small patches of grass. The next objective was the famous oasis of Soda Springs, in Idaho. To reach Soda Springs you had to travel *southwest* from the Little Sandy at least as far as the present town of Granger. After Old Gabe built his trading post you usually went even farther to the southwest, to Fort Bridger. Here the trail made the great bend that so galled the California-bound. It struck northwest to Soda Springs and went on to Fort Hall (for convenience, the present city of Pocatello, Idaho). . . . There was plenty of water on this stretch; the grass was usually abundant; and though there were mountains to cross, they were comparatively gentle and the canyons were open. . . . Beyond Fort Hall, the trail to Oregon took a long westerly course along the Snake River — and here was where, traditionally, the California trains left it for good. (By '46 there were several routes, used only occasionally, which crossed to the south of Fort Hall, going west by Soda Springs, by Raft River, or by Bear Lake — but they all made for the established route and reached it before it struck the Humboldt.) They turned southwestward, beyond Fort Hall, and by a route sufficiently difficult with lava, alkali, sagebrush, and dry drives, but nevertheless a safe route, they reached the Humboldt River almost exactly where a line traced due west from Fort Bridger would have reached it.

That was precisely the trouble — that possible due-west line from Fort Bridger. The established trail moved from Fort Bridger to the Humboldt along two sides, northwest and southwest, of a right-angle triangle whose due-west hypotenuse stretched straight past the southern end of Great Salt Lake. . . . Late June at Fort Laramie, the South Pass journey still to come, and beyond it that long, laborious, and apparently senseless detour, several hundred miles long, to Fort Hall. Anyone who studied a map at Fort Laramie, intending to go to California, would look with loathing on that detour. On June 27, 1846, no map ever drawn had filled in the country between Fort Bridger and Great Salt Lake — no map showed what the Wasatch Mountains were like. And no map filled in the country between Great Salt Lake and the north bend of the Humboldt River — which included the Salt Desert.[27] . . .

June 27. There was visiting between the trains, and no doubt Nancy Thornton was a genteel hostess again, though her linen would be dingier. No doubt Margaret Reed and Tamsen Donner botanized among the cottonwoods, Virginia Reed rode her blooded horse at a gallop for the admiration of young Minneconjou bucks, and the children gazed at hundreds of painted Indians and their dogs and lodges and herds, the marvels learned in books along the Sangamon now magically made real along the Platte. Owl Russell had his big drunk, and so did the Taos trappers, and M. Richard, the hangers-on of Fort Bernard, the dusty, tired emigrants, and the Sioux. Furniture, clothes, surplus food, were traded to the Taos men for what little they would bring, or just abandoned. Hammers rang on iron as tires were reset and shoes refitted to horses. Laundry bloomed on the cottonwoods, to dry in desert sun. The Sioux yowled and galloped and, as night came on, got drunker still, pounded their chests, counted *coups,* fell to quarreling, drew their knives, felt their hearts going bad. A big night in the desert, a big night at Fort Bernard.

Lines of campfires dotted the wagon trains, their flames gilding the cottonwoods and shining in the Platte. And at one fire, Jim Clyman says, "several of us continued the conversation until a late hour." Jim had met a messmate of the Black Hawk War, James Frazier Reed, who had sat by him at other campfires, with A. Lincoln. He met some of Mr. Reed's friends and companions. Edwin Bryant and Jessy Thornton and Governor Boggs for certain were at that fire, Owl Russell probably, and by inference George and Jacob Donner — the responsible minds of the two trains. He and his companions met a good many other emigrants, and told them all the same story.

For Jim and the others felt a heavy responsibility. Some of them tried to modify the emigrants' vision of the golden shore, speaking of sparse rain and ruined crops, speaking of the low quality of Americans resident there. Bryant grunted in disgust. He was for California, and it was clear to him that these trail-stained travelers, Clyman in particular, were lying, for some reason not on the surface. He was not credulous enough to believe plain liars but he perceived that many of his associates were. Thornton, who was for Oregon anyway, was detached and believed them.

The wagon train grew quiet but this one fire was kept blazing — a carmine splash against the blue-velvet night, the desert stars near above it, the white bow of a wagon top behind, and, farther away, the singing of drunken Missourians at the fort and the screaming of drunken Sioux. Clyman talked on. He knew Hastings' plans, he knew what Hastings would tell these innocents near South Pass. And he had just crossed — with Hastings — from the bend of the Humboldt to Fort Bridger by way of the Salt Desert, Great Salt Lake, and the Wasatch Mountains. A Sioux yipped, the barking of coyotes ringed the sleeping caravan, and Jim told his listeners: take the familiar trail, the regular, established trail by way of Soda Springs and Fort Hall. Do not try a cutoff, do not try anything but the known, proved way. "It is barely possible to get through [before the snows] if you follow it — and it may be impossible if you don't." Shock and alarm struck the travelers and made them angry, who were still far short of South Pass, whose minds could map that weary angle from Fort Bridger to Fort Hall and back again to the Humboldt. Tense and bellicose, Reed spoke up (Jim records his words), "There is a nigher route, and it is no use to take so much of a roundabout course." Reference to Lansford Hastings' book, Jacob Donner's copy bought at Springfield, back in the States, now scanned by firelight at Fort Bernard, a well-thumbed passage marked with lines. *The Emigrants' Guide to Oregon and California*, page 137: "The most direct route, for the California emigrants, would be to leave the Oregon route, about two hundred miles east from Fort Hall; thence bearing west southwest to the Salt Lake; and then continuing down to the bay of San Francisco. . . ." Proved. And someone would spit into the fire.

(When Lansford Hastings wrote that passage he had never seen the Humboldt, or Great Salt Lake, or the Wasatch Mountains, or the Salt Desert; neither he nor anyone else had ever taken the trail here blithely imagined by a real-estate man who wanted to be President or mortgagee of California.)

Yes. But Jim has just traveled that route, and if they would save their skins, they will not take it, they will go by way of Fort Hall. "I . . . told him about the great desert and the roughness of the Sierras, and that a straight route might turn out to be impracticable." Told him about the glare of the salt plain under sun and without water. Told him about the Diggers lurking outside the camps to kill the stock. Told him about the chaos of the Wasatch canyons which Jim Clyman and Lansford Hastings, who were on horseback and had no wagons and so no need of a road, had barely got through.

In the tents or in the wagons Tamsen and Elizabeth Donner and Margaret Reed fell asleep. The children slept. All the women and children and most of the men of these two trains were asleep by now, all the men who were not listening to the argument or helping make the noise that sometimes surged through the darkness from Fort Bernard. A tired, strained, bewildered company hemmed in by desolation, the shade and waters of their homes almost forgotten, the dream become more real than memory. Islanded in mountain night, islanded in awe and the unknown, ringed round by drunken Sioux. The cottonwoods rustling, the night cold.

Clyman talked on, repeating his warnings and threats — the mountain man, the man who knew, the master of this wilderness, pleading with the tenderfeet. Till there was no more to say, the fire was only embers shimmering in the dark, and they separated, to lie awake while the coyotes mourned and the Sioux screamed — and think it over. In the desert, where Laramie Creek empties into the Platte: a moment of decision.

Next morning they had made up their minds. Bryant was not deterred. He would take the way he had decided on, and rightly so, for he would travel by pack train and could travel fast. The unappreciated orator Owl Russell would go with him, and the eight original volunteers were steadfast. (Though a few days later Clyman's words seemed sound sense to Mr. Kirkendall, and he rejoined the Oregon train — to soften Thornton's troubles and suffer hardship on another cutoff.) Governor Boggs and Judge Morin, however, had been convinced. They sought out Clyman, before he moved on, and told him they would follow his advice — would go to Oregon by way of Fort Hall. Not Reed and the Donners. Their impatience had not been scotched. They would go on their determined way, and if any cared to join them, they would be welcome.

So be it. Jim repeated his warnings, but he had his own trail to follow and late in the morning he led his party eastward.

Another chapter in the outline of American history, which now had only a few more to go before the peace and satisfaction of its last years. Eastward, in the direction of Scott's Bluff, with Chimney Rock to come, and Ash Hollow, and the crossing to the South Platte. But American history in the person of Jim Clyman had told the Donner party not to take the Hastings Cutoff from the California trail.

VII
"Cain, Where Are Thy Brothers?"

ON May 1, meeting at Petersburg, Menard County, the Whig Convention nominated A. Lincoln to represent the Seventh Congressional District of Illinois, thirty-seven years old, "a good Whig, a good man, an able speaker, and richly deserves the confidence of Whigs in District and State." His Democratic opponent was to be the middle border's mightiest man of God, Peter Cartwright, presiding elder of the Methodist Church, the greatest of the circuit riders. For nearly forty years Elder Cartwright had fought the devil through the prairies, bearing on his own shoulders unnumbered thousands of souls back from the pit that flamed at the foot of his pulpit, pricking uncounted frenzies of guilt to release in barking, yipping, jerking and rolling on the ground toward the peace that passeth understanding, cursing liquor and jewelry and gambling and profane swearing and pride and fornication in a brazen voice that clanged across the sacred grove and silenced the roistering of the ungodly at the groggeries beyond. He and A. Lincoln were to campaign till August but little of their oratory has come down to us. Both respected the policy of that wayward summer: to say nothing about slavery, to avoid the war but to praise it when it could not be dodged, and to keep silent on all issues that either would have to face in Congress. Mr. Cartwright appears to have attacked Mr. Lincoln as an infidel and a slave of the liquor interests. But this was no camp meeting and when the votes were counted the infidel had the largest majority on record in Illinois and was the one Whig his state sent to the Thirtieth Congress. And the man of God carried a grudge all the rest of his life.

He was still older in 1859 when his grandson, Peachy Harrison, was tried at Springfield for the murder of Greek Grafton, who had been a law student with the firm of Lincoln & Herndon. Mr. Lincoln had grown in reputation when he took Peachy's case but there was arrayed against him a bouquet of lawyers whose fame made a greater sum than his, and the Court was biased. So biased that Mr. Lincoln got mad. "Mad all over," Herndon says, "terrible, furious, eloquent," like the Reverend Mr. Cartwright battling with the devil, and "the scoring he gave that Court . . . was terrible, blasting, crushing, I shall never forget the scene." No use. So Mr. Lincoln called to the witness box the prisoner's grandfather, whom he had defeated for Congress thirteen years before. He had Cartwright tell the jury how he, who had prayed above so many sinners as they died, had bent down to hear the last words of Greek Grafton. Sandburg quotes them: "I am dying; I will soon part with all I love on earth and I want you to say to my slayer that I forgive him, I want to leave this earth with a forgiveness of all who have in any way injured me." Following that testimony, A. Lincoln need only speak a quiet phrase to the jury, some intimation of malice toward none and charity for all, and the boy was free.

The Washington press heard that our troops on the Rio Grande were well supplied, chiefly by the Mexicans, and were safe. That there would be no collision with the Mexicans. That desertions had been ended by Taylor's firmness (which looked like cruelty to Congress). But sometimes, depending on which mails were in, it heard some of the rumors that the army itself had heard, exchanges from Texas promised that there were skirmishes, and the opposition editors speculated about the chance of a border incident.

Congress passed this year's pension bill for veterans of the Revolution in the sum of $1,400,200, and began to debate the appropriation for the Military Academy at West Point. The Academy was annually charged with "abuses," and this year, as every year, there were proposals to abolish it. For could a democracy tolerate a body of professional officers? George III still threatened the Congress of the United States, and had not George III maintained mercenaries? Was not an officer caste repugnant to our institutions? Who knew but that the officers might some day make a *coup d'état?* Moreover, was not the expenditure of public moneys on West Point an unjustifiable waste? Was it not known that Morgan's Rifles and the Minute Men of Middlesex would spring to arms at need?

On May 1, Vice President Dallas told President Polk that he was for 49°. Unhandsome of a subordinate, but a warning. On May 3 Senator Benton at last said that he would not claim beyond 49°, and moreover he thought it wise to get the Oregon question settled before taking up Mexico, with whom, he made it clear, he wanted no war. Mr. Polk wanted no war but was preparing "an historical statement of our causes of complaint against Mexico," which he would transmit to Congress. On May 5, the Cabinet discussed a possible collision between Taylor and the Mexicans but had no word from the General later than April 5. The next day Taylor's dispatch of April 15 arrived but had no news in it, but on May 8, Mr. Slidell was back from Mexico at last with the opinion that we must take the "redress of the wrongs and injuries" into our own hands and "act with promptness and energy." Possibly Mr. Slidell meant something other than war by that, and so possibly did Mr. Polk when he agreed and promised to communicate Mr. Slidell's frustrations to Congress. The next day, May 9, the Cabinet agreed that Polk must recommend war if the Mexicans should commit any hostility against Taylor — and that did not go far enough. For Polk went on to poll them on the question whether, in the message he was now preparing for Congress, he ought not to recommend war anyway. Mr. Buchanan said that he would be better satisfied if we had a hostile act to go on but felt that we had ample cause without one and would recommend war. So would all the others except Mr. Bancroft, who held out for that hostile act.

Very well. Mr. Polk would ask Congress for war, and Mr. Buchanan would please prepare the supporting documents. So the President sat down to write a war message. He could talk about the unpaid American claims, the failure of Mexico to acknowledge the true boundaries of Texas, its refusal to receive Mr. Slidell, and quantities of bellicose, rhetorical defiance. It would have needed a strong bellows to blow that up to war size, but Polk seems to have been confident of its acceptance by a Congress where the opposition had now succeeded in disciplining itself and the majority was breaking up in factions. However, he did not need to make the trial.

He was arranging his characteristic, precise formalities in a request for war when, about six in the evening, the Adjutant General came to the White House and told him that the Southern mail had just arrived, bringing a new dispatch from General Taylor. The Mexicans, Taylor reported, had crossed the Rio Grande on April 25, and had killed or captured all of two companies of Dragoons under Captain Thornton. So he would not complete the subterfuges of his message. He called the Cabinet for half-past seven, Mr. Buchanan and Mr. Bancroft would help him draft a real war message, and the word had got round Washington fast, for here were Senators and Representatives crowding into the White House, "greatly excited." He wrote hard the next day, though he had to take time out to go to church (in a city that had begun to run a fever) and to temporize with the first Congressmen who aspired to high military command,

Haralson of Georgia and A. Lincoln's closest friend, Edward D. Baker of Illinois. There was a furious note-sending to committee chairmen and majority leaders, and all the secretaries copied documents late into the night. "It was a day of great anxiety to me." So was May 11 — not least anxious in that Benton, summoned to the White House as chairman of the Committee on Military Affairs, though he assured the President that he would vote the required men and dollars, reminded him that he had not favored sending the army to the Rio Grande and would not favor aggressive war.

At noon he sent his message to the Congress. After an assertion that the Rio Grande was "an exposed frontier" and a recital of events up to April 25, "the cup of forbearance had been exhausted even before the recent information from the frontier of the Del Norte [Rio Grande]. But now, after reiterated menaces, Mexico has passed the boundary of the United States, has invaded our territory and shed American blood upon the American soil. She has proclaimed that hostilities have commenced, and that the two nations are now at war."

Wherefore, "As war exists, and, notwithstanding all our efforts to avoid it, exists by the act of Mexico herself . . . I invoke the prompt action of Congress to recognize the existence of the war." And to provide the arms and money to prosecute it.

The message found the Senate still debating whether to abolish West Point. It put that dilemma aside for the moment and took up the President's bill authorizing and financing an army, but did not pass it on May 11. Such unpatriotic delay convinced Polk that his personal opponents in the Democracy had joined the Whigs in order to discredit him, and from that moment on he saw the war with Mexico as primarily a factional contention in the Democratic Party. He had always regarded a difference of opinion as a political attack on him; from now on he regarded one, quite honestly, as a species of treason. The last Southern politician of the second period was outlining the Southern politician of the third period. . . . But they were sounder men in the House. After listening for an hour and a half to the supporting documents that accompanied the message (and contained the evidence), they dispensed with the remainder and voted Mr. Polk his men and money in thirty minutes, 173 to 14.

On May 12 the Senate kept up its treasonous debate, trying to determine whether there was a war if Congress had not said there was, and how far into his own country you could chase an enemy without abandoning defensive warfare. Mr. Webster was not in the Senate when the division came, and the one-man Calhoun Party abstained from voting. The bill passed 42 to 2. The muse of history does not sleep: that day an organization of superintendents of insane asylums convened in Washington.

The entry in the President's diary for the next day, May 13, is informative. General Winfield Scott, the commander of the army, calls with the Secretary of War and presents a plan for allocating volunteers among the states. Mr. Polk does not regard him as in all respects suitable for the command of the army to be raised (he was a Whig) but knows that he must have it and so confers it on him. The Secretary of War makes a requisition on the governor of Missouri for a thousand mounted troops for Colonel Kearny, to protect the traders who are en route to Santa Fe. This is the first step toward the conquest of New Mexico and plain proof that one campaign of the war had had some planning. Then in the evening, at a meeting of the Cabinet, Mr. Buchanan, to the President's stunned horror, wants to memorialize foreign courts and declare that in making war we do not intend to acquire New Mexico, California, or any other portion of Mexican territory! (Mr. Buchanan's best spur-of-the-moment guess about the shortest distance between war and the Democratic National Convention of '48. A bad guess and an impudence to his chief.) Mr. Polk sets him right: we will take California and such other lands as may be necessary to indemnify us. If this be made known, Mr. Buchanan protests, then we shall have war with England certainly and very likely with France too. Mr. Polk thinks not, but would accept war with "either England or France or all the Powers of Christendom" rather than make this pledge "that we would not if we could fairly and honourably acquire California or any other part of the Mexican territory which we desired." The meeting generates heat, the rest of the Cabinet assail the Secretary of State, and the fight lasts for some two hours. Not take California? Then why all this labor? And Mr. Polk ends matters by striking out the offensive paragraphs in Mr. Buchanan's memorandum and substituting some forthright language of his own, which he orders the Secretary to use instead. So to bed, "much exhausted after a day of incessant application, anxiety, and labour."

During the day he had signed the bill which recognized (not, as the *Diary* says, declared) a state of war, and had issued the necessary proclamation. So the United States had its war at last on May 13, 1846, though it had begun in April.

On May 13, Clyman was traveling up the Humboldt River, toward its big bend. At sunrise Francis Parkman, having drunk Colonel Kearny's Madeira the night before, finally jumped off for the Oregon trail. Edwin Bryant's wagons reached the fork of the Santa Fe trail in a pounding rain and turned off for Oregon. Some distance behind him, Jessy Quinn Thornton crossed the boundary of the Indian Territory and caught up with Lillburn Boggs.

And on May 9, at Klamath Lake in Oregon, Lieutenant Gillespie of the United States Marines caught up with Captain Frémont — and Zachary Taylor fought the engagement known as the battle of Resaca de la Palma.

Colonel Ethan Hitchcock was the most intelligent officer in the highest ranks of the army.[1] He had written in his journal that if Taylor were to succeed, it must be by accident.

Following the capture of Thornton's command, Taylor had gone on occupying his almost indefensible position at Fort Brown, opposite Matamoros, and exhibiting the serenity of a man of the plain people. He strengthened the fort's defenses but neglected to supply it with ammunition from his base at Point Isabel. He had not yet secured the Texas Rangers, though some of them, under the celebrated Walker, were at Point Isabel, but he did send patrols seven miles down the road his supplies must come up. Not far enough. The Mexicans crossed the river both above and below his position, unopposed and even unperceived. Finally, on May 1, he learned about them. He could understand that his base was in danger, and, leaving a garrison in Fort Brown, he got back to it — fast. The town of Matamoros saw his army moving out and printed some broadsides celebrating the first great Mexican victory.

Arista's idea was first-rate. He designed to pinch off the American expeditionary force, cutting its communications and attacking it in its unfavorable position. He had troops enough and they were good enough. But, like all Mexican commanders throughout the war, he could not maneuver them fast enough and had to combat the volcanic jealousies of his subordinates. He lost a week and Taylor got safely to Point Isabel. Arista took up a position on the road, waited for him to come back, and ordered the batteries at Matamoros to open on Fort Brown. So at Point Isabel on May 3 a young lieutenant of the 4th Infantry heard the cannonade and knew that the war which he regarded as a conspiracy of slaveholders had begun. "I felt sorry," Lieutenant Ulysses S. Grant wrote, "that I had enlisted."

They kept on pounding the fort for four days. The garrison, however, got the bombproofs finished under fire and suffered only a few casualties, one of them Major Brown, the commandant. They had too little ammunition to risk a full counter-bombardment, and toward the end they began to get jittery.

Taylor spent a week at Point Isabel building the earthworks he should have finished a month before, then, on May 7, started back to relieve the fort. His West Pointers begged him not to take the

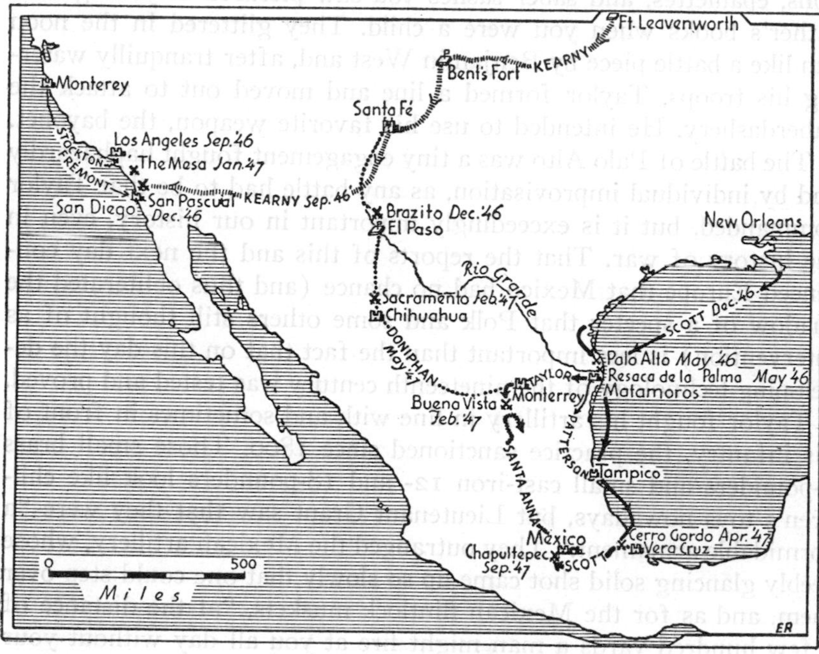

The Mexican Campaigns

massive train, which could be brought up later in complete safety, but he had no patience with textbook soldiers. . . . Well, what did he have? A sound principle: attack. A less valuable one which was to serve him just as well in this war: never retreat. Total ignorance of the art of war. And an instinct, if not for command, at least for leadership. He had been hardened in years of petty frontier duty, he had no nerves and nothing recognizable as intelligence, he was afraid of nothing, and he was too unimaginative to know when he was being licked, which was fortunate since he did not know how to maneuver troops. Add to this a dislike of military forms and procedures and a taste for old clothes and you have a predestinate candidate for the Presidency. The army and even some of the West Pointers worshiped him.

On May 8 at a place called El Palo Alto Taylor's army, on the way back to Fort Brown, came in sight of Arista's army in line of battle. Throughout the war the Mexicans had difficulty in getting soldiers who could shoot and greater difficulty in supplying them with food and powder, but their armies were always beautifully costumed. These are the shakos, pompons, plumes, buckles, aiguillettes, pennons, epaulettes, and saber sashes you saw pictured in your grandfather's books when you were a child. They glittered in the noon sun like a battle piece by Benjamin West and, after tranquilly watering his troops, Taylor formed a line and moved out to attack the haberdashery. He intended to use his favorite weapon, the bayonet.

The battle of Palo Alto was a tiny engagement fought haphazardly and by individual improvisation, as any battle had to be that Taylor commanded, but it is exceedingly important in our history, even in the history of war. That the reports of this and the next day convinced Europe that Mexico had no chance (and thus obliterated the shadow of a specter that Polk and some others still thought of as intervention) is less important than the fact that on this day the developing technology of the nineteenth century was tested and proved.

Taylor fought his artillery in line with and sometimes in front of his infantry, the practice sanctioned since 1800. Those small brass 6-pounders and small cast-iron 12- and 18-pounders look like children's toys nowadays, but Lieutenant Grant saw that they were "a formidable armament." They outranged the Mexican artillery, whose feebly glancing solid shot came up so slowly that one could step over them, and as for the Mexican flintlock muskets, "at the distance of a few hundred yards a man might fire at you all day without your finding it out." In his first engagement Lieutenant Grant had a happy moment of command when his captain made a reconnoissance and a happier one when he personally captured a colonel in braid and buttons. But also he got the first chapter of a lesson which was to sink deep. So far as the Americans were concerned, Palo Alto was almost entirely an artillery action. Colonel Childs, Major Ringgold, and Captain Duncan maneuvered their batteries as if they were platoons of cavalry and fired them almost as if they were pocket pistols. All afternoon they took at least an eight-for-one toll from the Mexicans, who could never get near them. So a function had been found for "light artillery" and Lieutenant Grant had learned about fire power. In four years of the Civil War he only twice forgot the superiority of metal to human flesh. He imparted the lesson to William Tecumseh Sherman, and a great part of the defeat of the Confederate States of America was inflicted in the muggy Mexican sun on May 8, 1846. For the far more brilliant Lee, who had as much chance as Grant to learn the lesson, never learned it. He remained confident that the courage of the Southern infantryman could prevail against the Northern barrage and sent them against it too often — at Gettysburg pushing the best part of his army against a semicircle of guns that unhurriedly went on shooting them down as they came. There is no reproach in that fact: the texts show that a full year of the first World War had passed, and half a million men had been killed in their tracks, before any commander learned about the power of massed fire what Ulysses Grant, whose campaigns all of them had studied, learned in the six hours of Palo Alto.

That the Mexican troops faced such fire and stayed on the field is ample evidence that they were good troops. Few of them, here or later, could shoot straight. Government policy, taking account of revolutions, had forbidden the citizenry to bear arms. Mostly, too, they were pressed men — gathered up by gangs from among the peons, to eke out the standing army, which was at least disciplined if poorly supplied and preposterously over-officered. There was little reason why they should fight at all. Did it matter which Mexican faction or which invader was quartered on them, raped their women, drove off their cattle, and levied on their crops? But they did fight, at Palo Alto and most other battles, with heroic doggedness. If one day of battle was frequently enough for them, so that on the second day they broke and ran, part of that routine flight may be ascribed to the usual failure of the commissary to bring up supper and breakfast, and the rest to their general officers who, by the second morning, were either panic-stricken or betraying one another.

Both commanders notified their governments that they had won a victory. Early the next morning, May 9, however, Arista withdrew from the field, where both armies had bivouacked in sight of each other's fires and within hearing of each other's wounded. He thus weakened the morale of his troops and, after an idle morning, Taylor took up the pursuit, his bands playing. The regulars moved across a prairie strewn with the corpses of men and horses and of one woman, described as richly dressed and "singularly beautiful" — and learned to praise their artillery. It was not so useful to them when they caught up with Arista toward four o'clock, however, for he had taken a position in the bed of a former channel of the Rio Grande, wooded and choked with chaparral.

The action that followed was a good deal more of a battle. It is known as Resaca de la Palma. It was a fierce, bloody, and obstinate confusion in the underbrush, with the Mexicans fleeing here and charging there, the Americans doing likewise, and no one to do staff work or make order of the attack. Since no one above the platoon leaders could see far enough to exercise command, some pretty local duels developed. For a long time it was a near thing. The Mexicans rushed into the thorn bushes with an admirable fierceness and, less admirably, their cavalry charged artillery — and nearly took it. That seemed a good idea to Taylor and, to the horror of his staff, he ordered Captain May's Dragoons to charge a Mexican battery. It was his principal contribution to the battle and, alas for the textbooks, it worked. Pretty soon the Mexicans, who had bent at one flank already, broke and ran. Fort Brown was saved and Taylor had won two battles.

Or his army had. Colonel Hitchcock, who was right about their commander, was proved wrong about the troops and they were entitled to the admiration which Lieutenant Grant accorded them. The American soldier had won his first battle against civilized troops since January 8, 1815, by the merits which tradition had emphasized, marksmanship, steadiness under fire, and individual initiative and courage. A good many subalterns who would be general officers in the Civil War had had their first taste of battle. And before the guns were swabbed the newspapermen were sending the news to the folks back home. The two engagements, Grant wrote, "seemed to us engaged as pretty important affairs but we had only a faint conception of their magnitude until they were fought over in the North by the press and the reports came back to us."

Old Rough and Ready moved on, in a welter of collapsing transportation, all the way back to his former position, and in less than ten days was ready to cross the Rio Grande. His West Pointers had been frantically urging him to pursue the retreating Mexicans, whose army had degenerated to small groups and was in full flight. Why should he? He had his victory, he was willing to attack (with bayonet) any enemy who might appear, and let no one suppose he was afraid. The West Pointers could not even get patrols sent out. But it would be pleasanter in Matamoros, so Taylor crossed the river on May 18 and the Americans had occupied a foreign city at last. Here, though he could certainly have ended opposition in the northern provinces and might even have ended the war, he sat down and did nothing whatever for six weeks.

Well, he was not altogether inactive. The correspondents were present and in Matamoros Taylor accepted the invitation which Jessy Quinn Thornton was currently breathing into the Kansas air. He opened his campaign for the Presidency.

Some patches of snow still lingered round the sheltered roots of the great pines on the shore of Big Klamath Lake, and Benton, on the basis of what his son-in-law wrote about it, was to interpret that snow to the Senate as a fierce winter storm that endangered the Pathfinder's life and turned him back again to the settlements. Frémont could also have found ice in the bottoms of northward-sloping ravines.

It was a picturesque scene on the edge of Klamath Lake, in southern Oregon. The Pathfinder enjoyed the splash of firelight on the dark, the columns of enormous evergreens growing dim above it. "How Fate pursues a man!" he wrote. Fate, on horseback, had taken the persons of William Sigler and Frémont's former blacksmith, Sam Neal, riding hell-bent through the night. Hooves sounded afar off through the forest silence and, tumbling into the firelight, the messengers told Frémont that an officer of the marines with dispatches for him was on his trail — and they thought the Indians were following close behind him.

It was a tense night and at dawn Frémont was off with ten picked men to meet and perhaps rescue the dispatch bearer. At sunset they met at the lower end of the lake, Childe Harold nobly longing for great deeds and Lieutenant Archibald Gillespie of the marines with dispatches dated at the end of October, '45, and also with an eyewitness account of the popular enthusiasm at Mexico City which had followed the bellicose Paredes' accession to power in early January, four months ago.

So there was another, more important campfire at Klamath Lake, in "a glade or natural meadow, shut in by the forest, with a small stream and good grass." May 9, 1846. A hero's hour had struck.

All the accounts which Frémont later gave of this meeting are in the tone forbidden by Hamlet, "we could an we would," and they are contradictory. But only once, and that once flatly contradicted by many other passages, does he get altogether out of intimation and into assertion. "Now it was officially made known to me that my country was at war," he says in his *Memoirs*. His best biographer, Mr. Nevins, all but repeats the assertion when he says that Gillespie, having had on February 22 at Mazatlán information from Mexico City of about February 10, could tell Frémont "that Taylor had advanced to the Rio Grande, where fighting was expected at any time."

Both statements are wrong. As for Mr. Nevins': Taylor's orders to advance to the Rio Grande were issued at Washington on January 13, he received them on February 3, he moved out of Corpus Christi on March 8, he reached the Rio Grande on March 28, and nothing was known about his orders or his movements at Mexico City on February 10 or at Mazatlán on February 22. As for Frémont's: not only was there no unofficial information in Gillespie's possession that there was war between Mexico and the United States, not only was the "official" information in his dispatches based on Polk's October confidence that there would be no war, but the dispatch which he repeated to Frémont expressly stipulated that California was to be pacified.

The deliberate implication of Frémont's private and public testimony (in his court-martial and in the hearings on the claims of the California Battalion) is that, on May 9, he received orders to go back to California and produce an incident. The deliberate but more veiled implication of Gillespie's testimony and depositions is the same. But whenever either of them is brought to an unequivocal issue, each flatly declares that there were no such orders. The repeated insinuation that there were secret instructions invariably dissolves when facts are approached. There were no secret instructions from anyone. Frémont was lying.

Frémont ultimately rests on the private letters from his wife and from Benton (neither of them qualified to give him orders or in this instance even advice), which, he says, were in a kind of family cipher. (This cipher, we are to understand, consisted of oblique allusions to earlier conversations.) It all boils down to the fact that Benton again advised him to watch out for foreign intervention in California if war with Mexico — which Benton did not favor and did not expect — should break out, or if the negotiations over Oregon should reach a crisis (as he did not think they would). Unquestionably the chairman of the Committee on Military Affairs wrote just that to his son-in-law. But it was not a solicitation to act, it was not official, and it was written at a time when Benton was shut out from the secretive Polk's confidence. The final bit of "official" evidence is a letter and memorandum furnished to Frémont forty years later by George Bancroft, then eighty-six years old. The two documents say nothing directly to the point, are at variance with the demonstrable facts, contain much ambiguity, and, in short, are the untrustworthy recollections of an old man who was remembering fierce controversy through the fiercer passions of the Civil War.

Polk's attitudes and motives are clear. His policy, though not farsighted nor intelligently statesmanlike, is equally clear. He wanted California. He would go to war for it if necessary but, in October, '45, believed that he would not have to. He thought he could buy it; if he could not buy it, he would get it by influence — by fomenting a revolution in a province known to be ripe for revolution, and then attaching it by the leverage of common interests. He expected to get it in the latter way, even if events should produce war with Mexico.

So much for what Polk thought. What he did is conclusive. He sent to his secret agent, Consul Larkin, the dispatch that Gillespie carried, the only "official" document Gillespie had. It directed Larkin to conciliate the Californians and to work for the President's unequivocally stated goal, a revolution which would detach them from Mexico. (The only instructions which Gillespie could possibly have carried to Frémont would have been to co-operate with Larkin to that end, not to make that end impossible.) Meanwhile there might be war with Mexico. So Polk instructed Sloat to seize the ports, if war should come, and to hold them. This seizure was directed against Mexico and also against the possibly interested foreign powers — and Sloat was directed to explain it as such to the Californians, in the interest of conciliation. Finally when war did break out and Polk did determine to take California by conquest, he entrusted the conquest to Stephen Watts Kearny. Kearny's orders contained no mention of Frémont whatever . . . Frémont had no instructions from Polk to produce an incident or to begin a conquest.

From Polk's *Diary* for March 21, 1848: —

The Senate of the U. S. having passed a Resolution calling for a letter addressed by the Secretary of State to Mr. Larkin, U. S. consul at Monterey, in California, in October, 1845, it was a question submitted for consideration [in the Cabinet] today whether it was compatible with the public interest to comply with the call. The letter was read. It was confidential and had for its object the protection of American interests and the prevention of Brittish and French interference in California. All agreed that the letter should not have been called for, but that as it had been called for a refusal to furnish it would lead to erroneous inferences, prejudicial to the administration. A false impression is being attempted by the administration in Congress, to be made, to the effect that this letter to Mr. Larkin contained instructions to produce a revolution in California before Mexico commenced the War against the U. S. & that Col. Frémont had the authority to make the revolution. The publication of the letter will prove the falsehood of such an inference.

The true explanation of the decision reached at that campfire by Klamath Lake was made some thirty-three hundred miles to the eastward. At about the time when Frémont was reading his letters under the tall pines, or within a few weeks afterward, Ralph Waldo Emerson, at Concord, Massachusetts, a mile and a half from the gentler evergreens of Walden Pond, sat down to read the Pathfinder's book. When he had finished it, the seer wrote in his journal: —

> The stout Frémont, in his Report of his Expedition to Oregon and California is continually remarking on "the group" or "the picture," etc., "which we make." Our secondary feeling, our passion for seeming, must be highly inflamed if the terrors of famine and thirst for the camp and for the cattle, terrors from the Arapahoes and Utahs, anxieties from want of true information as to the country and the trail, and the excitement from hunting, and from the new and vast features of unknown country, could not repress this eternal vanity of *how we must look.*

Klamath Lake by night through the trees and firelight gave Frémont a group and picture and his passion for seeming was highly inflamed. A Childe Harold, Destiny's courtier, and a messenger who had seen the Mexicans in a patriotic frenzy when their no-appeasement government went in. Surely their martial ardor would precipitate the war which everyone had expected for so long. And Frémont had talked for weeks with visiting *americanos* at his camps, daring, worried, some of them conspirators or actors in various local upheavals. And he had no chance for fame in the war which would be fought and no doubt finished before he could get back to it. And there was another, intolerable picture — of the hero retreating from Gavilán Peak after his brave stand and braver rhetoric, while the contemptible greasers rejoiced in having made him turn tail, while his own hard-bitten men talked behind his back in derisive whispers.

Fishing, a native proverb holds, is good in roily waters. It is good to be shifty in a new country. As Emerson perceived, Frémont saw pictures that might still be made. On the great stage he heard his cue spoken. He walked out and began to play his part.

The Pathfinder reached a decision while he sat by the dying fire after all the others were asleep. To go back to California and do a great deed, for honor and glory. To seize California for the United States and wrap Old Glory round him, to give a deed to the greatness in him. To seize the hour, take fortune at the full, and make his cast. To trust that the war which was certain to come would transform an act of brigandage into an act of patriotism, would transform the actor from a military adventurer, a freebooter, a filibuster, into a hero.

He was a hero from that moment on until he died, but always with the lines just out of drawing. Time, circumstance, and destiny always co-operated with him for a while, and always betrayed him in the end.

He went to bed at last and his course was determined. In the excitement he had neglected to post a guard. You must not, in Indian country, neglect to post a guard. And excitement had bemused Kit Carson, who not only did not remind his commander but went to sleep with his rifle unloaded. So the Hot Creek Modoc, who had been hanging on Gillespie's trail, crept into camp and woke them all by tomahawking Basil Lajeunesse and the half-breed Denny. There was a swift, short struggle, one of Frémont's Delawares was killed, the Modoc chief was killed, and both parties took cover to shoot at each other through the rest of the night. The whites were in a savage mood, the next morning, and when the rest of Frémont's party joined him they all went hunting Modoc, Klamath, and any of their neighbors who might be found. They hunted them violently for several days, killing a good many, burning a village, and riding down whatever skulkers they could find. The lieutenant of marines must have found these days fully as impressive as his stay in Mexico City.

Committed to his role, Frémont took his party back to California, heading toward Sutter's. On May 24 he reached Lassen's and learned that the U. S. sloop *Portsmouth,* Commander Montgomery, was in San Francisco Bay. So he sent Gillespie to it with a requisition for supplies, though the ample ones he had laid in before starting north could hardly have been exhausted in a month. The first three items on his list are: American rifle lead, 300 pounds; powder, 1 keg; percussion caps, 8000. . . . Three hundred pounds of lead would make 9600 bullets and he was already supplied for an exploring trip. What did he want them for?

"The people are no worse since they invaded Mexico," Mr. Emerson told his journal, "only they have given their will a deed."

The people had a war now and so did Mr. Polk. The people had gone fishing for chubs and caught a shark; Mr. Polk had lighted a firecracker and had a bomb explode in his face. The insufficiencies of a narrow intelligence, however firm, and the handicap of habitual suspicion, however patriotic, now made themselves felt on the destinies of the President and the nation. Among the bewilderments that settled over the United States for the ensuing fifteen years, not the least important was the demonstration, which would be memorably clear to eleven seceding states by '65, that if you are going to have a war you need a big man at the head of it.

In the spate of troubles that inundated the President, some surface meanings were hideously plain. We have seen Congressmen Haralson and Baker demanding commissions before the war message was written. So here is James Shields (who had once challenged A. Lincoln to a duel), Polk's commissioner of the General Land Office, calling at the White House to explain that he will go at once to Illinois and raise a regiment of volunteers. Polk angrily argues that it is the commissioner's duty to stay in Washington and do his job, but duty has no force when glory may be won, and Shields is off to glory, a wound, a Civil War command, and Senatorships from three states. Here, in a different order of problems, are Winfield Scott, commander of the army, and Wool, one of his senior generals, and Jones, the adjutant general, intriguing with Congressmen, editors, the prominent, and the strategically placed, to make sure that they (and the Whig Party) shall control the hundreds of army appointments. Here is Scott, when the administration proposes to commission new generals, writing to the Secretary of War, "I do not desire to place myself in the most perilous of positions, a fire upon my rear, from Washington, and the fire in front from the Mexicans." (Insubordinate and injudicious; it effectively kept Scott out of the early campaigns; but it was first-rate prophecy.) And, in still another order of problems, here on Polk's desk are many hundreds of applications for commissions in the new regiment of Mounted Rifles which can have, below its lieutenant colonel, only forty-four officers. Forty-four appointments: therefore hundreds of certain enemies.

As an illustration of Polk's ability to deal with wartime problems, see how he will solve this last one. Persifor Smith, who had served well against the Seminoles and returned to civil life, will be made colonel of this regiment, which (at the moment) is designed to police the Oregon trail, with an eye on the Mormons. Brevet Captain Frémont, from whom nothing has been heard for a long time, will be appointed lieutenant colonel, because he knows the country where the Mounted Rifles will serve — and, be sure, because the goodwill of the chairman of the Senate Committee on Military Affairs is belatedly seen to be valuable in wartime, after all. Now, over a hundred army officers have applied for commissions in the regiment, but Mr. Polk is determined to appoint all its officers from civil life. Why? Because every officer in the army who is not selected will be jealous — and will make trouble! No other consideration, Mr. Polk feels, will hold . . . Except one. He sends his secretary to interview various Whig Senators and Congressmen to get the names of acceptable Whigs for one majority and three or four lieutenancies in the Mounted Rifles. The rest of the forty-four vacancies will be filled by Democrats, preferably from the Western states.

The President and the nation had a war now, and neither was up to it. This book is to touch briefly on certain campaigns and their backgrounds which are related to our central purpose, but it has space to treat the war only in general terms.

The conquest of a foreign nation was the biggest enterprise on which, up to then, the American people had ever embarked. The war required a large-scale organization and an integrated effort for which no experience had fitted the Americans and which were, as a matter of fact, beyond their current ability. Since Mexico was what it was there was never any danger that the United States would lose the war. But it must infallibly have lost the war if it had been waged against a power of industrial, military, or financial resources even remotely comparable to ours. Our industrial and financial systems were flourishing but wholly unprepared for such a strain as they must now bear, our military system was the worst possible, and our system of government, as events were quickly to make clear, had reached a crisis in which its interior conflicts were making it impotent.

One way to win the war would have been to confide its management to a board of specialists, chosen for their effectiveness in management and without reference to their politics. Such a conception was altogether alien to the 1840's, to the stage of American party government then evolved, and in general to the nineteenth century. Feebly approximated in the government of A. Lincoln by 1863, after blood and despair (never approximated in the government of Jefferson Davis), it had to wait for 1917 and Woodrow Wilson. Besides, in 1846, there was not in America the kind of management required. Neither public nor private enterprise had ever undertaken such a job, and the wonder is not that it was done so badly but that it was done so well. While our narrative centers on other things, the reader should hazard some guess about the resources and organizations required to equip, transport, supply, and maintain blockading fleets in foreign waters and armies not only invading Mexico from three directions at distances of several thousand miles but also, in several columns, traversing the wilderness of the Great

American Desert. He should think in round numbers of the components of such an effort — hundreds of ships, tens of thousands of wagons, hundreds of thousands of draft animals and beef cattle, ordnance, small arms, haversacks, hospital supplies, food, blankets, all the *goods* that make a war. That they were supplied at all is the amazing fact, the demonstration that in the last handful of years the developing industrial system had grown altogether beyond what was currently understood about it. Time after time the extemporized organizations broke down. No army was ever as well equipped or as well supplied as its necessities demanded. Lacks and weaknesses which might have meant defeat if our enemy had not been Mexico repeatedly showed themselves. Millions of dollars were wasted, months were lost, vast if indeterminable hardships that might have been averted were inflicted on troops and citizenry. As always, the republic paid more in suffering and death than it ought to have paid. And yet, for all the ignorance, ineptitude, and delay that stopped the fighting for months at a time, bored and finally frightened the nation, and made the leaders both heartsick and suspicious, a kind of efficiency at last prevailed — and the first modern or industrial war somehow found a pattern and succeeded. As a rehearsal for a deadlier one to come.

There was one other way to win the war. It was adopted belatedly and with a scabby intention not to let it succeed too well, when Polk had already lost the country's support and when, be it remembered, Zachary Taylor, a Whig, was clearly getting popular support for the Presidency. There was one man in the United States capable of fighting the war. If he had been allowed to fight it from the beginning, no such elaborate effort would have been required, for he would have destroyed the Mexican armies and occupied a paralyzing part of Mexico before the volunteer enlistments had expired. Winfield Scott was the last of the American equites, a relic from an age of nobler sentiments and grander attitudes. His egoism was colossal, his vanity was monstrous. At a time when all public men were tainted with literary exhibitionism, he wrote the most fatal letters. His intrigues vindicated the common conception of military operations as a department of political opportunity. But he was a great soldier. The campaign he was permitted to make was brilliant and victorious. He won the war.

Polk could not measure up to the needs of public leadership in wartime. He felt that the greatest of the burdens he was called upon to bear was the necessity of fighting a war with Whig generals. Once war came, his mind burned fiercely — with the fire of a small backwoods partisan. He seethed with resentments, could see the breakup of his own party only as the lust of his subordinates to succeed him, and could see in the fundamental opposition to this war that was a turning point in our history only the scramble of other politicians to discredit him by wrecking his foreign policy. And if he saw devils, he also saw ghosts. He would not believe that a Whig could fight a battle except as a step toward winning an election. When Taylor's individualists won some victories for Taylor, Polk promptly began to whittle him down in the name of patriotism. In the name of patriotism, which he sincerely thought meant the maintenance of the Democratic Party, he would not let Scott fight the war. When he had to let him fight it, in the name of patriotism he would not support him and ended by deliberately disgracing him. . . . Some small part of his distrust of Scott, however, was grounded in an American fear that went back a long way. Scott was indeed running for the Presidency from the beginning and so, the moment he got his name in the papers, was Taylor. It was traditionally conceivable that our political generals, which is to say all our generals, might use the war and their commands to effect, in native terms, a military dictatorship by means of newspaper dispatches and the ballot box. Such a conception was in fact preposterous: the event would need a more terrible crisis, like the Civil War, and a genuine diabolist, like Ben Butler. But in Polk, who felt the fear, there was, besides the spooks of his own fantasy, the last vestige of the spirit that had made the fathers fear kings and professional armies.

Polk thought with admirable realism about tariffs, the treasury, and the routine of domestic policy. He thought with astonishing shrewdness about the necessary political maneuvers of government. But he thought badly about war. He was willing to make war on either England or Mexico, if he should have to in order to accomplish his purpose. But he believed that if there should be a war it could be won easily, probably without fighting, and certainly without great effort or expense. Deliberately carrying twin torches through a powder magazine from March 4, 1845, to May 13, 1846, he made no preparation for either war. He had no understanding of war, its needs, its patterns, or its results. The truth is that he did not understand any results except immediate ones. He did not know how to make war or how to lead a people who were making war.

He was not, however, behind his nation or his colleagues in public life. A generation had lived and died since the last war, and the generation of the first war had not been dead quite long enough.

The generations in between had had the spread-eagle emotions of the expanding nation without any need to refine them under the test of fact. What was thought to be the Spirit of '76 blazed across the entire country when word came of Thornton's capture. Under the headline "To Arms! To Arms!" A True Yankee Heart wrote in the *National Intelligencer* an epitome of a thousand editorials, all of which came down to "Young men . . . fly to the rescue of your country's rights, and save her brave little band from a savage foe! . . . now, my friends, is the time for you to show the world that you are all chips of the old Revolutionary block, that you are made of the true Yankee stuff even to the backbone. . . . Come out,* young men, one and all, and you will stand in bold relief before the world." They came out by the thousand, before there was any organization to receive them, more than any organization could receive. . . . It was '76 all over again in the people's thought. Hardly aware of it, they had been spoiling for a war; here it was and the Americans could lick the world. They were all Washington, Greene, Morgan, barefoot Continentals staining the snow of Valley Forge with their blood, foreheads bandaged, banners tattered, tootling a fife in a heroic painting. Or McDonough, Oliver Perry, Decatur, Tom Boyle's *Chasseur* boarding the *Lawrence,* Charles Stewart's *Constitution* taking *Cyane* and *Levant.* And a renewed anger at the massacre of Texans rose up and it was not only the defeat on the Rio Grande that we must avenge but Goliad, the Alamo, and years of forays. Not only Mejía and Ampudia were hated in mass meetings and burned on a hundred village greens, but the author of all infamy, Santa Anna — at the exact moment when Mr. Polk, hoping to substitute bribes for bullets, directed Commodore Conner to let him pass through the blockade to Mexico.

Then word of Palo Alto and Resaca de la Palma arrived and, on the word of the Baltimore *Patriot,* speaking the words of a thousand other sheets, "Blood of the men of '76 has not degenerated in our veins." Lieutenant Grant meant these demonstrations that "every officer and every soldier behaved like a hero" when he made his remark about the stories in the newspapers. It was true, then, that the eagle's children were irresistible, springing to arms from behind the stone walls of Concord Village, we were a nation of heroes, and "Look at the wounded! Look at the dead!" Farm boys and city clerks looked at them, from Maine to Florida, from Delaware to Missouri, and were off to the Halls of Montezuma.

* In this decadent age, it may be proper to remind the reader that this is a revival phrase.

The social militia put on their pink harem drawers and blue and scarlet swallowtails, eighteen-inch shakos, and epaulettes of Napoleon's Guard — the Tigers, Grays, Rifles, Terrors, Hotspurs, and the like, metropolitan or Southern mostly. Flags went up in village squares and the volunteers came tumbling in. In Congress it was suddenly clear that the Academy at West Point, so lately a despotism undermining democracy, had vindicated itself on the Rio Grande. Everybody was putting it "above praise and above censure," especially its graduates in engineering. In the House Representative Jefferson Davis of Mississippi, who looked like a statue of A. Lincoln done by Phidias, stood up to sing an aria about his alma mater. It got so bombastic that Mr. Sawyer rose to a point of privilege and reminded his colleagues that both Washington and Jackson had lacked the illumination of West Point training, but the orator swam on through swelling metaphors till he had found Jeff Davis in transfiguration. Then he resigned and was off to command the First Mississippi Rifles and, in exactly five days of action, to become the one military strategist whom Robert E. Lee was never able to defeat.

Even in New England the people were for this war, now it was here, and that made uncomfortable democracy's loyal opposition in Congress. The Whigs, like the country, had drifted into war, making the most perfunctory opposition and caught in a cruel dilemma. Here was a Whig Congressman on the floor of the House, wearing a colonel's uniform and shouting down his colleagues with a command which they knew their constituents would back up, that they vote the means of war. And "Mr. Webster told them how much the war cost," Emerson's journal remarked, "that was his protest, but voted the war [rather, the bill for volunteers and money], and sends his son to it [the son died in it]." That was both the easy and the immediate way out, for the most powerful of sentiments had been roused. . . . In 1861 one of the fourteen who voted against war in '46 was in Congress again, after an enforced vacation in private life. Would he oppose war now, he was asked, in this greater crisis? No. He had voted against war once, he said, and had learned his lesson.

The Whigs had the bitter knowledge that most wars increase the power of the party that fights them. They cried out, taking the ground that the Executive had usurped the war-making prerogative of the Legislature. It was a poor abstraction to offer an exultant people, some of whose sons were now being listed as casualties. So perhaps it would be better to follow Webster's lead: recognize the war, support it, and later blame the President. A. Lincoln took that stand, and it retired him from public life, even from politics, for six years. Then let us fight the war defensively, interpreting the defensive, if need be, as the right to chase the Mexicans all the way to their capital to prevent invasion, then later find out that the majority had deceived us. It was a time-serving, myopic policy, which offended even their supporters, who, though they were in no mood for analysis, were hardly to be seduced by legalities. The administration's case, however, was on no higher intellectual level: in May we were making war to repel invasion, but by August we were making war to obtain indemnity for claims and injuries and to overthrow a government whose despotism menaced free institutions.

By August, however, the aimless crosscurrents of pure emotion had subsided enough to permit certain elementary perceptions, and as this war, like all wars, was seen to be something other than its beginning had made out, realism began to take the place of evasion. It was a surprising realism. It exploded in Polk's face and he felt that it was ominous. It was: far more ominous than he knew.

But meanwhile an exultant people had their glory, at little risk. They had drifted into war without understanding even their own assent, with a bland feeling that any war the Americans might want to fight was both an easy one to win and a righteous one in motive. They had doggedly evaded both its immediate and its collateral issues and had refused to look at its implications. But now the awareness that is the forerunner of realism began to disturb certain persons who would eventually find ways of making a nation look at facts it had refused to see and at necessary consequences.

Realism is the most painful, most difficult, and slowest of human faculties. Mr. Seward, who was some years short of discovering that there was a higher law than the statutes and that an irrepressible conflict was eroding the nation's core, condemned the new war but was in favor "of plenty of men and supplies once it was started." William Cullen Bryant found it "not practicable" to oppose the war, "though he detested its objects and tried to terminate it as soon as possible." They and their kind lacked Ulysses Grant's, and Ethan Allen Hitchcock's, soldierly forthrightness — but there were those who didn't. Something was beginning to get rearranged. A number who had loved the middle way, holding, they supposed, to the course of progress, were suddenly arm in arm with fanatics who, they had supposed, were impeding it. Men of goodwill who for a long time had been looking at a composite, a complex, of social irreconcilables were now beginning, a few of them, to understand what they saw. Human wills that had been divided by doctrine or theory found themselves blending. With eager or reluctant hearts they achieved understanding and hardened toward purpose.

Just last summer Charles Sumner had found a career by committing, on July 4, a windy oration on universal peace. There was wind enough now when he chanted "Blood! Blood! is on the hands of representatives from Boston. Not all great Neptune's ocean can wash them clean" and "unquestionably the most wicked act in our history" — but even fastidious hearers got his point. Greeley's language was clearer: "unjust and rapacious," "a curse and a source of infinite calamities." Thus virtue's eternal tabernacles, but less neurotic integrities felt that something momentous and unworthy had come upon us. There was no one to describe the tides of the sun's pull — no one to say that the nation was bent out of shape not only by unsolved conflicts within itself but also by the explosion of forces new to the earth. There was no one, even, to call Mr. Polk's war the military phase of the Oregon trail. They could not, and no one blames them, dissect out causes. So, as they began to see effects they attributed them to personal devils no more credible than those which Polk was trying to exorcise. One of these was the slavery conspiracy: the idea that this war had been produced for the extension of slave territory. Speaking as Hosea Bigelow and speaking for a good many besides himself, James Russell Lowell was voicing this notion within a few weeks after Congress voted the war. He probably got it from Theodore Parker — and Parker, better able than most to define the effects he saw, was, like most, withheld from separating out their causes. He did not understand that the slavery crisis, which he now saw sharpening to a point, was one of the effects, had been produced by the tidal forces. Still, Parker could give effects a name.

It was a great speech that Mr. Parker made at the Melodeon on June 7, just five months after the Twenty-eighth Congregational Society of Boston, believing that the city was entitled to hear a man whom the churches feared, had installed him there as their minister.

I maintain that aggressive war is a sin; that it is a national infidelity, a denial of Christianity and of God. . . . Treason against the people, against mankind, against God, is a great sin, not lightly to be spoken of. The political authors of the war on this continent, and at this day, are either utterly incapable of a statesman's work, or else guilty of that sin.

Fools they are, or traitors they must be. . . . Considering how we acquired Louisiana, Florida, Oregon, I cannot forbear thinking that this people will possess the whole of this continent before many years, perhaps before the century ends. . . . Is it not better to acquire it by the schoolmaster than the cannon, by peddling cloth, tin, anything rather than bullets? . . . It would be a gain to mankind if we could spread over that country the Idea of America — that all men are born free and equal in rights, and establish there political, social, and individual freedom. But to do that we must first make real those ideas at home. . . .

When we annexed Texas we of course took her for better or worse, debts and all, and annexed her war along with her. I take it everybody knew that, though some now seem to pretend a decent astonishment at the result. Now one party is ready to fight for it as the other. . . . The eyes of the North are full of cotton; they see nothing else, for a web is before them; their ears are full of cotton and they hear nothing but the buzz of their mills; their mouth is full of cotton and they can speak audibly but two words — Tariff, Tariff, Dividends, Dividends. . . . Now the Government and its Congress would throw the blame on the innocent and say war exists "by the act of Mexico!" If a lie was ever told, I think this is one. Then the "dear people" must be called on for money and men, for "the soil of this free republic is invaded," and the Governor of Massachusetts, one of the men who declared the annexation of Texas unconstitutional, recommends the war he just now told us to pray against, and appeals to our "patriotism" and "humanity" as arguments for butchering the Mexicans, when they are in the right and we in the wrong! . . . I am not at all astonished that northern representatives voted for all this work of crime. They are no better than southern representatives, scarcely less in favor of slavery and not half so open. They say: Let the North make money and you may do what you please with the nation . . . for though we are descended from the Puritans we have but one article in our creed we never flinch from following, and that is — to make money, honestly if we can, if not, as we can! . . . How tamely the people yield their necks — and say "Take our sons for the war — we care not, right or wrong." . . .

Focusing Theodore Parker's intelligence on some effects, the Americans thus clearly observed a relationship among them. Emerson confirmed Parker: "Cotton thread holds the union together; unites John C. Calhoun and Abbott Lawrence. Patriotism for holidays and summer evenings, with music and rockets, but cotton thread is the Union." The seer found that fact leading to a conclusion he had reached by many avenues before: "Boston or Brattle Street Christianity is a compound of force, or the best Diagonal line that can be drawn between Jesus Christ and Abbott Lawrence." The cold judgment seemed infertile, useless, and Emerson's mind restlessly probed the relationships he had perceived. He had to feel, for sight would help him no farther. The Marcys, Buchanans, Walkers — the President's Cabinet — they were village attorneys, saucy village talents, not great captains. America seemed to have immense resources, land, men, milk, butter, cheese, timber, and iron, but was still a village littleness. Village squabble and rapacity characterized its policy. . . . Here, quite suddenly, the antennae of that restless mind, whipping the dark, touched something solid. "It is," he said, "a great strength on the basis of weakness." There, for a time, he stood.

His friend Henry would stroll in from the Walden cabin, these summer evenings, walking eastward against his needle's natural set, and they would talk in Emerson's garden while the light died on Revolutionary Ridge and Mr. Alcott's elms. The earth's longest diameter stretched between this green bottomland with its white houses and the chaparral of Resaca de la Palma, but the ether between was a continuum, the two Yankees were ligatured to Zachary Taylor's dead. . . . The state, the government that was the "unscrupulous and energetic" Polk's instrument — yes, what about the state? Emerson was not sure. The state was "a poor, good beast who means the best: it means friendly. A poor cow who does well by you — do not grudge it its hay. It cannot eat bread, as you can; let it have without grudge a little grass for its four stomachs. You, who are a man walking cleanly on two feet, will not pick a quarrel with a poor cow. Take this handful of clover and welcome. But if you go to hook me when I walk in the fields, then, poor cow, I will cut your throat." So the elder friend counseled Henry Thoreau. For we do not impeach Polk and Webster but supersede them by the Muse. To know the virtue of the soil, we do not taste the loam, but we eat the berries and apples.

Precisely. Loneliness in the resinous, still air of Emerson's pinewoods on the Walden shore had sharpened Henry's perception beyond his counselor's. Precisely there the point stood out. It was not the loam these two had been tasting but the proof, the berries and apples that sprang from it — and Henry's teeth were set on edge. He was of the opinion that the poor good cow had gone to hook Henry Thoreau when he was walking in the fields.

In the Presidency of Polk, Henry watched a war between red ants and black ones on the sandy ground upward from Walden water. He picked up a chip on which three ants were fighting to the death, took it in a cabin and put it under a tumbler, watched it through a reading glass, and "the dark carbuncles of the sufferer's eyes shone with ferocity such as war only could excite." At the end he had seen "the ferocity and carnage of a human battle before my door." It must be thought about in the forest silence. . . . Hoeing the beanfield back of his cabin, he could look up from labor and see the small imps of the air laying their eggs, hawks soaring on motionless wings, spotted salamanders coming out of stumps, or wild pigeons going by "with a slight, quivering, winnowing sound." And sometimes borne to his beanfield on the summer air other sounds came up from the far end of town, faintly as if a puff ball had burst or as if somebody's bees had swarmed and the neighbors were beating on the most sonorous of their domestic utensils to call them down into the hive. Hoeing his beans, Henry knew that on July Fourth the village of Concord had fired its big guns to celebrate the birth of Liberty, and that on another day its militia had mustered — for war on Mexico. "I felt proud to know that the liberties of Massachusetts and of our fatherland were in such safe keeping." Sometimes there was music. "It was a really noble and inspiring strain that reached these woods, and the trumpet that sings of fame, and I felt that I could spit a Mexican with a good relish — for why should we always stand for trifles? — and looked round for a woodchuck or a skunk to exercise my chivalry upon."

That savage and noble sneer moves on the momentum of the new realism that was beginning to well up here and there in America. What is momentous in it is not only the realism but the intensity. For it was a long while since anyone but fanatics had so passionately desired to renew the definition of human freedom. What, Henry wondered, what is the price current of an honest man and patriot today? The rich man, he saw, is always sold to the institution which made him rich. There was talk of the Spirit of '76: a relevant subject, and just what was that Spirit? Was it the citizen who fell asleep after reading "the prices current along with the latest advices from Mexico"? If not, just what and where? And, pointedly, what was its duty to that poor good beast whom Waldo called a cow? Good? no; poor? yes. Or poor but less a beast than a machine — a machine, he was constrained to think, which organized oppression and robbery. It had not "the vitality and force of a single living man." He pressed the image farther, into a clear, unmistakable perspective — and was beginning to move from effect to cause: "it is a sort of wooden gun to the people themselves: and, if ever they should use it in earnest as a real one against each other, it will surely split." . . . Omen of Biela's comet.

In those noon woods and beside those midnight waters, hour by hour of patient thought slowly pulled Henry Thoreau nearer causes. And nearer decision. This poor good cow, this wooden gun, this government, "*It* does not [will not] keep the country free. *It* does not settle the West. . . . The character inherent in the American people has done all that has been accomplished; and it would have done something more if the government had not sometimes got in its way." And its abettors were not far off, "not a hundred thousand politicians at the South but a hundred thousand merchants and farmers here, who are more interested in commerce and agriculture than they are in humanity, and are not prepared to do justice to the slave and to Mexico, *cost what it may*." Suddenly he was over the edge: to him personally came the realization that "you must squat here or squat somewhere, and raise but a small crop, and eat that soon." It was up to Henry Thoreau: the cow had hooked him while he was walking in the fields. "When a sixth of the population of a nation which has undertaken to be a refuge of liberty are slaves, and a whole country is unjustly overrun and conquered by [our] foreign army and subjected to military law, I think it is not too soon for honest men to rebel and revolutionize."[2]

On July 23 or 24 he went into the village to get a shoe which he had left at the cobbler's to be mended. Meeting a town officer, he received a final demand for his poll tax. Emerson had told him to give the poor cow its handful of clover, but he would cut its throat. He refused the tax — time for an honest man to rebel. So Sam Staples locked him up in Concord jail, and "it was like traveling into a far country, such as I had never expected to behold, to lie there for one night." . . . That was the extent of his rebellion, a refusal to "recognize the authority of the state," and at the extremity he was human clay, went scot-free the next morning when his aunt paid the tax, and was almighty mad at Emerson for not hurrying to bail out the revolutionist even earlier than that. No matter. The ripples of that pebble cast in Walden Pond were widening out, and the America of '46 had at last seen a cause attached to an effect in the nakedest light. "They calculated rightly on Mr. Webster," Emerson wrote. "My friend Mr. Thoreau has gone to jail rather than pay his tax. On him they could not calculate."

One by one, as the days went on, there would be others whom the calculations would no longer fit, coming more slowly than Thoreau, perhaps with greater pain, certainly with less clearness of mind, to stand in their various ways beside him. In August some of them would sound an alarm bell in Congress, the bell that long ago had roused Thomas Jefferson from his rest. In August a tide was making inland sluggishly that would go on flooding for fifteen years.

Yet only a few saw that they were moving down the diagonal between Mr. Emerson's perception that the people had given their will a deed and Henry Thoreau's perception that you must squat here or squat somewhere. Even these moved down it in bewilderment, with a sickness of heart also very difficult to understand. A sickness of heart which got a good many diagnoses besides the right one and which, so far as it affected the great middle order that is America, was altogether new to our national life.

It was a faintness, a shrinking back while the feet moved forward in darkness, a premonition more of the lower nerves than of the brain. Something had shifted out of plumb, moved on its base, begun to topple down. Something was ending in America, forever. A period, an era, a social contract, a way of life was running out. The light artillery at Palo Alto had suddenly killed much more than the ardent, aimless Mexican cavalry, and it was intuition of this death that troubled the nation's heart.

No one can be sure he knows the mind of John C. Calhoun. It was a maze of metaphysical subtleties too fine for anyone but Calhoun to understand; tides of destruction he did not understand and could not govern compelled it; it was beyond normality in most qualities, especially in hate, vanity, and trance. No man had willed the event longer than Calhoun, but when it happened he repudiated his agency, shrinking from the deed he had helped produce. The same sense of approaching doom that oppressed lesser minds took hold of his, and he said in the Senate: "I said to many of my friends that a deed had been done from which the country would not be able to recover for a long time, if ever; and added, it has dropped a curtain between the present and the future, which to me is impenetrable . . . it has closed the first volume of our political history under the Constitution and opened the second and . . . no mortal could tell what would be written in it."

Thus the metaphysician of political desire. Mr. Emerson had an earthier image: "The United States will conquer Mexico but it will be as the man swallows the arsenic which brings him down in turn. Mexico will poison us."

INTERLUDE

World of Tomorrow

NOT only war was fixing the destiny of the United States in May, 1846. In the last week of the month the bill to extend American jurisdiction over Oregon came up in the Senate, and Thomas Hart Benton rose to speak about it. He talked for three days, and the passages of analysis must have exhausted such of his colleagues as sat them out, for Old Bullion could be windy and achingly dull. But it was a great speech nevertheless, and when it was over Benton's longest study had come into fruition and the republic was nobly served by its great expansionist. His speech gave final substance to a lifetime's love and vision and when he finished it everyone knew that, when the Oregon question should be reopened, as it was about to be, nothing beyond 49° would be asked for. Also, during this month from time to time the bill establishing the Smithsonian Institution kept coming up when either house had a moment to spare, and at last something was to be done about the funds which the Englishman James Smithson had bequeathed to democracy for the "diffusion of knowledge" and which, unhappily, had been invested in state bonds now in default. Hitherto Congress could not agree on what kind of agency would best diffuse knowledge, but agreement neared. The bill was finally passed in August. Fifteen Regents were appointed, among them Robert Dale Owen, Rufus Choate, and Richard Rush. And since the government had need of Matthew Maury in his present place, it called our other first-rank scientist, Joseph Henry, from Princeton. Too bad that in making him an administrator it put an end to his researches.

More striking, however, was the National Fair, which opened in Washington on May 22 and taxed the boarding houses with additional crowds besides those that had swarmed in for military appointments and contracts. Mr. Polk visited it on the second day and, thin-lipped, thought the exhibits "highly creditable to the genius and skill of our countrymen," but was sure that the manufacturers had organized it "to prevent a reduction of the present rates of duty imposed by the oppressive protective tariff act of 1842." The President was maneuvering to repeal that act, and there was doubtless something in his suspicion. Certainly the Whig press exhaustively derived protectionist morals from the show. Democratic editors were cool toward it, except the tail-twisters, who found it horridly pro-British in sympathy and concluded that it was financed by British gold.

If it was, the British had been shortsighted. . . . Let us simply sprawl into some lists. The city of Lowell's products which so rudely transgressed the Brook Farmers' theories: calicoes, satinets, cambrics, cashmeres, muslins, balzarines, bed quilts, blankets, carpetings, laces, silks . . . Parchments, wrapping papers, glazed and colored papers, wallpapers, window shades, oilcloths . . . Binders' leathers, cordwainers' leathers, saddlers' leathers, harness leathers, military leathers, trunks, valises . . . Alum, epsom salts, rochelle salts, copperas, quinine, morphine salts, nitrate of silver . . . Mustard, chocolate, "prepared" cocoa, rice flour . . . Puddled boiler-plate iron, bar iron, rod iron, hoop iron . . . Steel pens, gold and silver pens, brass wire, steel wire, door latches, coffee mills, stair rods, locks, nails, saws, augurs, house bells, church bells, school slates, candelabra . . . Ice-cream freezers, sausage cutters, meat cutters, honing mills, washing machines, forges, hot-air furnaces, parlor stoves, cooking ranges, plows, scythes, shovels, spades, bullet molds, platform scales, water filters . . . Portable steam boilers, portable steam engines, a hydrostatic valve. A wheat fan, a seed and grain planter, a "tubular steam penetrator." Jackson Roberts' wheat-threshing machine . . . Bath heaters, patent refrigerators (ice water circulated through hollow shelves), welded wrought-iron tubes, tobacco presses . . . Hussey's reaping machine, McCormick's reaping machine. Cotton looms. Spinning frames. Patent weaver's shuttle. Card-making machine. Rotary backing-tool. Revolving stand premium pump . . . On and on for pages.

If you have observed certain goods that were extending the American empire southwestward, hauled in the wagons of the Santa Fe trade, be informed that the energies signified by the above list had, just last summer, produced an iron durable enough to be used in the axles of those wagons. Such axles were a startling innovation, which was already spreading. In 1846 William Kelly of Pennsylvania discovered that he could make malleable iron and steel from pig iron with no intermediate stage by blowing cold air through it when molten. The discovery was so revolutionary that his friends and family wanted him certified as insane, but it happened to anticipate the process of Henry Bessemer.[1] In 1846 the mills at Lowell were being repowered with a significant new engine, Uriah Boyden's water turbine which had the undreamed-of efficiency of 82%. In 1846 at Dover, New Hampshire, the schoolmaster Moses Farmer (who had invented a machine for manufacturing some of the window curtains listed above) was tinkering with a model electric railroad. It ran by a motor powered from a wet battery and he demonstrated it publicly the following year.

In 1846 the *Sea Witch* slid down the ways, was rigged and fitted, and on December 23 weighed anchor on her maiden voyage, out of New York, bound for Hong Kong. She made it in 104 days, and homeward bound reached New York 82 days from Whampoa. She was a sharp model, very beautiful, and her figurehead was a Chinese dragon with open mouth and partly coiled tail ending in a dart. Three years before, the *Rainbow* had been built for the same carriers, the first exemplar of the theories of design fathered by John W. Griffiths to which all the clippers were built, and in '46 John Currier built *Ariel* at Newburyport. All three were less extreme than the ships which Donald McKay and his followers were to be building in just a few years more for the California trade — and, in building them, were to make the most beautiful objects any American artists have ever made. But *Sea Witch* was a clipper right enough, and her times outward and homeward bound mark the beginning of a new era in transportation. If it was to be Donald McKay's era, it was also John W. Griffiths', who had created the theory of design and rigging, and Matthew Maury's, who had worked out the mastery of winds and currents. The American scientist, the American artist, and American technology had collaborated in a climax, a decision.

In 1846 Richard M. Hoe perfected and patented his method of attaching printers' type to a rotating cylinder, and in 1847 the Philadelphia *Ledger* installed the first of his new presses. It had four of these cylinders grouped together, and printed eight thousand newspapers in an hour — four times as many as the fastest press before it had been able to turn out. So the penny papers got an instrument that enabled them to reach their audience. The center of American journalism shifted to its foredestined place. The *Union*, the *National Intelligencer*, *Niles' Register*, and the like no longer kept the center of editorial opinion so dangerously close to the center of political power. Greeley, Bryant, Bennett, and Raymond came into their own. Democracy had gained a new weapon and a new tool. . . . Two years after the *Ledger* installed its new press, a technologist in England proved conclusively that type could not be made to hold to a rotating cylinder.

Look at the Patent Office. U. S. Pat. No. 4,464, April 18, 1846, to Royal C. House. A printing telegraph. Thus, two years after there was a public telegraph, long before there was a typewriter, there was a teletype. But what was significant in House's invention was the exquisite, exact, automatic production of successive operations in fixed sequence. Or U. S. Pat. No. 4,704, August 20, 1846, to Thomas J. Sloan. A simple thing: a wood screw which had a gimlet point and so turned itself into the wood instead of having to have a hole bored for it, the screw you used yesterday to put up a wall bracket. Or patent to Washburn Race of Seneca Falls, N. Y., for a self-acting register for stoves. Or patent to Erastus B. Bigelow, power loom for two- and three-ply ingrain carpets — next year he will patent looms for tapestries and Brussels carpets. Or a double handful of patents improving the textile machinery of Lowell, self-acting mules, new Jacquard Frames for figured fabrics, till one is dizzy making notes. Patent for hat-body machinery to H. A. Wells — and there are shifts and regroupings at Danbury. Patents to F. Langenheim of Philadelphia, W. A. Pratt of Alexandria, Virginia, and several others — improvements in the materials, processes, and mechanics for making reproductions by daguerreotype.

And U. S. Pat. No. 4,750, September 10, 1846, to Elias Howe. Covering three basic features of the first sewing machine: a grooved needle with the eye at the point, a shuttle operating on the opposite side of the cloth from the needle to form a lock stitch, and an automatic feed.

Bearing in mind what was to come out of Elias Howe's patent, one may glance back over the exhibits at the National Fair and understand how far, in 1846, the United States had already advanced in the World of Tomorrow. If you had spoken the phrase, "The American System," to Mr. Polk or any of his supporters or opponents, it would have meant to him the domestic policy fathered by Henry Clay and supported by the Whig Party, inherited by the Republicans, and maintained by them until usurped by the Democrats. That is, strong centralized control, development of the internal market, systematized public works, and the protective tariff. But in England and Europe the phrase had already acquired a different meaning. It meant a kind of factory production new to the world, which had made a large share of the manufacturers' exhibits. It meant: the displacement of hand labor by machine labor to an ever-increasing extent, the application of machine labor to successive operations, increased precision, the production of finished objects by such exact duplication of parts that the parts were interchangeable and so independent of the finished object, the progressive rationalization of processes and techniques, and the development of straight-line manufacture and automatic machine tools. It meant that, by 1846, the American industrial order had so matured that it was manufacturing tools for the manufacture of the goods exhibited at the Fair — specifically that in various places, especially the Naugatuck Valley and along the banks of the Connecticut River as far north as Windsor, Vermont, the modern machine-tool industry was well established. (Such men as Richard Lawrence, Frederick W. Howe, and Henry D. Stone, gunsmiths by training, were making machine tools in '46, had already developed jigs, dies, presses, planers, drop hammers, profile machines, and milling machines which are still serving their craft, and in a couple of years more would develop a turret lathe.) It meant that when Elias Howe put his sewing machine into production, he could manufacture it in a factory which, in the rationale of processes, was essentially any factory of today. It meant that Eli Whitney, by the exercise of what was primarily a Yankee passion for economy, neatness, and logical order, had made the world over.

As, in the summer of '46, Samuel Colt found out. From 1836 to 1842 Colt had manufactured about five or six thousand of his patent revolvers, the first successful repeating firearms. Bad financial management — outside Colt's control — had forced the closing of the factory and he had gone on to experiment with electrically controlled submarine mines and had laid the first successful submarine electric cable. But his revolvers had been tested in the Seminole War and had worked into the possession of the Texas Navy and the Texas Rangers — and of Santa Fe traders, such mountain men as Kit Carson, and other practical men who had to deal professionally with the Plains Indians. They had promptly worked a revolution in warfare comparable to and more immediately important than that heralded by the American light artillery at Palo Alto. They had proved themselves the first effective firearm for mounted men,[2] and had given the Texans and other frontier runners the first weapon which enabled white men to fight with Plains Indians on equal or superior terms.[3] Nearly all of the primordial five or six thousand had, by 1846, gravitated to the place where they were needed, the Western frontier. Most of the journals quoted in this book speak admiringly of their use and value in the West; nearly every writer who discusses outfits for emigrants recommends them.

As soon as Taylor was ordered to the Rio Grande, officers of his who had used Colt's revolvers in Florida began clamoring to have them made standard equipment, and the demand was supported by the Texas Rangers when they were incorporated in the army. The War Department bought up all those available in secondhand shops and brought Colt back to the armament industry with a contract for one thousand revolvers, which was supplemented with a second contract for the same number before the first was completed. Colt had kept none of his revolvers and could not buy one, and so had to make his model from memory. He improved it by simplifying it, which is emblematic of the American System, but more striking is the progress that had been made in four years. When his factory closed down in 1842 there remained many operations which had to be performed by hand. In 1846, when he began manufacturing again, it proved possible to perform nearly all of them by machine.

He went to the Whitney Arms Company, just outside New Haven, where Eli Whitney's son was carrying on and developing the methods of his father — and was helping the government switch the army from muskets to the "Harpers Ferry" percussion-cap rifle. (Though far from fast enough to equip the troops now necessary for the war.) With Whitney, Whitney's toolmakers, and Colt himself collaborating, new machine tools were designed. They passed into Colt's possession at the completion of the first contract, and the factory which he then set up at Hartford was the most advanced application of the American System so far seen. It was so advanced that when, a few years later, Colt set up a factory in England he could not satisfy his sense of commercial diplomacy by employing local industry and workmen. No foreign machines of the necessary precision could be found or made, and he had to bring them in from the United States. Bringing them in, he could not find mechanics sufficiently skillful to operate them, or sufficiently habituated to thinking in terms of complex machines to be trained. There had been a complete reversal in less than a generation, since the Lawrences and Lowells had had to smuggle out English mechanics to design their textile machinery. The Yankees now led the world.

The establishment of the Colt's Patent Fire Arms Manufacturing Company thus concentrates in a single item the full significance of the National Fair of '46. Colt or Elias Howe — or Cyrus McCormick, who got three hundred of his reapers made for him this year and would presently move to the Middle West and erect his own factory — signify the extreme spearhead of the industrial drive. They merely inherited, however, what the remaker of societies, Eli Whitney, had put into motion before the turn of the century. For if Whitney's cotton gin had dramatically reversed social trends and created an economy, his long-term revolution in manufacture (arrived at simultaneously, be it remembered, by another gunsmith, Simeon North, his neighbor twenty-odd miles away) was reorganizing the world. That revolution had been quietly accelerating all along, so that when, for instance, the clockmakers of Connecticut learned how to make brass works for their products, fully fifteen years before our period, they could apply the American System and achieve the mass production of identical, serviceable, cheap articles. But the further point is that by '46 that acceleration had become from one point of view prophetic, and from another, catastrophic. No Henry Adams attended the National Fair to spin an elegant metaphysical meditation into a theory of physical force. Since none did, it would have been extremely intelligent of Mr. Polk, or his supporters, or more especially John C. Calhoun, to spend laborious hours studying the exhibits and meditating on the future of the United States.

This text has several times taken an image from astronomy and spoken of energies which were drawing the United States out of shape, as theory tells us the earth swelled out in a lump when the moon was born. They are all in now. From astral space a dispassionate Martian might have seen the First Republic in process of transformation to the Empire by forces which moved within a parallelogram. He would have noted the armies working south, the fissures raveling across Congress, the American System building the factories of Elias Howe and Samuel Colt and Cyrus McCormick, and a long line of now-faded white-tops moving west.

VIII
Solstice

IN early June the command of Brevet Captain Frémont of the Topographical Engineers had come down the Sacramento Valley, where we left them on May 24, to the Marysville Buttes, sixty miles north of Sutter's Fort. As a military organization they were to go through several phases, but at this period they looked strikingly like some militia known to American humor as the Tallapoosy Vollontares.

Word of Frémont's return from Oregon spread over the countryside. Comandante Castro, whose quarrel with Governor Pico had at this exact moment reached the point where he was raising horsemen for a demonstration (which might have been the beginning of the very revolution for which Larkin had been sedulously working) — Comandante Castro heard about it and reached the not unjustified conclusion that an American invasion was beginning. Consul Larkin heard about it and innocently wrote to Frémont, inviting him to exchange news and reproaching him for not having kept in communication during his absence. And all the resident Americans heard about it. All supposed that something was beginning and most of them believed that they could guess what it was. Many of them rode in to the camp at the Buttes for information — or orders.

However you care to interpret what followed, you can get supporting evidence at the source. Frémont had come back to California to initiate a movement which should seize it for the flag — whether as an act of war against Mexico or as a safeguard against Great Britain did not matter to him and should not matter to us. He was promptly surrounded by men who had long wanted to seize California, who were both annoyed and anxious because the expected war had not developed, and who clearly understood the significance of his return. The expected was now going to happen and the only question is how far Frémont was an instigator of it.

This appears to be a reasonable judgment. If it could be arranged for some of the Americans who had the least to lose to get themselves attacked by Castro, then Frémont could come to their protection, and if Castro should thereupon attack him, then all the rest would follow in strict accordance with the usages of nations. It was a shifty plan. It worked.

After repeated conferences with Frémont, in the course of which he angered some of them by being too shifty and others by withholding his counsel too long, a band of Americans rode out on a raid, from the vicinity of his camp. They were acting on their own or they were acting under his instructions. General Castro, as we noted some time back, had sent a requisition to General Mariano Vallejo at Sonoma, for horses to be used in the demonstration against Pico. Nearly two hundred horses, herded by Castro's secretary who was named Arce, a lieutenant named Alviso, and eight humble privates, were on their way to Castro at San José. They would cross the Sacramento near Sutter's Fort. The raiders set out to get the horses. And Frémont moved down the valley and made a camp much nearer Sutter's.

There were ten or twelve of these marauders and they picked up four recruits on the way. They were led by a former mountain man named Merritt, huge and very tough. They included several other mountain men, a Yankee schoolteacher whose mind fermented with notions straight out of Brook Farm, and an ex-sailor who was wanted for murder. On June 10, at Murphy's ranch on the Cosumnes, they surprised and captured the general's horse herd. They released the herders and drove the horses back to Sutter's. Arce hurried to Castro and reported, with the strictest accuracy, that his horses had been stolen by American highwaymen. Castro at once prepared to fight the invasion which this raid appeared to confirm. He began to fight it, necessarily, by issuing a proclamation and by raising troops.

In the course of a few days the highwaymen were delighted to find themselves a vanguard of empire. If the raid was not robbery, then it was war. If it was war, then the laws of strategy required them to clear the surrounding countryside of enemy troops. There were no troops but, at the microscopic hamlet of Sonoma, there was the California equivalent of troops, a general. This was Don Mariano Vallejo, already mentioned, who in theory commanded the northern frontier for Castro and who had a few antique arms in his custody. He was perhaps the most considerable citizen of California. He was known to favor American annexation and had been suspected of conspiring to bring it about.

Later, Frémont claimed that he gave the orders for the capture of Sonoma. He thereby outraged some of its conquerors. They accused him of wanting to hog the glory after refusing to take the risk — if any. No matter: thirty-three strong now and including William Todd, the nephew of Mrs. Abraham Lincoln, the American revolutionaries reached Sonoma before dawn on June 14. In the reports which Senator Benton was to trumpet to an admiring nation the town figured as a fortified, garrisoned, and formidably armed presidio. That is what Old Bullion gathered about it from his son-in-law's letter, but Sonoma was a tiny little cluster of adobe houses and could have been captured by Tom Sawyer and Huck Finn. The conquerors found General Vallejo asleep.

They gathered in not only this general but a lieutenant colonel and a captain to boot. They told Vallejo that he was a prisoner of war. He had some difficulty understanding what war he was a prisoner of and set out brandy for his captors, so that they could talk it over. Conquerors and conquered wrote out a formal statement of terms, and by its third paragraph, the product of good native liquor, the California Republic was born.

To some of the army outside the house conquest began to look rather like a drunk. Others wanted to plunder the town. Still others, in cold morning air, began to wonder if high spirits had not carried them too far. The new republic nearly died of second thoughts, but it was saved by the Yankee schoolmaster, William Ide. He made a noble speech, and from then on was, for a brief but appealing time, chief of state. . . . There had to be a republic. Otherwise there was no sovereignty and the prisoners were being held simply by thugs; otherwise supplies seized for the army would just be stolen.

They sent the prisoners to Frémont, in camp near Sutter's Fort, and at Sonoma began mustering the Americans who rode in as the news traveled, scared or glad to be getting along with the revolution at last. President Commander Ide, calling upon his memory of speeches made from Yankee bandstands on Lexington and Concord Day, poured out his soul in a proclamation. He recited the grievances that a revolt must have if it is to gather in the shadow of Thomas Jefferson; there weren't any grievances but he made some good phrases. He summoned all native Californians of goodwill to rally to the free government now conferred on them at Sonoma. He sketched out the policies it would adopt. He closed with allusions to the bravery of his followers, all forty of them, to the native American hatred of tyranny, and to the favor of heaven.

When Josiah Royce came to narrate these events, in the study that remains on the whole the best one, he could find no solemnity adequate to describe this scene of a handful of exceedingly tough customers brushing a varnish of classical American rhetoric over a mere foray by brigands. He alluded to the Hunting of the Snark and let it go at that. There is a neater allusion in the works of W. S. Gilbert but one is deterred from making the parallel. For another parallel comes to mind. Here were some American settlers in California, some of them legitimate immigrants and others just adventurers on the loose, announcing in the morning sunlight to some amiable, peaceful, and extremely bewildered Californians that they were creating a new Texas on the golden shore. Comic enough. But in a study in the White House, on the plane of international affairs, with all due circumstance of diplomatics and phrased in better English than Conquistador Ide used, a new Texas was precisely what the President of the United States had envisaged.

They had a Republic, California model, by proclamation, out of Lexington and Brook Farm. So while they went about giving it substance they ought also to set up a standard to which honest republicans might repair. William Todd obliged, women's patriotism assisting him. The wife of one revolutionist sacrificed a chemise and the wife of another one a petticoat, and Todd made a flag. Red flannel stripes across a white (or at least unbleached) field. He painted in red a crude five-pointed star in the left-hand corner and, facing it, an animal standing on its hind legs, doubtless remembered in emergency from the state seal of Missouri. A realist, or he may have been an adept of symbolism, described it as a hog, but Todd meant it for a bear. Underneath, in ink or pokeberry juice, he lettered in the legend: California Republic. He left the *i* out of the last syllable and made a blot painting it over again, but the one-village nation had the ensign that has come down to glory.

All California north of Monterey quivered with alarm or curiosity. The amazed Montgomery, of the navy's sloop *Portsmouth,* hurried to proclaim that neither he nor the United States had or wanted any part in the creation of this commonwealth. The one accredited representative of the United States, Consul Larkin, realized that if any hope of fulfilling his instructions had remained after Frémont's drama on Gavilán Peak, this gaudier drama had extinguished it. In resignation he also disavowed the Republic and told the California authorities that he would help them bring its proprietors to justice. More Americans rode in to join the founding fathers, others rode in the other direction to join Frémont, and the Californians rode in all directions, taking counsel.

Frémont received General Vallejo and his companions and ordered them confined at Sutter's Fort, which he now seized, inaccurately, in the name of the United States. . . . Thus began the downfall of

John Augustus Sutter, emigré, fantast, true empire-builder, and the end of his amazing principality in the new world. At the very moment when the heroes raided the horse herd Sutter had a man out, once more, trying to locate the best site for a sawmill on the American River. The project had been interrupted before this; when at last it should be completed, James Marshall, some Indians, and some veterans of the Mormon Battalion would finish what Frémont had now begun.

The first stage of any California action had to be rhetorical, and the veterans easily surpassed the amateur Ide's proclamation. Castro told his fellow citizens "to rise en masse irresistible and just," and assured them that he would be the first to sacrifice himself. "Duty leads me to death or victory. I am a Mexican soldier and I will be free and independent or die with pleasure for those inestimable blessings." Farther to the south Pico outdid his *comandante,* rising to this peroration: "Fly, Mexicans, in all haste in pursuit of the treacherous foe; follow him to the farthest wilderness; punish his audacity; and in case we fail, let us form a cemetery where posterity may remember to the glory of Mexican history the heroism of her sons, as is remembered the glory won by the death of that little band of citizens posted at the Pass of Thermopylae under General Leonidas. . . ."[1] Neither Ide nor Semple could compete with that and the American oratory must win or lose with John Charles Frémont.

But the California orators meant what they said and had at least the dignity of men who were defending their lives and independence. If their language was overblown, it was spoken against an attack on their country, which had harmed no one, neither the head Conqueror himself nor any of his collaborators.

A little order began to come out of the miscellaneous riding. Certain improvised bands came together and Castro made plans to recapture Sonoma, the capital of the Republic and so far its entire domain. Commander Ide, who now had a flag and a proclamation, was receiving volunteers, was offering a square league of his future conquest as a bonus for enlisting (thus repeating the leitmotif), and had organized his forces into the First Artillery and the First Rifles. He had made prisoners of war of the town's alcalde, a simple-hearted and extremely bewildered young man, and thirty or forty other citizens. He invented a service of supply and information — and had to combat the foul rumor that he was a Mormon or a Mormon agent. A dispatch from Frémont arrived, to be forwarded to Montgomery at San Francisco Bay. Ide called on the versatile Todd to become a courier. Todd was valorous but unacquainted with the principles of military security. He ran into one of the bands of wandering horsemen and now the Californians in their turn had a prisoner of war. At once they had two more. For Ide sent a couple of his recruits, Fowler and Cowie, to procure a keg of powder for the Republic's army and they also met some horsemen on the public road. These were more excitable horsemen: if there was going to be a war, let it begin here. They shot Fowler and Cowie. Since they were enemy horsemen, this was clearly against the laws of war. (It was promptly, and erroneously, rumored that they had dismembered the bodies.)

Word of these captures, though not of the murders, reached the Republic, and Ide sent out his lieutenant, Ford, with a dozen and a half irregulars to retake the prisoners. On June 23 they met some horsemen at the hamlet of San Antonio and took four of them prisoner. The next morning they blundered into a party of fifty campaigning Californians who had stopped for breakfast at Olompali, halfway between Santa Rosa and Petaluma. This was the first of three detachments which Castro intended to send against Sonoma but the only one that got across the Bay. It was led by Captain Joaquin de la Torre, who was mightily surprised to find himself under fire. The Americans were equally startled but gamer. They took cover, killed one Californian, wounded another one, and presently had de la Torre riding hell for leather down the back trail to San Rafael. Ford went on to his original destination and recaptured William Todd, then rode back to Sonoma. . . . End of the military history of the California Republic.

Meanwhile Captain Frémont, commanding sixty American freebooters of his own and nearly as many irregular recruits, had become an open ally of the Republic. He was imprisoning at Sutter's Fort all peaceful wayfarers his men encountered — including certain Americans who could not understand that what they took to be a violation of the public peace was an honorable warfare to liberate the enslaved. Also he was in a literary phase, spouting letters of explanation, manifesto, and deception — to Montgomery, to Larkin, to Senator Benton — describing the purity of his intentions, the extreme peril of his situation, and the wakeful resolution of his heart. . . . No one could look ahead to the summer of 1864, to a time when history's stage manager would make him, for a while, a candidate for the Presidency against not only A. Lincoln but George B. McClellan as well. He had McClellan's talent for believing himself surrounded by irresistible hordes of enemies and for calculating his chances at something like one in ten thousand. So now he peopled the countryside with marching masses of murderous Mexicans — hundreds of them and all thirsting like the Indians of ten-cent fiction for the hero's gore. Moreover, he was somehow being insulted as well as hunted down, and one of his letters announced that, besides defeating the Californians, he intended to force an apology from them.

Word reached him at Sutter's of Castro's intention to attack Sonoma. The Republic was in danger! So gallop, gallop, Frémont *au secours!* Eighty miles he took his cavalry at full speed and at the end found himself in extreme danger — of being fired on by the garrison of Sonoma, who had been weakened by the dispatch of Ford's expedition but would nevertheless sell their lives dearly when hooves came pounding through the night. Good playwriting saved the Conquistador just as the lighted match was arching to the breech of Sonoma's cannon. Frémont, as senior officer of guerrillas, now took command of the Republic's military establishment, and the next day Ford got back with word that de la Torre had escaped.

Even the topographical engineers knew that pursuit was called for. Frémont took his army — it had grown to about 130 — off to San Rafael, toward which de la Torre had been fleeing when Ford last saw him. He was not there when Frémont arrived. (He was farther down the Bay, desperately afraid that he would not get boats before the *americanos* caught up with him.) But another enemy appeared.

Across the Bay, General Castro, still hoping to urge his forces into action against Sonoma, was wondering what had happened to de la Torre, his spearhead of attack. Two young men, brothers, volunteered to cross over and try to take a message to him. An old man insisted on going with them, the father of Sonoma's alcalde. He had heard that the *americanos* had imprisoned his son, and wanted to see if the rumor was true and if he could do anything about it. A fourth man offered to row them across the strait. They got across, the rower turned back again, the two messengers and the anxious old man started up the shore. And here was Captain Frémont, watching them come on. He was having a moment of being the Conqueror, pacing by himself, like Hannibal and Napoleon. He ordered Kit Carson and two others to intercept this enemy. They did so. Kit reported to Napoleon and asked for instructions. The Conqueror's mind swarmed with enemies, this was war, and he must be stern. "I have no room for prisoners," he said, possibly thinking of biographers unborn. So Kit Carson and his corporal's guard killed them.

De la Torre was no great soldier, possibly, but he worked the hoariest ruse in warfare and let a dispatch bearer be captured by the Conqueror, with plans of an attack preparing on Sonoma. Frémont galloped back again and de la Torre crossed his command to safety. But three days later Frémont performed another feat of arms. The ship *Moscow* was anchored in the Bay; back in March its captain had offered Frémont refuge at the time of the show on Gavilán Peak. Now Frémont, with Gillespie as adjutant, told him that he was acting on orders of the government and requisitioned his help in reducing the enemy fortress on the far shore of the strait, the site of San Francisco. Captain Phelps supplied a longboat and some sailors to row the party of assault on its desperate mission.

Another daring venture at midnight when graveyards yawn. On the way, Frémont resumed his outgrown role of geographer long enough to give the strait its name, the Golden Gate. They reached the far shore at dawn and stormed its defending fortress, El Castillo de San Joaquin. There was no one there: no one had been there for a generation. The cannon were rusting away into eternity but the Conqueror spiked them nevertheless — ten popguns that had been cast early in the seventeenth century to arm some Spanish galleons — and so brought to a glorious end the first phase of John Charles Frémont, military genius. He had done his first great deed.

As the curtain falls on this act, the performance may seem below the standard of great drama. But if the hero's role has been trivial, let Hubert Howe Bancroft remind us what he had achieved. He had made himself, by his actions so far, Bancroft sums up, "a popular hero, a Senator of the United States, a candidate for the Presidency, a millionaire ad interim, [and] a major-general."

Bancroft adds that he was a lucky fellow. Right — so far. How lucky he was is apparent when one considers what would certainly have happened to Frémont and his guerrillas if, civil war having been precipitated in a California which was slow to act but could have annihilated the revolutionists, the news of the outbreak of the Mexican war had not now reached responsible men who had instructions to act. That news arrived at about the time when Frémont captured his empty fortress. The one-town California Republic ended its sovereignty and the conquest of California began.

The marine band played in June dusk on the White House lawn, and here were dispatches from Minister McLane saying that Her Majesty's government would propose to settle the Oregon boundary at 49°. So the administration faced an embarrassment. The President, however, had prepared an exit: to submit the proposal, if it should come, for the advice of the Senate and thus escape the odium of having to withdraw from the extreme position. The levy and supply of armies for the Southern excursion made it all too clear that the extreme position would have to be abandoned, that the British offer would have to be accepted. But it was also clear that the oratory for 54° 40′ was going to be remembered.

The Cabinet agreed that the exit would have to be used. Except that Mr. Polk was by now completely surrounded by candidates for '48, and the strangest belligerence had seized Mr. Buchanan. Having for a full year protested, moaned, and all but wept at the President's firmness in the matter, having pleaded for the amelioration of many dispatches, having held out for 49° from the beginning and once demanded that Great Britain be given anything more that she might ask, he now held out for 54° 40′ and would bleed for it as gallantly as General Cass. He was ranging ahead to the national convention of '48 and the delegations of disappointed Western states, as the President immediately understood. Polk wrote that Buchanan's about-face "excited" him: he meant that it made him tearing mad, reasonably enough. His patience held for a day or two, then he loosed his formidable rage on his Secretary of State, who collapsed like a punctured bladder and would accept 49°.

Pakenham, the British Minister, drove up to the White House and made the expected proposal. Polk duly forwarded it to the Senate, where the warhawks bellowed with outraged anger. But for one thing Thomas Hart Benton's erudite analysis had convinced his colleagues, and for another, even a warhawk had to admit that one war at a time was enough. After two days of debate, the Third War with Great Britain became just something that *Niles' Register* had asked questions about in January, we were not going to twist the lion's tail, and the warhawks could muster just twelve votes against thirty-eight. Senator Allen of Ohio, however, had meant the orations that had annoyed Herman Melville: on the spot he resigned as chairman of the Committee on Foreign Relations.

The vote of June 12 was to instruct the President to accept 49°. Three days later Mr. Buchanan and Mr. Pakenham signed the convention that settled the Oregon question forever. . . . At this point it is wholesome to recall once more the rates of communication, since they governed the management of armies as well as the tidings of peace. The convention was signed on June 15. At once an express left Washington to notify the Oregonians that they were American citizens after all and need not, as some of them were at that moment proposing to do, commit a Bear Flag maneuver against the Hudson's Bay Company. It went to Vera Cruz and followed in Gillespie's tracks across enemy soil to Mazatlán. The first boat out was bound to China by way of the Sandwich Islands, and at Honolulu the dispatch was put on board the bark *Fawn,* which crossed the bar at the mouth of the Columbia on November 12. Five months after the signing of the convention, the *Fawn's* supercargo was rowed to shore with the great news. He was nine days behind unofficial dispatches from Honolulu on the *Toulon.*

Mr. Polk had now achieved the first of his four objectives. But at some cost. Allen had become an enemy of the administration, so had Hannegan (he was almost incoherent, in fact, applying polysyllabic but barbed epithets to the President who had let him down), and the support of such men as Cass, Atchison, and Jarnegan could no longer be counted on for anything. The internal tensions of the Democracy had been stepped up still farther, nearer the breaking point.

And to the westward, where thousands of Bill Bowens had supposed that oratory meant what the words said, subtle shifts and movements within the submerged Republic began to set in a new direction, toward a far-off event. One of the strongest cohesive forces in the United States, one that had long seemed a law of nature as firm as the law of falling bodies, was the implicit alliance between the South and West. Lines of strain showed on its surface now and, once more, the tug of vast bodies was pulling the nation out of shape. Whatever diverse things expansionism had meant, Manifest Destiny had been thought of as a common purpose. Now the South had Texas and it also had a war which, Bill Bowen knew, would bring in other square miles of unsettled land. But Bill Bowen, looking by the thousand at that vote of 38 to 12, may be excused for interpreting it as the South abandoning him when it had got what it wanted.

The sole practical preparation for war that had been made was the order for Commodore Sloat to seize the California ports if he should learn that war with Mexico had broken out. There had been some conversations between department heads and the appropriate committees of Congress. They had anticipated a war with Great Britain, however, and little action had come from them. Although Polk and his Cabinet had envisaged the possibility of war with Mexico from March 4, 1845, on to May, 1846, they had done nothing to prepare for it. They suffered the illusions of a nation that had not fought a war since 1814, had fought foreign wars only with the navy, and had never fought a war of conquest. They expected the irresistible sharpshooters of Yorktown and New Orleans to spring to arms: in Robert Dale Owen's phrase, "two companies of Kentucky rifles" could do the job. In June of '46 the Americans were springing to arms all right, far more of them than could be used, but no one had any idea what to do with them.

The army had no general staff to plan campaigns. It did have a military genius, Major General Winfield Scott. But Scott made no plans in advance of the war, and his first act after its outbreak was to disqualify himself by an act of insubordination toward his commander in chief. Polk retired him from command for a time and would probably have done so anyway, for he thought that Scott was too "visionary and scientific" — that he knew too much about his business. Scott wanted to equip and train an army before trying to use it, whereas the President wanted quick victories and a short war and no nonsense about logistics or discipline, which were unnecessary. And as for Polk himself — in the preparation of grand strategy he had a small army on Mexico's northern frontier, some maps, and an overwhelming ignorance not only of the conditions under which armies must operate but of the country through which his particular armies must operate. By the grace of God and the ultimate return of Winfield Scott, this equipment served him very well indeed.

They were poor maps; if they had been good ones, probably even the amateur strategists would have been deterred. If their innocence had been tarnished by knowledge of the country they proposed to campaign across they might easily have lost the war.

They were, however, passably informed about the internal politics of Mexico. So a plan of strategy developed: part desire to make sure of California (the true begetter of the war), part the hope that no fighting would prove necessary, and part a notion that the northern provinces would revolt. . . . From the Atlantic westward, these were Tamaulipas, Nuevo León, Coahuila, Chihuahua, and, on the Pacific, Sonora. North of these and a special problem were New Mexico and California. All the northern provinces were supposed to be ready to rebel against the federalist government of Mexico. Demonstrations had, in fact, occurred in some of them; Santa Anna had called attention to the shaky loyalty of Nuevo León and Tamaulipas; at the outbreak of war disturbances in Sonora were reported and they were expected to spread to Chihuahua.

So Polk decided to occupy the northern provinces and hold on, meanwhile blockading the seaports. That might do the job — with the assistance of a bribe fund, Santa Anna, civil war, and the luck of the American arms. Tamaulipas had already been invaded when Taylor occupied Matamoros. Just beyond the end of its southern coastline was Tampico, the second largest port of Mexico. Commodore Conner of the blockading squadron was ordered to occupy it; he did so and Taylor, after bungling his instructions to support Conner, finally sent some troops. As for Nuevo León and Coahuila, it was natural to expect Taylor to attend to them, for whether he should move overland or up the Rio Grande they would be square in his path. Eventually they were both occupied, when Taylor took Monterrey and Worth, back in the army with his grievances and his goose quills, took Saltillo.

So much was obvious, and Mr. Polk's gaze moved across his map to Chihuahua. (Always remember that this province was the principal market of the Santa Fe trade.) The volunteers who were pouring in so fast would be concentrated at three places, the mouth of the Rio Grande, New Orleans, and somewhere in Texas, say San Antonio. On the map a mere forefinger would reach from San Antonio to the city of Chihuahua, the capital of the province. Good: we will take Chihuahua. So General John Ellis Wool, a veteran but neither senile nor a letter writer, was ordered to lead an expedition against it down that finger-length of paper from San Antonio. Wool, an excellent officer, cold, a martinet, undertook the job but it proved impossible. After great expense, a waste of material, transport, and supplies, after a dangerous waste of time and dispersion of force, and after much hardship unnecessarily inflicted on green troops, the expedition failed. Wool had to cross not a map but a countryside — and it detoured him in a vast arc so that, when he was recalled, he was little nearer Chihuahua than he had been at San Antonio.

The Chihuahua expedition was preposterous and a failure. The expedition against the special case, New Mexico, was little less preposterous as a military conception but it did not fail. It was Polk's own ewe lamb; he had been thinking about it as far back as he had been thinking about New Mexico. And he had the assistance of knowledgeful realists, Benton and a large part of Benton's constituency, those who were interested in the Santa Fe trade. The Western press had been advising such an expedition for months, and there were those at hand who knew how to get it started.

On May 13, the day when Polk signed the war proclamation, the governor of Missouri was called upon to supply a thousand mounted volunteers (he had anticipated the summons and already had the machinery working), and Colonel Stephen Watts Kearny, commanding the First Dragoons at Fort Leavenworth, was ordered to protect the freight caravans understood to be en route to Santa Fe. But it was, or immediately became, clear to Polk that New Mexico was the true key to California and by May 16 the protection of the Santa Fe trade had become the conquest of New Mexico. Kearny was put in command of the volunteers being raised in Missouri and ordered to undertake another of Mr. Polk's bloodless conquests. (The President was supporting it with diplomacy, hoped to support it with bribes, and called in specialists in the Catholic religion to organize a propaganda arm.) By May 30, the conquest of New Mexico had become the conquest of California. Kearny (given discretionary power — apparently because he was not known to be a Whig) was ordered to organize New Mexico after he had occupied it, to determine whether he could reach California this year, and if he thought that he could, to do so. Thus the conception of an ambitious and potentially decisive campaign was fully developed in seventeen days.

It looked simple when you studied the map. It turned out to be almost as simple as it looked.

The First Dragoons were the crack regiment of the army and had been habituated to frontier service. Kearny was not only a practised frontier commander but one of the most skillful and dependable officers in the army. In the vaudeville show of swollen egoism, vanity, treachery, incompetence, rhetoric, stupidity, and electioneering which the general officers during the Mexican War display to the pensive mind, Kearny stands out as a gentleman, a soldier, a commander, a diplomat, a statesman, and a master of his job, whose only superior was Winfield Scott. He did the jobs assigned him. Since one of them involved reducing John C. Frémont's heroic dislocations, he aroused the enmity of a fiery hater, Thomas Hart Benton, and so has had less than his due from history. But he wrote no letters to the papers and he could even address his superiors in respectful prose.

Exactly two weeks after Francis Parkman drank wine with him at Fort Leavenworth, he received his first orders. At once he got to work, acquiring arms and munitions, buying transportation and supplies, arranging to send them ahead of his expedition. A frontiersman, he knew what was ahead of him; in fact, as we noted earlier, he had traveled the Oregon trail to South Pass and the Santa Fe trail from Bent's Fort back to the settlements, the preceding summer. He began forwarding supplies to Bent's Fort. But he could not buy enough of them and could not organize the service fast enough.

When he got his expedition moving, his troops were ahead of their rations most of the time.

His orders to protect the Santa Fe traders were soon supplemented by orders to stop them and to arrest some of them — Governor Armijo's wagons and those of Albert Speyer, which were known to contain powder and arms. He hurried out two companies of his Dragoons, but the traders also knew that the war had begun and were too far ahead. They were urged on by a double incentive: the blockade would insure them high prices in Mexico, since it would cut off the usual British and German competition, and the duties would be discontinued as soon as New Mexico should be conquered, so they must sell out before their competitors could get there with the army. As they hurried their trains down the trail they confidently expected New Mexico to be conquered, expected no New Mexican interference with the trade, and expected, like Mr. Polk, that the country would not rise.

Meanwhile volunteers were pouring in on Kearny at Fort Leavenworth. . . . Just as, in the same headlong eagerness, they were swarming to New Orleans and would soon be inundating Texas and Taylor's bases. The regular officers were frantically trying to do what they could without arms or equipment and without discipline. For the problems of a volunteer army were acute. The depots and bases filled with whores, sutlers, and gamblers, were already a continuous jamboree and vicious with crime. The regular officers were too few to control the volunteers and their own officers, holding their jobs by the suffrage, had little disposition to try. Already there were indecorums at Matamoros, which would presently become an unsystematic but recurrent pillage and murder. Taylor, who was running for the Presidency, lacked Scott's willingness to impose martial law and so destroyed any chance there may have been of the conquest of the northern provinces by persuasion.

A Maryland regiment on the way to the Rio Grande by transport fought with fists and knives, was sometimes on the edge of mutiny, and suffered attrition from delirium tremens. Arrived at its base it was soon quarreling with an Ohio regiment, went for its muskets, and lined up to settle matters with the Buckeyes for good. Quick work by some officers prevented the slaughter but there was not even a court of inquiry, though Taylor spoke of one as the proper procedure. The occurrence was to be duplicated or approximated many times. Lieutenant George Gordon Meade watched the arrival and behavior of the volunteers and his precise mind was shocked. "They (the volunteers) have killed five or six innocent people walking in the streets, for no other object than their own amusement; to be sure they are always drunk, and are in a measure irresponsible for their conduct. They rob and steal the cattle and corn of the poor farmers, and in fact act more like a body of hostile Indians than of civilized whites." Presently two members of the West Point Class of '46, George Brinton McClellan and Thomas Jonathan Jackson, who were in this much alike, that they thirsted for glory even more intensely than Frémont, would go beyond Meade's apprehension to contempt. It was McClellan, though it could easily have been Jackson, who spoke of the "cursed volunteers" and was always seeing them "from the general down to the dirtiest rascal of the filthy crew" as "scared out of their wits (if they had any)." By autumn there was not only a cleavage but a feud between regulars and volunteers. And on the whole the regulars were right. Lieutenant Meade summed up at Saltillo, after a Kentucky regiment had been ordered to the rear in disgrace, for rape and, following the Mexican civilians' retaliation, indiscriminate murder: —

> Without a modification of the manner in which they are officered, they are almost useless in an offensive war. They are sufficiently well drilled for practical purposes, and are, I believe, brave and will fight as gallantly as any man, but they are a set of Goths and Vandals, without discipline, laying waste to the country wherever we go, making us a terror to innocent people, and if there is any spirit or energy in the Mexicans, will finally raise the people against us, who now are perfectly neutral. . . . They cannot take care of themselves; the hospitals are crowded with them, they die like sheep; they waste their provisions, requiring twice as much to supply them as regulars do. They plunder the poor inhabitants of everything they can lay their hands on, and shoot them when they remonstrate, and if one of their number happens to get into a drunken brawl and is killed, they run over the country, killing all the poor innocent people they find in their way, to avenge, as they say, the murder of their brother.

Kearny escaped this kind of trouble. His volunteers were a homogeneous lot and he could give them the discipline of the Santa Fe trail. He was able to work them so hard and move them so fast, and through such a barren country, that the amusements of single men in barracks had to be forgone. The kind of work he had to do did not require the West Point ritual of close order and tent-peg severity, and his ego did not trouble him. . . . A correspondent of the St. Louis *Reveillé* saw him go up the gangplank of a steamboat at Fort Leavenworth and instruct the sentry to prevent the volunteers from following. No use; they had to see what was going on and rushed the sentry. One of them apologized, slapping his commander on the back: "You don't git off from us, old hoss! for by Ingin corn we'll go plum through fire and thunder with you. What'll you drink, General? [He had been promised promotion but his commission was not yet signed.] Don't be back'ard! Sing out!" If the invitation had been made to Lieutenant McClellan or the chrysalis of Stonewall Jackson, there would have been hours of full-pack drill in the sun, if not a general court. But Kearny, the correspondent says, tried for only a moment to look grave, had to laugh, and ended by asking the Missourian to drink wine with him. Wine, in the opinion of the soldier, warn't worth shucks, was only fitten for women. And another gaping youth chimed in, "Why in thunder don't you go for the corn juice, General? It's the only stuff for a military feller to travel on." . . . There is a distinct foreshadowing of Lee's Army of Northern Virginia or Sherman's Army of the Tennessee.

They were mostly Missourians, though a sprinkling of recruits from the Eastern and Southern states drifted in on the tide. They were mostly farm boys, though the towns and cities sent their share. The Ladies' Aid gave them a pie supper on the lawn, the mayor or the schoolmaster quoted classical hexameters at them and sprayed them with tags from Sam Adams and Patrick Henry, they wandered down back lanes for a last half hour with Lucy in June dusk, and they were off for the Halls of Montezuma. Ignorant, eager for glories which had only the haziest definition, they were the frontier democracy taking a military phase at the moment when their cousins, in another phase, were toiling up the Oregon trail toward Fort Laramie.

Kearny had written to Lieutenant Colonel Ethan Allen Hitchcock, asking the philosopher to be his inspector general. But Hitchcock, on leave in St. Louis, was still being treated by Dr. Beaumont, thought his army career was over, and buried himself in Spinoza, Swedenborg, and Strauss's *Vie de Jésus*. (He would recover by the end of summer, join General Scott, and make himself invaluable in the campaign for Mexico City.) The recruits arrived with horses and in the formations given them on the village green but otherwise unorganized and unequipped. Kearny had his officers equip and drill them, teach them to make camp, give them on this gentler prairie some of the lessons they would desperately need later on.

Meanwhile he was concentrating his own regiment, the First Dragoons, which had been dispersed in frontier cantonments. The War Department got part of it away from him, including Lieutenant Richard Ewell, a blend of Buffalo Bill and the Chevalier Bayard who would have fitted the Doniphan expedition perfectly but instead got himself celebrated under Taylor and Scott. (And carried out of this war a remembrance which made him, in 1861, the only Confederate on record who hoped aloud that the Federals would not turn up a chap he had watched in Mexico, a man named Grant.) But Kearny was in time to arrest the theft of Troops B and K, at Fort Atkinson and Fort Crawford, which started for Fort Leavenworth under their respective commanders, both "unexpressibly disappointed" at being ordered on what they took to be a sideshow outside the big tent. One of them concerns us, Captain Philip St. George Cooke, who was another reason why the First Dragoons were the best regiment in the army. A Virginian, Cooke was the brother of John Rogers Cooke the constitutional lawyer, and of Dr. John Esten Cooke, the celebrated antagonist of Dr. Drake at the Louisville Medical Institute. He was an uncle of Philip Pendleton Cooke, the ill-starred romantic poet, John Esten Cooke, the novelist, and, by marriage, John Pendleton Kennedy. He fathered one Confederate general, John R. Cooke, and his daughter married Jeb Stuart but Cooke was to stay in the Union when the time came. Something of the family's poetic impulse had accompanied him through years of chasing Indians on the frontier. He had made his adolescent journal into a book which is full of gothic moonlight, sentiments that Frémont would have found noble, and a literary pathos hard to associate with as hard-bitten an officer as the army had. He did not know it but he was going to take charge of some Mormons.

Pretty soon Kearny had enough soldiers to shape the regiment he had been ordered to organize, the First Missouri Mounted Volunteers. As volunteers, they were entitled to elect their officers. Fine! a ballot box in the Halls of Montezuma. Lacking stumps, the orators climbed ammunition cases and promised their constituents to fix the sutlers' prices, look tenderly to the rations, keep the moral tone high, and resist the tyrannies of West Point. Then they were off in the voting procedure of the emigrant trains, lining up behind their candidates. The town of Liberty, Missouri, had been providing free tavern breakfasts to advertise its leading citizen, a private of Company C who had once been a militia general. His principal opponent "had been a lieutenant-colonel in the Florida [Seminole] war and had not won a very enviable name for himself; and when he came to mention his name in connection with that war [during which some Missouri militia had run away], some one from the crowd informed him that it would have been better to keep that fact a secret. The vote was taken and was given almost unanimously in favor of" the town of Liberty's candidate. The First Missouri Mounted Volunteers had found their ideal colonel in Alexander W. Doniphan.

They elected as lieutenant colonel Charles F. Ruff, and as major, William Gilpin, either of whom the West Pointers would have been glad to see in Doniphan's place. Ruff had been for five years a lieutenant in the First Dragoons, and now had ahead of him a distinguished military career. Gilpin was an amazing man who, like Doniphan, had inevitably gravitated to leadership in the frontier democracy. Educated in England and the University of Pennsylvania, tutored by Nathaniel Hawthorne, he had gone to West Point, where he was tutored by George Gordon Meade and Montgomery Blair, and had served in the Seminole War. He resigned from the army and practised law at Independence. He was a frontiersman by instinct and a museum specimen of expansionism. He vibrated with the premonition of empire, saw the great central valley as the focus of all future civilization, predicted and charted the future of Kansas City, and so competently understood the westward currents that he had insisted on accompanying the second Frémont expedition. His campaigns under Doniphan will be noted here but we cannot describe his bloodier campaign down the trail in '47. After the war he lived further romance. His visions of the great valley swelled out in a kind of aurora borealis, which produced two books of an amazing mixture of incantation and inspired prediction comparable to nothing in our literature except Dr. Drake's earlier treatises. He was a tireless agitator for the Pacific railway and became the first governor of Colorado Territory, where he mightily served his nation by organizing a regiment which helped save the Southwest for the Union. His administration was shadowed by financial manipulations not ascribable to him, which got still farther into the imagination of Wild West fiction. After it he came back to Kansas City and still gaudier dreams of empire, and he appears in the autobiography of our last link with the age of heroes, William Jackson, the pioneer photographer, who married his daughter, as an old gentleman boring everybody with monologues about a railroad to Alaska which was to subjugate the whole world to his home town.

At last Kearny got his command organized: the Army of the West. The core of it was six troops of his own regiment, the First Dragoons. The rest were, in Cooke's phrase, "all raw volunteers." Doniphan's First Missouri was 856 strong, eight companies, when it left Fort Leavenworth.[2] The rest of the Missourians had been organized into a battalion of infantry, 145 men in two companies; two companies of light artillery, about 250 men; and a spare troop of cavalry from St. Louis, 107 strong, called the Laclede Rangers. There were the usual staff troops and a detachment of topographical engineers.

A detachment of the First Missouri left Fort Leavenworth on June 16, convoying a hundred wagons and eight hundred cattle toward Bent's Fort. On June 22 two troops of the Dragoons and two of the First Missouri sprinted down the trail to join the pursuit of Speyer and Armijo. On June 26 the real start was made, Ruff taking four or five companies in the advance, Doniphan following with two companies which were to gather up all the traders' wagons. The topographical engineers set out on June 27, and on the next two days all the troops remaining at the fort got under way, Kearny commanding them in person. On July 6, two troops of Dragoons that had been upriver hurried out to catch up with him. The army did not come together as a whole till they reached Bent's Fort.

These are the troops who gave substance to Polk's fantasy. No other troops except supply trains would go down the trail till Sterling Price took the Second Missouri to Santa Fe. We will pick Kearny up a few miles to the southwest, but we must first turn back to another officer of the First Dragoons, Captain James Allen of Company I, whom Kearny had detached to enlist some soldiers from the Mormons.

All through 1845 Brigham Young had had agents in the East, soliciting aid for Israel's emigration. They had got contributions from many private citizens who were appalled by the Burnings, but persistent efforts had not succeeded in interesting the government. Over a year ago, interviewed by the Illinois Congressmen, Polk had spoken consoling generalities and refused action. Now, however, Polk was moving upon California — and so were the Mormons.

The energetic, rhetorical, and ambiguous editor Samuel Brannan had been instructed to take Eastern Mormons to California by sea. In January he went to Washington to solicit government help for Israel. In Washington there is always a Man to See, and in '46 this insider was Amos Kendall. The model of all Brain Trusters, Kendall had been one of the intellectuals (George Bancroft was another) who had given Jacksonian democracy its program. A member of Jackson's Kitchen Cabinet, author of many of Jackson's state papers, ringmaster behind the scenes, Postmaster General when a scandal had to be cleaned up, for years one of the most influential of Democratic editors, he had thrown his support to Van Buren in '44 and so had had no favors from Mr. Polk. So, setting a model that was to endure, he had begun to practise as a collector of claims against the government, and more recently had insured his old age by becoming the fiscal manager of Samuel F. B. Morse. Arriving in Washington, Brannan ran foul of an adventurer named Benson, who saw an opportunity and explained to him the stern purpose of the administration to prevent the Mormons from going west. Governments can be manipulated by those in the know, however, and for a consideration Mr. Benson would take charge of the Mormon interest. He would see the Man to See.

There followed a series of consultations from which Brannan emerged with a conviction (or possibly a story to tell Brigham) that the government had been manipulated, a contract drawn by Amos Kendall, and Benson's assurance (or again a story to tell Brigham) that the President of the United States was a sleeping partner in a land fraud. The contract represented that the government would permit and assist the emigration and protect the Mormons from their enemies — and stipulated that when they should be granted government land in Upper California (where in January the government had no land), every alternate section and town lot was to be the property of the contracting syndicate, Benson, Kendall, and the sleeping Polk. Brannan forwarded the contract to Brigham Young, wrote that Israel now had a listening post and interested friends in the center of the government, and sailed for Yerba Buena with nearly 250 Saints on February 4, the very day when Israel started crossing the Mississippi from Nauvoo. Brigham, however, had not been born yesterday. He understood Mr. Benson at a thousand miles, and the Council voted no contract.[3]

The situation had changed fundamentally by May, when Elder Jesse C. Little, head of the Eastern States Mission, set out for Washington from New Hampshire on Brigham's order, bearing letters of introduction to George Bancroft. He was instructed to apply for any kind of help the government might be pleased to offer. He was to suggest that the Mormons might volunteer troops for the occupation of California, might employ their teams and wagons transporting army supplies, might erect forts in the Indian country and garrison them, or might build roads and operate ferries along the trails. Brigham was eager to milk Mr. Emerson's poor, good cow, even while he was fulminating against its persecutions.

On his way to Washington, Elder Little attended to his priestly duties, convening special "conferences" (the Mormon term for church conventions) of the Saints. So the Lord inspired a young Gentile with curiosity, and Thomas Leiper Kane, out for a morning walk, strolled into the Conference at Philadelphia. Elder Little was a mighty exhorter and the young man's heart was moved. . . . He was a romantic and neurotic young man, a sentimental humanitarian, the kind of miniature Gerrit Smith who loved all good works and by the hundred obstructed the path of serious reformers, and he would have greatly enjoyed himself at Brook Farm. He was the brother of Elisha Kane, who as an arctic explorer and leader of heroic last chances would be the Henry Stanley or Charles Lindbergh of the 1850's. More to the point, his father was John Kenzer Kane, the attorney general of Pennsylvania, leader of the bar and elder statesman of the Democracy, friend and political ally of Polk, who would elevate him to the federal bench before the end of June.

Young Kane listened to the sufferings of the Saints and at the end of the meeting took Elder Little home and sought further instruction. The Lord gave the missionary eloquence and two days later Kane announced that he would go west, share Israel's tribulations, and accompany Brigham to the Rocky Mountains. Pity jangled his unstable nerves and he fell ill. Little cured him by prophecy, the cure smelled of miracle, and in the end he set out with Little to visit Israel. He reached it at Council Bluffs and here his emotions boiled over and he again fell ill. The Saints nursed him back to health but he lacked strength for the migration. (He later claimed to have convinced Young, at this time, that Great Salt Lake Valley was the best place for Zion. The claim is absurd.) He presented a dagger to Porter Rockwell, the great Danite, and it may be that Brigham baptized him into the faith. Thereafter he was not only a propagandist but an agent for Mormonry in high places. He took to the lyceum circuit with a lecture which was the best propaganda the Church had ever had. And in 1857 when James Buchanan, President at last and taking no joy of it, sent Albert Sidney Johnston's army against Utah, Kane hurried west and worked out a compromise which permitted both the President and the Prophet to save a certain amount of face.

But in May of '46 Kane's importance was that his connections could open doors to Elder Little. Little carried to Washington a letter to Vice President Dallas, who put him in touch with various members of Congress, Buchanan, Secretary of War Marcy, and finally Polk himself. The opportune Mr. Benson showed up again and trotted out his Amos Kendall, who showed Little the wonders of the telegraph and the National Fair and got him the privileges of the floor in the House of Representatives. Polk gave him encouragement and finally led him, after a grandiloquent letter in which Little recited the loyalties of the Twelve Apostles, to suggest that a battalion for the defense of California be enlisted from the Saints. The President welcomed the patriotic offer, the Cabinet expressed satisfaction, Little hurried off a message of congratulation to Brigham, and all Mormons who could vote this year would vote Democratic.

A typical Polk maneuver. The President neglected to tell Little and his sponsors that, a week before he accepted the offer of Mormon volunteers, he had instructed Colonel Kearny to enroll "a few hundred" Mormons in his Army of the West. Polk had taken thought of that large body of emigrants who were on the right flank of his invasion and had no reason to love the United States. He made sure that Kearny should not take enough Mormons to endanger his command, but it was desirable, as his diary explicitly says, "to conciliate them, attach them to our country, & prevent them from taking part against us." Little's petition gave him a chance to deserve the gratitude of the Saints, and he got it. The most fulsome adjectives distinguished him from other recent Presidents, all of whom burned in hell every Sunday morning, till the expedition of 1857 prodded Brigham to represent the enlistment of the Mormon Battalion as just one additional persecution in the long list of Satan's buffetings.

Kearny was gratified by the order because it would add some infantry to an army which, Missourians being averse to service on foot, was topheavy with cavalry. Just before he left Fort Leavenworth with the Dragoons, he had an interview with Kane and sent Captain James Allen to take the offer to Brigham Young, who had reached the Missouri at Council Bluffs.

It reached Brigham with his central quandary still unsolved. It had become quite clear that he could not get the whole Church over the mountains this year — on May 21 eight hundred men reported that they had less than two weeks' provisions — but he and the Twelve were still laboring to work out some plan that would get a considerable party to Zion. Clearly, many would have to stay at the permanent camps that stretched across Iowa from the Mississippi, and many more would have to stay on the Missouri. But the daily agitation was to form a party of picked specialists, perhaps five hundred strong, to send them "over the mountains" and to get other parties farther along the trail than the Missouri, to prepare the greater migration of '47. The party of specialists was to find a resting place for Israel in the Great Basin or, if none could be found there after all this planning, might go on to California, where Brannan would be and whither many of the Saints still thought they were all going. It was also to consider setting up another outpost like Brannan's, on Vancouver Island. The other parties might occupy such places as Grand Island on the Platte where they, like the advance party, could plant crops for next year's movement.

The proposal of an advance emigration to the Great Basin this year divided the Twelve and agitated the faithful. It kept up without cessation or settlement and Brigham, who put his full strength behind it, had to deal with a more effective public opinion than ever opposed him again. Sometimes the proposal was to devote Israel's goods to supporting an advance of five hundred families; more often the specialists were to leave their families behind for Israel to take care of till next year. Both ideas brought consternation to the Saints, and the alternative one which developed, that a smaller party headed by the Twelve should go, was just as alarming. There was the most serious division of opinion, doubts about the future, and inability to see how any satisfactory program could be worked out this year — or even next year.

Brigham required little time to understand the importance of the government's desire for volunteers and to readjust all his plans. He saw at once that the Mormon Battalion would both prohibit any large emigration this year and save Israel. He professed to find oppression and serious danger in it, but he was merely bargaining for official permission to camp, build blockhouses, cut timber, and raise crops in the Indian lands. Allen assumed the authority to grant such permission, believing that Brigham's consent hung on it, but it was only a tip. For Brigham had decided. The government Israel was fleeing from would take Israel to its sanctuary.

That, the free transportation for five hundred men and the sum in cash for their pay and allowances which would solve the financial problem of the main emigration, was unquestionably the weightiest reason for Young's decision. Almost as important, however, was a basic reason of strategy and diplomatics. The outbreak of war made it certain that Zion, the land of Israel's inheritance, would be under American jurisdiction, not Mexican as it had been when the preparations for the exodus had been made. It would be of the greatest importance for the Church to locate there by the encouragement and permission of the United States and after answering a demand for patriotic service. The Mormons would not only be the "old settlers," the first arrivals, the ones who broke the wilderness and so could dictate to those who followed after, but they would have the United

States considerably in their debt for the conquest of this very country.

Nevertheless, the withdrawal of five hundred men, among the most active of the Church, would create the most serious problems. It at once forbade any large-scale attempt to get "over the mountains" this year. (Young still intended to get someone there, and as late as July 14 repeated his orders to his farthest outpost, Bishop George Miller's party, to make the trip, though he rescinded them on August 1. Even then, however, he still hoped to send a small party under the Twelve to locate Zion.) And also, the withdrawal of so many men put not only the care of their families but also the performance of their duties as teamsters, farmers, hunters, and priests on those who stayed behind. A more stringent co-operation was called for, and Young sent out letters and messengers to accelerate the work of the way stations and to prepare the final evacuation of Nauvoo, which he still expected would not have to occur till the following spring.

So he started raising volunteers. The Saints began to love the government when they were bidden to, but they required some psychological adjustment after years of robustly cursing it. Was this Gospel? "I confess I was glad to learn of war against the United States," Hosea Stout's journal says, and other journals say the same thing more venomously, "and was in hopes that it might never end untill they were entirely destroyed for they had driven us into the wilderness & was now laughing at our calamities." Furthermore, families already strained with fatigue, disease, and malnutrition, and on the eve of the unknown passage of the desert, were not eager to send fathers or sons on a military expedition far away. Brigham set up a flag, had the Apostles act as recruiting agents, and—got only a handful of volunteers. He announced that this new plan was really Gospel, hurried epistles saying the same thing to Mount Pisgah and Garden Grove, and finally lost patience. He ordered the Saints to volunteer. If the young men did not come forward, he announced, he would draft old men, and if he could not get enough of them he would fill up the ranks with women. Grace was given his flock and the Mormon Battalion was formed, five companies, a little over five hundred men. A good many wives went along, some entire (and large) family organizations, a number of grandfathers, and a flock of children. The Battalion was an excellent organization for the service asked of it, on the whole, but when Cooke took command, after Allen died, he had to weed out so many cripples, invalids, and old men that it was reduced nearly a third.

Young diffidently offered to name the officers. Offer accepted, and by July 18 the Mormon Battalion was ready to march from Council Bluffs to Fort Leavenworth to be mustered in. Young gave them his sacerdotal blessing and promised them, quite safely, that none would be killed in battle. He even pledged his right hand that all would return alive — if they obeyed counsel. It would be wise, however, to wear the holy Temple underwear, which was invulnerable to hostile weapons. Let them treat prisoners civilly and avoid taking life except as a last resource. Do not dance with Gentiles, burn your decks of cards, carry a Bible and a *Book of Mormon,* do not preach in public except when people desire to hear, keep your observances, obey the priesthood among you. Be humble, teach charity, eschew profanity, and every man who accepts counsel will return alive. . . . Counsel turned into a dancing party and the daughters of Israel were, in Thomas Kane's eyes, extraordinarily comely and decorous, in neatly darned white stockings, bright petticoats, and starched chemisettes. "Light hearts, lithe figures, and light feet had it their own way from an early hour till after the sun had dipped behind the sharp sky-line of the Omaha hills. Silence was then called, and a well cultivated mezzo-soprano belonging to a young lady with fair face and dark eyes gave with quartette accompaniment a little song, the notes of which I have been unsuccessful in repeated efforts to obtain since — a version of the text, touching to all earthly wanderers, 'By the rivers of Babylon we sat down and wept, we wept when we remembered Zion.' "

On July 21 and 22 they marched for Fort Leavenworth, the Army of the Lord in the oddest phase it had yet had. Their commander knew of no route to California from Santa Fe and supposed that they would be back here presently to go by way of South Pass.[4] They would come dangerously close to their enemies, the Missourians, and they wondered if their enlistment as American soldiers would stay the enmity of the Pukes. Rumors reached them that the Pukes were indeed arming to receive them, but their apprehension was much less than that which their approach produced. The Missouri border, sufficiently excited by the summer's development, got a new panic, and a flood of warnings and petitions poured in on Polk, Marcy, and Benton. Even the governor of Missouri solemnly warned the administration that Missourians and Mormons hated one another much more intensely than they could be brought to hate Mexicans, and predicted an outbreak of mobbery and insurrection. But, humble men who were quite willing to shift from the land-seeking to the military phase of expansion at the prophet's command, they trudged southeastward to an accompaniment of miracles that strengthened their hearts. They reached Fort Leavenworth on August 1 and were made soldiers of the United States.

Back at Council Bluffs Brigham Young attacked the job of reorganizing a migrating people who had given up five hundred able-bodied males, preparing for the winter, gathering in the crops and laying in supplies, battling hunger and disease and discontent and heresy, and fitting together an organization for next summer's travel to the Great Basin. The job strained even his genius for management, but now he could go about it with assurance. Out of the hands of the enemy he had snatched safety. He had sent agents to receive the volunteers' commutation allowance for clothing, more than twenty-one thousand dollars, and would send others to intercept the march at Santa Fe and elsewhere to collect their pay. (Perhaps fifty thousand dollars more, though by no means all of it went into the common funds.) And if five hundred laborers had been taken from the vineyard, still there would be so many less to feed this winter and transport west next summer. The ways of the Lord were mysterious altogether, and it was not for Brigham Young to question them. Israel needed wagons, stock, supplies, clothing, money, and if the Lord pleased to provide them by government subsidy, Brigham could see the joke. Some of his pious following had already been vouchsafed a miracle of quails, and now here was manna.

IX
The Image on the Sun

ON June 5, three weeks before he got his expedition moving from Fort Leavenworth, Colonel Kearny sent Captain Moore with Companies C and G of the First Dragoons hurrying down the Santa Fe trail to detain some traders who had left Independence two weeks before. Tom Fitzpatrick went with them, Jim Clyman's old messmate and brigade leader, once Jed Smith's partner, once a partner in the Rocky Mountain Fur Company, Carson's instructor in the mountain craft, twice Frémont's guide. He was one of the greatest mountain men, perhaps the greatest. Carson was the focus of Frémont's book and so got the publicity, and Jim Bridger was about to begin the service in yellow-back novels that would insure his immortality along with Kit. But Fitzpatrick was fully as skilled in the craft and perhaps had more intelligence than either. He was an extremely valuable addition to the Army of the West.

The day after Moore's detachment set out, Kearny learned from Captain Waldo of the Missouri Volunteers, who was a Santa Fe trader, that one of the outfits Moore was pursuing belonged to a brother of Armijo's, the governor of New Mexico, and had some $70,000 worth of the governor's goods. Along the Missouri frontier there was a belief, supported by the traders who had wintered in Santa Fe and had now returned, that Armijo would not oppose the invasion, and this looked like a chance to assist his pacific impulses. So Kearny hurried out Lieutenant Noble with fifty more Dragoons to bid Moore hurry even faster. On June 22, as soon as the volunteers could be equipped and given the rudiments of drill, he dispatched Companies A and D of Doniphan's regiment, under Waldo, to reinforce Moore.

Moore traveled fast but could not overtake Armijo. A number of other wagon trains traveled far enough ahead of the army to outdistance the pursuit. They had been leaving Independence since early May and most of them had been moving fast. Moore ordered those he passed to rendezvous at Pawnee Fork and wait for instructions, and hurried on. He chased his quarry as far as the

Cimarron Crossing (where they turned down the Cimarron Fork of the trail), then gave up the pursuit and went back to the Pawnee Fork, where he camped, chaperoned the arriving trains, and waited for the army to catch up with him.

Santa Fe was nearly eight hundred miles out from Independence, or about a hundred and fifty miles farther than Fort Laramie. The journey, however, was much easier. The route was mostly through plains country, there were mountains to cross only in the last stage, and though there were deserts and bad ones, they were on the last leg and (except on the Cimarron Fork) were not so difficult as those the emigrant trail had to cross. Water was not often out of reach, there was abundant grass, and the route was fixed — had even been surveyed — so that there were few detours or cutoffs.

On the other hand, the Santa Fe trail had had blood on it from the beginning. Early in the eighteenth century a Spanish expedition had been massacred on its central marches, and from then on Spaniards, Mexicans, New Mexicans, Frenchmen, Texans, and Americans had regularly perished at one another's hands or those of the Indians. Parts of it had been the disputed frontier between Texas and New Mexico. New Mexicans and the *Comancheros,* whites who traded with the Comanche in stolen Texas horses and stolen Chihuahua and Sonora mules, had plentifully sprinkled it with blood. Guerrillas of both sides raided one another along the trail, freebooters and filibusters fought along it, and all of them fought the Indians.

The southern end of the trail was within striking distance of the Apache, a vigorous and cruel race, the eastern stretches were under claim of the Pawnee during the days of their vigor and ferocity, before whiskey and smallpox had tamed them. The rest of it was more dangerous, in that it was a no man's land where many tribes raided. The southern Arapaho, more populous than their northern kin and fully as dangerous, might be encountered at any time. The southern Cheyenne were also here, a powerful and valorous people, but in our period they were not troublesome, having been pacified by the Bent brothers, with whom they kept their word. There remained the most terrible savages of the plains, the Comanche. The Comanche were not better horsemen or better warriors than other plains tribes: probably the Blackfeet, the Sioux, or the Cheyenne would have defeated them in the ultimate battle to the death which history, so prodigal of Indian wars, omitted to bring about. But they had organized marauding on a larger scale than any other tribe, and they were not only professional marauders and murderers, they were also practising sadists. Their raiding parties regularly went hundreds of miles into Mexico and Texas, cleaning out the border, depopulating the settlements, and taking back horses and cattle by the thousand. These herds were the staple of their trade with whites and Indians alike, but they also did a profitable business in white captives, Mexican, Texan, and American, whom they brought back by the score from their raids. These they held for ransom or sold into slavery; when they could not turn a profit on them, they enjoyed themselves. No one has ever exaggerated the Comanche tortures. The authenticated accounts fill thousands of pages, and some are altogether unreadable for men with normal nerves. They had great skill in pain and cruelty was their catharsis. In short, the Comanche killed and tortured more whites than any other Indians in the West, stole more horses and cattle, were a greater danger. With their allies, the Kiowa, they were for many years what the title of a recent book calls them, a barrier to the settlement of the plains.

There was never a time when the unwary might not be attacked by Comanche on the Santa Fe trail, but in '46 they were comparatively quiet there. The war made their customary victims, the Texans and Mexicans, even more vulnerable and they raided southward. Their herds prospered, they got many women to rape in gangs and many children who could be entertainingly dismembered. In May, while the great raid was actually in progress, commissioners from Polk signed a treaty with them at the Brazos River, and they sent a delegation of chiefs to view the white man's medicine lodge in Washington and to pay a number of ceremonial calls on their White Father. And a few months later Zachary Taylor had to raise new companies of Rangers to shove them back toward the border of Texas. They were back on the trail again in '47, more profit-minded than ever and, since the army supply trains were staffed by tenderfeet, more daring.[1]

Apart from the Indian menace, travel on the Santa Fe trail was necessarily easier than on the Oregon trail for it was conducted by professionals. This was the commerce of the prairies, not a migration of individualists, and the best procedures were enforced. The techniques were adapted from those of the mountain men, who, in fact, had first organized the trade. The wagon trains were more closely directed than those that traveled the northern trail, discipline was semi-military, the routines were established and there was seldom any reason to vary them. Competition between traders sometimes produced incidents at a ford or a water hole, and once the mountains were crossed it was every man for himself, but in general the relations of the trail were amiable. Beyond Council Grove trains traveled in close formation, in two parallel lines usually, in four lines where they could. The corral was formed at night, and messes were organized on a caste basis. The trip was so short — between forty-five and fifty days from Independence to Santa Fe — there was no danger of supplies running out. No trader stinted his employes and much of the route was buffalo country. Business sagacity supplied ample replacements of oxen, mules, and horses. Late or early crossings might be uncomfortable and occasionally hazardous, but in the season anyone who could take heat and sandstorms in his stride and was on the alert for Indians need not suffer.

In '46 the trade was stimulated by the war, rather than hampered, though the trains were six months later than usual in arriving at Chihuahua and the towns beyond it. The vast wagons, twice the size of the emigrant wagons, crawled down the trail behind the blubbering oxen quite as usual, except that there were more of them, they were under military guard, and the traffic was increased by the army supply trains. (Military freight wagons were small.) The Santa Fe trail was much busier than it had ever been before: the regular trade, Kearny's army, his trains and those of his supports, Price's Second Missouri, the Mormon Battalion, the developing service of supply, scouts, surveyors, couriers, expresses, ambulances, detachments of discharged and invalided soldiers. In this area Manifest Destiny took the shape of a large-scale freight operation.

When the Laclede Rangers, a hundred St. Louis volunteers, arrived at Fort Leavenworth it was too late in the day for them to be mustered in. Colonel Kearny invited the officers to dine with him but could not entertain the whole outfit — and army regulations forbade the feeding of civilians. As heroes, they were willing to die in the Halls of Montezuma but they wanted to live to get there. So the officers, returning from an excellent dinner, found their command preparing to take the post apart. Fast thinking was called for and Captain Hudson, the lawyer who had raised the company, made an oration. He waved not only the flag of freedom but the silk guidon stitched by fair fingers in the homeland, and the Rangers cheered. "Yes," he bellowed, "we shall knock at the gates of Santa Fe as Ethan Allen knocked at the gates of Ticonderoga, and to the question 'Who's there?' we shall reply 'Open these gates in the name of the great Jehovah and the Laclede Rangers.'" Tumultuous applause. The captain soared on, "But suppose the fellows inside should call out, 'Are you the same Laclede Rangers who went whining round Fort Leavenworth in search of a supper?'" Hudson knew his Missourians and there was no mutiny.

This reminiscence, by Lieutenant Richard Smith Elliott of the Rangers, gives the tone of the Army of the West. It was the damnedest army. It could do nothing well except march and fight, and would not do those by the numbers. For a while, till they learned to respect the unalterable, the West Pointers who had to oversee it would willingly have murdered most of its components. Kearny made his subalterns keep their shock within bounds but even he was sometimes startled out of wisdom. He was once injudicious enough to reprove Captain Reid's company for not wearing coats. Since they had been on half-rations for weeks it was not an auspicious moment, and Captain Reid replied that they had enlisted to fight for their country, not to dress for it. Kearny held his peace, and the army never bothered about the externals of discipline. They were not its forte.

They were volunteers, they were farmers mostly, they were incredibly young, they were Missourians and frontiersmen — close kin to the Big Bear of Arkansaw. All good armies grouch; probably none has ever bellyached so continuously as this one. They groused about their officers, their equipment, the food, the service regulations, the climate, the trail, the future. They would accept direction or command no more easily here than at home, and were always assaulting their noncoms on the ground that Joe's stripes could not neutralize his native stupidity and did not sanction him to put on airs. They howled derision of the officers whenever it was safe and frequently when it wasn't, made fantastic plots against the most inflexible of them, and when a vacancy occurred resolved to elect no one except from the rank of private. They abominated neatness, they hated the routine of guard duty and the care of horses, they straggled worse than any other troops in history that would fight. Till the army was concentrated at Bent's Fort, its component parts were just where whim took them — a battalion strung out for five miles while the individual soldier wasted ammunition on imaginary antelope, or three quarters of it marching in a clump with the guard just to see what the country was like.

They were extremely uncomfortable till they learned the mechanics of soldiering. Patriotic dedication and the bright dream of glory got smothered in the first day's profanity. Their equipment was incomplete and faulty. Boots didn't fit and blisters burned one's heels but were no worse than the sores made by pack straps. Saddles were rudimentary, made running sores on the horses' backs, and seemed designed to split the rider lengthwise. The cavalry saber was a purely decorative weapon, useless against any possible enemy, which was always whacking one's back or head. The first few days saw the only rain they would encounter till they reached the mountains and initiated them in the pinch of sodden saddles, daylong drenching, water-soaked blankets, cold food, and muddy underdrawers. Captain Fischer's artillery company, which had been recruited from German immigrants in St. Louis, was particularly inept, always in difficulty, and lurched across the prairies under a canopy of half-literate complaint. It never really learned its job, had to be left on guard duty at Santa Fe, and was the butt of everyone's derision. But other organizations needed time to become more expert or less dolorous.

The West Pointers moaned over the simple awkwardness of boys who were grappling with strangeness, and had to retreat upon the simple assumption of all military life, that though soldiers may be fighting men they are also children. Issued a day's rations at dawn, they would eat it all for breakfast, grouching about having to do their own cooking, or throw away what they could not eat and then, at night, curse God, Polk, Kearny, and Doniphan who required patriots to go supperless. Some would replace the water in their canteens with whiskey, sip it through torrid hours, and have to ride retching in the wagons. Or they would drink bad water till their bellies swelled, and have to crawl into the grass and lie foundered for hours. They knew the management of horses on farms but resented the cavalryman's subjection to the well-being of his mount, and took such wretched care of theirs that the officers had to hold classes of instruction. Kearny anticipated that, coupled with the probable failure of supplies, this bad management would give him an army of infantry from Santa Fe on.

However, he had a job to do and he drove them hard. He was fortunate in having Doniphan, colonel by suffrage of free electors, a drawling uncle to farm boys who were far from home, seldom or never in uniform, unfenced by discipline, always approachable, forever calling privates Jim or Charlie, a master of impromptu exhortation. The boys looked at the colonel, lounging his huge frame beside some poker game or amiably explaining that Joe had to go on guard tonight because Elmer had done his stint last night, and didn't yield to that fantasy of running a West Pointer through. They dug in and marched. Fifteen miles was a standard day's travel on the prairies but it was too slow going for Kearny. He demanded twenty miles a day, twenty-five, twenty-eight, thirty, sometimes thirty-two. The troops keened but took it — took it, in fact, better than the horses, which weakened on grain and developed the vicious ailments of their species. And the infantry took it best of all. Companies A and B customarily forged ahead of the cavalry they were attached to and, though they cursed the inhumanity of their officers, took pride in their mileage. Their lips parched in the prairie wind, the sun nauseated them, the wagons and ambulances were always picking up some who had not stood the pace, they were sure that Kearny was a tyrant, but they made camp some hours before the cavalry and turned out to boo them in great content when the tired beasts sagged in at twilight. Their legs swelled at the shin with a queer distemper, which turned out to be periostitis, the common splint they were accustomed to treat in plow horses. College athletes who are worked too hard are familiar with it today, and the red-hot band it clamped along the shin made no holiday of the march.[2]

Most of the expedition struck the Santa Fe trail at Elm Grove or Willow Springs. (The first rumor of the enemy's approach had occurred on the Waukarusa, seven hundred miles from the nearest Mexican.) From there on they took the hard-packed, familiar road of the traders — Council Grove, Diamond Springs, the Arkansas at Great Bend, Pawnee Rock, the Pawnee Fork, the lower crossing (which they did not make), Chouteau's Island. After the rains the country dried out so that wagons and caissons got mired only at the streams, which dwindled and were farther apart. They left the high grass behind and timber with it, so that part of the duty of the soldier was to collect buffalo chips during the last hour of marching. This was another strangeness and some thought the fires stank abominably but others found that they gave a welcome tang to the salt pork and corned beef. So many things were strange: jack rabbits, antelopes, and especially the buffalo, the great legend now gaped at by these rural youths, who tried to hunt it and sometimes succeeded. The country was unimaginable, plains on a scale they had not dreamed of diminishing one to a dot that seemed to travel on the bottom of a bowl, the vast heave of the swells that seemed like the swells of the ocean they had read about, many miles long. Most of all the sun. Missouri sun is nothing amateurish but the sun of the plains flattened the life in you, filled your eyes with the color of blood, and baked you to the bone — with sudden overheated winds and violent dust storms making it worse. The boys kept going and began to stink.

There were rattlesnakes by the hundred, killed on the march, buzzing from beside the buffalo chips you stooped to pick up, slithering into your blankets at night. There were the mosquitoes, much deadlier than the snakes. There were swarms of buffalo gnats to choke the nostrils and cluster under the eyelids of men and horses. The country began to break out in patches of "saline incrustation," alkali. Like the emigrants to the northward, the army drank corrosive water and got violently physicked. And not only by alkali; the curse of armies, dysentery, had begun to flourish. Nor was the scummy standing-water of the buffalo wallows any better for them, when it was all they got to drink at nooning, crawling with infusoria and noisome with buffalo urine. The less fit began to break. As the oxen collapsed from heat and either died or had to be driven up by night, some of the troops found that they could go no farther. Here is a man discharged and sent home for d.t., another for bad eyes, another for general debility. As the trains fell farther behind and rations shortened, scurvy appeared. Measles traveled with them. The wagons filled with sick; some of them died. A grave had to be dug at Pawnee Rock and from there on burial parties were no novelty. They had come for a patriotic summer while the eagle screamed, but for some of them the great adventure was ending in a short agony and a shallow grave filled with such stones as could be gathered to keep the wolves away.

On the approach of war, Senator Benton had sent word to Independence, directing one of the traders, as soon as he should arrive there from Chihuahua, to come to Washington by the fastest means. James W. Magoffin got that message on May 25, and on the evening of June 15 Benton was introducing him to the President at the White House. Polk, hoping for a bloodless conquest, thus got the services of the most sagacious man in the province he intended to invade. For twenty years Magoffin had engaged in the trade to Santa Fe and Chihuahua and he had made a fortune from it. He had been consul in Chihuahua and Durango, had built up rich properties there, and in Santa Fe had married a daughter of the native gentry. He knew more about the country, probably, than anyone else who could have been found. Two years before, when his wife died, he had moved his residence to Independence again but he was still active in the trade. He was a good deal of a man — tall, opulent in looks and behavior, an epicure, a wit, extremely companionable, and much admired by the Mexican officials, who liked his wines and anecdotes and called him "Don Santiago."

The President met him at a crowded and difficult moment. The House was harpooning Polk with the zest of Congressmen who have been denied commissions as brigadiers. Washington swarmed with the unclean who were clamoring for contracts. Someone had at last realized that the conquest of California would probably need more than the handful-and-a-half furnished to Commodore Sloat and General Kearny — so there was a discord of plans and ideas and no great confidence that troops could be raised. The Senate was boiling with the warhawks' resentment of the Oregon settlement: Polk could get no appointment confirmed and wondered if he could force his war measures through.

He welcomed Magoffin as one who might have a conquest in his pocket. When the President had a secret he kept it even from his diary, so we do not know what was said when he, Marcy, and Benton met with this cosmopolite. Polk says only that Magoffin could be useful in furnishing supplies and conciliating the people of New Mexico, and Benton's account was a part of his campaign to discredit Kearny. But Magoffin must have confirmed the consuls' and traders' reports of disaffection in New Mexico, must have described the helplessness of the province, and must have been quite clear about that miniature of Santa Anna in all but intelligence and courage, General Manuel Armijo, the governor. At any rate, from that conference he posted back toward Santa Fe at full speed, instructed to do what he could and bearing a letter which ordered Kearny to facilitate his mission. He was to work in what we have come to call the fifth column, resident Americans, Mexican traders, more especially the officials, and most especially the governor. Magoffin traveled fast. He was back at Independence in early July and started down the trail sometime before the fifteenth. Never a man to skimp his comforts, he supplied his light equipage with the latest sleeping bags and other gadgets and the best wines and cigars. It was hard, however, to get good brandies at short notice, and Don Santiago had to start with a stock so small that he was afraid it would be exhausted before he could reach Santa Fe. . . . He carried the letter from Jessie Frémont to her husband quoted in our first chapter, and presently picked up a friend and fellow merchant, José Gonzales of Chihuahua.

Meanwhile, on June 11, the spring caravan of his firm had left Independence in command of his partner and younger brother,

Samuel Magoffin. So Susan Shelby Magoffin, not yet eighteen but a bride of six months, who had been honeymooning in the East, found that the first house she could call her very own was a conical tent made in Philadelphia, very luxurious, furnished with tables, cabinets, and stools, and a carpet of sailcloth. The bride's first meal in her mobile house was a supper of "fried ham and eggs, biscuit, and a cup of shrub, for I preferred it to tea or café." Her familiar combs and mirror were at hand, her Bible, her journal, and some improving books, and she slept on a camp bed made up every night with sheets, pillows, and counterpane.

Susan was pregnant and she was very much in love. The details of her husband's business were enchanting; the prairie voyage was really a continuation of her honeymoon. Samuel was taking fourteen wagonloads of goods and the train included a baggage wagon, the proprietor's carriage, a dearborn for Susan's maid Jane, and a *remuda* of about 200 all told, oxen, mules, and saddle horses. Twenty men staffed it, three of them Mexicans. The bullwhackers' profanity stunned her but she gratefully found that it diminished on the Sabbath.

Otherwise the bullwhackers were fascinating and so was the routine of prairie life. Her dog Ring was with her, a greyhound "of noble descent," who, she felt confident, protected her from "bruens" and Indians when she strolled off the trail. The seminary had taught her to botanize and she pressed flowers in her Bible, faithfully listing them in a gentlewoman's misspellings. There were wild raspberries, gooseberries, and "plumbs." There were exciting gallops through the grass. There were indolent noonings when she could lie on her cot and think of love in terms of Stephen Foster's songs. There were streams to fish in while the train halted to extricate a mired wagon, though she caught nothing. She recovered from the cold she had taken in Independence and found herself growing strong and gay — "I shall be fit for one of the Oregon pioneers." Not even the deluge of mid-June could discourage her, for it was cozy to sit like a tailor on her cot with sewing and writing implements round her and listen to the drumming on the canvas roof, though one night the tent blew over in a cloudburst and she had to shiver till dawn in Jane's dearborn. The mosquitoes were bad and got worse, sometimes kept her awake all night, and increased from hundreds to thousands to millions. Snakes made her scream and a crawly prairie bug was loathsome. "I never walk in the grass without holding my dress up high, from fear that its long arm may chance to grapple me." After the rains, the heat was monstrous even at night, so that once "I had to pull all but my chemise [off], and even that would have been sent off without regret had not modesty forbid me," for a gentlewoman must not sleep naked.

She was altogether a darling, and in nothing more so than the penitence that oppressed her whenever she remembered her religion. That was usually on the Sabbath, which prairie travel tended to profane, in so much that Susan would take her pleasure on horseback or even labor at her "kniting." Then she remembered that it was "appointed by my heavenly father for a day of rest," and "Oh, how could I ever have been so thoughtless, so unmindful of my duty and my eternal salvation!" She grew mindful of them as the Indian country neared and was piously pleased to see that nature was mindful likewise — on Sunday even the birds were quiet or "reverential in their songs." So she meditated on her blessings and the Creator's wisdom, then spread a buffalo robe in the shade of the carriage and took a siesta.

At Council Grove they met the train of Samuel Owens. Here also was John M. Stanley the artist, who would presently join Kearny's engineering detachment under Lieutenant Emory and make the drawings that embellish his report. Charles Bent, coming eastward up the trail, met them twelve miles out from Diamond Spring and Susan was able to send Papa a letter. They had been joined by other trains and the caravan was growing. Colonel Owens' wagons were usually near when they camped, and most days now they saw soldiers on the trail. They passed the Cottonwood and the Little Arkansas, and now the mosquitoes were worse than ever. They maddened the mules, when Susan stepped out into the grass her dress filled with them, at night they sounded like rain on the roof, and she was made sick by the stings. Oxen were dying from the heat and had to be driven at night; Susan never felt refreshed till after dark. But there was fresh buffalo and she contrived a miracle of cuisine. Supper one night was boiled chicken (from the noisy crate lashed to the baggage wagon), soup, rice, and "a dessert of wine and gooseberry tart."

One evening, catching up with Owens again, they found him burying a Mexican employe who had died. This and a violent storm with "vivid and forked lightning quickly succeeded by the hoarse growling thunder" reminded Susan of God's magnanimity. That was near Pawnee Rock, the prairie register where, seeing the many names carved in soft sandstone, she desired to engrave her own. She made a hasty job of it for the site was notorious for Indian attacks and she began "to tremble all over." Samuel and Jane were on guard, however, and there were no Indians. So they rode on to catch up with the train, which had crawled ahead, and Susan and Samuel got into the carriage. A mile or so farther on they came to Ash Creek.[3] The stream could be dangerous when flooded but was now shallow. The banks were steep and Samuel and Susan intended to cross on foot. Before they could tell the driver, however, the carriage was over the edge. It teetered, slid, and crashed to the stream bed in a litter of "books, bottles — one of which broke and on my head too I believe — guns, pistols, baskets, bags, boxes, and the dear knows what else." Samuel succeeded in clasping her in his arms and so probably saved her life, partly fending off the carriage top when it collapsed on them. But the top or the bottle knocked her out and she knew nothing till the aroma of whiskey roused her and she found her distraught husband rubbing her face. The carriage had been ruined and they had to go on in the dearborn. That night they camped at the Pawnee Fork, among the wagon trains that Captain Moore was detaining there. It was the Fourth of July. And Samuel Magoffin might worry about the effect of the day's mishap on his pregnant bride.

On July 4 most of the Army of the West was still behind the Magoffins. It was the hottest day they had had so far. Back at Fort Leavenworth the anniversary was commemorated in fitting military style, with parade and formal guard mount, the bands playing and everyone given liberty at noon. That day the artillery, farthest to the rear, were only a few miles out, competing with the baggage train in the still mugginess of the fords. Captain Fischer's Germans were all thumbs, so helpless that Kearny's staff had to explain how to water horses. Camping at Elm Grove, they were able to buy some liquor from the sutlers but were too tired to have much fun. The infantry, caught between two streams, had to march after dark, many were prostrated by the heat, and they were straggling in for hours after camp was made thirty miles from last night's bivouac. They hardly remembered it was the glorious Fourth, and the Laclede Rangers, who had chosen this torrid day to lose the road, were also done in. Farther ahead Company C of Doniphan's regiment labored toward Council Grove. John T. Hughes, the bachelor of arts, who had already jotted down the parallel with Xenophon's Ten Thousand, faced another classical obligation. "Our bosoms," he says, "swelled with the same quenchless love of freedom which animated the breasts of our ancestors of '76 and caught inspiration from the memory of their achievements. Ever and anon the enthusiastic shout, the loud huzza, and the animating Yankee Doodle were heard." The huzzas were mostly oaths, probably, and only the advance guard under Captain Waldo, which was hurrying to join Moore at Pawnee Fork, had a reasonably good time. Waldo had brought a keg of whiskey with him. He issued it at breakfast, "each man drank his fill," and the twenty-five miles they covered that day were not troublesome. But rations had to be reduced a third and Private Robinson of Company D, though he liked the whiskey, wrote lugubriously that "if we cannot overtake the commissary wagons we shall have nothing to eat but our own horses."

In the conquered town of Matamoros, Taylor's army had a better time. There were oratory and salutes, the *cantinas* were gay, no one went hungry or thirsty on Independence Day. The Mexicans made an admirable conquered people, amiable and polite, and their cookery, religious observations, and social customs had the Americans agape. The army enjoyed itself while Taylor called for reinforcements and wondered what to do. The volunteers kept coming in from the north and the staff exhausted itself trying to improve communications and supply. The correspondents, who had no new battle, went on inflating Palo Alto and Resaca de la Palma. They filled their space with atrocities, all Mexican, and heroisms, universally American. The hated foemen stripped and mutilated the American dead, lanced the wounded, fired on their captors after surrendering, and were running at the first fire so commonly that there was trouble describing the battles as famous victories. They were, however, and the folks back home read how Lieutenant McIntosh had stopped midway of a charge to fix a tourniquet on the arm of a dying soldier before hurrying on, how Kirby Smith had straddled a captured cannon and held off a counterattack with his sword, how Private Dudley had taken two prisoners barehanded, how Lieutenant Dobbins had split a perfidious Mexican's head with one blow of his bowie knife. And so on. But Old Rough and Ready was getting mad. The administration had made him a major general but no official thanks for the victories had reached him. Must be politics.

In the harbor of Monterey, California, the flagship *Savannah,* which had arrived on July 2, greeted Independence Day with the salute prescribed. So did *Cyane* and *Levant,* anchored in line with her. Commodore Sloat had sailed from Mazatlán on receipt of news that war had begun. He was afraid that the English squadron, which had the same news, might get there first, and his orders were to seize the port. But, arriving well ahead of the British, he began to fall apart from internal conflicts. He was old, sick, and a navy fussbudget, and the responsibility of seizing a foreign province was a heavy one — the heavier in that it had had an unfortunate dress rehearsal. Four years before, Commodore Ap Catesby Jones, in harbor at Callao, had heard rumors of war and seen a British ship acting suspiciously, and had hurried off to Monterey and run up the flag. The Secretary of the Navy had had to disavow the act and relieve Jones of his command. Sloat had that embarrassment to think of and here was Consul Larkin, horrified by the Bear Flag uprising, passionately arguing that his orders were to conciliate the Californians and could still be obeyed. It was not till July 7 that the discreet desperation of his subordinates prodded Sloat to land 250 men, plant the flag on the customhouse, and announce that the town was occupied by the United States. The natives were bewildered but politely acquiescent.

But there was one glorious Fourth on the golden shore. The one-village California Republic still lived. Captain Frémont got back after being outwitted by de la Torre and storming the empty fortress of San Joaquin. So there were salutes to the flag and to the blended petticoats as well, and that night there was a fandango. The music of guitars drifted through the purple dark, to the continuing bewilderment of the Californians. Next day Frémont went on organizing his men and the forces of the Republic for further service. On July 9 Lieutenant Revere of the *Portsmouth* arrived, on Sloat's order, and took possession of Sonoma in the name of the United States. Thus the great Republic went down, passing from light opera into history.

Francis Parkman was still in camp at the mouth of the Chugwater, yearning for the Sioux, who still delayed their rendezvous at La Bonte's. Riding back from Fort Laramie on June 28, he had found Shaw and Chatillon returned and Chatillon's squaw dead. Some mountain men arrived and pitched camp with them and Parkman lay in the shade, weakened by dysentery, and listened to the epic of their wars and wanderings. "I defy the annals of chivalry to furnish the record of a life more wild and perilous than those of a Rocky Mountain trapper." On July 4 three Indians came into camp bringing with them on a mule a wretched Negro who had strayed from Richard's camp on Horse Creek thirty-three days ago, "and had been wandering in circles and starving ever since, without gun, knife, moccasins, or any knowledge of the country or its productions. We seated him in the midst of a circle of trappers, squaws, and children — the wretch could scarcely speak. The men considered his escape almost miraculous." On the same day Parkman noted that "the squaws [they were the wives of the trappers and traders] are constantly laughing. It is astonishing what abominable indecencies the best of the Indians will utter in presence of the women, who laugh heartily."

A couple of days later Parkman and his party started out at last for the rendezvous at La Bonte's. There was suspense, for the fickle Indians appeared not to be keeping their appointment. But at last they came, the Whirlwind's village still smoking hot for war. Chatillon's brother-in-law, the Bull Bear, got Parkman entree to the most select circles, his notebook filled with jottings, and in the corresponding passage *The Oregon Trail* attains its first ecstasy. For here he was, at last a resident of an Indian village, they were rehearsing war, and they were the real thing.

Dysentery prostrated him again. He suffered "the extremity of languor and exhaustion." Sometimes he could not move off his blanket. Opium accomplished nothing; he seemed to improve on a diet of one ship's biscuit a day, then collapsed again. Swooning, he studied the Oglala, for while he still lived he must think of the books he had planned. . . . And the Indians let him down. They whooped and charged in belligerent, sham exercises, but also they maintained the interminable ceremonies that made tribal life a blend of a sewing circle and a high-school debating club. So suddenly the caprice changed and they weren't going to La Bonte's, they weren't going to take the warpath against the Shoshoni, they were going hunting. They boiled off toward the Laramie Mountains and, impaled on his disappointment, Parkman had no recourse but to accompany them. Spoonfuls of whiskey swallowed at intervals enabled him to sit his horse.

The next day a trapper caught up with them dispatched from Fort Laramie by Bisonette, a mountain man, with word that not all the Sioux had abandoned the warpath. Ten or twelve villages would keep the rendezvous at La Bonte's and Bisonette would meet Parkman on the way there. Hope revived and he led his little company away from the Whirlwind's village. In great pain, he rode toward La Bonte's across a "dreary monotony of sun-scorched plains, where no living thing appeared save here and there an antelope flying before us like the wind." They reached Horse Shoe Creek at noon, green-banked, beautifully timbered, and there they camped. "I was thoroughly exhausted and flung myself on the ground, scarcely able to move. All that afternoon I lay in the shade by the side of the stream, and those bright woods and sparkling waters are associated in my mind with recollections of lassitude and utter prostration. When night came I sat down by the fire, longing with an intensity of which at this moment I can hardly conceive for some powerful stimulant."

Our emigrant trains had been traveling close together since leaving Fort Laramie and were now plodding up the last marches along the Platte, through a writhen, volcanic desert that was a warning of worse ones just ahead. Laramie Peak was behind them now and the trail hugged the twisting river, here narrow and swift. The country was a succession of great bowls brimming with vacancy, the scale increasing, the buttes and obelisks bigger, the hills deeply gullied, the skyline toothed and jagged, the distance sometimes purple and white with glimpses of the Wind River Mountains. It got greener for a space near where the city of Casper, Wyoming, now stands, and the trains camped there within sight of each other on the night of July 3. Now Bryant and Russell came riding in, having been stopped, up ahead, by the need to replace Mr. Kirkendall, who had pondered Jim Clyman's warning and decided to go by way of Fort Hall. Thornton had the last watch that night and "fired my rifle and revolving pistol at the dawn of day, in honor of the Declaration of American Independence. The pulsations of my heart were quickened as I heard the morning gun and saw the banner of my country run up to the top of the staff and thought of the rejoicings of the nation."

They were a long way from the rejoicing cannon that woke Mr. Polk to a rainy dawn, that day, the crowd that filled the White House for his noon reception, and the two processions of Methodist Sunday Schools that upset his afternoon. They were far from the lush pleasures of Matamoros, but they were hardly more than sixty miles from Francis Parkman, weak on his buffalo robe at the mouth of the Chugwater. The two trains joined for a celebration. The ladies did their best for a "collation." There were sentimental and patriotic songs, a volley of musketry for each toast, and, after a procession, a reading of the Declaration and — inevitably — an oration by Colonel Russell. That gorgeous voice boomed in the emptiness under the white-hot sun, and then the Oregon train moved on. The good-byes had been said and these friends would never be all together again. But the California wagons lingered awhile and James Frazier Reed produced some fine wines and liquors which he had brought from Springfield for just such an occasion. They pledged one another, the Reeds, the Donners, Boggs, Bryant, Russell, in a moment of fellowship deep in the badlands. They shook hands. Bryant and Russell rode off through the stench of hot sagebrush, taking Hiram Miller with them, who had been a teamster for George Donner. Bryant noted the yellow cactus flowers. He would hear no more of the Donners till word of their extremity should reach him in circumstances now altogether beyond imagining. At last the California train yoked up and the shrill clamor of the wheels began again. Red Butte and Independence Rock were ahead of them, the Sweetwater, and the long plane rising toward South Pass.

In the opinion of the First Missouri, this country would be hard to farm, if not impossible: there was no timber. The army had said so in eastern Kansas and repeated the judgment with emphasis as they neared and crossed the hundredth meridian and pushed on through increasing aridity. At Pawnee Rock, Captain Reid's column was scattered by buffalo, which charged through it and scared the horses into a stampede. The army blazed away at them, killed a few, and scared the horses still worse. From there on, small or large herds were frequently in sight. Some of the troops acquired a superficial connoisseurship in buffalo meat. Also they now heard rumors of the Comanche but they met none — fortunately, for not even fear of the Comanche could discipline their marching.

Grouchy and hungry, they reached the Arkansas at its great bend. There was water in the river, which was by no means a constant condition. In these parts it is a muddy and rather odorous stream which runs in trickles through a wide bottom choked with cottonwoods and brush. Under its opaque water and between the rivulets quicksands are common, and in summer some stretches are almost dusty.* Farther west it narrows to a more certain bed, like the Platte, and as it gets nearer the mountains has more water in it. The trail followed its general direction, touching its crazy course at the nodes, and the freighters were accustomed to camp on certain timbered islands as a defense against the Indians.

The country grew more severe now, the scale infinitely extended, the swell longer and the pitch steeper, the wind stronger, the sun hotter, the dust more inexhaustible, water scarcer and less drinkable. If there was little water, there were millions of flowers; if the

* Phrase by courtesy of a Montana Highway Commission road sign.

steady wind blistered their faces and sudden torrid gusts sandblasted them with alkali, the infinitely blue sky produced cloud effects the most magnificent. They trudged through prairie-dog towns a mile wide, jack rabbits by the hundred streaked away from them, the nights were full of wolves. The horses grew weaker but the men slowly toughened. Kearny watched them and applied more pressure. They howled and lustily hated all officers, in so much that accusations of malingering and inefficiency now circulated about even the venerated Doniphan. The West Pointers did their best to make the march orderly and sometimes briefly succeeded. Moore was especially tough: anyone who broke ranks in his outfit had to march on foot for the rest of the day. The adjutant who enforced the order got well cursed, but the order stood.

The oldest trail went to Bent's Fort and thence south over Raton Pass. The traders, however, had come to prefer the shorter though more dangerous route which left the Arkansas at the Lower Crossing (near the present Dodge City) or the Cimarron Crossing, twenty miles farther west, and struck through desert for the usually waterless bed of the Cimarron River. Most of the horror stories of the trail, especially those of thirst, belong to that stretch. The army did not take it but kept to the Arkansas in less precarious but equally dreary country. True desert, sandy, sparsely vegetated, beginning to break up into foothills, but supplied with drinking water of a sort at safe intervals.[4] They crossed the river at Chouteau's Island and, since it was here the international boundary, became an army of invasion at last, though they would cross again to American soil before they reached Bent's Fort.

Inconceivably, the weather got hotter still, but one day a storm passed near enough to cool the air. The nights were always cold, campfires were just buffalo chips, and rations were slim and bad. Then the unpredictable country got green for a space and even produced some patches of trees and finally, at the Big Timbers, a substantial belt of them. Then more desert, more siroccos — and then the infantry came over an incline to a flat stretch and on the western horizon, thin, dark, cloudlike masses were suddenly recognizable as a culminating wonder, the Rocky Mountains. The twinned blur to the southwest was the Spanish Peaks, Wah-To-Yah which Lewis Garrard would poetically translate as The Breasts of the World. To the northwest, equally indistinct and amorphous and much farther away, was a wavering phantom under cloud and snow which the knowing told the incredulous was the monument of their story books beheld at last, Pike's Peak. The doughboys yelled in delight and suddenly realized that they had come a long way from Missouri. A hell of a long way! They took up the march across a last stretch of parched sand and sagebrush and sometime before noon saw the walls of Bent's Fort rising from the plain. Two miles from it they reached Moore's detachment camped by the river, made their own camp, and started to dig a well. It was July 28 and the infantry had beaten everyone except the advance guard to the rendezvous.

Five hundred and thirty miles out from Independence, on the north bank of the Arkansas again, they had reached the first permanent settlement in what is now Colorado, Bent's Old Fort or Fort William, at a crossroads of the West. It was on the mountain branch of the Santa Fe trail; a few miles to the southwest that trail forked, and the other fork went to Taos. Westward a trail led up the Arkansas to the Fontaine Qui Bouille and on to the trappers' paradise, South Park. Northward stretched an immemorial Indian warpath and trade route to the Platte. Except for Fort Union, the American Fur Company's headquarters at the mouth of the Yellowstone, Bent's was the largest of all the trading posts, and it had perhaps the most varied and adventurous history. Its thick adobe walls made a rectangle a hundred by a hundred and fifty feet inclosing a central patio, two of them were two stories high, and there was a walled corral beyond. It was a complete factory for the Indian trade — warehouses, smithy, wagon shop, storerooms — and it had dormitories and such incredibilities as a billiard table and an ice house. Bent & St. Vrain, its owners, kept as many as a hundred and fifty men permanently employed here, many with Indian wives and families. Many mountain men wintered among its comforts; usually at least one village of Indians was camped by the river, three hundred yards away. They were usually southern Cheyenne, whose trade the firm monopolized, but might be Arapaho or Ute or even Kiowa or Comanche. The post's daily life was an adventure story and the yarns it heard are our lost history.

There were four Bent brothers in the trade, grandsons of the Silas Bent who had led the masqueraders when they threw the taxed tea into Boston Harbor; one of them was dead now and two more would die within a year. There were two St. Vrains, Ceran and Marcellin, St. Louis French, aristocrats, lovers of fine living, and Ceran had married into the New Mexico gentry. So had Charles Bent; and William Bent, the resident manager of the fort, was married to Owl Woman of the Cheyenne. The marriages were important, for they attached important loyalties in Santa Fe and Taos to the

American cause, and they kept the Cheyenne peaceful. These were mighty men, whose will was prairie law, who could sway whole tribes, who knew Indians and Mexicans as few others did. They freighted their own goods from Independence and their Indian trade reached far to the north, west, southeast, and southwest. They maintained smaller posts in the Indian country and agents of theirs lived with various bands. They had great influence with all the tribes for hundreds of miles, and through William Bent they held the southern Cheyenne in the hollow of their hand.

Here, on the heat-tortured plain flickering with mirages and cooling to the freezing point at night, with the spectral mountains on the far horizon, Kearny assembled his army in the last days of July. He left the infantry near the fort, to swim in the river, guzzle Taos Lightning and other liquors at twenty-five dollars a gallon, exhaust the firm's supply of clothing, and gape at Mexicans, mountain men, Arapaho, Cheyenne, and Ute. He took the Dragoons and most of the First Missouri ten miles farther on, hoping to condition the horses with rest and grass. The sick were to be weeded out, equipment to be repaired, something done about the collapsing commissary.

Major Clark arrived to take command of Weightman's and Fischer's artillery. He was the oldest son of William Clark and was named Meriwether Lewis for his father's great companion; his half-sister was Kearny's wife. Messengers, couriers, expresses kept arriving. Some supply trains creaked in. Suspicious-looking Mexicans were arrested as spies and freed again to magnify the size of the army, going home. The two delayed companies of Dragoons rode in under Sumner and Philip St. George Cooke, for whom a job was ready. Also the freighters were being concentrated and organized as the trains came up to add their noise to the confusion at the fort and extend the vast circle of used-up grass. There were more than four hundred of their wagons now.

Susan Magoffin noted the white tents of Captain Moore's detachment along the river when she arrived at the fort, July 26. She had not been happy since her accident. Ominous symptoms had appeared and a dread possessed her. Samuel halted his train on Pawnee Fork for several days to let her rest, but neither her spirits nor her health improved. They went on through massive heat. Near the Coon Creeks there were a big herd of buffalo, which amused her for a while, "ugly, ill-shapen things . . . and they look so droll running," but she was frightened when Ring chased them. Samuel joined his wagons with those of Manuel Harmony, Cornelius Davy, and Edward Glasgow, and two of Kearny's supply trains lengthened the caravan. Susan grew sicker and there was a flurry of alarm. Samuel rode ahead to another train to bring back Dr. Masure of St. Louis, "a polite delicate Frenchman" with a reputation in the treatment of women's ills. Susan was comforted but did not get better. A sudden storm brought the tent down on her, one night, and the next day there was an Indian scare. They got to the fort and William Bent cleared a room for his friend's wife. Susan was moderately comfortable but everything was strange — the Mexican ladies combing their hair in public and saturating it with grease, the painted Indians, the uproar and confusion of the troops.

She wrote to Papa and her sisters. Dr. Masure watched her carefully, the officers made formal calls on this gentlewoman in the wilderness, there was the changing pageant of the fort. Susan tried to be interested but religious gloom obsessed her. Thursday, July 30, was her eighteenth birthday. Samuel wanted to celebrate it properly but now it was plain that Susan was very sick. "Strange sensations in my back and hips. I am obliged to lie down most of the time, and when I get up to hold my hand over my eyes." It was said that Kearny was going to order them forward and the thought of those jolting wagons was more than she could bear. She lay in bed and "there is the greatest possible noise in the patio." Horseshoeing, children crying, servants quarreling, Arapaho singing their chants.

That was her birthday. The next morning premature labor came upon her and before midnight she had a miscarriage. It was a near thing but Dr. Masure brought her through, and "I sunk into a kind of lethargy in *mi alma's* arms." After a long agony, she had lost her first child. At the same moment, on the dirt floor of the room underneath her, a trader's squaw "gave birth to a fine healthy baby . . . and in half an hour after she went to the river and bathed herself and it." Susan had that casual papoose to think of when her lethargy lifted for brief moments.

She mended slowly. The clamor of the army's preparation continued and Susan reflected on this methodical preparation for bloodshed. "The follies and wretchedness of man! . . . sinking himself to the level of the beasts, waging warfare with his fellow man even as the dumb brute . . . striving for wealth, honour and fame to the ruining of his soul and loosing a brighter crown in higher realms." While she was there the army started out for Santa Fe.

In the next day or two the traders followed it. On the eighth day she was able to leave her room — just twelve days since she had reached the fort — and on the next day Samuel got his wagons started. Susan was glad to go but she wondered what dangers might be ahead. They could hardly be worse than what she had experienced already, but the thought struck her that perhaps she would never see "the fair and happy America" again.

While Susan lay unconscious, her brother-in-law James Magoffin reached Bent's Fort and Kearny hurried him on to Santa Fe. Her journal does not mention his arrival but he must have come to the door and looked at her pale face before hurrying on to obey Mr. Polk's orders.

Kearny had been working hard to sift rumors. All the traders who had passed Bent's Fort from Santa Fe this year had predicted that New Mexico would not be defended. This agreed with the assurances Kearny had from Polk. But here at the border of the province to be invaded, the general could see clearly just how precarious the project was. His cavalry would have been better off dismounted. Sixty per cent of the artillery horses had died or become useless. The service of supply had failed badly; rations had been reduced already and would have to be reduced further. The line of communications was six hundred miles long and in constant danger from the Comanche. The route to Santa Fe lay through the mountains and any skillfully led troops could close it to Kearny's command; a reasonably large force could probably annihilate the A.E.F. In spite of the assurances that there would be no opposition, other circumstantial rumors said that Governor Armijo had raised an army, had been reinforced from Chihuahua, and would offer battle in the mountains. The two agents before Magoffin whom Polk had sent to Santa Fe had learned little and done nothing.

Well, Kearny had his orders. From Bent's Fort he issued a proclamation annexing the province of New Mexico east of the Rio Grande to the United States. (Thus using the old, shadowy claim of Texas, and sheathing his advance in a diplomatic envelope of peace.) He sent this in with some of the spies he had captured and also sent a copy to Taos, to propitiate the Pueblo Indians. And here was James Magoffin, from the President. Kearny detached Captain Cooke with twelve Dragoons to take the secret agent to Santa Fe, and had him carry a letter and a copy of the proclamation to Armijo.

He told the governor that his purpose was peaceful but resolute, referred to the force he commanded and the reinforcements traveling down the trail behind him (they were just starting from Fort Leavenworth), and invited Armijo to submit gracefully to the inevitable. He would confide the rest to James Magoffin's talents.

Philip St. George Cooke was still mourning his lost chance of glory on the Mexican battlefields. (In so much that he got his metaphors mixed: "at a plaintive compliment, that I went to plant the olive where he would reap a laurel, the general endeavored to gloss the barren field of toil.") But he was a Virginian on the most generous scale and Magoffin was a Kentuckian on the same scale. Calling on Bent's ice house and personal mint bed, they made a pitcher of juleps the first act of their mission. The army was setting out at the same time and Kearny was pushing it so hard that they took several days to get ahead of it. Cooke's old sergeant was amazed but prideful. "If regulars were to straggle so," he said, "they would be considered as mutinizing."

The stretch from Bent's Fort to the summit of Raton Pass was the most difficult of the entire trail. Cooke and Magoffin saw it through a pleasant haze. Magoffin's fear had proved correct: the brandy had run out. He had plenty of claret, however. The two gourmets nooned in the shade of piñons, and when they took to the saddle again there would be more mirages than usual on the horizon. Magoffin was the most amusing man Cooke had ever met, huge, jovial, courageous, incapable of anger, a master of plains travel and of taking his ease. He laughed much, apostrophizing his pocket corkscrew, exchanging jests with José Gonzales, the Chihuahua merchant whose country he hoped to betray, discoursing with Cooke on the pleasures of gentlemen, and bragging about the virtues of his cook. The cook was a Mexican and Magoffin's praise seemed justified daily, but once he went too far. Someone caught a small turtle at a water hole and that night there was soup. Magoffin enjoyed it but Cooke had to spend a day in his new friend's carriage, languorous with opium but interested in the ruins of Pecos pueblo and still fit for claret.

Pressing hard but solaced by Magoffin's wine chest, they got over the Raton and crossed the violently colored country to San Miguel, to the Pecos pueblo, and on to the last canyons. In the adobe hamlets they encountered only the touching courtesy of the little people who had been cowed by two and a half centuries of Mexican and Indian oppression. On August 12 they rode into Santa Fe, a handful of dirty foreigners, and so surprised the guard that it howled aloud.

Cooke mistook the noise for an alert, hastily tied a handkerchief to his saber, and "announced my mission in a sentence of very formal book Spanish." There was a sudden thought that the outriders of invasion might be roughly handled.

No: only a difficulty of etiquette. The Mexicans had not prepared for a guest and there was the same embarrassment when, a few minutes later, Cooke rode down the twisting, garbage-littered street and came out into the historic plaza. His bugler sounded off but for some time no one answered the summons, though the windows must have been crowded with gaping faces. Mr. Polk's Southwestern vicar felt both foolish and angry at the anticlimax. Finally an officer appeared and led him into the ancient Palace of the Governors, where Armijo welcomed him in a gorgeous uniform. Cooke and his men, the governor explained, would be cared for in the palace; then they could meet officially. Magoffin had slipped away to make his own preparation among his friends, the cavalrymen were billeted across the way, and the wife of Captain Ortiz was turned out of her room in the palace. At once some American merchants came out of the ground, Señora Ortiz found cake and whiskey for their entertainment, and, the ceremony over, Cooke hastened to make himself as presentable as possible. Shaved, washed, brushed, his shoulder straps and saber knot rubbed as bright as possible, he was formally conducted to Armijo. . . . The will of the war President had found its instrument and in the person of Captain Philip St. George Cooke, First Dragoons, Manifest Destiny was calling on its first objective to surrender.

The army of invasion moved out from Bent's Fort on August 1 and 2. Kearny had done his best to tighten its organization, had left about seventy-five on sick call to rejoin him at Santa Fe or be carted back to Fort Leavenworth, and had clamped down such discipline as was possible. He had enlisted William Bent and a number of his trappers to range ahead as scouts. With Bent was Francis Preston Blair, Jr., the son of the great editor whom Polk had forced out of the *Globe*. Young Blair had spent the summer of '45 with Bent & St. Vrain to improve his health, and was at the fort again when the army reached it. Now he was beginning a career that would be momentous.

The traders followed, and, army and traders, it was a formidable caravan. One census makes it 1556 wagons and nearly twenty thousand stock all told, oxen, beeves, horses, mules.[5] A long column moving through the most intense heat yet encountered and the worst desert of the trail. For four days there was almost no grass for the horses and little grass for anyone. Lieutenant Emory's thermometers showed 120° and the sirocco never died across the sand. The troops tied handkerchiefs over their mouths, to no avail. They got nosebleeds from the altitude and dysentery from the alkali. The wagons laboring behind, rations had to be cut. They could not be controlled at water holes, where the first ones spoiled the drinking for the rest. The horses were even worse; Captain Johnston observed that when the water was scarcest they were most apt to urinate in it. Private Marcellus Edwards of Doniphan's Company D said of one small pool they passed on August 4 that it was "so bad that one who drank it would have to shut both eyes and hold his breath until the nauseating dose was swallowed. Notwithstanding its scarcity, some men allowed their horses to tramp through it, which soon stirred it up to a thick mud; and to give it a still greater flavor, a dead snake with the flesh just dropping from his bones."

Rear guards of detachments saw wolves trotting with them just out of rifle range. They were waiting for the horses to drop. They fed well and it looked as if Kearny's wish for infantry might be granted right here. A number of the volunteers died too, the Halls of Montezuma proving just six feet of desert earth. The volunteers were now accusing their officers of every villainy, from malingering to selling water for cash, and their complaints swelled to a sustained bellow. The West Pointers thought that morale had failed, but this was only the army exercising a freeborn American's right to express a grouch. The moment they reached the mountains, they were skylarking again.

All this time they were angling toward the mountains; the Spanish peaks grew higher every mile and the main range of the Rockies stretched its abrupt bastion out of sight, north and south. At last they struck the Purgatoire near the present site of Trinidad, Colorado, and it proved to be a stream out of paradise, swift, cold, poetically timbered. They drank till all were surfeited and some vomited, they bathed, they washed their clothes. One of them went mad, several died from the now ended strain, but game was shot, some supplies caught up and beef could be butchered, and the West Pointers had been wrong about their morale. The next night the campfires slanted upward at a steep pitch: they were in the Raton Pass. Here was the first place where an alert enemy could have destroyed them, but in spite of the daily rumors no enemy appeared; the one alarm was just some Doniphesias [6] wasting ammunition for the fun of it. Raton Pass is a long, twisting, arduous grade and they did better with it than the horses, which were now punch-drunk. They reached the top and looked out on one of the continent's great views, all New Mexico spread out below in the molten gold of Southwestern sun. They clambered down the other side and found that the molten gold was hot.

Now Bent's scouts were bringing in various Mexicans and others were coming in to see for themselves. Spies probably, and Kearny sent more of them home to report that he was irresistible. They had proclamations by Armijo and others, the usual proclamations, and they brought notice of trouble ahead. Two thousand troops were assembling to oppose the invasion, then five thousand, eight thousand, twelve thousand. Kearny closed up his intervals, posted scouts, and kept on. At the Mora they found another beautiful camp ground and the first settlement since Fort Leavenworth, a half-dozen adobe huts and "a pretty Mexican woman with clean white stockings, who very cordially shook hands with us and asked for tobacco." Every few miles there were more huts, where the streams made a green thread across burnt plains, and the Doniphesias could buy mutton, corn, vegetables. They could also feel a hearty Protestant contempt for Popish superstitions and, gaping at the Mexicans, marvel at the extremity of poverty, dirt, obsequiousness, and desire to please the conquerors.

The daily captives told conflicting stories. Either there were no preparations to resist or the whole province had risen. Americans from Santa Fe came in and the best thought was that Armijo would fight at Apache Canyon, fifteen miles from the city. Beautifully uniformed lancers brought a letter from Armijo, suggesting that the commanders meet to the eastward of Las Vegas and negotiate. That was August 14. Kearny kept on, Armijo was nowhere, and the army camped a mile outside the town.

Las Vegas was the largest village they had seen so far. They heard that the Navajo had raided it since Captain Cooke passed through, a week before. They bought some sheep, scorched their palates with the native stews, and stole some corn for themselves and their horses. Kearny promptly won the villagers by promising to pay for the corn, which was not the custom of any other troops who had ever passed this way. There was a growing murmur: some of the Missourians were remembering that the Texas Expedition of 1841 had been attacked and slaughtered in the canyon just beyond Las Vegas and that at San Miguel, a few miles farther on, General Salazar had shot some of the prisoners. That night word came that a Mexican force had reached that same canyon and was fortifying it.

Word of the expected battle went far back on the trail and Captain Weightman of the artillery, coming up after convalescing at Bent's Fort, rode all night to take part in it. He reached the army at reveille and Major Swords was with him, the quartermaster, bringing Kearny's commission as brigadier general at last. Kearny made combat dispositions, spare ammunition was issued, some of Doniphan's officers reminded their men that, on General Taylor's word, Missouri volunteers had not distinguished themselves at the battle of Okechobee,[7] so maybe they had better wipe out that stain. Keyed up, the army marched through town and halted while Kearny, from a roof top, announced to the villagers that they were now Americans. He did it skillfully, reminding them of the oppressions they had suffered, promising them security in their property and religion, and assuring them that the United States would defend them against the Indians as in two centuries no one ever had. There is no record of what they felt, a humble folk whose entire history had been misery, paupered by all governments, preyed on by brigands, and called by the Apache the mere herders who raised stock for them. They knew no way of life that was not constant oppression and intermittent massacre. Probably the promise of protection from Indians warmed them a little, though it was not to be kept for half a century. Probably also they cared no more than anyone else to acknowledge another conqueror. However, much experience of conquest had taught them that courtesy was best. They smiled, bowed, cheered, gave fruits and wines to the guards, and took the meaningless forced oath of allegiance in the best of humor. "But listen! he who promises to be quiet and is found in arms against me, I will hang."

The first formal occupation made, Kearny prepared to drive the enemy out of the narrow canyon that today bears his name. He sent the infantry with a couple of dismounted companies of the First Missouri over the foothills to the right. He formed the rest of the Doniphesias and the artillery behind the Dragoons, took his place at the head of his old regiment, pushed out a cavalry point, and ordered the army forward. The Dragoons trotted, then broke into a gallop. There was a shine of sabers in the sunlight, the pound of hooves and the long lift of the charge — and the guidons were fluttering in the empty pass. No enemy, just another rumor, and the army rejoiced in its first battle.

That afternoon at Tecolote Captain Cooke rode in. His opinion was that they would be unopposed, but Armijo's forces kept on growing in the stories of most arrested Mexicans, though some cynics held that the discharge of one American cannon would suffice. If there was to be any fighting it would come at Apache Canyon, and you could choose any number up to twelve thousand enemies. The next day Kearny swore in another, larger town, San Miguel, and among the day's pickups was the son of the General Salazar who had slaughtered the Texans. On the following day they passed the ruins at Pecos that had once been the largest town of the Pueblo Indians. Stephen Watts Kearny had intersected a conquest of his predecessor, Coronado. The First Missouri scattered to carve their names on the fallen adobe of that pueblo and the ruined Christian church beside it, much impressed by antiquity and the promptly circulated information that what they called the sacred fire of Montezuma had burned here through the centuries till eight years ago. But they could not realize the blood which, through those same centuries, had soaked these ruined bricks — the screams and ecstasy of human sacrifice, the generations of war with wandering tribes, generations of conquest by the Spaniards and revolt against them, decimation and submission, the long darkening of the Pueblo hope, and at last the Comanche coming in raid after raid till the handful of survivors had fled to pueblos better protected by the mountains. Mr. Polk's brigadier had taken over a harvesting whose last yields are not yet in, and today at Taos or Tesuque or Santo Domingo any tourist may catch a glimpse, making what he can of it, of blood and cruelty remembered for centuries and not yet resolved. The shaping of that memory began with Coronado and the Spanish search for cities named for the buffalo, which were said to be paved and roofed with gold. . . . Most Western tribes have a myth that describes mysterious, godlike Indians whose skins are white. No one has ever fully explained it. With the Pueblo it took the form of prophecy: some day the fair gods would come from the East and deliver the village-making people from the slavery that the Spanish had riveted on them. They talked of this promise in the *kivas* when the army was nearing New Mexico and wondered if General Kearny might be this deliverer. Well, he was — in a way.

That same day, August 12, all messengers and prisoners said that Armijo had fled his position in Apache Canyon. So the road was open and Captain Johnston, of Kearny's staff, wrote in his journal, "here is the end of the campaign." . . . In Santa Fe there had been little will to oppose the Americans, and no hope. Why should there be? The disintegration of Great Spain was at its worst in New Mexico, and though there were castes and the exploitation of castes, there was no society. The mass of the people were inexpressibly poor and harried by their betters. Though the padres and the rich men told them that Kearny was coming to steal what they had and to debauch their women, the threat was little worse than the reality of two centuries. And at least the mountain men and the traders whom they knew had money to spend. Moreover, there was only a handful of regular troops, and they were not fighting men. The governor was a general but by courtesy only. He was also the scourge of the poor, formidable only in the stealing of sheep, a coward, and either bought or terrified by Polk's agent. Just how James Magoffin worked on him [8] is not known, but certainly he convinced him that it would be both safer and more profitable to let the conquest proceed unopposed. Magoffin found more resistant material in Diego Archuleta, the lieutenant governor, who was a brave man, a patriot, and an experienced Indian fighter. It seems probable that Magoffin, who had had no more of Mr. Polk's confidence than anyone got and was acting in good faith, successfully argued that the conquest would stop at the Rio Grande, the claimed boundary of Texas, and that Archuleta could maintain and defend the rest of New Mexico. At any rate, Archuleta did not force a stand and the handful of determined men who wanted to were not enough.

Armijo posted off to Apache Canyon with his personal retinue of dragoons. Some three thousand militia, forced peasants, and Indians gathered there. They felled trees across the narrowest point, placed some minute cannon there, and dug trenches. It was only a showing for the record, and Armijo at once announced that all was lost. Several of his officers pleaded for a fight but he ended by threatening them with his cannon. There was nothing to do but to go home. The extemporized army went home, greatly relieved, and with his bodyguard Armijo spurred southward. He rode hard and long. . . . Near Durango, Lieutenant George Frederick Ruxton of Her Majesty's 89th Regiment, who was making a pleasure trip northward through Mexico toward the States, met this "mountain of fat" conducting his private freight caravan along with Albert Speyer's. Lieutenant Ruxton gave himself the pleasure of calling General Armijo to his face an arrant coward.

Tuesday, August 18, a cloudy morning with occasional showers. The army marched before dawn, twisting through the defile. They reached the abandoned fortifications and decided that a few hundred men could have held them off, though the engineers thought that the position could have been turned. Out of the canyon to sagebrush flats, arroyos, foothills, small canyons. By midafternoon they were trudging across the high plain above Santa Fe, a slow line of dirty, ragged men on foot or riding emaciated horses.[9] They halted and waited for the laboring artillery to come up, while the clouds thickened and the sun sank lower.

They were tired and hungry, but below them lay the Royal City of the Holy Faith of Saint Francis. The sudden wealth of trees hid its full extent and the adobe houses were dingy against overcast skies. To most of the army it seemed a miserable and dirty town, but it was a capital city and older than any settlement in the United States. The Sangre de Cristo peaks stood up beyond the hills on which the army halted, westward were the Jémez peaks and southward the bare Scandia. A strange landscape, very beautiful, one that had a dark and bloody history reaching down from Peralta's time, who had founded it in 1609, invoking the blessing of the gentle saint who preached to his brothers the birds. El Camino Real here ended its reach from Mexico City, and every mile of that road had been bought and rebought with Indian and Spanish blood. The town's sleep was troubled with memories of flogged and murdered Indians, massacred friars, soldiers and colonists who had died for Holy Faith. The altar had been desecrated and its church made into a *kiva* when for twelve years the Pueblo Indians won the town back. Then De Vargas had taken it again after a vow to the Virgin, whose small image is still carried in procession every September to commemorate the victory that she gave. Then just the slow passage of years in a hard country which had to be held, as it had been won, with blood.

Late in the afternoon the conquerors were ready. Two subofficials had come out to profess submission and, sending his artillery to a hill that commanded the town, Kearny rode back with them and his staff, the army following in column. Bridles jingled and scabbards clanked in the little, twisting, dirty streets, between the brown adobe houses. There was a low wailing behind shuttered windows where women cowered in terror of the rape and branding which the priests had told them the Americans meant to inflict. Soldiers filed into the Plaza of the Constitution, which has always been the center of the town's life. The infantry stood at parade rest, the tired horses drooped, in the silence one heard the rustle of cottonwoods and the silver music of the creek. The ranks stiffened and the muskets came to present arms, Kearny and his staff raised their sabers, the bugles blared down those empty streets, and the flag went up. As it touched the top of the staff, the artillery on the hilltop boomed its salute, and for the first time in history the Americans had conquered a foreign capital. And they had done exactly what Mr. Polk had instructed them to do: they had taken New Mexico without firing a shot.

X

Sonorous Metal

ON July 16, Her Majesty's Ship *Collingwood,* Rear Admiral Sir George Seymour, made Monterey. Her officers began paying calls of ceremony on the American flotilla, and one of the anxieties of Commodore Sloat abated. He had forestalled by nine days the possible hoisting of the Union Jack over the custom-house, where the American flag now flew with the entire acquiescence of the natives. In fact there had been no possibility that the British would make trouble before or after the occupation. Their mood was a cool professional interest in the technics of empire.

The Royal Navy knows how to enjoy shore leave and made the most of the pleasant town. Its spectacle was tepid till late afternoon of the nineteenth, when Lieutenant Walpole of the *Collingwood,* who had read Cooper, found the familiar confronting him. A cloud of dust showed north of town and there came marching out of it a body of horsemen in column of twos. Almost two hundred of them, with a *remuda* of three hundred besides. The advance guard consisted of sailors who sat their saddles none too well, but the rest was first-rate pageantry. Riding alone came the commander, who had, Lieutenant Walpole says, "such an eye!" — the eye of a Conqueror. Then five Delawares, whom Walpole took to be a personal bodyguard, savage and painted, unmistakably the image of Uncas. Then a wilder, more savage troop, "many of them blacker than the Indians," to the number of 160 in all, thirty-nine of them the Conqueror's own, the rest "loafers picked up lately." The thirty-nine took the believing British eye, for they were authentic trappers. Cooper had told him about them and he was so awed that he even dressed them in buckskins, as an alert costumer ought to have done for him.

To any eye, the army of the deceased California Republic, now a force without any standing whatever, looked tough. The vernacular had not yet coined the phrase which later remarked of Ben Butler that he could strut sitting down. But the Conqueror, riding alone between his sailors and his Delawares, could swagger in the saddle, and his filibusters swaggered through Monterey, to make camp in a wood beyond the town. Walpole saw "the rifle held by one hand across the pommel of the saddle," and gaped in the knowledge that one of the invaders was Kit Carson who, he said, was as famous in these wilds as the Iron Duke was in Europe. Colton, the American chaplain, noted their black beards and gleaming teeth and felt the town shake as they passed. He then composed a tableau while dusk came up and the campfires shone against the woods.

A recognition stirs, different from Walpole's instruction in Cooper. This column of bearded horsemen with white teeth parading the street of Monterey, this carefully spaced display of the Conqueror riding alone on a cheap errand while the audience cheers, this arrangement, this camera angle — it is labeled. The dramaturgy of Captain Frémont had changed its medium. The Conquest had got into the movies, where it was to stay.

Scared stiff that he might have exceeded his instructions, Sloat had nevertheless had the flag raised at Yerba Buena, Sonoma, Bodega, and elsewhere, and had issued a decent and proper proclamation. He had, remember, been told to occupy the California ports, proclaim the occupation a deliverance from tyranny, and invite the consent of the natives. Events, particularly the Bear Flag opera, had made his instructions obsolete, but Consul Larkin still hoped that his own intrigue could succeed. To Larkin the Bear Flag incident seemed a venture in outlawry, which is what it was, and he yearned to get Frémont under control. So did Sloat, though he also hoped that Frémont was acting under orders, in which case he would feel much better about his own episode in imperialism. (He kept remembering Ap Catesby Jones.) Neither Pico nor Castro accepted his invitation to come in and collaborate with him, and Castro, who was moving south and losing troops by desertion as he went, inquired what he made of the Bear Flag filibuster. Sloat longed for Frémont, who was supposed to be pursuing Castro. Frémont, marching toward Monterey by routes which could not possibly have intercepted Castro, was eager to join Sloat.

For Sloat was the duly constituted commander of the United States forces in California and could legitimatize Frémont. When they met, Sloat asked what authority Frémont was acting under, and the Conqueror was forced to admit that he had no authority. The admission shocked the commodore and strengthened his determination to get out of here fast, letting others bear the responsibilities of empire. He was old, sick, irresolute, and a long way from Washington. But he refused to co-operate in Frémont's proposed march against Santa Barbara and Los Angeles, which was to complete the Conquest, and refused to muster Frémont's battalion into the service of the United States.

This was embarrassing. The Conquest remained illegitimate and the Conqueror's status was that of a thug. The sense of grievance burst into flame and Frémont would presently write to Senator Benton an account of these events that lay somewhere between falsehood and hallucination. Also, with his province yanked from under him, he had the sick thought that this might be the best time to go home.

But a different commodore arrived, to whom Sloat joyfully turned over command and responsibility. This was a d'Artagnan part, played by Robert Field Stockton, an energetic, imaginative personage cast as a sea dog. Commodore Stockton needed only to survey the situation in order to understand the cinematic requirements. He supplied them. He commissioned Frémont (it is a little hard to see by what authority) as a major in the army, made Gillespie a captain, and mustered in Frémont's irregulars as the Navy Battalion of Mounted Riflemen. That is, in strict accuracy, as the Horse Marines. He furiously prepared to conquer the rest of California and, be sure, he issued a proclamation.

The touch of paranoia Frémont suffered from had magnified actual events, just as the desert mirage magnifies actual objects. Much of Frémont's career in California is explained by the fact that he was seeing mirages — delusions. But Stockton was not suffering delusions — he was lying. . . . If there had been hope of conciliating Castro, Pico, or the Californians in general, he destroyed it with his proclamation of July 29. Quite properly, the Californians had made some impromptu opposition to Frémont's filibuster but, so far, they had not at all opposed the forces of the United States. Nevertheless Stockton accused Castro of "lawless violence" and an intention to "with the aid of hostile Indians keep this beautiful country in a constant state of revolution and blood" — which was not only a lie but absurd as well. Castro also was "a usurper, has been guilty of great offenses, has impoverished and drained the country of almost its last dollar, and has deserted his post now when most needed [!]." And so on. Therefore, Stockton said, moved by "reports from the interior of scenes of rapine, blood and murder," and "as the only means to save from destruction the lives and property of the foreign residents and citizens of the country who have invoked his protection" — he was going to drive the criminals and usurpers out of California and restore peace and prosperity.

There was no rapine, pillage, or murder, no one had invited his protection, and those he was calling usurpers and criminals were the constituted authorities. And Stockton was not only falsifying the situation, he was disregarding the purposes of his government. Frémont was not the only one who could see a main chance, and the commodore was off for glory. He knew his Hollywood.

Frémont's memoirs show that he was not happy in having to accept a superior commander, but as Major Jinks of the Horse Marines he was at last legitimate. Stockton embarked the Navy Battalion of Mounted Riflemen on the *Cyane,* July 26, and sent them off to occupy San Diego. Kit Carson's most poignant journey followed: he got seasick and so did his messmates, who had just finished a big drunk. Frémont raised the flag at San Diego on July 29, and after impressing horses started north to join Stockton on August 8. The Conqueror's record remained untarnished; he had not yet faced a hostile force in California. He never did.

Stockton made up a landing force of 360 marines and sailors and sailed in the *Congress* on August 1. He stopped to raise the flag at Santa Barbara and reached San Pedro on August 6. Larkin, who was with him and still hoped to abate the show of force, got in touch with Castro and Pico, whose pathetic efforts to raise a defensive army were failing. They would have been happy to declare a truce and meet Stockton for negotiations. A rout is more glorious than a treaty, however, and Stockton refused with a ruffle of drums which proved that the navy was as good as the army at soliloquy. So the governor and the *comandante,* oozing a rhetoric that is no less absurd in that it expressed the genuine emotions of conquered people, gave up the struggle for which they could rouse no popular support and abandoned their fragmentary forces. Castro rode away for Mexico and Pico, after hiding for a month near San Juan Capistrano, escaped to Lower California. There was now not even a mirage of opposition. On August 14 Frémont's command joined Stockton's and the land army of sailors occupied Los Angeles. This was five days before Kearny entered Santa Fe, and the Conquest of California, Major Frémont second in command, was completed . . . for a while.

Stockton sat down to write his report, or shooting script, to the Secretary of the Navy. (It would come into the hands of Mason, formerly Attorney General, who took the place when Polk made Bancroft Minister to England.) He told his chief that in less than a month he had "chased the Mexican army more than three hundred miles along the coast, pursued them thirty miles in the interior of their own country, routed and dispersed them and secured the Territory to the United States, ended the war, restored peace and harmony among the people, and put a civil government into successful operation!"

What war? What army? What harmony? What civil government? But it was a practical treatment for the movies and the Secretary of the Navy was in Washington.

The treatment, however, left out of account some facts and potentialities. Stockton, head of the military conquest and *de facto* governor, began to prepare a constitution and a plan to organize California as a territory of the United States. He gave it up — which was just as well since the Californians had something left to say and since the President had charged General Kearny with that job. So his thoughts turned toward an attack by sea on Mazatlán and Acapulco — a sound idea. He began to put California in condition to spare his genius. He ordered Frémont to recruit the Horse Marines to a strength of three hundred. He sent Kit Carson overland with dispatches, on August 28. Reaffirming martial law as the code of his territory, he reorganized the military.

By orders of September 2 he divided California into three military districts. He put various subordinates in command of various small areas, where they promptly began granting paroles to Californians presumed to have been in armed opposition. He made Gillespie commander at Los Angeles, which was a mistake. And he made Frémont commandant of the whole territory, which, though all he could do, was a worse mistake.

In northern California various resident Americans hurried to form various semi-military organizations, or vigilance committees. Various other Americans began the speculation in real estate which had always been one promise of revolution. And the first immigrants from the East began to come down from the Sierra.

Through the summer President Polk was forced sometimes to remember that he had a war on. The necessity, which was national, greatly irked the head of the Democratic Party, which had gone local. He had his Oregon Settlement and his Independent Treasury now, and while Congress heaved and rippled with dissents he was trying to force through his bill for the reduction of the tariff of '42. It was vehemently opposed. Polk scented corruption and his resentment flowed steadily in his diary. He had to compromise with the Democratic ironmasters of Pennsylvania, though he told them their state was agricultural. The compromise got the bill passed but the November elections were to show that he had lost Pennsylvania. He had lost New York, too, though no one yet understood why.

Those November elections were never out of anyone's mind. Polk had gloomy apprehensions when he vetoed not only a bill for the repayment of the French Spoliation claims, the sustenance of an ancient lobby, but also that checking account of Congressmen, the rivers and harbors bill. The activity of pressure groups for various candidates grew obscene, but was only one part of the political turmoil. All summer long Mr. Buchanan yearned to be a Justice of the Supreme Court, as a further step toward the White House, but shrank from the fight he would surely have to make to be confirmed. Every angle and shadow of this appointment had to be considered in relation to the pressure groups. Polk was embarrassed in his maneuvers but on the whole relieved when Buchanan decided to stand pat and keep the State Department. He got little other relief. Few Democrats measured up to his standard of selfless subordination, none had a passion for anonymity, the party press was fractious, the Whig press was in full cry, revenues fell off when the tariff reduction took effect, the Treasury found no brokers who would take a war loan, and Congress, boiling and bucking toward adjournment, was not so much in rebellion as in a coma. It would have been a bad time for any administration, it was disastrous for a war administration.

But something had to be done about the war and it seemed to be up to Polk. No one had a plan but slowly, haphazardly, under pressure of events, politics, and chance, one began to form by accretion. Bile spurted in the President's diary at what he took to be a conspiracy — anything was a conspiracy that did not square with his ideas. There was Taylor. Since the engagements which he spelled "Palialito" and "Resacka," Taylor had apparently wanted to do nothing whatever. . . . The victor sat in his attakapas pantaloons under a tent fly and grew great. He wrote to his son-in-law Dr. Wood that "I greatly fear that the [any further] campaign will be a failure which will break down the individual who conducts it," but he summoned publicity to prevent the breakage. He established the friendliest relations with newspaper correspondents, who knew copy when they saw it. Brave, benignant, stupid, as common as your Uncle Bill, he dealt gently with the excesses of volunteers, assuring them that whoever might be responsible for disease, inaction, and bad food, Old Rough and Ready was not. While the political brigadiers kept a stream of letters going home where they would do the most good, Taylor also enlarged his correspondence. Bliss, his chief of staff, corrected the spelling, Taylor being of the opinion that, in our perfected system, a President did not need spelling or much else.

Polk foresaw Taylor's candidacy even before Taylor did and it made him furious. He could get neither plans nor information from Taylor, who had none. His hard mind bogged in the softness of what cannot be called Taylor's intelligence. He saw that Taylor, who unhappily could win battles, intended to carry out orders, not plan campaigns. Polk had no orders to give him — and the worst was that any campaign he might conceive for Taylor would only glorify the Whig candidate. There was no alternative to Taylor but Winfield Scott, the head of the army, and Scott was doubly damned. Not only was he a Whig and a perennial candidate, but he had opposed Polk's ideas. What was worse, he insisted on preparing to fight before fighting. He had warned Polk that it would take at least till fall to create an effective army. That proved his ignorance of political necessities or else meant a Whig plot to discredit the administration. He wanted to drill troops, arm them, work out logistic problems, gather shipping and transport — in short, he was scientific and visionary. He would not do. Polk longed to turn the war over to one of the Democratic orators whom he had made brigadiers. Any of them would have done, say Shields, who was lately of the Land Office, or Judge Quitman, who was a leading Mason, or Robert Patterson, who had nominated Jackson for the Presidency, or the venal Gideon Pillow, who claimed to have made Polk President. His favorite, however, was William Orlando Butler, who was probably the best military man of the lot. But the Cabinet had to inform him that he could not entrust the war to amateurs, and in this simple fear that votes would be lost the republic was saved. Polk gave in but went on despising Whigs and military science and by election time would achieve the most preposterous military suggestion ever made by a President.

It was Scott who kept the war going — Scott, and Jesup, the Quartermaster General, and Marcy, the Secretary of War. In a shambles of ignorance, inefficiency, graft, and political intrigue, they somehow got a prodigious job done. They turned loose a gigantic productivity and got some of it under control. Troops were raised, arms and munitions were manufactured, transport was achieved. It cost the Treasury hugely, the waste was incalculable, the failures were innumerable, but the job was done. And Scott, who was a soldier, was thinking toward the military end. He kept his temper, he wrote no more damaging letters, he began to make headway. He bade a friend "imitate the example of that heathen who touched his hat to the fallen statue of Jupiter, saying 'Who knows but that he may be replaced upon his pedestal?' "

Polk's secret war developed, the affair of Santa Anna. From Havana the great brigand was directing the efforts of his conspirators to undermine the Paredes government in his fatherland. They were succeeding. As early as January Paredes had written, "Order is precarious, peace insecure, and the nation, in the midst of the anarchy which consumes it and the chaos which surrounds it, moves toward dissolution and the fear of death." It had got steadily worse. His associates were either treacherous to him personally, café-table intellectuals, or grafters. He himself was honest and patriotic but stupid and given to drink. There were few revenues. The army had magnificent uniforms, incomplete equipment, and no pay. Besides, it was far from loyal. Various provinces were in chronic revolt, one was declaring itself independent, full-scale revolution was ready to break out. Paredes and such assistants as he could get dealt badly with the increasing anarchy — and had against them, in Havana, the master of treachery who was also the idol of the people, or of some of them. By mid-July Santa Anna had Mexico ready to long for some more of his liberation.

And Polk, who had agents in Mexico encouraging anarchy, now sent a messenger to inquire whether the earlier arrangement still held. On Santa Anna's word, it did. The brigand was going to reappear as a Liberator and, with the assistance of the United States, would deliver his unhappy country from the tyranny of its monarchists. When he returned to power he would accept Polk's offer to suspend hostilities. He would make a treaty ceding enough land to indemnify the United States for its war expenses. (Here, as elsewhere in Polk's dream, the United States was to pay for the ceded territory. In other words, the indemnity was to consist of the profit following a rise in real estate.) He would assist in determining a permanent boundary and make sure that the harbor of San Francisco was north of it. In order to preserve the appearance of coercion, which his bemused but patriotic countrymen would require, he suggested that the ports of Vera Cruz and Tampico be occupied. (By this time Polk had also got round to thinking of them.) He assured the messenger that the army of occupation would find the climate healthy. And he ended with a solicitous reminder: let the President see to it that the personal publicity of Santa Anna in the American press was conducted in the most favorable terms.

Good! The President renewed his undercover arrangements. He got to work again on the secret Executive fund of two million dollars that was to buy a treaty by underwriting the pay of the Mexican army. And in the serene belief that he had arranged a peace for the warring countries, he ordered Commodore Conner to pass the Liberator through the blockade. He had bought his gold brick.

The Liberator acted. On August 3 Vice President Bravo, Santa Anna's man, overthrew Paredes, and the garrison of Vera Cruz and other parts of the army made a *pronunciamento*. This ceremony, a tradition, consisted of a formal announcement, accompanied by oratory and salutes, that someone else had bought the army or was expected to buy it. Its symbolic value was considerable and even in the disaffected northern provinces detachments put their new loyalty on record. On August 8 Santa Anna left Havana on the steamship *Arab*. On August 16, under the arranged chaperonage of a captain of the British Navy, who reported to Conner that she carried no contraband, the *Arab* passed the blockade and anchored at Vera Cruz. In demonstrations of wild enthusiasm — gunfire, confetti, and a blizzard of engraved resolutions — Santa Anna landed and began a progress of state to his hacienda at Jalapa.

Napoleon was back and as much unity as Mexico was capable of answered his return. He told his countrymen that he desired no political power but hoped only to drive the invader from Mexican soil. He notified Mr. Polk that the American proposals for an armistice and the negotiation of peace could be considered only by the Mexican Congress, which would not meet till December. Then with the superhuman energy that was his one valuable characteristic he began transforming the pressed soldiery from a mob to an army.

President Polk had been as shrewd as possible and American diplomacy had achieved a triumph.

Taylor sat under his grapevine at Matamoros and could not have had a better press. Clearly the country appreciated his victories but the administration sent no official praise. The holy cause of Whiggery, about which Taylor had no clear ideas, was probably being degraded by the Democrats. Taylor cultivated his acquaintance with Congressional Whigs in letters which show Bliss's editing. The President and the War Department kept annoying him with incomprehensible demands for information. They wanted to know what the country around him was like; he made no effort to find out. They wanted to know what ideas for further conquest the commanding general in the field was working out; he wasn't working any out. The administration's ignorance and the commander's stupidity interacted, and the confusion was increased by the sloth of communication. It took between three and four weeks to deliver a dispatch, but neither headquarters thought of establishing a courier service. (Polk usually heard of developments in the war from the British embassy before reports came through from the army.) But for that matter, neither headquarters thought to put its dispatches into cipher.

Volunteers kept arriving till Taylor had some twelve thousand troops, twice as many as he could supply or maneuver. The military system had enlisted them for periods ranging from three months to a year; some had to be sent home as soon as they arrived. They lost their morale and their health at base camps, dying by the hundred. Most of the regulars had been acclimated in lower Texas and had been disciplined a little; it was the volunteers, especially those from the Northern states, who sickened. The problems of supply by sea and transport by land now became acute, and remained so for the duration. Taylor's officers did what they could but most of them were novices. The quartermaster general succeeded in getting several thousand wagons to Matamoros. They were almost useless for the country ahead but Taylor, if he knew that fact, had neglected to inform Jesup or Marcy. It therefore became necessary to get mules. Mexico was full of them but Taylor had not tried to locate them and when the army finally moved it had about half as many as it needed. Ammunition was short, medical supplies were short, food was not short but was frequently bad. The army, which had come to fight, found itself going to hospital instead. Hundreds went over the hill, many of them putting such training as they had had at the service of Mexico.

Lieutenant George Gordon Meade was depressed. He had a mathematician's mind and he was a soldier. He had not favored this war but any war should be conducted efficiently, and all that reassured him was the equal inefficiency of the Mexicans. He admired Taylor as a fighting general but could praise nothing in the conduct of the campaign. Soon after the occupation of Matamoros he saw that the next logical step was to take Monterrey,* but he had no conviction that it could be done. He continued to resent the volunteers, who had "to be taken care of as you would so many children." A third of them were sick, most of them, including the officers, were helpless. He disliked the Texans, who were vindictive and, though the bravest of men, careless and stupid in action, squandering their ammunition

* This name is universally spelled Monterey in American texts. I use the Mexican spelling so that the reader may distinguish it at sight from the Monterey in California.

and being forced to retire, leaving their sick and wounded on the field. He did not think that the Mexicans would offer formal opposition in the field, but believed that they would conduct an effective and possibly disastrous guerrilla war. When he heard that Santa Anna had landed, however, he changed his mind. "He is the master-spirit of this country, far beyond all others in talent and resources . . . we may look for a long and severely contested war."

Independently of the administration and by some process which must not be thought of as cerebral, Taylor decided to do what Polk was hoping he would do — advance into the northern provinces. He organized the largest force he could supply, about six thousand effectives — and then had to stop for the reconnoissance and preparations that should have been attended to long before.

His probable objective was Saltillo, beyond the mountains in Coahuila, and on the way to it he must take Monterrey, the capital of Nuevo León. A march overland turning out to be impossible, he started a flotilla of river steamboats up the Rio Grande on July 6. Some two hundred and fifty miles up the river, the mouth of the San Juan was the head of navigation, and a few miles up the San Juan was the small city of Camargo. Through July the army crawled toward Camargo and the advance guard took it without opposition on the thirty-first. It was notoriously the unhealthiest place in the region and Taylor determined to make it his base. The army now got really sick — and sat down while Taylor took thought.

He had acquired an unshakable conviction that the administration was trying to kill his candidacy by procuring his defeat in the field. He knew, however, that a candidate had to go on winning victories. On August 19 he started his advance toward Cerralvo, sixty miles away. (Under Worth. Achilles had returned to the war on hearing the news of Palo Alto. He had brought his inkstand along and went on sending letters to his lobby. But he was incomparably the best soldier in this army.) The early part of this march was terrible with heat, bad water, and bad roads. But higher altitudes brought cooler weather and the army's health improved. The advance reached Cerralvo, a beautiful town in the foothills, on August 25. Anticipations appeared to have been justified, for the populace welcomed the invaders. Here were good food, abundant water, a lovely countryside, and an agreeable conquest. Morale rose.

So far there had been no hostilities, hardly even the glimmer of lances on the horizon. Another hitch would take Taylor to Monterrey, and here Ampudia had concentrated the fragments of his defeated army and was getting reinforcements. At this moment the

New Orleans *Delta* heard that the Mexican troops were chiefly "the lowest classes of the cross breeds, who have been taken in chains to the capital and there, in their half-naked state, they are furnished with a musket and taught roughly and toughly how to load, aim, and fire." The Mexican press described Taylor's army in similar terms. But if either army supposed that the other would not fight, Lieutenant Meade assured both that they would learn otherwise.

On September 18, with Hays's Texas Rangers riding ahead and Taylor losing his lethargy as action became likely, the army came down into the valley of the San Juan again after a detour, and found itself within cannon range of the green and white city of Monterrey, with the foothills beyond it rising to the peaks of the Sierra Madre. Taylor promptly considered his favorite maneuver, a bayonet charge, but the Mexicans opened on him with cannon and he had to stop and do some thinking.

To Taylor, as to many other American generals in the succeeding hundred years, a battle consisted of some preliminary work and a splendid finale in what was called cold steel. Just how he had acquired his vision is not known, since his principal campaigns had been against the Seminole, whom no bayonet ever touched. But in obedience to it he had solved the problem of inadequate transport by leaving most of his artillery behind. His engineers reconnoitered Monterrey on Saturday, September 19. The eastern and northern approaches were heavily fortified. West of the town, the road to Saltillo, which was the line of both reinforcement and retreat, was commanded by lighter fortifications but the terrain they dominated was formidable. The engineers reported that Monterrey could be turned and the Saltillo road cut. They thus suggested the tactics that won the battle.

The battle began late Sunday afternoon, September 20, when Taylor sent Worth with the Second Division (mostly regulars) and Hays's Texas Rangers to take the Saltillo Road. They did not quite reach it and had to bivouac in a driving rain. But the next day, September 21, they began the operations that saved Taylor for glory and made the battle of Monterrey a technical victory for the American Army.

Worth won his battle because he was able to co-ordinate his attacks and give them sequence. The lesson of Palo Alto was repeated on Monday, when the insufficient American artillery broke up a heavy charge of Mexican lancers so handily that the Rangers could turn it back with little loss. This cleared the road and Worth had won his battle right there, for the Mexicans in Monterrey could neither retreat to the interior nor receive reinforcements or supplies. But Worth knew war and, not content with a paper victory, began to attack the city from the rear. He formed an assaulting force under C. F. Smith, who was to live long enough to repeat this decisive action at Fort Donelson. They had to cross a river, they had to work up a hillside nearly a thousand feet high, they were under artillery and rifle fire, but they had competent officers and plenty of guts. Reaching the crest, they were able to charge the first bastion with the bayonet, though probably it was empty when they reached it. By midafternoon they had the whole ridge, at slight cost, and were turning captured cannon on the next stronghold. This was another height, across the river and nearer the city. Worth prepared to attack it but his skirmishers had got no farther than the base of the hill when night fell. Another violent storm set in. Most of Worth's men had not eaten since Sunday morning and none had blankets, but they had won a battle.

Meanwhile, to the eastward, Taylor had not got near enough Monterrey to use his favorite weapon. Many eyewitnesses say that his courage was an inspiration. It was just as well, for his intelligence and his professional competence were not. Garland was commanding the First Division, the quarrelsome Twiggs being ill, and Taylor sent him out to take the eastern forts with the bayonet. Garland led his command past some of the redoubts and into the nearest city streets, where artillery from the forts promptly blew them to pieces. Garland withdrew to re-form and Taylor, who lacked Worth's skill at coordinating attacks, sent in Butler's division over much the same approach. The Fourth Infantry, including Lieutenant Grant, had a bad time and something less than half of it was left when, after a few minutes, it also had to get out again. A brigade under Mr. Polk's appointee, General Quitman, was still fresh, and Taylor sent it in farther to the south. Quitman also was met with a decimating fire and his troops began to melt away. But the Mexicans in the forts were beginning to be discouraged by the enemy's insistence on coming back, and their commander was scared. He withdrew some of them and others fled at the crucial moment. So Colonel Jefferson Davis of the First Mississippi Rifles, who for three happy and heartbreaking months in 1835 had been Taylor's son-in-law, was able to wave his sword, lead his men into one of the redoubts, and so prepare the defeat of the Confederate States of America. The Mississippians took another redoubt also and withstood a concentrated fire from the other forts.

Taylor was trying in person farther to the north, and inspiring with his courage a lot of soldiers whom the Mexican artillery, some of it served by American deserters, blew back three separate times. They could not get close enough to thrust with Old Betsy. When they got into the outskirts of the town, the Mexicans slaughtered them from the roofs. No one had thought to bring scaling or storming weapons, and they died by scores. Taylor thought that a small battery ought to advance and shoot it out with the heaviest fort but the commander sensibly refused. So, late in the afternoon, Taylor had to pull all his army out of range again except the volunteers, mostly Davis', in the captured redoubt. He had lost about six times as many men as Worth was to lose in three days of fighting. He had taught a number of his subordinate commanders a lesson he could not learn himself. And he had so used up his army that they would do no fighting the next day, though the Mexicans withdrew by night to the center of the city.

On Tuesday the twenty-second, however, they occupied the abandoned earthworks and appreciatively watched Worth's troops win the remaining heights west of Monterrey. Worth conducted this operation with spirit and intelligence — and without help or information from Taylor. His Mexican opponent received reinforcements which any attack by Taylor would have prevented, and prepared an assault. The Mexicans attacked with great *élan* but Worth caught them in the flank, drove the survivors headlong into the city, and concentrated the captured guns on them.

By Wednesday the twenty-third Taylor's subordinates had sufficiently reorganized his battered army for him to try again. They had made plans for street fighting too, and so the troops made their way from block to block toward the grand plaza in the center of Monterrey. It was terrible work and they were cruelly shot up but they kept going. At midafternoon ammunition failed them. Lieutenant Grant, who was a quartermaster, rode frantically back to organize the supply. But Taylor, for no reason, ordered the whole force back again, all the way out of town. They went back, protesting, and the Mexicans shot them up as they went.

Worth had no orders from his commander. His batteries threw shell into the city and his attack was ready. When he heard the noise of Taylor's battle he sent it in — two columns down main streets.

Pause while one of history's emblems is created. Many of Worth's troops were Texans, and some had worked the great herds of Texas longhorns. As, heads down against the musket fire, they pelted along those two avenues toward the first barricades, they began to shout. They produced a cry of the cattle range, a wild, unnerving sound deep in the bass which climbed to a full-throated, deafening falsetto. They would go home again after the campaigns in Mexico and peace would come for a while. Then on July 21, 1861, some of them would be under arms again behind the brown stagnant watercourse called Bull Run Creek, facing McDowell's army of Northerners, and would produce that screech again. It was the Rebel Yell.

They had almost as bad a time as Taylor's troops, fighting from house to house, but they would not be stopped. Their engineers, chiefly Lieutenant Meade, taught them to pierce adobe walls and throw grenades through the holes. They mopped up, square by square, fighting desperately, swearing like Texans, posting sharp-shooters, bringing cannon up dismounted and training them down the streets. They were just one square from the plaza when night fell. Worth did not call them back.

He had won Taylor's third victory. Ampudia had had enough and, before fighting could begin on Thursday morning, asked for terms. Taylor proposed unconditional surrender but consented to a meeting of commissioners. As a result, Ampudia was permitted to withdraw his army intact, with six of his field pieces and all his small arms and equipment. The Americans were to occupy the city but were to remain east of a line drawn a few miles beyond it for eight weeks, the Mexicans also agreeing not to cross that line. This amounted to an eight weeks' armistice. Taylor had no authority to grant an armistice.

Badly shaken as the army was — casualties amounted to twenty per cent of the effectives — Taylor could have destroyed Ampudia's army with another day of fighting. That is, Worth could have destroyed it. If he had done so, Santa Anna's preparations to the southward would have been jeopardized or even paralyzed. But Taylor was outtalked by his opponent, knew that he had forfeited the respect of his principal subordinates, and, besides, was making an unfamiliar essay in political war. He needed at least eight weeks to restore his army — and maybe the Santa Anna intrigue, which he vaguely knew about, would mature in that time. Or, if he did not wound Mexican pride by destroying the army, maybe the northern provinces, maybe even the national government, would make peace.

His political thinking was as bad as his generalship. When word of Monterrey reached Washington, Polk, as commander in chief, had to disavow the armistice, and, as head of the Democratic Party, understood it to be a Whig stratagem to bring the war into disrepute. He began to whittle down the Whig candidate.

No use. Though Worth was writing letters again as soon as the fighting stopped, though many other politicians in the army also told their correspondents the details of Taylor's ineffectiveness, he had won another victory. Worth and the courage of the private soldier had won the battle, but the glory was their commander's. Nothing could keep him from the White House now, though his subordinates were to give him a fourth, dubious, unnecessary victory. With some nine hundred Americans killed or disabled in three days, the newspapers had plenty of copy. Stories of heroism went out for an exulting nation to read. The relatives of the dead could get what satisfaction they might from a bravery that accomplished nothing. For the battle of Monterrey should not have been fought and did nothing to advance the war.

Polk learned about the battle on the evening of October 11, and the next day he ordered the armistice terminated. But the dispatches that arrived in October arrived in a United States that was rounding a decisive turn. That turn had begun in August and we must go back six weeks before the battle of Monterrey.

Nothing is more fragile than the secrets of diplomacy. Rumors of Polk's deal with Santa Anna had reached the army, as we have seen. They also traveled across the United States, gathering picturesqueness as they spread. Before Santa Anna landed in Mexico the Whig press was airing them. They temporarily cured the schizophrenia of the Whigs, who on the one hand had had to denounce the war and on the other had had to praise the valor of those who were fighting it. In the public mind they mingled with other rumors, especially those which magnified the army opposing Taylor and anticipated for him disasters that were in no danger of occurring. There were casualty lists now, also: the dead and wounded of the first battles, of the guerrilla raids, of the camp fevers. By August a discouragement typical of this stage of all our wars had undermined the enthusiasm of May. And finally, Henry Thoreau's laborious thinking at Walden Pond had been prophetic of his countrymen. A good many had caught up with Thoreau, with Theodore Parker, and with Hosea Bigelow. What, Hosea had asked on June 17,

> *Wut*'ll make ye act like freemen?
> *Wut*'ll git your dander riz?

. . . As early as July 9 the Baltimore *American,* a Whig sheet, had learned, it said, what portions of Mexico the administration intended to seize as the spoils of war. The rest of the party press was soon publishing the *American's* findings. To wit: all Mexico to the line of Tampico; all California; parts of Jalisco, Guadalahara (meaning Guanajuato), and Zacatecas; all of Sonora, Durango, San Luis Potosí, "New Leon," Chihuahua, Coahuila, and Tamaulipas.

It must be said flatly: no such plan was in anyone's mind. Immediately after the declaration of war jubilant cries had gone up from the most extreme expansionists, eagle-screamers like Walter Whitman, and a few who would have been members of the slave conspiracy if there had been a slave conspiracy — cries which welcomed all Mexico to the liberation of the United States. Sometimes they added in the Central American states, sometimes the rest of the hemisphere. They had, however, soon subsided. Such a conquest was obviously impossible and few Americans knew enough foreign geography to have clear ideas about it. Toward the end of the war, when strains had been quadrupled, a desire to seize all or a great part of Mexico would awaken again, but in August of '46 none contemplated and few desired it. The most extreme expansionist in official life was Walker, the Secretary of the Treasury, and he said nothing. Polk himself wanted what he had always wanted, New Mexico and California. He carefully left the door open for further expansion, repeatedly telling his diary and his callers that "perhaps something more" was not unlikely, but that was a contingency, not a plan, and it hinged on a simple calculation of the costs of war.

Nevertheless, by August the expeditions against Santa Fe, Chihuahua, and California had notified everyone, if nothing else had, that this was a war of conquest. The United States was going to acquire a lot of land. Nearly everybody wanted that land but now there was no way to avoid thinking about it. Implications, relationships, began to force their way into consciousness.

At the beginning of August Congress, which would adjourn in ten days, was in one of the angry, resentful moods that always precede a re-forming of the lines. Mr. Polk, detecting candidacies in every move it made, was stubbornly following out his plans. On the third he vetoed the seasonal pork, the rivers and harbors bill. On the fourth the House tried and failed to pass the bill over his veto. And on the fourth also he sent to a Senate which had lost its pork his proposal for a secret appropriation of two million dollars.

Once more, here is what Polk intended by this step in his deal with Santa Anna. Mexico owed citizens of the United States a considerable sum, duly adjudicated. Mexico had no money and could pay only by ceding land. Santa Anna, Polk thought, would make the cession. But no Mexican government could make such a cession unless it kept the support of the army. To keep that support, Santa Anna would have to pay the army, but Mexico had no revenue. The two million dollars, an advance on the ultimate payment in full, would enable Santa Anna to pay the army, conciliate his country, and actually make the cession of New Mexico and California which in turn would enable Polk to end his war. This, Polk thought, was a simple, straightforward way to peace. Nobody could have been more honest in that belief. Or more blind.

The proposal went to the Senate in Executive (secret) Session. At once it focused much opposition, resentment, and maneuvering that had been aimless. Polk and his whips worked hard, but in the bars and boarding houses where the unofficial steering committees met there was a flurry of purposeful preparation. Heads got together, expedients suggested themselves, and here was a big chance. The Whigs had him in a vise and would not vote his appropriation unless he also asked it of the House — which was equivalent to making it public and giving the show away. Polk refused to give in, worked furiously, had to give in. The money was asked of the House as an appropriation for foreign negotiations.

(*Voted:* to adjourn at noon of August 10.)

On August 8 Polk went to the Vice President's room in the Capitol, to sign the miscellaneous bills that drop out of the machine in quantity at the end of a session. The day wore on. Polk heard that a bill appropriating two million dollars for "extraordinary expenses" originating in the intercourse between the United States and foreign nations had been introduced in the House. He did not promptly learn what followed, but he began to hear that the gentlemen of the Congress were celebrating the imminent adjournment. "Several members . . . were much excited by drink," Mr. Polk, a temperate man, disapproved, and of course Daniel Webster was one of them. The President left the Capitol at eleven-thirty.

A little before 7 P.M., in the House Chamber, lamplit, moist with the terrible still heat of August in Washington. About a hundred people in the spectators' gallery, among them the majestic commander of the armies, General Scott, in dress uniform. Several speakers rose to defend the President's request, or to suspect it in Whig sneers. Mr. Winthrop of Massachusetts was specific: he felt a dilemma like the one that had forced him to vote for war, and he was sure that the President was asking Congress to sanction an increase of Southern territory, slave territory. Mr. Grider of Kentucky succeeded him. Then Mr. Wilmot of Pennsylvania, who had been busy during the five o'clock recess, stood up. Mr. David Wilmot, Democrat, in his first term, who had been wholly orthodox in his conduct so far, so orthodox that, alone of his delegation, he had supported Mr. Polk's tariff reduction.

(August 8, 1846. Taylor's army had occupied Mier, beyond Camargo, but had not started for Cerralvo on the road to Monterrey. Kearny's Dragoons stayed in camp on the Canadian River, while Doniphan's First Missouri and the artillery came down from the Raton to the parched New Mexico plain. Twenty-five miles out from Bent's Fort Susan Magoffin, just alive, saw no blade of grass but "with anxious eyes and heart to gain first the long wished luxury" saw her first "false ponds" or mirages. Francis Parkman, on his way south from Fort Laramie to the Pueblo, was in camp with Bisonette, had heard from an Indian that there was war with Mexico, and made a note on "the gross indecency" of some Indian names. Frémont started north with his captured mules from San Diego to join Stockton, who was preparing to take Los Angeles. Bryant had come out of the Salt Desert into the greasewood barrens west of it, and on this day saw grass again and cottonwoods, and with a lifting heart reached the Humboldt. There came to Fort Hall, where Boggs and Thornton were camped, one Jesse Applegate, a famous man, bringing word of a better route to the settlements in Oregon. At Fort Leavenworth the Mormon Battalion was getting equipment. At a crossing of the Weber River, near the mouth of Echo Canyon, the Donner party had sent James Frazier Reed ahead to find a road where no road was. Anxiously awaiting his return, they could ponder a message from Lansford Hastings which told them that the way he had chosen for them to travel to Great Salt Lake could not, he found, be traveled. . . . But Mr. Wilmot is speaking in the House.)

Speaking about the President's request. Mr. Wilmot says that he did not think this a war of conquest when he voted for it and does not think it one now. He will support the President, but just why does the President want this money? Since we will not pay for land we claim to be ours, that is up to the Rio Grande, there must be an intention to acquire more land. Mr. Wilmot approves our acquiring territory on the Pacific, including the Bay of San Francisco, by purchase or negotiation. But he is opposed to the extension of the peculiar institution. Slavery existed in Texas, so Mr. Wilmot accepted it there. But if, now, free territory comes in (and Mexico was free soil) God forbid that we shall plant the peculiar institution in it.

Mr. Wilmot, not being an orator, speaks easily, clearly, quietly. He moves an amendment to the bill:—

Provided: That as an express and fundamental condition to the acquisition of any territory from the Republic of Mexico by the United States, by virtue of any treaty which may be negotiated between them, and to the use by the Executive of the moneys herein appropriated, neither slavery nor involuntary servitude shall ever exist in any part of said territory, except for crime, whereof the party shall first be duly convicted.

This is the Wilmot Proviso. It fastened the slavery question to Polk's request for two million dollars for the purchase of territory.

At 8:20 P.M., Saturday, August 8, it fell, not explosively, into a House which was disorganized, inattentive, and in some degree drunk. The Southern nerves were lax; only a feeble opposition could be improvised, though a whisper ran through the city, the gallery filled, and the Secretary of State, the Postmaster General, and the Secretary of the Navy hurried into the lobby to watch the maneuvering. After the customary substitutes and motions, the Proviso was amended to apply specifically to a treaty of peace. Then the House passed the bill and adjourned into cavernous heat.

On Monday, August 10, the Senate took up the House bill, an hour short of noon, and Lewis of Alabama moved to strike out the Proviso. Over Sunday something of its importance had been realized, groups had met hurriedly, angry plans had been formulated. But time was inexorable: the First Session of the Twenty-ninth Congress would end at twelve noon — and the House clock was seven minutes faster than the Senate's. Senator John Davis of Massachusetts got the floor, began to talk, and would not yield. It is not known whether he intended to let the bill come to vote in the last minute — Lewis' motion would surely have passed — or whether he intended to talk it to death. At any rate, while the clock was still short of twelve, word came that the House had adjourned. Mr. Davis was still talking but Mr. Atchison, the president pro tem, declared the Senate adjourned.

Polk was furious. He considered the Proviso "a mischievous & foolish amendment," to be explained as factional intrigue only. He wrote in his journal, altogether honestly, "What connection slavery had with making peace with Mexico it is difficult to conceive." He shared that difficulty with his kind and with, it is certain, a majority of his countrymen. But the limitations of his tight, shrewd mind show nakedly in that sentence, and that particular kind of limitation had now been started toward oblivion. His blindness was his country's evasion, and evasion was now going to end. Slavery was out of the closet, and it was going to stay out. By December the nation would be rocking in the storm which was to last nineteen years. David Wilmot, safeguarding the conquests of his party's war President, had made A. Lincoln President of the United States.

It has become conventional to explain the Wilmot Proviso as something other than what it was. True, into the hasty plans that produced it and the debates and maneuvers that followed it up to 1850 there went a complex variety of motives and interests. That the Democratic Party was in process of breaking up to re-form on a simpler base has certainly not gone unmentioned here. Polk's handling of the war had made enemies in his party. His handling of Oregon had displeased some, his veto of the annual pork had angered others, his tariff policy had cost him the support of still others, especially in the North. He had made enemies by his stubbornness and secretiveness, by his loathing of office seekers, by his appointments and his refusals to appoint. Moreover, the old tensions inside the party had increased. Some Democrats had become Whigs, others were on their way toward Free Soil principles. There were anti-war Democrats, anti-expansion Democrats, high-tariff Democrats, Old South Democrats, New South Democrats, pan-South Democrats, anti-South Democrats, anti-slavery Democrats. The pressures strained the containing skin and the Democracy needed only a touch to fly apart.

If the Democracy was a chaotic contradiction, it made more sense and order than the Whigs. They also were in process of disruption. For nearly every Democratic faction there was a corresponding group of Whigs who held much the same beliefs, at whatever cost in logic, and there were other factions. Only the tariff and opposition to the war were keeping them a national party. Otherwise they were a series of local institutions, interests, and machines, riotous with contradictions and heading for the complete extinction of '52. That there were pro-war Whigs, extreme expansionist Whigs, low-tariff Whigs, and pro-slavery Whigs only added to the violence of the storm that would begin before December.

Finally, there had occurred the fission between the South and West that overturned an established security. The war had increased the strain of a deficit economy. And Oregon and California were further stresses breaking the equilibrium.

Now, no doubt all this, and more besides — anti-rent sentiments, the pressures of candidacies, a sudden sharpening of agitation — can be found in the maneuvering that preceded and followed the Wilmot Proviso. That being said, the fact remains that David Wilmot, on his own behalf or acting for others, to better his position in the party or to assert a belief — David Wilmot, in a ten-minute speech, sounded the brazen alarum in the night that had sometimes waked Thomas Jefferson in terror. For twenty-six years the nation had refused to face the paradox at its core, the unresolved conflict at the base of its economy and its politics. If it had faced that conflict steadily during the preceding years, the death and destruction now ahead of it might have been modified or even averted. It had not. Now it would have to. So the collapse of parties was not a disease but the symptom of one. Repression begets neurosis and Congress was only faithfully mirroring the profound disturbance underneath. The motives of David Wilmot and his supporters do not matter. The thing he did must have been done by someone at some time — but he did it here and now. He broke the repression.

XI
Continental Divide

THE Whirlwind's people howled and gashed their arms to mourn Henry Chatillon's squaw, and killed her horse because she was lame and would need it to cross the prairies to the spirit land. But the warriors posed — motionless on horseback, arms crossed, or standing like statues in blacked robes, or sitting with robes draped in marble folds round their shoulders. Only in the Vatican had Francis Parkman seen "such faultless models of the human figure." Free and noble attitudes, bow in hand, quiver slung at the shoulder — Parkman knew why Benjamin West, on first seeing the Belvedere Apollo, had exclaimed, "By God, a Mohawk!" The Oglala looked beautiful and male to a young man so weakened by dysentery that he staggered when he tried to walk. Nothing would break the disease. When he grew stronger for a day or two, hope would come back; then a worse attack would stretch him racked and gasping on his robe.

Suddenly the Whirlwind's caprice was to hunt and he took his village beyond the Black Hills. Parkman would make one last attempt to see the savage in action and led his friends and hangers-on to the mouth of La Bonte Creek, where the war parties were still supposed to rendezvous. They reached it and found no Indians there. Quincy Adams Shaw decided that he had taken enough frustration from Indians; he would go no farther. While Parkman lived, however, the will of his ancestors forbade him to relinquish a purpose. They sent Delorier back to Fort Laramie with the cart and baggage. With Henry Chatillon, Shaw headed for the Laramie Mountains to hunt, but the first night he slept in poison ivy and his aristocratic limbs swelled so badly that he had to head for the fort, where Parkman had arranged to join him on August 1. After a midnight attack of dysentery that seared his bowels, Parkman started out with Raymond, the cheerful nincompoop, to find the Oglala. Perhaps some of them might still take to the warpath. If not, there would be some solace in watching a hunt, in the Medicine Bow Mountains.

They traveled the desert for three days. The desert of Isaiah: the cormorant and the bittern possessed it, the owl also and the raven dwelt in it, the satyr cried to his fellow and the line of confusion was stretched out on it, and the stones of emptiness. Under the sun's burning-glass, Parkman reeled in his saddle, all strength gone from his knees, his mind a spate of mirages. Raymond made all possible mistakes, let the horses escape, lost his rifle, saw many imaginary dangers but could not see the real ones — and the wonder is that the two of them did not die here of pure ineptness. New England kept rising into Parkman's feverish reverie: a green, cool land, a land of grass and trees and white-tumbling waters. The Coos Meadows, the lakes of the Connecticut — how many lakes and rivers! — Winnepesaukee, Memphremagog, the Winooski, Otter Creek, and a hopeful, strong young man paddling down them while he planned to write of Pontiac, Major Rogers, the noble Montcalm. Remembered in alkali dust that turned the sun white, the stench of sage, dead earth crawling with black crickets, metallic whir of locusts — and that last sound meant childhood in the Medford Fells. Once he thought of his strong, hale friend Tom Crawford — at his notch in gentler mountains, near more fragrant pines. "I lay for some time, scarcely able to move a limb. . . . The whole scene seemed parched with a pitiless, insufferable heat . . . a man armed to the teeth but wholly unable to fight and equally so to run away, traversing a dangerous wilderness on a sick horse."

The Medicine Bows were cooler, shadier, more hopeful, but Raymond was scared for here they might meet Shoshoni, or Arapaho, or even Blackfeet. His partisan ordered him on, and on July 16 they came down the far slope and saw the lodges of the Oglala. "Never did the heart of wanderer more gladden at the sight of home than did mine at the sight of those wild habitations."

So, joining Big Crow's lodge and taking Red Water for his friend and adviser, Francis Parkman began his life as an Oglala Sioux. It lasted just seventeen days while the village killed buffalo, dried meat, turned back to the Laramie Mountains, and cut lodge poles, but it was the historian's one ecstasy. All his life it would remain a splash of color and desire, unbelievable but real, much more real than anything that occurred in the years of suffering and despair, blindness and unrelenting will, on Chestnut Street.

Through those years on the walls of that Chestnut Street study hung lance and pipes and medicine pouch, war feathers, arrows, a strung bow, the pitiful mementoes of '46. There were days when he could not work at all for fear of bringing on the agitation that seemed to mean insanity. There were days when the use of his eyes was rationed at five minutes by the clock, or three minutes, or one minute. Days when he could not move his arthritic legs and would have himself taken in a wheel chair to his woodpile and chop kindling till he was exhausted. Days when, blindfolded, he guided his pen along the wires of a frame to write his histories. Days when he listened to a secretary reading the archives of France or Quebec which he could not read. On such days Francis Parkman could touch the buckskin or the feathers with his fingers, smell sagebrush, taste alkali, and remember a young man's courage and exaltation among the Sioux.

But he was so sick![1] One afternoon, waking from an hour's sleep, he found that he could not stand and could not saddle Pauline, though he must ride on with the village. "Then for the first time it pressed upon me as a strong probability that I might never leave these deserts." The historian might die among the Sioux. The code of his ancestors told him that it was better to die in the saddle than to "drag out life . . . in the helpless inaction of lingering disease," and he had himself lifted to Pauline's back and kicked a spur into her flank. But he saw his Sioux through fever. A quality of phantasmagoria comes into this, the best section of his book, and Parkman on the Indians is Parkman in the shadow of death.

His admiration grew but at the same time he fell out of love, confessing disenchantment. They told such marvelous stories—and their minds were so pointless and absurd! They looked so magisterial, so antique Roman at the council fire—and they gabbled like old women, reasoning with an illogic it would have been kind to call infantile. Their ceremonies had a dignity of ancient tradition, of profound belief—and were incrusted with superstitions evil and abhorrent to a reasoning mind. Their cruelty was perhaps explicable but aimless, spasmodic, irrelevant. They had virtues, family virtues mainly and the affections of the hearth, which the Puritan must admire—but what must a Puritan make of their gluttony, their laziness, the coarseness and obscenity of their talk? They lacked purpose, they had no steadfastness—and that was worst of all. No intention held for them, their bright parrot minds were the thickness of film only, impulse dominating them, fad and whim and the moment's fancy overcoming even self-interest—and this was stupidity. They could not think, they had a culture but no character, they were helpless against the world and even in selfhood—and they must go down. They were, the realization phrased itself, and many of Parkman's successors down to now would have been wise to follow it, they were — savages. End of Rousseau for a young historian.

But how admirably fierce, strong, tireless, and male! How splendidly shaped to function! The Panther, a young buck, gallops his horse, pursuing an antelope while the village yelps its admiration — and here, existing absolutely in the moment, mastery of life reproaches the impaired historian. The Hail Storm, a mere boy, chases a plunging buffalo and turns to laugh in pure ecstasy while the great beast's eyes glare red and blood gushes from his nostrils. . . . Parkman watched the Hail Storm put away boyhood and become a brave in the course of a few weeks. He slew his buffalo, killed a deer, was admitted to hunting parties, learned to wear his blanket with a grace irresistible to maidens, strutted before squaws with an ear cocked to their admiration, made conquests in the bushes, found out how to be imperturbable and stern, needed only to count a *coup* in warfare. And, Parkman admiringly realized, would have counted *coup* on Parkman to become a man, if he had got a chance.

Here are the buffalo hunters, stripped to the G string, sitting bareback and lashing their unbridled horses to the gallop. The long line charges on the herd. The shock strikes Parkman's bared nerves. Under dust and clamor the dark beasts go down. Frenzied, the squaws and boys and unmounted braves cut up the carcasses, while the hunters move out of sight, still yelling, still shooting single arrows clear through a buffalo's forequarters. They rip out the liver, the gall bladder, portions of the intestines, the tripe, and gobble them. Blood, marrow, and grease drip from their chins, from their forearms, from their knees. Big Crow comes in from hunting, a male who has killed. His squaws take off his bloody moccasins and bring bowls of water to wash his bloody hands. They give him fresh-boiled buffalo to eat and the functional killer, the fulfilled warrior, sleeps.

By campfires, how their eyes glitter! What heroisms, cruelties, and violence they have wrought, undergone, and survived! Crawling through brush at midnight to stampede a herd, strutting in front of barricaded enemies to utter taunts, dueling with fleshed arrows shot under the necks of galloping horses, rushing unarmed into a melee to touch an enemy before the next-fleetest can come up. These talkers by the campfire have passed a knife under the topknot and ripped scalps from skulls. They have fought shrieking with Arapaho, Pawnee, Shoshoni, Cheyenne, Blackfeet. Big Crow himself, Parkman's uncle pro tem, is covered with scars truly received in war, has killed fourteen enemies and tells Parkman all his *coups*. Once, having killed a Shoshoni,[2] he chased another one, wounded him, caught up with him, and scalped him alive. Then Big Crow and his companions made a fire and, first severing the tendons of the captive's wrists and feet, threw him into the flames, held him there with long poles, and watched him burn, screaming. . . . Horrible, but — good God! — how strong.

There is a good deal more than a trace too much of this. They were, you are to perceive, powerful, reckless, and not impaired. Their eyes were good and their bowels wholesome. Weakness did not enervate their knees, an objectless panic did not surge up in them, their minds had no depths of self-suspicion, they felt no dread that they might not be whole. As far back as Francis Parkman could remember a dread of impairment had lurked on the margins of his mind. It was assuaged by these extremities of violence and his admiration masks a simple envy. Cruelty was abhorrent but an inability to inflict cruelty was even more abhorrent. If the books he wrote in his maturity sometimes reveal too much gusto in scenes of torture, be sure he paid cash for it in detestation of the weakness he feared was his.

Yet even here the Sioux could let him down. White Shield rides about camp singing a war song and challenging the bravest to ride out with him to find the Shoshoni and avenge the wrong which the Oglala have forgotten. A valorous buck, the White Shield, yearning for glory, smarting under the communal injury, who cannot live unless it is avenged. But there prove to be reasons against valor. He has given away some war arrows, some of his young men have had bad dreams — and one morning White Shield comes down with a sore throat. He mopes round the village, sniffling, wailing, complaining, just any countinghouse clerk with a cold. No enemy scalps for White Shield.

In sum, they were savages, a neolithic people, an anachronism embedded in the eighteen-forties and being extinguished from that decade. Parkman came to accept them as spectacle. Always the fires, the tales, the pipe passing, the invocation to innumerable gods. Red Water, the admirer of the whites, telling how he had hidden in a beaver house and learned that the beaver, the wisest of animals, were also the white men. The squaws erecting lodges, waiting on their masters, instructing the children, making pemmican, giggling over smutty stories, scolding the dogs they were about to kill and cook. Love songs, medicine songs, war songs. Big Crow finding the buffalo herd after his little friend, a cricket, had told him where to look. Big Crow's lodge and everyone feasting everyone else, giving feasts for Parkman, Parkman giving feasts and making admirable orations while the connoisseurs of eloquence grunt their critical satisfaction. A fight boils up when Tall Bear does not repay Mad Wolf's present. Sudden shots and yelps split the camp, two lines of warriors form at once, shooting wildly, and here is Mad Wolf, "the most dangerous man in the village" with his bow bent and arrow "quivering close to the breast of his adversary"—and Tall Bear, not in the least scared, his knife dripping blood of the horse he had just killed, awaiting the attack. Parkman and Raymond run out of the line of fire. Old Red Water, the ancient, grabs bow and arrows with one hand and his knife with the other, runs out yelling to join the fight, trips over something, and sprawls peacefully in the dust. Shots pepper nothing in particular for a moment, then the village police end the riot.

Or from a ridge high above a canyon, watch the village pour through the Black Hills toward the camp where it will get lodge poles. The travois bump over rocks and sagebrush, the squaws yelling. Pack horses in long files, the herds dimpling and stringing out, boys riding the flanks. White shield-covers catch the sun, lance feathers shake in clear air, bronze-yellow faces wear a powder of dust. Dogs howl and pant, horses snort, balk, plunge. A brass bracelet shines on a copper arm. Out on the plain again the poles rise and grunting squaws tug the skins over them. The herd dips over a hill to grazing land. The braves form their senate to smoke, counsel, and despise the squaws.

Or the village in midafternoon. The naked sun has softened the plain's nakedness with seven veils of mirage, but a skin lodge with an open flare at the top and raised dampers along the edge is, after all, an air conditioner. The whole tribe has withdrawn into the lodges to escape the bowl of fluid sun. The ramparts of the Laramie Mountains, black with the cedars that gave them their first name, are flattened and without substance. "A profound lethargy, the very spirit of indolence," has ended all activity and all but little sounds. Stretched on a robe in Big Crow's lodge, his shoulders cushioned in a net of rawhide, Parkman can hear the chirping of locusts or a tiny complaint of children, or some girl giggling at a whispered confidence in a near-by lodge, or his uncle snoring in a dream of *coups*. He can smell hot sagebrush and juniper, hot dust, the nearness of cool water running through cottonwoods. Desert emptiness, desert hush. Parkman's mind is a panorama of things seen since he left Westport, moving before a backdrop of New England pines. The pictures merge, he succumbs to the desert and falls asleep. During many white nights on Chestnut Street when fear of "inflammation of the brain" will not let him sleep, he will remember drowsing to Big Crow's snores.

Parkman had found the West.

Time shortened, he was due at Fort Laramie, and he had as much as he could ever get of what he had come for. Before dawn he and Raymond rode ahead, young Hail Storm going along to guide them through the mountains. But a delay occurred and so they rode with the village for another day. They passed another Western spectacle, immense brush fires on the mountains. That smoke would make an impalpable haze over the sun hundreds of miles away and give the air a prickling pungency that, wherever encountered, means summertime to those born in the Rocky Mountains. A different Indian rode with them the second day, and was able to name all who had passed their old camp at the Chugwater, where they spent the night. The Indian left without ceremony while they slept, the sun came up copper from the forest fires, and, breasting a hill, Parkman could see ten miles away the whitewashed adobe of Fort Laramie. It was August 3.

Shaw, Chatillon, and Delorier came out to meet him. After the Oglala, they seemed tinted with qualities of the archangels. Parkman stretched out on buffalo robes in Papin's room; he had returned to civilization on Laramie Creek. Shaw, whose taste had coarsened in the wilds, complained that he had no "shongsha" (kinnikinnick, willow or dogwood bark, arrowroot, or similar aromatic herb) to mix with his tobacco. Parkman had brought some, but for his part civilization was best. He spent the afternoon reading *Childe Harold.*

The next day they took the trail again, leaving Fort Laramie for good — Parkman, Shaw, Chatillon, Raymond, Delorier, and a couple of trappers who were joining Bisonette. They traveled south, on the old trade route east of the main chain of the Rockies. They were making for Bent's Fort by way of Cherry Creek, Pike's Peak, and Pueblo. From Bent's Fort they would take the Santa Fe trail to Independence.

By circuitous paths Parkman had found the West and now he turned homeward by a circuitous path. Promptly his health improved.

Edwin Bryant's horseback party, with Hiram Miller taking Kirkendall's place, made excellent time from Fort Laramie. A Kentuckian named Buchanan joined them from a train which they met near the Red Buttes, and another recruit named McClary brought their strength to eleven. They hurried through fantasy land. They saw many dead oxen, Bryant treated invalids at the trains they passed, he himself fell ill with mountain fever. Independence Rock and Devil's Gate on July 8. Two days later on the Sweetwater they saw the snowy peaks of the Wind River chain and met a solitary horseman dangerously riding these wilds, a Mr. Bonney who was carrying a letter from Lansford Hastings to the emigration. They traversed South Pass and drank Pacific waters on July 12, and it was Owl Russell's turn to be stricken by mountain fever. On to the Little Sandy, acres of lupine and clouds of mosquitoes, and to the Big Sandy on August 12, overtaking some Shoshoni who were going home from the buffalo range. They told the Indians that the Sioux were singing war songs against them, and the Indians boiled away westward. (Bryant notes a "very beautiful young female" in pantaloons, tastefully decorated, and expends an emotion on her face and figure. Phenomenon of bachelor life on the trail.) They reached Green River on July 15 and Black's Fork on the sixteenth. The next day they went a mile or so farther and pitched a tent for the first time since leaving Fort Laramie. They had reached Fort Bridger, and their tent went up beside the camp of Mr. Hastings and Mr. Hudspeth, who had just traveled a new route from California which shortened the distance "from one hundred and fifty to two hundred miles." The partners were gathering a big wagon train to lead over that new route.

Fort Bridger had filled up since Jim Clyman passed it on June 7. Besides Hastings' party and the gathering emigrants, there were Taos traders and rival traders from near Bent's Fort, come to dicker with the emigrants and the Shoshoni. There were five hundred Shoshoni, who struck their lodges and swarmed westward as soon as Bryant's party repeated their information about the Sioux. Neither Bridger nor his partner Vasquez was there, but Bryant met another master mountain man. This was Joseph Walker, one of the canniest and most weathered of them all. He had had a miscellaneous, exhaustive experience in the trade, had been Bonneville's guide and lieutenant, and had broken one of the trails to California when Bonneville sent him there to look for beaver — or for routes of invasion. The presence of Carson, Fitzpatrick, Godey, and other favorites on Frémont's third expedition (of '45) has tended to obscure Walker's service to that expedition, as his slaughter of Diggers seems somehow to have overshadowed the importance of his earlier trail-breaking. But he was Frémont's real guide west of

Great Salt Lake and may be given credit for the successful passage of the Salt Desert. Also he headed the main party which Frémont sent over the Sierra by a southern pass, the party which the Pathfinder kept awaiting in his letters to Castro. He had stayed with Frémont till the episode of Gavilán Peak was finished, when he resigned, contemptuous of the heroics. Then he began his own conquest of California by rounding up a big herd of horses from the ranches. He drove them east, for sale to the emigration, and had reached Fort Bridger.[3] The facts about "recent occurrences in California of considerable interest" which he told Bryant probably had to do with the siege of the Gavilán.

Joe Walker did not think highly of the cutoff which Hastings was selling to the companies that kept driving up to Fort Bridger. He said so, and made rather more headway than Jim Clyman had been able to. Mr. Curry and Mr. Holder resigned from Bryant's group, to take the Fort Hall route. Trains split up and regrouped, following their example, but Hastings went on making converts. Bryant thought hard.

"Circles of white-tented wagons may now be seen in every direction, and the smoke from campfires is circling upwards, morning, noon, and evening. An immense number of oxen and horses are scattered over the entire valley, grazing upon the green grass. Parties of Indians, hunters, and emigrants are galloping to and fro, and the scene is one of almost holiday loveliness. It is difficult to realize that we are in a wilderness, a thousand miles from civilization. I noticed the lupin and a brilliant scarlet flower in bloom."

Hudspeth was to go ahead of the train that was forming, taking three men from it to familiarize them with the route. He agreed to accompany Bryant's party as far as the edge of the Salt Desert. So Bryant and his companions held to their decision to take the Hastings Cutoff. They would travel on horseback (or muleback) and they had no wagons, families, or responsibilities. But Joe Walker had at last convinced him, and so he wrote several letters to his friends in the train he had abandoned, advising them not to take the cutoff but to travel the old trail by Fort Hall. He addressed them and left them at Fort Bridger, for delivery when the train should come up. They were never delivered.

The train which Hastings was forming at Fort Bridger is known as the Harlan-Young party and the three members of it who went with Hudspeth were Kirkwood, Ferguson, and Minter. These scouts and Bryant's party left Fort Bridger on July 20. Six days later they had crossed the Wasatch and emerged in Great Salt Lake Valley.

They had barely made it. Narrow, brush-choked, and boulder-filled canyons, precipitous divides, stretches many miles long of almost impenetrable brush, and above all the course of the Weber River between vertical mountain walls that rose straight from the water's edge, had almost defeated them. And they were on horseback, whereas Hastings' recruits would have to bring wagons and ox teams through.[4]

On July 26 Bryant's party camped in the valley of Uinta, where the Weber River breaks through the westernmost wall of the Wasatch. After detouring the upper canyon of the Weber, Hudspeth had gone back through it to determine whether wagons could be brought through. The others climbed mountains for the view, waiting for him to get back, and Hiram Miller caught trout in the Weber in stretches where the author of this book, who grew up there, was never able to. The oak brush on the mountains was on fire over wide areas and the sulphur-yellow smoke dulled the valley colors. Hudspeth was back on July 29 and they moved southward along the lake, making not too good time to the site of Salt Lake City. (July 30, a year less six days before Brigham Young.) The sagebrush plain was fantastically hot, ashes from the burning oakbrush sifted down on them, and Bryant marveled at the sunset colors of the lake. They headed round the southern end of the lake and on August 2 made what preparation they could for their worst hazard, the crossing of the Salt Desert. At dawn Hudspeth pointed toward it and said, "Now, boys, put spurs to your mules and ride like hell." He turned back to pick up his companions. Bryant's party began their crossing.

They followed, roughly, the trail made by Hastings and Clyman this year and by Frémont the year before. They made the best crossing ever made. That fact is eloquent, for the crossing of the Salt Desert was a severe test of strength, intelligence, sanity, and character. . . . It still is. In a century men have learned that desert and, in small numbers, are at home there. But to this day carelessness or mistakes or the hazards of weather can produce catastrophe. . . . It was choppy and broken at first, then absolutely flat. The rising sun made it a white hell and produced violent mirages. Cities, forests, battlements, cathedrals, lakes, and fountains slid and undulated before their tortured eyes. Wraithlike objects rode parallel with them and later became a party of horsemen. These figures, they thought, might be Frémont coming back to the States, but they grew gigantic and eventually dissolved. Puffs of wind raised columns of pulverized salt and filled the sky's bowl with a white mist. They choked and gagged, could see nothing, strung out and began to straggle. The mule which carried all that was left of their provisions wandered away; Bryant found it and drove it on. Dark came up. They had had no food and their only drink was the two quarts of coffee made last night from brackish water which they carried in a powder keg. It was past ten o'clock when Bryant could see the crusted salt (a few inches thick, above a repulsive salt mud) beginning to yield to sagebrush and felt the ground beginning to slope upward underfoot. He rounded up his party and they kept on till they found — on Pilot Peak — a spring of celestially pure water. They had been half dead from thirst but, with water at hand, felt no great need of it. They made camp. Bryant estimated that they had traveled seventy-five miles — and was five or ten miles short. They had made a two-day journey in thirty-one hours.

They had run their risk and survived the worst that the country could bring against them. There is no point in detailing the rest of their journey. It is true that the Nevada desert from Pilot Peak to the Humboldt is worse than the Wyoming deserts. It is true that the route down the Humboldt and on to the crossing of the Sierra was usually the most difficult stretch of the migration, made worse by the failure of stock and equipment, cumulative fatigue, the shortening of the season, and the end of human endurance. . . . As evidence. This was a small party, unencumbered, traveling much faster than a wagon train. They were friends, their association was voluntary and congenial, they had a common purpose and a common sense of achievement. Yet four days after they crossed the Salt Desert two of these friends cocked rifles at each other "about a very trivial matter of dispute." Bryant got them stopped and invoked the desert law: anyone who made trouble would be forced to go it alone.

Back on the trail again, near the mouth of Bishop's Creek they met Lindsey Applegate and some companions, on an errand which we will pick up farther on. (Jesse Applegate, Black Harris, and others had ridden ahead of the party to Fort Hall.) Diggers hung round them, begging, stealing, awaiting a chance to make trouble. They went on through nightmare land and their provisions dwindled. They reduced the daily ration but seemed likely to fall at least a week short. They caught up with the very tip of the emigration, two Missouri wagons which had outdistanced their train. Messrs. Craig and Stanley, their proprietors, had little to spare but the trail's democracy held and Bryant's party replenished their supplies and were not permitted to pay for them. Later the wagons caught up with them for a while and one of the party had broken under strain and gone crazy. They pushed on past Humboldt Sink and the hot springs where Clyman's spaniel had died, on to the Truckee and up that gallant river to a sudden stunning shock — forests, great tall pines and firs, leafy shade, perfumes of fertility, the high country, the Sierra. Then Truckee Lake and a cabin at its western end where fragments of old newspapers were strewn about, one of them a Philadelphia religious weekly. A letter written at Morristown, New Jersey; another one, franked by a Congressman to Dr. John Townsend, Bloomfield, Indiana. Truckee Lake would soon get a different name.

They crossed the divide on August 26 and were on westward-flowing waters, little brooks that drained into the Yuba. Bear Valley on August 27 (whence we saw Clyman and Hastings moving east), and the next day breakfast and supper each consisted of a cup of coffee. On August 30 they saw their first natives, who might be the bloodthirsty California army which Hastings had described but turned out to be only some Indians gathering acorns for flour. They went on and saw their first private house, Johnson's ranch, on the rim of the great Sacramento Valley. Two local trappers came up and they got news of the war which they had heard about on the bank of the Kansas River. General Taylor, they were told, had won four battles, had killed fifty thousand Mexicans, and was now dictating peace in Mexico City. Late in the afternoon Johnson himself — ex-sailor and perennial conspirator — came in with the first issue of a new newspaper, the *Californian,* Bear Flag Captain Semple, editor.

So on September 1 nine men in rags came down to the American River, forded it and went on to New Helvetia. The Stars and Stripes floated from its flagpole, Indian sentries were walking post, and the sally port was populous with men oddly costumed in buckskin breeches and blouses of the United States Navy. Sutter came out and explained that his fort was now a military post of the United States.

They must have been an odd sight to the army, or navy, of occupation. They were as skinny as their mules, whose ribs were sharp under slack hides. The fairer ones were burned red and their hair was bleached the color of new rope; the brunets were black as Mexicans. Their clothes were ragged and loathsome; their outfits were held together with twine, sinew, and willow withes. They were half starved, they smelled rancid, and their ways and manners showed a desert taint. But, nine villainous looking men, they were fulfilling a good many dreams — John C. Frémont's, Lansford

Hastings', Thomas Hart Benton's, James K. Polk's, Henry Thoreau's, and Bill Bowen's.

For on September 1 the emigration of '46 had reached California.

Behind them the intending President of California staged his dress rehearsal of catastrophe. The train of sixty-six wagons * which he formed at Fort Bridger is known as the Harlan-Young party, though Harlan and Young were the captains of only two of the four fragmentary trains that went into it. Some of these had originally been with the great Owl Russell train at Indian Creek. (On the Sweetwater, Stanton, of the Donner party, had noted five segments of that company camped within five miles of one another.) Like the Donners, many of them were educated and well-to-do — and one wonders if the intelligentsia were not especially sensitive to high-pressure advertising.

Hastings had told them that his new route was four hundred miles shorter than the Fort Hall trail, that it was less mountainous and easier on man and beast, and that the Salt Desert was only forty miles wide, just half its width. It is clear that he was not crazy, so he was lying. He now broke a wagon trail, and to the meadows west of Echo Canyon, where Bryant had detoured the upper Weber Canyon, the going proved no worse than Jim Clyman had foretold. Hastings got them through so far with not too much delay. Hudspeth and he had decided against the only route they knew, the one they had taken eastward from Great Salt Lake in early June. Unlike Hudspeth, however, he blithely led his charges into Upper Weber Canyon.

First prophecy. The Weber is a commonplace mountain stream. Some of its stretches are more open than most of the rivers of the Wasatch. But through much of its two western canyons the present highway has been blasted through rock which, in '46, rose straight from the water. In some places the Harlan-Young party had to take their wagons down the bed of the stream — round great boulders, across slanting rock ledges, sometimes careening off the short bank, sometimes among willows and cottonwoods. In other places they had to cut a road through trees and along the edge of the canyon, a hundred feet or more above the water, prying boulders downhill,

* Apparently about forty wagons went with Hudspeth. Others followed up to the sixty-six mentioned in the text — the number usually given. One account makes the total eighty wagons.

leveling where they could, achieving a steep path the width of a wagon tread which the failing oxen must climb and descend as they could. Sometimes neither river bed nor bank nor canyon wall was possible and with ropes, windlass, men grabbing at spokes, women tugging at ropes, they had to go over a shoulder of mountain. When a mountain is better traveling than a canyon, you have reached the worst. Once, where the canyon makes a horseshoe curve exactly the width of the river, a place called Devil's Gate, they had to take their road high over sheer cliffs, and, seeing the scar today, no one can conceive how wagons made that passage and held together.

Oxen died. One wagon broke the ropes that held it and crashed down a cliff, killing its teams. They made a mile some days, more days a half mile, but they got through at last to the little valley of Uinta where Bryant had preceded them. They were the first emigrant wagons ever to reach Great Salt Lake Valley, the inheritance promised to the Mormons. They supposed that they had surmounted their difficulties now and, after repairing their wagons, held a feast. The music of frontiersmen, minstrel shows, the Scotch border, and the Methodist hymnbooks drifted through the cottonwoods in the valley of Uinta. It was premature.

Second prophecy. They went on, taking Bryant's trail to the point of the mountains at the southern end of Great Salt Lake, and here John Hargrave died, worn out by the crossing of the Wasatch. The promised land got its first emigrant grave, a Gentile's. Leaving a note in a cleft stick for his next batch of victims, the realtor led the party on to the Salt Desert. They crossed it in two days and a night.

Third prophecy. Many oxen died. Many wagons had to be abandoned in the salt. They merged outfits, forming teams of the survivors and salvaging what they could. Hastings had promised them water by the end of the first day. Some of them reached it, barely alive, toward the end of their second day. They carried water and grass back to the others, saved some crazed oxen, and went into camp on Pilot Peak. They stayed there, going back into the salt to round up surviving teams, jettisoning their possessions, repairing wagons. After "many days" (Sam Young's phrase), they were ready to move on and try to reach the trail at the bend of the Humboldt — "with the loss of most of their stock, worn out, and greatly discouraged."

Hastings got them over the Sierra about October 5 (a little more than six weeks behind Bryant). Only one of them had died and not all of them had been bankrupted. Taking an average of the other trains, perhaps they had not lost more than three weeks on Hastings' fine new route. But while they labored in the Wasatch and across the salt, every California-bound wagon that took the Fort Hall trail came comfortably over the divide and down to the American River. They were the last ones in. The California emigration of '46 ended when those merged outfits creaked down the western slope. Too bad the California Republic had become history and there would be no empire for Lansford Hastings.

But he had played his dress rehearsal through. Now the curtain could go up in earnest.

Jessy Thornton left a bundle of tracts with Mr. Bordeau at Fort Laramie. The Sioux, very cocky now that they weren't going to fight the Shoshoni, bade the emigrants form large trains so that neither they nor the Indians whose hearts were bad would attack them. The emigrants didn't. They kept on dividing and regrouping while the wagons lurched past Independence Rock, Devil's Gate (which pulled the plug of Thornton's rhetoric again), and on up the Sweetwater. Mr. Bonney, the lone rider whom Bryant had met, came up with Hastings' letter just as they reached the river.[5] Many of them were sick with mountain fever, Nancy was prostrated, and Thornton himself was spitting blood. Oxen were dying, the exhausted ones and those that had drunk too much alkali. Thornton had four yoke to pull his wagon and a spare yoke for replacements. He lost his first one here, just short of the divide, "Old Brady," who fell ill and could not rise. The next day Thornton plodded back to see if he had recovered but found his skeleton cleaned by wolves.

They crossed the divide a little before sunset on July 18, six days later than Bryant, and camped at Pacific Spring, where the waters of the western ocean begin. The next day many fragments of trains mingled in camp on the Little Sandy, and on the morning of July 20 the Thorntons said good-bye to their California-bound friends. Since all other chroniclers quote Thornton's words, they may be repeated here. "The Californians were generally much elated and in fine spirits, with the prospect of a better and nearer road to the country of their destination. Mrs. George Donner [Tamsen] was, however, an exception. She was gloomy, sad, and dispirited, in view of the fact that her husband and others could think for a moment of leaving the old road and confide in the statement of a man of whom they knew nothing but who was probably some selfish adventurer. (Mercury at sunrise 46°; sunset, 52°.)"

The Donners went on to Fort Bridger. The Oregon fragments took a route known as Greenwood's (for Caleb) or Sublette's (for Bill) Cutoff, which shortened the road by by-passing Fort Bridger. With Boggs and other friends Thornton joined a company captained by Kirkendall, who had left Bryant's party and who was to be infinitely kind to the genteel invalids. Thornton had lost his drivers and had to manage the team himself. He was inept and grew weaker. Neighbors, the captain, sometimes Nancy, had to do the work. He found the Wyoming desert — it was really Oregon at last, now that they had passed the divide — unspeakably dreary. It remains an ugly desolation today, but it had more grass and eventually more water than any of the alternative routes they could have taken. They passed a train which was burying a Mr. Campbell, who had died of exhaustion. Along cliffs and across divides, Mr. Kirkendall or Mr. Perkins or Mr. Burns took the team for him. They reached Bear River, a beautiful stream, crossed it, and kept coming back to it till they struck it at the most famous oasis of the entire trail, Soda Springs.

A storage dam across the Bear has backed up water over many of the famous springs now, but that valley is still beautiful. In the years of the emigration it was life-giving. Deep grass, clear water, cottonwoods, timbered hillsides, made a living landscape in a country that had been dead for six weeks' travel. Less spectacular than the valley of Fort Bridger, it was always appreciated much more. Wagons were parked under the trees. Washing bloomed on the oak brush. Children whooped around the bubbling soda-water fountains, the miniature geysers, the springs of quaking mud. Horses and oxen could get back a little flesh; the river was deep enough for swimming, as none had been for weeks; though buffalo could not be found there was abundant game of other kinds. Everyone's spirits rose; it was suddenly realized that much was behind, that to reach here intact was a considerable achievement.

There was a new kind of mist in early morning, the powder blue that means approaching autumn in the mountains. Sunsets were smoky and with evening a chill wind came out of the hills. In early August they remembered pumpkins on the stoop in New England, shocked corn in the prairie states, the feeling of harvest.

Then a soberer realization: how far, after all, it still was to the Willamette Valley.

The next leg was short, a four-day haul through sage beginning to be broken by plains of black lava, to Fort Hall. Thornton's party reached it on August 7 and went on a few miles farther. The next day Jesse Applegate, an Oregon pioneer, came into camp at the head of a small party that included Jim Clyman's old messmate, Black Harris. Applegate also was in the road-shortening business — but with a difference. He had been sent out by the Oregon settlements to do the job which the War Department had ordered Frémont to do in '45. Nearly all the earlier Oregon emigrations had foundered on the last stretch of the trail, either in the Cascade Mountains or along the Columbia River. Applegate had just completed his survey and was recommending a route to the settlements that avoided this stretch altogether and entered the Willamette Valley from the south.

Lansford Hastings' letter was addressed, "At the Headwaters of the Sweetwater. To all California Emigrants Now on the Road." The burden of this famous letter was simple: that the Californians would probably try to keep the emigrants out, that the emigrants should form one large party for defense, and that they should save time, strength, and effort by using the new road, which was at least three hundred and fifty miles shorter than the old.

As we have seen, most of the emigrants ignored the ad, exercising a hard-minded skepticism. That the Donner party acted on it appears to have been a triumph of literature. Hastings had written a book: he must be right.

The Donner party, which could as properly be called the James Frazier Reed party, really formed at the Little Sandy on July 20. We had better list it.

In Chapter V we described the nucleus, the families and retainers of George and Jacob Donner and of Reed, and also Patrick Breen and his family and his friend Dolan. Since then Reed's mother-in-law, Mrs. Keyes, had died and Hiram Miller, one of George Donner's teamsters, had joined Bryant's party. There remained: —

George Donner, his wife Tamsen, and five children.

Jacob Donner, his wife Elizabeth, and seven children.

John Denton, a companion of the Donners, and Noah James and Samuel Shoemaker, teamsters for the Donners.

James Frazier Reed, his wife Margaret, and four children.

Baylis Williams, his sister Eliza, Milton Elliott, James Smith, and Walter Herron — all employes of Reed.

Patrick Breen, his wife Peggy, seven children, and their friend Patrick Dolan.

At the Little Sandy, a waif named Luke Halloran who was dying of tuberculosis joined the George Donners, having roused Tamsen's pity. Here also the train organized with George Donner as captain. Most of the additions had been in the original Indian Creek train or in trains it had neighbored with along the Platte. They were: —

William Eddy, from Illinois, his wife Eleanor, and two children.

Lavinia Murphy, a widow from Tennessee, and her four unmarried children. Also her two married daughters and their families. These were Sarah Murphy Foster and her husband William Foster and one child; and Harriet Murphy Pike and her husband William Pike and two children. Mrs. Murphy is supposed to have been a Mormon who had left Nauvoo to seek employment in Warsaw, Illinois, and was working her way west as cook and laundress.[6]

Lewis Keseberg of Westphalia, Germany, his wife Phillipine, and two children.

Karl Burger from Germany, driver for Keseberg.

——— Hardkoop, from Cincinnati but born in Germany, traveling with Keseberg.

Joseph Reinhardt and Augustus Spitzer, from Germany, partners, probably traveling with Keseberg.

——— Wolfinger and his wife. Their Christian names are not known.

Charles T. Stanton, from New York State by way of Illinois.

"Antoine," a herder; it is not known whom he worked for.

At Fort Bridger, George Donner hired another teamster, Jean Baptiste Trubode. Also the train was joined by: —

William McCutchen, from Missouri, his wife Amanda, and one child.

This completes the party that left Fort Bridger. It consisted of twenty-six men of eighteen or over; twelve women of eighteen or more; six boys between the ages of twelve and eighteen and four girls of similar age; six boys between six and twelve and three girls of similar age; eight boys and nine girls under six.

The Graves party, who joined them in the canyons of the Wasatch, may as well be listed here. This party consisted of Franklin Ward Graves (usually called "Uncle Billy"), lately from Illinois but originally from Vermont, his wife Elizabeth, and eight unmarried children. Also their daughter Sarah Graves Fosdick, her husband Jay Fosdick, and a teamster named John Snyder. They had started west with the train mentioned in Chapter VI as being scattered by the Pawnee; the Mr. Trimble whom the Pawnee killed had traveled with them. They had been associated with various companies on the way to Fort Bridger, where — incredibly — they pushed on alone, catching up with the Donners in the first stage of their disaster. Thirteen in all, they brought the total to eighty-seven. That completes the roster of the Donner party as history knows it, except for two luckless Indians who were brought up from California to meet it near the Sierra.

When the patriarch George Donner was elected captain at the Little Sandy, these people had comfortably survived the emigration so far. Mrs. Keyes had died at the Big Blue but since then they had experienced routine health and satisfaction and no more than routine hardship. They were entirely representative of the emigration, from the wealthy Reeds and Donners down to the invalid Halloran and the teamsters and hangers-on. Note the earlier pioneering ventures of the Donners, Reed's European background, the Yankee strain in Graves and Tamsen Donner, the fact that the majority were from Illinois and Missouri, the fact that they included Irish, immigrant Irish, and immigrant Germans.

George Donner got his train to Fort Bridger on July 28, and on the way there from the Little Sandy had one final warning. Joe Walker, driving his stolen horses eastward, met them and repeated what he had told Bryant. They had become resentful of croakers, called him a Puke, and moved on. Arriving at the fort, they found that Hastings had broken the promise made in his grandiloquent letter. He was not here, would not personally conduct them to the Humboldt, had gone ahead with the Harlan-Young train. Bridger and his partner Vasquez had returned, however, and these two seasoned mountain men confirmed Hastings' advertisement. The new trail to the southern end of Great Salt Lake, they said emphatically, was open and easy and much shorter than the Fort Hall road. This is the heaviest sin charged against Old Gabe in his entire career. Also Bryant's letters of warning were not handed to them.[7]

They stayed at Fort Bridger for four days, a reckless delay justified only by Hastings' advertising. The stock needed rest after the Wyoming deserts and the wagons had been so wrenched and shaken that much blacksmithing was required. The McCutchens joined them here and the thirteen-year-old Eddie Breen broke his leg in a fall from a horse. Frontier medicine prescribed amputation but his mother would not consent and the boy could agonize in splints while the wagon careened through the canyons. He was walking again when they reached the Humboldt.

They left Fort Bridger on July 31, eleven days behind Bryant.[8] On August 6 they came out of Echo Canyon to the valley of the Weber. (They had thus followed the route of the Harlan-Young party, which differed from that taken by Bryant, who had detoured Echo Canyon and all the stretch east of it from the Little Muddy.) So far the going had been difficult — more difficult than any they would have encountered on the Fort Hall road — but by no means impossible. They ought, however, to have made it in four or five days, instead of six and a half. Still, here they were and no damage done at the place which the Mormon emigrant route was to call "the crossing of the Weber." It is approximately the site of the present village of Henefer, Utah.

Here, thrust in a cleft stick, they found a letter from Hastings, directed to anyone who might be traveling his road. Hastings had apparently ridden back from the Harlan-Young company, which he was taking through Upper Weber Canyon, after Hudspeth rode back from Bryant's party at the mouth of Lower Weber Canyon to tell him what the last part of the new trail was like. The letter announced that the Weber route was bad, and directed the victims to camp at the crossing of the Weber and send a messenger ahead to find Mr. Hastings. Mr. Hastings would then come back and personally show them a better route through the Wasatch. His routes were always better.

So while the season shortened, while a richer purple got into the mountain shadows and frost crept farther down by night on the peaks, the Donners went into camp by the Weber River. They sent Reed, Stanton, and McCutchen ahead to find Hastings. Perhaps they spent their leisure factoring an equation which could express dwindling supplies, the approach of winter, and some wild *x* representing the country ahead of them.

Five days later, August 11, Reed came back. Stanton and McCutchen were not with him. Their horses had broken down — an omen of the Wasatch crossing. Lansford Hastings was not with him, either. Mr. Hastings had decided to hurry the Harlan-Young party over the Salt Desert. But in the kindest way he had accompanied Reed to the top of a divide east of Great Salt Lake and, tracing his finger across the blue space above the ridges that could be seen from there, had sketched a route which he thought preferable to the Weber Canyons for the party he had promised to lead in person. It was the route which he, Hudspeth, and Clyman had traveled in June, though there was no way for Reed to know whether he was keeping to it. Reed had blazed some trees and set up markers on the route he had taken, leaving his companions when their horses failed and pressing on. Maybe he had come by the sky map of Lansford Hastings, maybe not. At any rate, they would now try Reed's trail. In fact, they must.

When the money paid to the Mormon Battalion as commutation of clothing reached Israel on the Missouri River, Brigham Young wrote to his soldiers that it was "a peculiar manifestation of the kind providence of our Heavenly Father at this time." It would buy food for the winter and equipment for the Exodus. But the prophet found that the Battalion had privately forwarded part of their bonus to their families. This impeded the socialization of Israel's wealth. He secretly dispatched John D. Lee, his son by adoption in the mystical Temple relationships, to intercept the Battalion at or near Santa Fe. Brother John would collect the Battalion pay and turn it over to Brigham for consecration unto the Lord. Private generosity, the prophet thought, signified that some of the Battalion had not hearkened to counsel, and they would get into trouble.

They already had. Passing in apprehension down the western fringe of Missouri, the land of their enemies, they arrived at Fort Leavenworth on August 1 and were outfitted for the march down the Santa Fe trail. But they were still in the midst of the enemy. The War Department was beginning to understand the size of the proposed conquest of the West and had ordered reinforcements for Kearny and Doniphan. Missouri had raised another regiment of mounted volunteers and here it was at Fort Leavenworth, under command of Sterling Price. Price was a politician (lately in the House) with a voice as beautiful as Owl Russell's — and he had commanded the Missouri jail where the prophet Joseph Smith had been imprisoned. These troops, the Second Missouri, were to prove rowdier and less controllable than Doniphan's — or Price was less gifted at leadership — but they were just as chary of the Mormons as the Mormons were of them. The Saints could not understand that, however, a band of mostly unwilling conscripts far from Israel, still in the shadow of persecution, and commanded by their prophet to serve the nation which for years they had been commanded to despise. They were frankly afraid of the Pukes. They remained afraid of them till they had put Santa Fe behind them and taken the trail to California.

They spent their time at Leavenworth drilling, performing the ceremonies of the Church, and inhaling rumors. The greater part of Price's regiment took the trail ahead of them (some detachments were behind them), and on August 13 the Battalion was ordered out. They marched without Lieutenant Colonel Allen, their commander, who had fallen ill at the fort, and in a few days they learned that he had died. Already there had been evidence that the Lord was displeased with them, for a good many had been taken sick and an old woman and her husband, traveling in the family of an officer, had died. It had been necessary to convene them as Saints and preach to them. A violent storm was evidence of Jehovah's anger, and they were bidden to "obey the word of the Lord and the counsel of His servants." The high priests laid their hands on the sick, anointing them with the sacred unguents, and then resumed their function as soldiers in the hope that the Lord would bless the work. But some of the brethren were buying whiskey from the sutlers at six dollars a gallon.

The death of Allen seemed a catastrophe. They had liked him, or now thought they had. He had been kind to them, had sanctioned the establishment of their families on the Indian lands, and had not interfered with their rites. Moreover, the prophet had acknowledged him as commander of the expedition, which deputized him in the authority of the priesthood, the succession of which was broken by his death. The prime source of the trouble his successors experienced was the fact that they held commissions only from James K. Polk, not from Brigham Young.

Now the Battalion was alone in the wilderness and counsel was far away. A very troubled soldiery tried to solve the problem by oracle. The Battalion knew in its heart that the priesthood should lead, but the officers, who were lower in the sacred hierarchy than some of their command, took thought of worldly things. They sent word to Polk in Washington — and the War Department ordered Captain Jacob Thompson from Jefferson Barracks to take command, but he never caught up with them. They also notified Brigham Young, who was too far away. When Allen died the commandant at Fort Leavenworth sent Lieutenant Andrew J. Smith of the First Dragoons to, in the words of the Saints, "tender his services to lead the Battalion to Santa Fe," with the temporary rank of lieutenant colonel.

As captain of Company A, Jefferson Hunt was senior among

the officers of the Lord, and Lieutenant Dykes had been consecrated adjutant. Hunt was a sagacious man and a good soldier, who later was to become one of the best frontiersmen in Zion's deserts. With Dykes he prevailed against the judgment of the priesthood, who were for keeping U. S. officers out of the Lord's military forces. They pointed out the principal threat that Price, just a few days ahead, might try to bring the brethren under his command, if the new commander was not received — and Price was a Puke and an enemy. Furthermore, if the brethren did not accept government leadership, they might have trouble getting rations — and even, Hunt pointed out, pay. That settled it and after a formal negotiation with the new commander, Hunt telling Smith exactly the terms on which they would recognize him, the priesthood yielded to the secular arm. For a moment Smith seemed to justify their abdication, for he requisitioned from Price twelve days' rations which, Hunt was convinced, the Pukes would not otherwise have given up.

Most of the Battalion, however, felt that this yielding to authority was a kind of betrayal. They kicked openly and rebelled secretly, generating the aggrieved and righteous obstinacy which the Mormons have always known how to put to the best use. When Brigham Young learned what had happened, he was furious. They had had a chance to escape Gentile control, and they had muffed it. They might have conducted their affairs according to the Lord's leading — and the prophet's orders. They might have ended their year's service at Bent's Fort, and Brigham began to convince himself that they were not obligated to go farther than that. (As a matter of fact, the Battalion did not go near Bent's Fort. At the Arkansas crossing Smith took it down the shorter, thirstier route to Santa Fe, the Cimarron branch of the trail. Price's Second Missouri also took this route.) At Bent's Fort, of course, they would have been in a position to assist the Exodus next spring, compared to which their contract to conquer California amounted to nothing. Young sent a rebuke southward with Lee. But he saw also that he now had an alibi; so he used it. If any of the Battalion should suffer hardship or disease, if the holy union suits should fail to protect them from Mexican bullets, let them not cite the prophet's promise. They had disobeyed counsel: be the punishment on their heads.

They began hungry, and in fact were not often to be well fed till they got to Santa Fe. Mr. Polk's expeditionary forces were always in advance of their commissaries, though the War Department had by now organized a prodigious freightage. The garrison at Santa Fe was not to be satisfactorily supplied till the late spring of

'47, and the Mormons, Kearny, and Doniphan were never to get supplies in satisfactory quantities. The Saints blamed their half-rations on their commander, who was a Gentile and therefore must be conspiring against the children of God. He joined the enormous corps of specters who, in Mormon belief, have inflicted malign cruelties on the chosen. From the beginning up to now all Mormons have always been able to discover a plot to bankrupt, harry, and kill them in the most innocent conversation or facial expression of the most complete nobodies. Theirs is the world's most hair-trigger martyr complex. The events that first begot it were real enough, God knows, but its survival in our time gives the archeologist a kind of living fossil to marvel at. The peaceful towns of Utah are, in Mormon fantasy, likely to erupt at any moment with the gunfire of Gentiles sworn to put God's people to death. The Saints cannot understand the complete indifference of the world to the forms and content of their religion: the inability is perhaps a compensation for that religion's essential dullness.

So there was martyrdom in every order that Lieutenant Smith gave, and the Saints made their daily march in a fever of suspicion and mulish antagonism, employing Israel's talent for insubordination against him and against their own officers, who, they thought, were toadying to him when they wanted his orders obeyed. Nothing on the record shows that Andrew Jackson Smith was anything but a good man trying to do a hard job in difficult circumstances. He was a first-rate man, a first-rate soldier. His Civil War service was brilliant. He had four years of hard and various action, rose to command a corps, and once defeated Nathan Bedford Forrest—which, it will be recalled, few others ever contrived to do.

But remember that the Mormons were lately from a genuine persecution and that they suffered a daily apprehension of the Missourians ahead of them on the trail. Alone in the desert, far from the warm security of a dictator's will, they naturally cherished the mania of persecution. The snare of the fowler, the digged pit of the enemy, was forever at their feet. But even if Smith had been able to understand this communal neurosis, he would have found his job no easier. He was a West Pointer and had had eight years' service with the army's crack regiment, the regiment of Stephen Watts Kearny and Philip St. George Cooke. Orders were to be obeyed, not referred to a priesthood for interpretation in the light of gospel and debated according to private inspiration. Military duties were to be performed as they arose, and he but vaguely understood the offense when they sometimes interfered with ordinances and ceremonies related to the eternal glories. He took this to be a detachment of the United States Army, and did not understand that it marched under a canopy of revelation, that prophetic dreams and signs from Heaven took priority over the regulations of the high command. He did not understand that he himself was without claim to their obedience, a man outside the law, one of the tribe marked for destruction — as John D. Lee called him, "a poor wolfish tyranicle Gentile who was a second Nero." He was Nero when he told them to close ranks, mend their pace, or pitch their tents in a place which he thought proper. So daily and hourly he butted into either the voluble argument or the mute refusal to obey orders of a secret society of very righteous men. They had no drill, no sense of military function, no knowledge of how to march — and when he tried to teach them, elders, priests, high priests, Seventies, and men gifted in the interpretation of the holy languages of Heaven invoked either prophecy or the writings of the martyred Joseph to put him in the wrong.

Moreover, he was marching not only soldiers but some daughters in Israel as well. Seven large families and a miscellany of gaffers had been sent on to Pueblo when the Battalion turned south at the crossing of the Arkansas. About twenty-five women remained. Army regulations permitted the enlistment of four laundresses per company. In peacetime frontier garrisons this euphemism looked to the comfort of single men in barracks. But the regulation had enabled some of the officers to bring their wives — and their wives' mothers — and a few of the enlisted men had contrived to do likewise. The comfort, whims, and prudery of these females had to be considered on the march, and the unhappily wifeless had an additional envy and regret. Clearly the War Department ought to have considered the sacrament of celestial marriage and, like the Mexican Army, permitted soldiers the assuagements of the marital couch.

Furthermore, prayer, counsel, and confession of sins had not amended all the impiety of the Battalion: they continued to get sick. In fact they got sicker, especially with mumps, as they traveled the desert trail in violent heat, drank bad water, and neglected their hygiene. The few wagons and ambulances filled with the disabled. And Gentile tyranny had put a murderer in a position of power. This was Assistant Surgeon George W. Sanderson, christened "Captain Death" by the Battalion and so known in Mormon history ever since. In fact, Mormon history has always treated the march of the Battalion (when not treating it as a desperate adventure which saved the United States) as primarily an episode in attempted poisoning. Sanderson appears to have been a good doctor as doctors went in that, the darkest age of American medicine, and Edwin Bryant, whose judgment was excellent, spoke of his scientific attainments with great respect. But he had no faculty of command or persuasion. With considerable justice, he felt that the Saints were sabotaging the expedition, and he interpreted most of their illnesses as malingering. His prescriptions were the familiar ones of army medicine: give him a CC pill or paint him with iodine and mark him duty. And he had no leverage for obedience except a military one. The Saints found themselves assailed with a profanity such as they had heard only from the mouths of Pukes. Whereas, they well knew, God had reserved cursing as a prerogative of the faithful.

In the light of science, they were right to refuse Sanderson's calomel. But the light they refused it in was the doctrine of healing oils and the laying-on of hands. Sickness was a jurisdiction of the priesthood, medicine was precisely the mortal error which Mary Baker Eddy was later to make of it, and the elders would "minister" to their flock. Army regulations made no allowance for such exorcisms, however, and Sanderson, bawling his oaths, made them line up and swallow calomel by the spoonful. When they spat it out, Lieutenant Smith had no recourse but to call them insubordinate and to assess penalties — which was further evidence that the Gentiles were conspiring against them. Those who recovered had been cured by the priesthood; those who died, mostly the grandsires but a few enlisted men, had clearly been murdered.

This fear of murder and this holy resentment of tyranny chiefly occupy the journals that have survived. One gets from them, besides, only the daily sense of miracle; the rest is Sanderson or his conspiring master, Smith. The countryside went all but unnoticed and they took strangeness in their stride. (Though Private Bliss notes a proof of the *Book of Mormon* when they pass through Pecos pueblo, the ruins of an "old Nephite city.") But, considering how many of them should never have been enlisted, how many were frail, how many elderly — they made a pretty good march of it.

Before the middle of September they caught up with most of Price's Second Missouri, thus demonstrating, as Kearny's infantry had done, the superiority of footmen to horse soldiers on such a march. They were, however, on the verge of mutiny, and before long John D. Lee arrived from the prophet, with his faithful friend Pace and his fellow avenger Howard Egan. They learned with pleasure that Young would uphold them in rebellion, and they filled Lee's ears with their intolerable injuries. (They had acquired a new fear, that the wives and grandams might not be allowed to go on with them from Santa Fe.) Lee gave them counsel and then, as representative of God's representative, rebuked Smith, their commander, bidding him mend his intolerable ways. Lee was a Seventy (just below the high priesthood in the organization) and he was also one of the Sons of Dan, one of the prophet's Gestapo. In both capacities he informed Lieutenant Smith and Dr. Sanderson that if they did not "cease to oppress my brethren" he would cut their throats. The lieutenant had to take it, but that night Jefferson Hunt, who was scandalized and better informed about the power of the United States, told Lee that he would order him under guard if he did not stop counseling mutiny. Lee saved that up to report to Brigham, Hunt's future in the Church was damaged, and Howard Egan was diligent to steal Sanderson's two skinny mules when he started home. (Somehow that theft shocked Lee.)

Still wearing his shoulder straps, however, Smith kept them going. Beyond Las Vegas, he separated the healthy from the sick and the halt, and hurried them ahead. The rest had to march ignominiously in and out of the company of the Missourians. The advance got to Santa Fe on October 9, the rest three days later. No mutiny. But some of Price's command were there ahead of them.

An old friend of the Mormons was in command of the town, Colonel Doniphan. Private Hess at once appealed to him not to violate the sanctity of marriage by sending the private's wife home. The saintly Doniphan at last agreed, though even Adjutant Dykes was disgusted by the plea, and permitted Hess to accompany his wife to the Pueblo. However, the Battalion's malingering was going to end abruptly now, for it came under a different kind of officer. Kearny, en route to California, had called on his best captain to command the Mormons and had advanced him to a lieutenant colonelcy. From now on the Battalion would take orders from Philip St. George Cooke. Also it would obey them.

No Battalion diarist reports visions, dreams, or signs in the heavens on September 17. But on that day the valorous wolf-hunters of Illinois finished their job at Nauvoo.

Less than a thousand Saints were left in the City of Joseph. All spring and summer the families had been crossing the Mississippi and taking to the trail, as fast as they could sell their property at five cents on the dollar and buy outfits. Class lines established themselves: the wealthiest and those highest in the priesthood went first, others followed in the order of salability of their real estate. By July so few remained that the mobbers felt secure. They began to fill the little newspapers with threats and indignation again. They rode by night and sometimes even by day, little gangs of armed thugs brave enough to raid outlying farms and kill a widow's chickens under her very eyes. They had deputies arrest Saints under all the old accusations. Here and there they shot someone who didn't have his friends with him. Finally they decided that it was safe to hold the wolf hunt.

No reason. Governor Ford says they were afraid that Mormon votes might turn the Congressional election again. Such Mormons as dared to exercise the franchise did in fact vote Democratic in August, in understandable if unjustified gratitude to James K. Polk. But August was over and, besides, there were not enough of them for any politician to fear.

That is exactly the point. Nobody was afraid of the Mormons any more. The thugs could abuse anyone they cared to. An aroused savagery does not soon abate and years of anarchy had sanctioned some questionable gratifications. Responsible citizens were cowed, public leaders were absorbed in politics or absent with the volunteer army. It is possible to explain the earlier mobbings of the Nauvoo Mormons: there was reason for them, they grew out of things past, they were probably inevitable. But the September climax can be even more easily explained: these mobs were just swine. It had come to be fun to torture a Mormon, so they had fun.

We need not detail the weeks of terrorism. It began to intensify. What the swine called posses grew into sizable mobs. They increased in daring, coming nearer and nearer Nauvoo, with heavier armament, louder noise, and more spectacular riding. Finally, with various pieces of small artillery, they attacked the city itself, producing in these all but deserted streets such scenes as the army of the United States was about to produce in the formally attacked, formally defended enemy city of Monterrey.

Apart from some committees of high-ranking Saints delegated to sell real estate and direct the migration, there were left only the sick and the very poor. They were joined in the defense by the "New Citizens," the thrifty who had bought the Mormons out and intended to take a profit on their foresight. Thus Bill Hickman, the Black Avenger of the Spanish Main, found himself fighting side by side with a Methodist parson who had been one of the most tireless agitators of hate but now had property here. Hickman, whose taste was experienced, admired the divine's profanity as he loaded and fired at the attackers, prominent among whom was a Campbellite minister. . . . No census is reliable, but probably the entire garrison of Nauvoo, including women and children, numbered less than a thousand and none of them were warriors. The mob has no census, either, but there were fifteen hundred or twenty-five hundred hard, tough, loud-mouthed gunmen, all of them, in the circumstances, brave. By discretion of the attackers, the battle was maintained at fairly long range. It lasted several days and a number were killed on both sides. Back of the mob various peace-lovers organized and finally an armistice was arranged — on the Mormons' promise to forget the contract signed with them ten months ago and to get out now, all of them, at once.

The mobbers whooped into the city and began to amuse themselves with the terrified. They stole what they wanted, broke what was breakable, converted the Temple floors into latrines (and, Kane says, vomitories), yelled at children, and flourished guns at women. It was their pleasure to beat up some Saints and to baptize others in parodies of the sacred ordinances. They had an enjoyable time and the Saints hauled their sick into the brush to escape lynching, gathered what possessions they could, pleaded unavailingly for time and mercy, and got out. Some died of fright, others of shock and injury, others still in premature childbirth.

Most of them got out in crowded boats during the afternoon and night of September 17. The next day the victors made a good job of it by expelling the New Citizens too.

Some six hundred and forty huddled on the Iowa shore, in the marshes, with the rains coming and the chills-and-fever season at hand. They built brush shelters, made tents of sheets and wagon covers. The brethren at Garden Grove, Mount Pisgah, and Winter Quarters hurried to send what help they could — it was little enough. "I came to the camp of the poor, sick, and persecuted Saints," says Luman Shurtliff, who led one of the relief parties. "Many places where there had been camps were now desolute and without inhabitant. [At] Others a ragged blanket or quilt laid over a few sticks or brush comprised all the house a whole family owned on earth. [Some] Among the occupants lay stretched on the ground either sick or dying, others perhaps a little better off had a few boards laid up on something and had [were] more sick than well. . . . I was not a little surprised to hear them relate the blessings of God in the deliverance from disease, death, and starvation."

In the course of ten weeks, they were all moved out to various way stations on the trail, where they fared a little better. Meanwhile there was never enough food, never enough shelter, and never any comfort at all. They ate what they had brought with them, what they could find, what they could beg or buy in the vicinity, what the succoring wagons could haul to them. Ague, typhoid, dysentery, pneumonia, ravaged them. But, of course, beyond them in the sunset somewhere was Israel's inheritance.

In the Mormon memory this swampy pest hole is known as "The Poor Camp," and no wonder. They died like flies.

At Santa Fe Susan Magoffin had her own house, a very foreign one with floors of hard-packed clay and adobe walls covered with gay calico. Susan found herself the belle of the occupation. Brother James Magoffin had, of course, arranged a final dinner for her before he hurried on to Chihuahua to set up another Trojan Horse. He had hunted up oysters and unlimited champagne, and his and her husband's friends paid extravagant court to her. Some were New Mexican gentlemen, some were American gentlemen with New Mexican wives, and the women loved Susan but had the strangest manners and dismayed her with the most intimate curiosity when they called in state. General Kearny, who seemed very much like dear Papa, paid her courtly compliments and squired her in public with staff and retinue. The general was a Kentucky gentleman and behaved not only toward her but toward his conquered province, Susan thought, with admirable courtesy. He took her to Fort Marcy, the stronghold which his engineers were building above the town. He took her riding through the parched, outlandish country, Susan's skirt falling in a great curve from her sidesaddle while the scabbards of the general's aides made a brave sound. He donned a full-dress uniform and took her to church, to stand holding a lighted candle while the priest muttered a heathen ritual. Susan's pious, evangelical heart revolted from the abysmal superstition of these kneeling peasants. She was sure that the priest did not understand the Latin he mouthed, and she was shocked to find the same little orchestra playing the offertory (and playing it rather like a hoedown) that had played waltzes and boleros at a ball a few nights before.

That was the general's ball, too, and Susan could not approve the abandon of those dances in which the women were so fervently embraced. She was not reconciled to the native costumes which, though prettily colored, were not reticent about a woman's limbs and exposed so much of the bosom that Susan turned her eyes away from what she considered open incitation of the baser instincts. All the women smoked corn-shuck cigarettes, too, and fat priests drank wines and *aguardiente* and displayed an unclerical mirth that distinguished them sharply from the parsons she knew. But worst of all La Tules was there, Doña Gertrudes Barcelo, a handsome, urbane female. Everyone seemed to like her although she owned and personally managed the town's biggest gambling hall. She had, the distressed Susan wrote down, "that shrewd and fascinating manner necessary to allure the wayward, inexperienced youth to the hall of final ruin."

There was the officers' ball for their general, a mixture of fandango and regimental hop in the big hall of the Governor's Palace. A native artist had painted a mural in which Stephen Watts Kearny was handing to an Orozco peasant the scroll of a constitution lettered *libertad,* before a background of plow, cross, and cannon. They draped the flag in front of it and at least five hundred people danced to the languor and melancholy of the native tunes. The demobilized native officers in their effulgent uniforms quite dimmed our own. But the Americans admired the displayed "forms" of the native women, were sure that they lacked chastity, and poeticized Susan as purity added unto loveliness. The enormous Doniphan spun her in a frontier waltz — she must have been sixteen inches shorter than he — and Captain Moore was intoxicated but complimentary. Volunteer or regular, they gave her a rush.

They kept on giving her a rush. A beautiful, well-born girl holding open house in a sun-baked village of foreigners, she realized in rosy flesh the phantasy of soldiers far from home. She smiled over her embroidery, she patiently instructed the little maids who did her housework, her white fingers hovered above a table of chocolate and confections, and they adored her. Major Swords, Major Clark, Captain Moore, Captain Johnston, Captain Burgwin, Captain Turner, Lieutenants Emory, Hammond, Gilmer, Peck — all of them, in procession. They brought her word of the occupation, the patrols, the new fort, Taos, the Indians of the frontier. They discussed the native food, superstitions, customs, industries. They sang for her and paraded their gentilities in learned conversations about Literature and Foreign Thoughts. They bowed over her hand and some of them could deplorably be in liquor — Susan remote of course, disapproving, forgiving, calling on Samuel to intercept the noisier ones. To a man they openly envied Samuel Magoffin, the proprietor of these charms when the door shut behind them.

The merchants called too, and the grandees, their enormous wives swathed in priceless laces, who instructed her in domestic economy and, too much, in the decorum of privacies. They gave dinners for her, beginning at two o'clock and lasting through the afternoon, with Susan collecting recipes as the courses multiplied. She did not like the severe separation of sexes at table and all the meats were strange. She would not smoke cigarettes, naturally, but Samuel Magoffin had taken care to tutor her in wines and she found these excellent. The general rose: "The United States and Mexico — They are now united, may no one think of separating!" Translation by one of the omnipresent Robidous, and, traders and grandees, they were on their feet shouting "*Viva!*" The ladies withdrew to one of the big rooms that always had benches but never a rocking chair for Susan.

Admiration could not altogether protect purity from its equivalent on a lower plane. One day a stranger tapped at the door. Susan thought him a teamster seeking employment from her husband and so admitted him. Alas, he was in liquor and, her frozen horror discovered, mistook this for a different kind of house and her lovely self for a kind of female whose existence she had heard whispers about. Righteousness faced the inconceivable with a terrible dignity and the venturer got out somehow, but that night doubtless she wept in Samuel's arms.

It was a crowded, gay, strange month, September in Santa Fe, with those amazing colors at their best and pageantry outside her door all day long. The Flag was flying over the Plaza and she had forgotten the agony and heartbreak of Bent's Fort. Then suddenly the visits of officers redoubled, they called in twos, threes, half-dozens, and they were making their farewells. They fervently pressed that small hand, made their best speeches, and bowed out with a jingle of spurs. The army was moving on.

It had done a good job and, on the whole, had enjoyed itself.

A lot of them were sick, to be sure, and there was never a time when all of them had enough to eat. Scurvy kept breaking out and they had brought the measles down from the Raton to this conquered capital. So the measles spread among the children who, the first peacemakers, crowded the camps and drills. A long series of funerals followed, a little uncoffined corpse dressed in such cheap finery as its parents could afford carried through the streets behind Popish symbols, with a fiddle playing gay tunes while mothers sobbed under their shawls and fathers stolidly told their rosaries. The Missourians got a lesson in broad-mindedness.

Other lessons followed. Few had any awareness of the past, Great Spain, or the glory that Nuevo Mejico had been in many minds. They could summon up no ghosts of hard, desirous, noble, brave, or cruel men who had lived, fought, and died to hold these uplands for Christ and the King. Coronado, de la Cruz, Oñate, Benavides, Peñalosa, Peralta, de Vargas, Escalante, Dominguez — they did not even know those names and could not have pronounced them. They were wholly ignorant of that older and far bitterer conquest. If they had known of it, they lacked the sense of sword and cross and they would not have seen a war of gods as well as men. They had heard of Zebulon Pike and would meet Kit Carson — and such names were comfortable, such a conquest was adapted to their understanding.

But they began to shed some of the indurated provincialism they had brought here. At first they just gaped at the unfamiliar. It was laughable but it was nicely colored. The town was full of Indians, some of familiar types, others very strange. There were the Pueblo people, fat, docile, and tamed — or, as at Santo Domingo, warlike, haughty, bearing themselves with an ineffable contempt. Ute, Apache, Navajo, came in to investigate the conquerors and calculate the chances. All these in scarlet, green, purple — and the New Mexicans also violent in color. Men in breeches slit to show their drawers, operatic with cloaks, musical with spurs and silver ornaments. Women also in primary colors, barelegged, short-skirted, low-waisted. The Missourians were shocked by the paint on their faces, their familiarity and easy laughter, and, the truth is, by the charm they gave to what had to be considered vice. They showed their breasts and, it was believed, in fact it was soon proved, they could be easily possessed — for pay, for kindness, or for mere amenity. An instructed prudery showed itself: sex ought not to be decorative.

New Mexico did not experience such sexual terrorism as Taylor's volunteers were by now inflicting on the northern provinces. The Army of the West had a gift for international goodwill. But propitiation took time and a few of the boys were violent. They learned, however. This was a simple, childlike, gay people, given to fandangos, feasts, parades. One joined them at first derisively, then with the simplicity of boys on a holiday. So the frail girls could be frail charmingly, and Inez glancing over her shoulder at Mass turned out to be much like Betsy when the fiddles were playing a hoedown at a corn husking back home.

Similarly with other things. The farm boys began by laughing at an alien way of life but pretty soon were taking to it with the readiness of all Yankee armies. They were lofty toward alien agriculture — irrigation, intensive cultivation, a French valuation of manure and waste. It was comic of the foreigners to work their women in the fields, of the women to carry baskets on their heads. The jackasses no larger than St. Bernards, with produce piled high on their backs, were funny. The communal herds were funny, goat's milk was funny, the children herding the goats with hugs and kisses were funny. Then they weren't funny any longer. The Missourians decided that they would never understand these people and no matter. They crowded the Plaza with them, evenings and Sundays, shot dice and played monte with them, were rolling cigarettes and learning to eat chili without tears. They played with the children, dropped in on Juan or Jesús of an evening and jabbered with him and his wife and his aunts and aunts-in-law in a mixed jargon which no one understood. They swarmed to innumerable fandangos. They learned some good addresses.

While thus getting a little Mexican gloss themselves, they busily Americanized the town. In some things, too much so. Food was not easily come by but the liquor supply never gave out. They learned to drink the coarse wines of the district, resinous and sharp, much inferior to the superb vintages that were still being produced at the haciendas of Chihuahua. They never liked mescal or tequila, though willing to take them if nothing else was offered. The brandies of the region were something else, and the legendary voltage of Taos Lightning, they found, had not been exaggerated. Santa Fe began to roar more than a little. When the boys seemed to be getting out of hand Kearny shifted them to horseherd duty miles away or found marches for them to make. Doniphan cracked down too. They beefed at their officers, pulled down their tents, went AWOL and made orations when guards rounded them up. There were some knifings and a couple of shootings. Summary courts followed; offenders were drummed out of camp; some were laid by the heels. Kearny gave them more work to do.

They hauled a huge, antique press down from Taos and began to publish a newspaper. They organized debating societies, legislatures, glee clubs. The city slickers of the Laclede Rangers set up a theatrical company — and the New Mexicans could now raise their eyebrows at a barbarian morality which dressed up blond young lieutenants in women's clothes.

Stephen Watts Kearny was a good soldier and a good conqueror.

He was organizing the conquest and preparing the future. His proclamation was hardly dry when he began reducing the taxes that had sweated these people for two centuries. He made every possible demonstration of peace, courted the fat, powerful priests, was brisk and kind to the humble. He took half his force on a rapid tour of the Rio Abajo, the southern settlements of New Mexico. He was ceremonious with the Pueblo people. The Santo Domingo charged down on him in their complimentary mock warfare, then feasted him in the pueblo, where he avoided offending a single god. On to Tomé, Bernallilo, Isleta, Peralta, Albuquerque. There was a great fiesta at Tomé. Kearny was punctilious at Mass, fireworks flamed in the violet sky, and the Doniphesias were badly outridden by the natives in mounted games. Kearny broke bread, made speeches, granted privileges, accepted the kindly honors heaped on him, commanded the presence of raiding Indians whom he ordered to make treaties, memorized the protocol and details of local administration. He came back from his tour convinced that the conquest was complete, that the conquered had accepted their new estate and would make no trouble. Probably they would have made none if Kearny or Doniphan could have stayed.

Kearny had delegated to Doniphan a task which Polk had imposed, of organizing the civil law. A frontier lawgiver, Doniphan could create a state offhand. Whatever help he might need was at hand in his own regiment. He called on Francis P. Blair, Jr., the amateur scout, Captain Waldo the trader, the historian John T. Hughes, and a private of Captain Moss's Company C who had successfully stumped Missouri for Mr. Polk, against Doniphan, in '44. This last was a twenty-six-year-old genius named Willard P. Hall, a Yale man removed from Baltimore to Missouri. Eventually he would lead the stormy "provisional" government of Missouri during the Civil War, half bolstering and half hindering A. Lincoln's involved manipulations in that vital, tortured state. Now he sat with Blair and Doniphan in a sunny room of the Governor's Palace and practised the peculiarly American art of making a government. They produced a constitution and a code, which Kearny proclaimed the law of the commonwealth. Later, in the chaos that headed up in 1850, Congress would find that Polk, through Kearny, had exceeded his authority and would rescind part of them, thus giving Boanerges Benton another shot at the man who punctured his son-in-law Frémont. But, in their essentials, they governed New Mexico up to statehood, and large parts of them govern New Mexico today.

Not a bad achievement for soldiers taken from barracks duty to build a state — and another way in which this conquest was strange to a much conquered people. One day while Hall worked in his low-ceilinged room, Colonel Doniphan came in with news that the folks back home had elected Hall to Congress. His discharge from the army followed, but he had no taste for abandoning a job. He attached himself to Philip St. George Cooke as an unofficial aide and went on to California with the Mormon Battalion.

The New Mexican sun gentled with September. In the high peaks willows and popple put on the bright yellow of autumn. The fierce colors of the mesas grew fiercer in leached air, the nights sharpened, and the aromatic smoke of piñons hung above the town. The army had learned to like the grapes and melons and even the outlandish breads and stews. It was badly fed by its government, which had as yet got no paymaster this far and was unable to keep supplies coming in. The horseguards — up in the hills where there was grass — got scurvy. They, the outlying patrols, and the garrison all howled a healthy complaint continuously. Lacking money, the army found its brass buttons worth from ten cents to two bits as currency and used them, having long since exhausted its credit with the sutlers. (It could not commandeer supplies from the New Mexicans. They were Americans now and must be paid in coin. No coin was sent but only Treasury checks which no one would honor. Part of the expedition was financed by a loan from La Tules, the faro dealer, whom Captain Johnston squired prodigiously at a fandango.)

They had lost their contempt of the ingratiating, poor folk whom they had invaded. Six weeks proved enough to reconcile them to the furriners, though they would never understand Catholicism and the frontier plenty they were accustomed to blinded them to the simple fact that a universal poverty had organized this way of life. They had come to like the furriners, who liked them in turn and would have gone on liking the gringo conquerors if Price's troops had behaved as well as Kearny's. When Price entered Santa Fe he fired a wonderful artillery salute, which broke most of the few windowpanes in town. It furnished a good symbol of what was to come.

Kearny's last business in New Mexico was to do something about the Indians. The Navajo had been raiding the frontier settlements and almost up to Santa Fe. The Apache, too far away to be handily admonished, had not interrupted their vocational theft and murder. Both tribes professed to understand that the American war on New Mexico had sanctioned their destruction of a common enemy. Both sent representatives to look over the Long Knives in Santa Fe.

Kearny warned them and sent out a force to bring in the Ute, who were accustomed to raid from the north. He told them to behave themselves and sent them home. But the Indian problem had to be left to Doniphan.

For Kearny had to go on to the other conquest required of him. He named a civil government of New Mexico, with Charles Bent as governor and young Frank Blair attorney general. Then on September 25, with three hundred of his Dragoons and with Tom Fitzpatrick for guide, he took the lower trail to California.

The next day, September 26, hundreds of miles away, General Wool's army left San Antonio to begin Mr. Polk's map-calculated conquest of Chihuahua. It was this invasion that Kearny ordered Doniphan to converge on at the city of Chihuahua.

Doniphan, Kearny's order read, was to turn over the command of Santa Fe to Price, as soon as the Second Missouri should arrive. But first he must clean up the unfinished business. He must round up the Indians, exhort them, and make treaties with them. It sounded simple enough: he was just to pacify the overlords of New Mexico.

The Army of the West had finished its holiday. The farm boys would now do some campaigning.

INTERLUDE

Friday, October 16

UNDER the Bulfinch dome of the Massachusetts General Hospital, the young gentlemen of the Harvard Medical School shuffled their feet, wondering what was up and why it didn't happen. It was certainly important, for the biggest men in their profession were gathered round the professor of surgery, Dr. John Collins Warren. Here were Dr. Henry J. Bigelow, Dr. J. Mason Warren, Dr. Samuel Parkman, Dr. Gould, Dr. Hayward, and Dr. Townsend, all dressed in the morning coats proper to the practice of their profession. Dr. Warren looked angry, kept glancing at his watch, and muttered something to Dr. Haywood and Dr. Bigelow. He was saying waspishly that since Dr. Morton had not arrived it must be presumed that he was otherwise engaged. But the young gentlemen in the amphitheater seats could not hear that and went on discussing the array of notables. They paid no particular attention to the patient who had been prepared for operation, a young man named Gilbert Abbott who was in the red plush chair with a sheet thrown over it, his arms and legs strapped down. It was just any operation, apparently. The young gentlemen had seen many before it in this well-lighted room with its ancient mummy case and its white cast of Apollo.

Dr. Warren put up his watch again, decisively this time. But another gentleman, whom some recognized as Dr. William Morton, a dentist, came in hastily and murmured an apology to Dr. Warren. Dr. Morton was carrying a piece of philosophical apparatus, which he explained in low tones to Dr. Warren. The young gentlemen saw it as a glass globe with projecting tubes or arms. It was about half full of a colorless liquid.

Dr. Warren came forward and addressed the medical students. He said that there was a gentleman present who claimed to have made a discovery which would produce insensibility to pain during surgical operations. As the class knew, Dr. Warren had always regarded that condition as an important desideratum in operative surgery. Therefore he had decided to permit the experiment they were about to witness.

The patient, Dr. Warren explained, was suffering from a vascular tumor of the neck on the left side, occupying the spaces from the edge of the jaw downward to the larynx and from the angle of the jaw to the median line. They could see it and diagnose it from where they sat.

Dr. Morton, the experimenter, put the long tube of his apparatus in the patient's mouth, told him to inhale, and asked one of the notables to hold his nostrils shut. Tension came into the airy room. The doctors bent forward; the students felt their muscles getting tight; Dr. Morton crouched before the patient, watching him closely. In between four and five minutes the patient, after some heaving and struggling, seemed to go to sleep. "Dr. Warren, your patient is ready," Dr. Morton said, and withdrew the apparatus. Dr. Warren made an incision about three inches long over the center of the tumor, through the skin and subcutaneous cellular tissue, and removed a layer of fascia which covered the enlarged blood vessels. He then passed a curved needle, with ligature, under and around the tumor and exerted considerable pressure. The growth came out and Dr. Warren closed the incision.

The patient appeared to be sleeping quietly, but just before the operation was completed moved and twitched a little and muttered indistinctly. Presently he awoke. He was asked if he had suffered any pain. No, he said, but he had felt a dim sensation, as if his neck were being scraped with a blunt instrument.

The class sat back and flexed their muscles. "Gentlemen," Dr. Warren said, "this is no humbug."

XII
Atomization

THE power of religion and the fascination of psychology are that they try to explain character. What gives men standards of responsibility, called honor? What is it that, in extremity, forces some men to betray those standards in the hope of escaping death, and what forces other men to hold by them, let death come? Why does danger paralyze the will and intelligence of some men, and why does it vitalize the will and make purposive the intelligence of others? Why, when death must be faced, do some personalities disintegrate whereas others abide by the qualities of resolution, fortitude, and courage which have persuaded the human race that it has dignity? Why, at the inexorable test, do some men yield to the suddenly loosed primordial terror that is our inheritance, whereas some are able to hold the monsters in check and act as their God has promised them they will? What are self-command, hardihood, gallantry, audacity, and valor?

It would be helpful to know the answers to such questions when we look at a train of twenty emigrant wagons parked near the crossing of the Weber River on the evening of August 11, when James Frazier Reed gets back to them from Great Salt Lake, not accompanied by Lansford Hastings. For the long, inexorable testing begins here.

There is no point in devoting to the Donner party the space it receives in this book except as it provides one of the varieties of frontier experience. It has been a favorite story of historians and novelists because it is concentrated, because the horror composes a drama. But the reader of this book will understand that the disaster which overtook the Donner party was part of the trail's *if,* one factor in the equation of chance under which emigration across the mountains and desert traveled. The fate of the Donners or its equivalent was, as a hazard, part of the equipment packed in every white-top that pulled up the slope beyond Fort Laramie, this year, the years before it, and for some years still to come. Whether the risk was to be taken successfully or unsuccessfully depended on chance, weather, skill, intelligence, and character — all inscrutable.

No part of the tragedy is unique. There is more horror in the Mountain Meadows massacre of September, 1857. An armed band of Mormons led by John D. Lee, and under the superior command of William Dame and Isaac Haight, murdered one hundred and twenty men, women, and children. (In the entire history of the West no massacre by Indians was so large-scale or so complete.) Equal folly and suffering, and equal heroism, can be found in the story of the "Jayhawkers" and the Bennett-Arcane party who, in the autumn of 1849, tried to find another shorter way to California. Jefferson Hunt, of the Mormon Battalion, was guiding them by a safe route which had been blazed to escape the Salt Desert where the Donners foundered, but they left him and wandered off to disaster in the region which, because of them, has ever since been known as Death Valley. The Donners were not the only emigrants who disintegrated in panic, and the fact which the public chiefly remembers about them, their cannibalism, was no novelty in the West. It had occurred along the route they traveled, and when, in the last days of 1848, Frémont's fourth expedition stalled in the San Juan snows, Bill Williams' detachment probably killed and certainly ate one of their companions. Kit Carson remarked of Bill Williams that in starving times no man should walk ahead of him on the trail, and old Bill shared that reputation with numerous others. In fact, the last resource of starving men is a commonplace.

It is as the commonplace or typical just distorted that the Donners must be seen. Beyond Fort Laramie every stretch of the trail they traveled, at some time during the history of emigration, saw one or another party just escaping disaster, and a number of stretches saw some parties not altogether escaping it. Just west of the Salt Desert the Donners crossed the trail of the Bartleson party of 1841 (mentioned earlier in a footnote), who had no trail at all across the Sierra, wandered lost for weeks in the mountains, starving, and just contrived to live till they could reach the universal succorer, John Augustus Sutter. The cabin which some of the Donner party camped in at the foot of Truckee Lake had been built two years before, in November, 1844, by the Stevens-Murphy party in the fear that they might have to spend the winter in the snow. One member of that party, Moses Schallenberger, did in fact spend the winter in that cabin alone. The others got across the divide which the Donners could not cross only because they had a master mountain man with them. Old Caleb Greenwood got them over by a heroic feat of will, intelligence, and ingenuity. And we have seen how close the Harlan-Young party, under Hastings' personal direction, came to disaster in the Salt Desert. . . . Finally, there is not much difference between dying of starvation in the snow and dying of exhaustion, as some of their former companions had done before they reached Truckee Lake, or dying of pneumonia in the Oregon rains, as others of their former companions did a month after the Donners turned back from the divide. Death on the trail was a hazard of emigration. You took your chances. Our concern with the Donners comes from the fact that the common chance turned against them.

The Wasatch are one of the most beautiful of Rocky Mountain ranges, but not among the highest. Characteristic of them are small, narrow, twisting canyons which have no logic except the laws of flowing water. These canyons are adventurous for mountain climbers but their discouraging attribute for those who travel them seriously is the way they lead into one another. The Union Pacific Railroad takes the one direct pass through the north and south main chain of the Wasatch, Weber Canyon, which we have seen Bryant and the Harlan-Young party traveling — but takes it by virtue of dynamite. All other passages of the Wasatch are circuitous, by small canyons which lead into other small canyons, sometimes widen into circular valleys off which a number of canyons lead (only one of which will be the right way onward), and by degrees take their streams westward round cliffs, the base of peaks, and the jutting ends of spinal ledges. Modern highways cross the Wasatch by such oblique routes now. The Donner party had to find such a route when, on the morning of August 12, they started out from their five-day encampment a little west of the mouth of Echo Canyon.

Fifteen days later, on August 27, they reached Salt Lake Valley, having covered a distance estimated, but probably underestimated, as thirty-six miles. In the meantime, Stanton and McCutchen, who had not been able to keep up with Reed, had rejoined the party, and the Graves family, thirteen altogether, with three wagons, had caught up with them from the east.

They had had to make a road for wagons, by a route which no wagon had ever taken before. With two of the able-bodied men absent and at least four other men disqualified by age or sickness, they had had to chop through aspen and popple and cottonwoods (and the underbrush that is just as bad) which choked the small canyons. They had to dig tracks and fell trees and level off centers high up on mountainsides, pry boulders out of their course, riprap swampy patches, sometimes bridge brooks that could not be crossed otherwise, grunt and strain and curse while the oxen heaved the wagons up inclines, over ridges, and around spurs of rock. Every ridge they topped showed a haze of further ridges beyond it. Every canyon that opened out closed in again. Every canyon that might be the last one ended in another one that might also be the last. Three times they found that they could go no farther, had to go back over part of the road they had built, and, abandoning it as wasted, try again, chopping and shoveling a new road. When they camped at the end of the fifteenth day they were almost out of the last canyon, the narrow defile which the Mormons were to call Parley's Canyon. The next morning they decided that they could not get through a tortuous place where the canyon walls almost met and the notch between was choked with loose rock. So they retraced their way up Parley's Canyon and the gulch by which they had entered it, and took the wagons straight up a mountain, over the ridge, and down into what is now called Emigration Canyon, and out, at last, into the valley of the lake.[1]

Edwin Bryant, who left Fort Bridger on July 20, reached the valley of Great Salt Lake on July 26. The Donner party, leaving Fort Bridger on July 31, reached the valley on August 27. That difference in traveling time states the first circumstance of their disaster but does not reveal all that had happened to them in the Wasatch. Their morale had begun to break. The morale of any emigrant train can be judged by its success in solving a fundamental conflict. On one hand there is any American frontiersman's impulse to go his own way, make his own choices, reap the rewards of his own intelligence and skill, and pay the penalties for his own mistakes. On the other is the co-operation enforced by the wilderness, which requires choices to be made in the common interest, assesses against the group penalties for every mistake made by individuals, and pools intelligence and skill for the use of everyone. We have seen the wagon trains breaking up and re-forming. Every new grouping was an attempt to establish a small social system which would function effectively; a successful passage along the trail meant the creation of a group spirit.

The feeling of being members one of another cracked in the Wasatch. They had to have a scapegoat and Hastings was not enough. James Frazier Reed began to be the focus of blame. He was responsible, or could be thought responsible, for the route they took; also, Stewart points out, he was now being paid back for his superior wealth and his aristocratic bearing. Furthermore, in fourteen days of heartbreaking labor some had begun to resent the weakness of companions who could not do their full share, and some had refused to do their share, accepting the common labor without putting into it all they had. The membrane that incloses the primordial inheritance was thus wearing through, and an even more dangerous pressure had been put on it. They had thought that Big Mountain was the last ridge that they must cross, but Stanton and McCutchen rejoined them just as they got down from it and told them that it was not. Then, Eliza Donner Houghton says, "Sudden fear of being lost in the trackless mountains almost precipitated a panic, and it was with difficulty that my father [George Donner] and other cool-headed persons kept excited families from scattering rashly into greater dangers." They had at last realized the danger they were in, and the realization was centrifugal, tending to drive them apart. It would dominate them from now on.

Overstrained and fearful but less exhausted than their stock, with the wagons jolted and shaken into a universal brittleness, they headed for the south end of Great Salt Lake and the Salt Desert beyond. One of George Donner's wagons stopped in blistering sun, and Luke Halloran, the consumptive, died, his head in Tamsen's lap.[2] They examined his possessions, which he had bequeathed to George Donner, and found $1500 in gold coin and the insignia of Masonry. The other Masons in the party convened a lodge and tossed the symbolic evergreen in a grave dug in salt mud. It was not far from the grave of Hargrave of the Harlan-Young party, and the Land of Canaan had claimed its second life from the emigration of '46.

There were eighty-six of them now, and twenty-three wagons. They toiled on, hurrying as fast as the condition of the oxen permitted, and in five days reached the last oasis east of the Salt Desert, Skull Valley. Here they found fragments of paper tacked to a board. Tamsen Donner gathered them up and pieced them together, and they proved to be a note from Hastings. The author of their ills was confessing another enthusiasm. He had originally said that the Salt Desert was no more than forty miles wide and could be crossed in one day. Now he was telling them that the crossing would take two days and nights.[3]

It took them six days and they traveled all or most of every night.

Here is where the membrane broke, where the group was atomized to individuals. The blinding glare, the burning blue sky with the insolent peace of bellying clouds, the horizon of mountains blue and purple and amethyst, the reds of sunset and the greens of dawn

— the cruel beauty of the death-giver could be observed in irony. Twisting whirlwinds or high walls of salt blew past them. Mirages offered them lakes and streams or showed them fields of grass blowing in the wind. William Eddy saw a file of men moving across the distance; they were himself repeated twenty times. Others saw similar processions and once some of them cried out, for this must be Hastings, the deliverer, coming back to help his victims. But none of this mattered for fear and the pit were upon them. They might die . . . here . . . now. The social system disintegrated. Some drove their oxen to the uttermost exertion, some tried to conserve their strength, some merely went on. Following the tracks of Hastings' wagons, they strung out across the white hell, under sun or full moon, formless, disorganized, at random, the stock failing, men and women with death in their hearts, all of them forced to observe the stoic, uncomprehending agony of the children.

The heavily loaded outfits of Reed and the Donners fell to the rear, where shrewdness would have put them anyway in a crisis of *sauve qui peut*. But too much had been required of the oxen in the Wasatch, and by the third night there was no water left in the casks. Men and stock must have water or die in the salt. Reed rode ahead, passing most of the others. Some had abandoned their wagons, driving the teams toward the water that was somewhere ahead. Others, frail, black-faced, stolid, were trying to keep to the wheel tracks. At the end of the fourth day (if he had slept at all, it was during part of the first night) he got to Pilot Peak and its springs. William Eddy and the Graveses had got there before him, first of all. Eddy, taking water to an exhausted ox, went back a few miles with Reed, who again in the moon's unreality passed down the frayed line of specters. He met his own teamsters, who had unhitched the oxen and were trying to get them and his horses to water in time. Then the Donners, driving their stock and some wagons. Then an abandoned Donner wagon and at last, toward dawn, his wife and children and some employes. One of the employes took Reed's horse back. The others waited for the drivers and the oxen.

They sat there in the salt, under the sun, blistered by wind, all the next day. No oxen and no drivers came. . . . The herd, maddened by thirst, had stampeded into the wasteland and would never be recovered. . . . So at the end of the day, Reed carrying the three-year-old Tommy, the others packing some food from the wagons and the remaining gills of water, they started out to walk it. When the children could go no farther, they made a kind of camp. An insane ox charged them and they got up again and went on. They reached

Jacob Donner's wagon, Reed heard that he had lost his teams, and, leaving his family, hurried on. Nearly everyone was getting to Pilot Peak now, some with their wagons, some with only their teams, some staggering in alone. The last day stretched out its agony, Jacob Donner came in with Reed's family, and, with no one dead, they had crossed the Salt Desert in six days. September 8.

Thirty-six oxen all told, just half of them Reed's, had died or stampeded into emptiness. As soon as they had drunk and let the surviving oxen drink, they started back to round up any stock they could find and bring the wagons in. When at last they had finished, the extent of disaster was clear. Those of high degree had been cast down, Reed altogether. They had futilely cached most of his possessions and abandoned two of his wagons, one of them the great van which his stepdaughter Virginia was to call the Pioneer Palace Car. He still had one ox and a cow; he hired two oxen from others and yoked the two teams thus formed to his remaining wagon. The surplus food supplies he had carried were distributed among his companions, who would presently refuse to share them with his family. Jacob Donner also abandoned a wagon, and so did the opulent Keseberg.

There were few spare teams left now, and all the stock was dangerously worn down. No more dangerously so, however, than their owners. The Salt Desert had accelerated the collapse which the Wasatch had begun.

They started toward the Humboldt. They had no way of knowing how to get there except by following Hastings' tracks — and the booster had taken the Harlan-Young party on a wide detour instead of using the trail which Clyman had found for him three months before.[4] Instead of taking a straight line, then, they tacked westward by long north and south courses which added at least a week to their traveling time. The oxen weakened and some of them died, and the wagons kept falling apart. The travelers repeatedly lightened their loads, sometimes making caches in the dream that they would be able later on to come back and open them, sometimes just leaving the stuff there in the desert. The process of doubling up had begun as the oxen failed: your remaining team and my wagon, whichever looks stronger, and as much food as we think we can carry.

Now they realized that it wasn't enough food. To the terror that they might not get across the Sierra before the snow came (now stimulated by a typical September snowstorm) there was added the terror that they might starve before they could freeze. So they did what the desert-bound in these parts always did: they resolved to appeal to Sutter. After a debate in which the nakedest suspicions must have found utterance, two who had previously served them volunteered and were accepted, the bachelor Stanton and the tall, powerful McCutchen, who would leave a wife and child behind him. On September 18 they rode ahead, hoping to bring supplies back from the Sacramento Valley in time. There was the plain danger that they might not get through to Sutter's. But in the minds of those they left behind, what assurance could there be that, if they should get through to food, comfort, and safety, they would commit the folly of coming back?

The going was dreadful all the way to the Humboldt. Even on the trail the Nevada stretches were always felt to be the worst of all. Except for occasional dry drives there was always water, and the double-teaming, the struggle with narrow gaps of rock or sudden and insane vertical hills or knife wedges of rock or stinking quicksand, was by now so routine that no one noticed. But it was here that the reserves of physical strength and moral stamina were exhausted. Here the cumulative strain of emigration precipitated trouble for man and beast and outfit alike, if it was going to. And here, if you were going to, you encountered the Diggers, their half-gram brains vibrating with the remembered murders of hundreds of kinsmen and with desire for oxen and other plunder.

The term "Digger" is an epithet, not a classification. It was properly applied to Indians who, being unskillful hunters or residing in country where game was scarce, lived on roots. But it came to mean certain degenerate bands of various tribes who can be exactly described as the technological unemployed. Unable to stand competition with hardier Indians, they had been pushed into the deserts and, living there on the subsistence level, had lost their culture. Many of them were physically decadent. The weapons of all were crude. Mostly they lived in caves or brush huts. Some had lost the use of fire. Some "Diggers" were Bannack or Shoshoni in origin; those in Great Salt Lake Valley were Paiute and Gosiute; fragments of other neighboring tribes also degenerated, and the Indians who harassed the Donners probably belonged to the Kuyuidika band of the Paviotso. But the whites who used the term meant no particular tribe; they meant only that they hated skulking, theft, and malicious mischief. From Ewing Young and Joseph Walker on, they had massacred Diggers idly, for fun, or in punishment for theft. The Diggers remembered . . . If they had not, they might have succored the Donners in the snow.

Hastings' route followed down the valley of the south fork of the Humboldt and the Donner party reached its junction with the main trail on September 30. They had come back (just west of Elko) to the road from Fort Hall which they should have taken from the Little Sandy or Fort Bridger. Exactly a month before, on August 30, Edwin Bryant had come down to Johnson's ranch on the far side of the Sierra.

The party split in two, one group forming round the Donners, whose outfits had survived in the best condition and could travel faster. The division was made on the theory that they could thus make more efficient use of the sparse grass. But it was really an act of anxiety, further evidence that the bonds of the community had been broken.

Some Diggers who came into camp seemed amiable and they were fed and allowed to spend the night. They were gone in the morning and so were two oxen. Some of their kin got a horse presently, and others began shooting arrows, not yet fatally, into the hides of oxen. And on October 5 the constraints of human association snapped apart. Note that in approximately the same place Bryant had stepped between two companions who were bent on killing each other.

It was double-teaming up one more of a thousand slopes that did the business. The Reeds had by now merged their small remaining outfit with Eddy's. Reed's teamster, Milt Elliott, who was driving the single wagon, had hitched Pike's team to it for the ascent. Elliott got into a quarrel with John Snyder, of the Graves party, over precedence up the hill. Snyder flamed into a rage and became violently abusive. Reed intercepted his threats. Snyder began to beat Reed over the head with his bull-whip, gashing him badly. Reed drew a knife and stabbed Snyder, just as another blow from the whip knocked him down. Snyder died almost at once. And at once this band of pilgrims traveling the frontier of death were atomized to armed men threatening one another. The Graveses demanded Reed's life. Keseberg, whom Reed had once insisted on temporarily banishing from the train for rifling an Indian grave and thus risking all their lives, propped up his wagon tongue — they were sufficiently veteran to know that this was how you hanged a man on the trail. Reed, supported by Eddy and Elliott, would not be hanged without some shooting first. When due fear of loaded guns had made itself felt above the blood lust, the party convened as a court, Reed's wounds bandaged and his wife's face showing the bruise where Snyder's whip had struck her. Sentence: on promise of the others to take care of his family, Reed must hereafter travel alone. And unarmed.

Such a verdict could not have been reached if the more stable Donners had been with this half of the party. Not only the cruelty but the grotesque folly of the sentence shows what inroads fear and exhaustion had made on their intelligence. They were depriving themselves of their strongest personality.

Prevailed on by his family, and by the thought that he might bring help to them all, Reed rode ahead the next day. Someone — either Virginia Reed or William Eddy — defied the common will by taking his rifle to him and so giving him a chance to survive. He overtook the forward section and had breakfast with George Donner. One of his teamsters who was traveling with them, Walter Herron, joined him and they went on. They carried a letter from George Donner to Sutter, asking him to send help and containing Donner's promise to pay all the expenses that might be involved. So there were now two pairs of messengers ahead of the divided train.

As the rack twists, certain of these people are seen to be more resistant than the others. In that inscrutable area of the personality which we call moral, Reed and his wife, George and Tamsen Donner, Mary Graves, Stanton, McCutchen, and William Eddy had a greater richness than their companions. It goes into the total sum for what it is worth. It proved to be worth much.

They were six days along the Humboldt stretch of the trail when the quarrel occurred. It took them the entire month of October to travel that stretch, go up the Truckee, and reach Truckee Lake just east of the final Sierra crossing. They had ceased to be a group long since. Some of them now ceased to acknowledge membership in the human race. Obeying the law of avalanches, the daily disasters grew worse.

Hardkoop, who was more than sixty years old, had been traveling with Keseberg and had suffered badly from the desert. One morning he could walk no more. Keseberg, with the limpid logic of the German mind, would not take him in a wagon, condemning the unfit for the preservation of the strong. Eddy was at the end of the caravan that day — it was of course no longer a caravan but only an irregular line. He saw Hardkoop, promised to take him in after crossing a difficult stretch, found the stretch longer than he had thought, and forgot Hardkoop. That night he did not come in, and that night and the next day Eddy, Elliott, and Pike would obey the

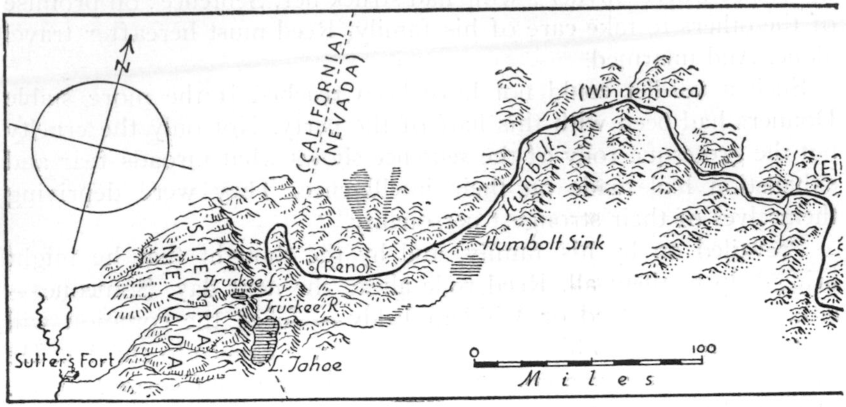

Route Taken by the

obligations of humanity and go back for him. But they had no horse to ride. Those who had horses would not lend them for such an errand. Let him die. He died.

They caught up with the section that had been leading — at a place where a member of the Harlan-Young party had been killed, and his grave rifled, by Diggers. At once the Diggers ran off Graves's horses. The next night they got eighteen oxen and a cow. The following night they playfully shot arrows into some oxen without killing them. The third night they shot twenty-one oxen, and those which were not killed were useless. . . . If there had been one mountain man along, the Diggers would not have struck more than once.

The last massacre of cattle occurred at the Sink of the Humboldt. Other horses and oxen had been dying. Wagons were abandoned. The dreary process of combining outfits and caching possessions in the hope of sometime reclaiming them went on. Wolfinger stayed behind one day to cache some of his wealth. Probably he wore a money belt. His countrymen, Reinhardt and Spitzer, stayed to help him, and Keseberg was also making a cache that day. When Keseberg, alone, caught up with the rest, he was suspected of having killed Wolfinger, but that was one offense Keseberg refrained from committing. It was Reinhardt and Spitzer who murdered Wolfinger, got his money belt if he had one, and reported that Indians had killed him and burned his outfit.

Many of the oxen killed by Diggers had belonged to the Donner

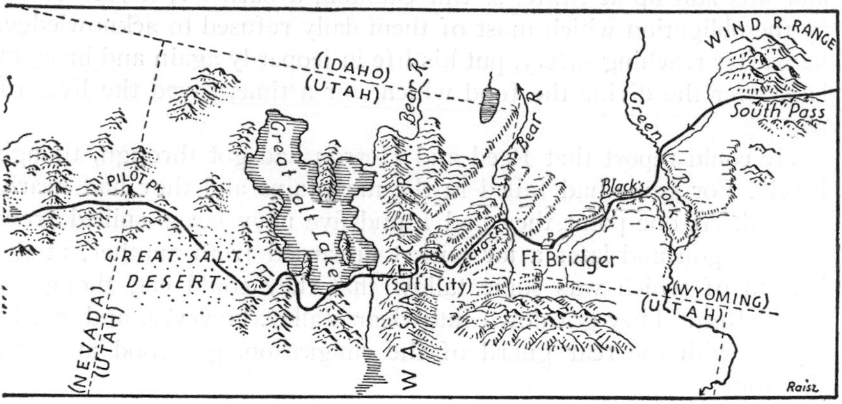

Donner Party

brothers, and serious inroads had now been made on that opulent outfit. Tamsen had dreamed of founding a polite academy for girls in the never-never land of California. Now a great crate of books designed for its library was buried in the desert. They would come back and get it sometime. . . . Neither Eddy nor the Donners could help Mrs. Reed and her children. All of Eddy's stock was finished and he could get none from anyone. He had smashed the lock of his rifle. No one would take his three-year-old son or the year-old Peggy into a wagon. He made a pack of some powder and bullets and three pounds of sugar. His wife carried the baby, he carried the three-year-old. On the last day in the desert the children nearly died of thirst. When they came into camp, old Patrick Breen, whose casks were full, refused them water. Eddy announced that he would kill Breen if he interfered and got some water for the kids. The next day, with a borrowed gun, Eddy killed nine geese. He distributed them among the families. The Diggers killed some more oxen.

At the end of that desert was the Truckee River. They rested for a day. Reinhardt and Spitzer came in and told their Wild West romance. The widow Wolfinger attached herself to the Donners, who crawled ahead of the rest again, and Eddy could get no food for his children. They headed up Truckee Canyon. And then, on the third day, October 19, Stanton came riding in from the west with seven pack mules and two Indians driving them. Sutter, whose mules and Indians they were, had not failed them. Nor had Stanton and McCutchen failed them. McCutchen had given out on the crossing and was laid up at Sutter's. But Stanton, a bachelor, moved solely by the obligation which most of them daily refused to acknowledge, had, after reaching safety, put his life in jeopardy again and brought back over the divide the food which, for a time, saved the lives of all.

He could report that Reed and Herron had got through, though barely. For game had failed in the mountains and they had nearly starved. At one point they had found five navy beans spilled from some wagon and later a tar bucket discarded from another, at the bottom of which was some tallow that they could eat, though it puked Reed. They got down into Bear Valley, however, and, catching up with the rear guard of the emigration, got food and met Stanton.

So, besides Stanton, Reed and Herron had reached the golden shore. From now on the man they had banished to die alone was the focus of their hope.

And why should Stanton, whose strength was restored and who had five strong mules and two Indians in his charge, stay on and share their journey? There was only one reason but it sufficed. He stayed on, and he died for it.

Also he took Mrs. Reed and her children under his protection. They came up to the Truckee Meadows. Here they were all together again — something over a dozen decayed wagons, and the oxen and the cows that were yoked with them all but dead. They were a tangle of fear, hatred, family love, friendship, fortitude, panic, and desperate hope. Ahead of them was the worst ascent of all, to the divide above Truckee Lake. If their teams had been sound they could have made it in at most three days. But their teams were hardly alive. They had to rest their stock at the Truckee Meadows — but there had been a number of snowstorms already and the sky above the pass was leaden with the threat of winter. The two dreads made a cruel dilemma. They solved it — though no longer in the orderly, debating-club process of the long vanished days when Owl Russell's big train had put Indian Creek behind them — by lingering to recruit the teams. They were thus following Stanton's advice. Stanton had been told at Sutter's, where the best judgment was to be had, that they could expect nearly a full month more before the snows would begin to block the pass.

They could not even be careful now. William Pike, the husband of Harriet Murphy, handed his pistol to his brother-in-law, Foster, and the gun went off. Pike died. Naomi and Catherine were father less.

There was another snow. It scared them and, without decision, merely as they could, they started for the pass, traveling in three rough sections. When the first section made camp, the first evening, a Digger skewered nineteen oxen. Eddy killed him. October 25. (According to Stewart's authoritative calculation. Thornton says October 22. The party itself had been unable to keep an accurate account of time.)

Back of them in the last section, one of George Donner's wagons broke an axle and overturned, nearly killing Georgia and Eliza. While they were making a new axle Jacob's chisel slipped and gashed George Donner's hand. The wound was eventually to save him from dying of starvation.

The peaks above them were blanketed with snow, and clouds hung round the summits. The advance party reached the lake — or rather a couple of miles short of it, a mile from the Schallenberger cabin — on the evening of the last day of October. It had taken them just three months to get here from Fort Bridger. Three and a half or four months would have been about right for a normal crossing from Independence to the Sacramento.

The terrible cold of the high places wrapped them round. On November 1 they tried the ascent. They found five feet of snow in the pass. They came back to the Schallenberger cabin, which the Breens pre-empted. They decided to stay there. On November 2 it rained all day. The middle group, Stanton traveling with them, came up. Stanton found them in the apathy of despair, but roused them, or most of them, to try again on November 3.

Even when there was no snow wagons were taken up that terrible slope only by an all-out labor of man and beast, by doubling teams, prying with crowbars, blocking wheels with stones and drags, all hands manning ropes. Before they reached the ascent, before they had even passed the lake they saw that the snow was impassable. They abandoned the wagons, packed what they could on the backs of oxen, tied the now crippled Keseberg to a horse, shouldered the children, and drove the stock ahead of them, to pack down a trail through the snow.

Stanton and an Indian got to the divide . . . and could have gone down the western slope. He came back. To help the others.

But they had reached the extremity and he could not rally them. No more. Don't call on the outraged flesh or the defeated soul for what is beyond its power. Evening was coming up and they made a fire and stayed close to it, quarreling. Make the effort, don't make it, stay here for the night, don't try till morning. They stayed here.

So it came on to snow. Strange weights woke them, their companions were sitting up from white mounds and the cattle had disappeared. They understood. The next morning, while the snow fell steadily, they straggled back to their abandoned wagons and on to the little cabin at the lake.

That snow caught the rear guard, the Donner families, a few miles farther east. They turned up Alder Creek Valley, made camp, and hurriedly felled trees for cabins. There was not time enough for cabins, brush huts must do. The snow fell, almost continuously, for eight days. Little Georgia and Eliza Donner loved the whirling storm. "It made pictures" for them . . . "it gathered in a ridge beside us upon the log; it nestled in piles on our buffalo robe; and by the time our quarters were finished, it was veiling Uncle Jacob's from view." Pictures, no doubt, of whirling snow in a farmyard of Sangamon County and children running through it from the barns of steaming cattle and on to the house, where they would stand at windows watching dusk come up through the storm, while firelight shimmered on the ceiling, and overhead was the children's room with the pitch of the roof sloping down.

Not more than thirty miles to the west, on the far slope of the divide, Reed and McCutchen with a pack train struggled toward them ever more slowly through the same snow, and at last were stopped. They had come up from Sutter's to Johnson's ranch with two Indians and thirty-one horses packed with food. Ignorant of what had happened since they left the train, they expected to meet their families on the way down from the divide, doubtless very hungry but out of danger. They thought of their desperate journey as one of alleviation only, not rescue. The only refugees they found, however, were a man named Curtis and his wife, emigrants who had quarreled with their companions as their train came down from the Sierra, weeks before, and had foolishly decided to spend the winter in Bear Valley. Reed and McCutchen left them supplies, horses, and one Indian, and labored on upward. The next day they made three miles to the head of Emigrant Gap. That night their remaining Indian deserted, fled back to the winter-bound Curtises and, gathering up his companion and three of the horses, vanished. Reed and McCutchen kept going for another day, snow to their shoulders, snow so deep that sometimes they had to dig the horses out of it. Finally it stopped them. They could go no farther. The Sierra and the snow had defeated them on the western slope, as they had defeated the sufferers on the eastern slope. And while their families and former companions, hardly thirty miles away, built shelters in a realization that the long snow had brought the winter in, Reed and McCutchen, with the same realization, turned back to lower altitudes. They got down to Bear Valley, picked up the forlorn Curtises, cached their provisions for a later attempt at rescue, and pushed on to Johnson's and finally Sutter's. Sutter told them that this premature snow had made it impossible for them to do anything till February.[5]

The Breens and Dolan reoccupied the Schallenberger cabin. Keseberg built a lean-to against one of its walls. The Murphys (including the Fosters and the widow Pike and her children) and the Eddys built another log cabin, not far away. Another double cabin was built, one half of it for the Graveses and Mrs. McCutchen and her child, the other for the Reeds, John Denton and the surviving teamsters, Stanton, and Sutter's two Indians. These were crude log structures, the roofs being merely poles covered with whatever would turn water, or partly turn it.

They were better than the huts which the Donners were able to build in Alder Creek Valley. George Donner built a semicircular hut of boughs and canvas against a tall pine, interlacing small branches and covering them with quilts and wagon covers. It was divided into two crude rooms and had a hole in the ground for a fireplace. Mrs. Wolfinger lived with the George Donners. Jacob Donner built a similar but even cruder structure, across the brook from George. The four teamsters had a Digger-like tipi of brush. There were twenty-one people here at Alder Creek, sixty at the lake.

Perhaps Reed and McCutchen would get through to them. Perhaps Sutter, the friend of the starving, would be able to drive a pack train through the snow by the sheer authority of his name. They could look up to the crest above them when the snow paused and the clouds withdrew: any help that might reach them would come from the west. But they could not depend on help. They must prepare to pass the winter here without help. The only food they were certain of was the surviving cattle — the last of the supply that Stanton had brought was gone. They saw clearly that they did not have enough for more than half the winter. They tried to catch fish: the trout of the mountain lake would not bite at this season. They tried to hunt: practically all the game had gone down to lower levels. Eddy, tirelessly roaming the snow with his borrowed rifle, killed a coyote, an owl, two ducks, a gray squirrel, and finally a grizzly. Most days he killed nothing.

Here in the snow, with the shadow of death stretched over them, they could still traffic and barter with their thoughts on the future in California. When one of Graves's oxen died, he would sell it to Eddy only on a promissory note for twenty-five dollars, which Eddy later paid to his heirs. Pat Breen, who was now the millionaire, being spacious in the possession of oxen, took Fosdick's gold watch for two of them. When it was proposed to kill for food the mules which Stanton had brought, Graves successfully prevented the butchering (he was a Vermonter), on the ground that Sutter would expect payment for them. They killed most of the oxen, some of which were dying anyway. The snow and cold, they hoped, would preserve the meat — all of it, intestines, hooves, horns.

Successive storms, some of them several shrieking days long, steadily deepened the snow at the camps. The refugees got weaker and more lethargic, making relentless inroads on their stores. The Donner women, Eliza says, had to do a man's work; all the women had to. But in this camp of slowly approaching death, one thinks most painfully of the children.

On November 12, thirteen men and Mary Graves and Sarah Fosdick tried to get over the divide. It was a question of those most able to go, not only for their sakes but for the sake of the children as well — they might be able to get relief for those left behind. Of course, both Eddy and Stanton made this attempt. They fell a full three miles short of the divide. The snow "was soft and about ten feet deep." They were back, defeated, by midnight.

After more storms it was possible to make another attempt on November 21. Eddy and Stanton again led the endeavor; there were twenty-two all told, six of them women. They were weaker than they had been before and could not allow themselves even so many of the meager slices of thin beef as they had previously taken. This time, on a firmer snow crust, they actually got over the divide, where Eddy measured the snow and found it twenty-five feet deep, and started down the far side. They were barely strong enough to gather wood for fire but spent the night in the snow. And spent part of it, the two most resolute, Eddy and Stanton, fatally disagreeing. They had been using Sutter's mules to break a trail; the mules were done in and must be abandoned. Stanton would not go on without the mules — they belonged to Sutter and the sacred rights of property required him to return them. Eddy pleaded the imminence of death, in a great gust of rage. No use. The next day they went back over the divide to camp. "Mrs. Eddy and her children were very weak but exhibited great courage and fortitude."

Another storm lasted more than a week, while everyone's strength waned. When it was over, all the oxen and horses that had remained alive were dead and lost beyond recovery under the snow. So were Sutter's mules, which Graves had not let them kill for food and Stanton had refused to abandon beyond the divide. December had come in during the storm which, Eliza Donner says, made fires unsafe, froze all the water, and shut out the light. At the other camp Graves and Stanton, who were Easterners, were showing their companions how to make snowshoes, out of split oxbows and strips of oxhide. There was another storm, which lasted for five days. It was almost impossible to get firewood.

At the upper camp Baylis Williams died; he had been one of Reed's teamsters. Others were obviously failing. They went faster at Alder Creek. Before the storm ended old Jacob Donner, Shoemaker, Reinhardt, and another of Reed's teamsters, James Smith, were dead. They buried them, more or less.

At the lake the snowshoes were ready, fourteen pairs of them. A party of seventeen prepared to start out: ten men, five women, and two boys. The three who had no snowshoes would trudge behind the others, in the trail they hoped to make. They took a rifle and an axe, a blanket apiece, and minute rations which they expected to last for six days. Stanton and his Indians and William Eddy were again the dominant spirits. Uncle Billy Graves, fifty-seven years old and the principal author of the snowshoes, went along. Mrs. McCutchen left her year-old baby in the care of the invalids and joined the party. Their principal hope was Stanton and the two Indians, who knew the route. December 16 was a clear day after a night of vicious cold. They started out.

It took them a full day to get to the upper end of the lake, about four miles. Two Murphy boys and Burger, Keseberg's teamster, were the three who started out on foot. Burger and one of the boys gave it up and turned back. That night they made a crude pair of snowshoes for the other boy and he kept on with them. On December 17 they got over the divide, all but dead. They could go down the far slope now but they were eating an ounce of food a day and the sun gave them snow blindness. Their movement was slow and agonizing, the travel of the half dead. Stanton, besides being snowblind, was weakening. On the march he fell behind, coming in to the campfire at night. There were brief, wild, swirling snowstorms. Their feet froze. Mary Graves had a hallucination. They had seen no game.

On December 20 they camped far down, beyond the Yuba Bottoms, about five miles, Stewart makes it, from Reed and McCutchen's cache of food at the Curtis wagon, near the head of Bear Valley. Stanton came in late to that campfire too. And Stanton was done.

December 21. That morning, going through his little pack, Eddy found half a pound of bear meat which, unknown to him, his wife Eleanor had put there, taking it from her own small store in order, her note said, to save his life in extremity. And when the others prepared to set out, Stanton sat quietly smoking a pipe. They asked him if he were coming. Yes, he said honorably, he would be along. He sat there, smoking.

It was up to William Eddy now.

XIII
Trail's End

IN the fifth decade of the twentieth century, the American cultural heritage is richly established. People who freely draw on it in writing books are usually indifferent to and nearly always ignorant of many important contributors to it. A triumph of the advertising business establishes anyone in posthumous esteem if he wrote a novel good enough to go into a third printing or appeared at enough literary gatherings to be mentioned by diarists. The gatherings did not matter when they occurred but were fully as important as the novels. But today inheritors of the literary tradition will solemnly appraise both salons and novels while ignoring men who built up the knowledge which establishes the habits of millions of Americans, shapes their businesses, and in fact makes possible the way they live.

Clarence King survives as a name to be mentioned in appraisals of our civilization through his friendship with a literary person of considerably inferior intelligence, Henry Adams, and through a rumor of scandal that has been attached to him, but what he added to our civilization is not mentioned. If King counts so little, why should literary values recognize an obscure geologist, even if he is named Ferdinand Vandiveer Hayden? He mapped thousands of square miles, topographically, for natural resources, for the census of timber and the habits of wild life. He built up the Geological Survey which has, tediously no doubt, put all that can be known about our land at the disposal of everyone. Appraisers of our culture will use its maps to locate the studios of sixth-rate essayists without wondering how there are maps, and you will not find Hayden's name in literary indexes. John Wesley Powell was a director of the Geological Survey and he was the begetter of the Bureau of Ethnology and the Reclamation Service as well. A few critics understand that he showed a kind of courage in navigating the Colorado River, they do not know what he did for our culture, and an odd scale of values has placed above this innovator, this prime intelligence, such names as, shall we say, Sarah Orne Jewett, Ambrose Bierce, or Thomas Bailey Aldrich, who edited the *Atlantic*. Still less should a subaltern of Powell's be known, Clarence Edward Dutton. He laid the basis of what is known about a large American area and, while doing so, incidentally taught some literary persons how to look at the Grand Canyon. Some of them — Charles Dudley Warner, John Muir, John Burroughs — copied a number of Dutton's pages verbatim but were too absorbed to inclose them in quotation marks. But they were serving literature, literature is known to be important, and, for instance, Charles Eliot Norton is civilization but the *Exploration of the Fortieth Parallel* is only produce from the Government Printing Office.

Such reflections occur to one on behalf of scores of never-mentioned captains and lieutenants of the United States Army who, at the head of small detachments, over three quarters of a century, traveled the American wilderness, making maps and recording observations of Indians, languages, religions, animals, trees, grasses, weather, rocks, ores, fossils, soils, and drainage. Those observations have passed into intelligent use but are not cultural. . . . On behalf of, for instance, a little group of topographical engineers starting out from Santa Fe with Brigadier General Stephen Watts Kearny on September 28, 1846. Even the *Dictionary of American Biography* can say of Lieutenant William H. Emory little more than that he served knowledge and diplomacy well, that his career was honorable for military virtues, and that his Civil War record was distinguished: a soldier's epitaph. Emory commanded Kearny's detachment of topographical engineers. He had one of Susan Magoffin's loyal admirers, Lieutenant Warner, and a handful of civilians, among them John Mix Stanley, a painter who would perhaps have a larger fame in indexes if the fire which burned down the Smithsonian Institution in 1851 had not destroyed all but five of the 151 paintings which he had made of the West. It is without literary importance that this little group observed the weather and resources on the day's march and set them down, that Stanley's drawings of plants were the first made in this region, that Emory gave the region its first scientific scrutiny and made the first map, an exquisite map which is extremely useful still.

As for Kearny, he was only a reliable officer of Dragoons doing a job set for him by a President who understood nothing whatever about it. He did the job so well that it has never had much comment by anyone.

Doniphan was in charge at Santa Fe. Price was coming up. So was the Mormon Battalion, which would go on to California. Kearny was further informed that another regiment was being sent to San

Francisco by sea. He wanted to take four hundred troops with him, a hundred more than his Dragoons numbered. So he had Captain Hudson of the Laclede Rangers try to raise and equip a hundred volunteers from the Santa Fe garrison; they were to be called the California Rangers. But a hundred horses or mules fit for desert travel, in addition to those which the Dragoons got, could not be found. They could not have been paid for anyway, since no paymaster or quartermaster funds, in coin, had yet reached Santa Fe. The California Rangers disbanded. The five companies of Dragoons with which Kearny started out were mounted mostly on mules—mules described as half starved, half broken down before the start was made. Kearny gathered a herd of the horses that had survived so far and headed them back toward Fort Leavenworth. A sentimental apostrophe of Captain Cooke's reveals that some of them had served the First Dragoons for thirteen years! From now on Kearny would try to buy or requisition horses and mules from every tiny settlement they passed and every band of Indians they met.

They started out down the Rio Grande, through hamlets which Kearny had visited on his earlier reconnoissance. On October 2 an express from Santa Fe caught up with them, reporting Price's arrival and informing Kearny that Lieutenant Colonel Allen, the commander of the Mormon Battalion, had died. He detached Philip St. George Cooke, the Virginia martinet, to command the Battalion, making him a lieutenant colonel. The next day, learning that the Navajo had raided a village only twelve miles from his army, he sent orders to Doniphan to hurry up his Indian campaigns.

What is remarkable in Kearny's march from here on is only the absence of remarkable events. Good management of expeditions, we are told, forestalls adventures. Kearny was a master of frontier craft and he had his own Dragoons, not only professional soldiers but veterans of the West. His one hard problem was how to maintain them as cavalry.

They passed through the little towns of the Rio Abajo, haggling with natives for food, forage, and horseflesh and holding councils with bands of Apache, the ill-favored suzerains of the region. And on October 6, just out of Socorro, they met Kit Carsòn, now a lieutenant in the United States Army by appointment of a naval officer. With a small party which included Frémont's Delawares, Lieutenant Carson was riding hell for leather to carry to Senator Benton, President Polk, and the War Department news of the conquest of California.

Carson had left Los Angeles on September 5 and was trying for a record passage with his news. He described to Kearny the condition of the golden shore when he left it: native generals in flight to Mexico, all ports and principal towns occupied, people pacified and reconciled, Frémont "probably" civil and military governor. Kearny understood that the job set for him had been done by the navy, assisted by his young friend Frémont and resident Americans. He had only to go on, take command of the conquered province, and, as in New Mexico, carry out his orders to establish a government. If this development deprived his Dragoons of their chance for war service, it also simplified his immediate problem. One of the duties negligently given him by Mr. Polk was to locate a wagon road. Even before he met Carson, it had become likely that he would not be able to take the company wagons down this trail. Moreover, the sparse grass and the frightful condition of his mounts made it desirable to reduce the size of the expedition, which Carson's news had now made safe. Kearny detached three of his companies of Dragoons, combing out their best animals for the remaining two companies, and sent them back to Santa Fe. With them he sent Tom Fitzpatrick, who was still his guide, to carry Carson's dispatches to Washington. Fitzpatrick was not familiar with the Gila trail, whereas Carson had not only helped to open parts of it years ago but had just traveled it. The honest, outraged Kit, who had not seen his family since joining Frémont in the spring of '45, contemplated going over the hill by night, but finally obeyed orders and turned back with Kearny.

Carson confirmed Kearny's judgment that the wagons could be got to California along this route only by months of labor, if at all. So Kearny got packsaddles and sent the wagons back to Santa Fe, ordering Cooke, who was to follow with the Mormons, to locate a wagon road. The Dragoons would pack mules, horses, and even their few oxen. They did, and it was hard on livestock. Presently, Emory wrote, "every animal in camp is covered with patches, scars, and sores made by the packs in the unequal motion caused by the ascent and descent of steep hills."

They left the Rio Grande and headed for the Gila, keeping mainly to the established trail, the lower and newer of the two by which the Spanish had communicated with California. The route led through the enchanted chaos of the Arizona deserts, a country mostly of naked rock in mesas, peaks, and gashed canyons, painted tremendous colors with brushes of comet's hair. Frequently it was a giant-cactus country — saguaro by designers of modern decoration, cholla by medieval torturers — or a country of yuccas and the yucca's weirdest form, the Joshua tree. Sometimes it was even a grass country. And through most of the route it was a country where occasionally you could find the characteristic oasis of the Southwest, a little, hidden arroyo with something of a stream in it, choked with cottonwoods, green plants blooming only a rifle shot from desolation.

They were on rations hardly half-size by any decent standard. There were enough tents when they started — though there were no tent poles — but some of them could not be packed and the others wore out or tended to be left beside the trail. The animals wore down steadily, could not be recruited, had to be abandoned, had in part to be eaten. It was a march without glory, little more than attendance on a demon-possessed herd through a desert with no end. But the journals of Emory and Johnston and the letters of Turner, by which chiefly the march can be followed, contain little mention of sickness, exhaustion, or even annoyance. The Dragoons were doing a disregarded job authoritatively.

Through October and November they pegged along, not making very good time except in relation to their emaciated mounts and the two howitzers. These were two "light mountain guns" of brass, cumbersomely mounted on small wheels, which were always far to the rear and sometimes had to be taken entirely apart before they could be moved. Mostly they were on, or not far from, the swift, clear Gila. As they approached its great bend they reached a country whose ghosts were Father Kino, the great priest, and the Hohokam, the prehistoric people of whom a shadowy memory has tinged many Indian myths. More to the point were villages of the Pima and Maricopa, jovial, sedentary Indians who had established about the best social adaptation to this country that has so far been worked out. After the Apache and the itinerant Mexicans whom they had met, these people with their irrigated farmlands supplied an emotional lift. They had cantaloupes, watermelons, corn, wheat, honey, any amount of foodstuff, even a couple of bullocks for beef, but no horses to sell. They practised the communism of the desert: asked the price of their cornmeal cakes, they said "Bread is to eat, not to sell, take what you want." Their sport was bartering, however, with loud laughter for Major Swords, the quartermaster, or for themselves when someone made a bad trade. They found Mr. Bestor's eyeglasses extremely amusing (he was a topographer), and in fact liked all their white brothers. Captain Johnston summarized the general verdict on their superiority to "the Apaches who bayed at us like their kindred wolves." Emory decided that they surpassed many of the Christian nations in agriculture, were but little behind them in the useful arts, "and immeasurably before them in honesty and virtue."

They took the officers to the mysterious ruined dwelling of the Hohokam now known as Casa Grande, and recounted their version of a widespread myth. Myth of rain, genesis, and fertility. A beautiful maiden of the god-people lived in a green valley — a valley of cottonwoods, flowers, and the smell of water — where all men courted her in vain. She was vowed to chastity, and she stored the increase of her lands to be distributed to the valley people when the drouths came. But one day she lay asleep and the clouds passed and a drop of rain fell in her navel. From this conception her son was born, founder of the Ancients . . . Bear of the West, blue woman of the West, I ask your intercession with the cloud people.

The army lingered for a day or two, trading with these hospitable mystics and letting the herd rest, then moved on. The country got peeled down to naked rock and the *jornadas* — stretches without water — lengthened. The mules and horses grew more brittle, some of them died on the trail, and the First Dragoons had become infantry who had an added duty of veterinary nursing. So they came out to where the Gila empties into the Colorado. Twenty-one miles to reach that confluence on November 22, a hot day, the cavalry staggering on foot in the torrid dust and General Kearny, his horse exhausted, kicking his spurs into a mule's flanks. Here they found a recently abandoned camp. There were signs of about a thousand horses and Carson, making a scout, estimated that there had not been time for them to go more than ten miles. The first guess, that this was a party of Indian horse thieves, changed to a guess that it was Castro coming back from Mexico with an army for a campaign against the conquerors of California. Emory made a reconnoissance, found the herd and its proprietors, and brought them in.

They really were Californians but whether they were rebels gathering up horses for their comrades in rebellion has never been determined. But they were accomplished liars and Kearny could make little of their stories. One refrain was consistent, however: there had been fighting in California since Carson left it and something had gone seriously wrong with the American cause. The next day, while Kearny was fitting out his Dragoons with half-wild horses from this herd, Emory made another scout. On the way back he picked up another Mexican, who represented himself to be one more humble horse-herder on peaceful business but turned out to be a courier. He was carrying dispatches from California to Castro and others who, in Sonora, were gathering forces for the maintenance of what the First Dragoons could now get a fairly clear idea of, the reconquest of California.

. . . For the shooting script of the Rover Boys in the Halls of Montezuma had got impaired. In early October there was a great reception for Commodore Stockton at Yerba Buena, with both the victors and the conciliated making fiesta and that new Californian, Owl Russell, filling the sky with oratory. Stockton also made a speech, a typical one. He had come back to these parts on business connected with his new picture, which involved enlisting a thousand Americans, transporting them to Mazatlán by sea, and thence marching them across the heart of Mexico to join Zachary Taylor, who would probably be waiting just outside Mexico City for him to arrive. (Frémont, recognizing the dreaming of a kindred genius, was out drumming up recruits for this new conquest.) But it now developed that the Army of Hollywood would have to let Taylor conquer Mexico unassisted for a while. Stockton learned that the conquered race had driven the conquerors out of the southern towns and he would have to begin all over and conquer them again. He made a start, between relays of the fiesta banquet, by loosing on the air, in reply to Owl Russell's flowers, a speech of such gore-thirsty courage that it should have ended the war right there.

What had happened to the southward was simple. The Pueblo of Los Angeles, though populated by greasers whom Stockton knew to be cowardly and baseborn, had got bored with Lieutenant Gillespie's arrogant ways and had driven him out. Even if Gillespie had used common sense his job would have been hard enough, conciliating both the tough malcontents and the orderly society of the region, who had lost a country in humiliation. But association with stars like Frémont and Stockton had had its effect: Gillespie thought of himself as representing the *hochgeboren* Anglo-Saxon race. By a series of arbitrary regulations and by the kind of personal strutting now attributed to the bite of the lens-louse, he had contrived to consolidate resentments against him. Surreptitious disorder and sabotage produced some gangs. These coalesced into larger ones and became openly aggressive. There was some armed skirmishing, suddenly a lot of people were in revolt, and Gillespie found his small command besieged. A force of California irregulars under "General" José María Flores and others who had been paroled by Stockton offered him battle or evacuation with the honors of war. On October 4 he took his command to San Pedro and embarked them on a merchant ship in the harbor. Los Angeles was Californian again and, in a snow of proclamations, the victors cleaned the American naval army out of Santa Barbara and San Diego as well.

Stockton got busy. He began summoning Frémont, who gave his recruiting assignment a new twist. The emigration had poured down from the Sierra. Frémont got recruits for the California Battalion to the number of three companies of emigrants. Among them were Bryant, Owl Russell of course, Hastings, Hudspeth, and James Frazier Reed. (Offered the captaincy of one company, Reed would accept only a lieutenancy. He had first to make his attempt to take food to his family and, while he headed toward the snow with McCutchen, was also on detached duty, advertising for enlistments.) There were also present in the Sacramento Valley some Wallawalla Indians who had come here on the unfinished business, reparation for murder, that Jim Clyman had tried to settle as their representative a year ago. They nursed their grievance but were patient and it was not till '47 that the affair boiled over and their Cayuse cousins massacred Marcus Whitman's mission at Waillatpu. Meanwhile they were willing to spoil the Californians; so they and some of the local Indians joined up with Frémont. No one ever doubted Frémont's personal courage but as a commander of troops he set a high value on the delayed attack. It took him nearly two months to prepare his little army. He marched it south on November 30 — all the other conquerors had been vociferously calling for him for weeks — and he moved it with a most strategic deliberation. It was not his fortune ever to meet armed opposition in California. He did not reach this war till it also was over. But he was in time to make trouble.

Stockton had sent Captain Mervine with the *Savannah* to recapture Los Angeles. The force which Mervine landed at San Pedro numbered, with Gillespie's men who were added to it, about four hundred. Something like a hundred Californian horsemen kept them from Los Angeles, with a small cannon and some homemade powder. Sailors and marines on foot could not compete with the irregular cavalry. They were stalled between Los Angeles and its port when Stockton — still denied the help of Frémont — reached San Pedro on October 27. He was under the same handicap, that there were no horses, but considering that he had at least eight times as many men as the revolutionaries were ever able to get together at any time, it seems odd that he did not take Los Angeles at once.

The navy is not gifted at operations inland, however, and besides, Stockton had Frémont's gift for multiplying the opposition by twenty-five whenever he calculated his chances. The Californians, who were having a fine time and extending their little revolution throughout the south, practised on him all the hoary tricks of guerrilla deception, and after a few days he re-embarked his expeditionary force and sailed to San Diego. After three weeks on a whaler in the harbor, the American garrison there had perceived that the Californians were not occupying the town and had gone ashore again. Stockton intended to operate against Los Angeles from there but the revolutionaries had swept the countryside clean of horses. He spent November sending out patrols to find some, while the Californians rode about in a boisterous humor, taking long shots at any Americans they saw. Toward the end of the month he got some horses, and a few days later learned of Kearny's approach. . . .

On the far side of the California desert, Kearny could not learn the details of this revolt. He could make out only that fighting had begun again and the conquest was in danger, if not already overthrown. He foresaw that he also would have to do some fighting — having sent back to Santa Fe, on receiving word that California was pacified, three fifths of his force. He had about a hundred and twenty-five men. He tried to mount them from the big herd he had intercepted, but the horses were unbroken and unused to desert travel.

On all trails to the West the last stretch was the hardest going. Beyond the Colorado River, which the army forded on November 25, ten miles south of the confluence with the Gila, the California desert began. It was one of the innumerable deserts called *Jornada del Muerte* by the Spanish, who also referred to the trail across it as the Devil's Highroad — ample indications. Much of it is below sea level, and a great part of it has been reclaimed by the irrigation projects of the Imperial Valley. The Dragoons tied grass for the first day behind their saddles and got their first water at the end of thirty hours by digging out and deepening an old well. A fifty-four-mile *jornada* followed and they made it in two days, remarkable time for horses and mules so broken down. Many of the mounts died on that crossing and some were saved only "by one man tugging at the halter and another pushing up the brute by placing his shoulder against its buttocks," to get them over the last stretch to the spring. They entered a country of cactus and bitter yucca and the weather was stifling. (An army post established here some years later appears to have originated the folk tale of the soldier who, having died and gone to his reward, wired back to the commandant for his blankets.) "The day was hot," Emory says, "and the sand deep; the animals, inflated with water and rushes, gave way by scores." He calls it a feast day for the wolves.

As always, human flesh had stood two months of desert travel better than horseflesh. The army was in excellent health and spirits. It was not, however, decently clothed. When Kearny sent the wagons back he had had to leave his meager quartermaster supplies with them. Cactus had ripped the uniforms to shreds and rimrock had done the same for boots. For some time there had been nothing to eat but unseasoned horse. "Meat of horses may be very palatable," Emory remarks, "but ours are poor and tough." No wonder that seven of his men ate a sheep at one meal, when they got to the first outpost of decency on the California side, Warner's ranch.

They reached that oasis, which served the same function for travelers of the southern trail as Sutter's in the north, on December 2, looking so much like Indians that the ranch crew started the herds precipitately toward the foothills. Warner himself — an American gone Californian in a lavish way — was reported to be a prisoner, and Kearny could learn little from his foreman. A neighboring English rancher named Stokes could tell him that the revolutionaries were in control of the situation and that Kearny was close to some of their forces. Stokes also reported Stockton's presence at San Diego, and Kearny sent him there with a letter telling of his arrival and asking for information about the state of affairs.

Kearny also heard of a California reserve of mules and horses fifteen miles away, and sent a detachment to bring it in. They brought it in, but again these were nearly wild horses and almost unusable. So on December 4 Kearny marched his small command toward San Diego. The next day they met a detachment of thirty-five of Stockton's sailors under Gillespie, Lieutenant Edward Fitzgerald Beale, and Midshipman Duncan, with information, military theories, and a tiny brass field piece to be added to Kearny's howitzers. That day, December 5, was rainy and foggy, and that night in the fog Kearny sent Lieutenant Hammond out to reconnoiter. Hammond found a body of Californians holding the road to San Diego at a hamlet called San Pascual. They would have to be cleared out. The opinion of Gillespie and of Carson was that the Californians would not fight. Well, they would have to find out — Kearny's force was too small to do anything but attack. He caught up with the Californians at dawn of the following day, December 6, and attacked them at sight. The opinion of Gillespie and Carson proved erroneous.

The action of December 6, known as the battle of San Pascual, lasted only a few minutes. The revolutionaries were California horsemen, the best in the world, riding their own well-trained, fresh horses and armed with muskets and long lances. The American force was mounted on the surviving, dilapidated mules and horses, not only starving but less than half-broken, and a quarter of it was on foot. The night of rain had made firearms all but useless. A small advance guard surprised the Californians but was ridden to pieces and its commander, Captain Johnston, was killed. The main body, led by Kearny, drove the Californians away and began a pursuit. The half-dead horses strung out in a long line and the Californians turned and came back. For something like five minutes there was a vicious melee of cavalry sabers and clubbed muskets against lances. When the howitzers, dragged all this way from Santa Fe for just such a use, came up the Californians rode away. They got one howitzer, however, for its team stampeded.

The little fight was as desperate as it was brief. At the end of it eighteen Americans were dead, including Captain Benjamin Moore whom we first saw rounding up the Santa Fe caravans at Pawnee Fork, Captain Johnston, and Lieutenant Hammond. Kearny had been lanced twice and Lieutenant Warner, Emory's second, had three lance wounds and four more rents in his blouse — an accurate gauge of the action.

For the rest of the day Captain Turner had to exercise command. He made camp on a hill and the surgeon got busy treating the wounded. "Our provisions were exhausted," Emory says, "our horses dead, our mules on their last legs, and our men, now reduced to one-third of their number [he means reduced by one third] were ragged, worn down by fatigue, and emaciated." That night they buried the dead on the cactus-covered hillside while wolves howled. Turner sent Alexis Godey and two other mountain men (who had arrived with Gillespie) to San Diego, forty miles away, calling on Stockton, who had about eight hundred effectives, for reinforcements and ambulances. They got to San Diego but were captured on the way back, bringing Stockton's message that, for the time being, he could not help out. Just why he thought he could not has never been made clear.

Kearny resumed command the next morning, weakened by loss of blood, and started his force toward San Diego. The remaining mountain men had built travois and the wounded were placed on them, to agonize while the trailing poles jolted over the ground. They got about ten miles to San Bernardo, the ranch of another Englishman, where the wounded were fed. Just beyond it the Californians, who had been hanging on the flanks and riding across the front just out of range, suddenly occupied a hill and seemed likely to start a fight. A small party under Emory drove them out and camped there. It was obvious that if the march kept up the free cavalry of his enemy must eventually capture his horses, his remaining howitzers, and even his wounded. So the next day, December 8, when he learned that his messengers had been captured, he determined to stay forted up where he was. That night Kit Carson, Lieutenant Beale, and Beale's Indian servant crept out of camp to take another summons to Stockton.

Their midnight crawl through the lines of a vigilantly patrolling enemy — who, Sabin says, were expecting Carson to do exactly what he did — ranks high among the exploits of the master mountain man, whose life was packed with desperate exploits. The three of them were on their bellies most of the time till dawn. Repeatedly they were nearly discovered. When at last they were past the besiegers' lines, they had lost the shoes which they had tied round their necks and had to travel barefoot through cactus toward San Diego. They separated, to increase their chances of getting through. All three did get through late the following night, Beale collapsing and having to be carried in. His health was broken for two years by the strain and fright of that adventure, and even Carson was in bad shape for several days.[1]

Back on the hill, the others ate mule and waited for news or help. Emory's notes have a moment. One of the wounded, the interpreter, old Antoine Robidou, would probably die tonight, with the temperature four degrees below freezing. But he woke Emory and asked him for a cup of coffee, which, he said, would save his life.

> Not knowing that there had been any coffee in camp for many days, I supposed a dream had carried him back to the cafés of St. Louis and New Orleans, and it was with some surprise I found my cook heating a cup of coffee over a small fire of wild sage. One of the most agreeable little offices performed in my life, and I believe in the cook's, to whom the coffee belonged, was to pour this precious draught into the waning body of our friend Robideaux [*sic*]. His warmth returned and with it hopes of life. In gratitude he gave me what was then a great rarity, the half of a cake made of brown flour, almost black with dirt and which had, for greater security, been hidden in the clothes of his Mexican servant, a man who scorned ablutions. I eat more than half without inspection, when, on breaking a piece, the bodies of the most loathsome insects were exposed to my view. My hunger, however, overcame my fastidiousness. . . .

They got better food the next day when they killed some fat horses which the Californians drove through the camp in an attempt to stampede the *remuda*. The surgeon reported that most of the wounded would be able to ride the next day and the others able to walk. It was assumed that Carson and Beale must have been captured or killed and Kearny decided that there was nothing to do but fight his way through. He would make the sortie at dawn, but before dawn a hundred and eighty of Stockton's command came up and the siege was over. On December 12 they got to San Diego. Kearny had reached Stockton, on the strength of whose dispatches he had left behind him the two thirds of his command that would have dissuaded the Californians from fighting and so have prevented the bloody action of San Pascual.

Meanwhile the Oregon emigration of '46 had reached the end of the trail. We left it a few miles west of Fort Hall, in southeastern Idaho, on August 8, when Jesse Applegate met Thornton and Boggs.

The destination of these people, the Oregon of Bill Bowen's dream, was the valley of the Willamette River, between the Coast Range on the west and the Cascades on the east. The valley was Oregon to dwellers in the States, or at least it was the Oregon that had been advertised for soil, climate, trade, and the hope of the future. To be sure, far to the eastward was the Walla Walla Valley, where the Whitman mission was and, by '46, a few settlers had located. There were also Astoria and Fort Vancouver, infinitesimal and still mostly British settlements up from the mouth of the Columbia. But of the seven thousand emigrants who had gone to Oregon, practically all had settled in the Willamette Valley or on the Columbia eastward from the valley's end.[2]

In '46 the southernmost house in the Willamette Valley was near the site of the present city of Eugene. Passing down the valley from there, one came to a kind of settlement, of which Lieutenant Howison, of the U. S. schooner *Shark,* reported this year that "too little exists to be worthy of an attempt at description." This was Salem, the real-estate development which the Methodist missionaries had by now substituted for their venture in saving Indian souls. Fifty miles farther downstream was the head of navigation — of such navigation as there was — where the Willamette, half a mile wide, tumbled over a forty-foot ledge. Here was Oregon City, the center of settlement and development, capital of the Iowa-model republic which had been floating in space ever since 1843. That republic had a governor, a judicial system, and five counties, in the tradition of frontier communities, and it had no legal connection whatever with the United States. (Presently we shall see how Polk's maneuvers for settlement of the Oregon country, the chaos in Congress, and the rounding of the year's decisive turn had killed the most recent efforts for relief.) In '46 there were well over a thousand people in the vicinity of Oregon City, though the town itself had less than a hundred houses. It had, however, a brisk trade, both internal and foreign, flour mills, sawmills, a foundry, environs already moderately rich in grain and richer in cattle, and the blessings of an evangelical culture. (It had been founded by Elijah White, another missionary who turned speculator in real estate.) These included a circulating library, a lyceum, a newspaper, a debating society, and the Oregon Temperance Society which was eight years old and had already made itself noisome advocating prohibition. Oregon City was the nerve center of Oregon, and the source of the puritan mores still discernible today in the sovereign state. Twelve or fifteen miles downstream, about the same distance from the mouth of the Willamette, was the town of Portland, which would have been Boston except that the coin fell tails, of perhaps a hundred people in '46. Nearer the mouth was a still smaller place called Linnton, for the great expansionist, and there were a few other hamlets here and there in the valley.

It was from these settlements that Applegate had set out, in June of '46, to prospect a better road for emigrants than the established trail from Fort Hall. A better route was vital both to the settlements and to emigrants. The established trail, the Oregon trail properly so-called, belonged to the mountain fur trade; parts of it, even, had been traveled by Lewis and Clark. It had been laid out to reach the American Fur Company's Astoria and the various posts of the Hudson's Bay Company, Astor's conqueror and successor and for many years the law west of Fort Hall. This trail, serving the needs of commerce in furs, was perfectly adapted to that business and to the methods of transport used in it. But in the service of the fur trade wheeled vehicles got no farther than Fort Hall, and in the service of Whitman's mission in the Walla Walla Valley, they got no farther than Fort Boise. The trail reached the Willamette settlements by an intolerably roundabout course, and it traveled country through which wagons could cross only with interminable labor and hardship. As every annual emigration so far had found out.

From Fort Hall the trail ran southwest, west, and northwest across the present state of Idaho. Most of this distance it was near the Snake River, though not often near it vertically, since this, one of the most beautiful of American rivers, here flows through sunken canyons. The country was desolate, sagebrush flats or stretches of jagged black lava, always breaking up into hills and ravines. There was little or no game but there was dust in daily clouds worse than anything encountered earlier. A detour down the Boise River reached the Snake again at Fort Boise. Fording (later ferrying) the Snake, the trail then struck overland northwest to the present Vale and thence north to the present Huntington,[3] thence up the Snake again to Powder River. It went up Powder River to about the present Baker, then turned north through fragmented mountain chains, which were really part of the Blue Mountains system, and came down into the magnificent valley called the Grande Ronde, whose center is the present city of La Grande. The land-hungry emigrants could have satiated their appetite here, where the soil was as fertile as any in the West, the climate equable, and the country rich in water and timber. But they reached the Grande Ronde with their supplies and equipment exhausted, the mission in the Walla Walla Valley was too feeble to support them through the winter, and they had to go on to the Willamette. Settlement of the great valley was not possible for years.

From the Grande Ronde, the earliest emigration got to The Dalles by heading straight north to the Walla Walla River and following it to the Columbia, the later ones by striking northwest to the Umatilla and descending it to the Columbia. Either route had to cross the main chain of the Blues, difficult and precipitous mountains whose western wall was almost vertical. Most trains got into difficulty by the time they reached the Blues, where snow was not uncommon, and practically all of them needed relief by the time they reached the Columbia. As far as The Dalles the land route down the Columbia was not particularly hard going, relatively to what had been experienced already, though those who went by water commonly ran into trouble. But at The Dalles an already exhausted and destitute emigration — toward which, from 1843 on, relief parties were usually hurrying from the Willamette settlements — faced the worst stretch of the entire two thousand miles between Independence and the Pacific. This was the sixty miles between The Dalles and the mouth of the Willamette — sixty miles, that is, by water but considerably more by any possible route across the Cascade Mountains. The fur traders had gone down the river, using the big native dugout canoes, and usually their expert native pilots, and portaging the worst rapids. But canoes would not suffice for the possessions of the emigrants and there were few boats. They had to build boats or rafts of their own and conduct them down one of the most dangerous pieces of river in the world, part of it quite impassable. Or if they resolved not to sacrifice their wagons or their herds (many of the earliest emigrants were hoping to become stockmen in Oregon), they had to take them across the Cascade Range, in early winter, past Mount Hood, through country where there were no roads at all.

The Indians of this part of Oregon were also a menace — to property usually, not to life. The Cayuse would wipe out the Whitman mission in '47, but up to then they and their relatives contented themselves with selling their services at exorbitant prices and exercising a fine skill at theft.

The Columbia or the Cascades, that was the dilemma, and up to '46 either choice had meant disaster. The emigration of '43 — the (first) Great Migration — had gone to pieces at the Cascades, some trying to make the river passage on rafts, some trying to build a wagon road over the mountains. Most of the fatalities were among the former, but all suffered exceedingly and they were succored mostly by the Hudson's Bay Company, which they had come to displace from its possessions. A few were winter-bound east of the Cascades. The emigration of '44, which was nearly fifty per cent larger, was delayed by muddy prairies and swollen streams in the early stages of the trail. The crest of it did not reach Fort Hall till the middle of September — five or six weeks later than Thornton's late arrival there in '46 — and had to send out its first call for assistance from that far point. (This was the year in which Clyman came back to the mountains. His messmate Black Harris was blamed by the greenhorns for many of their hardships but did heroic service in their relief.) They met snow in the Blues, many had to stay in the Walla Walla Valley through the winter, and the rest disintegrated in the Cascades. Not many died, but practically all arrived destitute in the settlements.

But the emigration of '45 had to undergo sufferings far greater than anything before it. It was the largest emigration so far, fully three thousand strong. Those who held to the difficult, established trail reached the settlements with about as much hardship as their predecessors had experienced, some loss of life, and a great loss of property. (This portion of the year's emigration produced one of the classics of the trail. Joel Palmer's *Journal of Travels over the Rocky Mountains*.) But at Fort Boise [4] a large party were induced to try a new road designed to avoid the Blue Mountains and the descent of the Columbia and to discover a better passage of the Cascades. The Lansford Hastings of this escapade, which cost almost twice as many lives as the Donner tragedy, was Elijah White, the ex-missionary who by this time had made himself thoroughly loathsome to his fellow Oregonians. His agent, who was to guide the experimenters, was Stephen Meek. Meek was a competent mountain man. Blamed by the emigrants for their catastrophe, he nevertheless was chiefly responsible for the survival of those who did survive. Nor was the proposed route absurd in theory. (For that matter, the Hastings Cutoff to California was, in theory, perfect.) He designed to lead his party — between 150 and 200 wagons all told — up the Malheur River and so across what is now central Oregon, into the Willamette Valley by a supposed pass well toward its southern end. His intention was to follow trails which were supposed to mark old routes of the mountain fur trade.

But Meek could not stick to his predetermined route. The party wandered aimlessly in a desolate region to the southward. The Malheur Mountains broke them and, in the vicinity of the Deschutes River, panic, mass frenzy, starvation, and the cumulative collapse of outfits struck them all together. From there on their experiences were all but incredible. Black Harris again and various relief parties from Oregon City got them down to the mouth of the Deschutes, to The Dalles, and finally to the Willamette. They are the "Lost Immigrants" of Oregon legendry and about seventy-five of them died.

Considering the emigrations thus summarized, it should be clear that a better road from Fort Hall to the Willamette was both a physical and a psychological necessity. The settlements knew that their increase and their trade depended on the establishment of one. The emigrants of '46 knew what had happened to their predecessors, and the stories had lost nothing on the way to them. The obvious solution was to locate a practicable road into the Willamette Valley from the Humboldt section of the California trail, if such a road could possibly be located. If one could be, it would avoid the Blue Mountains and the Columbia River altogether. The southern Cascades were less formidable than the northern part of the range, and if a good pass through them could be found, the terrors of the last stretch of the road to Oregon would be entirely eliminated.

This problem was also important to the War Department, which might have to oppose a British occupation of California based on Oregon. A survey of the trail from the Willamette settlements to California was one of the objects set for Frémont on his expedition of '45, and with it, if possible, the discovery of a better route to Oregon from the Humboldt trail. Instead of going back to California with Gillespie from Klamath Lake, Frémont should have been doing the job which Jesse Applegate's party did.

In May of '46 the settlements sent out an exploring party to locate the much needed southern entrance to the valley. It was insufficiently equipped, however, and the attempt was repeated in June by a party of fifteen men. No more intelligent, experienced, and resolute group could have been found. Notable among them were the veteran mountain man, Black Harris, David Goff of the '44 emigration, and Levi and John Scott of '43, all of them the highest type of pioneers, and Lindsey Applegate and his brother Jesse, who was then and long remained the first citizen of Oregon. The expedition was of great public importance and they were resolved to be deterred by nothing till they had found a satisfactory route into the valley from the south. Jesse Applegate, the effective leader of the party, had the strongest possible determination, having had a son drowned and a nephew crippled on the passage of the Columbia in '43.

Both the achievements and the good faith of this party must be stressed, for the principal eyewitness account of the portion of the '46 emigration that took their new road is Thornton's, and Thornton gave them a lambasting that would have been more applicable to Lansford Hastings. Thornton's experiences were so painful that he was unable to exercise his usually impartial judgment on the new route.[5]

The Applegate party did in fact locate a practicable wagon road into the Willamette Valley from the Humboldt section of the California trail. It became the standard route into Oregon, though, of course, use and further exploration changed details of it. They took the regular route southward down the Willamette Valley by which journeys to California were made. (Such journeys as Clyman made in '45.) They followed it as far as Grant's Pass in the canyon of the Umpqua, and kept within range of it to the valley of the Rogue River, where they began their tack to the southeast. They found the greatly desired pass over the Cascades and came down to Klamath Lake, camping where Frémont and Gillespie had determined on their adventure and fought the Modoc. (Thus Frémont had been within a few miles of achieving one of the objectives set him.) From here they crossed into the desolate wilderness of northwestern Nevada by way of Lost River, Pothole Springs, Goose Lake, Lassen (Fandango) Pass, High Rock Canyon, Soldier Meadows, and the Black Rock Mountains. Here they divided and explored the desert, hoping to locate a route across it with shorter intervals between water holes than their first trace. But they exhausted their supplies before finding such a course and went on by Rabbit Hole Springs to the California trail. Jesse Applegate, with Black Harris and two others, went to Fort Hall to get supplies and advertise the road to the emigration, and we have seen him meeting Thornton's party on August 8. The others continued up the trail, intending to locate a route from Bear River south of Fort Hall, and it was this group whom Bryant, fresh from the Salt Desert, met on August 9.[6]

They had done their job. The two largest Nevada deserts, the divide north of Klamath Lake, and the Umpqua canyon were desperately hard going. But they were no worse than several stretches of the trail both east and southwest of Fort Hall, and certainly they were far easier than the worst stretches of the upper Oregon trail. The suffering of the '46 emigration was not repeated. From '47 on, the principal trouble was Indians, not privation.

Applegate and Harris did what they could to reduce the difficulties of the people they proposed to lead over their new route. They pointed out the importance of traveling as rapidly as possible, and they ordered the emigrants to travel in groups large enough to discourage the Indians. Then they hurried ahead with some volunteers, to make the trail a road.

But, on a smaller scale, something of the same demoralization that was overtaking the Donner party overtook the Oregon emigrants. The reserves of morale had been exhausted. No organization was left, and little trail discipline. The trains had been fragmented. A good many of those who had left Indian Creek together in Owl Russell's big train and had split up were now together again, but not as units. There were only knots of wagons traveling more or less together, sometimes because their owners were friends, sometimes because outfits had combined as cattle died, but mostly because similar stages of exhaustion had long since yielded to doggedness. They were querulous and quarrelsome, they were near the end of their strength.

Kirkendall had been the last "captain" of the little group that included Thornton (he was the member of Bryant's party who had been convinced by Clyman). He went ahead with Applegate's roadmakers and on into the settlements, where he turned back with supplies. The consumptive Roby died. Presently Mr. Burns died, who three weeks ago had been vigorous enough to drive Thornton's outfit down into Bear River Valley while Thornton lay helpless in the wagon. They reached the Humboldt on August 22 and soon the

Diggers were skulking beside them. So we come to one of the terminal points of American history, the last recorded killing of an Indian by a Boone. Daniel would have been shocked by his grandson Jesse's effeminate reliance on a shotgun.

In little groups they moved on down the Humboldt, at a crawl. They found this stretch longer than they had expected — emigrants always did — and they and the stock grew wearier. Applegate's roadbuilders pulled farther ahead of them, and Goff, who was waiting at the road fork, had to wait there longer than anyone had counted on. When Lillburn Boggs's wagons reached that fork Boggs decided that it was safer to go on over the Sierra than to risk the Oregon mountains, and so became a California pioneer after all. Most of the others went with Goff into the Black Rock Desert, where some oxen died and the rest weakened. They toiled on to Klamath Lake and on the next divide, Thornton says, had to hitch as many as twenty-three yoke of oxen to a wagon in order to get over it.

But now, however exhausted, cynical, and rebellious, they could see that they had reached the land of their desiring. Eyes tortured by months of sagebrush and greasewood looked on trees again, and the world which had been sterile had regained fecundity. There was the sound of brooks and creeks and these grew to rivers; sweet clear water flowed in them and they would not sink out of sight. The mountainsides were covered with trees bigger than they had ever seen. It was altogether different from the shape and color it had had in last winter's dreams, but it was a living and a fertile land. Their hearts lifted.

Prematurely, however. They had lingered too long, moved too slowly, and spent too much strength. Many of them were without food. The passage of the Siskiyou Mountains killed many oxen, Thornton's among them. He jettisoned some of his possessions and hired companions to transport the rest — on shares. Others were doing the same. . . . After a century it is hard to recover the feelings of a family who had carried their household treasures eighteen hundred miles of increasing labor and anxiety, and now had to heave them off into the underbrush in order to get themselves whole to the new country.

They got down into the valley of Rogue River and met one of Applegate's party coming back from the settlements with cattle for their relief. So they had food again and this was a beautiful valley with grass for the exhausted teams. They stayed here for the better part of a week. Too long. The rainy season of the Northwest opened on them, and from here on it was a contest between death and endurance.

The Thorntons were typical, or more fortunate than most. They carried a sack of clothing apiece and some remnants of food. Jessy had his knife and rifle. Their greyhound, Prince Darco, ranged and whimpered beside them. The London-educated, Virginia aristocrat, at best a semi-invalid, walked on with his invalid wife. Or waded. For the creeks were over their banks and the narrow canyons filled from wall to wall. They passed the abandoned goods of those who had preceded them: "household and kitchen furniture, beds and bedding, books, carpets, cooking utensils, dead cattle, broken wagons and wagons not broken but nevertheless abandoned" —the rubble of a fleeing army. They passed despairing or frenzied movers, too. Here are the Smiths, she "thinly clad and the covering for her head [in the daily deluge] was an old sunbonnet," her child as badly off, and her husband sunk in a lethargic despair. Thornton rallied him and the Smiths took up the march again, with "about a pound of food." And here were a group standing aghast above the body of their father who had just died on the trail.

There was no escape from the rains in forest, canyon, or open flat. They waded one creek forty-eight times in three miles, and Nancy went blind and fainted. Jessy thought she was dying but she revived. They came upon their old companion, the Reverend Mr. Cornwall, who could go no farther and had put up a tent, waiting for relief or death. They had a little good tea left and some crackers; that night Jessy slept sitting on a puncheon bench and Nancy on his shoulder. Their food was altogether gone on November 12, but the next day Kirkendall and others who had been sent out from the settlements rode in, driving horses and cattle. Starvation ended and Thornton bought a horse for his last remaining suit of clothes. The rest was easy, though a few miles behind them one of the original Indian Creek party was killed by Indians. On November 18, "just seven months from the time of entering on our journey [at Quincy, not Independence]," they came down into Willamette Valley. Thornton was stripped clean. He had a rifle, a knife, some odds and ends of spare clothing, and a greyhound. Wagon, oxen, household goods, law library, botanizing notebooks, all the habitual possessions that make the envelope of a man's life were gone, and naked he entered his new world. Still, by February he was Judge of the Supreme Court of the government which by now knew that it was American, even if it was not an American territory. And before long he was superintendent of a Sunday School.

Behind him the rest of the emigration lingered longer and fared worse in the Umpqua Mountains and along Elk River. By groups or families they camped in brush shelters, or toiled a few muddy miles a day, or simply sat till relief parties from the settlements could bring them food and get them out. Thornton had reached the Willamette by the middle of November, but it was February when the last of them came in.

Mostly they came in like Thornton, stripped. From the Missouri to the Platte, up the Platte to Fort Laramie and beyond, through South Pass to the Little Sandy and Fort Hall, down the Humboldt and over Black Rock Desert to Klamath Lake and the last mountains. From the States to Oregon. It had been a long way. Let us not forget it had been a hard one.

And on January 30, 1847, one hundred and three days after leaving Santa Fe, the Mormon Battalion reached trail's end at San Diego.

The second chapter of the Battalion is routine. Like Kearny's march it was remarkably successful and for the same reason, the effectiveness of its commander. Its importance is that, in obeying Kearny's order to find a wagon road, Cooke had to go a good deal south of the first half of the trail which Kearny had followed, in the states of Chihuahua and Sonora. The road he located (mostly using Mexican and Indian trails) proved to be the most practicable route for a Southern railroad to the Pacific: it is followed by both the Santa Fe and the Southern Pacific. So when some unfinished business left over from the treaty of Guadalupe Hidalgo was settled, enough territory to secure this route was bought from Mexico. Cooke made the Gadsden Purchase desirable.

Otherwise there is nothing notable about the march. The Mormons, who are accustomed to gild all their works with miracle, have celebrated it in prose and marble as the cruelest suffering and the most patriotic service on record anywhere. But there is nothing remarkable about thirst, exhaustion, or a successful passage of the desert. Even allowing for the detour to the south, the Battalion did not make as good time as Kearny's Dragoons, and — despite Cooke's anxiety and the howls of his men — they had more to eat. But it was a difficult job, and the three hundred and fifty-odd who came down to San Diego had proved themselves tough, ready, and adaptable. They still simmered with resentment of wholly imaginary persecutions, they still consulted the priesthood rather than the military for orders, and they still stiffened their necks against Gentile authority with the awful righteousness of a people whose leading is on high. Nothing would give them discipline and the marvels of Heaven attended their slightest act, but they were soldiers and the desert had seasoned them.

There were 486 of them when Cooke took command at Santa Fe on October 13. From the Great Bend of the Arkansas, Smith had already forwarded the volunteer grandfathers to Pueblo, where a company of Saints from Mississippi were to spend the winter. He had sent with them most of the families who had tried to travel to Zion with the military arm. Many remained, however, who were too elderly or too infirm to make the desert passage. Cooke described them as "invalids," and from Santa Fe sent fifty-eight of them to Pueblo. Though the brethren howled about Gentile tyranny, he also disposed of the "laundresses," the wives of Israel who had come this far, promising them that the government would pay the expense of their journey to Zion next year. Twenty of them had to go to Pueblo. Even so, he had to accept the company of five women, two the wives of captains, three of sergeants.[7] When the bad health of the Battalion continued after they left Santa Fe — it was augmented by an epidemic of influenza — he sent back "fifty-five of the sick and least efficient men."

It proved impossible to equip them satisfactorily from government stores in Santa Fe, and Cooke felt the same lack of hard cash that handicapped Kearny and Doniphan. (They lacked, for instance, greatcoats.) Farther along, however, he had more success than Kearny in persuading the natives to take orders on the government. He disposed of most of his oxen early; after trying to make pack animals of them, he sent some back to Socorro and butchered others. Doniphan, Price, and Kearny had bought up all usable oxen and skimmed the mule market. It was mules, and not good ones, that Cooke had to hitch to his wagons — twenty wagons when he started, five when he got to California — and such supplies as could not be hauled were packed on muleback. He was able to renew his herd from time to time, though he had to break many of the remounts to harness, and so the stock did not break down till they reached the California desert.

Food was always an anxiety but actually was seldom scarce. The worst stringency came at the beginning in New Mexico, where the natives had sold much of their harvest and had recently been raided by Apache and Navajo. Private Bliss of Company B remembered eating roast oxhide here; and, near some ruins of the ancient Nephites which proved the authenticity of the *Book of Mormon* once more, Private Standage of Company E says forthrightly, "I eat guts today for the first time though many have eat them before." But when the Battalion got to Chihuahua and Sonora, friendlier and somewhat wealthier natives kept them decently supplied. Cereals were frequently short and once there was a period of two weeks when no meat ration was issued, not even the army salt pork. But Cooke succeeded in gathering a small herd of beeves and a larger one of sheep, and the Battalion did not suffer from hunger.

They took up the march on October 19. They went farther down the Rio Grande than Kearny had gone, left it above Rincón, and crossed Chihuahua (now southern New Mexico), piercing the "American backbone" near (but not by) the San Guadalupe Pass. From here they crossed straight to the San Pedro River, followed its valley for five and a half days (perhaps sixty miles) and then turned west to Tucson. From Tucson they crossed straight northwest to the Gila, striking it at the Pima villages. Thereafter, except for unimportant variations, they were on Kearny's route. Cooke's map makes this southern detour 474 miles. He was locating a road for the Gold Rush as well as the best gradients for railroad engineers.

Cooke had made his predecessor, Smith, assistant commissary officer. He had with him another captain of Dragoons and Lieutenant George Stoneman, West Point, '46, who would become a famous cavalryman in the Civil War, as well as two surgeons. One of these was Sanderson, still "Captain Death" to the Mormons, without his mules but laying up for himself more vengeance of the Mormon God by still feeding poison to the sick. Of the Mormon officers, Jefferson Hunt was conspicuously effective and so was his first lieutenant, George Oman. Chiefly because of them, Company A was the crack outfit. Company D, however, was a marching madhouse — chiefly because the malcontent Dykes was returned to it after being deposed as adjutant and because it contained high dignitaries of the priesthood. Company D could do little efficiently and had to be badgered into doing anything.

Cooke, the gourmet and romantic, was also a West Point precisian. At intervals his journal explodes over the "stolidity, ignorance, negligence, and obstinacy" of Israel's host, who began by both fearing and despising him. Sometimes, as at the crossing of the Colorado, the explosion attains a moving eloquence, and there must have been education in hearing Lieutenant Colonel Philip St.

George Cooke express himself. He had a gift of tongues which was little like that vouchsafed the faithful at fast meeting, but he must have reminded them of the prophet Brigham in a holy rage. But he was a splendid officer. He held them to the job and he slapped punishments on malingering or carelessness, but also he kept them fed and he kept them going. And if holy obstinacy galled his nerves, he learned a boundless admiration for the spirit, good humor, and guts of his command. In their turn the Saints appreciated his fairness and came to admire his leadership. The colonel's counsel proved to be practically as inspired as the priesthood's; almost he might have been a Seventy. They ended by liking him and he is one of the few Gentiles who have come down to the present in Mormon esteem.

They got through the mountains after severe labor and came out into the cactus and chromatic rock of the Arizona desert. It was Arizona winter too, occasional bitter spells but usually warm days and freezing nights. They kept meeting Lamanites, mostly of the Apache nation, who were robbing Sonora to sell to New Mexico, so that the Comanche in their turn could carry on the trade. They found good going along the San Pedro and could add mountain trout to their rations. Then they got beef from an unexpected source, herds of wild cattle. Private Bliss, filling his belly to a fine repletion, pronounced it "fat & tender the best beef I ever eat." On December 11 a large herd of these beasts, which were as deadly as grizzlies,[8] actually charged the Battalion. They thundered down on the column and scattered it. They gored some mules and wounded several of the brethren, who, however, shot enough of them for a feast. Cooke named a near-by creek Bull Run and, as it turned out, this was all the fighting that the Battalion had to do. Except that at Los Angeles they once were ordered out to massacre the town's innumerable, bloodthirsty dogs.

They pulled and pushed the wagons through impassable places, whole platoons grunting together, and gradually the wagons disintegrated. Still seeking a practicable route for them, Cooke left the valley of the San Pedro and headed across lots to the Sonoran village of Tucson. There was a small garrison here and visitors told the Battalion it was four or five times as large as it actually was. So Cooke gave the brethren some drill and target practice, told them they must neither bully nor plunder the inhabitants, and led an advance party to a possible attack. None was needed. The little garrison had withdrawn, the inhabitants were scared and kindly, and the Battalion got some much appreciated flour. It got little else except cigars and pomegranates.

Near Tucson was the great, half-ruined edifice of San Xavier del Bac. The Franciscans had completed it in 1797, nearly a century after Father Kino, the great Jesuit, first dreamed of a mission to the Pima. The Pima and the Apache made that century bloody and now the mission was abandoned, a desolate monument to the cross and sword of Spain, whose southwestern passion play was underscored by the passage of these heretics in the service of a different empire. But to the brethren it was one more Nephite monument, a memorial of those earlier Mormons of twenty-odd centuries ago who had built great cities in the desert before they declined from the faith.

At Tucson the Battalion had a comic night alarm and Cooke heard a rumor of the revolt in California but did not believe it. He struck northwest for the Gila and there was a forty-mile *jornada* which gave the brethren a thirst premonitory of what was to come. They reached the Pima and were back on Kearny's route near the Pima villages. Like the Dragoons, they found the Pima and Maricopa jovial, generous, and admirable. Cooke made an oration to the Maricopa chief and liked the country and Indians so well — so well, that is, in relation to the peculiar genius of his command — that he proposed this place as a possible colony for the Mormons. Captains Hunt and Hunter agreed with him and conferred with their brethren. They were prescient but premature. Settlement in these parts had been proposed and rejected before the Church left Nauvoo and it was not till Israel reached Great Salt Lake Valley that Brigham came to understand the importance of an Arizona outpost.

Near the Maricopa village they met a Mexican named Franciso, whom Kearny had sent to guide them on the trail, after he learned about the California revolt but before the action at San Pascual. Cooke had to hurry on for possible action, and his anxiety about short rations increased. He sent the young state-maker Willard Hall and a small party posting ahead to report to Kearny, and hurried down the valley of the Gila. Getting a blurred rumor of San Pascual, he considered taking half his command ahead by forced marches, but the condition of the animals and the helplessness of the brethren when he was not with them made it impossible. He made an unfortunate attempt to take some of his baggage and commissary down the river in boats made of wagon boxes. The river was too low, Lieutenant Stoneman knew less about navigation than he claimed to, and the Battalion lost some precious food.

They reached the mouth of the Gila on January 8 and turned down the Colorado a dozen miles to the place where Kearny had crossed. Cooke thought that the Colorado resembled the Missouri, and he remembered that "at the first fountain of this river, in Oregon, the First Dragoons encamped eighteen months ago." That was the military reconnoissance mentioned in our first chapter, which had reached the Colorado watershed at South Pass. The Dragoons had been foreshadowing the empire then; now the Battalion was helping to achieve it.

Franciso could tell him how bad the going was beyond the river, and could not possibly exaggerate it. Cooke started them crossing the Colorado on January 10. It took them all night and part of the next day and they did it badly. The six-day crossing of the California desert that followed was their worst ordeal. Cooke was desperately afraid of disaster and had reason enough — they gave out by the score, black with thirst. Water holes were twenty or thirty or forty miles apart and could be made to yield water only when wells had been dug in them. Sometimes they had to go down twenty feet before a thin seepage could be induced. Two of the remaining wagons had to be abandoned, the mules began to die, and now the stout boots with which the Battalion had been outfitted at Fort Leavenworth were going to pieces. Some had to wrap their feet with fresh rawhide or old shirts, some made buskins from the legs of the last oxen, which died here. Some fresh mules, sent back by Hall, met them on the last day but, in the desert, they had to stop and spend two violent hours breaking them to harness. The day before had been intolerably hot but clouds and winds moderated the final stretch (one more miracle), and they came past the minute oasis of Palm Springs to a place called Vallecito where there was water and some grass. The ordeal was over. They came in staggering, sunken-eyed, and completely exhausted. But Cooke held a dress parade and presently the Saints were fiddling and singing.

On the desert Cooke had received word of San Pascual. At Vallecito a message from Montgomery at San Diego came in, telling him that Kearny had apparently retaken Los Angeles (as he did, on January 10), and saying that he might expect skirmishes with the galloping Californians. Cooke moved on, ready for a fight, to Warner's ranch, where all the Battalion's troubles ended. Plenty of beef, if no salt; easy marching, if much rain. They went on toward San Diego. They caught a glimpse of "the great Pacific sea" which their hymns had celebrated as the destination of the faithful, and a rash of poetry breaks out in the journals, including Cooke's. They had arrived. God had watched over them, the prophet Brigham's vision had been true, and they swaggered. "We have endured one of the greatest journeys ever made by man at least in America," Private Bliss wrote, setting the tone of all subsequent Mormon allusions to it, "& it is by the faith and prayers of the Saints that we have done it." On January 29 the first of them reached San Diego, and the rest came in the next day. Cooke addressed them in a general order of sonorous congratulation. "With crowbar and pick and axe in hand we have worked our way over mountains which seemed to defy aught save the wild goat, and hewed a passage through a chasm of living rock more narrow than our wagons. . . . Thus marching half naked and half fed, and living upon wild animals, we have discovered and made a road of great value to our country. . . ." The Saints loved it and have gone on loving it. But Private Bliss turned his mind to the realities; he went out and gathered "some of the best mustard I ever saw for greens."

They had reached the golden shore and done their job, abundantly serving both their country and their Church. Cooke reported them to Kearny and, with five months of their enlistment left, they settled down to garrison duty here, at Los Angeles, and in various other towns, where they were eventually to establish the terminus of Israel's corridor to the sea. Soldiering was over for them, though they were once paraded in the expectation that Frémont, who was currently refusing to obey Kearny, might attack the troops of his commander with his Horse Marines.

They had heard nothing from the prophet since his last emissaries had collected their pay at Santa Fe. The vast distance between them and their families oppressed them and so did the lack of guidance and exhortation from the priesthood. Israel's destination had not been settled when they left Council Bluffs in July, and they had not heard of the debates and decisions since then. Perhaps Israel was coming to the great Pacific sea of the hymnal, and as late as May 23 Private Bliss complained that they had no "certing intelligence," though he had heard that no Saints would be coming over the mountains this year. They eventually met some of the brethren who had come round the Horn with Sam Brannan and were now settling in the San Joaquin valley and near San Francisco. (Brannan himself, who would soon apostatize because Brigham refused to bring the Church to California, was now posting eastward to meet the emigration.) They wondered, worried, and consulted the priesthood and the omens of dreams. Again, army officers would recommend this country for colonization (thinking of it as an armed American buffer against Lower California), again they would reject the counsel, and again Brigham would see that the officers were right. Here he anchored his corridor, protecting a supply route to Deseret and looking westward toward the Sandwich Islands, whither Mormon missionaries had already gone and where he would presently organize a stake of Zion.

As the slow months of their enlistment ran out, there were interior stresses to be alleviated. From the beginning there had been conflict between the Mormon officers, who exercised military command, and the priesthood who outranked them in ecclesiastical authority. On the march and while there was any possibility of action there had been no recourse but to subordinate the priesthood, even the Seventies, to the military — Cooke, like Smith, would not understand celestial discipline. Now in California the priesthood moved to resume command. Such realists as Captain Hunt bore in mind that, whatever the Saints might be in the structure of eternity, the Battalion was still a military organization and as such was subject to the regulations and penalties of the United States Army. But the officers had no chance; the soldiery were Saints and the priesthood won. There were meetings, exhortations, confessions, professions; the excitements of the Latter-days were roused again; and there was lighted at Los Angeles the first of the holy illuminations which that mystic region knows so well today.

But Israel did not altogether humble its heart — these were, after all, veteran soldiers. Guard mount and barracks routine were not onerous, the priesthood could not fill all their time, and the genial California air has undermined much puritanism in its time. The Saints learned to fill their canteens with the pleasant native wines, pagan sports like cockfighting tempted them, and Captain Hunter sneered at the priesthood that they had better raise up a prophet in their midst. "This morning," Private Standage wrote, "I met with the 70s as before appointed. Singing and remarks by Pres. St. John on the evils arising in the Battalion, to-wit: drunkenness, swearing and intercourse with the squaws."

XIV

Anabasis in Homespun

WE have come too far forward in time and must make our longest backtrack, to Santa Fe and the autumn of '46.

The reader will remember that when Kearny entered New Mexico, at Las Vegas, the first town he occupied, he told the inhabitants that one of the benefits the Americans were conferring on them was protection from the Indians. Since the Indians had been robbing, enslaving, and murdering the New Mexicans for more than two centuries, he could have made no more resplendent promise. His countrymen, however, needed a full half-century to keep it. . . . At a time when Lieutenant General Philip Sheridan was commanding the Department of the West, the telegraph brought word of one more massacre of helpless ranchers by the Sioux. Sheridan wired the commandant of the nearest army post to get his squadron out and surround the murderers. Out on the plains a harassed major of cavalry read the yellow flimsy to which the great name was signed—and this major, suddenly, had had enough. He wired back an insubordinate realism. How, he asked, how did one trooper surround fifty Sioux? . . . That is why it took fifty years.

Busy as he was in Santa Fe, reconnoitering his conquest, organizing it as a territory, and preparing for the march to California, Kearny nevertheless undertook to make good his promise. Understanding that the New Mexicans were intimidated and disorganized by the conquest, the Apache and Navajo had redoubled their raids. Even before Kearny started for California, he sent detachments to find the tribes, order them to behave themselves, and make treaties with them. He sent another detachment to the Ute on the same errand; they had been behaving themselves but had sent scouts to determine how bad medicine this general might be.

All these detachments were from Doniphan's command. With Price's Second Missouri coming to garrison Santa Fe, Doniphan would be free for any use Kearny might find for him. Kearny ordered him to march to Chihuahua, which Wool was supposed to be occupying, as soon as he had pacified the Indians. Then Kearny left for California and, when he was a week out of Santa Fe, got word of serious Navajo raids on southern New Mexico. (One wealthy rancher alone lost six thousand sheep.) He sent Doniphan orders to put teeth in the pacification — to invade the Navajo country, release captives, reclaim stolen property, and either awe or beat the Indians into submission. Kearny took up the march again and presently, meeting Carson with his report on the conquest of California, sent back three fifths of his Dragoons. This detachment, most of whom ended up protecting the encamped traders at Valverde, also got into trouble with the Navajo and for a while joined the pursuit.

The job thus casually set the First Missouri was a sizable assignment for farm boys. They had done pretty well so far. They had added many thousand square miles to the domain of the United States. They had established an advanced position which would make the conquest of California secure. They had, or seemed to have, conciliated a conquered people. How much had any other army done in four months?

But from now on to the end of the chapter they were going to work in the prodigious.

The story of the detachments sent out by Kearny himself is short. Captain Fischer, of the ineffective German artillery company, rode out beyond San Ildefonso, rounded up some Apache, and brought them in to Santa Fe. The Apache sunnily promised Kearny to be good Indians, collected their presents, and went home to organize some raids. William Gilpin, the dreamer of empires, took two companies north to Abiquiu and thence led eighty-five men on a beautifully managed, swift march a hundred miles northwest of Taos to the headwaters of the Chama at the continental divide in southern Colorado.[1] He did not meet the Ute but sent out couriers who brought in a large band of chiefs and sub-chiefs. Gilpin took them to Santa Fe, where Doniphan, who was now in command, made a treaty with them. (It had the value of any treaty with Indians.) Gilpin then went back to Abiquiu, where he was in camp when Doniphan's order for a more serious expedition reached him. Meanwhile a third detachment, successively commanded by Ruff, Parsons, and Jackson, marched into the Navajo country from Albuquerque and camped near Cebolleta (Seboyeta). They had picked up a genial Navajo chief whose name was rendered Sandoval, a mendacious and antic conversationalist much appreciated by the soldiery. They sent him looking for his people with an invitation to come in and make a treaty. By the time the new orders arrived Sandoval had come back saying that the Navajo reported their hearts pure but preferred to have the Americans come into their country and make the treaty there.

Doniphan had set out to obey his orders, which were to settle the Indian problem permanently. He ordered portions of Price's regiment to relieve Gilpin at Abiquiu and Jackson at Cebolleta, so that their forces could invade the Navajo country. Gilpin was to go in from the north and Jackson, whom Doniphan would accompany, from the south. Meanwhile Jackson sent out a party of thirty picked men under Reid and, when the Navajo brazenly raided his horse herd, another party of sixty under Parsons.

Prodigy can be described simply but it requires understanding. It is easy enough to set down that in October and November Gilpin led his force, augmented by some New Mexican guides and servants, up the Chama again, over the continental divide, down the San Juan to the Tunitcha Mountains, westward over their crest into the rock wilderness of Arizona, on to the brink of the Canyon de Chelly, and back to the appointed rendezvous near the present Gallup, New Mexico. But such a march at such a time would be prodigious for the best trained and best equipped troops of modern warfare. Gilpin's command had left their tents behind and the quartermaster service had been unable to equip or supply them. They were supposed to be cavalry but their horses had been half starved and their pack mules were in no better condition. At the end they had about half as many of each as they had started with. Their boots had not been replaced, nothing like a uniform was left, they were dressed in native New Mexican or native Indian costumes. Winter had come to the mountains. Arctic blasts hammered them in the canyons. Blizzards blew up over the ridges. They would wake, some mornings, and find themselves curiously warm and snug, then understand their comfort as the result of eight or ten inches of snow that had fallen during the night. Their beards got matted with icicles, packed mules slid down glare-ice mountainsides to eternity, they labored many miles through snow to their waists. They had to range far even for firewood, but they found it and the nightly campfires flamed in narrow gulches or on windswept naked rock. No wonder the Navajo whom they met agreed to come in and talk peace. They could have massacred this band of adventurers in a few minutes, at their ease, and with complete impunity. But maybe-so better not. The Navajo had not heard that there were white men like these. . . . From the Canyon de Chelly Gilpin hurried on to meet Doniphan at Bear Spring. About

180 strong, his whole command, except those who had died of cold, got there by November 22.

Their buddies had been doing similar work. Reid, who had proved himself the best of the captains, had taken his detachment of thirty men into the heart of the Navajo country, the Chusca Mountains and Laguna Colorado at their base, and had rounded up five hundred awed, and very likely scared, Navajo. Private Robinson gives a convincing explanation of the detachment's size: "it was not thought advisable for any more men to go with nothing to eat." They were in lower altitudes and did not have to battle snow. Sandoval was with them and could find adequate grass for their horses. Moreover, they could get food from the Indians they met. But this handful of amateurs, of course, traveled under suspended sentence of massacre. Hundreds of Navajo were on all sides of them, sometimes traveling and camping with them, and the Navajo were not soft Indians. What saved them was the very audacity of their venture; it vindicated the rumor now traveling the whole Indian country, that this breed of whites had better be respected.

As Reid's thirty got farther into the country, the Navajo came in by the hundred to look them over, and they returned the scrutiny. The Doniphesias had danced with some Pueblo over Navajo scalps; now, finding a party with some fresh Pueblo scalps, they shuffled and hi-ya-ed in the vengeance dance. They joined the Navajo games and gaped at the sham battles. They traded their rachitic horses for fresh mules, got buckskins to replace their tatters, and by night sat at the campfires while hundreds of their hosts danced, sang Injun, or related the interminable histories of their valor. . . . Reid finally collected more than eight hundred Navajo, harangued them, and got their promise to meet Doniphan and make a treaty. He then returned to the encampment, which had been moved from Cebolleta to Cubero. The Navajo who had agreed to follow him took up the trail but met a band of cousins who predicted that Doniphan would massacre them and so turned them back.

While they were gone the camp had been raided by another band of Navajo, who ran off forty-odd horses. Jackson sent out Parsons and sixty men in pursuit. They made a brilliant march, going clear to the Zuñi pueblo, rounded up about half of the stolen herd, and came back, Private Edwards says, without having changed their clothes or washed their faces in twelve days. Doniphan, marching toward the rendezvous at Bear Spring, received word (there was nothing in it) that the traders' caravan, which had gone into camp at Valverde, was threatened by a Mexican army from Chihuahua.

The three companies of Dragoons under Captain Burgwin which Kearny had sent back on meeting Carson were hurrying to Valverde, but Doniphan sent three of his companies to help out.

Doniphan reached the Bear Spring rendezvous on November 21. Hordes of Navajo came in to listen to the Long Knife. There followed the slow, stately, and preposterous ceremonies by which Indians and army officers were accustomed to reach agreement — parades, feasts, drama, and endless oratory. The Navajo claimed alliance with the Americans, who had come here to make war on the New Mexicans and appeared to be illogical when they asked the Indians not to do likewise. Doniphan got that point cleared up and the New Mexicans classified as Americans who must not be robbed or murdered from now on. A treaty as formal as one with a major power was drawn up. By its terms the Navajo agreed to cherish not only the New Mexicans but the Pueblo as well. Doniphan, Jackson, and Gilpin signed it on behalf of James K. Polk, the father of these good children, and no less than fourteen Navajo chiefs scratched their crosses underneath. It was impressive and affecting. Doniphan then made a detour to the pueblo of the Zuñi, thus once more touching Coronado's dream, and got a treaty with them also. It was worth a little more, for the Zuñi were less warlike.

On December 12, Doniphan was back at the Rio Grande, where his various organizations were disposed between Socorro and Santa Fe. Some of them now got the $42 clothing allowance they should have had in May, the first pay they had received and the last they were to get while on active service. Doniphan began to prepare them for the rest of the campaign.

A good many of them had died in the Indian country or on the way back, more had fallen sick. The job had had to be done without preparation, with inadequate supplies, poor food, no shelter against the weather. The Doniphesias were baying their resentment — but with a difference now. They had always beefed and bellyached, they always would, but now their complaints had a new tone, the confidence of tested men. They had done the unparalleled, and had done it easily. They were veterans.

Susan Magoffin had said good-bye to her little court, beginning with Kearny himself, who was so much like Papa. William Magoffin, the third of the brothers to come down the trail this year, had reached Santa Fe. (On his way out from Independence, his train stopped to exchange information with a small party moving east, which had Francis Parkman in it.) The town was still gay, with the dramatic club flourishing and a frantic rush at ten o'clock when the garrison had to get back from fandangos, gambling hells, and plain saloons. But it filled with rumors about disasters to Kearny, to Taylor, and to James Magoffin, who had gone on to repeat his work at Chihuahua. Susan's health remained delicate but she was glad to be active again, when they started south on October 9. Even though it meant going into dangers which the rumors increased tenfold. All three divisions of the Magoffin wagon train united and they moved on toward the camp at the ruined hacienda of Valverde where the entire Chihuahua trade of this year, more than three hundred wagons, had been concentrated. More rumors: Brother James robbed by Apache, General Wool capturing Chihuahua, a trustworthy one that Stockton had taken California. Then word from Valverde that the Mexicans were coming up from Chihuahua to attack the wagon camp. This was the rumor that had taken Burgwin's Dragoons and three of Doniphan's companies to the rescue, and it reminded Susan of her religion. She dosed herself with the Scriptures and Methodist sermons, and continued the treatment daily from now on. Short of Valverde, she took a fever and the train camped while she lay ill in a friendly house for two weeks. November 25 was the anniversary of her wedding, celebrated in this humble dwelling, among these courteous small foreign folk. Susan had been married for a full year, and had been traveling all that time, though it seemed a very short time, looking back, and "I shall be contented if all we pass are like it."

December brought worse alarms. (They had joined the traders by now.) Brother James had been imprisoned at Chihuahua and was to be tried as a spy. General Taylor had barely won a battle at Monterrey and General Wool, ordered to join him, was not going to Chihuahua after all. So the Mexicans there could come up and plunder the camp at their leisure.

(We get a glimpse of the camp at about this time, from Lieutenant George F. Ruxton of Her Majesty's 89th Regiment who, disdainfully flaunting the British insignia of long yellow mustaches, had made his way up from Vera Cruz among guerrillas, highwaymen, and casual murderers whom he simply could not take seriously. He was heading for the buffalo country where he had greatly enjoyed himself, while on leave from his regiment when it had been stationed in Canada. He thought more highly than Susan did of the encampment's defensive strength. It could defy any Indian or Mexican attack, he said, and spoke with respect of the "wild-looking Missourians" who inhabited it. Across the river and three miles upstream he visited one of the camps of the Doniphesias and saw

Doniphan himself. The British soldier's professional sense was outraged. He granted that the tents were in line but could grant no more. There were no regulations, there was no cleanliness or sanitation, not even the offal of slaughtered cattle was removed. "The men, unwashed and unshaven, were ragged and dirty, without uniforms and dressed as and how they pleased. [!] They wandered about listless and sickly-looking, or were sitting in groups playing at cards and swearing and cursing, even at the officers if they interfered to stop it — as I witnessed." They did not even keep proper guard against Indian cattle thieves, and all told they had nothing in common with Her Majesty's troops, they would not do at all. But Lieutenant Ruxton knew fighters when he saw them and, against all the articles of his faith, had to acknowledge that "they were as full of fight as a gamecock." [2])

News got gloomier and Susan thirsted "to see the face of the Lamb that sittith in Judgment." All of Doniphan's command was coming in, and a detachment of Price's Second Missouri also. This was "The Chihuahua Rangers" under Lieutenant Colonel Mitchell, whom Price had sent out in an unavailing effort to make contact with Wool. The traders had grown riotous and divided. They were frantic to get on and complete the year's business — it should have been finished long since. Some were resolved to go on and run their chances that the manufactured goods would mean more than war to the Chihuahuans. A few even tried but were promptly herded back by the army. Some, Susan's husband among them, could foresee only disaster if Wool had not taken Chihuahua.

Then on December 16 Susan heard that an advance guard under Major Gilpin had plunged into the dreaded *Jornada del Muerto,* just to the southward. Three days later a most reliable man, known personally to Samuel Magoffin, came fleeing from El Paso with news of disaster. Gilpin's three hundred, the bearer of evil tidings reported, had been captured and sent as prisoners to Chihuahua. Seven hundred terrible Mexican dragoons were hurrying up. Samuel walked the floor waiting for more news. Susan feared that "I shall be torn from the dearest object to me on earth, perhaps both of us murdered, or at best he will be put in prison." She summoned up the consolations of her faith. "Christ himself warns us that we must not fear those who can kill and in any wise injure the body, and can do nothing to the *immortal* soul. But he says, 'rather fear Ye him who after he hath killed hath power to cast into hell.' "

Just rumors. The army was enjoying itself. Its howls still rose to heaven but it had begun to do some soldiering.

For Doniphan, with 856 effectives, was off to keep his rendezvous with Wool at Chihuahua. His artillery was still in Santa Fe, where Price, suddenly surrounded by rumors of revolt, was reluctant to let it go. A captain of the First Dragoons and a lieutenant of regular artillery had joined him to brush a faint gilding of military procedure over his operations. Furthermore, since they were going to invade Chihuahua, Doniphan was done with the regulation which forbade him to requisition food. He sent out foraging parties who receipted for what they took but took what they wanted. They brought in several hundred beeves and thousands of sheep, and from now on the army would eat regularly. Some powder — far from enough — had come in. Medical supplies remained scanty. Some of the troops had got buckskins from the Navajo, others had bought clothes from the natives, a few from the traders, many wore the shreds of their original outfits.

Doniphan's objective was the city of Chihuahua, where he still expected to find Wool in command. If he was to meet opposition on the way it would come from the source of all the recent rumors, the town of El Paso del Norte, the ancient bastion of El Camino Real, where the Rio Grande breaks through the mountains to the high plains. On the way to El Paso he must take his command across the *Jornada del Muerto,* Dead Man's Journey. It had justified its name in nearly three centuries of travel, beginning with the conquistadors. But at this season the army could count on water at various holes that would be dry in summer, and in fact this ninety-three-mile desert proved less arduous than narrower ones beyond El Paso.

Doniphan started his advance guard under Gilpin on December 12 (half their year's enlistment had been completed on December 10), and the rest of his command followed in two sections. Most of the traders at Valverde broke camp and went with the army or just behind it, an anxiety and a ghastly inconvenience. The veterans did the *jornada* handily. The weather had turned cold and there was nothing but dry grass and soapweed for the nightly fires, but the only real hardship was experienced by those who tried to soothe their way with canteenfuls of *aguardiente.* There was much night marching, especially by the teamsters, who had to swear their wagons through the sand. Between December 19 and 23 they came together again at Doña Ana.

Here rumors of great armies coming up from El Paso thickened. The camp was reconnoitered by night, a couple of spies were shot, and many hoofprints were found by day. Arms were inspected, powder was issued, Doniphan told his men that the camp had better make less noise at midnight. On Christmas Eve the camp was again under investigation by Mexicans, but no one felt alarmed and no one thought to push the scouts out farther, the next morning.

They welcomed Christmas with gunfire and band music, then took up the march in excellent spirits. The camp had not been well made or closely guarded and much of the stock had strayed, so that Doniphan's trains and a third of his regiment were strung out for miles behind him. The boys sang and joked their way for eighteen miles, then pitched camp toward three o'clock, at a place called El Brazito. It was not far from the present hamlet of Mesilla, New Mexico, and about thirty miles from El Paso. It looked like a good camp site and, rejoiced to be let off with a Christmas march of only eighteen miles, the greater part of the army whooped off to water their mounts and gather firewood. During the march some scouts had brought in a beautiful white stallion. It caught the appreciative Missouri eye. Doniphan and several of his officers spread out a blanket and sat down to a game of loo to determine whose horse it was. The cards ran Doniphan's way and he had just got a hand which would have ended matters, when he looked up and saw a Mexican army forming a battle line half a mile away. Cursing the interruption, he buckled on his saber and prepared to improvise a battle.

It was an army somewhat larger than Doniphan's total force and had been gathered at El Paso by a temporary general named Ponce de León after earlier recruiting efforts had failed. It was adequately equipped and clad in the gorgeous uniforms that no Mexican force ever failed to acquire, but it lacked fighting men. Properly primed with rhetoric, it had ridden out from El Paso to annihilate the gringos, whom it despised with the universal Mexican contempt of blonds. It had a piratical black flag with two death's-heads lettered "*Libertad ó muerte,*" and a punctilious officer carried this banner forward to invite Doniphan to surrender. Doniphan, who had got his side arms on, returned the answer traditional to the circumstance, and the pause allowed most of the wood gatherers to come in, shouting.

Doniphan formed them, perhaps four hundred all told, into a kind of line as infantry. The Mexicans began bleating at them with a two-pound howitzer loaded with copper slugs, then fired continuously but wildly from their whole line. The First Missouri were under fire at last, six months out from Fort Leavenworth, and were pleasantly stimulated. Curious about the howitzer, which was posted on a flank, some Company G boys ran out and took it. The Mexicans knew that battles were won by charging and, infantry and lancers alike, trotted forward, firing as they came. Doniphan had his men lie down and got most of them to hold their fire. At about a hundred yards he gave the charge two volleys. The charge stopped and the Mexican army began to run away, except that a couple of hundred lancers veered off to a flank and tried to attack some of the wagons. The efficient Reid, however, had got some twenty of his company mounted and launched them at the lancers, who joined their companions to the rear. Reid could not catch up with them and they galloped on to El Paso, where they reported that the war was lost.

It had taken less than thirty minutes. Stragglers hurrying up the road at the sound of gunfire got there too late for the fun, and in fact not all the wood gatherers got in. Doniphan reported forty-three Mexicans known to be killed and 150 wounded. Seven of his Missourians had flesh wounds which they could flourish at less fortunate companions. Arguing violently about who had done the most execution, they went out to gather in the commissary. They got sizable stores of bread and cigars and a great quantity of wine. It was excellent wine; so, veterans also of gunfire now, the First Missouri settled down to celebrate Christmas.

But in the excitement the white stallion had bolted.

Christmas Day, 1846.

The White House was closed to callers, in order to give the servants a holiday. Mrs. Polk attended church but the President stayed in his office to draft for his message to Congress some paragraphs that would propose the silliest of his war schemes. He had begun his reduction of Zachary Taylor, in part because it was clear to everyone that the war could not be won from the north or by Taylor, more particularly because Taylor's candidacy was developing, as we have seen. Taylor himself, Scott, and the Secretary of War had all separately suggested that the true route to victory was an invasion from Vera Cruz. Something obviously had to be done, for the war dragged on, the Democracy had lost the House, public spirit drooped, discouragement and opposition were increasing. So Polk had promised the Vera Cruz expedition to Scott. He was able for a while to contemplate the aggrandizement of another Whig, but by now the prospect had become too painful. Consequently, quite unknown to Scott, on Christmas Day he was drafting a request for Congress to revive the rank of lieutenant general. If Congress did so, he would be able to get the victory back into Democratic hands. He would be able to advance over both Scott and Taylor his former antagonist who had by now become his close friend, a master of oratory, a Senator and a "Colonel," Thomas Hart Benton of Missouri.

Edwin Bryant had a dreary day with Frémont's California Battalion, which was still marching toward the war by a roundabout route and had got past San Luis Obispo. A violent rainstorm was blown at them through a gale that was almost a hurricane, as they came down the side of a mountain and tried to bring a brass howitzer with them. Everyone was extremely uncomfortable but Bryant and his mess got a fire going and a tent set up. He stripped naked and tried to dry his clothes. . . . In the Sierra, that rainstorm was a blizzard.

At San Diego Kearny, who was unable to convince Stockton that the administration could have contemplated any commander in California except Stockton, was trying to organize an expedition — under joint command — to retake Los Angeles, and had no time for Christmas cheer. The Mormon Battalion had reached the upper Pima village, didn't know it was Christmas, and didn't care.

On the day before Christmas, in the Sierra, westward from the divide, the fourteen survivors of the party which had left Donner Lake on December 16 labored in agony through snow that fell steadily all day long. Stanton had died honorably three days before; since then they had depended on Sutter's Indians to find the landmarks that would take them down to Bear Valley and safety. Without knowing it, they had lost the trail and were wandering. Nine days out, they had eaten nothing since the last daily mouthful was used up two days before. Months of exhaustion had eroded their strength before they started; now they had been nine days in the snow, a mile and a half high. Suddenly they reached an end. Eight men, five women, and twelve-year-old Lemuel Murphy had got so far, but now a conviction of fatality gripped them. All the men except Eddy announced that they would go no farther. There was some raving talk of going back to the lake. Nine days out, snow falling, no food — even the starving could recognize that the notion was insane.

An assertion of human will followed. Eddy, the strongest-hearted of them, insisted on continuing the effort while life was left to them.

The two Indians agreed. So did all the women. "I told them," Mary Graves said, "I would go too, for to go back and hear the cries of hunger from my little brothers and sisters was more than I could stand. I would go as far as I could, let the consequences be what they might."

Mary Ann Graves, twenty years old, born in Illinois of parents who had emigrated there from Vermont. An undistinguished item in the year's migration, one dot of Manifest Destiny, who had set out to find the West with her parents, five sisters, two brothers, and a brother-in-law. A person of no moment making the western traverse. The children of her children in California today are also commoners of the Democracy. Tradition says that she was beautiful and was engaged to marry the John Snyder whom Reed killed in a quarrel on the Humboldt. A further legend says that Stanton also had fallen in love with her. There is nothing remarkable about Mary Ann Graves, except that mankind can be staunch. "I would go as far as I could."

The will prevailed. But also it precipitated another decision. To go on they must live, to live they must eat, but there was no food. But there was food. Patrick Dolan, whose very presence on this desperate venture was a heroism, since he was a bachelor and owned more than enough of the oxen at the lake to keep him through the winter — Patrick Dolan voiced the thought which they had so far kept from voicing. Let them draw lots to see which one should be killed. Eddy agreed, Fosdick refused. Then Eddy, in revulsion, proposed a manlier solution: that two of them, selected by lot, take revolvers and shoot it out. "This, too, was objected to." In a moment the obvious became obvious to them. They were all near death. Someone would die soon. They groaned on through falling snow.

They stopped when dusk came and, with their single small axe, got wood for a fire — which they built on little logs on top of the deep, crusted snow. Now the Mexican herder, Antoine, died. Eddy knew that he was dead when he did not withdraw his hand, which had slumped into the fire. Suddenly, toward ten o'clock, the snowstorm changed into a blizzard. A tornado-like wind drove whirlpools of snow at them. All the wood they had been able to cut was used up. Trying to cut more in the midnight blizzard, they lost their hatchet. The fire began to sink through the snow. It made a deep hole but they succeeded in keeping it going for a while, water welling up round their legs. Finally it went out and the yelp of the blizzard was round them.

Most of them were moaning or screaming in the dark, Uncle Billy Graves was dying, and all but Eddy were willing to die. All would have died if it had not been for Eddy. He remembered an expedient of the mountain men in such storms as this — such a storm as Jim Clyman and Bill Sublette had survived in the Wind River Mountains, in our second chapter. They had their blankets. Eddy spread some of them on the snow and had his companions sit on them in a circle. He tented them over with the remaining blankets and closed the circle himself. This was shelter of a kind, and presently the blizzard covered them over and they could live. But not Uncle Billy. He reminded his daughters of their mother and brothers and sisters at the lake, told them they must get through to Sutter's for their sake, bade them eat his body, and died.

In that mound of snow, Graves's corpse upholding its part of the tent, they stayed all through Christmas Day, while the blizzard howled on and made the mound bigger. That morning delirium came upon Patrick Dolan and, screaming, he broke his way through tent and snow. Eddy went out into the blizzard and tried to bring him back but could not. He came back after a while, and they held him down till he sank into a coma. As dusk seeped through the blizzard, he died.

The storm kept on through Christmas night, with two corpses in the mound now, and through the morning of the next day. Eddy tried to make some kind of fire inside the blankets but blew up a powder horn and burned himself severely. Mrs. McCutchen and Mrs. Foster also were burned. In the afternoon the snow stopped. They crawled out of their mound, made tinder of the cotton lining of a mantua, struck a spark in it, and got a dead pine tree to burn. So they cut strips from the legs and arms of Patrick Dolan and roasted them. Eddy and the two Indians would not eat. Lemuel Murphy had been delirious for hours. The food could not revive him. That night he died, his head in the lap of Mrs. Foster, his sister. There was a moon. Moonrise would bring back this scene to Sarah Foster through the rest of her life.

The next day, December 27, they butchered the bodies of Graves, Dolan, Antoine, and Lemuel Murphy and dried at the fire such portions as they did not need now, packing them for the journey still to come. The Indians would eat this meat now, but Eddy still refused, though his strength was ebbing. After three days more here, when the bodies of their companions had restored their vitality a little, he got them into motion again, on December 30. In the literature of the Donner party, these people who made the venture over the divide are called "the Forlorn Hope," and this bivouac in the blizzard has the name they gave it, "the Camp of Death."

Of the huts at Alder Creek Eliza Donner Houghton wrote, "Snowy Christmas brought us no glad tidings." And at the lake the invalid Patrick Breen, who had begun to keep a diary on November 20, made this entry: "[December] 25. Began to snow yesterday, snowed all night, and snows yet rapidly; extremely difficult to find wood; offered our prayers to God this Christmas morning; the prospect is appalling but we trust in him." Breen, a Catholic, had lately begun to read the Thirty Days' Prayers. He read them and the Bible aloud by firelight in the murky cabins, and his faith *in extremis* sank into the childish heart of Virginia Reed. She made—and kept—a vow. If God would save her family she would seek baptism as a Catholic.

Milt Elliott, who was one of Reed's teamsters, and Noah James, who was one of the Donners', had started out on December 9 to get news of the Alder Creek camp, and Elliott got back to the lake on December 20. He reported the deaths of Jacob Donner and Samuel Shoemaker and James Smith and Joseph Reinhardt. They had not starved for some food was left, they had just died. (Before he died, Reinhardt confessed to George Donner that he and Spitzer had murdered Wolfinger.) At Alder Creek they were trying to locate the frozen bodies of the oxen by thrusting poles into the snow, but they were not succeeding. They were catching the field mice that crept into the huts and eating them. And they had begun the diet that was to be the staple here and at the lake. Strips of oxhide were singed to remove the hair and then boiled for hours, or days, till a kind of glue was formed. (They had some pepper left to season it.) They boiled the bones also till they were soft and could be swallowed, and a faint taste of meat was imparted to the water. Tommy Reed, three years old, grew up to have no stomach for calf's-foot jelly or similar foods, and it was among the memories of Eliza Donner, also three, that she had chewed the bark and young twigs of pine to ease the pain in her stomach.

Likewise she remembered that one day her mother Tamsen took her up the snow steps to where the dazzling sun shone on the snow and blinded her, and led her to a hole from which smoke was floating up. Uncle Jacob lived there, Tamsen said (but he didn't live there any more), and they must go down and see Aunt Betsy and Eliza's little cousins. Eliza peered down that blackness and was afraid. She called to her cousins to come up instead—and was more frightened when they did. They had grown skinny and white, they were strange, suspicious, feral. "So I was glad when my mother came up and took me back to our own tent, which seemed less dreary because I knew the things that were in it and the faces about me."

They had buried the dead in the snow, which froze over the bodies and then deepened as more storms came. At the lake no one had died since Baylis Williams gave the Forlorn Hope an omen for their departure. The huts at the lake were a little better off than those at Alder Creek — in that there were more hides to make glue of, some frozen meat still, a couple of handfuls of flour from which Mrs. Murphy could make gruel for her granddaughter, the infant Catherine Pike. Catherine had been weaned when Harriet Pike went over the divide with the Forlorn Hope, weaned on spoonfuls of water a little thickened with this hoarded flour. There were, or had been, four other nursing babies at this camp.

One thinks especially of these and the older children on Christmas Day, the Donners, the Reeds, the Murphys, Breens, Kesebergs, Graveses, Eddys. They could remember firelight on friendlier snow, Sunday School classes with scrubbed faces, hymns in warm rooms, going to bed at night, the inexplicable behavior of grownups on Christmas Day, the myth of a fat man who brought gifts. They could remember the Christmas of the vast America far to the eastward of this mountainside where trees cut down for firewood left twenty-foot stumps in the snow and death came slowly to families trapped by Lansford Hastings' ambition.

Nevertheless there was one Christmas feast at Donner Lake. In her end of the double cabin whose other half was occupied by the remaining Graveses, Mrs. James Frazier Reed had taken thought long before of her children's memories. When she bought four oxen from the Breens and Graveses, she had cleaned the tripe of one and hung it low outside the cabin, where snow would conceal and preserve it. She had also contrived to store away through nearly eight weeks a quantity of white beans amounting to a cupful, half as much rice, half as much dried apples, and a two-inch square of bacon. On Christmas Day she took them from the hiding place and made a stew of them. While the storm that was killing Dolan and Graves on the far side of the ridge buried the cabin still deeper, the children danced round that bubbling pot. Thirteen-year-old Virginia; Patty Reed, eight years old; Jimmy, five, and Tommy, three. There was once more a perfume of the kitchen in the hut, and diced cubes of tripe or bacon jigged on the bubbles while the children shouted. Thinking of her husband, possibly dead, possibly alive somewhere beyond the hurricane of snow, Margaret Reed could nevertheless speak the warning of all mothers on Christmas Day, "Children, eat slowly, there is plenty for all."

Another Christmas must not be forgotten, Bill Bowen's, who had come down to California or Oregon. The loss and alteration it may have cost his family has been made clear, but he had done what he set out to do. He had reached the new country — and had brought with him the core of American belief and habit, differentiated in two and a quarter centuries from the belief and habit of Europe that had accompanied the first of his predecessors when they began the westering which he had now brought to its farthest bound. Let the part of that core of feeling which made his Christmas American stand for the rest of American feeling. Stripped to little more than his skin, a stranger in the land of his desiring which proved more strange than he had imagined when he started, he would now make his new home in the West. It would be his old home modified not only by the new conditions but by the experiences of his crossing. He had come a long way, and at the eastern end of it was the old home. Great distances were a part of his mind now, the distances he had traveled, the distances he tinily lived among. He had given the nation its continent and perforce something continental formed the margins of his mind. It was a centrifugal, a nation-breaking force that had sent him out, but in the end it was a centripetal, a nation-making force he was changed into. He was a counterweight, the nation traveled was his nation and lines meant less to him; he was more a nationalist, less a sectionalist already and from now on. The ribbon of the trail bound the nation more tightly together — and the time was not far off when the United States would need that strength. So he had found the West and given it to the United States; now he faced the labor of subduing it and building in it a farther portion of the United States. To that labor would be addressed the rest of Bill Bowen's life and the lives of his children and their children. Christmas along the Sacramento and the Willamette, the Bay of San Francisco, the lower Columbia, was Christmas in a strange land firelit by memories of Christmas back home in the States but also heightened by the realization he had achieved. Beside these waters that fell into the Pacific there was a hope about the future that has become a deed within our past.

"These Mexicans," wrote Private Jacob Robinson of Captain Reid's Company D, the day after Christmas, "are a singular people:

but yesterday in arms against us — today every man says *omega* or friend."

Robinson made his contribution to linguistics in the now fallen city of El Paso del Norte.[3] Doniphan marched into it after the affair at El Brazito, commissioners coming out to pray that the conqueror would not lay it waste. They supposed that farm boys who could lick armies between meals must be carnivores. As a matter of fact, they now had one carnivore with them, James Kirker having ridden in to enlist, the day after Brazito. Kirker was an Irishman on permanent retainer from the government of Chihuahua to act as a destroyer of Apache. He had collected an elite guard of retired mountain men and the Ishmaels of the plains, the dispossessed Delaware. With this posse of specialists he ranged Chihuahua gathering Apache scalps and was paid fifty dollars per scalp, half price for women and children. (He appears by name in one of the best Wild West novels, Mayne Reid's *Scalp Hunters*, and is really the model of that romance's prettified gothic hero with the beautiful daughter and the heart of bitter fire.) Doniphan added him to the platoon of mountain men which was now captained by Thomas Forsythe. Disdaining to eat Chihuahuans, he did excellent service as a scout.

The army was not at all carnivorous. The boys had learned Spanish, or thought they had, and practised it on a citizenry who were eager to say "omega." They had arrived at a considerable city. El Paso was the last outpost of the Great Spain that had found New Mexico beyond its strength. More than ten thousand people, a more vigorous stock than the New Mexicans, lived in the beautiful town in its green valley, and an ancient culture flourished there. The churches were impressive though idolatrous. The ranchos supplied abundant food — Doniphan was now paying in government drafts which had better be accepted, or else. For centuries the haciendas of the valley had been producing notable wines. There was plenty to eat, plenty to drink, and a comfortable surplus of *señoritas,* some of whom the boys even married.

The army ought to have had a good time but did so too spasmodically. As a matter of fact, this is their low point and they show symptoms of ebbing morale. They had reacted from the exhilaration of Brazito, they had too little cash for pleasures, they were bored and grew quarrelsome, and there was an undercurrent of anxiety. It was now known that Wool's expedition to the city of Chihuahua had been abandoned and his force ordered to the support of Taylor. Rumor promptly gathered a crushing Mexican force at the city Wool was to have occupied, and at intervals the First Missouri were sent running out in their shirt tails to form battle line and repel an imaginary attack. The air vibrated with secret conspiracy. Another persistent rumor, which had more behind it, whispered that trouble was preparing at Santa Fe, which could cut the army off from its base. The precarious situation of a handful of conquerors a thousand miles from home, deep in a hostile country, was quite clear. So the army bragged, swaggered, dissipated, and sometimes bullied the inoffensive Mexicans. The wines were potable, there were plenty of stills, Missouri drank much and behaved accordingly. Native gambling games were everywhere; the boys got so interested in them that, tired of falling over monte banks in the public street, Doniphan ordered them cleaned out. There were cockfights, fandangos, fiestas. Brawling among themselves, the boys were willing to include any bystanders. They retaliated on native profiteers and, on January 12, the diary of John T. Hughes, our A.B., notes that three of Captain Hudson's company are "to be court-martialed for ravishing a Mexican woman."

Doniphan had more serious problems than those of an unruly organization in an enemy town. He had to recruit his outfit and, now more than ever, keep it at fighting pitch. Though a trickle of supplies came from Santa Fe, getting there down the trail from Independence to which the Comanche were now beginning to devote their attention, the quartermaster service was in collapse. The army had been living off the country ever since San Miguel — back in August — and had to provide even its own munitions. That at least proved easy: Doniphan's patrols picked up ten tons of gunpowder at El Paso, five hundred stands of small arms, a magazine full of cannon balls (not much good), four cannon (tiny), and a museum of culverins, swivels, and other medieval armament. (He took what he needed and sank the rest in the Rio Grande.) Except for a little scurvy and hundreds of hangovers his regiment was healthy, but horses fit for cavalry service were hard to find and the requisitioned boots and shoes were bad. A wagonload of medical supplies came down from Santa Fe but it was far from enough.

Moreover, at the end of a thousand-mile line of communication, two thousand miles from the War Department, he did not know what to do. The White House had arranged for Wool to take Chihuahua. Relying on the high command, Kearny had ordered Doniphan to join Wool. Doniphan now knew that the trivialities of terrain and command which the White House strategy had disregarded had broken up the pretty plan. (Happily he did not know that Missouri, hearing that Wool had turned back, supposed that its Mounted Volunteers were lost forever and was now mourning them.) Rumor had Taylor badly licked and perhaps a prisoner; it also had southern Chihuahua and its neighbors rising en masse to destroy its invaders. What was he to do? Councils of war produced conflicting advice — the army, if consulted, would have turned back, Private Robinson said — and finally Doniphan put an end to debate. The hell with it: he would go on and do Wool's job.

He sent for his artillery but at Santa Fe Price, who had extinguished one revolt just as it got started, was wary. He would release only Major Meriwether Lewis Clark and the battery of Captain Weightman, and wanted some time before releasing them. Doniphan cracked down on the traders, who had been an annoyance all along and were a burden from now on. Some of them had set up shop in El Paso and were doing an excellent business. Some bolted ahead to Chihuahua to run their chances and, though Doniphan sent a posse after them, most of these got away. Others held back intending to wait till the invasion was settled one way or the other, or to detour it at their convenience. They were, however, a possible source of man power, and Doniphan got tough. He called in his patrols, who had been looking for Chihuahua troops or chasing Apache for the inhabitants. He filled up his trains, commandeered what he wanted, drilled the farm boys in the school of the soldier, and got ready to march again.

He also arrested the principal local priest, Ramón Ortiz, with whom he had had trouble ever since he occupied the town. Ortiz, known to the First Missouri as the kindly protector of the Texans who had been captured on the abortive Santa Fe expedition of 1841, was the head conspirator of an underground nativist movement. An accomplished and intelligent man, he was a fiery patriot who could not love the conquest and was directing a widespread opposition. Doniphan took him and several other prominent citizens as hostages. It was just as well, for a few days after the army started south it got word that trouble had broken out in Santa Fe.

This was the brief but bloody uprising known as the Taos Revolt. There was a group of New Mexicans who had not tranquilly accepted the conquest of their country. Among them, probably the most forceful, was Diego Archuleta, the lieutenant governor who had wanted to oppose Kearny's entrance and whom James Magoffin had persuaded with a promise that the conquest would not extend farther west than the Rio Grande. He and others who had both courage and patriotism formed an underground organization which planned an uprising. Kearny left Santa Fe convinced that the province was pacified, but Doniphan, Price, and Charles Bent (the governor appointed by Kearny) became aware of the smoldering ground fire. They were confident, however, that the American force was large enough to prevent any outbreak of violence. They were alert and when Price became military commandant, on Doniphan's invasion of the Indian country, he instituted much more stringent regulations for both the troops and the civilian population.

They were certainly needed. For a large part of the blame must rest on the Second Missouri, the regiment which Price had brought down the trail. Doniphan's command — whether because they had experienced both the risk and the satisfaction of conquest or because Doniphan had some faculty of leadership that Price lacked — had not antagonized the natives. But the Second Missouri, in effect, had turned Santa Fe into a roaring Wild West town, full of jubilation, offensiveness, and personal insult.

The conspirators arranged an uprising in Santa Fe for December 26, with elaborate plans for the seizure of the governor and commandant, the capture of the artillery, and synchronized attacks on various portions of the garrison. The American officials got word of it, however, seized all the principal conspirators except Archuleta and his first assistant, Tomas Ortiz, and issued a proclamation denouncing the revolution. They believed that they had prevented violence, but they miscalculated. There were deeper and deadlier hatreds at work than they realized. For one thing, the blood lust of the Pueblo Indians had been aroused. The fair god from the east who had come to restore their ancient liberties had by now somehow got identified in their dark minds with the conquistadors.

This lust was heightened by the conspiracy and its suppression at Santa Fe. Trouble broke out at Taos, whither Governor Bent had gone to visit his family, in the belief that the crisis had passed. On January 19, 1847, a mob composed mostly of Pueblo killed Bent in his own home, and five other Americans. In other parts of the province other Americans, about fifteen all told, were killed, sometimes with revolting cruelty, and bands of insurrectionists formed rapidly. A wave of thoroughly justified alarm ran across New Mexico.

Price acted promptly and effectively. He marched north from Santa Fe with part of his regiment and a company of volunteers led by the Bents' partner, Ceran St. Vrain, and won a bloody skirmish at La Cañada. He was joined by more of the Second Missouri and a company of Kearny's Dragoons from Albuquerque under Captain Burgwin. (One of those that had hastened to protect the traders' camp at Valverde.) Nearly five hundred strong now, through a spell of bitter cold, they came over the mountains, won another skirmish, and finally blew in the pueblo of Taos itself on February 4. It made a bloody end to a bloody campaign — Burgwin was among those killed — and New Mexicans and Pueblo would think hard before making another conspiracy. Most of the ringleaders had been killed in battle. Price arrested others and the talents of Francis Preston Blair, Jr., lately occupied in drawing up a civil code for New Mexico, were now engaged to prepare a prosecution.[4]

The news of this revolt traveled surprisingly slowly and Doniphan had started south when it reached him. Clark had arrived with Weightman's artillery on February 1, and a week later the First Missouri took up the march again. The unruly traders were now commanded to form themselves into a military battalion and take part in their own defense. They did so and Samuel Owens, the half-brother of one of A. Lincoln's fiancées, was made their major. Over two hundred of them were enrolled and they had more than three hundred wagons. The arrival of the artillery had brought Doniphan's strength to 924 effectives.

They were caught between an unknown enemy in Chihuahua and a revolution in New Mexico, but they were marching again, the job they did best. They left the Rio Grande and soon reached a difficult two-day desert. "Traveling through these *jornadas* in a cold night," Private Edwards says, "brings many to the recollection of warm houses, the soft feather beds, and the cool springs at home." It brought worse discomforts than the memory of home, and the second day nearly did for them. The train stuck in deep sand, had to cut loose many oxen, abandon a couple of wagons, and jettison four tons of flour and much other food. Even the traders threw away some of the merchandise that usually outvalued the lives of their employes. That second day was torrid and near the end of it the Doniphesias were close to stampeding. A providential rainstorm lightened the last miles, however, and saved the dying horses and oxen. They camped for a day just beyond the desert. Then they went on to Carrizal and, on February 21, to Ojo Caliente. This abandoned hacienda was named for an enormous hot spring, where the whole army, including its commander, got a bath.

Beyond the hot spring they made a fifty-five-mile *jornada* and, on the far side, got themselves into a prairie fire. One of Gilpin's campfires spread into the mountains, where it burned beside them throughout a day's march. Lieutenant Gibson remembered an old song, "Fire in the mountains! run, boys, run!" and that night they had to run, when a gale drove the flames down to their camp. There was a wild half hour while the army set backfires, galloped the horses and wagons about, and swore at one another in pyrotechnic light till the show was over. Still another kind of campfire had been added to their memories.

Doniphan had been keeping them in military formation the last few days and his reconnoissance parties — under Reid, Kirker, and Forsythe — had seen evidence of preparations ahead. On the night of February 27 he camped some fifteen miles north of a creek called the Sacramento, which was about the same distance north of the city of Chihuahua. His scouts and some stragglers who had come into camp had told him that the Mexicans had gathered at the Sacramento and were prepared to fight him there. The information was accurate; the First Missouri was going to have a battle.

Chihuahua had raised and equipped a sizable force, after floundering through the period of factionalism, jealousy, and treachery that attended every part of the Mexican war effort. It amounted to about three thousand organized troops and perhaps a thousand additional pressed peons who were armed principally with machetes. It did not have Santa Anna to drill it, however, and he was the only one who could make marksmen out of peaceable, oppressed people not used to bearing arms. Its general was a trained engineer but neither he, his soldiers, nor the supporting population had acquired any respect for their enemy. Throughout the war Mexican armies were always being half paralyzed at the beginning of an action by the discovery that the cowardly gringos would fight. As scouts reported the approach of Doniphan's command, an exhilaration seized Chihuahua. Battle rhetoric in newspapers, broadsides, and the sermons of priests promised everyone an overwhelming victory. About a thousand people went out to make a bleachers at the expected battleground, and the army took with it a thousand prepared ropes. They would make a coffle in which to lead the captured Americans to Mexico City.

Conde, the commander, had prepared a fortified position near the crossing of the Sacramento, where the hills came in and narrowed the approach. He was a first-rate engineer and brought against the First Missouri the science of fortification which reached back all the way to Roman times and had been maturing ever since. The works would have edified Uncle Toby and should have been impregnable to assault. Conde failed to consider only one eventuality:

what if the Americans did not know the textbook approach?

He should have considered it for, after reconnoitering the position, Doniphan and his staff saw no reason why they need come by the route prepared for them. It was a pretty little battle, the action of February 28. An orthodox analysis would find that Sacramento reinforced the lessons of Taylor's battles and once more proved the virtues of artillery. For the six small cannon which were divided between Clark and Weightman outranged and outshot the Mexican artillery and were decisive. They broke the Mexican lancers, battered in the redoubts, and shot concentrations of infantry to pieces. So by the texts technology won the battle.

But the texts must be thrown away and the victory allocated to two things: frontier craftsmanship and the readiness of the private soldier to improvise tactics as required. . . . On the morning of February 28 they started out from camp, Clark's band rendering "Yankee Doodle." On the way to the Sacramento Doniphan gave them a battle formation new to the art of war but excellently adapted to the circumstances. He formed his train and the wagons of the traders in four parallel columns — the moving fort of any caravan on the Santa Fe trail when it was on guard against Indian attack. In extremity the wagons could have formed a corral, within which the army could have held off many times its number. He put his cavalry, infantry, and artillery in the intervals between columns, where it was ready to deploy at need. The classical American symbol, a train of white-tops, moved compactly toward the Sacramento. Approaching the fortifications, Doniphan took his formation to the flank, half turning the Mexican position instead of coming from the front as he was expected to do. On the way to the flank there was an arroyo and the Mexican lancers might have cut a disorganized train to pieces. But this train was not disorganized. The high art of the bullwhackers scored a military triumph in getting the wagons across swiftly and in order, to the orchestrated profanity that was appropriate.

It was a wild and stimulating time. The now frustrated redoubts opened fire at long range and the panoplied lancers formed under banners. Doniphan ordered his troops out into line and Clark's artillery shattered the lancers before they got well started. Thereafter for an hour the artillery commands banged at each other. Clark had made his battalion (part of it was a St. Louis militia organization of honorable traditions) first-rate artillerists. Though the fuses were faulty and many shells exploded prematurely, he put down a successful barrage. The Mexican pieces were old, their powder was bad. The solid shot they fired came up visibly, bounding and ricocheting. The farm boys watched them come, yelled their appreciation of the show, made bets with one another, and dodged so successfully that the only casualties were horses.

The Mexicans made another charge, at the rear and the wagons this time, and the traders who could shoot as well as the army beat it off without trouble. Doniphan moved his lines nearer the half-turned redoubts and musketry fire blazed everywhere. The Missourians were shooting in earnest but the truth is that the Mexicans, who had had no practice with arms and had been battered by artillery, mostly contented themselves with hoisting their pieces over the parapets and discharging them at the horizon. Doniphan, who sat on his horse and cursed with the homespun eloquence of his culture, watched the army work up to within four hundred yards of the redoubts, and then launched three companies of cavalry and Weightman's artillery in a charge at the Mexican guns. It started out gaudily but his adjutant, DeCourcy (who was rumored to be drunk), halted two of the companies halfway across. Doniphan got a bad scare and the halted companies stood cursing with fire coming at them from two directions. Weightman galloped his two howitzers halfway to the redoubts, unlimbered, and began to fire again. Owens, the trader, with two companions galloped down the front of the redoubts and got himself killed. Reid had not obeyed the order to halt but took his company up to the parapets and over them. The two companies that had halted joined him and the forts were carried in a few minutes of chaotic battle. The Missourians used their sabers, their clubbed muskets, convenient stones, and even their fists. The few minutes were gory enough to provide them with a lifetime of reminiscence — beheaded Mexicans, Mexicans split lengthwise, Mexicans shot down on the run, Mexicans locked in death grapples with their assailants, scared horses stampeding, roar of artillery, mountain men on one knee drawing beads, and the boys from home acting much as they did at a turkey shoot.

The Mexicans broke and ran. Some of them tried to rally on the other hill, but simultaneously Gilpin's wing swarmed over those fortifications and now everyone was running. The First Missouri, an army of victorious individualists, milled round for anybody's horse that was handy and began a pursuit. They sabered Mexicans on the run, they chased them down the river, they chased them into the hills where some Apache who had taken box seats for the spectacle killed a number, and a big moon came up and the Mexicans were still running. Some of them ran the full fifteen miles to Chihuahua. The Americans came straggling back to the battlefield by moonlight, found the surgeons of both armies gathering in the wounded, and answered the yells of their officers, who were trying to bring the victors together again as an army.

They had been fighting for more than three hours. Owens, the trader, had been killed. (Legend says that he had some romantic reason for wanting to die and had dressed in white clothes before the battle.) A sergeant had received a wound from which he died, and seven others had minor wounds. On their part, they had killed more than three hundred Mexicans, wounded at least as many more, taken forty prisoners, and permanently broken resistance in the state of Chihuahua. While the wounded screamed in the mesquite, the First Missouri ranged over the field to gather in the spoils. They were considerable, for Chihuahua had done well by its defenders. The Doniphesias got ten cannon and a miscellany of antique trench pieces, hundreds of small arms, many tons of powder, seven elegant carriages belonging to generals and their guests, Conde's field desk, scores of wagons and carts, hundreds of horses and mules and beeves, thousands of sheep. They got the ropes in which they were to have been marched to Mexico City and the black pirate flag with death's-heads that had been flaunted at El Brazito. They got a paymaster's box with $3000 in copper coin and they got an amount of silver which may have been $5000 or $50,000 but was carefully not reported to their officers. They loaded their pockets, belts, and haversacks with loot and came back to report themselves.

So they had still another kind of campfire, victorious under a big moon with the wounded moaning near by and Missouri two thousand miles from home, pounding one another's backs, wringing the officers' hands, and beginning to tell the stories that would bore their grandchildren. The fires blazed up and the boys cooked a meal, a big meal. The spoils had included a quantity of bottles, kegs, and skins of Chihuahua wine. Missouri settled down to celebrate not only the defeat of a hostile army but its total dispersion.

The next day, March 1, Doniphan sent Mitchell and an advance guard to occupy Chihuahua and on March 2 rode at the head of his column into this, the principal city of northern Mexico, which had fallen to a handful of ragged boys from the prairies. Forgive him if he swaggered, "not unlike a strutting gander," and forgive the boys, frowsy, ill-smelling, and unshaved, if, with the bands producing "Yankee Doodle" again and "Washington's March," they told each other that they had kept their oath and captured the Halls of Montezuma. A populace which had been promised the complete destruction of the invading heretics was panic-stricken, gaped at the conquerors in terror mingled with disbelief, and hurried out the prettiest *señoritas* with melons, tortillas, and more wine. The resident Americans, who had barricaded their houses in fear of a mobbing, rushed out to welcome their deliverers. They couldn't believe what they saw, for no one ever looked less like heroes than the First Missouri. Some of them hurried back and nailed the doors shut again, convinced that these were some Apache whom Doniphan had sent ahead to prepare his coming. The army swaggered and yelled behind its bands — past the mint, past the great cathedral, round the plaza, and on to ceremonies of capitulation. Private Robinson, nineteen years old a few days back, wrote in his diary a good soldier's summary: "We rode through the principal streets and public square, and on a rocky hill on the south side of the city fired a national salute in honor of the conquest, stole wood enough to get supper, and went to bed as usual among the rocks."

At the Cabinet meeting of May 4 Polk heard Secretary Marcy read "Col. Donophan's" report on Sacramento, and spoke of it in his diary as "one of the most decisive and brilliant achievements of the War." He was occupied with the quarrel between Kearny and Frémont or would unquestionably have said more about Sacramento. What he did say is not open to question. Eight months after the administration strategists had laid out this campaign in the Executive office, an improvised organization had fulfilled the President's intent, deep in enemy country, without support from the War Department, by application of their native talents to the task at hand. Frontiersmen easily changing phase, farmers becoming soldiers, they had conducted a probably impossible campaign to victory and made secure their portion, a large one, of a foreign conquest.

In a year of decision they had produced a decision. Chihuahua, one of the "Northern Provinces" of Mr. Polk's concern, had been made secure for the duration. New Mexico was also secure; after Sacramento there would be no revolts like the one at Taos. Since New Mexico was secured, California also was secure. Doniphan's work buttressed that of Sloat, Stockton, and Kearny, and the pieces of Mr. Polk's objective in the Far West now made a map. Moreover, the southwestern Indians, the Navajo and the Apache, though far from dissuaded, had at least learned to be cautious. The western end of the Santa Fe trail and the southern route to California suffered no such massacres as the Comanche perpetrated on the eastern portions throughout 1847. Finally, by its mere presence in Chihuahua the First Missouri had turned a balance farther to the east. On February 22 and 23 Taylor's subalterns won the battle of Buena Vista — but barely won it. It was a bloody battle and the excellent army which Santa Anna had raised lost it by an extremely narrow margin. If Santa Anna could have had the troops which faced Doniphan at Sacramento it is likely that Taylor's army would have been chased in fragments through the state of Coahuila.

Susan Magoffin stayed at El Paso in great distress. Only her heavenly Father could protect her now. To the north the Taos revolt had filled the land with danger, and to the south her friends and courtiers in the army had disappeared into a terrifying silence. Susan read her Bible and did little charities for the servants, dressed in her best and dined with the "Dons," clung to her husband and pretended that she did not see how anxious he was. Day by day worse rumors came out of the south. It seemed certain that Brother James would be executed as a spy, and there was always news that Chihuahua had annihilated the army. In tribulation Susan formed the habit of attending Mass and wondered if this made her an idolatress. The ceremonies seemed to comfort her a little, so she decided that her protestant heart was not corrupted by the images. Suddenly a subdued, arrogant triumph flared across El Paso. It must mean that Doniphan had been defeated. Susan and her husband were now almost certain to be murdered by the mob. Then on March 5, "we were struck with consternation about 12 o'clock today while quietly talking with our friend, Mr. White, Don Ygnacio Rouquia suddenly steped in at the door, with hair somewhat on ends and features ghastly. At once our minds filled with apprehensions lest the dread sentence [of death for James Magoffin] had been passed. Without seating himself and scarcely saying good morning, he took Mr. Magoffin by the hand and led him out of the room in haste and with tears in his eyes told him that 'he was a Mexican and it pained him to the heart to know that the American army had gained the battle and taken possession of Chihuahua.'" She gave thanks to God, but there was no word from Brother James.

Susan's alarm about James Magoffin was not justified. Don Santiago had saved his skin — with an expenditure of champagne closely calculated by his old companion, Philip St. George Cooke, at

3392 bottles. Mexican gourmets would not let a good host die, and the officer who got documentary proof of his treason courteously returned it to him. But they would not let him go. When Doniphan neared Chihuahua, they sent Don Santiago on to Durango as one of the consolations of defeat, and he was kept there, angry but still buying champagne, till the war ended.

At Doniphan's approach, Chihuahua had, however, released other Americans who had been kept in custody for various reasons, including some of the traders who had hurried down the trail from Independence ahead of the army, last May. A group of these, among them Dr. Wislezenus, the romantic scientist, had spent six months under guard at a little silver town named Cosihuirachi. Wislezenus had been dreadfully bored there; the mines were in barrasca, the town was poverty-stricken and rotten with syphilis and "*lepra*." He tried to botanize but it was barren country. He observed the natives' fatalism when the Apache raided their herds and killed the herders, and grinned at their futile, discreet belligerence when they sent posses to ride a safe distance after the marauders. One ranger company, he decided, could clean out the Apache for good, but there wouldn't be a Mexican ranger company. For months he expected Wool to raise the siege but Wool didn't come and the doctor stoically heard all American armies obliterated in rumor. The battle of Sacramento freed him from boredom and captivity. He rode to Chihuahua and was shocked by the First Missouri's rags. Still, "there was some peculiar expression in their eye, meaning that they had seen Brazito and Sacramento and that Mexicans could not frighten them even by tenfold numbers." He joined up as a surgeon and completed the great march.

Sacramento and Chihuahua made the high moment of the First Missouri. From then on life was pleasant enough but an anticlimax of garrison duty, drill, abortive expeditions, rumors, rioting, and finally the march to the Rio Grande. They occupied Chihuahua through March till nearly the end of April, while Doniphan tried to get orders from the War Department or any superior officer. He had to protect the traders, who at last opened the commerce they had been anticipating for ten months. (By now the army was fed up with its wards and did not relish guarding them.) He had to negotiate customs arrangements for their protection and otherwise to conduct a civil government on behalf of the native officials. He had to arrange a future for his command, whose enlistment would expire in June, and held repeated councils of war with his officers. They could reach no agreement — whether to join Wool or Taylor, whether to go back the way they had come, whether just to sit here and wait for the government to remember them. Gilpin, still dreaming empires, conceived an idea that this handful of troops could go down El Camino Real to its terminus and take Mexico City for Mr. Polk, whose chosen instrument seemed unable to take it. Some younger officers agreed with him, and, on the showing so far, the First Missouri would probably have undertaken the assignment with confidence.

The troops took their ease in the capital city. It was the biggest city most of them had ever seen, and by far the oldest and richest. A beautiful city too, as the lush spring came on with smoky air and vistas of fruit blossoms. Doniphan could drill them, harass them with guard duty and target practice, and prod their officers to keep them busy, but there was plenty of time. Bullfights, much bloodier cockfights, gaming tables even on the sidewalks, cantinas and willing *señoritas* everywhere — they knew how conquerors should behave and Doniphan was afraid they would disintegrate. When money got short again (they were still unpaid) they formed an easy habit of taking it where they found it. They conceived a distaste for the wormlike, hairless dogs of the town, tied firecrackers to their tails, and roused many a scared citizen by night with an uproar that seemed to mean pillage but was only the persecution of his pet.

They got the news of Buena Vista and made the town reverberate. At last one of Doniphan's patrols got through to Wool at Saltillo and came back with orders from Taylor to join him there. The night those orders came, Chihuahua rocked. "Every one to express his joy got drunk. There were hundreds fought and 'twas dangerous for a little fellow to poke about much. A fellow would hit his neighbor a thundering love pat and a fight would ensue, but [they would] soon be friends again. Such a motley crew of drunken men as the courtyard of the *fonda* presented I suppose never were together before. Some were crabbed and surly, others lively and good-humored; some for peace, others war; some making speeches, others remaining perfectly mute and sullen. This was not confined to the privates but [extended to the] officers of all grades." The conquerors had caught up with the United States again, on the far side, and intended to tell the world about it.

Some of the traders prepared to stay at Chihuahua, others to go back to Santa Fe, still others to march through the interior with their custodians. Doniphan released his prisoners and discharged his governors, turning the city back to its officials. He got the First Missouri ready to move again. A few farm boys went over the hill to marry their *señoritas* and make homesteads in this valley. A few *señoritas* put on breeches and prepared to follow their farm boys. And on April 25, 26, and 28, in various divisions, the army left Chihuahua, heading south and east.

They had a diversified march to make — more *jornadas,* more mountains, more green valleys. But they were certainly the best marchers in the world by now and though, as always, some sickened and a few died, they put their shoulders into it. Dust, sand, swamps, summer heat, lizards, scorpions, snakes — nothing mattered now that they had turned east. Doniphan laid the gad to them and all their records toppled. As they marched they learned of Scott's landing at Vera Cruz, the beginning of the campaign that ended the war, and his first inland victory at Cerro Gordo. They foraged liberally but also they chased Apache and Comanche for the natives, Mitchell and the indefatigable Reid riding the flanks in sweeping forays. As they got down into Coahuila they reached country where Taylor's invasion had raised up guerrillas who harried Americans and Mexicans alike. And one day, "a Mexican courier came to the colonel with news that Canales [a guerrilla chief] had made an attack upon Magoffin's train of wagons, and that Magoffin and his lady were likely to fall into his hands. A detachment of sixty men under Lieut. Gordon was quickly sent to his relief. They anticipated Canales' movement."

(Susan does not even mention this alarm. She has been too exhausted to write in her journal — the attempt to keep up with the marchers was back-breaking and heart-breaking. "Many nights I have layed down not to sleep for my bones ached too much for that, even had I had the time, but to rest an hour or two prior to traveling the remaining and greater portion of the night to get a little ahead of the command." The Magoffins went to Saltillo with the First Missouri, then said good-bye to it at last and from there on were under the protection of other troops, as Samuel traded toward the Rio Grande. It was an endless anxiety and a long pain. James was reported killed, though at last they knew that he was free. Samuel caught a lowland fever. Susan was ill repeatedly. They moved through the backwash and along the periphery of the war, scared, stubborn, persevering. In August she knew that she was pregnant again and they crawled on through the fetid summer and ended their long journey at Matamoros. There Susan caught yellow fever and a son was born to her while she was sick. The infant died very soon. Brigham Young would have told her that she had come up through much tribulation.)

The army came down to the beautiful oasis of Parras and for the first time encountered a population who had learned to fear and hate American soldiers, a lesson they had taught no one. "Wherever we encamped, in five minutes women and children would roam through the tents to sell different articles, never meeting with insult or injury." Wool's and Taylor's troops had given the natives wholly different emotions, and from now on the Doniphesias would see an ugliness of war that was strange to them. The West Pointers claimed that it was the volunteers' fault, and it was at least the fault of the volunteer system, which prevented discipline. Also, of course, Taylor did not care to tarnish his candidacy.

Another hitch brought them to Saltillo and on to the battlefield of Buena Vista and the headquarters of General Wool. Doniphan tried to brush and curry them a little but it was no use. Drawing full rations at last, after eleven months, some of them refused soap, explaining that they had no clothes to wash. Doniphan got them into line long enough for Wool, the precisian, to review them, but again it was no use — they gaped and lounged and made remarks. Wool tried to re-enlist them for another year, which showed optimism. Even Meriwether Lewis Clark made comments on the way the War Department had treated them, and when Wool said he would take care of them Clark remembered out loud that they had heard the same story at Fort Leavenworth.

They got a chance to stare at Taylor too, near Monterrey, and found that they loved him and his great-commoner act. They left their sick here — lowlands and tropical weather were cutting them down — and marched on to the Rio Grande. At Cerralvo they saw some Texas Rangers execute a guerrilla who, they felt, was a brave man and entitled to protection as a combatant. The officers had difficulty restraining them from expressing their belief. Thereafter they did not like the "Texians," though admitting that their habitual cruelties were justified by years of border raids. And as they came into contact with regular army outfits they fervently added their antagonism to the old quarrel. Finally, a few miles from Reynosa, they lost a sergeant to guerrillas and exacted a thorough revenge, in the manner of the Texians.

At Reynosa they had reached navigable water — by marching almost exactly three thousand, five hundred miles from Fort Leavenworth. Here, ending a feat of arms without parallel, they awaited transports in rain, swamps, and muggy heat. They were dirty, they were lousy, they had practically no clothes left, and they acquired a new set of grievances against the war. The government could not send their horses home by boat but would try to drive them overland — and could not transport their outfits. They burned their saddles and blankets and crowded aboard bad transports, to eat weevily hardtack, be seasick, and find themselves with as little drinking water as if they were making another *jornada.* So they came to New Orleans and down the gangplanks, some of them wearing only greatcoats, some just their drawers, all long-haired and bearded and burned black.

New Orleans, which was near enough to the war to recognize heroes at sight, went wild over them. They fed to repletion on good American food at last, though they were apt to get out their case knives and go for the roasts with both hands. They read newsprint about their adventures and perfected their reminiscences. They got paid, after twelve months — though paid less than they thought they had been promised. In the last week of June, '47, they were discharged and started home to Missouri.

Missouri outdid New Orleans. St. Louis — where they found friends who had grown rich from the war, as they assuredly had not — broke out its bunting and illuminations and deafened the heroes with as much cannon fire as they had heard at Sacramento. They came off the river steamers and marched through hastily erected arches while the packed streets roared at them. Old Bullion loosed his oratory and Doniphan and his officers got a chance to resume the same art. Skyrockets, Roman candles, transparencies, mottoes, champagne, and good corn liquor — the boys were home from the war.

It was the same when dwindling little squads reached their home towns and the villagers made the most of them. The Ladies' Aid baked cakes again, who had made their company guidons, and here was Betsy to walk with in the evening. They were heroes in their home town, the newspapers printed their adorned stories, the ecstasy lasted for a while. Then they were just farmers again.

Memory took over. They had made their march, thirty-five hundred miles of it, from Fort Leavenworth to the Rio Grande by way of Santa Fe and the Navajo country, El Paso, Chihuahua, and Buena Vista. As long as they lived, the twelve-months march would splash their past with carmine — prairie grass in the wind, night guard at the wagons, the high breasts of the Spanish Peaks and all New Mexico spread out before them from the Raton, fandangos at Santa Fe, glare ice above the Canyon de Chelly, the hot gladness of the charge at Sacramento, the grizzly that wandered through our camp that night, tongues swollen by the *jornadas,* Jim dying in the snow, the ammonia stench of the buffalo wallows, the campfires glimmering in a slanting line of rubies all the way up the pass, the *señorita* who looked in the wagon that day when I was sick and "oh the beauty of the exquisite Spanish word *pobrecito* when heard from such lips, the sweetest of all sounds."

They remembered the campfires most of all, though Missouri has not chosen to memorialize them in the murals of its First Mounted Volunteers at Jefferson City. A campfire burns in the submerged memory of the Americans all the way west from Plymouth Beach, and the First Missouri had sat round three hundred and fifty campfires on their way. The fires illuminate the composite memory of the March of the One Thousand — thirty-five hundred miles of prairie, desert, and mountain, the faces of your squad ruddy in that light and some of those faces you would not see again, stories by firelight more memorable than any stories you would hear in Missouri, the ease of stretching out by the flames after the day's ride, buffalo hump to eat or maybe just charred cakes of cornmeal, and sleeping under the peaks before dawn came up and the heat mirage began to shine.

They too had found the West and left their mark on it, an honorable signature.

XV

Down from the Sierra

SEVENTEEN members of the Donner party had composed "the Forlorn Hope" when it started from the huts at the lake on December 16. Two had turned back during the first day. Stanton had died on December 21, and Antonio, Dolan, Graves, and Lemuel Murphy during the Christmas storm. That left ten of them: Sutter's Indians, Luis and Salvador; William Eddy, William Foster, and Jay Fosdick; Sarah Murphy Foster, Sarah Graves Fosdick, Harriet Murphy Pike, Mary Ann Graves, and Amanda McCutchen. Eddy was thirty years old, Foster twenty-eight, Fosdick twenty-three. Mrs. McCutchen, whose husband was at Sonoma trying to organize a rescue party, was twenty-four and had left her year-old daughter at the lake. The two Murphy girls, Sarah Foster and the widowed Harriet Pike, were twenty-three and twenty-one, respectively. Harriet had left two children behind her and the Fosters, one. The Fosdicks had no children. Eddy's three-year-old son and year-old daughter were with his wife Eleanor at the lake.

Their story after leaving what they called "the Camp of Death" must be told briefly. A little strength restored to them, they started off again on December 30. They knew they were off the trail now but the good weather that succeeded the storm held. Furthermore, the snow was crusted hard enough for them sometimes to travel without their crude snowshoes and gradually they got down to where patches of bare ground showed through. "Gradually" is a word: the meaning is men and women who were all but dead falling forward step by step through a white desolation, the risk of tumbling into oblivion disregarded, their minds dim and submerged in terror. Five or six miles a day, a mile or two when the flame burned weaker. Fosdick was almost dead. The dried flesh of their companions was gone. Getting down to country where bare ground was common enough to justify it, they made another meal: they cooked and ate the rawhide of their snowshoes. After that there was nothing to eat. Everyone but Eddy wanted to kill the two Indians. Eddy would not; he told the Indians what was being considered and they silently disappeared.

Eddy and Mary Graves had more strength remaining than the others. He determined to strike out ahead, as well as he was able to. In panic and despair the others begged him not to but he took the gun — they had been carrying it by turns — and made a trial for the preservation of them all. Mary Graves went with him, the two of them staggering a little faster than the others could and gradually getting out of sight. So Eddy killed a deer. His frontiersman's craft enabled him to identify a place where one had bedded for the night. He and Mary knelt and prayed, and pretty soon they saw it. He could not hold the rifle steady enough to draw a bead but finally contrived the swinging snapshot which frontier gaffers used when their strength was gone. He wounded the deer, crawled toward it, and cut its throat. He and Mary cooked the guts and that night slept soundly, within gunshot of the others.

Farthest of all from him, the Fosdicks heard the shots that Eddy fired to hearten them. Jay Fosdick correctly interpreted them. If he could get to Eddy and the meat, he said, he would live. But he died and Sarah wrapped his body in their remaining blanket and lay down beside him to die. She did not die but woke again in the morning and started out alone, only to meet some of the others who were coming back to find the Fosdick corpses — to get meat. Specifically, "with instructions to get Mrs. Fosdick's heart." They got Jay's heart instead and Sarah saw it roasted on a stick. Eddy called them in and they spent the day drying as much venison and human flesh as they had not eaten.

There were two men left now and William Foster's sanity had lapsed. The next day when the new food was exhausted he began to plead with Eddy to kill one of the survivors. Mrs. McCutchen was his nominee — he said she was a nuisance and was delaying them. Eddy refused, reminding him that Amanda was a wife and a mother. Then kill the sisters, Sarah Fosdick who was a childless widow, and Mary Graves, who was unmarried. Eddy refused, and suddenly his revulsion could not be stayed. He picked up a club, struck it against a log to make sure it was sound, tossed it to Foster, and told him to defend himself. Then Eddy started toward him, drawing a knife. Four pitiful wraiths of women fell upon Eddy and disarmed him. He mastered his rage but told Foster that he would kill him if he renewed the suggestion or made any move against the women. If any member of this party had to die in order to keep the others alive, William Eddy said, he and Foster would fight it out.

Thornton calls their bivouac that night "the Camp of Strife." The next day they saw bloody footprints in a patch of snow and knew that Luis and Salvador must have made them. A little later they found the two Indians stretched out on the ground, dying. Foster could not be denied now and Eddy protested with words only, for it was no longer rational to protest. He took three of the women a little way ahead, out of sight, and left the gun. Foster shot the Indians, they butchered the bodies, and that night they ate again. But Eddy ate only grass.

Thereafter they traveled and slept in two groups, Foster with his wife and her sister, Harriet Pike, Eddy with Amanda McCutchen, Mary Graves, and her sister Sarah Fosdick. They often saw deer, some at close range, but Eddy could not raise the rifle for a shot. They rested every quarter of a mile, Eddy had to use two hands to climb over a log, the smallest hummock threw them, and "the women would fall and weep like infants and then rise and totter along again."

It was on January 12 that they found strange footprints in the mud — it had been raining for two days — and came at dusk to the brush huts of a tiny Indian village. Lowly Diggers lived there but the squaws wept at sight of these living dead and the children wailed with them. All that the Indians had to eat was acorns. They gave the specters some but Eddy could not eat them. Next day, through another rainstorm, the Indians helped them to another village, where there were more acorns and some acorn meal, and through two more long days, half carried from brush village to brush village they went on, the Indians touched by the sight of suffering to the residual pity at the heart of life. Eddy was still living on grass, and acorn bread would not save the others.

But at last a mangy chief gave Eddy a handful of pine nuts, and they made all the difference. It was January 17, a bright blue day, and after one mile of going the others had at last reached the uttermost limit. Their feet were only pulp wrapped in shreds of blanket that were sodden with mud, and the remaining filament of strength that held them up broke. They lay down to die. But his handful of pine nuts had brought Eddy back from his "dream of combats, of famine and death, of cries of despair, of fathomless snows and impassable mountains." He refused to die. One Indian was still helping him and they met another one whose help could be bought by a promise of tobacco. Supported on their shoulders, Eddy left bloody footprints across six miles of rough ground and came, an hour before sunset, to a little shack on the edge of Johnson's ranch, the first outpost of settlement, at the eastern wall of the Sacramento Valley. The shack belonged to M. D. Ritchie, an emigrant of '46, one of a number who had settled near Johnson's for the winter. Young Harriet Ritchie came to the door and Eddy asked her for bread.

Harriet Ritchie burst into tears. But she got him to bed, got bread for him, and ran out among the other shacks, summoning help. Before long, four Americans were hurrying back to find the six survivors whom Eddy had described, and were able to find them by following his bloody footprints. The Forlorn Hope had reached the succor of their own kind, seven of the fifteen who started out, thirty-three days after the beginning of the effort for which they had laid in six days' rations of two mouthfuls a day.

Now the settlements could learn the truth about the Donner party, of whom they had known only, on Reed's and McCutchen's reports, that they were caught in the snows with enough cattle to see them through the winter, and that they could probably not be reached till February. February was two weeks away.

At Johnson's there was a small cluster of emigrants who had crossed this year, some of them in the very train the Donners had started with from Indian Creek. Notably, from that great train that elected Owl Russell captain when the dew was still on them all, there were Acquilla Glover and Riley Septimus Mootrey. The latter is Moultry in most of the literature but he was Mootrey to Jessy Thornton and it was as Mootrey that we saw the Reverend Mr. Cornwall marry him to Mary Lard, one June Sunday beside the Platte. Among such men as these, men who had shared the trail with the Donners and safely passed the hazards that had overcome them, there was no question of doing whatever could be done to save them. There was only the question of how best to go about it.

At Johnson's they at once prepared to send help. But there were too few of them and only Glover, Mootrey, and a runaway sailor named Sels volunteered. They sent word to John Sinclair, a Scotchman who was an associate of Sutter's and the alcalde of these parts, and to Sutter's Fort, where Edward Kern, Frémont's artist and cartographer, now commanded for the United States Navy. Sinclair and Kern called a meeting of such men, this year's emigrants mostly, as had not gone out with the California Battalion or with the even more irregular detachments that were now riding the countryside in its troubled state between peace and war. As a result of this meeting the rescue party known as the First Relief was organized. But also Sutter sent his "launch" down the river with a letter from Sinclair which told the story of the Forlorn Hope and summarized Eddy's description of what they had left behind. This got to Yerba Buena — San Francisco, now — just as the effort of Reed and McCutchen to raise rescue parties was beginning to be successful.

Reed and McCutchen, when they rode out from Sutter's in late November to raise help in the settlements, had found them nearly empty of men. McCutchen had ended up at the late republic, Sonoma, and Reed at San Jose. The countryside was full of rumors and armed bands, native and American. Till some kind of tranquillity could be restored no one could be spared for the relief of starving emigrants far away in the snow. Reed had to join a company of horsemen at San Jose and ride out on guard duty as the quickest way to help his wife and children. (Remember that he knew of them only that the snow had cut them off and that there was no one but Milt Elliott to defend them against the hate roused by his own fatal quarrel with John Snyder.) So through December he was an active home guard, a "lieutenant," and as such on January 2 took part in what was called the battle of Santa Clara, which was practically bloodless but ended the guerrilla war in these parts. It took another month to rearrange the hashed society tolerably, and finally on February 1, Reed was able to go to Yerba Buena bearing demands from San Jose that action be taken to rescue the Donner party.

Yerba Buena was commanded by the navy, whose officers would not commit the government to the project officially but would help out in their private capacity. They called a mass meeting on February 3 and Reed found there a number whom he had traveled with on the plains and others he had soldiered with more recently. Called on to speak, he burst into tears and could not. But the Reverend Mr. Dunleavy, first of all to lead a group of seceders away from Owl Russell's wagon train, spoke for him. The parson was able to guess exactly where the Donners must have been stopped and he needed no gift of fiction to describe their plight. He roused the horror and pity of his audience: Yerba Buena would do what it could. Thirteen hundred dollars was raised to equip and pay a relief expedition. A recent arrival in California, Passed Midshipman Selim Woodworth, was put in charge. That was a mistake.

Woodworth was the son of Samuel Woodworth, a journalist who is still remembered as the author of "The Old Oaken Bucket" and "The Hunters of Kentucky." He had been sent to Oregon in April, '46, with dispatches notifying settlers there that joint occupation had been terminated. Francis Parkman had met him at St. Louis and again at Westport and had not been impressed. Woodworth, a man gifted in the appreciation of his own qualities, had voiced a Stockton-like plan to raise some volunteers and capture Santa Fe — presumably on his way to the Columbia by the northern trail — which Parkman understood as brainless. Later Parkman's notebook records, "I rode to Westport with that singular character, Lieut. Woodworth. He is a great busybody and ambitious of taking a command among the emigrants. . . . Woodworth parades a revolver in his belt, which he insists is necessary." Doubtless he paraded it all the way to Oregon and doubtless the comparative sobriety of life along the Willamette was what had brought him down to California. He made a splash there, talking himself into a considerable reputation. So now he was going to contribute some additional disasters to the Donner party and their rescuers.

While Woodworth talked and Reed worked furiously preparing his expedition, Sutter's launch arrived with Sinclair's harrowing description of Eddy and the Forlorn Hope. Horror stimulated the preparations and now here was Caleb Greenwood coming in from Sonoma, where McCutchen also had got action at last. Greenwood was gathering a rescue party in Napa Valley, spurred on by an offer of $500 reward from Mariano Vallejo, lately the prisoner of the Bear Flaggers.

We have met Greenwood a number of times in this narrative, and at last there had come into the preparations for relief a man who knew and knew how. In November of 1844, by the exercise of a mountain man's intelligence and skill, he had saved from the fate of the Donners, and in precisely the same place, the last emigrant party of that year. He had, that is, got the famous Stevens-Murphy party over the divide just as the snows came. (That was the party to which Moses Schallenberger belonged, who built the cabin in which the Breens were now living.) Last April, following Clyman, he had crossed the Sierra through the snows, and last September, guiding the Aram party to California, he had actually got from Diggers a vague anonymous rumor of the Donners' troubles in the Salt Desert and had ridden eastward from the junction of the trails for a full day to find them. Greenwood was eighty-three years old but was made of parfleche, and he had lived in the mountains forever, his career going as far back as the Astorians. Last December Edwin Bryant had met him at his hunting camp in Napa Valley, where he was recruiting his strength on bear meat after the puny fare of "bread, milk and sich-like mushy stuff" which he had had to endure with the "emigrators." Bryant had relished his profanity and that of his fellow mountain man, John Turner, "who could do all the swearing for our army in Mexico and then have a surplus." Old Greenwood tried to make a census of his children for Bryant but there were too many of them, mostly the issue of his Crow wife, and one was named Governor Boggs and another, who would join the relief, was Britton.

Blasting his profane encouragement, Caleb Greenwood got to work too. His would be a party of professionals, mountain men, among them his son Brit and John Turner. Accordingly, leaving Woodworth to organize and finance bases and supporting expeditions, Reed rode off with Greenwood to prepare an advance party. From this came what the literature knows as the Second Relief. But meanwhile the First Relief had left Johnson's and headed toward the snow.

Let it be understood: any man who went to the assistance of the Donners knew that he was risking the fate he was trying to save them from. Down in the great valley the California spring was riotous, the opulent loveliness that stirred Jim Clyman's heart when we first met him. But in the Sierra the snow was thirty feet deep and the worst storms of the winter, worse even than the Christmas blizzard, were still to come.

When the First Relief rode out from Johnson's on February 4 it numbered fourteen, among them William Eddy of the intrepid heart, who had had less than three weeks of rest. He could not go all the way but he got to the high ridge well up in the mountains where, at Mule Springs, they made a base camp. He and another were sent back from here with the horses, since the rest of the going would have to be on foot. Two others were left to guard the camp (one of them was a half-wit), and ten men set out from Mule Springs, each one carrying as heavy a pack as he could manage, seventy-five pounds perhaps. The snow was already higher than their knees. Four days later, at the foot of the vertical wall that drops down from Emigrant Gap, three of them had had enough — Jotham Curtis (whom McCutchen had had to bully so, last November), Ritchie (to whose shack Eddy had been dragged by the Indians), and a German who was known only as Greasy Jim. No one may blame them for turning back: they had ahead of them the Sierra and the storms. But there were seven who would not turn back.

Reaching this insistence of naked valor, George Stewart, the historian of the Donner party, for the second time quotes the words in which George McKinstry (lately of the Harlan-Young party, now sheriff of the lands surrounding Sutter's) reported the First Relief: "I will again give you a list of their names, as I think they ought to be recorded in letters of gold." The seven were: two ex-sailors, Sels and Ned Coffeemeyer, and five emigrants of '46, Acquilla Glover, Reasin Tucker (called "Dan"), Riley Septimus Mootrey, and the Rhoads brothers, John and Daniel. The last two were among the very few Mormons who, maintaining a seemly reticence about their faith, had crossed to California last summer with Gentile trains. Tucker's son George, a boy of sixteen, had been left at the base camp at Mule Springs.

It had taken them eleven days to get to the base of that high cliff —through violent rainstorms, over swollen mountain streams which they sometimes had to bridge, and at last through snow. They had been drenched and chilled, they had had repeatedly to stop and dry out the food they were carrying, sometimes they had slept in snow water, sometimes they had not slept at all. Now they started into the snow which, at the divide, had been deepened by another storm. With great daring they left the emigrant trail which they had been following (and which the Forlorn Hope had missed) and broke a new one to the Yuba Bottoms, where they made caches of food for the return trip. Single file. One man breaks the snow as well as he can, the others following behind him till he is used up. Then he falls to the rear and it is the next man's turn. Bright weather, snow dazzle, steel air. A short snowstorm. They stop and make snowshoes. The storm ends. . . . If it hadn't, they would have died.

They camped at the western end of the pass on February 17, just fourteen days out from Johnson's. The next day they went over it on their snowshoes, with Glover and Dan Rhoads barely able to cross as their lungs heaved in thin air and their hearts pounded. They were all day coming down the barrier that the Donners had not been able to get across and following the silent, white lakeside to the huts. They could see no smoke, they could not even see the huts, since they were buried deep, till they came right up to them at sunset. They shouted, wondering if anyone were still alive, and something like a woman came up out of a hole in the snow. (It was Mrs. Breen, who had started to take Mrs. Reed outside to whisper her belief that Virginia Reed was dying.) The others crawled up the ramp of frozen snow to mew at the seven men from beyond the mountains, in the crimson sunset and the violet shadows of the woods. They looked like mummies, their wailing was cracked and tiny, their cries broke into lunatic talk. Around them at the top of the ramp, in the sunset, lay the bodies of those who had died since the last storm, dragged so far and left uncovered.

Life in those buried huts since December 16, two months before, when the Forlorn Hope departed, is hardly to be understood. Over them were the storms and the sunny, bitter days and the sunny, gentle days. Around them was fantasm, whose figures were both real and unreal. Their minds peeled down to anger and dread out of which bubbled the primitive delirium for which physicians to the diseased soul probe. Besides those tempests were the exterior dreads of what sanity remained to them, as the cattle hides they lived on ran out. No clue told them which of the figures they saw and the voices they heard were hallucinatory and which those of their companions. The mind grew monocular, its vision flat. Up from childhood came the figures of the Old Testament, and from a far more distant past the figure of Lansford Hastings by whose act they had become animals that died in apathy and animals that lived on sodden with their personal filth. Abraham and Hastings and one's own children with dim eyes lying silent till they died — all mingled together in the reeking huts.

The indomitable Margaret Reed (it seems superfluous that she had always suffered from migraine) had, just after New Year's, made an attempt fully as resolute as her husband's. She left one of the youngest children in each of the three huts. ("We told them we would bring them back bread," Virginia Reed says, "and then they were willing to stay.") Then, taking Virginia and Milt Elliott and Eliza Williams (whose mind had dimmed to childhood), she made a desperate ascent of the ridge, between storms. They were gone five days, missed the trail, and got back just in time. (Virginia: "I could get along very well while I thought we were going ahead, but as soon as we had to turn back I could hardly walk.")

Breen was reading his Bible and keeping his diary, one of the most soul-shocking documents in our literature. It details the weather and the deaths, not much language spent on suffering or despair. The great winds, the great snows, how the hides and bones were holding out, sometimes a prayer remembered from the Mass or the litany, and who died — that is what Patrick Breen put down. How the Graveses confiscated the hides that Margaret Reed had bought with promises, how Milt Elliott made good his demand that Margaret be given a hide — the Keseberg baby died last night — "Eddy's child died last night," February 5, with Eddy climbing toward Bear Valley in the rain to save little Margaret's life. Then Mrs. Eddy is growing weaker — Spitzer dies — Mrs. Eddy dies —

Keseberg never gets up from bed (Breen had his suspicions of Keseberg and listed the valuables he hoarded, which might not have been his at first) — "Milt Elliott died last night at Murphy's shanty," the last friend of the Reed family gone — John Denton, the English gunsmith, growing weaker — Mrs. Graves takes back the hide that Milt had got for Mrs. Reed (title to it really vested in John Augustus Sutter) — "wind SE all in good health Thanks be to Almighty God Amen" — and the First Relief arrives.

The seven gave them a little food — it was not safe to give them more — posted a guard over the packs, and got their first full night's sleep in a week. The next morning, three of them went on down to Alder Creek. None had died there since the report Milt Elliott brought back, but George Donner appeared to be dying. Tamsen was still strong. Her small body had the toughness of her Yankee forbears. She would not leave and neither would Elizabeth, Jacob's widow. So the rescuers took four of the older children, Tamsen's daughters Elitha and Leanna and Elizabeth's sons George and William Hook. They also took Noah James and the widow Wolfinger. They left the Donner women and the younger children with one man to take care of them, the worthless Jean Baptiste Trubode. They were counting on the Reed-Greenwood relief being just behind them, and surely Passed Midshipman Woodworth, that staunch commander, would be sending other relief parties with ample food. They went back to the lake, where their companions were trying to decide which of the babbling, cursing survivors could or should attempt the trip.

That left eleven at Alder Creek. Elitha and Leanna had a piece of blanket over their clothes — good, substantial clothes, for the Donners had been richly outfitted. They were in great pain and they kept sitting down in the snow to cry. Those left at Alder Creek had only one hide remaining. As the party started out Tamsen said staunchly that if food did not come by the time it was used up, they would begin eating what they had refrained from eating.

At the lake the seven made their decision. All the Reeds were to go and their surviving hired girl, Eliza Williams, by now an innocent. Only Edward, thirteen, and Simon, nine, of the Breen family — who had plenty of hides. William, Eleanor, and Lovina Graves; their father had died on the Forlorn Hope (the rescuers carefully lied, saying that everyone who tried the crossing had survived), Mary and Sarah had got through, their mother and younger brothers and sisters would wait for the next rescue party. William Murphy, eleven, who had started with the Forlorn Hope but had to come back, and his sister Mary — leaving their mother, feeble and going blind, and ten-year-old Simon, and the Pike baby and little George Foster, Mrs. Murphy's grandchildren. She would also try to take care of James Eddy, William's surviving child. Mrs. Keseberg was to go, with the surviving Ada, but Keseberg was too sick to make the attempt — and, if later suspicions were correct, he had his eye on the property of the dead. The dying John Denton would start, too, and John Rhoads would carry Naomi Pike, daughter of Harriet Pike of the Forlorn Hope and granddaughter of the widow Murphy.

Seventeen from the lake, leaving seventeen there, and six from Alder Creek — twenty-three all told started with the seven rescuers on February 22. The calm weather still held. They had not gone far when it became obvious that three-year-old Tommy Reed and his eight-year-old sister Patty could not make the journey and were endangering the lives of the whole party. Glover, the real leader, told Mrs. Reed that they must be taken back to the huts. She had no recourse but she swore him on his honor as a Mason to come back for them if their father could not. "That was the hardest thing yet," Virginia's account runs, "to leave the children in those cabins — not knowing but they would starve to death. Martha [Patty] said, 'well Mother, if you never see me again, do the best you can.' The men said they could hardly stand it: it made them cry." That must have been Mootrey and Glover, who took the two children back to the huts, and Patty told them that she was willing to care for her brother but knew she would not see her mother again. The Breens refused to take them in. Mootrey and Glover had to make detailed promises of reward and at last had to supplement them with threats. Even so they doubted if the children could survive the unwatched charity of the Breens.

We need not detail the progress of children and adults through the snow. The first day Denton failed on the trail and had to be carried into camp. The next day he failed altogether. They built a fire for him and left far more than his share of food, wrapped him in a blanket, and left him to his courage. When they reached the first cache, it had been rifled by martens — and now there was exceedingly little food for anyone. There was nothing to do but to send the two strongest ahead, Mootrey and Coffeemeyer (the latter's snowshoes had been eaten, overnight, by one of his charges). Glover and Dan Rhoads had to go with them; they were exhausted, of no further use. They would either meet another relief party or raise one of the remaining caches and bring back food. That left

Sels, Tucker, and John Rhoads to bully and exhort the twenty survivors, give them a shoulder for a few rods, cajole and carry the children by turns. They built fires on log platforms by night. At evening on the fifth day Mootrey and Coffeemeyer came in with packs replenished from the cache at Bear Valley. But they brought also the terrifying news that they had not met any of the other parties who by now should be here.

The packs were replenished — two packs. A little beef, a little bread, and clearly no further help to be counted on. In the morning they started out again. They must be seen in a line stretching westward below the peaks, among the evergreens, in the snow and silence of the heights. So James Frazier Reed saw them, who was hurrying his Second Relief forward, having met Glover and Dan Rhoads the night before. "Left camp on a fine, hard snow," Reed's curt record says, written by firelight in fifteen feet of snow, "and proceeded about four miles, when we met the poor, unfortunate starved people. As I met them scattered along the trail, I distributed some bread that I had baked last night. I gave in small quantities to each. Here I met my wife and two of my little children. Two of my children are still in the mountains. I cannot describe the death-like look all these people had. 'Bread!' 'Bread!' 'Bread!' 'Bread!' was the begging cry of every child and grown person. I gave all I had to give them and set out for the scene of desolation at the lake. I am now camped within twenty-five miles of the place, which I hope to reach by traveling tonight and tomorrow."

Margaret Reed fainted when the cry came down the straggling line that her husband was here, but Virginia ran and fell and ran again over crusted snow till she was in his arms. They had last seen each other on the Humboldt, with Snyder buried and Milt Elliott cocking his rifle lest Keseberg should prop up his wagon tongue again for a desert hanging. But Patty and Tommy were at the lake, with the unwilling Breens. . . . Reed told the saved that behind him the swiftly organizing Californians were building a series of way stations for them, bountifully supplied with food. The vigilant, resolute Passed Midshipman Woodworth would take care of them. They were, his diary says, "overjoyed." He led his party on and the saved took up the trail again.

Two days later they reached Mule Springs, where by now Woodworth had come up and made a camp. Military man's camp, with brandy to drink and strikers to rub the commander's feet with snow, lest they be frostbitten. The victims of winter thought tenderly of his risks and discomforts, and the next morning mounted the horses that had been brought here for them and rode down toward green earth and warm weather. Virginia Reed was not yet fourteen years old but this was a frontier community they were coming down to, after all, and one of the emigrants who was shepherding them had an eye to the needs of the commonwealth. He looked at this skinny child and proposed marriage. By that token Virginia, giggling an unpractised refusal, knew that the ordeal was over and they had come in. (Three months later she wrote her cousin Mary, back in Springfield, "Tell the girls that this is the greatest place for marrying they ever saw and that they must come to California if they want to marry." Before the year was out she was married.) On March 4 they reached Sutter's and the nursing of Mrs. Sinclair.

When Reed, at the head of the Second Relief, met the First Relief coming down, his party had dwindled to ten. They had left old Caleb Greenwood at Mule Springs in charge of cattle and a base camp. McCutchen was with Reed, the great, powerful man who had crossed with Stanton to Sutter's long ago and fallen ill. He had seen his wife Amanda, of the Forlorn Hope, and when he met the First Relief he learned that their year-old daughter had died at the lake. But McCutchen would do his part, he would go on. Also with them was another emigrant responding to the need of his kind, Hiram Miller, who had been one of George Donner's drivers as far as Independence Rock and thence had ridden ahead with Edwin Bryant. The other seven were Greenwood's men, all but one of them trappers, young, sturdy, and experienced, several of them mountain-man French and among them Brit Greenwood and John Turner of the mighty oaths.

The incompetent Woodworth had missed all the meetings he had arranged with them, but men like Reed, McCutchen, Miller, Turner, and the Greenwoods did not need help or rely on it. So far they had come on their own, triumphantly, and they hurried on toward the lake. On the way they passed the frozen corpse of John Denton, sitting wrapped in his blanket at the foot of his tree. He had not needed the food in his pockets but before the end a strange need had come upon him. Dying as a man of honor in the snow, he had taken out his memorandum book and pencil and had written a poem. Reed and his companions did not find it when they passed but William Eddy did, a few days later, and here it is, from the hour of death in the snow.

O! after many roving years,
How sweet it is to come
Back to the dwelling place of youth —
Our first and dearest home: —
To turn away our wearied eyes
From proud ambition's towers,
And wander in those summer fields,
The scene of boyhood's hours.

But I am changed since last I gazed
Upon that tranquil scene,
And sat beneath the old witch-elm
That shades the village green;
And watched my boat upon the brook —
It was a regal galley,
And sighed for not a joy on earth
Beyond the happy valley.

I wish I could once more recall
That bright and blissful joy,
And summon to my weary heart
The feelings of a boy.
But now on scenes of past delight
I look, and feel no pleasure,
As misers on the bed of death
Gaze coldly on their treasure.[1]

Reed had pushed three of the youngest ahead, Clark, Cady, and Stone. The day after the meeting with the First Relief these three got to within two miles of the cabins, where they saw some Indians. (Diggers, probably from Winnemucca's mangy little tribe, who had been afraid to investigate the huts closely and had been further scared by reports from their most resolute scouts that the white men were eating one another.) They had no arms, wondered if the Indians had killed the survivors, and camped without a fire.

Early in the morning of March 1, Clark, Cady, and Stone went on down to the first hut. They distributed a little food and Clark and Cady pushed on to Alder Creek. The others came up at noon and Reed found that Patty and Tommy were alive. The little boy did not know him but Patty's disbelief was cured; presently she had the duty of distributing one biscuit apiece to the living. At the Murphy cabin they found Stone washing the children's clothes. They took off their own clothes — need one remark that there were lice? — and began to bathe little James Eddy and George Foster.

They needed the bath: for two weeks they had not been moved from the bed. Finishing this sanitation, Reed and McCutchen began to bathe the disabled Keseberg, who once had propped up his wagon tongue to invoke the justice of the trail on Reed.

Just outside the hut was the dismembered, recognizable body of Milt Elliott, Reed's driver and the protector of his family. It was nine days since the First Relief had left the lake, and in that interval the survivors had reached the extremity. Breen's diary, six days earlier, stated: "Mrs. Murphy said here yesterday that [she] thought she would commence on Milt and eat him." She had. The conscientious Thornton adds, "Half consumed limbs were seen concealed in trunks. Bones were scattered about. Human hair of different colors was seen in tufts about the fireplace."

And at Alder Creek the same. Clark and Cady got there at a moment when Trubode, sent by Tamsen to borrow a meal from Elizabeth, was returning with a leg of Elizabeth's husband, Jacob, and the message that the best of neighbors would be able to spare no more. At sight of the rescuers, he tossed the now unneeded leg back on the butchered corpse. Jacob's surviving children "were sitting upon a log, with their faces stained with blood, devouring the half roasted liver and heart of the[ir] father, unconscious of the approach of the men, of whom they took not the slightest notice even after they came up."

Elizabeth had not eaten the food her children fed on, and she was nearly dead. George Donner, Reed's old friend, with whom he had shared the dream of California in the long planning of an earlier winter — George Donner had a few words of friendship for him but seemed to be dying. Tamsen, keeping her resolution, had kept her strength also. Reed could see the bearded face of his other old friend, Jacob, in the snow, the head cut off from the body and the brain opened.

Tamsen would not leave her husband. George, pointing out that he was dying, bade her go. But the honor of marriage sustained her. She would stay beside him while he died.

Reed decided that the younger children also must stay here. Surely Woodworth would arrive in two or three days at most, and he was able to leave food enough to last a week. So Tamsen's three youngest daughters, Frances, Georgia, and Eliza, and Elizabeth's two youngest sons, Lewis and Samuel, would stay at Alder Creek, waiting for the largest and best supplied of all the relief parties, as Woodworth's would surely be. Reed left Cady and Clark to care for them and took Elizabeth's three remaining children with him. At the lake he chose Patrick and Margaret Breen, Mrs. Graves, and eleven children. That left the two helpless adults, Keseberg and Mrs. Murphy, and three children, Simon Murphy, James Eddy, and George Foster. Stone was left to care for them, and Woodworth with many men and much food must come down from the pass any day now, perhaps tomorrow.

Woodworth was not coming; he never came. He was taking his comfort in camp and nourishing what, compared with the courage of the others, can only be called an ignominious cowardice. So the return of the Second Relief, which should have been the most successful, constitutes the final catastrophe of the Donner party.

Like the First Relief, Reed's men had been scrupulous not to allude to the deaths of the Forlorn Hope, and Mrs. Graves was taking to her dead son-in-law, Jay Fosdick, the violin she had watched over for him at the huts. Patrick Breen played on it for hours, the first two nights out, serene in the belief that they were safe at last. That music is a bizarre touch for already the Second Relief were in ghastly danger. They had counted on traveling faster than it was possible to travel with so many children, most of whom the seven rescuers had to carry in turn. And they were counting on meeting Woodworth, who was not coming.

Even before they got over the divide Reed sent three of his best men ahead — Turner, Gendreau, and Dofar — to bring back food, whether by lifting the nearest cache or by urging Woodworth on if they should meet him. The four remaining rescuers got their seventeen charges over the divide and down to the head of the Yuba, camping where the First Relief had camped. The three who had been sent ahead should join them here if they found the first cache intact. But it had been rifled by animals and they had had to go on.

On March 6 just such a storm as the Forlorn Hope had had to live through struck the Second Relief. From Reed's diary: "The men up nearly all night making fires. Some of the men begin praying. Several of them became blind. I could not see the light of the fire blazing before me nor tell when it was burning. . . . The snow blows so thick and fast that we cannot see twenty feet looking against the wind. I dread the coming night. Three of my men only able to get wood. 'Hungry,' 'Hungry,' is the cry with the children and nothing to give them. 'Freezing!' is the cry of the mothers who have nothing for their little, starving, freezing children. Night closing fast and with it the hurricane increases."

The storm lasted two full days and three nights. At one point Reed himself nearly died but they brought him back and his dauntless will revived. Once the fire was blown out altogether but McCutchen and Hiram Miller, demonic in the gale, got it blazing again. During the last night five-year-old Isaac Donner died quietly, unnoticed, lying between his sister Mary and Patty Reed. When the wind dropped and the snow ceased on March 8, they had to make their last try. The four rescuers could travel. They would take the two Reed children and Solomon Hook (Elizabeth Donner's son) and Mary Donner. The Graveses could not travel. The Breens would not — Patrick's will to survive had gone out and Reed's pleas and commands would not budge him. They cut wood for the eleven they were leaving behind and started off, Miller carrying Tommy Reed. That afternoon Patty seemed to be dying. Her father had saved about a teaspoonful of crumbs in the thumb of his mitten. He gave it to her, he warmed her with his own body, and the child came back. Her heart rose too: "God has not brought us so far to let us perish now," she told them. She is a slightly formidable child, this eight-year-old with an ancient fatalism and an ancient hope, but she was holding them to the job. The first night after the storm they camped beside the Yuba. The feet of several were frozen, notably Brit Greenwood's. No sign of Turner, Gendreau, and Dofar. No sight of Passed Midshipman Woodworth. But while they were rubbing their feet with snow beside the blazing fire, two men came down from the pass and joined them. Cady and Stone, who had been left to take care of the starving. They brought no one with them, not even a child. But they had a pack of table silver, silk dresses, and other valuables that had been the Donners'.

(It is not clear what had happened. Either fear broke their morale or they had planned robbery before they left the settlements. As soon as Reed and his company left the lake, Stone had forsaken his charge and joined Cady at Alder Creek. Clark was away, hunting a bear. There either Tamsen offered them five hundred dollars, or they demanded it, to take her three young children out. Tamsen washed and combed Frances, Georgia, and Eliza, dressed them in rich, warm clothes from the chests packed on the Sangamon, and made up the bundle of silk and silver that might buy the orphans a little care in California. She led them to the bed where George Donner still lived and they said good-bye to their father. "I may never see you again," she told the little girls, "but God will take care of you." Stone and Cady started out with them, took them as far as the huts at the lake — and left them at the Murphy cabin, striking out alone. The storm drove Stone and Cady back to the lake again. In the Murphy cabin, Keseberg was wild and hideous. A child cried out for bread and Eliza Donner heard a man's voice, Keseberg's, "Be quiet, you crying children, or I'll shoot you." Once she woke to find six-year-old Frances — Eliza was not yet four — forbidding Keseberg to pick her up, screaming that he wanted to kill her. The storm ended. Back at Alder Creek Elizabeth's three-year-old Lewis had died. Stone and Cady, who had been in the Breen cabin, now empty, started out again and in one day got over the divide and down to Reed's campfire. On the way they passed the pit where the fire made for the Breens and Graveses was sinking down through the snow.)

As Stewart says, "The sheriff's writ did not run in the mountains of California." Nothing could be said to men who had broken their trust: whosoever chooses to save his own skin is entitled to. In the morning they started off together, and another fraction of the Donner party were leaving bloody footprints on the snow. Late in the afternoon they found some food hanging from a tree at the end of a rope. Turner, Gendreau, and Dofar had hung it there, finding a little left in the second cache. They struggled on. They camped for the night, building another fire. Cady and Brit Greenwood, their toes frozen, pushed on a little way. They shouted to the others. Their shouts were answered — from the wrong direction. The tip of another relief party had reached them. Howard Oakley and John Starks, of that party, came to the fire with food. Later, Midshipman Woodworth, here making his farthest venture toward the pass, came up. Later still the two men appeared who had shamed, threatened, and bullied Woodworth to this effort. They were William Eddy and William Foster of the Forlorn Hope, who two months before had been murderously attacking each other in the snow.

Reed and those with him were safe now. But there were the Breens and Graveses back in the snow, and there were the others at the lake and Alder Creek. Woodworth's band had the sight of those drained men to make them thoughtful, and moreover had met Turner, Gendreau, and Dofar, who were in as bad shape or perhaps worse. Eddy and Foster were blazing to go on but at first could get no companions except John Starks, who had come up with Woodworth, and the staunch Hiram Miller, who had just come down with Reed. Eddy and Foster pleaded with the others and finally determined to go alone. Reed persuaded them against suicide, got them all to go back to Woodworth's luxurious base camp in Bear Valley, and there renewed his pledges of high pay. Howard Oakley volunteered. So did another of Woodworth's men, named Thompson. So did Starks and Hiram Miller. So did the recreant Stone. Hiram Miller, Thompson, Foster, and Eddy would go on to the lake. Starks, Oakley, and Stone would bring on the surviving Breens and Graveses from their camp in the snow. On March 11, the Third Relief really got going. Let it be remembered that Foster and Eddy had been with the Forlorn Hope, and Hiram Miller had just escaped death on the Second Relief.

It was at Woodworth's camp that Patty Reed revealed the secret she had kept throughout this last journey of cold and agony. Before leaving the huts she had wrapped up her treasure in a little bundle. Doubtless it had sustained her through the days after her mother left her there. Doubtless it had been a solace through long days of dust along the trail last summer and she had cherished it when the wagons parked at night beneath twisted buttes or when she came footsore to bed in the Wasatch or when the grownups argued or despaired along the Humboldt. Leaving the lake she had hidden it under her dress, knowing that the men would make her throw away the slightest weight, even so slight a weight as this. There was a tiny glass saltcellar, one of those jewels that are precious to children. There was a small wooden doll with black hair and black eyes. And there was a lock of gray hair, her grandmother's hair. When Mrs. Keyes had died, way back at the Big Blue, Patty herself had snipped that lock before they buried Grandmother, before John Denton, now dead below the Sierra, chiseled her name in stone. She had wrapped them all in a shred of lawn dotted with blue flowers. Now she was safe in California and could bring out the treasure and settle down to play.

It was due to the will of Eddy and Foster that Woodworth had nerved himself to come as far as this. Coming back to Johnson's ranch with the horses which the First Relief had had to abandon, Eddy had stayed on there, recruiting his strength. So had Foster, whose sanity returned. The two men were friends again, companions in anxiety. The return of the First Relief with its starving refugees informed Eddy that his wife and daughter were dead but that his son and Foster's were still living when the refugees left. When the last storm ended the two got horses and rode furiously toward the mountains, knowing that the Second Relief would be in terrible danger but believing that Woodworth would be hurrying to rescue them. Reaching Woodworth, who bandaged his cowardice with innumerable justifications, they had cursed him and his five men as far as the camp from which they had heard the shouts of Reed's party.

Now the seven of the Third Relief, on two errands, were starting off on the morning of March 11. Late in the afternoon of the twelfth they reached the survivors in the pit which their sinking fire had made — twenty-five feet deep, bare ground at the bottom. It was the fifth day since Reed had left here. Little Isaac had died before that. Since then the five-year-old Franklin Graves had died and so had his mother. Her year-old daughter Elizabeth, when the rescuers got there, "sat at her side," Thornton says, "one arm on the body of its mangled mother, and sobbing bitterly cried 'Ma! Ma! Ma!' " The mother's body was indeed mangled, for the Breens had cooked her breasts and most of the meat from her arms and legs. Nor was there much left of the little bodies of Franklin Graves and Isaac Donner.

The Relief had thought that more than these would be dead, and Stone and Oakley were for leaving the Breens there and taking the rest down. Starks refused. He was a big man, as big as McCutchen, and nothing was too hard for him. It is due to his efforts principally that all these came through. (Though little Elizabeth Graves died, after reaching safety.) Oakley and Stone took one child apiece and made a quick trip down. Starks carried, jollied, bullied, bribed, and promised his flock through three and a half days — one of the biggest achievements of the whole story. Then Eddy and Foster with their party caught up with him, coming down from the pass, and almost at once another relief party, coming up, reached them all. For the undaunted Glover, Coffeemeyer, and Mootrey were coming back again — and had shamed Woodworth into coming, at least this far, with them.

Eddy, Foster, Thompson, and Miller, after leaving the camp whence Starks was taking his charges down, were able to cross the divide in a few hours. It was still early morning when Eddy and Foster sprinted ahead and reached the huts at the lake. Mrs. Murphy, nearly blind and almost dead, answered their question with a single word. George Foster and James Eddy were dead. The terrified Donner children thought then, and thought throughout their lives, that Keseberg, now a mere sac of bestiality, had killed little George Foster. They were probably right. Whether they were or not, Keseberg could stand there in the hut and remark to Eddy and Foster that he had eaten their sons.

Besides Keseberg and Mrs. Murphy, there were still alive in this room littered with filth and butchered corpses the three Donner girls, Simon Murphy, and — Tamsen Donner. Tamsen had come here from Alder Creek desperate for word about her children — for Clark had seen them here, though for days she had supposed they had been taken safely over the pass. She had become dazed before she could reach the huts and Simon Murphy had led her in.

She had strength left, however, and God knows she had the will that endures. She could have gone over the divide with this, the Third Relief. But George Donner, her husband, somehow had not yet died when she left Alder Creek. Moreover, she supposed that Clark and Trubode were there, and she had a duty to tell them the rescuers had come. Eddy pleaded with her, setting out the logic of her going with him. But no. If they would wait while she went back to her own huts at Alder Creek (Elizabeth was dead, everyone was dead but George and Elizabeth's little Samuel) it might be that they would find that her husband had died. Then her duty would be discharged and she could save her life. Also, they could tell Clark and Trubode to bring Samuel. William Eddy rightly said no. The trip would consume another full day and they could not wait. They had no food for an extra day, they could not risk the coming of another storm. So Tamsen shook her head. She said good-bye once more to Frances, Georgia, and Eliza. She would go back and sit beside George Donner and, when the time came, close his eyes.

Two hours after reaching the huts, the Third Relief — merely four men of stout hearts — started back. Mrs. Murphy obviously could not be taken. Neither — if anyone cared — could Keseberg. They did what they could for the dying widow Murphy and then took charge of a child apiece. Miller carried Eliza but the others could mostly walk by themselves. They reached the foot of the pass and camped for the night. . . . And Clark and Trubode joined them, Clark carrying a heavy pack of loot, instead of Samuel Donner, whom he might have brought from Alder Creek.

The rest is the memories of children. On the second day Hiram Miller's kindness cracked and Eliza remembered that he bribed her to walk with a promise of sugar which he did not have. Then he punished her. She was lonesome for her mother. Frances stormed at Eliza's persecutor. Eddy found a bundle beside the trail, and when they opened it at the evening fire it proved to be the spoons and silks which Cady had abandoned when his feet swelled. So Thompson, who had previously made some moccasins for Frances, got out his needle again and from the fine silk dresses made sleeping bags for the three little girls. They wore them on the trail too, the next day — the dove-colored silk for Frances, the light brown for Georgia, and the dark brown for Eliza. Eliza remembered passing a dim, wailing line of children and John Starks setting two down from his shoulders beside the trail and going back for two more. Then there was shouting. They had met Glover, Coffeemeyer, Mootrey, and Woodworth. It was March 17 and their mother had been right. God had taken care of the children who had been told always to say that they were the children of George Donner.

"Often we looked at each other and exclaimed 'How good to be here instead of up in the snow.'" Thus Eliza Donner, remembering Sutter's, the universal inn and hospital at the end of the California trail. And Virginia Reed, writing from the same place to Cousin Mary back home, "It is a beautiful country. It is mostly in vallies and mountains. It ought to be a beautiful country to pay us for our troubles in getting to it."

The survivors were brought down to Sutter's as soon as they could travel, and there they might grow from death to life and to the expectation of a new home in the West. Two families had come through intact, the Reeds and the Breens, the most complex nervous systems, one thinks, and the simplest. The others were variously reduced. All the Donners were orphans (Hiram Miller would be appointed their guardian) and William Eddy had lost his entire family. Everyone who has written about the Donners has remarked that the women had withstood the trial better than the men.

Back in the mountains there were George and Tamsen Donner, their nephew Samuel, Mrs. Murphy, and Keseberg. Woodworth, the titular head of the entire relief enterprise, should have kept on after Foster and Eddy met him coming back — should have taken his fresh men over the divide to save any of the five who could be saved. Passed Midshipman Woodworth was just no damned good. His stomach would not take danger, and besides the audience was in the settlements. He turned west again and if the commander would not undertake another relief, who should? The men went back with him to Sutter's — but McKinstry ordered Woodworth back to his job. He had no difficulty getting volunteers — John Rhoads, Starks, Coffeemeyer, Sels, Tucker, all veterans of the reliefs, and William Foster again, and even young William Graves, who had been down out of the snow only two weeks. They started about March 23 but got no farther than Bear Valley. Woodworth was timid and with slack leadership the men were slack. They knew that George and Samuel Donner would be dead by now and that if life remained to Mrs. Murphy she could not be brought out. No one cared what might happen to Keseberg and Tamsen Donner had made her choice. So when another great storm blew up, the Fourth Relief turned back.

The final expedition differed from the others. It was made primarily to salvage the property of the survivors, and it initiated a bickering that was to last for a long time. It was headed by Thomas Fallon, who seems to have been a Canadian mountain man and was just back from marching with Frémont. Five veterans of the reliefs joined him, Sels, Coffeemeyer, Tucker, John Rhoads, and the now tireless William Foster. There was also a novice, an emigrant named Keyser from Johnson's. They left Johnson's on April 13 and found no snow till they reached the head of Bear Valley, whence they went in, like all their predecessors, on foot with packs. They thought that Tamsen and Keseberg might still be alive but found no one at the lake, which they reached on April 17. They did find a scene which shocked Fallon, whose nerves were probably strong. He mentions the body of Mrs. Eddy, "the limbs sawed off and a frightful gash in the skull," and other "sights from which we would have fain turned away." They went on to Alder Creek, which looked worse. The Donner property, broken open by Keseberg and probably by Diggers as well, was scattered all about, "books, calicoes, tea, coffee, shoes, percussion caps, household and kitchen furniture." At the mouth of a hut — the snow had mostly melted away — was a kettle full of pieces of the body of George Donner. They judged that, amazingly, he had been dead no longer than four days. They noticed that legs of oxen, reclaimed from the snow that had preserved them, had not been eaten.

They made up packs of valuables and four of them started back to the lake. There they found Keseberg, whose tracks they had seen in the melting snow and who had been keeping away from them. He was "lying down amidst the human bones, and beside him a large pan full of fresh liver and lights."

Like a monomaniac squirrel, Keseberg had filled his noisome burrow with possessions of the Donners. Fallon was a curt man; he put the rope to Keseberg's neck and commanded him to reveal where the money was — on behalf of the Donner orphans and of Thomas Fallon also. He got $517. Cady and Stone had got as much before. No more of the thousands of dollars in cash which the Donners brought with them is known to have been found.

Fallon and his veterans could discover no liking for Keseberg.

A century later it is difficult to discount their suspicions. His story was that Tamsen had come to the lake in delirium after George Donner died. She was raving, her babble of children, the pass, her dead husband. Keseberg said he warmed her and put her to bed and the next morning found her dead. The salvage party could identify no trace of her body, unless there might be fragments of it in the pan or in "the two kettles of human blood, in all supposed to be over a gallon." Since she had been in excellent strength three weeks before, in fact a little corpulent, they believed that Keseberg had killed her. He denied it and went on denying it through the rest of his life. But there in the cabin he told them that "he ate her body and found her flesh the best he had ever tasted. He further stated that he obtained from her body at least four pounds of fat."

They could not identify any fragment of Mrs. Murphy's body, either, but Foster, her son-in-law, could recognize Landrum Murphy, "who had been dead about three months, with the breast and skull cut open and the brains, liver, and lights taken out." . . . One final testimony to the degeneration of human personality under stresses that had hardened others into nobility. "We asked Kiesburg [Fallon's spelling] why he did not use the meat of the bullock and horse instead of human flesh, he replied he had not seen them. We then told him we knew better and asked him why the meat in the chair had not been consumed, he said 'Oh! it's too dry eating!' the liver and lights were a good deal better, and the brains made good soup!"

(Edwin Bryant, passing here with Kearny two months later, says that at Alder Creek they found George Donner's body decently wrapped in a sheet. If so, then this last party, perhaps at the behest of Foster who had come down the trail with him, had done this final decency.)

They took Keseberg with them when they started back on April 23, as they might have taken an abandoned dog from the scene of a friend's disaster. The snow in the pass was only six feet deep. On the twenty-fifth they were back at their horse camp. The episode was over, and so was the work of Lansford Hastings. There had been eighty-two of them when they reached the Sierra, after five had died this side of the Wasatch. Thirty-five of these had died and, besides them, two of the rescuers, Luis and Salvador, the Indians. Forty-seven had come through to the end of the trail and might now set about fulfilling the dream that had started them toward Independence on this journey, in April just a year before Fallon brought Keseberg down to Bear Valley.

XVI

Whether It Be Fat or Lean: Canaan

ON November 24, 1846, Hosea Stout, the captain of Israel's guard, moved into his new house at Winter Quarters. It was not much of a house — "neither door nor windows not even but a few of the craks was yet stoped up and a hard North wind blowing." But it was about as good a shelter as any in this town and better than most. Hosea remarked that it would be hard to burn the Saints out, so many of them were living in dugouts, caves in the bluffs, or log shacks roofed with dirt. But John D. Lee, coming back from Santa Fe with the Mormon Battalion's pay, looked at those hundreds of buildings and was proud. "No other people but the Saints of God," he said, "has ever been known to accomplish so much in so short a time."

The accomplishment had had a price. Shivering through the first night in his cabin, Hosea Stout remembered that there had been no roof over his family since he left Nauvoo, nine months and fifteen days before.

> During which time we have under went almost every change of fortune that could be imagined. One half of my family so dear to me has been consigned to the silent grave & we who yet remain have often been brought to the verge of death often in storms & rains have I stood to hold my tent from uncovering my sick family expecting every moment to see them exposed to the rain & wind which would have been certain death. . . . How often in sorrow & anguish have I said in my heart when shall my trials and tribulations end. But amid all these adverse changes, these heart wrending trials not once yet have I ever regretted that I set out to follow the council of the people of God & to obey the voice of the spirit to flee from the land of the Gentiles.

One of Hosea's wives and three of his children had died on the way to Winter Quarters. The death of little Hosea, the father's favorite, had been particularly horrible, for a devil had entered into the child's body, twisting and contorting it. The priesthood cast out the devil so that the child's spasms and delirium quieted and he died peacefully. . . . Hosea had one child left now, one child and two wives. The child was to fall into a long stupor and die and one of the wives was to die in childbirth, before the winter was out.

It is the sheer bad health of Winter Quarters and the other camps that most impresses one who reads the journals of the Saints. (They themselves called the Missouri bottoms, "Misery Bottoms.") They were now paying in full for a year of terrorism and a summer and fall of forced migration. It amounted to another tax assessed by the mobbers and today, all the way across Iowa, you can find little clusters of graves, the winter's fatalities where groups of Saints had settled down. Winter Quarters was not only the largest but the richest and healthiest of the camps, and in Winter Quarters burial parties were always at work. The old wives exhausted their brews of prairie simples, the priesthood laid their hands on the afflicted and spoke the holy incantations. Even the indestructible John D. Lee sickened. His third wife, Louisa, lay and embraced him for two hours. (She only caught the infection.) Neither herbs nor a saleratus bath restored him. Finally he called on his father by spiritual adoption, Brigham Young. The prophet came and "laid on my breast a cane built from one of the branches of the Tree of Life that stood in the garden of the Temple." Then Apostle Woodruff rebuked the sickness and promised Lee that his earthly usefulness would continue and that "Heavenly visions of Eternity" would be opened to him. The disease withdrew but there was no physician to heal the physicians and both Young and Woodruff were sick repeatedly.

East of Winter Quarters the other camps were worse. They had been composed of the poor and the infirm to begin with and had the smallest granaries. No colony escaped disease and death but the six hundred Saints at Garden Grove had the worst time. They had stripped their small store for the relief of the Poor Camp — the refugees from the final mobbing at Nauvoo — and had taken in many of these invalids. The Twelve sent such supplies as they could from Winter Quarters. The local authorities detailed laborers to work among the Gentiles, scoured the countryside for help, and even sent missions as far as Kentucky and Ohio to collect any charity that might be had — a barrel of flour, a yard of cloth to make a child's dress, a side of bacon or a pig of lead. They lay and shivered in their sod huts. The autumnal agues lingered on. They were ravaged by scurvy and pneumonia. By April their food was gone entirely.

Winter Quarters had been established when it was finally determined that Grand Island would not do and could not be reached in force, anyway. Bishop George Miller's company, which had been in the lead most of the way to the Missouri and had several times been ordered to go on to the mountains (until Young finally made up his mind) — Bishop Miller's company pushed on to the Ponca village at the mouth of the Niobrara.[1] Here most of the group that had joined James Emmett (the scout whom Joseph had sent West) attached themselves to Miller and shared a winter of discontent that finally ended in apostasy.

There was another sizable detachment of Saints far from Brigham's control. They had started out from Mississippi in April under William Crosby and John Brown, instructed to pick up the main emigration of the Saints somewhere along the trail. Since the main body never reached the trail, they traveled it in ignorance till July 2. That day they reached Ash Hollow and met Jim Clyman, who was coming east. Clyman performed his last service to the emigration of '46 by telling them that there were no Mormons ahead of them anywhere on the trail.

They were dumbfounded by the information. After counsel, they continued up the trail, nineteen wagons, twenty-four men, a miscellany of wives and children, and five Negro slaves. They got to Fort Bernard and so were farther west than any other Mormons got in '46 except the Battalion and the obscure few who, like the Rhoads family, made the trip to California with Gentile trains.

At Fort Bernard, Richard, the bourgeois, advised them to winter on the upper Arkansas and, starting with some robes for Taos, offered to guide them. He took them to a trappers' winter stockade at the Pueblo (Colorado). "We were received very kindly," John Brown's *Autobiography* says, "and they [the trappers] seemed pleased to see us." They began to build cabins for the winter.

On August 20 Francis Parkman, coming down from Fort Laramie to Bent's Fort, reached the Pueblo and met his old friend Richard, who "entertained us hospitably in the little round room, the best in the fort, and gave us a good supper on the floor." Brother Therlkill, who had recently been mauled by a grizzly, dropped in that evening and asked Parkman some personal questions, eventually begetting another shudder in *The Oregon Trail.* Next day Parkman rode over to visit the Saints. His notebook says, "Found them at work upon their log houses but they suspended their labors to talk with us. Some of them completely imbued with the true fanatic spirit — ripe for anything — a very dangerous body of men."

They were just some devout Mormons far from home but their manners were too rude for Francis Parkman.

There at the Pueblo they were joined by the families of the Mormon Battalion that had been sent on from the crossing of the Arkansas.[2] On November 17 the laundresses and the "Sick Detachment," whom Cooke had sent on from Santa Fe, arrived under Captain James Brown and Lieutenant Elam Luddington. Later still the last detachment of Battalion invalids joined them. All told about three hundred Mormons spent the winter at the Pueblo.

Winter Quarters, Perrigrine Sessions remarked with satisfaction, was "surrounded by the Lamanites on all sides and over one hundred miles from the cursed Gentiles." The Lamanites were of the Omaha tribe, an unmilitary but thievish race who constantly stole the cattle of their Nephite brethren and kept running to them for help against the Sioux, Oto, and Potawatomi. Working out an Indian policy for use hereafter, Young tried every method from flogging to overfeeding but no method got results. Yet the Omaha have a uniqueness in history: they were a people who could endure more "counsel," harangues, and sermonizing than the Mormons.

Young had chosen to build his city on Omaha land several miles downriver from the first crossing. The site, today a suburb of the city of Omaha, was selected on the stated ground that it was favorable for defense by John Scott's homemade three-pounders. For terror of mobs and government lingered on, there were repeated rumors of impending destruction, and the U. S. Dragoons were always coming in force to arrest the Twelve. Little outpost groups were as much as twelve miles in the interior, and there were small settlements north and south as well as across the river in Iowa. But the principal group, about thirty-five hundred, was at Winter Quarters and built there a town of six or seven hundred rude structures. And John D. Lee was quite right: nobody but the Saints had ever done anything remotely like it.

The most important element in the preservation of the Church was Young's conversion of the dizzy sacerdotal system which Joseph Smith had created into a system of fiscal administration and control. It was a long process but the beginning was made right here. The Church was a delirious network of councils, committees, degrees, lodges, and societies, all based on eternal mysteries which multiplied so fast that there was never time to get any of them quite clear. They overlapped so badly that it is doubtful if the more exalted Saints knew themselves just which ones they belonged to or just how many holy prerogatives they possessed. Young was constantly getting entangled in the sacred red tape, and the journals of such honest subalterns as Lee and Stout record a bewildered effort to keep the jurisdictions straight that frequently ended in quarrels. But Young kept his mind centered on his goal: to save Israel here and now and to build up its inheritance in this world. He made Winter Quarters a town and a church. Civil and ecclesiastical organizations were coterminous. He was to simplify the organization as time went on but here, even before starting, he shaped the instrument that eventually conquered the desert.

Nothing in American history — not the ephemeral towns of mining rushes nor the hardier ones of real-estate booms — is like Winter Quarters. An entire people had uprooted itself and, on the way to the mountains, paused here and put down roots. The endless church government went on. Not only the other camps had to be managed from Winter Quarters but all the missions too, in the United States and overseas. Supplies had to be kept moving; hundreds of teams were out all the time, freighting grain, flour, beef, pork, hardware, dry goods. Brigham invested most of the Battalion's first pay, which Lee brought back, in foodstuffs which he sold to the Saints through his own firm. The money belonged to Battalion families in fact, though theory consecrated it to the Church. There was much grumbling and Brigham finally yielded to it, at least in part, but he turned an honest profit on the deal. (The grumbling was unjustified, for life at Winter Quarters was easier after the supplies arrived.) He also conscripted labor to build a gristmill from which he expected to make twenty dollars a day. He dispatched Saints to work for the Gentiles wherever jobs could be found. Others had to herd the thirty thousand cattle and innumerable sheep, which the desirous Omaha simply could not leave alone. Scores were on wood duty, gathering fuel. Some trapped, some hunted, some made baskets. Israel had to work in order to live and the prophet made sure that there was little time for the dangerous pursuit of leisure.

Well, Peletiah Brown had proved to be a profane swearer when he hired out to William Clayton, Zion's clerk. So no one was surprised when, on complaint of Apostle Woodruff, it appeared that he and Daniel Barnum and Jack Clothier had been out for fifteen successive nights with some of the girls, committing the crime of "adultery or having carnal communication." In the mores of a polygamous society there is no greater crime. The boys expected either death or castration when Colonel Hosea Stout and Marshal Eldredge came for them. But the Marshal let them off with a sound flogging. The punishment shocked Israel and so great a murmur rose that Brigham had to justify his police in open meeting. And the Word of Wisdom, which forbade strong drink, was disregarded to the extent of the available supply. Brigham's own freighting company imported whiskey which was sold over the counter in Brigham's own store. With that sanction, they used liquor who could buy or make it. Hosea Stout's guards and rangers needed solace, for they had to patrol the town in all weathers and were always riding out to scout imaginary enemies. One night three Apostles came to reason with the police, who had protested when their pay was cut. Hosea found the best solvent and Orson Hyde, Parley Pratt, and John Taylor, holy men all, took a grateful turn at the jug. Parley would know how to find protection from now on, he said, and Hosea spoke wisdom: "Parley, do you not know that some things in this kingdom are only spiritually discerned?" . . . The trouble was that such discernment might end in resentment of the priesthood. Eventually Brigham (though he made a regional wine from some wild grapes) had to denounce the traffic. But it kept on and, as they started west, the Lord Himself had to reprove His Saints for drunkenness.

There was, the truth is, a lot of denunciation at Winter Quarters. The Saints were afraid of the mob behind them and the wilderness ahead. They were sick and underfed. Their hovels were uncomfortable. They could not love the outbreaks of communism that levied on their goods for the poor. They hankered for more celestial fireworks than Brigham had time or willingness to give them. They but incompletely developed the holy docility that he desired for them. "It is the policy and intention to put down any spirit in the Camp of Israel that would seek to establish independence," Norton Jacob wrote, and loyally added, "I say Amen." Tirelessly pursuing transgression, Brigham scolded, fumed, denounced, derided, threatened, and rebuked. This people must find righteousness or they would be swept from the earth. Covetousness and insubordination must end or they would "all be destroyed by the Lamanites as were the Nephites of old." He summoned them to reform. He would bring them to grace by his own hand. And he warned them that when they started into the desert the "law of God in every particular would take full effect and that would cut the matter short, even as short as the man who went to cut a dog's tail off and by mistake he cut it close behind the ears." It was due notice and something of a revival answered it, the Saints hurrying to confess and be rebaptized in the icy Missouri for the remission of sins.

There was not enough revival, however, to slake the thirst of a millennial people for the glories Joseph had accustomed them to. There are times when Mormonism seems a single, sustained harangue. They outdid the Indians and the Germans in passionate love of exhortation. The innumerable holy orders kept meeting and preaching. They petitioned for more. Brigham was too busy. He preferred to discuss fiscal affairs — and even there set a limit to oratory, as, growing bored with the Omaha mourning their dead, he sent out guards to shut them up. So at the Council House he could put an end to talk. "The thing was talked out of countenance," Hosea Stout says, "and finally Prest. Brigham Young moved to have the whole matter laid over till the first resurrection and then burn the papers the day before."

But if the flavor of miracle was lacking and if the reformation loudly demanded by Heber Kimball proved fairly quiet, the thirst could be slaked at the daily meetings of the priesthood's divisions. Winter Quarters was not organized as a Stake of Zion (for doctrinal reasons and because there could be no substitute for a Temple), so the holy ordinances had to be suspended. But Brigham would make exceptions for his favorites, chief assistants, and spiritual family. Many faithful workers got the solace of young wives, sometimes the Twelve were permitted to reveal more of the celestial arcana, and there was always a sermon or a prayer meeting or an experience meeting or a fast.

If Israel always thirsted for three-hour harangues, it always hungered for the innocent pleasures of gregariousness. With the graveyard on the bluffs filling so fast that some of the dead could not even be given burial robes, the Saints still made as merry as they could. There were always parties, and a pan of hominy sprinkled with maple sugar was a "sweetmeat" acceptable unto the Lord. They gathered in the dugouts to pleasure themselves with frugal meals and the high spirits of the elect. The bands played every day. The children in dugout schools had games between sessions at Webster's spelling book, and their families had games, mock trials, elocution, singing classes, quiltings, all the diversions of the frontier society from which they came. About the turn of the year the improvement of transport made supplies more plentiful and a general rise in morale could be observed. The little private entertainments widened into a community program. The log Council House was turned over to various organizations, which were told to bring their "cakes, pies, sweetmeats &c" and praise God. "I will take the liberty of showing you how to dance before the Lord," Brigham had said. So, John D. Lee wrote, he "then bowed before the Lord, dedicated the hall to Him and asked

Him to accept of their offerings this evening, after which the band struck up a lively tune and in a moment the whole house appeared to me to be filled with the melodious sounds of the inspired harps of Heaven. Pres. B. Young led and went forth in the dance of praise before the Lord. About 10 Pres. B. Y. retired and about 11 the music ceased."

Over and above sickness, supply, doctrine, the administration of a fiscal and spiritual kingdom, and the refreshment of the weary — above all these was one paramount objective. Brigham was preparing the final Exodus. All through the summer and fall of '46 and the succeeding winter the prophet and his best minds examined its problems. Everyone who came down the river or eastward over the prairies was drained of his information. There were a good many of them, from Father De Smet, the great missionary who had spent a lifetime in the mountains, to casual strays from trading posts upriver. The Apostles learned what they could, made a census of Israel's resources, worked out minute calculations of what had to be done. The first fruits of this preparation — all that the faithful need know — were issued to a meeting of the Twelve at Heber Kimball's cabin on the afternoon of January 14. The Council was above Hosea Stout's station but, as commander of the guard, he was invited to attend nevertheless. His joy was great when he found that the Lord had taken this occasion to reveal to His servant Brigham the general orders for the migration.

This is the only formal revelation that Brigham Young ever issued, though of course he spoke by inspiration all his life long, as occasion might require. It is called "The Word and Will of the Lord," and it is a plan for the move west. The Lord did not require of the Saints more than they could accomplish. They were to maintain the organization of companies, hundreds, fifties, and tens which had served them so far. Each company was to determine how many of its members could afford the journey this year and was to prepare all the vehicles and supplies it could. It was to take its share of the poor and those whose providers were with the Battalion. It was to build houses and provide supplies for those who could not cross this year. Five Apostles and Erastus Snow, who was soon to become an Apostle, were named to head various companies. The Saints were instructed to grow in virtue, stop drinking, pay back what they had borrowed from neighbors, maintain their "testimony," and humble themselves. God repeated the long, long history of their blessings and tribulations — and of their enemies, who would destroy them if their faith should fail. And, putting aside the pen, the

Deity closed, "So no more at present." Brigham, the Lion of the Lord, could be trusted to attend to the rest.

As he starts west from Winter Quarters, we may remember that the Lion of the Lord was one of the nineteenth century's great men. The modern Church has lavished on Joseph Smith's birthplace at Sharon, Vermont, all the resources of pious commemoration. At Whitingham, sixty miles away, there is neither landscaping nor missionary service to do reverence to the man who saved the Mormon Church, brought the Kingdom in, and gave the Great Basin to the United States. There is only, on a bare hillside, above the waters of Whitingham Dam, a barbed-wire inclosure round an apple tree and a marker of native marble about the size and appearance of a gravestone. "Brigham Young," the inscription reads. "Born on this spot. 1801. A man of much courage and superb equipment." Stet.

Nothing, Henry Thoreau wrote at Walden Pond, nothing is effected but by one man. Brigham Young saved his Church when Joseph was lynched, brought it to the Missouri, took it to Great Salt Lake, gave it safety, wealth, and power. The state of Utah is his monument: or, if you like, the lives of hundreds of thousands. He was not a large man in stature, this seeking Methodist who found his fulfillment in the chaos of Joseph Smith's vision. In January, '46, he was five months short of forty-six, smooth-shaven, his eyes small but steady and severe, his body beginning to thicken. He grew fatter as the years passed and raised a benignant "wreath" beard that set the style for patriarchs in Utah. It did not wholly soften the chin, which stiffened as the iron came out of his soul, and he needed it for the insufficiencies of his people and the strain of defending them against their oppressors. He was a carpenter and glazier, a mechanic, a man who worked with his hands — and with his hands built the greater part of his own white cottage in Salt Lake City, just such a Yankee farmhouse as one might see in Whitingham. So he became the foremost American colonizer, the only man who succeeded in colonizing the desert in his century, it may well be the only one who will have proved to have colonized it successfully when all the bills are in. He had the genius of leadership, of foresight, of command, of administration, of effective will. He was not gifted at seeing into the mysteries of Heaven, except when a half-antic mood led him to indulge his people's love of sweets, but he saw into the making of society. His kingdom was of this earth. His God commanded him to establish Zion, to act where the great Joseph had only made promises. He was a great man, great in whatever was needful for Israel. Great in understanding, in will and fortitude and resolution, in finding the means which others could not find. Great in remembering also, in the command and management of men, in opposition and hostility and hate. A great leader, a great diplomat, a great administrator, and at need a great liar and a great scoundrel. He was one of the finders and one of the makers of the West.

It came to sending out a small pioneer party, as the Twelve had tried to do ever since the spring of '45.

But first proper obeisance had to be made to Israel's need of portents. So one morning as Brigham got out of bed a trance came upon him. A wife thought that he was dying and when the trance lifted he told her that he had been where Joseph and Hyrum were. "It is hard," he told the Saints next Sunday, "it is hard coming to life again. But I know that I went to the world of spirits but what I saw I know not, for the vision went away from me, as a dream which you lose when you awake. The next day I had a dream."

In the dream he saw Joseph sitting by a bright window with his feet on the lower round of his chair. Brigham took Joseph by the hand, kissed him on both cheeks, and asked why they could not be together again. Joseph said that they would be but must be separated for a while, and went on to speak of the Temple ordinances. He then gave Brigham further instructions in the ways of distinguishing the spirit of the Lord from the spirit of the enemy and in the highest order of mysteries, which Brigham was to teach his people at the proper time. A treasury on which Brigham could draw in moments of stress thus established, "I turned away and saw that Joseph was in the edge of the light, but where I had to go was as midnight darkness." So the venture westward was perfumed with marvel, and Brigham said pointedly, "I want you all to remember my dream for it is a vision of God and was revealed through the spirit of Joseph."

Pretty soon it was the holiest day, April 6, the day when the Church of Jesus Christ was restored to this earth in the Last Days. Seventeen years ago Joseph Smith and Oliver Cowdery, kneeling in Peter Whitmer's house at the village of Fayette in York State, had felt the power of the Holy Ghost poured out upon them and had ordained each other the first elders of the restored Church. With that ordination the Dispensation of the Fullness of Time had begun. Seventeen years, from York State to Kirtland, to Independence, to Clay County, to Nauvoo, and on to the Missouri River. At Winter Quarters on April 6, 1847, the second prophet addressed the Latter-day Saints in General Conference, looking still farther west, and the spirit was poured out again.

The pioneer party was almost ready to set out, but the timorous in Israel were shrinking back. Hearts that had been staunch so far began to falter, and half-dugouts in the Omaha bluffs, now sodden with the spring run-off, seemed preferable to the trail and the unknown mountains whither the Twelve were to journey. Panic showed itself and for a while Brigham ordered the ferries to take no one to the Iowa shore who could not show a passport from the priesthood. In the Iowa camps the fear was stronger. They were composed mostly of those who had to stop there because they could go no farther. Weak, sick, impoverished, scared of what was to come, a great many refused to set out again. Some had private revelations, illiterate copies of semi-literate originals, with God telling the head of a family that the Twelve had departed from the true faith, and then neighbors gathering by night and finding after prayer that this new light was true. Others simply fell away, returning to the Westminster Confession or just letting religion slide while they made a new beginning in the prairies. For years there was a state-wide belt across Iowa of tiny schismatic sects and mere apostates. Their descendants are there still.

At Winter Quarters the refractory Bishop Miller, coming down from his Niobrara outpost, had a revelation of his own. He wanted to uphold the hands of James K. Polk — to settle the Church between the Nueces River and the Rio Grande and "make a treaty with Mexico and have them give us the land." It was queer inspiration: to settle among Texans and in the army's corridor. (Miller had been one of the earliest advocates of founding Zion in Texas.) Brigham told him "that his views were wild and visionary, that when we moved hence it would be to the Great Basin where the Saints would soon form a nucleus of strength and power sufficient to cope with mobs." Miller preferred his own light and departed for Texas, where Lyman Wight's schism had established itself. It did not satisfy him; he ended at Voree and Beaver Island, with King Strang.

Miller's was the last apostasy. But there remained a sharp, an incurable anxiety. Israel's notorious tendency to grow muddleheaded when the wise were absent might prove fatal now. Brigham spent the entire afternoon of March 26 admonishing the assembled Saints. After he had started west, he said, "men would rise up and complain that the Twelve were not right and they themselves were the ones to lead and govern the people, and that he knew who it was, and plainly pointed out some who were now trying to raise up a party to themselves." The most sedulous dispatch of couriers between the pioneers and the Church could not relieve this fear, and on the way west Brigham's nightly meditation dwelt on the sheepfold, the wolves, and the silly sheep. He did not lose the fear till, leaving the pioneers beside Great Salt Lake, he hurried back over the trail and met Israel coming on.

Then they were off. Between April 7 and April 15 those who were to compose the pioneer party left Winter Quarters for the rendezvous at the Elkhorn River. They were to have made up the twelve times twelve chosen men of the Apocalypse but the true Scriptural formation was impaired when one of them proved too feeble for the trip. None of the sisters in Israel was to have gone along, but a wife of Lorenzo Young's was at last accepted in order to restore her health after the malaria of "Misery Bottoms." She took two children with her and, one exception having been made, Brigham permitted himself to take a wife and granted the same privilege to Heber Kimball, the Second in Israel. So the party which left the Elkhorn on April 16, 1847, numbered 143 men, three women, and two children. They had 73 wagons, 93 horses, 52 mules, 19 cows, 17 dogs, and some chickens. A stringent selection had been made and most of the party were from the upper ranks of the priesthood: 8 Apostles, 18 high priests, and 80 Seventies.[3]

We need neither name the ten companies of Mormons that left Winter Quarters later in the summer of '47 nor say anything about their experiences on the march. They numbered something more than eighteen hundred all told, and when the winter closed in the new Great Salt Lake City had a population of about twenty-one hundred. Nor need we say much about the pioneer party as emigrants. The experiences of the Mormons do not differ in kind from those of the emigration of '46 which we have followed or the considerably larger emigration of '47 which was on the trail while the Mormons were and whose fringes they were continually touching. The Mormons were less well equipped than most of the Gentiles — they were migrating on a frayed shoestring — but they made the passage in less time and with less hardship. Naturally, to move an eighth of the Church west in one summer was a more difficult enterprise than to take over the same trail any of the parties we have studied. That so remarkable a job was done so well depended on three things: the shorter distance they traveled, the preparation that had been made after searching study, and the authority of God's vicar, Brigham Young.

Reaching Great Salt Lake, the Saints were at trail's end, whereas at an equivalent distance those who were bound to Oregon or California had still to make the most difficult part of their journey. Through the preceding ten months, from books and maps, from mountain men and prairie travelers, they had learned what was ahead of them. They knew where Indians had been troublesome, where the main buffalo herds were usually encountered, what specific problems characterized each section of the trail. They had studied the trail, the grades, the fords, the passes, and the mountains. To an astonishing degree they had been able to provide in advance the right answers to problems which they actually encountered. Finally, individualism made no trouble in the Camp of Israel. The Way and the Will of the Lord provided a surface varnish of religion but its structure was military: though the "counsel" of the priesthood was expressed in a pious vocabulary, it was a military discipline. There would be no trouble about the nightly corral, guard duty, hunting, the order of the march, the distribution or conservation of supplies, double-teaming at a grade, or any other of the disagreements of freeholders that split, delayed, and frustrated the Gentile trains. Trouble might break out but it could last no longer than it took the responsible Apostle, bishop, or delegate of priestly power to get there on the run. The Saints had their hardships, they found the trail long and dry and painful, but there was clamped down on them a discipline which came straight down the channel of revelation from the Throne. It was enough.

After the pioneers reached the Platte (beyond the Loup Fork) they traveled up the north bank, thus establishing what is called "the Mormon trail." It was not a new trail and in fact they repeatedly met parties coming down it from the west, but the usual trail was up the south bank. The Saints took their new course for two reasons: grass would be more plentiful north of the river and they need not mingle with the Gentile emigration. They remained in deadly fear of persecution (as they still do in 1942) and preserved their illusion that innumerable mobbers, politicians, and especially Pukes were after them. There is not the slightest evidence that, by the summer of '47, anyone anywhere in the prairies or the Far West intended them any harm whatever — but it was good sense to avoid the opportunities of friction. (Later companies wandered widely from the trace made by the pioneers.)

They were pioneers in the strict military sense: they were preparing the way for the main body of the Church. So they made careful observations and recorded all the data they assembled. When the Apostle Parley Pratt was sent to the English mission late in the preceding summer, money for scientific instruments had been given him. They arrived in time and were turned over to Parley's brother, the Apostle Orson Pratt. Orson was the best educated of the Saints and one of the principal intelligences, a remarkable man who had been the faculty of the putative Nauvoo University as he was to be the faculty of the University of Deseret. He determined the latitude and longitude of the camp whenever observation was possible, and examined the terrain for all conceivable information. He soon found that his observations were more precise than those of Frémont, whose map they were using. Therefore, in collaboration with Willard Richards and William Clayton, two other trained minds, he proposed to make a new map. Eventually the data they assembled were digested by Clayton in *The Latter-Day Saints Emigrant's Guide.* Published the next year, it was the most accurate study of the trail before Stansbury's. Clayton, who had been detailed to compute distances, grew bored with counting the revolutions of a wagon wheel — 360 to the mile — and so Orson Pratt invented an odometer. Appleton Harmon carved its gears from planking and thereafter the distances were exactly known. At intervals a kind of logbook of the pioneers, together with all relevant information and the counsel of the Twelve, was deposited in a slotted board and set up where the next company would see it. They dotted the route with such "prairie postoffices" and occasionally set up signboards giving the total distance from Winter Quarters and other landmarks. These were the first mileposts ever erected on the Oregon trail. The pioneers also sent back letters and counsel by everyone whom they met coming down the trail.

At the very beginning they met Papin, the bourgeois of Fort Laramie, making his annual trip to St. Louis with robes and furs, as Parkman had done last year. They met others coming down the trail and pumped them all dry of information. They met a few Sioux and had an occasional Indian scare, though, as Norton Jacob said, "the Lord had turned the Indians aside." They lost an occasional horse. Last year's drouth was not repeated this year and they understood that the Lord was going before them. After time and powder had been wasted, Brigham restricted the hunting privilege to the Twelve and a group of expert marksmen. They traveled by the Way and Will of the Lord and the counsel of Brigham Young: strict herd guard, strict corral, strict night guard, advance party, outriders.

But they began to enjoy themselves too much. Too many practical jokes, too many mock trials, too much (womanless) dancing, too much frivolity of cards, dominoes, and checkers. A puritanism which was not typical of him and probably originated in his anxiety about the sheepfold at Winter Quarters suddenly afflicted the Lion of the Lord. Opposite Scott's Bluff he halted the train and gave them what-for. "My text will be the way I feel, as I do not feel like going any farther with all this company of men and with the spirit that now prevails in this camp." Expert vituperation loosed like thunder in the desert blew them into virtue, and we get the first hint of Brigham's realization that, hemmed in by the wilderness, there could be persuasions more pointed than oratory. "If anyone shall attempt to introduce anything that is unlawful, secretly, to carry their purpose into operation without permission, I swear they shall not return home." Brigham had talked that way to Gentiles, now he could talk that way to Israel, and let no one suppose that he was fooling.

He ordered them to renew their covenants. Separating into their priestly orders, they donned their priestly robes and went off into the hills for penitence and prayer. When they got back again a more seemly spirit prevailed.

On June 1 they camped opposite Fort Laramie and two Saints who had brought up their families from Pueblo crossed the river to greet them. These were Robert Crow and his son-in-law, that George Therlkill who had been wounded by a grizzly and had rudely questioned Francis Parkman. Their party numbered nine men, five women, and three children, with six wagons, richly outfitted, and a large herd. They reported four deaths and two births at Pueblo and said that the rest of their party and the Battalion's sick detachment were impatient to finish the pilgrimage. Brigham dispatched Apostle Lyman and three men to Pueblo to bring them in. (They were the second Mormon train to reach the valley.)

Crow and Therlkill, who had been at Fort Laramie for some time, had gathered information from several parties that had come down from South Pass. The Twelve got more information the next morning, when they crossed over to the fort. Bordeau received them amiably in the room that had wrought on the imagination of Parkman, rented them his boat to cross their outfits, and told them all he knew about the conditions ahead of them. He tipped them the by now customary gratuity of hard words about Lillburn Boggs, telling them large and comforting lies about Boggs's Missourians. The blacksmiths set to work reconditioning the wagons. Other Gentile parties came in, from the west, from Santa Fe, and from the east. The year's emigration had caught up with them. The Saints were astonished, for the Gentiles, even the Pukes, showed no hostility whatever. Must be some diabolical plot.

Here they began to make money from their enemies — it has remained their principal mundane pleasure. At the Crossing of the Platte, near Casper, they occupied both fords, usurping one with what amounted to force. The rains (they were miracle) had swollen the river and the fords had to be ferried. Gentile wagons were jammed up there and the Saints made a good thing of crossing them — for cash or, what was better, foodstuffs at Independence prices. So good a thing that they set up forges and did blacksmithing for the enemy as well and resolved to remain in business here. Brigham detached a party to run the ferries till the Church should come up. He gave it the proper sacerdotal organization, invoked the Lord's blessing, set the Lord's schedule of fees, and started the pioneers west again.

Independence Rock, the Sweetwater River, the first breath-taking vista of the Wind River peaks. Strangely, the Saints were not forced to shoot it out with any of the Gentile trains which they now met every day. (Between Fort Laramie and Fort Bridger they were following the established trail.) Instead there was a sweet, unbelievable neighborliness.

On June 26 Orson Pratt and several others, a few miles in advance, crossed the divide in South Pass and camped at Pacific Spring. When their fire blazed up, a party that had camped not far away paid a visit. At the head of them was Black Harris, fresh from Oregon on his way to meet the emigration and get his summer's employment. He had some Oregon newspapers and a copy of the *California Star* which, they were amazed to learn, Brother Samuel Brannan had founded at San Francisco, "beside the far Pacific sea." This also proved that the Lord was taking care of them. Harris stayed in camp the next day, when the rest of the pioneers came up, trading furs and telling Young all he knew about the Great Basin.[4] They were getting close to Zion now, wherever Zion might prove to be, and they questioned him exhaustively. Great Salt Lake Valley, he thought, was not too good, chiefly because there was little timber. Bear River Valley was little better. His judgment was that Cache Valley would be best. But "we feel that we shall know best," William Clayton wrote, "by going ourselves for the reports of travelers are so contradictory it is impossible to know which is the truth without going to see."

That was June 27, the day when most of the pioneers crossed the continental divide. Their hearts were angry and aggrieved. For just three years ago today Joseph and Hyrum had been murdered in Carthage jail.

They bought some robes from Harris and went on, leaving him in camp to meet the Gentiles who were not far behind.

The spectacle, as such, of Exodus is to the eastward of the pioneers with the companies now en route for Winter Quarters and those which were getting ready to leave it. With these eighteen hundred Saints going west is the pageantry which the summer of '47 has entered in our legends, the Children of Israel moving toward the land of Canaan and a pillar of cloud going on before. They are the miscellany of the Saints, all kinds and conditions, families, herds, miracles, the yearning and the heartbreak, the humor and the dream — the mural of a chosen people crossing the desert. . . . But the pioneers also had their moment of drama and should be allotted their panel in that mural, on Monday, June 28.

They came down out of the corridor of South Pass and presently they reached the fork where Sublette's or Greenwood's Cutoff left the rutted, iron-hard trail. On July 19 a year ago two trains traveling together had halted here for the last good-bye and Jessy Thornton had written in his diary that Tamsen Donner was "gloomy and dispirited" when her husband's wagons kept on down the California fork. The Mormons now took that same fork and some hours later made a nooning at the Little Sandy. Drab sagebrush, no timber, and the merciless Wyoming sun. After their rest they took the wagons across the little stream with a loss of two tar buckets. A mile farther on Apostle George A. Smith came riding back to the main party with a weather-worn gentleman whom he had met coming up the trail. They camped at once and held a "Council" with the Apostle's find. Drums should have rolled and trumpets sounded, or the supernatural stage management of this millennial creed should have provided signs from on high, for the Mormons had now met the master of these regions, their final authority. Apostle Smith had brought in Old Gabe, Jim Bridger.

Old Gabe was actually three years younger than the Lion of the Lord but he had grown up with the Great Basin. He was an Ashley man; with Fitzpatrick and Carson, he was at the top of the pyramid. He was one of the greatest of the great mountain men, already a legend then and still a legend in our day. While the fires blazed up and the sun sank behind the nondescript hills west of the Little Sandy, Old Gabe told these forerunners of Israel about the land they were to inherit. His memory was the map no one had had in the

White House of President Polk or the Council House of President Young. Through his stripped speech, whose idiom must have caused the Saints some trouble, ran thousands of miles with the wind and sun on them. His was the continental mind, like the mind of his messmate Jim Clyman, telling the Donners at Fort Bernard not to take the Hastings Cutoff. The pilgrims of eternity were children come a little way into the kingdom of Old Gabe. As a monarch he instructed them. (And had his pay, some years later, when they ran him out.)

They were bewildered, and why not?—his monologue made marches of a thousand miles, the names of innumerable deserts, gulches, peaks, and rivers jeweling it. They report him differently but all who report him at all say that he spoke favorably of Great Salt Lake Valley.[5] Much of what he said was unintelligible to greenhorns but William Clayton's journal entry is set down from notes which Clayton was making while Old Gabe talked. All the information recorded in that entry is exact. Run through it today and you will find nothing misrepresented in any particular whatever.[6] Jim spoke as one having authority. The only ambiguity is Clayton's note that "there have been nearly a hundred wagons gone on the Hastings route through Weber's Fork"—and here Jim was unquestionably talking about '46, not '47 (and had the number right). He went on talking, sketching in the entire map from the Grand Canyon to the Snake, from the Little Sandy to the far Pacific sea, and all its minerals, trees, shrubs, roots, rainfall, vistas, local gods. He took them into the big unknown and made it known, compressing into a few hours the whole function of the mountain man. "He said it was his paradise," Wilford Woodruff wrote. It was. His talk moved on to the resident Indians—Paiute, Diggers. The Saints need not be afraid of them, could "drive the whole of them in twenty-four hours." But Jim, a formally adopted Shoshoni brave, would not kill the Diggers; his counsel was to make slaves of them. Finally, "Supper had been provided for Mr. Bridger and his men and the latter having eaten, the council was dismissed, Mr. Bridger going with President Young to supper, the remainder retiring to their wagons, conversing over the subject touched upon."[7]

Observe that final, private conversation between Old Gabe and the Lion of the Lord. The hours of Bridger's exposition had cleared the obstructions from the channel of inspiration. Now, while Jim sat with Brigham in the patriarchal white-top and a candle burned in a bucket there, unquestionably the heavens opened. It may be that they talked some more about the Paiute, who were in greater force southward from Great Salt Lake than beside it. It may be that there was further talk about the canyons that broke through the Wasatch at the south end of the lake. Whatever they talked about, Jim Bridger became the oracle of revelation and when the time came, Brigham would be able to speak the Lord's will and say "This is the place."

Two days later while the pioneers were fording Green River another circuit was closed, when Sam Brannan in person rode into camp. The Saints had circumnavigated the United States — Brannan was coming from the colony which he had planted in San Joaquin Valley. Typically, he arrived in bad company, with a man who had been a counterfeiter at Nauvoo. Typically also, he had a rich stock of truth, rumors, and lies. "Old Boys [Boggs] is on the opposite side of the bay" from the colony, Norton Jacob understood, "and dare not come over for fear of the Mormons:" Sam had made this year's earliest crossing of the Sierra (not bad for a greenhorn) and, on his way, had met Fallon and the last relief party bringing Keseberg down. The Saints got their first word of last summer's catastrophe — it is surprising that Harris had not heard of it in Oregon — and began adapting it to fable.[8] The fable was to go on growing until it became a permanent part of Mormon mythology. For years (and occasionally now) the innocent victims of Lansford Hastings were murderers of the prophet or hirelings of the devilish Boggs who paid in the snows for having persecuted God's smuggest people.

Brigham had the satisfaction of learning that his most imperial move, the California outpost, was a success. But he had acquired a Native Son. Brannan was of the type that the golden shore has always furiously oxidized. He was boosting California and would presently have revelations about it. He could not argue Brigham into taking the Church there. Eventually he apostatized — founding a sizable fortune on gold dust from the mines and the tithes he had piously collected from the San Joaquin Saints.

At the camp on Green River mountain fever broke out. The Saints swelled, ached, and burned. Brigham sent back a party of five under Phineas Young to meet the oncoming Church with notes, statistics, counsel, and rebuke. The next day was July 4 and there was another reunion. Twelve outriders from the Battalion sick detachment, coming up from Pueblo, rode into the camp, to loud hosannas, almost exactly a year after Brigham had set up the flag and ordered them to volunteer.

On the way to Fort Bridger Apostle Woodruff's eye kindled, for some little whitewater brooks must surely have trout in them. He got out the rod he had brought all the way from Liverpool, attached a fly (he thought it likely that he was the first to use one in these parts), and sure enough there were trout. The pioneers camped within a mile or two of the fort on July 7. There was a congregation of mountain men and Indians there, so that the Saints got more intimate details about the route of revelation. The trace of the Hastings Cutoff led west from here, a mere wagon track. As they heard more of its story, the myth grew. The Donners were now from the abhorred Clay County, "a mob company that threatened to drive out the Mormons who were in California, and started with that spirit in their hearts. But it seemed as though they were ripe for judgment." Woodruff thought that he remembered baptizing Mrs. Murphy in Tennessee. She had apostatized and joined the mob, he decided, and in God's loving-kindness had been punished by being killed and eaten.

Nevertheless God had used the mobbers and apostates to prepare a way for His chosen, who took the trail the Donners had made. Taking it, they struck the Bear River on July 10, the first part of Zion which they knew by name. Here they met Miles Goodyear, who was driving a herd of California horses toward the emigration. He had just traveled the whole stretch of the Hastings Cutoff — had passed the cabins at Donner Lake, crossed the Salt Desert, and followed the Donner trail through the Wasatch. Moreover, he was the sole proprietor of Zion, having built a cabin and corral and put in crops on the Weber River, some miles above its mouth. Once more they interviewed a veteran mountain man. This one had real estate to sell but he did not sell it now (he did a few months later), for Porter Rockwell rode back with him to examine the direct route to Goodyear's holdings. This was the Weber Canyon route down which Hastings had taken the Harlan-Young wagon train. Porter needed only a glance at those chasms: the Saints would not go that way. He reported and Orson Pratt was ordered out with an advance party "to find Mr. Reid's route across the mountains." Mr. Reid, of course, was James Frazier Reed.

Mountain fever had stricken a good many of them. Now it afflicted Brigham, who was so sick that, stopping beside the trail, the priesthood had to minister to him. From here on the pioneers traveled in three divisions. While some of the priesthood, in their Temple robes, went up into the high place to pray for the sick, forty-two men with twenty-three wagons, under Orson Pratt and Stephen Markham, led the advance. Pratt rode a few miles into Weber Canyon, determined that Porter Rockwell's judgment had been sound, and set his men to work improving the Donner road. He could understand what his predecessors had endured. In spite of their more than two weeks of agonizing labor in brush, along mountainsides, and down the beds of creeks, "we found the road almost impassable and requiring much labor." He had his party supply the labor. They hacked the brush away, pried boulders out, leveled, graded, felled trees. He kept riding ahead to reconnoiter and sent his data back to those who were following. Through most of this scouting his companion was John Brown, of the Mississippi Saints, and after a Sabbath rest on July 18 it was these two who caught the first glimpse of the promised land. On July 19 from the ridge beyond Big Mountain which had thrown the Donners into their first panic they "could see an extensive level prairie some few miles distant, which we thought must be near the Lake."

But it was Erastus Snow, from the second group, who was with Pratt on July 21. (Now the time was the time of the first ripe grapes.) That day they followed the Donner road up Little Mountain and "looked out on the full extent of the valley where the broad waters of the Great Salt Lake glistened in the sunbeams." Seeing that land from the wilderness of Zin unto Rehob, as men come to Hamath — seeing it, Pratt says, "we could not refrain from a shout of joy which almost involuntarily escaped from our lips." They made their way downhill to Emigration Canyon, down that winding, gentle gulch, and out at last to Zion. They made a twelve-mile circle on the holy land before going back into the mountains. Pratt was back the next day with another Apostle, George A. Smith from the main company, and seven men. Young had sent instructions (unquestionably from the revelation unto Jim Bridger) for them to turn north for a few miles after reaching the valley. This brought them to the twinned creek where ground would first be broken. They rode carefully, examining the soil, thinking of dam sites and crops to come, ominously noting a profusion of black crickets. That night all the wagons except those which lingered with the sick prophet camped in Canaan. The next day, July 23, they sent a report to Brigham and moved the whole camp to the divided creek. "Here we called the camp together," Pratt says, "and it fell to my lot to offer up prayer and thanksgiving in behalf of our company, all of whom had been preserved from the Missouri River to this point; and, after dedicating ourselves and the land unto the Lord and imploring His blessings upon our labors, we appointed various committees to attend to different branches of business, preparatory to putting in crops, and in about two hours after our arrival we began to plow, and the same afternoon built a dam to irrigate the soil, which at the spot where we were ploughing was exceedingly dry."

There had lately been some showers in the Wasatch but they could not have greatly freshened the valley. In late July it is always a dry land weary with summer. When the Apostle Orson came over the ridge of Big Mountain he was in a zone where the ground whitened with frost at daybreak and the silver undersides of aspen had the first gilt tinge of autumn. But he came down past the benches of the prehistoric lake to a plain of sage and stunted oak brush smelling of dust under a brazen sun. Dust lay on the oak leaves, dust made a flour to the tops of their boots, the tar-and-turpentine stench of sage was in their nostrils, and the sky whitened with heat. They saw the valley as men coming from a far country to the promised land. It was the women whose hearts sank at sight of desolation — the empty plain, the line of the Wasatch stretching south with perhaps a few patches of snow left still like outcrops of chalk just below the ridge, to the south the more desolate Oquirrhs canting westward toward the end of the lake, and then those bright, amazing waters with peaks rising from them and the sun striking a white fire from them and from the whiter sand. Well enough for the Apostle Orson to fall on his knees and dedicate the land unto the Lord and give thanks. "Because the Lord loved you and because he would keep the oath which he has sworn unto your fathers hath he brought you out with a mighty hand and redeemed you out of the house of bondage." But to the women it was a stark and hideous land. The years of persecution and the long moving ended here — but in a desert. The ground crawled with crickets, a rattler slid into the sage, well out of rifle range a coyote loped and sat and stared and panted off into emptiness.

It has its hideousness, it has its beauty, nor are they separated in the depths of any mind that has known them. A hard, resistant folk had found a hard, resistant land, and they would grow to fit one another. Remember that the yield of a hard country is a love deeper than a fat and easy land inspires, that throughout the arid West the Americans have found a secret treasure. . . . There is one who remembers it below the Atlantic fall line, to whom east is always the direction where you will see the Wasatch ridge and west the house of the sky where the sun sinks into the lake. The cottonwood leaves flutter always beyond the margins of awareness. The streams come out of the mountains to a plain that was greener when one was young than when Orson Pratt found it. March starts the snows withdrawing up the peaks that have not changed much, sagebrush is a perfume and a stench, and at midnight there is a lighter line along the ridge where the sky begins. A stern and desolate country, a high, bare country, a country brimming with a beauty not to be found elsewhere.

The day they venerate is the next day, July 24. At five in the afternoon the favor of God was manifested by a shower of rain, but the end of a long journey had come earlier than that. On the twenty-third they had planted grain and parsnips; today they were planting potatoes and bringing water to them from City Creek, near the site of the Temple of the Lord. At two o'clock, accompanied by some white-top wagons that had had much trouble getting over Little Mountain, wagons held together by the expedients of the trail, wagons groaning and squealing (for the last time in this narrative) with dry axles and shrunken hubs, their tires held on by wedges and rawhide — the carriage of Wilford Woodruff came up to the camp at City Creek and, half-reclining in it, the convalescent prophet Brigham Young looked out at the site of Zion in the land of Canaan, toward the River Jordan flowing into the Dead Sea.

"In the name of God, Amen. We whose names are underwritten, ye loyall subjects of our dread soveraigne Lord, King James, by the grace of God, of Great Britaine, Franc, and Ireland king, defender of ye faith, etc. Haveing undertaken for ye glorie of God and advancemente of ye Christian faith, and honour of our king and countrie, a voyage to plant ye first colonie in ye Northern parts of Virginia, doe by these presents solemnly and mutually in the presence of God and one of another . . . "

No, that was a different covenant. The Apostle Wilford Woodruff: "Thoughts of pleasant meditation ran in rapid succession through our minds at the anticipation that not many years hence the House of God would be established in the mountains and exalted above the hills, while the valleys would be converted into orchards, vineyards, fields, etc., planted with cities, and the standard of Zion be unfurled unto which the nations would gather."

The prophet had less to say. What he wrote was an entry that gave the distance traveled, recorded the potatoes, and mentioned the shower. What he said from the carriage was that "we were on the spot where the city was to be built. He knew it as the place he had seen in vision. Said we might explore the mountains over and over again and each time return to this place as the best."

It was enough to say. But, though his mind focused sharply on those potatoes and the life-giving water that was flowing over them, though it was already ranging out to the mountains and valleys all about and on to the Pacific and back to Winter Quarters — nevertheless, Brigham Young must have permitted himself a moment or two to taste and savor such triumph as few have known in all our history. *The thing was done!* Fayette, Kirtland, Jackson County, Clay County, Nauvoo, the frozen Mississippi, Sugar Creek, Pisgah, Winter Quarters — and now Zion. Seventeen years, the angel and the golden plates, the prophet murdered, hundreds of Mormons dying in the passion of battle or the salt frenzy of flight or shaken by ague or starving at slackened breasts or just going down into the dark after too much strain at Misery Bottoms. The faithful and the recreant, the persecuted and the damned, the mobbers and the politicians, the oaths sworn and forsworn — Israel's fear had ended. "For thou art an holy people unto the Lord thy God: the Lord thy God hath chosen thee to be a special people unto himself, above all people that are upon the face of the earth." That promise made to the dispensation of Moses and repeated in the dispensation of Joseph had now been redeemed through the earthly agency of Brigham Young. He had saved his Church, he had brought his people out of bondage, and the gates of hell had not prevailed against them. Danger was over, the kingdom would now come in. He would drive a stake of Zion in the desert soil. Nothing could stop him. The hell with the Gentiles, the hell with the United States. God's people had reached their land. . . .

He was not a man to spend much time in the unprofitable business of prophecy or cursing — in anything unprofitable. Be sure that he did not long indulge himself with triumph but began to correct mistakes and urge the Saints to greater effort. In a few days more ground had been broken, explorers had been sent out, arrangements had been made to facilitate the coming of those who were on the trail and those who were to take to it through the succeeding twenty years, a city had been plotted, a site for the Temple had been chosen, a company was ready to leave for California, and another one was ready to go back to Winter Quarters. The prophet was already at work making his empire, his part of the American empire. It was named Deseret, a word which, we are told, means "land of the honey bee." Deseret existed from a corner of California well into Wyoming — for a while. The United States canceled it when Utah became a territory, and you will not find it on maps. But it is there still, an empire within the domestic empire, the commonwealth that Israel built, the life and function of the Latter-day Saints, a society of their own and like no other. Deseret began in July, 1847, and has gone on up to now, and Deseret is seen to be, as this narrative takes leave of it, what happens when Brook Farm comes into the hands of those fit to build Brook Farm. As such, Deseret was outlined in the sermon which Brigham Young preached on July 28, in Zion.

That sermon, essentially a plan for the self-sufficiency of Israel, would be our focus and taking-off if we had anything to do with Western history, but we have not. The end of the trail is the beginning of history in the West; we are not concerned with Israel's inheritance but only with Israel's reaching it. . . . If a people had found their land, a land had found its people. A history of the Mormons in the West would be the history of a hard, fanatical people bringing a dead land to bring forth life. Deseret was not the deep soil of the Willamette Valley with the great forests and the abundant rain. It was not the eternal summer of the golden shore. It was a land poisoned with alkali and dead for want of water, a land which could be made to live only by the incessant labor of a people shaped to a fit instrument by suffering, faith, and the domination of a prophet who spoke with the authority of Almighty God. It would be a history of a mad prophet's visions turned by an American genius into the seed of life, in the memory of suffering and the expectation of eternal glory, while the angels hovered overhead and portents flamed in the sky. . . . It would be quite a history. Someone should write it.

XVII

Bill of Review – Dismissed

THE largest of Mr. Polk's four objectives had been the acquisition of California: it was achieved. In California they were having trouble getting a government. That trouble was emblematic of graver difficulties to the eastward.

The fight at San Pascual, in which so many of Kearny's officers were killed and the general himself was wounded, took place on December 6, '46. Kearny joined Stockton at San Diego on December 12. In theory Frémont's California Battalion, with its accessions from the emigration of '46 and its delegation of Wallawalla braves, was marching down the interior. Even before San Pascual a force of Americans well in advance of it had been roughly handled by native horsemen (who had taken Consul Larkin as a hostage) at Natividad. Frémont brought his force southward with a wariness that would have prevented a surprise by overwhelming numbers of the enemy, if there had been any. The Battalion was uncomfortable in the rains, it lost many horses, sometimes it got out of hand, and it made wretched time. It never saw an enemy or smelled gunpowder. Though it was now a legitimate force, it retained the pattern of extempore war: whenever anyone had had enough rain or scorched beans, he went home.

The Battalion was supposed to be marching on Los Angeles from the north. Stockton and Kearny started toward the same place from the south. Since most of their force consisted of Stockton's sailors, marines, and volunteers, and since Kearny had not fully recovered from his wounds, Stockton commanded the expedition. On January 8 — Jackson Day — at the San Gabriel River they met the only sizable force of armed Californians remaining and drove them from their position. The next day they fought another skirmish and the Californians began to slip away. On January 10 they entered Los Angeles unopposed; the presidio was American again. The Californians melted northward and ran into Frémont, who accepted their eager surrender and made a set of peace terms. Formal and very elegant terms, which required no oath to the United States and extended amnesty to those who had violated their paroles. As it turned out, this amnesty had a good effect, though it ignored Kearny's authority, robbed the panting Stockton of a victory and a proclamation, and was contrary to the intention of both. But it signalized another shift in the career of John Charles Frémont. The great deed had had its surface marred by the native revolution and then, just when Frémont was marching to restore the veneer, a superior officer arrived. A change in his role was necessary. The Pathfinder and Conqueror became a politician.

The next two months would be good farce if one could forget that Stockton and Frémont were risking a serious danger: the paralysis of both government and military force in a conquered province whose people had been outraged by their arrogance, could revolt again, and might be supported from Mexico as the war went on. The tone is a good deal more sinister than the Ruritanian unreality of the Bear Flag Republic. The best interpretation that can be made of the two barnstormers, the best light they can be put in, is bad enough: that Stockton's egotism had been inflamed by his experience of power, that Frémont's always fragile intelligence had been overstrained, and that both had had too much publicity for the good of the United States.

Stockton's later career — in the United States Senate and in the Ku Klux Klan of the period, the American Party — contains nothing to weaken the judgment that he was a fool. He did not quite make the nomination for the Presidency. Frémont did, and in doing so jeopardized the Republican Party, as from then on he repeatedly jeopardized the United States. You cannot let him off so lightly as Stockton. He was worse than a fool, he was an opportunist, an adventurer, and a blunderer on a truly dangerous scale. He was foisted on the Republic in the hour of its peril by the power of publicity, the reputation erected on his career in California during '46 and '47. That was the career of a military adventurer, a filibuster, and an officer of the United States Army committing mutiny. In the Civil War, as in California, he made a play for every opportunity that would serve John Charles Frémont, regardless of its effect on the United States. Then, as in California, he created spectacle but bungled what he had started out to do. Only, in the Civil War he came into the keeping of men with stronger intelligences and clearer understanding of the forces at work who could use the symbol of John Charles Frémont for their private purposes. Their purposes were not pretty and Frémont did nothing to inconvenience them. That they did not destroy the United States was not their fault. Neither was it Frémont's. (It was in part the responsibility of a major general who in February of '47 arrived in California as a lieutenant of artillery, William Tecumseh Sherman.[1]) Technically and in the light of his own conscience, he was not a traitor to the United States in 1864. That this was not for lack of the raw stuff out of which treason is made was clear in '64 — and was clear in '47.

God and events were against Frémont. He tried to be a great man but something always happened.

Kearny arrived in California with orders from the President of the United States to take command of the land forces which were to occupy the province and to organize a civil government. The thousands of pages that have been written about the controversy have not altered the fact: Kearny had the authority of the United States and was carrying out the intention of the government. But Stockton regarded himself as the conqueror of California. On paper — and on paper only — he had organized a civil government. (His authority for doing so was the force of circumstance, and it ended at the moment when Kearny showed his orders.) He had named Frémont civil governor and a gentleman from the emigration of '46 secretary of state, Colonel William Henry Russell of Kentucky, a bosom friend of Henry Clay.

Stockton refused to acknowledge Kearny's authority. He withdrew the navy and marine detachments from Kearny's command.[2] This left Kearny with only his handful of Dragoons. He was under orders to take command of whatever armed forces might have reached California from the east and whatever armed forces might have been raised there. At the moment that meant, practically, Frémont's California Battalion. But when Frémont marched it into Los Angeles his instinct for self-aggrandizing treachery proved infallible. Stockton was going to make him governor, and in his judgment there was more to be gained from Stockton. So Lieutenant Colonel Frémont (his commission in the Mounted Rifles, now fighting in Mexico, had caught up with him) informed Brigadier General Kearny, his commanding officer, that he would not obey orders.[3]

Kearny had no recourse but to return to San Diego and await the arrival of unmutinous troops. Frémont began the series of appeals to his father-in-law, Thomas Hart Benton, that ended by defacing Kearny's reputation in American history. Stockton went on being a personage in ink, and there was no government in California. At the end of January the Mormon Battalion arrived — part of Kearny's command. He ordered it to garrison duty at San Luis Rey and elsewhere and went on waiting. Cooke, its commander, a very intelligent man and one of the best officers in the army, knew mutiny when he saw it and promptly gave it a name. His impulse was to give it the treatment that mutiny in wartime deserves. Philip St. George Cooke had a hard time holding his tongue and withholding his hand.

It must be realized that Kearny, Cooke, Turner, Emory, and the other officers of the constituted army of occupation were, as a result of Stockton's and Frémont's idiocy, in a position of extreme delicacy. The war was not over, Californians might take to the saddle again with this encouragement, adherents of Frémont might make it active mutiny, and the plain truth is that the United States Navy's *esprit de corps* was getting inflamed and might make a fatal division on behalf of its commodore. In the circumstances, Kearny and his officers did the only intelligent thing. They avoided forcing the issue and played for time.

It was a bitter dose, however. In private, Captain Turner longed for the decency of civilian life and began to believe that his chief was afraid of Benton. "Were I to behave as Frémont has done he would cause me to be put in irons and would pursue me with a bitterness that would drive me to desperation." Frémont, he said, deserved to be dropped from the rolls without even a trial. And Stockton was "a low, trifling, truckling politician."

Time did the job. Early in February a new commodore arrived, to replace Stockton. This was Branford Shubrick, who had a sense of reality. He recognized Kearny's authority but the two of them agreed that they had better await specific instructions from Washington. These arrived later in the month with Richard B. Mason, lately Kearny's second in command and now his successor as colonel of the First Dragoons. Kearny went to Monterey to meet him and found the President's orders unequivocal. Kearny was confirmed as commander and civil governor of California. He was to return to the States as soon as the province could be considered pacified and Mason was to succeed him. The California Battalion was to be mustered into the service, if this had not already been attended to, and was to be discharged as soon as possible. Frémont was to be sent east to his regiment as soon as he could be spared. (This was not intended to catch Frémont and Benton between the jaws of a trap, but it did.) Shortly afterward some more navy arrived and, a little later, a regiment of volunteers enlisted at New York for the purpose of colonizing, not conquering, California.

Kearny got to work. He began the pacification and government of California. His proclamation organized it under military command, pending the establishment of Territorial status by Congress. Also he sent orders to Frémont to have the California Battalion mustered into the service and to turn over his papers. Those orders produced the silliest act of Frémont's entire performance.

He appears to have told the Battalion that they could be mustered into the service if they wanted to be.[4] He reported to Cooke, whom Kearny had put in command of the southern district of California, that they declined to be mustered in. In the sworn judgment of Cooke — who was much more intelligent and much more honest than Frémont — there was ample "reason to doubt that steps were taken to allow the men of that battalion to decide, knowingly, upon their being mustered into the service." Frémont made a show of acting through Owl Russell, the secretary of state in Stockton's government, which had completely lost any standing it may ever have had. He refused to obey Cooke's orders and instructed his adjutant not to obey them and not to turn over to him any military property. He began to whoop up rumors of a vague but vast (and nonexistent) native revolt — he somehow contrived to represent it as at once directed against him and made in his support. He proclaimed that conflict between various of the military organizations was on the point of breaking out. (If any should break out, it would be at Frémont's instigation — which the cool-minded Cooke thought not at all unlikely. But Frémont's present yell about it had a purpose: he was planting it for use later when he could play his ace, the support of his father-in-law.) That was sinister enough but he picked up a more sinister tool: he permitted the circulation of talk that hostilities were on the point of breaking out between the Missourians in his Battalion and the Mormons under Kearny's command. There is strong reason to believe that he not only permitted the talk and helped to circulate it but actively tried to incite the hostilities. He was working in the area of politics, for his own advancement — and if the incitement of armed conflict between organizations of the United States Army is not treason, just what is the right name for it?

He also saw a chance for cinema and made a thundering ride from Los Angeles to Monterey. It has become part of the Frémont myth and let us be scrupulously fair: the movies have never surpassed it. At Monterey he blustered and spoke orations, galling Kearny almost to the limit. He tried to resign his commission — more raw material for Benton to use. His sensitive honor was wounded a number of times but not too deeply to prevent him from insulting Kearny and Mason. At last Kearny asked him whether he intended to obey orders, advising him to appraise the gravity of his decision and offering him an hour or, if he wanted it, a day for the appraisal. An hour turned out to be enough and he said yes. Kearny told him to go back to Los Angeles and obey the orders he had received.

Meanwhile, on Frémont's order, Owl Russell had started east by the southern trail. This mission had an extremely important object: to turn the mightiest Senator, the father of expansionism, loose on everyone who had marred the theater of John Charles Frémont. Meanwhile also, his adjutant, obeying his orders, had defied the authority of Cooke, had even refused to turn over to him a howitzer that belonged to the Dragoons. With some difficulty Cooke held to Kearny's policy of avoiding overt clashes. "I sacrifice all feeling or pride to duty, which I think plainly forbids any attempt to crush this resistance of misguided men. It would be a signal of revolt." But the Virginia precisian let off steam in his report: —

> My God! to think of a howitzer brought over the deserts with so much faithful labor by the dragoons; the howitzer with which they have four times fought the enemy, and brought here to the rescue of Lieutenant Colonel Frémont and his followers, to be refused to them by this Lieutenant Colonel Frémont and in defiance of the orders of his general! I denounce this treason, or this mutiny, which jeopardizes the safety of the country and defies me in my legal command and duties, by men who report, and say, that they believe that the enemy approaches from without, and are about to rise in arms around us.

Cooke had literary impulses but they did not equip him to appreciate the role which Frémont had written for himself. However, that role began to crumble now. Other Battalion subordinates obeyed Cooke and presently Frémont was back to begin the sad business of doing what he had been told to do. His honor got infected and he made himself as offensive as possible. Cooke held his temper but when the public hero sent Mason a challenge, the colonel of the First Dragoons was willing. He named "double-barrelled guns and buckshot cartridges," and would certainly have let the romantic drama end in such travesty if Kearny had not forbidden the duel. All through the court-martial Frémont kept trying to get the court to take cognizance of that duel, advertising it to the great public as a heroism still pending. But even here the effect cracked at the edge, for he could not help insinuating that the cowardly Mason was an expert with the shotgun.

This series of tableaus occupied the end of March, '47, and half of April. By the end of May Kearny regarded his job in California as finished and was ready to start east. It had not been difficult to tranquilize the province once an intelligent man was able to exercise authority. Practically all the riding of the Californians, north and south, had been a species of vigilante protection, natives who were afraid, for sound reasons, that their property and even their lives were in danger. They were afraid of such half or wholly irregular military forces as the Bear Flag stalwarts and the California Battalion, and they were afraid of the possible exuberance of the immigrants who were arriving in a disturbed society. The military needed no more than an intelligent commander, however, and the immigrants proved to be overwhelmingly well-disposed, peaceable, fair-minded people who had no desire to expropriate anything. (In that fact exists the entire absurdity of the Bear Flag affair and even the irrelevance of Mr. Polk's war.)

Kearny had a harder job than anyone would have had if Stockton had behaved intelligently in the beginning, if Frémont had had common sense, or if the Bear Flag uprising had not occurred. The emotions roused by such things as these left deep wounds, and in any event much injustice was unavoidable. But Kearny's government was another service of inestimable value to the Republic. He achieved much more than was to be expected in the circumstances. So did his successor, Mason. So did the commonwealth-building goodwill of the emigration. When Kearny left California the golden shore was peaceful, reconciled, and, the truth is, invigorated. He was justified in believing that it would go peacefully forward to the next stage, organization as a Territory of the United States. That it did not was due to the sum of forces much too great for calculation west of the Sierra. California had been acquired, Mr. Polk had achieved his principal objective, expansionism had broken the farthest frontier, the Americans had reached the Pacific, the dream had broken through its chrysalis, the United States was a continental nation . . . and a demand note covering the expenses was presented for payment.

A number of our characters were in the party that started east with Kearny from Sutter's on June 16, '47. There were Cooke, who had resigned his California commands in order to see service in Mexico, and Turner and Swords. There was Sanderson, the "Captain Death" of the Mormon Battalion. There was Willard Hall, who had accompanied it to California as a freelance and was going home to take his seat in the Thirtieth Congress; an item of Manifest Destiny, he would explain it to politicians who had merely watched it. There was Edwin Bryant, content to have his *Wanderjahr* reach its end; for the last three months he had served, on Kearny's appointment, as alcalde of San Francisco and was proud of the job he had done. There were thirteen members of the Mormon Battalion who had been brought up from the south to serve as a military escort. Among them were Daniel Tyler, who would presently be the historian of the miracles vouchsafed the Battalion, and our diarist, Sergeant Jones.[5]

And, traveling separately, there were Frémont and the remnants of his original exploring party, reduced from Caesar's Tenth Legion to a party of topographical engineers again. Frémont industriously laid up possible personal affronts to exhibit to the court-martial which he suspected was ahead of him — and, over its head, to the public. Kearny paraded the detachment at Sutter's, in order to inspect it and find out whether any cared to be discharged here: Frémont told the court that that was an attempt to expose him to the derision of a naval officer who happened to be there on business. One night he was ordered to camp at a site which was to the rear of the escort; since the escort were Mormons, he thought there was a chance to derive some advantage from the public dislike of Mormons. Kearny several times refused to let him go home by various routes — the Gila, by way of Great Salt Lake, across lots to Mexico from Fort Laramie. These requests were meant solely as ammunition for the court and the public exhibition beyond it: he could represent Kearny's refusals as vindictive and tyrannical. Some of those refusals were pursuant to the orders given Kearny and the court found that the others were within his discretion as a commander, but Frémont was a martyr in newsprint. In fact, anything would serve as fodder for paranoia and publicity: he even entered in the record, with all possible solemnity, a statement that, when he reached Fort Leavenworth, only one officer spoke to him over a period of several hours.

Reaching Donner Lake (another Mormon diarist called it Cannibal Camp) they found the ghastly scene which Brannan and Goodyear had passed before them, a rubble of scattered goods and half-dismembered skeletons, some with putrefying flesh still on them. (It was June 22.) Kearny ordered the bodies buried and the cabins burned, so some of the unfortunates got decent burial at last. But he appears to have burned only one set of the cabins at the lake and none of those at Alder Creek. A later detachment of the Mormon Battalion coming east and numerous members of the western emigration report the pitiful bones and skulls and abandoned goods still lying round. There would be souvenirs there for years to come.[6]

They went on, a small party making excellent time. The Truckee, the Sink of the Humboldt, the Humboldt, the junction where dim scratches made by wagons of the Harlan-Young party and the Donners came in from the east. (Jones wrote wistfully that they were only two days' journey from the Salt Lake, but it was a good deal more than that.) Kearny rejected the Hastings Cutoff; so did the whole emigration of '47, which took its moral to heart. Eventually the first half of it, from Fort Bridger to Great Salt Lake City, was to become the standard emigrant route. From the City of the Saints later emigrants would either strike north to Bear River or south to a Mormon-built variation of the old Spanish trail.

Kearny reached this junction on July 9: the Mormon pioneers were just setting out from Fort Bridger. His party met the outriders of the summer's emigration a few miles west of Fort Hall on July 14. Two days later, beyond Soda Springs, the Mormons got their first authoritative word of the Church, meeting a Gentile who had traveled east with Brannan. By the end of the week they were meeting emigrants in swarms. On July 24, as Brigham Young's carriage halted at City Creek, they crossed the divide and started toward the Sweetwater. And on July 29, just east of Independence Rock, the thirteen Mormons met their people at last — an advance party of the first company out from Winter Quarters under Parley Pratt. More emigrants, more Mormons, Fort Laramie, Chimney Rock, Ash Hollow, and at last, their rations exhausted, Fort Leavenworth. The thirteen Mormons had reached the end of their military service, and so had the Army of the West.

(Two months after them, Stockton and Gillespie also made the overland crossing. They can be glimpsed in various journals, Mormon and Gentile, but there appears to have been nothing important about their trip. Except that Stockton, the prototype of cinematic man, loosed a flood of publicity about the prodigies he wrought single-handed when some Indians got hostile.[7] They reached the States in November, in ample time for the court-martial. . . . And in mid-July the enlistment of the Mormon Battalion expired. "We bid good-bye to Unkle Sam having it to say You are the Most Exact Unkle we ever had." Mason was able to prevail against the priesthood sufficiently to enlist one company for another year of guard duty in California. A few stayed on to settle in southern California, the others organized themselves according to the Lord and under the priesthood, and in various groups started out to find their Church. A few dropped off in the San Joaquin, at Brannan's settlement. A few others got the priesthood's permission to hire out to Sutter, who always had jobs for everyone. The remainder moved over the Sierra.

(They passed the melancholy relics at Donner Lake and their

journals show more charity than the pioneer party had exercised when they heard of the tragedy. As they were moving eastward the next day, September 6, they met Sam Brannan coming west to rejoin his colony, and a little later Captain James Brown of the Sick Detachment lately at Pueblo. [Both parties had avoided the Hastings Cutoff, coming by way of Bear River.] Brannan was overcharged with rebellious counsel, denouncing the folly of the Twelve in selecting Great Salt Lake Valley for Israel's home, and inciting these veterans to return to the golden shore. [Brannan, like Hastings, was a predestinate Booster.] But Brown, who was on his way to find an officer with authority to muster out his detachment and pay it off, had counsel and a letter to the veterans from Brigham Young. The prophet told them that those who had no families in the emigration and wanted to spend the winter in California were free to do so — supplies at Great Salt Lake City were low.[8] So the veterans divided again. Some kept on eastward to Fort Hall. Here some went south to Great Salt Lake, others kept on till they met their families on the trail, and still others went all the way to Winter Quarters. Of those who turned back to California with Brown a good many stopped off at Sutter's and found employment.)

At Fort Leavenworth Kearny ordered Frémont to report himself at Washington under arrest, for trial. The court convened at Washington Arsenal on November 2 and reached its verdict on the last day of the following January. Captain Turner had been wrong in suspecting that Kearny was afraid of Benton, but might have devoted some thought to the officers who composed the court. For they permitted Frémont and Benton, who was his principal counsel, to turn a military trial into a political circus. Neither misuse of Senatorial power in the pursuit of advertising nor the creation in newsprint of a great public hero is an invention of our age, which has not seen any betterment of the technique that erected Frémont into a martyr and a man designed by providential forethought to save the American people from their governors. Here, at a trial designed to assess his actions on the fringe of empire, was created a figure of pure advertising that cost the nation heavily from then on, a creature of oratory and newsprint. That creation was almost enough to wreck the republic. It was enough to convince innumerable people born since the advertising stopped and its proprietors died, so that you will still find it in the instruction given our children. The report of that trial is a case study in the dynamics of reputation.[9]

The technique of the defense was to dramatize him to the American newspapers — not the court — as a pure and great man who was being martyred by jealous, vindictive incompetents. Benton could be a gigantic hater and his hate had already several times had a decisive effect in American history. It was now loosed on a man who had dared to oppose the husband of a beloved daughter. The Thunderer turned demagogue on an almost cosmic scale. Benton was a great man, he has a place in our history among the most honorable and most distinguished, he served the republic well, his shadow is long. But his attack on Kearny shall not be forgiven him. It was dishonest, it was absurd, and it was puerile. He looked quite as silly as his son-in-law and sometimes quite as crooked.

The witnesses testified: Stockton, Gillespie, Kearny, Cooke, Turner, Edwin Bryant, Owl Russell, and Willard Hall of those we have been concerned with. The Conqueror was presented as Sir Galahad clad in buckskins and wrapped in Old Glory. Permitted by a scared court the most harrowing deviations from both legal and military procedure, Benton hurled this hero at the people who would be asked to vote for him from now on. (The theory behind that vote henceforth was: that incompetence is courage, that self-seeking mutiny is statesmanship, that youth and purity of intention — if purity exists in the main chance — qualify a stupid man to lead armies and govern a nation, that martyrdom in headlines erases blunders and nullifies treason, that greatness is a loud noise.) Mr. Polk had lost a good deal in recent months: he saw himself losing much more as the trial went on, and he wrote some comments on Galahad in his diary that soothe the student's annoyance at a distance of ninety-five years. And the press co-operated with the designs of Benton. It had found a usefulness in Frémont that it would not lose throughout a generation and so tried the case on a country-wide basis.

But neither Benton nor the court's awe of him could reduce the facts. By verdict of a general court, Frémont was found guilty on three charges, supported by twenty-three specifications. The first charge was mutiny: "And the court does therefore sentence the said Lieutenant Colonel Frémont, of the regiment of mounted riflemen, United States Army, to be dismissed the service." Thus ended the first volume of a romantic trilogy. The same pattern was to shape the two sequels and both were to end in precisely the same mood.

Such a verdict encroached on high politics, and Mr. Polk's Cabinet discussed it repeatedly. The court had recommended executive clemency, and in high politics the President extended it. He threw out the charge of mutiny, sustained the other two charges (disobedience to the lawful command of a superior officer, and conduct to the prejudice of good order and military discipline), and approved the sentence. Then he remitted the sentence, released Frémont from arrest, and ordered him to report for duty. There was political pain in this, though there would have been as much in any other outcome, and the President lost Benton when he needed him most, with the peace treaty coming up for ratification. Three months later, Benton, once his confidant in strategy and his candidate for the high command, was willing to nod to him at a funeral, but reconciliation got no farther.

Frémont remained Childe Harold. While Benton blew enough trumpets to reduce a walled city, he resigned his commission and took up the preliminary publicity of the political arm, to which he was committed from now on. He prepared to vindicate himself by leading an exploring expedition over the main chain of the Rocky Mountains in midwinter. This would absorb publicity from the agitation for a Pacific railway, which had enormously increased now that California was ours. Also it would humiliate the United States Army which, by folly of its own act, was deprived of the Pathfinder's services. After a high-pressure advertising campaign he took his Fourth Expedition into the San Juan Mountains of southwestern Colorado. Kit Carson had refused to go with him and Tom Fitzpatrick was not available, having begun a distinguished career as an Indian agent. So the Pathfinder was without the two to whom the safety of his earlier expeditions had been due. The guide he got, the almost mythical Bill Williams, was wise in mountain craft but he could not impose his judgment on Frémont. So a little later, expeditions precisely like those that rescued the Donners were starting out from Taos to bring in the Pathfinder, who had overruled Bill Williams. They were caught in the San Juan snows — where no railroad has ever crossed. A dozen of them died; there was cannibalism; Frémont's unstable egotism had repeated a pattern. There is no more shocking or more unnecessary failure in the exploration of the West. . . . No matter. He was off to California, the Mariposa Grant, a fortune in gold, a Senatorship, the first candidacy of the Republican Party, two inept military campaigns in the Civil War (one of which was disastrous), and two crises of his own deliberate making, either of which might easily have lost us the war. But his conviction of greatness and martyrdom remained unshakable and the limelight never left him till he died.

Benton kept on bugling. Late in July of '48, while Congress

rocked in the stormiest session it had ever had, there was introduced a bill conferring the brevet rank of major general on Stephen Watts Kearny. Kearny had meanwhile been in Mexico, where he had served as governor of Vera Cruz and later of Mexico City, once more the quiet man keeping his head while he worked to tranquilize a far more turbulent society than that of California or New Mexico. Benton had never stopped exposing him as a villain and this bill brought him out on the roar. For the better part of two weeks he deafened the Senate whenever he could get the floor. Polk wrote in his diary that Senator Benton "was violent beyond what is usual even for him," and set down a sad, astringent memory that he had made Kearny a brigadier chiefly because of Benton's recommendation. Benton's thunder and even his threat to filibuster were unavailing, however, and the bill went through. The brevet commission reached Kearny at the home of Meriwether Lewis Clark, his brother-in-law, who had commanded Doniphan's artillery. He had come home an invalid, having taken fever at Vera Cruz. There, at the end of October, assisted by Benton's malice, the fever killed him. Before he died, he sent for Jessie Benton Frémont, once his friend, daughter of one man and wife of another man who had once been his friends. Jessie blamed him for as many injuries as her father and husband did, and alleged that he had killed her infant son. The beautiful virago (the noun is Lincoln's) would not visit that deathbed.

Because of what Benton said of him in that interminable speech, at the trial and in the newspapers, and in the *Thirty Years' View,* Kearny has never had his due. Besides the malice, prejudice, and blind rage in Benton's attack there were innumerable deliberate misstatements, misrepresentations, and misinterpretations. They were immoral acts of revenge and historians should contrive to get beyond them to the facts. Kearny's service to the United States at a decisive turning point in history is great — was itself decisive. He did the jobs assigned him, quietly, completely, authoritatively. He took New Mexico and organized it. He completed the conquest and began the organization of California. In that packed year his was a job rich with possibilities of failure — with just such possibilities as we have seen fulfilled by the stupidity, arrogance, carelessness, or egotism of other men. He succeeded at everything he set out to do: he was an expert. He kept his temper and he held his tongue. He wrote no letter to politicians or the press. He conducted no intrigues and was not interested in politics. Few of those in high places we have had to deal with were capable of putting the republic before themselves. Kearny served it without trying to serve himself. He was a man, a gentleman, and a soldier. The enmity of an adventurer's father-in-law should not be permitted to obscure his achievement any longer.

Meanwhile, Winfield Scott, half-betrayed by the commander in chief, half-inhibited by the military system, much less than half-equipped and half-supplied by the overstrained quartermaster department, and constantly intrigued against by politicians who held generals' commissions — Winfield Scott had won the war.

It has been made clear that though James K. Polk was, by a wide margin, the biggest man who held the Presidency between Jackson and Lincoln, he was not big enough to conduct a war. When Congress adjourned in August of '46, representative government in the United States had come close to collapse. Both parties were formless, without logic and almost without meaning. Finances were precarious: the administration had destroyed its principal source of revenue, the tariff, at the moment when it undertook a war that required the greatest expenditure yet made by the United States. (From the end of summer on, however, the finances improved rapidly. The bad luck of the Irish saved the credit of the United States. The famine overseas brought farm prices back to pre-'37 levels and beyond them. The exportation of cereals brought a boom in shipping. War manufacture accelerated the already accelerating industries. In '47 the nation roared into a war boom.)

If Congress adjourned in chaos, it was accurately reproducing the country's emotions. The period between August and December was absolutely decisive in our history. At the moment what is important about it is that bewilderment, resentment, and frustration began to head up. The intoxication of May and June ended. A lot of people found that they didn't want any war, a lot more that they didn't want this one, a few that they didn't want the next one. Those who wanted this war still did not like the way it was going. When they came to vote they canceled a certainty of political interpreters, they did not increase the power of the party in power. The Whigs would have a House majority in the Thirtieth Congress. It did them no good, it only increased the chaos and helped to show that a decisive turn had been rounded — and it laid a further load on the insufficiencies of Polk.

He did what he could. He had not been able to buy or bribe a victory. His peripheral campaigns had given him the West, all the principal Mexican seaports except Vera Cruz, and a fringe of territory in northern Mexico, but the Mexican government strangely refused to submit. Polk's idea had been to sit on a conquest of about this size and wait for submission. But by December it was obvious that such a policy would mean a long war and that the nation would not stand for a long war. There was no recourse but to increase the national effort and fight a decisive campaign. Specifically, to fight the campaign which Scott and a number of others had been urging on him: to take Vera Cruz and move on Mexico City.

But this involved decisions of great pain. It was clear that such an operation was beyond the talents of Zachary Taylor. Besides, it would make him President. That left Scott. Scott had been insubordinate, he was a trained soldier, and he was a Whig — three formidable disqualifications, the last almost insuperable. While Polk raised armies and tried to finance them, he was exhausting his ingenuity trying to get the high command into safely Democratic and safely amateur hands. As his counselors succeeded in convincing him that he could not entrust it to political generals, the autmun of '46 brought the brief, surprising period of his accord with Thomas Hart Benton. Out of that came the most preposterous military proposal ever made by a President, which we have seen him writing in his message to Congress on Christmas Day. He tried to have Congress revive the rank of lieutenant general, so that he could put Benton in charge of the war. Benton's ignorance of war was absolute, but that was rather a virtue than a defect in Polk's eyes, and Benton's appointment would be economical. It would have at least two inestimable results: it would prevent a Whig military victory and it would pull out the kingpin of the Van Buren faction of the Democratic Party.

All this time Scott was laboring at his job. The war effort, particularly the service of supply, was never equal to the needs of the armies but it succeeded better than there was any reasonable hope it could. That it succeeded so well, that it did not break down altogether, was due to Scott and the two men who worked with him, Jesup the Quartermaster General, and Marcy the Secretary of War. Marcy was a wheelhorse politician who had been appointed to the Cabinet for services rendered but the emergency had refined him into a first-rate Secretary of War. He had come to appreciate Scott's genius and, when it became clear that there was enough good sense in Congress to keep Benton out of the high command, he succeeded in bringing Polk to the abhorrent decision. There was nothing else to do if we were to win the war.

So finally Polk approved Scott's plans for the reduction of San Juan de Ulúa and the invasion of the heart of Mexico from Vera Cruz. He then put Scott in charge, with a set of instructions which told him quite openly that if he won it would be an administration victory and if he lost no one would share the responsibility with him. Presently Polk found himself actually pleased by this solution. He believed that he was spoiling the Taylor for President movement and he was confident — on ample grounds — that he could keep Scott's candidacy from blossoming. However, he found the idea of any success by any Whig general increasingly distasteful. For a full two months after he had started Scott toward Mexico with a promise of complete authority and complete support, he went on trying to make Benton lieutenant general. He came pretty close: the House actually passed one of the bills creating the office. But he finally lost this weapon and, to produce the necessary disgrace of Scott, had to rely on Worth and his own political generals, notably his former law partner, the confessed father of his candidacy, Gideon Pillow.

It was altogether impossible for Scott to raise an army large enough for the job set him; the first condition he worked under was to do the job with inadequate forces. He began by taking over about half of Taylor's army and ordering Taylor to confine himself to defensive activity. Since the battle of Monterrey in late September, Taylor had done nothing but occupy Saltillo, watch a number of aimless expeditions peter out (fortunately, they brought Wool down within supporting distance at Monclova), cultivate his press relations, and consolidate preparations for his candidacy. When Scott deprived him of troops necessary for the conquest of Mexico, Taylor had a blinding revelation of human perfidy. His mind was not large but it was violent. They were not going to keep Old Rough and Ready from either glory or the White House! There followed the instructive spectacle of the head of an expeditionary force in hostile country acting in defiance of his immediate commander and in disregard of the commander in chief, with the uproarious approval of his army and the sustained praise of the war correspondents. It cost a lot of blood and treasure to make Zachary Taylor President of the United States for sixteen months.

The battle of Monterrey had been a wasted battle, had accomplished nothing, but at least it was inevitable in the campaign Taylor had been ordered to make. Whereas the bloody engagement at Buena Vista was not only wasted, it was wholly a step in the advancement of a political candidacy. Taylor had been ordered to secure and defend the occupation of the north as far as Monterrey. Instead of that, in a sublime belief that he could take his reduced forces on to San Luis Potosí and perhaps to Mexico City, he concentrated his army at Saltillo, well beyond Monterrey, and prepared to go even farther. On February 5 he reached a position in the mountains a little beyond Buena Vista, where he arranged his troops in various positions and camped to await developments. They came on February 22, when Santa Anna attacked him.

Santa Anna had worked a prodigy: he had succeeded in raising a large army from a nation that was half in revolt against him, he had armed and equipped it, and he had made it a fine fighting force. It was a good army, it fought with sustained fury, it came exceedingly close to winning the two-day battle, and it might well have won it if Santa Anna's own courage had lasted long enough to send it into action on the third day. At the end of that day the Americans had broken every assault but had been pushed back, were disorganized, and had let the Mexicans work round their flanks within striking distance of their rear. However, the heroic defense, though it had not broken the spirit of the Mexican Army, had broken Santa Anna's nerve. On the morning of the third day, instead of attacking again, he was already in retreat. The retreat became a panic, the army melted away, and it was only by what amounted to another miracle that he raised an army to oppose Scott.

For the Americans it was a desperately near thing. It turned out a victory after all, a victory won by Taylor's subordinates and the courage of the private soldier. Everyone who has ever written about it has paid tribute to Taylor, sitting on his white horse, absolutely without fear or even concern, inspiring a whole army by his coolness, and giving history and the Presidential campaign of '48 a tagline, "a little more of the grape, Captain Bragg." But it was Captain Bragg and the other officers of artillery (T. W. Sherman, George Thomas, John Reynolds), it was Jefferson Davis and the First Mississippi Rifles, above all it was the anonymous platoons, who won the battle. The will of the individual soldier to stand his ground under fire and cavalry charge, to take enormous losses without fleeing, to go on shooting long after military logic would have had him running to the rear — that was what counted when the balance hung at dead center. Taylor may have inspired his troops: he certainly did not direct them. The company officers and the private soldiers improvised a rule of thumb defense on the spot as it was needed. The army was shot to pieces in two days of murderous fighting that was frequently hand-to-hand, but it was still full of fight — and it held the field. Thus ended the military career of Zachary Taylor. His former son-in-law had won the election for him.

And that son-in-law had advanced farther toward the defeat of the unborn Confederacy. It was a little after noon of the second day when a brigade of Mexican cavalry, grandly uniformed, charged the one remaining strong point that defended a flank and protected the road to Saltillo by which an American retreat would have to move. The troops of that strong point had been driven back and the Mississippi Rifles were coming up in support. Their wounded colonel formed them as a retracted flank, joining an Indiana regiment at a sharp angle. When the Mexican cavalry got within rifle range, it halted. Mississippi and Indiana blew it to pieces and there was no further attack in that part of the field. That refused flank is the *V* that comes down in history. By September Jefferson Davis was a Senator of the United States. In 1853 he was Secretary of War. In 1861 he was a President exercising the function of a military genius. The war was half finished when a Confederate newspaper put the grief of nations into a remark on that genius, "If the Confederacy ever perishes it will have perished of a *V*."

Winfield Scott, however, made an army and conquered a nation. He never had half the troops he needed; at best he had only two thirds of those definitely promised him, and never had as many as that at any one time. His little force was weakened by the necessity of sending home regiments whose enlistments had expired. Supplies were cut off for weeks at a stretch and he ended by abandoning his line of communications, living off the country, and capturing ammunition. He was hamstrung by the instructions given to a political commissioner who was sent to treat for peace. One of his best generals betrayed him in the end and his worst general, besides endangering his campaign, was betraying him from the beginning. But he clamped down on a formless mass the discipline and training that made them a fighting army. He curbed the disorders that Taylor had permitted for the sake of his candidacy. He dealt so equably with a conquered people that, before he left, responsible portions of them begged him to stay and establish a dictatorship. And, taking his army up the pathway of invasion established by a famous predecessor, Cortes, he fought one of the most brilliant campaigns in military history.

He had, of course, brilliant assistants. Twiggs was a first-rate fighting man, and Worth, the letter writer who gave Polk his chance to disgrace Scott, was rather more than that. Some of Mr. Polk's Democratic generals were excellent too: Persifor Smith, Quitman, and Shields (lately Commissioner of the Land Office) revealed a natural talent for war. Moreover Scott had a handful of brilliant engineers — Robert E. Lee who was effectively his chief of staff, Beauregard, Meade. The intelligence of Ethan Allen Hitchcock, his inspector general, was a mighty force. Finally, the Academy at West Point which the Senate had recently been so eager to destroy vindicated itself. Company and battalion officers whose names read like a list of Civil War generals, North and South, fought in detail the campaign that Scott conceived and directed.

This last was by no means the least important result of the march that ended with the American flag flying over the Halls of Montezuma. They got a schooling that enabled them to manage armies when the deadlier war came. It trained them as West Point could never have done, and some of the training went deep. The classic tactics of Robert E. Lee, the perfect battle of Chancellorsville, the converging attacks of Gettysburg, were all learned at the headquarters of Winfield Scott. When Ulysses Grant, to the horror of textbook soldiers and the derision of journalists and English critics, cut loose from his base and marched overland to take Vicksburg from the rear (thus foreshadowing the March to the Sea), he was able to recall the same horror and derision when Old Fuss and Feathers marched out of Puebla, abandoning his base.

It was March 29, '47, when Vera Cruz surrendered after the fortress of Ulúa had been battered in by the big guns landed from Matthew Perry's fleet and sited by Lee. (Perry, who was to negotiate the opening of Japan, had succeeded Conner.) On April 8 Scott advanced into the interior and on April 18, in the mountain pass at Cerro Gordo, he shattered an excellent army which Santa Anna had raised since Buena Vista. A brilliant reconnoissance by Lee made possible the turning movement that won the battle, and the bungling of Mr. Polk's law partner, Pillow, endangered it. (Pillow took a slight wound, went home to buttress Polk's distrust of Scott, and came back a major general.) The army occupied Jalapa the next day, and here Scott had to send seven regiments back to the States — which left him with six thousand men to conquer Mexico. Here also he quarreled ferociously with Nicholas Trist, the liberal philosopher and dreary letter writer who was Polk's peace commissioner. On May 15 the army occupied Puebla and presently Worth, its first governor, was converted into an enemy of Scott's, when a court-martial directed the commander to rebuke him for injudicious behavior. At Puebla, Trist and Scott settled their quarrel (though the reports of it were laying up trouble for both of them in Washington) and tried to negotiate a peace.

Their efforts failed and the campaign had to be resumed. Another political general arrived with a brigade of reinforcements at last. This was Franklin Pierce, who eventually would run a wound sustained by a fall from a horse on the field of battle into the Presidency. On August 7 Scott abandoned his base. On the word of the Duke of Wellington he also abandoned all hope of winning his campaign or successfully retreating from the defeats he was sure to suffer. He took the army over the last majestic mountains and down to the great central plateau of Mexico. On August 19 and 20 he won two brilliant and bloody battles, known as Contreras and Churubusco, that brought him to the gates of Mexico City. Again Lee found the key to victory, again Pillow's ineptness exposed the army to defeat, and again a first-class army outfought another first-class army whose generals lacked staying power and guts. Twiggs, Worth, Quitman, and Persifor Smith made up for Pillow's stupidity and Pierce's mediocrity, and Scott personally directed the tactics that U. S. Grant was later to call faultless.

Outside the capital, Scott again tried to negotiate a peace. (Neither he nor Trist knew it but both of them had by now been discredited at Washington. Malice, lies, politics, and bad communications had convinced Polk, who was longing to be convinced, that they were both out of sympathy with him, which made them traitors.) The negotiations broke down, for Santa Anna did not dare risk the domestic consequences of acknowledging the military situation, and after two weeks Scott terminated the armistice and prepared to attack the city. He first stormed a group of buildings known as El Molino del Rey, part of the fortifications based on Chapultapec. His information — which proved false — was that cannon for the defense of the city were being cast there. The action of September 8 was intense and the victory cost the Americans heavily, far more than it should have done if Worth, who was in charge, had learned the lessons in artillery which the whole war had been teaching. Five days later came the decisive battle, which has been known ever since as Chapultapec.

In proceeding against Mexico City, Scott had two alternatives. He could storm the heavily defended stone causeways that led to the city from the south across swamps, or he could storm a causeway that led from the west. This last was more lightly held but was much stronger naturally in that its defense could be based on the high hill known as Chapultapec. For once the reconnoissance and advice of Robert E. Lee were disregarded, in favor of a dissenting opinion by Pierre Beauregard, and Scott chose to attack Chapultapec. The hill was crowned by an immense stone palace, once the summer residence of the viceroys of Spain, now occupied by the Mexican Military College. Throughout September 12 Scott battered it with his heaviest guns. The cannonade accomplished little and the next day, September 13, assault groups from Worth's and Twigg's divisions of regulars set out to storm it. They clawed and shot their way up the almost vertical slope through a terrible musketry fire, climbed the palace walls with scaling ladders, and, after a savage bayonet action, drove the defenders out. (Among the Mexican troops were the young cadets of the Military College. Santa Anna had ordered them relieved but they would not go. Their stand richly deserved the monuments that commemorate it at Chapultapec.) The capture of the fortress opened the way to the city. Worth — Scott hoped to mollify his innumerable grievances by letting him finish the job — worked his way down one causeway. It was bitterly defended, Santa Anna commanding in person, but Worth got a little way into the city before digging in for the night. So did Quitman, down another causeway which was defended just as stubbornly. At daybreak of the fourteenth Quitman pushed on to the center of the city while Scott, Worth, and Hitchcock were talking to civilians who wanted to surrender on terms. There in the Plaza de Armas, at seven A.M., he raised the first American flag that ever flew above the capital of a conquered nation.

The five months' campaign from Vera Cruz to Mexico City, with its six bloody victories, was a tremendous feat of arms. Between George Washington and the maturity of two subalterns who watched Scott enter the national palace two hours after Quitman raised the flag, there was no American general who could have come anywhere near doing it. It remains a classic of generalship succeeding against all but impossible odds. Also it gave Mr. Polk his desire: it put an end to opposition in Mexico.

That ending came on September 14, 1847. On February 2, 1848, Nicholas Trist, deprived of power to make a treaty and ordered home in disgrace, nevertheless memorably served his country by signing the Treaty of Guadalupe Hidalgo. On February 18, Scott — who for five months had kept an idle and increasingly rebellious army in check and had smoothly governed Mexico — received orders relieving him of command and summoning him also home in disgrace. Worth and Pillow had collaborated in a job. Mr. Polk was arranging to keep the conqueror of Mexico from heading the Whig ticket this summer. He was preparing to turn a court of inquiry, which had been convened to investigate the lying of Gideon Pillow, into a public repudiation of Winfield Scott.

Through all this time the United States had been unable to provide a government for Oregon, which went on sustaining the unattached organization, like the free state of Franklin, which it had developed between 1843 and 1845. The United States had also been unable to provide governments for New Mexico and California, where the military organizations established by Kearny went on operating, or for Deseret, where Brigham Young was in no hurry for an exterior government.

The treaty of peace which the discredited Trist signed at Guadalupe Hidalgo on February 2, 1848, was ratified by the Senate on March 10. It was ratified in desperation, because the war had to be ended so that more serious business could, at last, be faced. The treaty confirmed the American possession of Texas, of California as it is today, and of New Mexico to the Gila River and down that river to the Colorado. (This last was ambiguous and unsatisfactory. The ambiguity was cleared up and the cession extended to include all of Cooke's wagon road and a route for a Pacific railway by the Gadsden Purchase of 1854.) So the West of Mr. Polk's original intention became American by treaty and was declared to be worth fifteen million dollars, here guaranteed to Mexico, above the costs of war and the assumption of the American claims.

And still there was no government for Oregon, New Mexico, California, and Deseret — for the West. Oregon was finally given Territorial status in August, 1848, and the first governor arrived there three years after Termination. New Mexico continued under military government till the great Compromise permitted it organization as a Territory in September, 1850. The same measure pared down Deseret from Brigham's claims, renamed it Utah, and gave it Territorial status. California never was a Territory. The military organization established by Kearny had to govern it till the same Compromise made it a state of the Union.

The three preceding paragraphs record a beginning.

This narrative has remarked that a decisive turn was rounded at some time between August and December, 1846. On August 10, the First Session of the Twenty-ninth Congress adjourned while

Senator Davis was discussing a measure, which had originated in the House and bore the name of David Wilmot, to exclude slavery from the territory to be acquired from Mexico. Senator Calhoun of South Carolina said that the first volume of our political history under the Constitution had been closed and the second opened, that a curtain had been dropped between the present and the future which was to him impenetrable. Prescience woke in the nerves of William Lowndes Yancey, however; he resigned his seat in the House and went back to Alabama; in the second volume of our political history he could predict no future under the Constitution for the Southern states. Likewise, when the Second Session of the Twenty-ninth Congress convened in December, John C. Calhoun was able to penetrate the impenetrable curtain for at least a little way. He was the last survivor of the first period of the Southern politician, and Yancey's resignation is the signal that the third period of that politician was taking charge. The survivor of a period when there were clearer and more powerful minds, aware that the thing had happened in the intervening months, aware that a curtain had not been lowered but that at last a curtain had been raised — John C. Calhoun thought he saw one way of saving the United States. It was a tolerably desperate way: the United States must enter again into the womb and be born a second time. Since the summer solstice of 1788 when by a vote of 57 to 46 the New Hampshire convention brought the number of states ratifying the new Constitution to the nine necessary for adoption — from that June day on, the whole course of the United States had been wrong. In the opinion of Calhoun, we must go back to the preceding September, reconvene the Constitutional Convention that then adjourned sine die, and start all over.

"The United States will conquer Mexico," Ralph Waldo Emerson had said, "but it will be as the man swallows the arsenic which brings him down in turn. Mexico will poison us."

The Second Session of the Twenty-ninth Congress convened in chaos and so accurately reflected the nation which, according to the provisions of the Constitution, it was to govern. That chaos was the reason why the United States could provide no government for Oregon till 1849 and none for New Mexico, Deseret, and California till 1850. When what is called the Compromise of 1850 was finally voted in Congress chaos had not been in the least resolved but a channel had been established which would contain it for just ten years.

Already in December of '46 Congress, exactly tuned to the

vibrations of its electorate, was more turbulent than any Congress before it had been. Seen against that turbulence, the human figures that expressed it do not matter much, and at this distance the patterns they wove, the passions that dominated them, the ideas and expedients and guesses and experiments and evasions they worked with are less than the overmastering fact itself. We need waste no effort in trying to determine whether war with Mexico was just or unrighteous. Even the long shadow which the war cast to the southward, a shadow which is only beginning to be dissipated after ninety-six years, is not within our purpose. The fact of the Mexican War is infinitely smaller to us than the fact, the complex of facts, which now had to be faced by the Congress and the people of the United States. And the facing of those facts is the basis of some other book than this one, which has endeavored to lead up to them and may now end with the statement that the West had been won.

Bill Bowen in Oregon could not be given citizenship, he could not even be protected from the Indians who on November 29, 1847, massacred Dr. Whitman and his missionaries — till it had been determined whether some abstractions called the Ordinance of 1787 and the line of the Missouri Compromise of 1820 ought to be effected on humble farmsteads along the Willamette River. There could be no Negro slavery in Oregon, and there could be none in New Mexico, Deseret, or California. But Bill Bowens of those territories could not be citizens till it had been decided whether or not boys who had died at Monterrey and Cerro Gordo had died to extend the political theory of a low-energy, gang-labor economy which was already altogether obsolete. Can Congress deprive any state of its right in any Territory? Can Congress forbid any citizen to take his property anywhere? Who shall decide whether California, Oregon, and New Mexico shall be free or slave? Who has the authority to decide? Who can constitute a Territory? Who shall make its laws? Can the citizens of a Territory exclude slavery? Can Congress exclude it from a Territory? Can Congress exclude it anywhere? Can any people exclude it anywhere?

In Oregon, California, New Mexico, and Deseret they broke the ground with plows. They tore out the sagebrush by the roots, felled the trees, brought water to the parched earth, bred their cattle, gathered honey, grafted slips on orchard trees, built wharves, set up water wheels, ground wheat and sawed timber. They built houses, sent the kids to school, gathered on Sunday to thank God for having brought them safe to a new land, and taxed themselves to prevent the curse of an illiterate ministry and to secure the blessings of liberty to themselves and their posterity. But to the eastward, breaking through increasingly ineffective subterfuges, fighting the whole thing out on an unreal question, the United States at last was facing the paradox and quandary at its core. The West had made the United States a continental nation. But the continental nation was under the necessity of resolving its basic contradiction.

The theorem of squatter sovereignty, the theorem of Dred Scott — both announced before 1847 ran out. Resolutions from nine states that all territory added to the area of the United States shall be henceforth and forever free. Resolution by the legislative body of Virginia that Congress (or the people) has no authority over slavery. *Voted:* to extend the Missouri Compromise line to the Pacific. *Voted:* to repeal the vote. Through the spring and summer of '48, while James K. Polk, the last man of Yesterday, began to fade into the shadow of abandoned unrealities where, a good, small man, he has existed ever since, there went on a violent struggle for the control of two political parties which meant less than was yet realized. The election, fought in the collapse of subterfuges, was itself one more, desperate subterfuge. No logic could be imposed on the Democratic Party. All but one of its pressures might have been angled into another such forced harmony as had made Polk its candidate in the now faraway, now innocent and hopeful year of 1844. That one pressure was the Territories — the West — and it was invincible. Martin Van Buren and his following withdrew — and this meant that a portion of the Democratic Party had announced that the extension of slavery would be a moral curse. That settled the Democracy for this year, and after this year it would be a different party. It nominated the most sedulous, the loudest of its candidates, Lewis Cass — and the Whigs won. The Whigs won with a subterfuge candidate, Zachary Taylor, who was a war hero and had no convictions about slavery. That finished the Whigs forever.

They had already lost the "Conscience Whigs" — those who were not wrapped in the cotton thread which Emerson said held the nation together. In 1848 some of these joined a variety of small parties which suddenly seemed much less crackbrained, much more respectable than they had seemed last week. More, however, shaken to find themselves in such astonishing company, voted for Martin Van Buren and Charles Francis Adams. It was an incredible vote for an unbelievable ticket and there it was, irrefutable evidence of what had happened since August of '46. Van Buren and Adams stood for free soil in Oregon, California, and New Mexico, where soil could not possibly be anything but free. "Free soil," their slogan said, "free speech, free labor, and free men." Stripped to the actuality: free West. It had happened.

Well, how? By the sum of many small and a few great things.

In part by this . . . He was a good boy. You remembered how he had laughed and chattered. You remembered being harsh to him, in the unforgivable stupidity of parenthood. One day he was playing with a tin sword or, with a wooden gun, shooting imaginary Indians round a corner of the barn. A day or two later his voice was not treble any more and it was not a wooden gun that was on his shoulder when the fifes shrilled and he marched off behind the silk banner which the ladies of the church had made. You saw his face when he waved to you at the curve in the road, and you wouldn't see it again. He had died of fever at Matamoros or of thirst on the way to Monclova, or a Mexican lance had done for him at Buena Vista or he had got halfway up the slope at Chapultapec. No children would spring from his loins as he had sprung from yours. So in Georgia you watched the upland where he had hunted squirrels turn brown with autumn, or in Ohio you saw the cows come in at milking time in still evening with someone else whistling to his dog. For what? For New Mexico and California. What did those three words mean? As day was added to day, slowly, insensibly, it was borne in on you that you had better find out.

But that is simple, easily dramatized, and too slight. Georgia or Ohio, as day was added to day, you were tugged at by forces subtler, more complex, more powerful, and more lasting than personal grief. A steelyard's arm had been lengthened and the counterpoise had moved out along it. Imperceptibly, the nation's consciousness was shaping to a new orientation, as the logic of geography, now acknowledged by the map, became the logic of economics. As, at a different level, the logic of desire achieved became the logic of daily expectation, and the logic of time became the logic of time continuing. The lines ran east and west more firmly than before, old constraints were broken through, new bonds were formed. Yesterday poised on the brink of disappearance. The center of gravity had been displaced. Imperceptibly, with an uncomprehending slowness, the nation began to answer to its new conditions.

But too slowly. On March 4, 1861, not enough Americans knew what the new President was talking about. "Physically speaking we cannot separate. We cannot remove our respective sections from each other, nor build an impassable wall between them. A husband and wife may be divorced and go out of the presence and beyond the reach of each other; but the different parts of our country cannot do this. . . . Suppose you go to war, you cannot fight always; and when, after much loss on both sides and no gain on either, you cease fighting, the identical old questions as to terms of intercourse are again upon you."

So Abraham Lincoln (who might have been governor of Oregon) had learned in the old West, and so, now that the counterpoise was at the far end of the lengthened steelyard, the old West and the new West were prepared to prove. Mr. Lincoln was telling his countrymen that the achieved West had given the United States something that no people had ever had before, an internal, domestic empire, and he was telling them that Yesterday must not be permitted to Balkanize it.

Too late. At some time between August and December, 1846, the Civil War had begun.

They had done that, the people of this book: they had brought in that empire and made that war inevitable. The soldiers who followed Kearny to Santa Fe and on to California, Doniphan's farm boys and the Mormons slogging along with Cooke under their canopy of dust and miracle, Brigham Young's dispossessed people, and Owl Russell, Edwin Bryant, Jessy Thornton, the Donners. The wagon trains pulling out from Independence in the mud and coming finally to the Willamette or the Sacramento. They had shifted the center of gravity of the nation forever.

From August '46 until the murky dawn of April 12, 1861, the war progressed through political and social phases. Then in that dawn Edmund Ruffin, the most honored Virginia secessionist, pulled the lanyard of a cannon on Morris Island that was trained on a fort in Charleston Harbor, and the military phase began.

The book ends here, for we are not dealing with Western history. That history exists, one may remember, and its spectacle might be touched upon almost anywhere. Already in 1847 Asa Whitney, the dreamer of railroads, was by no means the figure of cloud-cuckoo land which he had been a year before — precisely as the abolitionists had, in that year, somehow ceased to be madmen. The spectacle of Western history might begin with the railroads, or with the stage-coaches that preceded them, or the pony-express riders — or with tall masts coming into the Bay of San Francisco, taller masts than any seen there before, and a jubilant crew singing to Stephen Foster's tune, "Oh Susanna! Oh please take your ease, for we have beat the clipper fleet, the *Sovereign of the Seas*." Or it might begin with spectacle's curiosa: the airship that was to cross to California in three days but somehow didn't, or a nester waking at midnight to see against the copper circle of the Arizona moon the silhouettes of Lieutenant Beale's camels. Or with the wagons that kept on coming year after year till Asa Whitney's dream took flesh, and very little difference between any of them and those we have followed here. Or agony giving a name to Death Valley. Or the mines in the canyons where the Forlorn Hope starved, or the mines anywhere else in the ranges of the West. Or the Long Trail and its herds, its ballads, and its too much advertised gunfire. Or the vigilantes, the Sioux and the Cheyenne rising, the army on the march. Or anything else from an abundance of spectacle.

No Westerner, however, would begin the history of his region with spectacle. For the history of the West is the history of such people as we have seen here living out their lives in the new country, and watching their children and grandchildren grow up with that country. It is not a spectacular but a laborious history. One who once thought of writing it would have written it in terms of alkali, sagebrush, wind, and water — in terms of making a dead land bring forth life — and in terms of the mortgage held on it by other sections where a man's labor was permitted to secure his old age, since he gave value to the land he settled on, as the West was not permitted to do. It could not possibly be a spectacular story. But, whatever it might have turned out to be, that book not to be written would have begun where this one ends, with the internal empire of the United States achieved.

There remains one paragraph of this history. In 1861, following Mr. Lincoln's appeal to his countrymen, the Civil War went into its military phase. Yesterday would not yield to the future without appealing beyond Mr. Lincoln and human intelligence to arms.

It was Yesterday, of course, and the greatest tragedy of the war it fought was that that war was fought for an anachronism. The low-energy economy and the chattel slavery it consisted in had been slain by such men as Eli Whitney, William Kelly, Cyrus McCormick, Samuel Colt, Elias Howe, the gunsmiths who made machine tools, the proprietors of the National Fair, the city of Lowell, the Naugatuck Valley, Pittsburgh, the railroads, the telegraph lines, the turbines. These — but in collaboration with men who went West and made the nation a continent. It had become a nation which inclosed a journey from Baltimore to San Diego, or Charleston to San Francisco, or Richmond to Oregon City, that crossed no frontier and kept always within a common texture of experience and feeling. They had stretched out that commonalty to the Pacific, making the empire, and New Bedford sold its goods to Santa Fe through the entrepot of St. Louis from within, or Monterey sent its sons to the college at Cambridge still from within. In this continental nation the habit and expectation of thought had already realized the empire. Since that had happened, the expectation of the seceded states was already obsolete when they met in Montgomery to make a nation against Tomorrow.

What was done at Montgomery was to file a last Bill of Review against reality and, when the nation dismissed it, to appeal from the dismissal to the final court. That appeal might have succeeded, one remembers, working in virtual motions, in history's *if*'s. At least, in the course of human history such bills of review have sometimes been granted, the future has not always won when the past attacked it. This time the future won, Yesterday was overturned and rejected. Of those who have thought about that decision in our own time, a certain curious, gentle set of literary people have fallen in with their spiritual ancestor, Calhoun, and regretted the event, feeling that the past would have been better for us all. History is not properly concerned with them and could only call them fools; they had best be left to literary criticism, which may call them poets. At any rate, Yesterday lost out. On June 18, 1865, Edmund Ruffin, rising once more to the surface of events, acknowledged that A. Lincoln had been right on March 4, 1861. The admission made, he killed himself. In history's *if*'s that sacrificial acknowledgment need not, perhaps, have been made. Except that some people went west in '46, and so sentenced Edmund Ruffin to death.

Outline of American history, final chapter.

On Christmas Day, 1848, Jim Clyman sat down in Napa Valley, where he had spent the winter when we first met him, to write to a friend back in Wisconsin, whither he was returning when he left our narrative. "We left the west of Missouri on the 1st of May and arrived here on the 5th of September without accident or interruption of any kind worthy of notice," Jim said. "Matters and things here are strangely and curiously altered since I left this country."

For the waters of Manitou had worked their spell once more and Jim had crossed to California in '48. He had signed on to guide some emigrators west, the Mecombs from Indiana. He was fifty-six and he was going back to the golden shore. All the West was in his memory, and it was a mountain man who found nothing worthy of notice in that crossing. We must take his word, however, since there is no record. But Jim Clyman found at least one notable element in the passage west. She was Hannah Mecomb and on August 22, '49, she married him at Napa. The mountain man would now settle down. He farmed in various places and finally bought a ranch at Napa in 1855. Children were born to him. Some of them died. He and his wife adopted other children. He worked his land. He died on December 27, 1881. Grandchildren are working his land now. (Outline of Western History.)

When Clyman wrote in December, '48, that "matters and things" were curiously altered since he had left California in '46, he was alluding to the sequel of an event which he had heard of on his way west. It was an event which one would think "worthy of note." In August, '48, the Mecomb train was coming westward along the Truckee River. It may be that Jim was telling his greenhorns about the emigrators of '46 who had traveled this very stretch too late to cross the pass ahead, when they met a party who had just come down from that pass. God knows how often in his time Jim had halted on a trail to exchange information with a party met in the wilderness and traveling the trail the other way. But this was like no other meeting.

The eastbound were former members of the Mormon Battalion on their way to Deseret, where their twenty-six months' journey would end at last in the company of their families, the prophet Brigham, and Israel growing strong in Zion. We saw some of them, just eleven months before this meeting, turning back to Sutter's when they received the prophet's counsel that they might take jobs there for the winter and so ease the strain on food supplies at Great Salt Lake City. Henry Bigler had been with them then, and he was with them now, meeting the Mecombs and Jim Clyman by the Truckee. They had information to give Jim in exchange for any news about the Saints in Zion or on their way to it which he may have picked up in his long traverse. They could tell him that a former companion of his, James Marshall, a man who had come down from Oregon with him in '45 and then gone to work for Sutter, had finally located on the American River the sawmill site that Sutter had so often wanted located there. They could tell, and show, him what Marshall had found on that site six and a half months ago, on January 24 of this year.

If John Bidwell is right, Marshall was more than a little star-crazed. At least when he started in to build that mill — on shares — he had some notion of rafting lumber down the canyons of the American River. But, on Bidwell's word, he was a good millwright and built a good mill. Six of the Mormon Battalion, including Bigler, were working on it under his direction, besides three Gentiles and a number of Sutter's Indians. They got the wheel set too low, and so the tail race had to be deepened. They would dig during the day, then turn the water in at night to clean it out.

On January 24, 1848, there were still nine days to go before Trist and the Mexicans could sign their treaty at Guadalupe Hidalgo. Brigham Young was at Winter Quarters again, where he had at last had himself formally "sustained" as president of the Church of Jesus Christ of Latter-day Saints, and was preparing the emigration of '48. At Washington, the court-martial told Lieutenant Colonel Frémont that he might submit a written defense, and Mr. Polk wrote in his diary, in a crazy fear of an inconceivable rebellion, "The Conduct of Mr. Trist and Gen'l Scott, who seem to have entered into a conspiracy to embarrass the government gives me great anxiety. They have proved themselves [the man who won the war and the man who saved the peace] to be wholly unworthy of the positions they hold, and I most heartily wish they were both out of Mexico." Many soldiers, scattered in detachments in many places, heartily wished themselves out of Mexico, that day. In Congress they were quarreling about the bitterly felt but not yet understood. The Comanche were licking the wounds that a campaign by William Gilpin had cost them, and were preparing this year's slaughter. Scattered about America new Bill Bowens, not so many as in '46 or '47, were dreaming of spring, when they too would take to the trail.

On that Monday morning Marshall turned the water out of the tail race as usual, and toward midafternoon got down into it to see how much progress had been made. Not much, for they were down to bedrock. A few inches of water covered the granite shelf. Marshall saw something shiny under that water. He stooped to pick it up.

That was what Henry Bigler and his homing fellow Saints told Jim Clyman beside the Truckee in August, '48.

The past was not going to win the appeal to arms, the continental nation was not going to be Balkanized, it was going to remain an empire and dominate the future.

Notes

CHAPTER II

1. The Aricara, the Assinniboin, the northern Arapaho, and most of all the Blackfeet.

2. The opinion of scholars, which has changed before this, is again that the returning Astorians learned about South Pass and traveled it — from west to east. Such descriptions as they print do not closely describe South Pass, but it is neither my business nor my interest to question them. At any rate, the Ashley party under Jedediah Smith, certainly the first white men to travel the Pass from the east, were the effective discoverers. They made it known and the rest followed — from their passage, not that of the Astorians.

3. With Markhead, La Bonte, Hatcher, and the Seventh Baronet of Grandtully in Ruxton's *Life in the Far West,* 1848. This statement is tolerably arbitrary. Stewart himself published a novel called *Altowan* in '46, two years before Ruxton's book. Mike Fink and Rose had been celebrated in the magazines still earlier and various romances had introduced characters modeled on the mountain man. But genuine portraiture begins with Ruxton.

4. Stein's words in Conrad's *Lord Jim.*

CHAPTER III

1. This map reading, from Polk's *Diary* for February 13, is substantially repeated on February 16 and exhibits Polk's — but by no means Atocha's — ignorance of the country he was trying to acquire. The Colorado, of course, flows west only through a part of Arizona; mainly it flows south. The description could be given meaning only by concluding that Atocha meant to offer Polk everything he wanted except the southern half of the present state of California.

2. For a discussion of Joseph Smith's psychosis, see Bernard DeVoto, "The Centennial of Mormonism," in *Forays and Rebuttals,* 71 ff.

3. Certainly from 1833.

4. Speculation in real estate was a strong part of Mormonism from the very beginning. Under Young in Utah fictitious land values came to be capitalized as the society developed on its strong base, and so they were a legitimate instrument of colonization. But in the earlier periods in Ohio, Missouri, and Illinois, the Mormon enterprises in real estate were, quite simply, a theocratic phase of the westward-marching land

boom of the frontier. Remember that the promise of landownership was always the strongest appeal the Mormon missionaries had to make to Europe's poor.

5. Sterling Price, who also enters the narrative later on, was in charge of them.

6. Leaving the lake after his brief exploration of it, Frémont says nothing about the country thereabout as a place of settlement but does highly recommend Bear River Valley. "The bottoms are extensive; water excellent; timber sufficient; the soil good and well adapted to the grains and grasses suited to such an elevated region. A military post and a civilized settlement would be of great value here; and cattle and horses would do well where grass and salt so much abound. . . ." Practically everyone who had ever written about the Bear River had said the same thing, including Jim Clyman (who met the Mississippi Saints on his way east in '46). No one, in fact, could help making that observation the moment he saw the oasis of Soda Springs. Coming back to the Great Basin the following summer, Frémont got to Utah Lake but did not go back to Great Salt Lake. His report says, "In the cove of mountains along its eastern shore the [Utah] lake is bordered by a plain where the soil is generally good, and in greater part fertile; watered by a delta of prettily timbered streams. This would be an excellent locality for stock farms; it is generally covered with good bunch grass and would abundantly produce the ordinary grains." A couple of pages later he sums up his judgment of the entire Great Basin in a properly celebrated passage which accurately predicts its future.

A later controversy between Frémont and Brigham Young deals with an ambiguous passage (p. 273 of the report) in which Frémont seems to mistake Utah Lake for an arm of Great Salt Lake. It was certainly foolish of Frémont not to make the two-day ride which would have settled the matter. He answers Young's accusation in *Memoirs of My Life* but with the same mingling of vagueness and dishonesty that characterizes so much else of that book.

7. There is no dependable evidence whatever to support the attractive speculation that the hard-headed Young did in fact send out a small exploring party to the Great Basin in '46. I have always considered such a party one of the musts of American history, and between Young's arrival at Council Bluffs and the closing in of winter there was plenty of time for such a party to go to Salt Lake Valley and return. In Coutant's *History of Wyoming* the statement is made (and it has been repeated in newspapers and elsewhere) that such a party was in fact sent out under the guidance of two veteran mountain men, Jim Beckwith and O. P. Wiggins. Coutant's authority was two letters by Wiggins which are now in the library of the Nebraska State Historical Society. Not one of the six Mormons whom Wiggins names as composing the party can be identified in any of the Mormon rolls open to me, however, and various students who have access to the Church library are unable

to identify them there. The same students assure me that there is no allusion of any kind to such an exploration in any of the records of the Church. The idea must be dismissed as speculation. It remains true, however, that no man was ever more skillful than Young at keeping his left hand, even if that hand were the Quorum of the Twelve, from knowing what his right hand was doing. I shall not be altogether amazed if eventually it appears that someone did go to the valley in '46, like the six whom Joshua sent into Canaan, to spy out the land. The idea is herewith tendered to those who are making novels about the Mormons a leading American industry.

8. There were many respiratory diseases. Strain and exposure made the Saints an easy prey to pneumonia. An epidemic of whooping cough traveled with them across Iowa, killing many children. The "black canker" which so many journals mention was probably sometimes scurvy, sometimes diphtheria, and sometimes septic sore throat. Scurvy and other ailments resulting from malnutrition were, of course, extremely common.

9. This is the true Council Bluffs of Lewis and Clark, fifteen miles upriver from the present Iowa city of that name.

CHAPTER IV

1. Duly adapted in the City of the Lord, which Joseph Smith, Jun., and his city planners worked out on paper.

2. The date of Frémont's letter is in dispute. Camp concludes that it was written at this time.

CHAPTER V

1. An unfortunate vagueness in Clyman's journal makes it uncertain just whom the party consisted of. When they were all together again on April 28, several thought it was still "impracticable to cross the mountains at this time." Clyman says, "several of us are However verry anxious to try and assertain that fact," and the next day he and the party he continued with started out. Mr. Charles L. Camp, Clyman's editor, writes me that he believes that eleven or twelve men, two women, and two children stayed behind to make the later crossing (various later entries in the journal which need not be cited here support this reading), and that this party went by way of Fort Hall and is the one which will be mentioned later on. Mr. Camp believes that the seasoned old Greenwood, who was "going out to catch emigrants and was in no hurry," was among those who stayed behind. The important thing for our purpose, however, is that Hastings and Hudspeth were in the advance party — by this reading necessarily reduced to seven or eight men, one woman, and a boy — with whom Clyman traveled.

2. Like the log cabin, the covered wagon is a classic American symbol. But, Hollywood notwithstanding, it was not standardized. In any train, even a Santa Fe freight caravan, wagons were likely to differ widely. Nevertheless, by 1846 some evolution and standardization had occurred. Think of the Santa Fe freight wagon (which had the easier passage to make) as about twice the capacity of the Oregon emigrant's wagon, larger in all its dimensions, with longer and more massive tongue (jointed), higher wheels, wider tires, and heavier hubs and hardware. (Hubs might be sixteen inches wide, tires eight inches — or even more.) An average freight might be two and a half tons and an average team five yoke of oxen, though up to five tons or more and ten yoke or more were not unknown. It was unwise to load the lighter emigrant wagon (for which a three-yoke team was usual and a four-yoke team desirable) with more than three thousand pounds and two thousand was better. The lighter the load, the better chance of getting load, wagon, and team through to your destination. Emigrant wagons were likely to be brightly painted — for the first few days. The canvas tops were sometimes blue, green, or red as well as white, and frequently had slogans painted on them.

3. Generally given as either thirty-four or thirty-six. I can count only thirty-two at Springfield.

4. With equal or greater sophistication Polk's war message had said that the district had been represented in the Texas Congress and was incorporated in the United States revenue system.

INTERLUDE: *Doo-Dah Day*

1. No recognizable jubilee ("spiritual"), I believe, has been dated earlier than 1840. But the jubilee as we know it was a long time developing and came out of two centuries of Negro Christianity. It is a complex thing but its principal begetter was the "white spiritual," which in turn developed from camp-meeting songs, and if it shaped much of the singing in minstrel shows, the minstrel song helped to shape the jubilee. Note that the banjo was a Negro invention and became a musical instrument by way of the minstrel show.

2. Many of the chanties which we cherish developed on the clippers and so date from the 40's. One of the best of them, "Rio Grande," dates from this very year. Note also the *Zeitgeist* of a still finer one, "Shennydore," which was a chanty before it was an army song: it deals with an Indian chief, his daughter, and a trader who crosses the wide Missouri.

CHAPTER VI

1. This probably identifies him as the Romaine with whom Father De Smet traveled in that year. The name is unusual, De Smet's sketch of him resembles Parkman's, and he insisted that he was a practised plainsman. His name and those of the Chandlers are given in full in the notebooks. In *The Oregon Trail* they are mentioned only by initials.

2. After missing the trail they had been seeking, the trace made the preceding summer by the First Dragoons under Kearny, on the expedition to South Pass that has been referred to previously.

3. The correct name of the Indians with whom Parkman traveled is the Dakota; he spelled it Dacotah. Specifically they belonged to the most populous division, the Teton Dakota, and to the Oglala subdivision or "tribe." He called them Sioux in his notebooks, however, and that has always been their name for laymen. It will be used here.

4. Whom Parkman had met in St. Louis. His notebook speaks of "the impulsive, unobservant, ardent Kentuckian [Ewing] who lays open his character to everyone and sees nothing of those about him" and "the quiet, sedate and manly Jacobs, his companion." If he met Bryant, he does not mention it.

5. Mules for speed, on the prairies, and oxen for endurance. Since, besides, they were cheaper, it was therefore usually oxen. They had the added advantage that the Indians did not covet them. They must be young and, preferably, acclimated by a year's residence in these parts. Much bad stock was sold to the emigrants — and died during the earliest stages of the journey. Bryant should have bought a fourth yoke, for replacements. The price he paid was remarkably low.

6. This is the largest single herd I have found in the emigration of '46. It evidences one of the prime expectations in the early migration to Oregon. It was thought — and Frémont's report had endorsed the idea — that Oregon would be a stock breeder's paradise. Large herds had accompanied the emigrations of '43, '44, and '45. The effort to get cattle down the Columbia and over the Cascades, in fact, was a principal cause of the annual disasters.

7. I cannot forbear quoting a sample of Thornton's genteel sensibility: the exquisite kind of sentiment that flooded the gift books of the period and made the mail for St. Valentine's day of '46, so the Postmaster General said, the heaviest yet carried in the United States. On May 12, his heart "drank in the general joy" by way of some birds he saw. "Some were building their nests; one was pouring his love song into the ears of his beloved; and I almost fancied that I could see his eyes sparkle and hear his heart beat as with stooping wing he received a promise from his lady-bird that she would indeed be his." The next day he apostrophizes a mockingbird, advising him to get a mate before emigrating, "and concluded by expressing the opinion that, if he did not, he might have to pair with a blue-jay or perhaps even with a spar-

row hawk." The well-bred had such sentiments — which did not in the least impair Thornton's shrewdness or intelligence or keep him from the greatest usefulness in the new country.

8. The notion that the free lands on the frontier served as a "cushion" to our cyclical depressions is textbook economics. Only a small fraction of the dispossessed even "went west" at any time — they simply could not afford to — and the fraction grew smaller as the frontier got farther from the industrial districts. When a mill at Lowell or Patterson shut down in 1837, how would an operator raise the money to take his family to Illinois, Texas, or Michigan? How would he live there till he could raise a crop? By the time the free land was almost exhausted, however, it was possible for a few of the unemployed to ride the rods west and for greater numbers of them to be recruited by the railroad companies for settlement (under mortgage) on their land grants. Presumably this area of sophisticated railroad management is not what the textbook theory has in mind. (Land was not free till 1862.)

9. Quoted from a ms. in the Missouri Historical Society by Ralph P. Bieber in his edition of *Wah-To-Yah,* p. 356.

10. Indian warfare was conducted on two principles, superiority of numbers and surprise. The Indian wanted booty and glory, not heroic risk. He made war in swift forays.

11. Beyond the mountains the principal nation on the trail was the Shoshoni, who, like most Oregon Indians, were genuinely friendly. The only danger — but a serious one — came from the miserable, cowardly, infinitely treacherous Diggers.

12. The mountain men had anticipated Mr. Stefansson's observation. The meat of the buffalo was a complete diet, one of the healthiest recorded. They ate much of it raw, of course, and fairly swilled the fats and marrow.

13. The upper valley of the North Platte is greener today at all seasons than it was then. Irrigation. If you see it in August, however, you readily perceive how it looked in June of '46.

14. Bancroft's *Oregon* quotes some memoirs which say that the Dutchman was not Thornton's employe but his partner and was merely claiming his own. The story is unsound, on the evidence, and was probably a by-product of the resounding Methodist-Presbyterian row that Thornton got mixed up in later on, in Oregon.

15. Treatment for tires: if you were good at blacksmithing, cut out a part, heat, and weld them, and put them on again, drilling new holes; otherwise, slowly and profanely hammer in a series of whittled wedges between tire and felloe. Treatment for collapsed wheels: replace spokes if you had remembered to provide spares, otherwise buy or steal some hardwood and make new spokes with the tools at hand.

16. Bryant was right. The Sioux were big, tall, lithe, Roman-nosed Indians, among the most impressive of the tribes. As Clark Wissler points out, it happens that most of our popular iconography of the

Indians is Sioux — the Indian on the nickel, the war bonnet and lance and shield conventionally bestowed on all Indians, the characteristic dress, the characteristic tipis, robes, beadwork, etc. They got a good press early and have come to typify all Indians to most Americans. Probably the Indian most widely remembered in our time is Sitting Bull, who was a Hunkpapa Teton Sioux, and it was the Sioux who disposed of Custer.

17. We had better be explicit about this route and take it from the east, west — as the emigrants did. West of Great Salt Lake is the Salt Desert; before it, whether one travels round the north or the south end of the lake, is a steadily intensifying stretch of typical greasewood desert; west of the Salt Desert another such stretch must be crossed on the way to the Humboldt. The journey thus falls into three divisions. Jedediah Smith had traveled considerably to the south of the Salt Desert on his western passage to California in 1826 (the first ever made by the central route), but, returning in 1827, he had crossed to the southern end of Great Salt Lake, thus traversing the Salt Desert in a northeasterly direction, the first white man who ever set foot on it. In 1833, Joseph Walker, leading the party which Bonneville sent to California, moved through the badlands north of Great Salt Lake but turned northwestward to strike the Humboldt and so missed the Salt Desert. In 1841 the "Bartleson party," whose diarist was John Bidwell, abandoned the traditional trail at the northern bend of Bear River, struck overland to the head of Bear River Bay (the eastern arm of Great Salt Lake), moved round the north end of the lake, skirted the western edge of the Salt Desert, and, after terrible suffering, reached the trail again near South Fork. Frémont's route of 1845, which Hastings and Clyman traveled in reverse, led round the southern end of Great Salt Lake to approximately the site of Grantsville, Utah, and then took a due northwest course straight across the Salt Desert to Pilot Peak. As I have said earlier, Frémont deserves more credit for this passage than for any other part of his career as an explorer. He was really being a Pathfinder — Walker instructing him.

18. Frémont, however, remembered more wood and water and much easier going than he actually encountered. He did not, for instance, set down that some fifteen of his horses and mules gave out and had to be abandoned.

19. One of the pleasantest valleys in the West. Bridger's Fort was built on Black's Fork, a tributary of Green River, in fertile, wooded country with the Wasatch in sight to the west, the Uintas to the south, and similarly timbered peaks in the dooryard. It was especially delightful to the emigrants because they reached it, on the way down from South Pass, after a stretch of hideous desert. It was a humble stockade but the first post built west of the divide for the emigrant trade. Chittenden assigns its establishment in 1843 as the true end of the mountain fur trade. Taking the return of Lewis and Clark as the other limit, the era of the mountain man thus lasted thirty-seven years.

20. By this time word of his intention had reached the Oregon settlements. They hurried out agents of their own equipped with denunciations, manifestoes, corrective statistics, and a sizable propaganda of their own. These agents traveled farther and talked to more prospects than Hastings.

21. Probably old Caleb Greenwood was with this party. At any rate he rejoined Hastings and was still with him, looking for "emigrators," when, at the Green River, they encountered a train captained by Joseph Aram. Hastings gave them his sales talk, promising that they would save a month if they took his road, but Greenwood told them otherwise. They believed Greenwood and hired him to guide them by the Fort Hall trail. Just as this party reached the place where the Hastings-Frémont trail joined the California trail they heard from some Indians that the Donners were in trouble on the Salt Desert. They actually turned east to see if they could help but, meeting no one in a day's travel, turned back again and went on to California. . . . Presumably the Aram company were the "emigrators" about whose effeminate diet Greenwood was still complaining when Bryant met him in November.

22. Red Buttes, about twelve miles westward from Casper, Wyoming. Here is where the trail west began a dramatic passage from the still somewhat green and fertile valley of the North Platte to a stretch of bitter desert, on the way to the Sweetwater.

23. Parkman spells it Bordeaux. Otherwise Boudreau, Boudeaux, Bedeau, Bondeau, etc. He probably did not know how to spell it himself.

24. By this time the corporate name of the over-all company which had inherited the Astor interests was Pierre Chouteau, Jr., & Company. It embraced several management and operating companies. But the original name, The American Fur Company, lingered on, a symbol of power in the mountains.

25. He probably exaggerated. The Shoshoni were able to hold their own with either the Sioux or the Blackfeet and quite willing to take them on at any time. All Indians, however, had sudden mass panics or inexplicable second thoughts, and this may have been one of them.

26. The notebook shows that Parkman did not see the incident as his book suggests but learned about it several days later, at his camp.

27. The Humboldt had been so named by Frémont; in '46, however, it was still called Ogden's or Mary's River.

CHAPTER VII

1. During the Civil War he was summoned from retirement and attached to the War Department as a Major General of Volunteers. He was offered Grant's army just before the campaign for Forts

Henry and Donelson and the Army of the Potomac while McClellan was still hesitating to begin the Peninsula campaign. He refused the first on principle and the second on the ground of age and ill health. But he performed valuable services as Commissioner for the Exchange of Prisoners and in other capacities, not the least of them that of unofficial liaison agent between the War Department and the White House. I suspect that he was the reason why Lincoln's military ideas were frequently better than those of his commanders.

2. Mingled with quotations from what Thoreau wrote in the spring and summer of 1846, in the preceding two paragraphs, are quotations from "Resistance to Civil Government," which he did not write until 1848. It should be obvious, however, that the thought is continuous.

INTERLUDE: *World of Tomorrow*

1. Some authorities, however, date Kelly's discovery in 1847.

2. In the hands of cavalry they were, according to the official statements of U. S. Army officers, as effective as the rifled carbine at 100 yards and as effective as the musket at 200 yards.

3. This is the point made by Walter Webb in *The Great Plains*. A rather silly controversy has recently led to the publication of *An Appraisal of Walter Prescott Webb's "The Great Plains"* by the Social Science Research Council, in which this and other points are challenged. So far as the point repeated from Webb in my text is concerned, the challenge simply will not hold. Absolutely all the available evidence — it makes an enormous bulk and, to a bystander's diffident amazement, none of it is studied in the *Appraisal* — supports Mr. Webb's discussion of the effect of the introduction of the revolver in plains warfare. In fact, Mr. Webb would have been justified in making his conclusion more sweeping and more emphatic than he did.

CHAPTER VIII

1. Translations of Castro's and Pico's proclamations from Bancroft's *California*.

2. Since they were cavalry they should be called "troops," not "companies." But army nomenclature was not fixed and "company" was used indifferently to describe infantry, cavalry, and artillery.

3. Since this wild story rests principally on the testimony of Sam Brannan, it is extremely difficult to interpret. Brannan's dime-novel style and his fervent admonitions to secrecy may mean that he was taken in or they may mean that he was working for Sam Brannan as a participating party in the intended sucker game. It is not clear whether Kendall had any knowledge of the intended fraud. The rumor that Lansford

Hastings was acting in California for the Mormons rests on the fact that he was an agent by correspondence for Benson. Benson and Kendall had planned a kind of wholesale colonization of California, doubtless on a realistic calculation of the future. It was a wildcat real-estate scheme which would have profited from any emigration and any upheaval, especially a revolutionary one. Hastings got himself associated with it when he was in the East in 1845 and it unquestionably was a prime force in his activities of 1846. But when he returned to California he had no knowledge of the Mormons' intended emigration.

4. Another indication of the state of geographical knowledge, the more indicative in that Allen as a Dragoon officer had been to South Pass and even to Bent's Fort. He thus knew far more than the administration, which at one point actually proposed to send Price and the Second Missouri to California by way of South Pass in the winter months. Note that the Mormons had informed themselves thoroughly, and Orson Pratt knew of the trail which Kearny took west from Santa Fe.

CHAPTER IX

1. In the summer of '47, according to William Gilpin, who commanded a punitive expedition against them, the Comanche killed 47 men and burned 300 wagons on the trail.

2. It and other illnesses reported were probably complicated by the lack of salt, the necessity of which for sweating men was not appreciated. The army had no supply except what came with the pork.

3. East of Larned, Kansas. Not to be confused with the more famous Ash Hollow of the Oregon trail.

4. The army had reached what is now the Dust Bowl, in western Kansas.

5. Hafen and Ghent; *Broken Hand.* I do not know what their authorities are and the number of wagons and stock is far greater than I am able to account for. I doubt if so many all told moved down the trail that summer.

6. This came to be a prideful nickname. It had been invented by the Laclede Rangers, who, having been attached to the Dragoons, felt superior to the First Missouri.

7. December 25, 1837, in the second Seminole War. Old Rough and Ready had made his entire reputation there, and it was true that some of the Missouri militia had run away.

8. Thomas Hart Benton's intimation, in *A Thirty Years' View,* that Magoffin bought Armijo, presumably for $50,000, is almost certainly untrue.

9. The old trail came into Santa Fe not by the route of the corresponding motor road of today, Highway 85, but over the foothills to the east of it, past the site of the Laboratory of Anthropology.

CHAPTER XI

1. We badly need a competent clinical study of Parkman's ailments. A chapter in George M. Gould's *Biographic Clinics* presents all the details of the physical and mental symptoms. But Dr. Gould wrote at a time when such terms as "migraine" had little specific meaning, he lacked psychiatric understanding, and he was a monomaniac on the subject of "asymmetrical compound astigmatism." Obviously Parkman had a severe neurosis and a neurotic element is discernible in all his symptoms. A professor of ophthalmology whom I have consulted dismisses all his eye trouble as neurotic, pointing out that he was treated by the best specialists of the time. Yes: and some of the treatments they used are horrible to read about. But that the best specialists could not remove his symptoms by correcting errors of refraction does not prove that his eye trouble was wholly neurotic — as Dr. Gould has no trouble showing. Much of it probably was neurotic, and this element increased for many years, but also there was certainly some organic difficulty which the science of his age could not diagnose. The Dartmouth Eye Clinic, which specializes in aniseikonia, quite properly will not bring in a finding that he had it, and says merely that he suffered from severe and complex eyestrain — which is exactly where Dr. Gould left off in 1904. Nevertheless aniseikonia may well have been the basis of his trouble. Apart from the neurotic element in his anxiety about his eyes, Parkman also suffered from hypochondria, depressions, and periodic anxiety-storms. A competent psychiatrist ought, for history's sake, to try to chart the pattern of these symptoms. There remain other questions to be considered by a psychiatrist in collaboration with an internist. Was there a neurotic element in his arthritis? Was his heart trouble real? How much of his endless suffering would modern medicine or psychiatry undertake to cure?

Parkman attributed much of his later sickness to the exposure and hardship of his summer on the trail. Possibly his eyes were permanently injured by the desert sun, but I do not think so. All his later symptoms seem, in some degree, to have shown themselves before he went west. He recovered rapidly and completely from his dysentery and none of his later trouble can be attributed to it. The "general exhaustion" to which he sometimes referred his symptoms has no standing in modern medicine and should have had none in the nineteenth century, in relation to a young man of twenty-four. Let the interested psychiatrist observe how often bad attacks of dysentery and prostration follow some spectacular activity of the Oglala. My text hazards other suggestions about the roots of his neurosis.

2. The notebook says a Ute.

3. He must have found the trading slow for he took his time on the trail. Abert reports him on August 26 in camp a few miles from Bent's Fort with a small, residual herd of mules waiting to sell them to Price

(who was not coming that way). If he had come to Bent's Fort direct from the trail, then he traveled a few days behind Parkman.

4. Mr. J. Roderic Korns has worked out Bryant's route through the Wasatch with a fair degree of certainty. By the courtesy of Mr. Korns and Mr. Dale L. Morgan I print it here for, I believe, the first time. From Fort Bridger he followed the course of the present U. S. Highway 30S (approximately) to about 12 miles east of Evanston, Wyoming, where it strikes the Little Muddy. Thence west to Sulphur Creek and down Sulphur Creek to the Bear River. Thence north up the Bear River about 8 miles. Thence west about 6 miles and southwest about 3 miles to Seleratus Creek. Thence up Seleratus Creek about 5 miles and over a divide to Spring Creek, and down that to Lost Creek. Down Lost Creek to the valley of Croyden. Here the canyon by which Lost Creek makes for Weber River discouraged the party and they turned northeast and circled round to the Weber from that end of the valley. They started down the Weber but were deterred by Upper Weber Canyon (which contains Devil's Slide). They returned to the valley of Croyden and tried to get through the mountains north of Weber Canyon but parallel to it. This was impossible and they turned eastward again, all the way to Henefer this time. Here they started up Little East Canyon (as an Indian had previously advised them to do) and traveled up it to its head and over the divide and down into Dixie Hollow. Reaching the narrows in Dixie Hollow and thinking it impassable, they took an Indian trail up its west wall and down into East Canyon. They struck East Canyon at approximately the site of the present dam, and, still using the Indian trail (which held to the hillside, not the bottom of the canyon) followed it northwest to where it debouches in the valley meadows at Morgan. From here they followed the Weber River. They had detoured Upper Weber Canyon (Devil's Slide), but went through Lower Weber Canyon (Devil's Gate) to Great Salt Lake Valley.

Hastings took the Harlan-Young party through both Upper and Lower Weber Canyon. The route which Bryant followed from Henefer, up Little East Canyon, Dixie Hollow, and over the divide to East Canyon, was the one followed by the Donner party. Instead of turning northwest at the site of the dam and going down East Canyon, as Bryant did, the Donner party, however, turned south up East Canyon.

Note that Clyman, Hastings, and Hudspeth, on their way east, had traveled Dixie Hollow and Little East Canyon in reverse. They had reached Dixie Hollow from Great Salt Lake Valley by way of Parley's Canyon and East Canyon. Thus both Hudspeth and Hastings were familiar with the route eventually taken by the Donner party. Both were so dubious of anyone's being able to get wagons through it that, unquestionably by mutual agreement in advance, they led the scouts of the Harlan-Young party and the party itself by different routes *which neither of them had ever seen before*. Then, having traveled the Weber Canyon route in person, Hastings thought it even worse than the route he had taken eastward and warned the Donners away from it, directing Reed to follow his own eastward route. He had, however, taken the Harlan-Young wagons through the mountains by the Weber Canyon route. The decisions were extremely hard to make but there can be no question that Hastings ended by making the wrong ones. His judgment was just no good.

5. Hastings' letter was dated "At the headwaters of the Sweetwater," that is, east of the continental divide, and Thornton, who makes the most positive statement, says that Hastings had "proceeded as far as the eastern side of the Rocky Mountains and encamped at a place where the Sweetwater breaks through a canyon, at the point where the emigrants leave that river to enter the South Pass," and then returned to Fort Bridger. This is the statement usually repeated in the literature. But Thornton made it, not in his daily journal, but in his recital of the Donner tragedy, which was written more than a year later. It is not clear to me that Hastings came as far east as the divide, and both the known dates and the probabilities are against it. He may have come no farther than the Little Sandy.

6. There are contradictions, absurdities, or impossibilities in every account of the Murphys I have seen. My text repeats the commonest statement of Mormon historians, though the size of the Murphy outfit clearly rebuts it. The most factual statement, as well as the longest, is that of Daniel Tyler's pious *Concise History of the Mormon Battalion,* which is demonstrably wrong in practically everything it says and refers to Mrs. Murphy throughout as "Mrs. Murray." Later in my text, various rumors about the Murphys which were believed by the Mormons are repeated.

7. The presence of Bridger and Vasquez is established by a letter which Reed wrote home from Fort Bridger and which was printed in the *Sangamo Journal* of November 5, 1846. Reed calls them "very excellent and accommodating gentlemen" and says they "are the only fair traders in these parts." The other "independent trappers, who swarm here during the passing of the emigrants, are as great a set of sharks as ever disgraced humanity, with few exceptions. Let the emigrants avoid trading with them."

This letter concisely states the expectation which Hastings had produced. "The new road, or Hastings' Cut-off, leaves the Fort Hall road here, and is said to be a saving of 350 or 400 miles in going to California, and a better route. There is, however, or thought to be, one stretch of 40 miles without water; but Hastings and his party are out ahead examining for water, or for a route to avoid this stretch. [It could be avoided only by way of Bear Lake or Fort Hall.] I think that they cannot avoid it, for it crosses an arm of the Eutaw [Great Salt] Lake, now dry. . . . There is plenty of grass which we can cut and put into the waggons for our cattle while crossing it. We are now only 100 miles from the Great Salt Lake by the new route — in all 250 miles from California;

while by way of Fort Hall it is 650 or 700 miles — making a great saving in favor of jaded oxen and dust. On the new route we will not have dust as there are but 60 waggons ahead of us. . . . Mr. Bridger informs me that the route we design to take is a fine level road, with plenty of water and grass, with the exception before stated."

8. There are no journals and only very brief reminiscences by the members of the Harlan-Young party, and I cannot determine the exact date when they left Fort Bridger.

CHAPTER XII

1. Because the Wasatch are the country of my boyhood I have been interested, rather irrelevantly to our purpose, to state the various routes through it. By the efforts of Mr. J. Roderic Korns and Mr. Dale Morgan, I am able to print the route of the Donners more in detail than it is usually given. If the reader will refer to note 4 of Chapter XI, he will be able to see the differences. The best maps are the Fort Douglas Quadrangle of the Geological Survey, the "Wasatch National Forest" by the Forest Service, and the Salt Lake City sheet of the Sectional Aeronautical Chart.

In June, Clyman, Hastings, and Hudspeth had traveled eastward out of Great Salt Lake Valley by way of Parley's Canyon. (Camp's *James Clyman* says by way of Emigration Canyon, but Mr. Camp, in a letter to me, corrects the statement to agree with mine.) Clyman's language is obscure but certainly they left Parley's Canyon by way of Mountain Dell Canyon and very likely came down to East Canyon Creek by way of Little Dutch Hollow — that is to say, by exactly the route which the Donners used. (However, they may have traveled down Little Emigration Canyon instead of Little Dutch Hollow.) They followed down East Canyon Creek to Dixie Hollow, turned up that to the divide, and went down Little East Canyon to Weber River.

Bryant's party, in their effort to detour Upper Weber Canyon, had turned south at Henefer and gone up Little East Canyon, over the divide, and down Dixie Hollow. Whereas Clyman and Hastings had followed the bed of Dixie Hollow, however, Bryant and his companions, reaching the narrows, took an Indian trail over the western wall of the canyon, along the ridge, and down to the site of the present dam across East Canyon Creek (approximately). Here they turned northwest down East Canyon to the Weber again.

The Donners also left the Weber River at the site of Henefer, having perhaps camped rather farther south and west. They followed Bryant's route up Little East Canyon, over the divide and down Dixie Hollow to the narrows, over the canyon wall by the Indian trail and down to East Canyon. All this way, of course, they had been building a road that wagons could follow, whereas their predecessors had been on horseback.

At the site of the present East Canyon Creek reservoir (approximately), the route which Bryant had taken turned down East Canyon northwest to the Weber River. If the Donners had taken that trail (an Indian trail) they would eventually have reached the Weber at the Morgan meadows and could have continued west through Weber Canyon along a road which had been made passable, if barely passable, for wagons by the Harlan-Young party. Whether they might not have made better, even much better, time if they had done so is an unprofitable speculation. Presumably it would have been easier and faster to improve a road already built, however crudely, than to build an entirely new one, but Hastings had advised against their doing so and that settled it.

They turned south up East Canyon Creek, along the trail which Clyman and Hastings had followed in the opposite direction. They struck off to the right (southwest) up Dutch Hollow (Little Dutch Hollow on the Fort Douglas Quadrangle). At the head of Dutch Hollow they began the most formidable part of their labor, the ascent of Big Mountain — 8200 feet, a half mile higher than East Canyon Creek. Here is where the first panic occurred. The descent on the far side took them to Mountain Dell Canyon and they went down it to Parley's Canyon, which they followed almost to the mouth. Turning back, they went up Parley's Canyon and up Mountain Dell Canyon again, over Little Mountain, down into Emigration Canyon, and so down into the valley.

2. "Near the springs at Lakepoint, west of Garfield." (Charles Kelly.)

3. Stewart thinks that Hastings had posted this notice before taking the Harlan-Young party across. He argues that it had actually taken that party more than two days and that Hastings would not have sent back across the desert information he actually knew to be false. But the Harlan-Young party had actually crossed in just less than two days; the additional time was consumed in going back to salvage abandoned outfits. Kelly thinks that Hastings sent Hudspeth back with the note, after the two-day crossing, while the salvage was going on. If so, Hudspeth made three crossings.

4. Kelly suggests that Hastings took this route in the belief that he could not get wagons through Humboldt Pass.

5. Thornton, who got his facts from Reed and McCutchen themselves, tells the story of this first attempt at relief in considerable detail. He gets into it a note of macabre humor, one of the very few touches that lighten the tragedy.

CHAPTER XIII

1. The story is told in detail in several places: with Beale's own remarks in Stephen Bonsal's *Edward Fitzgerald Beale*. Beale was a first-rate man and his later career was important and picturesque. It was he who suggested and made the famous experiment, under Jefferson Davis as Secretary of War, of using camels in the Southwestern desert.

2. Joint occupation had dissuaded most Americans from settling north of the Columbia, though there was a tiny beginning on Puget Sound.

3. Some trains stayed by the Snake all the way to Huntington.

4. On the right bank of the Snake River (which here flows north), about eight miles below the mouth of Boise River. Not the site of Boise, Idaho.

5. It was Thornton's misfortune to provoke the hair-trigger dislike of Hubert Howe Bancroft who, though he admits the value of Thornton's book, succeeds in doing an injustice to its author. I find Thornton fully as valuable as Clyman for the events treated in this book, and I have no higher praise. He seems to me usually an intelligent, judicious, and trustworthy witness. His animus toward Applegate is flagrant but wherever else I can check him I find him dependable. Bancroft himself uses Thornton's account of the Donner party — which is at second hand, the work of a reporter, not of an eyewitness — as a primary source. So does George R. Stewart, the authority.

6. Once more, my thanks to Charles L. Camp for a detailed statement of Applegate's route from the Willamette on which the above summary is based. Note that the idea of finding a route from Bear River south of Fort Hall was sound. A good many such traces, from Soda Springs, from the lower crossings of the Bear, and from Salt Lake City had been found by the time the Gold Rush passed in '49. Some of them passed Bear Lake.

7. Cooke says five and Roberts, by far the best Mormon historian, repeats him. Golder names four women who completed the march. Cooke also says that he sent all the children to Pueblo and I find no mention of children in any of the Battalion journals I have read. But on December 20, Cooke's journal mentions "sheep, families, children" as taking up the march, and is apparently speaking of his own command.

8. These originally Spanish cattle belonged to the stock which gave rise to the famous longhorns of Texas, which were to be the basis of the Cattle Kingdom.

CHAPTER XIV

1. It is impossible to determine the exact route of this detachment or that of any of the others in the Indian country.

2. This is as good a place as any to express my regret at being unable to weave into this sufficiently complex narrative three stories of '46 — Abert's reconnoissance, Ruxton's trip through northern Mexico and eastward along the Santa Fe trail, and the wide-eyed adventures of Lewis Garrard. They would help to make a formal composition of this book, since they gather up a number of threads necessarily left dangling without them. Ruxton traveled with Garrard and with Abert, Garrard lived with the Cheyenne who were Charles Bent's relatives, stood siege at Fort Mann on the trail when the Comanche harried it in '47, and was brought back to the settlements by Owl Russell, a friend of his family, when Russell came east with dispatches from Frémont. Ruxton's comments on Santa Fe and the trail in '47 are enormously interesting, and Garrard's adventures with Long Hatcher, Blackfoot Smith and other mountain men, his account of New Mexico following the Taos revolt, and his description of the trial of the conspirators are of the first importance. If there did not have to be an end to all books, even of this one, all three stories would appear here.

As a matter of fact, this narrative did at one stage include Garrard's story. I put it in as a specimen of pure ecstasy in the West. I took it out because I could not do justice to it without giving it more space than pure ecstasy justifies. I can only say that Abert's report and the books of Ruxton and Garrard all add to the picture of the West in '46 and '47, that Ruxton's (it is called *Adventures in Mexico and the Rocky Mountains*) is an important and very interesting work, though less so than his fictionized account of the mountain men, *Life in the Far West,* and that Garrard's book is one of the very best ever written about the West. In fact, *Wah-To-Yah* is one of the unacknowledged classics of our literature. It has far more understanding of the West than *The Oregon Trail,* has just as much verve and gusto, and, all told, is a better book. Anyone who may learn about it in this book for the first time is advised to waste no time but to read it at once.

3. El Paso, known everywhere as "The Pass," was the present city of Juarez, across the Rio Grande from the Texas city of today. There were, however, some tiny settlements on the site of the American city, one of them clustering round the ranch of James Magoffin.

4. Word reaching Bent's Fort of the Taos uprising, a hastily gathere force of mountain men rode south through the winter mountains to j the fighting. Lewis Garrard accompanied it and this part of his b with his account of the trial of the ringleaders, achieves a fine iror excitement. Garrard pictures himself greasing the ropes with w guilty were hanged and reflects on the mockery of charging t treason.

CHAPTER XV

1. Reproduced from Thornton. It is impossible to determine whether Thornton may have improved it to agree with his ideas of appropriate gloom. In any event, it is a strange thing to happen in the snow.

CHAPTER XVI

1. About a hundred and fifty miles up the Missouri from Omaha. The Niobrara is the Eau Qui Court of the fur trade and the Running Water of the Mormon texts.

2. Crosby and Brown went back to Mississippi for the winter. Traveling east along the Santa Fe trail, they met the Battalion coming west on September 12. Apparently the Pueblo rendezvous was arranged at that time.

3. It is extremely difficult to identify all the members of this pioneer party, although their names and their division into "tens" (some of which numbered twelve or thirteen) have been published. The 143 included three Negro slaves (Hark Lay, Oscar Crosby, and Green Flake), who belonged to Saints whose last names they bore. By doctrine, Negroes could not be members of the Church. The party also included several others — I cannot make out how many — whom all the journals speak of as not being Mormons. On one occasion Brigham Young ordered those who did not belong to the Church to behave themselves. On May 29, a journal entry of Norton Jacob's says there were six of them; Appleton Harmon speaks of "one or two." No Mormon historian has ever cleared up the ambiguity. I conclude that they were either Saints lately in good standing who had neglected to be re-baptized before starting or relatives of Saints in good standing who were Mormons in everything except the formal covenants. Most, possibly all, of them were baptized in Great Salt Lake a few days after the pioneers got to the valley.

4. He "bought two rifles and some tobacco [!]. He paid in deer and elk skins." (Norton Jacob.)

5. There is a towering humor in the opinion of Howard Egan, who later became one of the best of Mormon desert runners, that "he spoke not knowing about the place." The Mormon God taught His people this complacency.

6. Including Bridger's doubt about the ability of the valley to grow rn. Serious Mormon historians (such as Roberts) have tried to cor- an ancient absurdity, which originated in Brigham Young's propa- bragging. They have been unable to correct it and many Mormon still repeat the idiotic statement that, in effect, Bridger offered 'oung a thousand dollars that corn could not be grown in the is in such contexts as this that the universal smugness of the

Mormon mind ascends into a vainglory which a pious people can find rebuked in the Old Testament.

Clayton, the best reporter, quotes Bridger as follows: "The soil is good and likely to produce corn were it not for the excessive cold nights which he thinks would prevent the growth of corn." Wilford Woodruff says that Jim "remarked that it would not be prudent to bring a great population to the Basin until we ascertained whether grain would grow or not." The unpublished "Manuscript Journal," which was always written by Young himself or under his eye, says (as quoted by Roberts — I have not had access to it): "Bridger considered it imprudent to bring a large population into the Great Basin until it was ascertained that grain could be raised; he said he would give $1000 for a bushel of corn raised in that basin." Precisely. This was an intelligent judgment by a man who knew all there was to know about the country and understood the problems of the Mormons better than anyone outside the faith could be expected to unless he had the continental mind. It expresses a doubt that corn would grow in the valley, a hope that it would, and a caution that they had better find out.

Note that Bridger told them that, in the lands south of Utah Lake, the Indians regularly grew corn as good as any "in old Kentucky." Finally, note that he was right about Great Salt Lake Valley. The Saints got there a month after they talked to him. At that moment the only corn growing in the valley, at Miles Goodyear's stockade on the Weber River, had not yet eared up. Corn was not grown in the valley with much success or promise of success until hardy, specially adapted varieties were introduced there. Even so, it cannot be called a corn-growing country today.

7. The journal of Norton Jacob contains a detail which I have not found elsewhere. It quotes Bridger as saying that during the preceding winter (and I find no record of his movements then) he had "found a country the best he ever saw." It was "bordering on the range of mountains that constitutes the southern boundary of the Great Basin." Jacob's description is too vague for positive identification, but this was obviously Utah's Dixie, possibly the Parowan country.

8. Norton Jacob: "Bro. Brannan fell in with a company of emigrants who by quarreling and fighting among themselves delayed time until they got caught in the snows on the mountains last fall and could not extricate themselves. The snows were much deeper in all this region than was ever known before. There sufferings were incredible. Many of them perished with cold and hunger. All their cattle died and they were compelled to eat the flesh of those that died among them. In fact they killed some and among the rest a mormon by the name of Murphy who formerly lived in Nauvoo. These people are in a wretched condition. [Note that Jacob understands they are still in the mountains.] There teams all gone and they cannot get away until assistance can be sent from Oregon. Quarreling is a common complaing [*sic*] among these emigrants unti

they all divide and subdivide into small parties. They can't agree to travel together in peace which fulfills Joseph Smith's prophesy, that peace is taken from the earth. These are the men who have mobed and killed the saints." Jacob had badly hashed Brannan's information but he made sure that a Mormon had been persecuted, drew an unctuous moral, and found that this, like all the tongues and testimonies of the earth, bore witness that Joseph was a prophet.

CHAPTER XVII

1. Who, when he saw Frémont in California, admired the costuming but was not stirred by the act. See his memoirs.

2. He also tried to suspend Kearny from command of the Dragoons. See the *Proceedings* of the court-martial, page 117.

3. At this point the situation becomes pie for Hubert Howe Bancroft: three American military men at odds with one another. In his satisfaction he is led to a grotesque judgment. Stockton was wrong, Bancroft decides, but Frémont was right in siding with him. For there must be honor among filibusters!

4. When the time came to make claim for their pay, they decided that they had certainly wanted to be, or at least certainly ought to have wanted to be.

5. Both Jones and Tyler record that, at a camp between the Stanislaus and the Sacramento, they were visited by a Mormon named "Rhodes," a Missourian who, they both say, had come to California the previous October. This was the father of John and Daniel Rhoads of the Donner reliefs. Their notation is important for there are exceedingly few records of the undetermined, necessarily very small number of Mormons who traveled overland with Gentile trains in the summer of '46. Several historians have said that the thirteen members of the Mormon Battalion were serving as an escort or guard of Frémont's party. Jones's diary makes quite clear that this is not so. Frémont's party was only occasionally in touch with Kearny's after both parties left Sutter's, and the Mormons were always with Kearny.

6. "To see the Bodys of our fillow beings Laying without Burial & their Bones bleaching in the Sun Beames is truly shocking to my feelings" — Robert S. Bliss. "We found what we took to be a woman's hand, it was nearly whole, it had partly been burned, the little finger on it was not burnt but the flesh on it was completely dried" — Henry W. Bigler.

7. Bancroft believes that Caleb Greenwood was their guide. If so, Stockton's yarn was even more absurd. But he was, of course, a seafaring man, not a prairie traveler.

8. Brigham's letter says that "some few have passed by a new route to California called Hastings cut-off . . . but it is not a safe route."

This is phrased clumsily; he must have meant Miles Goodyear and his horse herd, traveling east.

9. Senate Executive Documents, No. 33, 30th Congress, 1st Session, *The proceedings of the court martial in the trial of Lieutenant Colonel Frémont.* This is by far the most important source for Frémont's career in late '46 and '47. Recent treatments of Frémont have consulted but not studied it. . . . It is only fair to add that much of Frémont's reputation today issues from the campaign biographies of 1856.

Statement on Bibliography

A list of the books, monographs, periodicals, and manuscripts read or consulted in the preparation of this book would run to several thousand items and would be useless alike to the critic and to the student. Adequate bibliographies for most of the subjects treated here either exist already or can easily be assembled by any student. In view of these facts, I have chosen not to print a bibliography but to make a statement describing my use of sources and accounting to the reader for my principal debts to secondary authorities.

The purpose of the book is twice stated in my text. I have investigated the subjects it deals with so far as I thought necessary in order to fulfill that purpose. As the book leaves my hands, I am aware of no errors in it. Since I am acquainted with the usual fruits of industry, however, I am assured that there are many small errors of statement and interpretation, perhaps a great many. I have this to say of them: they do not issue from a failure to consult the material a mastery of which would have prevented error.

My preference is for the eyewitness, for an intelligent eyewitness if he can be found but for any kind of eyewitness if intelligent ones are lacking. When eyewitnesses cannot be found, and in order to supplement them when they can be, I like the accounts of experts contemporary with the events, official reports, and the accounts of contemporary newspapers. All the principal stories of my text and all the principal discussions and analyses are based on eyewitness accounts or accounts by intelligent contemporaries who set out to learn the facts. They are buttressed by government reports, by contemporary newspapers, and by a considerable miscellany of other contemporary material. I have submitted them to the criticism of all relevant works by modern historians. When my account differs from the accounts made by such historians, the difference is deliberate and for cause. And there are a good many places where no qualified modern historian has treated the material which I use.

In short, where facts are important, I have got them at the sources, and where judgment is called for I have tried to give my judgment authority by adequate research. In the use of unimportant facts, however, and in certain other passages where judgment is not called for, I frequently rely on secondary authority. Thus in, for instance, the history of California before my period, it would have been a waste of time to qualify myself in the sources. Everything I say about it (except in relation to the fur trade) rests on authority. Likewise, there are portions of the diplomatic and political background which I have explored no farther than modern histories, though I have gone to the sources for everything that bears directly on my purpose. Finally, in purely connective passages, I have used my own research or the treatments of secondary authorities as best suited my convenience.

Students who are acquainted with the field will find that some of my dates differ from those given by standard authorities. Well, one object of my book was to suggest, so far as possible, the simultaneity of various actions in it. I therefore prepared a careful, extremely detailed itinerary and time schedule of every journey described in the book. I then found that I had a master timetable of the West in 1846, and that its cross references allowed me to check dates and provided information or clues to information which allowed me to correct some of them. Mr. Mason Wade's discovery of Francis Parkman's notebooks, which he generously put at my disposal, was particularly helpful. All the dates which I use in connection with Parkman come from the notebooks.

So much in general. Several specific statements must be made.

Any agreement in judgment between what I say herein and what Justin Smith says in *The War with Mexico* either means a judgment too well supported for anyone to doubt or else is coincidental. The research behind Professor Smith's book is certainly one of the most exhaustive ever made by an American historian, and if it came to an issue of fact I should perforce have to disregard my own findings and accept his. But it is frequently — very frequently — altogether impossible to understand how Smith's conclusions could exist in the presence of facts which he himself presents. If there is a more consistently wrongheaded book in our history, or one which so freely cites facts in support of judgments which those facts controvert, I have not encountered it. Since the Mexican War was a master condition of my book, I consequently had to make an independent study of its politics, diplomacy, campaigns, and personalities. Frequently a few sentences about Taylor, Scott, Marcy, Trist, secondary commanders, miscellaneous figures, or leading events issue from a prolonged study of official reports, newspaper correspondence, journals, memoirs, and biographies which there is no occasion to mention in the text. Nevertheless, I rely on Smith in passages where unimportant facts could not be verified elsewhere without disproportionate labor. I gladly acknowledge that I lean heavily on Major Charles Winslow Elliott's *Winfield Scott.*

My portrait of Frémont rests on a laborious analysis of what he said, did, and wrote; on many eyewitness accounts; on many letters, journals, and memoirs; on the testimony, much of it sworn testimony, of those who were associated with him; and on later accounts by people who were qualified by position or intelligence to write factually. But also I have had at hand such treatments as those by Royce, Bancroft, Goodwin, Sabin, and Nevins, and I have not scrupled to let them decide matters which were unimportant to my purpose and had not come within the scope of my own inquiry.

This brings up the histories of Hubert Howe Bancroft. While actually writing this book I have referred to *California* and *Oregon* innumerable times, to *Utah* occasionally, to others infrequently. I cannot imagine anyone's writing about the history of the West without constantly referring to Bancroft. His prejudices are open, well known, and easily adjustable. A generation ago it was easy for historians to reject much of what he wrote; in the light of all the research since done, it is not so easy now. I have frequently departed from his reading of facts and a sizable number of the facts I use were not known to him, but I have found that you had better not decide that Bancroft was wrong until you have rigorously tested what you think you know. Throughout my treatment of California, the translation of Spanish texts is from Bancroft.

Of the private journals which are the principal source for my account of the Doniphan expedition, a number have been published by Ralph P. Bieber in the *Southwest Historical Series.* I am under a heavy debt to Mr. Bieber's annotation of them, of Cooke, and of Garrard.

James Clyman's journals, letters, and verses are published in Charles L. Camp's *James Clyman: American Frontiersman,* and Susan Magoffin's journal in Stella Drumm's *Down the Santa Fe Trail.* Both books are splendidly edited and both are prime sources. I owe more to *James Clyman* than to any other single book. No more careful work has ever been done in Western history; Camp's editing does almost as much as Clyman's text to make it one of the half-dozen classics of the field. My great debt to Mr. Camp is acknowledged elsewhere.

I owe much to George R. Stewart's *Ordeal by Hunger.* In order to fit the story of the Donner party into the story of the emigration as a whole, I have had to use most of Stewart's sources independently, and my narrative is usually synthesized from Thornton, McGlashan, and Eliza Houghton, and supplemented by contemporary newspaper stories and by the journals of other emigrants of '46 or '47. But anyone who writes about the Donners today necessarily owes much to Stewart and necessarily uses him repeatedly. I adopt all his dates west of Fort Bridger and all but one of his spellings; I rely on him for the identification of geography from Donner Lake on to Sutter's; and I depart only once from his statement of routes. In several places I follow Charles Kelly's excellent *Salt Desert Trails.*

There are practically no trustworthy authorities about the Mormons.* My text rests on only one Mormon historian, Brigham H. Roberts, rests on him only when he quotes from official documents not open to me, and never, I believe, rests on any Gentile historian. Everything I say about the Mormons and about the Mormon Battalion derives from the sources, and in the interpretation of Mormon experience derives from Mormon sources exclusively. What I say in judgment derives from an exhaustive study of the entire field. The journal of Henry Standage is published in Golder's *March of the Mormon Battalion,* and Charles Kelly has published *Journals of John D. Lee.* The journals of John W. Hess, Robert S. Bliss, Henry W. Bigler, and Nathaniel V. Jones have been published in the *Utah Historical Quarterly.* Most of the other journals quoted in my text were typed and deposited in various places, in Utah, at the Library of Congress, and in New York, by the Historical Records Survey. Material in my text from a good many other journals and autobiographies not directly quoted is also usually from the Historical Records Survey. Various other journals, quoted and not quoted, were put at my disposal by their owners.

In the emigration, I have tried to submit the individual experience to interpretation by means of the typical experience. My stories are of 1846 but the supporting material is from the entire history of emigration in the West before the railroads.

Though the actions of this book occurred nearly a century ago, some of them are still in dispute. To students who know the details of those controversies, I may say that sometimes, in the absence of evidence absolutely conclusive, I have chosen, after due consideration of all relevant material, to adopt, so far as possible, the account of the man who seemed to me the most intelligent man on the spot.

*I should like to exempt from this statement, formally and even vigorously, Dale L. Morgan and Nels Anderson. Their published work, however, has not yet covered very much of the material I deal with.

Three such men are conspicuous: Jessy Quinn Thornton, Ethan Allen Hitchcock, and Philip St. George Cooke. I believe that I have not followed any of them where there is good evidence against them. On the other hand, it would take exceedingly good and plentiful evidence to impugn their testimony.

BERNARD DEVOTO

Index

Sentry Editions

1 A Week on the Concord and Merrimack Rivers
by Henry David Thoreau

2 A Diary from Dixie *by Mary Boykin Chesnut, edited by Ben Ames Williams*

3 The Education of Henry Adams: An Autobiography

4 J.B. *by Archibald MacLeish*

5 John C. Calhoun *by Margaret L. Coit*

6 The Maritime History of Massachusetts: 1783–1860
by Samuel Eliot Morison

7 My Ántonia *by Willa Cather*

8 Patterns of Culture *by Ruth Benedict*

9 Sam Clemens of Hannibal *by Dixon Wecter*

10 The Great Crash, 1929 *by John Kenneth Galbraith*

11 The Year of Decision: 1846
by Bernard DeVoto

12 Young Man with a Horn *by Dorothy Baker*